WOMEN
AND THE
CRIMINAL JUSTICE SYSTEM

A CANADIAN PERSPECTIVE

SECOND EDITION

EDITED BY
JANE BARKER
D. SCHARIE TAVCER

emond · Toronto, Canada · 2018

Emond Montgomery Publications Limited
1 Eglinton Avenue East, Suite 600
Toronto ON M4P 3A1
http://www.emond.ca/highered

Printed in Canada.
Reprinted December 2018

We acknowledge the financial support of the Government of Canada.   Canadä

Emond Montgomery Publications has no responsibility for the persistence or accuracy of URLs for external or third-party Internet websites referred to in this publication, and does not guarantee that any content on such websites is, or will remain, accurate or appropriate.

Vice president, publishing: Anthony Rezek
Publisher: Mike Thompson
Director, development and production: Kelly Dickson
Developmental editor: Joanne Sutherland
Production supervisor: Laura Bast
Copy editors: Tara Tovell, Marg Anne Morrison
Typesetter: Tara Agnerian
Permissions editor: Alison Lloyd-Baker
Proofreader: Lila Campbell
Indexer: Andrew Little
Cover image: elwynn/Shutterstock

Library and Archives Canada Cataloguing in Publication

Women and the criminal justice system / [edited by] Jane Barker, D. Scharie Tavcer. — Second edition.

Includes index.
ISBN 978-1-77255-181-5 (softcover)

1. Female offenders—Canada—Textbooks.   2. Women prisoners—Canada—Textbooks.
3. Women criminal justice personnel—Canada—Textbooks.   4. Women—Crimes against—Canada—Textbooks.   5. Criminal justice, Administration of—Canada—Textbooks.   6. Textbooks.
I. Barker, Jane, 1965-, editor   II. Tavcer, D. Scharie, editor   III. Title.

HV9960.C2W64 2017   364.0820971   C2017-903548-7

Brief Contents

Contents

PART I Overview of Women and the Canadian Criminal Justice System

PART II Female Offenders in Canada

PART III Victimization and Criminalization

PART IV Women Working in the Canadian Criminal Justice System

Preface

Women in the Criminal Justice System: A Canadian Perspective was first published in 2009. We realized that it was time for a new edition in 2015, and began working toward making the second edition as updated and comprehensive as possible in its coverage of issues related to women and the criminal justice system in Canada.

The main objective of this textbook is to provide the reader with a thorough picture of women and the criminal justice system in Canada: women offenders, women victims, and women who work in the system. This book is divided into four parts. The first part is devoted to an overview of women and the criminal justice system and theoretical underpinnings of offending and victimization. The second part looks specifically at women and girl offenders, their distinct characteristics, what sets them apart from male offenders, and how the correctional system addresses their needs. The third part of this book addresses the victimization of women and girls, including the intersection of victimization and offending, offenders and their mental health, Indigenous women and girls, prostitution and sex trafficking, and the National Inquiry into Missing and Murdered Indigenous Women and Girls. The fourth part provides a generous overview of women police officers, correctional workers, women working in the courts, and the systemic and structural issues that they face. We hope that through reading each successive chapter, readers will develop a solid base of knowledge regarding women and the Canadian criminal justice system.

New to This Edition

There are a number of new features to the second edition. We have included four case studies; one begins each part of the book. We hope that the case studies will alert the reader to contemporary topics that relate to each of the four parts of the text.

There is a new chapter on prostitution and murdered and missing women in Canada. We included this new chapter because, in our discussion of women and the criminal justice system, ignoring prostitution and forms of sexual exploitation would not provide students with a fulsome textbook. Since the first edition, Canada's prostitution laws have changed. Our focus on murdered and missing women in the chapter was an imperative given our coverage of women's victimization. Women in Canada have been reported missing and have been found murdered for decades, while the federal government has only recently begun an inquiry into these missing and murdered women.

We have also included a number of "What Do You Think?" boxes. These boxes tackle issues in the criminal justice system, and will challenge and engage the reader to think critically as they work their way through each chapter.

Throughout each chapter, statistics have been updated, current examples have been utilized, and the focus of each chapter continues to be on important Canadian issues as they relate to women in the criminal justice system. We tried to put more of a national focus on the book by including examples and statistics from across Canada.

You will also note that we have expanded the list of "Additional Resources" at the end of each chapter in an attempt to provide the reader with as many relevant resources as possible.

Acknowledgments

This book could not have been completed without the contributions of many talented academics, applied researchers, and practitioners in the field of criminal justice. Walter DeKeseredy, a respected researcher and prolific author of many books, including a textbook on women in conflict with the law, provided comprehensive additions and support toward the reworking of the theory chapter and the victims chapter. Thanks also to Shahid Alvi, a well-known and respected researcher and author, whose expertise was greatly appreciated in his contributed chapter about youth offending. Franca Cortoni and Marie-Pier Robitaille, from the University of Montreal, experts in sex offenders, provided an up-to-date and empirically rich chapter on violent women. Jill Atkinson, from Queen's University, provided a thorough and comprehensive examination of the current state of correctional assessment, treatment, and reintegration needs of criminalized women. Jean Folsom, who has decades of experience working in the federal correctional system, contributed her experience and knowledge to the chapter on the mental health needs of women offenders. The unique expertise of psychologist Brenda Restoule (the first Indigenous counsellor in the psychology department at the Prison for Women) was very much appreciated in her chapter on Indigenous offenders. Thanks also to Alexandra Gault for her research assistance on Dr. Restoule's chapter. In addition, the contributions of Constable Kellie Woodbury added a real-world element to the chapter on policing. And, lastly, an esteemed colleague in the School of Criminology and Criminal Justice at Nipissing University, Greg Brown, completed the picture of women in Canada's criminal justice system in the chapter describing the challenges and issues facing women who work in policing. This book would not have been complete without the valued contributions of all of these outstanding individuals.

In addition to those who wrote individual chapters in this book, Mike Thompson at Emond deserves considerable recognition. It was Mike who enthusiastically worked with us to make sure that the proposal for the second edition moved ahead. He offered his expertise and continued to be a source of support throughout this project. He ensured that the whole process ran smoothly from start to finish. Mike, we cannot thank you enough for all of your assistance and guidance on this project.

To Joanne Sutherland, Tara Tovell, and Marg Anne Morrison, who supported us through their edits and guidance, and ensured we stayed on task, we offer our sincere gratitude. To Laura Bast, Kelly Dickson, and the rest of the team at Emond who had a hand in making this book a reality, we offer our heartfelt thanks.

Lastly, we are both very appreciative of each other's efforts and enthusiasm in bringing this project to fruition. If it wasn't for Dr. Tavcer contacting Dr. Barker in 2015 and graciously offering to assist with the production of a second edition of the text, we might not be where we are today. This project truly was a collaborative effort and for that we both wish to acknowledge the valued contributions of each other.

This kind of book is like a pot-luck dinner—you gather the experience and expertise of a group of people who work in related areas, and you look forward to tasting their signature dishes, while hoping they don't all bring a Caesar salad. Please forgive any repetition that might exist—we simply want to emphasize those important points. The following chapters provide much food for thought, and we hope all readers will benefit from reading this volume.

The authors and the publisher wish to thank the following people who provided feedback and suggestions during the development of this project: Chantal Faucher, Simon Fraser University; Judith Grant, UOIT; Catherine Huth, Langara College; Patricia O'Reilly, Wilfrid Laurier University; and Ron Taylor, UPEI.

Instructors' Supplements

For information on accessing the teaching resources available to instructors who have chosen this book for their courses, contact your Emond Publishing representative or visit the "For Instructors" tab on the book's website, www.emond.ca/WCJS2e, for more information.

About the Authors

Jane Barker (lead author and editor) is Chair and Associate Professor in the School of Criminology and Criminal Justice at Nipissing University.

D. Scharie Tavcer (lead author and editor) is an Associate Professor of Criminal Justice in the Department of Economics, Justice, and Policy Studies at Mount Royal University.

Contributors

Shahid Alvi is Professor in the Faculty of Social Science and Humanities at the University of Ontario Institute of Technology.

Jill Atkinson is Associate Professor and Chair of Undergraduate Studies in the Department of Psychology at Queen's University.

Greg Brown is Professor in the School of Criminology and Criminal Justice, and in the Sociology Department at Nipissing University.

Franca Cortoni is Associate Professor in the School of Criminology at the University of Montreal.

Walter S. DeKeseredy is Anna Deane Carlson Endowed Chair of Social Sciences, Director of the Research Center on Violence, and Professor of Sociology at West Virginia University.

Jean Folsom (retired) is former Director of Psychology and Rehabilitation Services at the Regional Treatment Centre, Correctional Service of Canada, in Kingston.

Brenda M. Restoule is an Indigenous psychologist who gratefully works with First Nation people on Indigenous mental wellness and is the Chair of the First Peoples Wellness Circle.

Marie-Pier Robitaille is a post-doctoral fellow in psychiatry at the Research Centre of the University of Montreal's Institute for Mental Health.

Kellie Woodbury is a police officer with the Ontario Provincial Police.

PART I

Overview of Women and the Canadian Criminal Justice System

CASE STUDY

Yvonne Johnson

D. Scharie Tavcer

In March 1991, Yvonne Johnson was convicted of first-degree murder of Leonard (Chuck) Skwarok in Wetaskiwin, Alberta. For three days in September 1989, while under the influence of alcohol, a fight broke out among several people in her home, and a man whom her cousin accused of being a child molester (Chuck) ended up dead. It was a gruesome death that involved hours of torture, forcible confinement, and assault.

The sequence of events those nights was fuzzy for each to remember while the police tried to determine if Chuck's death was planned and deliberate. Yvonne's husband, Dwayne Wenger, pleaded guilty to second-degree murder and Shirley Anne Salmon pleaded guilty to aggravated assault. Ernest Jensen and Yvonne stood trial. There was strong physical evidence against Jensen, but there was no physical evidence whatsoever against Yvonne. Instead the jury was convinced by Shirley Anne's contradicting testimony. Yvonne was convicted of first-degree murder.

In the 1990s, we still had the Faint Hope Clause. This law permitted those who were convicted of first-degree murder to make an application to the court asking that the 25-year minimum parole eligibility be reduced. If the court granted it, only then could an inmate apply for parole to the National Parole Board (now called the Parole Board of Canada). In addition to applying for Faint Hope, Yvonne petitioned the court to change the venue of the hearing because she believed racism would have impacted her hearing.

At the time, Wetaskiwin was a rural town with deep and long-standing rifts between Indigenous and non-Indigenous residents. It was known anecdotally as a jurisdiction where Indigenous people routinely receive tougher sentences than non-Indigenous (Wiebe & Johnson, 1998).

In March 2005, Johnson was successful on both fronts. After 17 years' imprisonment, Yvonne's application for day parole was granted in 2009. This required her to reside in a halfway house, which she did successfully (she followed all of her conditions) and in December of 2010, she was granted full parole. The National Parole Board ruled that Johnson was a low risk to reoffend. As with any life sentence, she will be supervised for the rest of her life.

Yvonne's story is unfortunately common for many Indigenous women who face the criminal justice system in Canada. She lived through years of physical and sexual abuse at the hands of family members, family violence as an adult, addiction, alienation, and racism. As an adult she was still a victim and struggling.

> Before my arrest, a lot of shit happened to me. If I had not been in prison for this charge, I would most likely [have] been in [prison at] some point thereafter, if I never got helped.

Or dead by suicide. My love for my kids kept me barely touching ground when I was just hanging onto existence and reality. ... I felt evil, nasty, and dirty and lost. ... I gave up trying to feel, except with my babies, I took to being so overly protective. Yet I still drank, I knew I was losing ground fast. ... Never in my whole life [have] I been to such a low level, with no will, striving, dreams, or hope ... it truly was the most dead time in my life. (Yvonne's journal, as cited in Wiebe & Johnson, 1998, p. 227)

Another example of the significant, albeit hidden role that prosecutorial discretion plays in murder cases is evident in Johnson's case. The result in her prosecution demonstrates systemic racism whereby Indigenous persons who are not the most significant actors in a crime, can often be given the lion's share of legal and punitive responsibility for a crime. She was denied the benefit of a plea bargain, even when it was extended to the other perpetrators.

Today Yvonne lives freely (but still under parole supervision) in Calgary, Alberta. She has reconnected with her children and raised her grandchildren while building a life for herself through school and work. She is 55 years old.

QUESTIONS TO CONSIDER

1. Read the book *Stolen Life: The Journey of a Cree Woman* and decide for yourself whether or not Yvonne (and the others) should have faced a charge of first-degree murder.
2. Read the case law and decide for yourself what charges Yvonne (and the others) could have faced in this case: *R v Johnson*, 2005 ABQB 221, available at https://www.canlii.org/en/ab/abqb/doc/2005/2005abqb221/2005abqb221.html.
3. Identify the criminogenic factors that Yvonne and the others had that may have contributed to the escalation of violence the night of Chuck Skwarok's murder.
4. What are your thoughts about the Faint Hope Clause? Was it fair? Was it too lenient? It was repealed and is no longer valid as of December 2011. (See Bill S-6: www.csc-scc.gc.ca/victims/003006-1001-eng.shtml.)

REFERENCES

R v Johnson, 2005 ABQB 221.

Wiebe, R., & Johnson, Y. (1998). *Stolen life: The journey of a Cree woman.* Toronto: Random House of Canada.

The Canadian Criminal Justice System and Women

Introduction: The Canadian Criminal Justice System

The criminal justice system in Canada comprises three interconnected agencies: the police, the courts, and the correctional system. A woman who comes into conflict with the law will likely interact with many individuals from each of these agencies, not all of whom will treat her with respect and dignity. Unfortunately, in the criminal justice system, as in our society as a whole, girls and women are sometimes the targets of abuses of power.

This chapter provides a brief description of the criminal justice system in Canada and a basic understanding of the structure and organization of the various agencies within it. A fairly cursory overview of the types of police agencies is followed by a brief introduction to the court system. A detailed account of the history of the correctional system's treatment of women illustrates how the needs of female offenders have historically taken a back seat to the needs of male offenders. The end of the chapter serves as an introduction to women as offenders, as victims of crime, and as workers in the field of criminal justice.

Policing

In Canada, policing occurs at three levels of government: federal, provincial or territorial, and municipal. In addition, numerous Indigenous communities have their own police services. For 2014/15, expenditures related to all levels of policing in Canada totalled $13.9 billion. Police spending has remained fairly stable from 2010/11 to 2014/2015. In total, 68,777 police officers were employed across Canada in 2015, representing a rate of 192 officers per 100,000 Canadians (Mazowita & Greenland, 2016).

Federal Policing

Canada's federal police service is the Royal Canadian Mounted Police (RCMP). The RCMP is responsible not only for enforcing federal statutes but also for providing a variety of resources to police, including forensic analysis, identification services, the Canadian Police College, and the Canadian Police Information Centre (CPIC). The *Royal Canadian Mounted Police Act* governs the organization of the RCMP. As such, the RCMP is headed by a commissioner who reports to the Minister of Public Safety Canada. The RCMP is organized into four regions (Atlantic, Central, Northwestern, and Pacific), each operating under the direction of a deputy commissioner. Other deputy commissioners are assigned to head up operations and integration, national police services, and corporate management and comptrollership (RCMP, 2017). In addition to the headquarters located in Ottawa, the RCMP is further organized into 15 divisions, most of which correspond to provincial or territorial boundaries. As of September 1, 2015, a total of 28,461 people worked in the RCMP. More than 6,300 people were employed as public servants, and 3,838 as civilian members. The bulk of the employees were constables (11,491 people) (RCMP, 2017).

Provincial and Territorial Policing

Canada has three provincial police services: the Ontario Provincial Police (OPP), Sûreté du Québec, and the Royal Newfoundland Constabulary. Provincial police services are concerned with the enforcement of the *Criminal Code* and provincial statutes in areas where no municipal force exists. It is not unusual to find an overlapping of police boundaries. For example, in the city of North Bay, Ontario, a municipal police force (North Bay Police Services) is responsible for policing in the city of North Bay, while the OPP patrols the highways that pass through the city. In areas of Canada without a provincial or territorial police service, the RCMP is contracted to provide this service.

Municipal Policing

Officers who are employed to conduct policing at the municipal level enforce the *Criminal Code*, various provincial statutes, and municipal bylaws. Some municipalities operate their own policing force; others combine with a neighbouring municipality to provide police services to both areas or contract the work to either a provincial police service or the RCMP (Reitano, 2006).

Areas of Canada that do not have municipal policing include Nunavut, Yukon, the Northwest Territories, and Newfoundland and Labrador. The provincial police force in Newfoundland and Labrador provides municipal police services to four municipalities (St. John's, Corner Brook, Labrador City, and Churchill Falls), while the rest of the province contracts the RCMP to provide municipal and rural policing services (Reitano, 2006).

Indigenous Policing

In June 1991, the First Nations Policing Policy (FNPP) was introduced by the federal government (Public Safety Canada [PSC], 2016). The purpose of the FNPP is to "provide First Nations across Canada with access to police services that are professional, effective, culturally appropriate and accountable to the communities they serve" (PSC, 2016, ¶ 1). Under the direction of Canada's lead department for public safety, Public Safety Canada, and Indigenous communities work with provincial, territorial, and federal governments to establish tripartite policing agreements that meet the needs of the communities they serve.

The Courts

The system of Canadian courts has been described as complex (Canada, Department of Justice, 2017). This complexity stems from the four levels of court and various types of courts that exist in Canada. Very briefly, provincial and territorial courts deal with the majority of cases. These are the "lowest" courts in the system. Next up the ladder are the provincial and territorial superior courts, where appeals from the provincial and territorial courts are heard, as are cases involving the most serious crimes. At the same level as the provincial and territorial superior courts is the Federal Court. This court has jurisdiction over matters in the federal domain. At the third level are the provincial and territorial courts of appeal and the Federal Court of Appeal. And lastly, the highest court in Canada is the Supreme Court of Canada (Canada, Department of Justice, 2017).

Provincial and Territorial Courts

Apart from Nunavut, every province and territory has a provincial or territorial court. Although their names may differ, the role and function of these courts are the same: they hear cases that involve provincial, territorial, or federal laws, the majority of criminal cases that come before the courts. These courts deal with criminal offences, crimes committed by young offenders, matters of family law (but not divorce), regulatory offences, traffic violations, and claims involving money. Also, all preliminary inquiries are held in provincial or territorial courts to determine whether a serious criminal case has sufficient evidence to warrant a full trial. Specialty courts also exist at this level. For example, some courts are mandated to hear specific types of cases, such as Toronto's Drug Treatment Court (DTC), which was established in 1998 to hear cases involving non-violent offenders who have come into conflict with the law as a result of their drug addiction (Canada, Department of Justice, 2017). For non-violent offenders who qualify, their drug addiction can be addressed through the option of treatment combined with judicial supervision. Other specialty courts include youth courts and domestic violence courts (Canada, Department of Justice, 2017).

Provincial and Territorial Superior Courts

All provinces and territories have their own superior court, and although their names may differ, their role is generally the same (except for Nunavut, where the Nunavut Court of Justice is concerned with both superior court and territorial court matters). These superior courts have "inherent jurisdiction" at the superior court level, which means they can hear any cases in any area unless the case is specifically limited to a different level of court (Canada, Department of Justice, 2017). These courts try the most serious civil and criminal cases, including those that involve large sums of money and cases of divorce. Provincial and territorial superior courts can have special divisions, such as the family division. The provincial and territorial superior courts are also the court of first appeal (Canada, Department of Justice, 2017).

Courts of Appeal

Appeals from decisions rendered at the provincial, territorial, or superior courts are heard at the court of appeal, where a number of judges (usually three) hear the cases as a panel. The court of appeal also addresses constitutional questions raised in relation to individuals, government agencies, or the government (Canada, Department of Justice, 2017).

Federal Courts

The Federal Court of Appeal and the Federal Court are basically superior courts that have civil jurisdiction (Canada, Department of Justice, 2017). However, the jurisdiction of these courts is limited because the courts (created by an act of Parliament) are permitted to deal only with matters specified in federal statutes. This authority differs from the provincial and territorial superior courts where the court has jurisdiction in all areas except where excluded by statute. Specialized federal courts have been established by the federal government to assist the courts in operating in an efficient and effective manner. For example, the Tax Court of Canada deals with matters pertaining to federal tax and revenue legislation. If a taxpayer exhausts all options under the *Income Tax Act*, then any dispute between the taxpayer (that is, an individual or a company) and the federal government will be dealt with at the Tax Court of Canada (Canada, Department of Justice, 2017).

The Supreme Court of Canada

The final court of appeal is the Supreme Court of Canada, which has authority over all private and public law in Canada. This court has jurisdiction over matters in all areas of the law, including criminal and civil law, constitutional law, and administrative law. The Supreme Court of Canada comprises a chief justice and eight judges. The judges, three of whom must be from Quebec (as specified in the *Supreme Court Act*), are appointed by the federal government. In addition to the Quebec judges, traditionally one judge is appointed from the Maritimes, two from the West, and three from Ontario (Canada, Department of Justice, 2017). The Supreme Court of Canada hears "as of right" appeals when a provincial or territorial appeal court has overturned an acquittal from a trial court, or when dissent about a question of law occurs at a provincial or territorial court of appeal. In addition, subcommittees of the Supreme Court can refer to the highest court in Canada cases involving legal issues that hold a particular relevance and cases of public importance (Goff, 2008).

The Correctional System

The correctional system in Canada is divided into one federal service, the Correctional Service of Canada (CSC), and 13 provincial and territorial services (see Table 1.1). In Ontario correctional services are subsumed under the Ministry of Community Safety and Correctional Services, while in Alberta these services are the responsibility of the Ministry of Justice and Solicitor General.

Pre-Confederation Corrections

In 1849, member of provincial Parliament (MPP) George Brown submitted the *First Report of the Commissioners Appointed to Inquire into and Report upon the Conduct, Economy, Discipline, and Management of the Provincial Penitentiary*, later known as the Brown commission report. This report was primarily a scathing condemnation of the warden of Kingston Penitentiary, Henry Smith, and of the abusive practices that were all too common at the penitentiary. The Brown commission report (Canada, Commission Appointed to Inquire, 1849) detailed the horrific living conditions endured by both male and female inmates. The prison food was abominable, the cells were reported to be overrun with bugs, and the inmates suffered from brutalities inflicted by staff. The women's area, located in the basement, was described in the following manner:

> The cells of the female Convicts are built of pine; have been many years in use, and are small apartments, with little ventilation. There seems no doubt that the cells have been overrun with vermin, and that the women suffered frightfully from them for years. (Canada, Commission Appointed to Inquire, 1849, p. 136)

The Brown commission report included descriptions of all manner of punishments inflicted upon the women at the Kingston Penitentiary. A detailed account of what

Table 1.1   Ministries Responsible for Provincial and Territorial Corrections

Province or Territory	Ministry Responsible for Corrections
British Columbia	Ministry of Public Safety and Solicitor General
Alberta	Ministry of Justice and Solicitor General
Saskatchewan	Ministry of Justice
Manitoba	Manitoba Justice
Ontario	Ministry of Community Safety and Correctional Services
Quebec	Public Security
New Brunswick	Public Safety
Nova Scotia	Department of Justice Correctional Services
PEI	Department of Justice and Public Safety
Newfoundland & Labrador	Department of Justice and Public Safety
Nunavut	Department of Justice
Northwest Territories	Department of Justice
Yukon	Department of Justice

happened to inmate Charlotte Reveille serves as a disturbing reminder of the atrocities that can occur in a civilized society. The length of her sentence is not entirely clear, but it was noted that although her sentence expired on February 14, 1849, she was kept incarcerated for longer because the warden and inspectors did not want to discharge her during "this inclement season." Charlotte Reveille was imprisoned longer than her sentence because of the weather!

According to the warden's punishment ledger, during Reveille's stay at the Kingston Penitentiary, between July 11, 1846 and October 7, 1847, she was punished on no fewer than 50 occasions for a range of behaviours, including but not limited to using bad language, refusing to walk, refusing to wear shoes, tearing blankets, "great violence," abuse, and cursing the matron. Her punishments, as listed in the warden's ledger, included being confined to her cell for 48 hours, being placed in a dark cell for 24 hours, being placed in a box on bread and water, and being given six lashes with rawhide. Reportedly not included in the ledger was the order by inspectors on April 5, 1847 for "Charlotte Reveille to be gagged, whenever it might be necessary to reduce her to silence" (Canada, Commission Appointed to Inquire, 1849, p. 206). Charlotte Reveille's case was thoroughly investigated by the Brown commission, which concluded that although Reveille likely arrived at the penitentiary in poor health and with a "predisposition to insanity," her condition was very likely worsened by the extreme punishments that she received (Canada, Commission Appointed to Inquire, 1849, p. 208). The Brown commission believed that the flogging of women was not an isolated incident at the penitentiary; the flogging of female inmates as young as 12 years of age had also been reported. The Brown commission report viewed punishing women in this manner as "utterly indefensible" (Canada, Commission Appointed to Inquire, 1849, p. 190).

The Brown commission found Warden Smith guilty of all charges levelled against him, including cruelty, financial impropriety, neglect of duty, falsifying records, and general mismanagement of the institution. As a result, the commission recommended Smith's immediate and permanent removal from the position of warden at the Kingston Penitentiary. Another recommendation specific to the needs of women was that "a suitable building must, however, be erected before any reform can be attempted with success" (Canada, Commission Appointed to Inquire, p. 296). The results of the Brown commission report are critical in the history of women's incarceration in Canada. Table 1.2 lists some of the commissions, reports, and key events related to women's corrections in Canada.

Provincial Corrections

An examination of the history of women's prisons in Canada suggests that public recognition of the plight of women prisoners has waxed and waned over the years. A pattern of collective ignorance about the state of women's incarceration has often been followed by a surge of interest expressed as outrage over the conditions of their imprisonment. Despite considerable improvements over the last century to the physical state of women's prisons, criticisms are still being levelled against the provincial and federal governments responsible for the care of incarcerated women. To fully appreciate the current state of women's corrections in Canada, the history of its development is needed.

Prior to the opening of Toronto's Andrew Mercer Ontario Reformatory for Females in 1880, women sentenced to incarceration in Ontario were housed in local jails alongside male prisoners (Strange, 1985). Their accommodations in these facilities were abusive at their worst and mediocre at their best. In small facilities, women were sometimes locked up with men. In larger jails, separate cells were sometimes reserved for women; however, these cells were reported to be overcrowded (Strange, 1985). In a review of women's prisons from 1874 to 1901, Strange noted that an increase of approximately 6 percent over the previous year in the number of females sent to jail in 1878 was seen as evidence by then Ontario Prison Inspector J.W. Langmuir that a separate women's prison was needed.

The Mercer reformatory was designed and built at a time when Canadian society was willing to entertain two ideological viewpoints: (1) that prisons should focus on reformation not punishment; and (2) that men and women were so distinct in nature that their correctional experiences should also reflect this "differentness" (Strange, 1985). Langmuir, in his lobbying of Ontario legislators, looked to the United States for examples of how a separate women's reformatory could be instituted in the social climate of the day. Central to this proposal was the assertion that an all-female staff at such a facility could provide the "maternal reform" that would enable those incarcerated to become respectable women. In both the United States and Canada, some members of the moralistic middle class believed that "fallen" women could be reformed by the maternal qualities of these middle-class moral guardians (Strange, 1985). Langmuir's vision was never fully realized, as the history of the Mercer reformatory can attest (Strange, 1985). The ideological axiom of reform over punishment received only weak support from Ontarians, and the obstacles to the application of such a "maternal reform" in a prison setting were considered insurmountable (Strange, 1985).

Table 1.2   Women's Corrections in Canada—Timeline of Commissions, Reports, and Key Events

Commission/Report/Event	Year	Main Recommendation/Description/Exact Date
Brown commission report	1849	Build a separate unit to house women at Kingston Pen.
MacDonell report	1914	Build a separate prison for the women.
Biggar report	1921	Amend the *Penitentiary Act* to allow women to be incarcerated in their own prison.
Nickle report	1921	Women should not be housed in a male facility.
Prison for Women (P4W) construction began	1925	
P4W open to all women	1934	All remaining women from Kingston Pen were transferred to P4W.
Archambault report	1938	Close P4W and arrange for women to be put in provincial jails.
Gibson report	1947	Move the women to provincial jails and turn P4W into a men's facility.
Fauteux report	1956	Keep one central women's institution for reasons of economy.
Canadian Corrections Association brief	1968	Prisons for women must be designed with the special needs of women offenders in mind.
Ouimet report	1969	Establish regional facilities to be shared by federal and provincial governments and appoint a woman to a position of leadership and responsibility with respect to women's corrections
Clark report	1977	Establish regional secure institutions for women who need a high security setting while other women would be housed in provincial facilities. An alternative approach was that provincial governments would assume responsibility for all women offenders.
Subcommittee on the Penitentiary System	1977	P4W described as "unfit for bears, much less women."
Joint Committee to Study Alternatives	1978	Keep one secure, central facility for women and maximize exchange of service agreements with the provinces.
Needham report	1978	Close P4W.
Task Force on Federally Sentenced Women (TFFWS) Creating Choices report	1990	Close P4W and build five regional facilities and a healing lodge in the Prairies.
April 22nd incident at P4W	1994	April 22, 1994
The fifth estate airs video of cell extractions.	1995	February 21, 1995
Arbour commission report	1996	Report released April 1996. CSC showed a "disturbing lack of commitment to the ideals of justice." (See link to report in What Do You Think? following Box 1.1.)
Nancy Stableforth is appointed the first Deputy Commissioner for Women.	1996	June 21, 1996
P4W is closed.	2000	May 8, 2000

Strange (1985) points out that around the time the Mercer facility was being planned, a number of economic benefits were associated with a separate reformatory for women. Among these benefits was an expectation that a women's facility would be far less expensive to operate than a men's jail because women were seen as being less dangerous and the associated security costs would therefore be lower. In addition, the women's reformatory was expected to contribute in kind to the government coffers through the inmates' work activities (laundry and sewing, for example). Another cost saving associated with a women's reformatory would come in the form of staff wages. An all-female staff could be paid less than a staff of men, which was customary at the time (Strange, 1985).

It should be noted that ultimately the establishment of the Andrew Mercer Ontario Reformatory for Females was not based on any type of intense public pressure for reform but instead resulted from some effective lobbying by Langmuir. He was able to convince the provincial government to earmark $90,000 from the estate of Andrew Mercer to build the reformatory (Strange, 1985).

Today, provincial and territorial facilities across Canada house female offenders. For the most part, offenders in these institutions serve sentences of two years less a day, although some federally sentenced women, who serve longer sentences, are incarcerated in provincial facilities. Within the Canadian penal system, an agreement between a province or territory and the federal government that allows for the incarceration of provincial or territorial inmates in federal institutions or vice versa is known as an **exchange of service agreement (ESA)**. Since 1973, ESAs have been in place between federal corrections and some provincial corrections to enable federally sentenced women to serve their time closer to home (Correctional Service of Canada [CSC], 1990). For example, in Quebec, prior to the building of a regional federal facility in Joliette, the Tanguay Agreement allowed federally sentenced francophone women to remain in Quebec. The 1982 Tanguay Agreement marked the first time the Correctional Service of Canada purchased guaranteed accommodation from a province (at the approximate cost of a $1 million capital contribution for five years with an option to purchase an additional five years) (CSC, 1990). ESAs have also been in place between the CSC and various psychiatric institutions across Canada to meet the needs of offenders with specific mental health issues. For example, the Institut Philippe-Pinel provides federal offenders with psychiatric care if the offender is referred by a federal institution (CSC, 1990).

exchange of service agreement (ESA)
Within the Canadian penal system, an agreement between a province or territory and the federal government that allows for the incarceration of provincial or territorial inmates in federal institutions or vice versa.

Federal Corrections: The Early Years

Historically, the federal correctional system has been at a loss for how to deal with female offenders. With the passing of the *British North America Act* (the BNA Act) in 1867 and the creation of a federal dominion, the "establishment, maintenance, and management of penitentiaries" came under federal jurisdiction as outlined in section 91, item 28 (*Constitution Act, 1867*). Kingston Penitentiary and a number of existing penitentiaries in the Maritimes came under this new federal jurisdiction (*Constitution Act, 1867*, 1867; Hayman, 2006).

As is the case today, at the time of Confederation, Canada incarcerated significantly fewer female inmates than male inmates. The *First Annual Report of the Directors of Penitentiaries for the Year 1868* indicated 67 women incarcerated as of December 31,

1867: 3 women were incarcerated in the Halifax Penitentiary, 1 in Saint John, and 63 in Kingston Penitentiary (Canada, Directors of the Penitentiaries, 1870). Although 29 women were being held at the Rockwood Asylum on January 1, 1868, none appears to have been a "convict lunatic." According to the warden's report for Kingston Penitentiary, only 20 male "convict lunatics" housed at Rockwood were on the penitentiary's register (Canada, Directors of the Penitentiaries, 1870). Interestingly, at that time, proportionately about the same percent of women were incarcerated in the federal penitentiaries as they are today. At the end of 1867, women accounted for approximately 6.75 percent of federal incarcerates (that is 67 women versus 925 men) and in 2014/15 approximately 7 percent of all federally incarcerated persons in Canada were female (Reitano, 2016).

In the *First Annual Report of the Directors of Penitentiaries for the Year 1868*, the directors of the three federal penitentiaries in Kingston, Saint John, and Halifax and the Rockwood Lunatic Asylum in Kingston made brief mention of the women under their control (Canada, Directors of the Penitentiaries, 1870). The medical superintendent of the Rockwood Asylum, Dr. John R. Dickson, afforded more detail in his report to the analysis of expenditures for the year 1868 than to the state of its inhabitants (Canada, Directors of the Penitentiaries, 1870).

Similarly scarce reporting of the condition or state of women inmates was reported by the directors of the Halifax and Saint John penitentiaries. The matron at the Halifax Penitentiary, Mary McGregor, noted that she was "happy to report that everything, in connection with the female department of this institution, is going on quietly and satisfactorily" (Canada, Directors of the Penitentiaries, 1870, p. 47). McGregor also expressed her exuberance concerning the behaviour of the women incarcerated in the Halifax Penitentiary when she stated, "I am happy to say that none of the women have needed, or received, punishment" (Canada, Directors of the Penitentiaries, 1870, p. 47). The language of the day is indicative of the attitude held toward the rights—or lack thereof— of offenders incarcerated in Canada around the time of Confederation.

In comparison with the other directors who filed reports for 1868, the director of the Kingston Penitentiary wrote the most detailed account of the state of the women's conditions of incarceration. The author of the report, Director Donald MacDonell, devoted a separate one-page section, "Remarks on the State of the Female Prison," to the situation of the incarcerated women. He included comments on the cleanliness and neatness of the facility, which was located in the basement. Although he noted that the basement was "very extensive," he did report that "a proper and convenient prison, for the female convicts, is much required" (Canada, Directors of the Penitentiaries, 1870, p. 22). This statement can be interpreted as one of the earliest recommendations at a federal level for the need to establish a women's federal prison. The matron of the female prison at Kingston Penitentiary, Belinda Plees, provided more detail concerning the makeup of the female inmate population. She concluded that the slight increase in the number of incident reports that year was "due to there being two or three exceedingly bad and turbulent women, who take delight in disturbing the prison" (Canada, Directors of the Penitentiaries, 1870, p. 22).

Unfortunately, this kind of sentiment was echoed more than a century later, in 1994, when a National Board of Investigation reported on the April 22nd incident that had occurred at the Prison for Women (P4W) earlier that year. According to the Commission of Inquiry into Certain Events at the Prison for Women (also known as the Arbour inquiry), the Board of Investigation report was deficient from a factual point of view because it downplayed the inadequate correctional response to the incident by overemphasizing the dangerousness of the offenders involved. The "April 22nd incident," as it became known, and the commission of inquiry that followed will be discussed in further detail later in this chapter.

With respect to the *First Annual Report of the Directors of Penitentiaries for the Year 1868*, the comment that can perhaps best provide a glimpse of how women offenders were viewed in the latter half of the 19th century comes from the director of Kingston Penitentiary, Donald MacDonell:

> The poor creatures, who are sent here, are generally of the unfortunate classes and of the worst temperaments. They are, here, taught the usefulness of labor, and those, well disposed, are allowed to learn the working of the sewing machine, so that, on their release, they may be enabled to obtain a livelihood. (Canada, Directors of the Penitentiaries, 1870, p. 22)

By 1914, the women at Kingston Penitentiary were being housed in a building separate from the rest of the population of the penitentiary. In their report (known familiarly as the MacDonell report), the Royal Commission on Penitentiaries noted that although the women at Kingston Penitentiary were being kept in a "new and suitable" building, the establishment of a separate prison would be desirable in that "the interests of all concerned would be best served if these few inmates were transferred to an institution for women" (Canada, Royal Commission on Penitentiaries, 1914, p. 9). The MacDonell report also mentioned the possibility that arrangements could be established with the provinces for the custody of the federally incarcerated women.

A Separate Federal Prison for Women

In 1921, the *Report of the Committee Appointed by the Rt. Hon. C.J. Doherty, Minister of Justice, to Advise upon the Revision of the Penitentiary Regulations and the Amendment of the Penitentiary Act* recommended that section 63 of the *Penitentiary Act* be amended to include a provision for women to be incarcerated in facilities separate from men's institutions. The Biggar report, as it became known, noted that the *Penitentiary Act* as it was written did not allow for women to be housed in a separate penitentiary, but permitted them to be kept only in a separate ward of a men's penitentiary (Canada, Committee Appointed to Advise, 1921). The Biggar report also noted that "one of the recognized elements of imprisonment is the deprivation of the convict of opportunities for association with the opposite sex" and that housing men and women within the same penitentiary would bring "this deprivation constantly to the minds of both male and female convicts" (Canada, Committee Appointed to Advise, 1921, p. 19). For this reason, the committee recommended that section 63 of the *Penitentiary Act* be amended to allow the possibility for women to be incarcerated in a separate institution.

In 1921, the Nickle commission report was the first to specifically address the needs of federally incarcerated women (Canada, Commission on the State and Management of the Female Prison, 1921). In the report, Nickle described the accommodations and daily lives of the women incarcerated at the Kingston Penitentiary and commented on the behaviour of some women. One of the major concerns of the commission was that housing women within a male prison contributed to inappropriate behaviour that could be avoided if women were held in a separate locale. Nickle painted the picture of a hapless female, a victim of her own pathological biochemistry, unable to control her insatiable urges:

> Without doubt some of the women, more particularly at certain periods, are thrown into a violent state of sexual excitement by the mere sight of the men, more often by their being or working contiguously to the female quarters and my attention was called to one instance of this group of cases where a sedative had to be given to soothe desire. (Canada, Commission on the State and Management of the Female Prison, 1921, p. 3)

Concern was also voiced that by housing the women in a male facility, the women were being placed at risk and their vulnerabilities could be exploited by both male inmates and staff. In addition, it was noted that some male staff were fearful of accusations by the women, which could have dire consequences:

> As a matter of fact to-day the male staff, from the warden down, view with apprehension the administration of the Female Prison. While the disclosures of the past year have shown how unscrupulous officers have taken unfair advantage of opportunities for flirtations, improprieties and indecencies that presented themselves, yet it can be truthfully contradicted that many decent officers are fearful, knowing that a few designing and crafty women might ruin a well-earned reputation. (Canada, Commission on the State and Management of the Female Prison, 1921, p. 5)

As a result of the Nickle commission report, construction was begun on the new Prison for Women in Kingston, Ontario (Hayman, 2006).

The Prison for Women

Construction of the Prison for Women began in May 1925 and was completed in 1932. At that time, considerable rioting had taken place at Kingston Penitentiary, damaging an area that housed some male inmates (Hayman, 2006). As a result, some men were transferred temporarily to the new Prison for Women building in 1932 (Hayman, 2006). Finally, in January 1934, after the men had been removed, all the women who had been housed in Kingston Penitentiary were transferred to the newly built, separate prison (Canada, Royal Commission to Investigate the Penal System, 1938). Four years after the Prison for Women in Kingston opened its doors, a royal commission recommended that it be closed (Canada, Royal Commission to Investigate the Penal System, 1938).

Early Reports and Commissions on the Prison for Women (1938–1956)

The *Report of the Royal Commission to Investigate the Penal System of Canada*, chaired by Justice Joseph Archambault, included recommendations specific to female inmates in Canada (Canada, Royal Commission to Investigate the Penal System, 1938). The Archambault report highlighted the relatively small number of female inmates compared

The Prison for Women (P4W) in Kingston, Ontario.

with male inmates in the federal correctional system. The new women's prison was designed to hold a maximum of 100 inmates, but in the decade prior to the Archambault report, the average daily population of female federal offenders was approximately 37 inmates (Canada, Royal Commission to Investigate the Penal System, 1938). During that ten-year period (1928 to 1937), the highest population of female offenders (51 women) occurred in 1932, and the lowest population (26 women) was seen in 1936.

The Archambault report, in the chapter entitled "Women Prisoners," noted that women made up only 1 percent of all federal inmates (Canada, Royal Commission to Investigate the Penal System, 1938). Furthermore, the authors asserted that most women were "of the occasional or accidental offender class" and were "not a custodial problem" (p. 147). As such, the authors recommended the women could be as effectively housed in reformatories as they could in a penitentiary. According to the Archambault report:

> There is no justification for the erection and maintenance of a costly penitentiary for women alone, nor is it desirable that they should be confined, either in the same institution as men, or in one central institution far from their place of residence and their friends and relations. (Canada, Royal Commission to Investigate the Penal System, 1938, p. 148)

According to the Archambault commission's conclusions and recommendations, the authors clearly did not perceive a need to build a separate women's prison in Kingston, Ontario. The commission report stressed the pecuniary savings from no longer incurring the operating expenses associated with the Prison for Women or having to transport women from the eastern and western provinces to Kingston. The commission recommended the Prison for Women be closed and arrangements be made with provincial authorities to provide custody for those federally sentenced women (Canada, Royal Commission to Investigate the Penal System, 1938). In 1947, the Gibson report echoed this sentiment with recommendations that the Prison for Women be converted from a women's institution to a male facility for classification and segregation of offenders (Canada, Department of Justice, 1947).

Most reports written on P4W recommended that it be closed and other arrangements made to meet the needs of women sentenced to federal terms of incarceration. One of the few reports that did not recommend the closure of P4W was the Fauteux report of 1956, which acknowledged that the geographic isolation of women from the east and west coasts was unfortunate and the consequent lack of support from family and friends in their home communities was also undesirable. However, the authors of the Fauteux report concluded that the existence of one central institution for women was preferable for treatment delivery. Because of their small numbers, keeping the women in one facility would allow for economical service delivery that could take the form of an intensified treatment program (Canada, Committee Appointed to Inquire, 1956). This sentiment was not echoed in future reports.

Reports and Commissions Recommending the Closure of the Prison for Women (1968–1996)

In 1968, the Canadian Corrections Association published its "Brief on the Woman Offender," a report prepared for the Royal Commission on the Status of Women, which addressed three key items specific to women offenders. The first item dealt with the criminal acts most often committed by women. The second focus was the problems experienced by women in conflict with the law at various stages of the justice process. The final concern was the detention facilities that existed for women. The authors of the brief sought recommendations specific to the needs of women in conflict with the law. Of particular interest was their recommendation that staff working with women receive training specific to working with women in prison. Additionally, the authors recommended that women's prisons be designed with the special needs of women of- fenders in mind and a variety of women's prisons be built to accommodate different kinds of female offenders. According to the brief, "prisons for women should not be patterned on male institutions but rather be planned on the basis of the special needs of women" (Canadian Criminology and Corrections Association, 1968, p. 42).

In 1969, the report of the Canadian Committee on Corrections (also known as the Ouimet report) identified a host of problems associated with having most federal female offenders serving their sentences at one prison. At the time of the Ouimet report, some women from the West (described as being drug addicted) had been incarcerated at Matsqui Institution in British Columbia. However, women from the rest of Canada were being sent to the Kingston Prison for Women. The Ouimet report identified issues related to geographic separation, lack of French-language programming, and the incar- ceration in one facility of women who differed with respect to "age, degree of criminal sophistication and emotional stability" (Canadian Committee on Corrections, 1969, p. 400). The report's recommendations specific to women offenders included the sug- gestion that the federal government consider purchasing the services of provincial government facilities in the larger provinces and the establishment of regional services that could serve the needs of both the federal and provincial regional governments. Clearly, the continued use of one central federal prison in Kingston was not fully sup- ported by the report. An additional recommendation in the Ouimet report was that the federal government "appoint a suitably qualified woman to a position of senior respon- sibility and leadership in relation to correctional treatment of the woman offender in Canada" (Canadian Committee on Corrections, 1969, p. 403). Interestingly, the establish- ment of the position Deputy Commissioner for Women did not occur until recommended by the Arbour inquiry (Canada, Commission of Inquiry, 1996), after which Nancy Stableforth, in 1996, became the first person to hold this position (CSC, 2008).

In 1974, seven individuals were appointed to the National Advisory Committee on the Female Offender; in 1977, they produced a report on their findings (known as the Clark report). The committee, which included representatives from stakeholder groups, such as the Elizabeth Fry Society and the National Parole Board, was tasked to:

> study the needs of federal female offenders and to make specific recommendations to the Commissioner of Penitentiaries and the Executive Director of the National Parole Service regarding the development of a comprehensive plan to provide adequate institutional and community services appropriate to her unique program and security needs. (Canada, National Advisory Committee on the Female Offender, 1977, p. 9)

The committee members chose not to limit themselves to only *federal* female offenders but also concerned themselves with the realities faced by *all* female offenders in Canada. At the time the Clark report was written, women comprised just less than 2 percent of all federal incarcerates in Canada. The percentage of provincially incarcerated women was higher, at about 7 percent (Canada, National Advisory Committee on the Female

Offender, 1977). Not unlike the previous reports, the National Advisory Committee recommended that the Prison for Women be closed. The committee members even went so far as to state their opinion that P4W should be closed "within three years from publication of this report" (Canada, National Advisory Committee on the Female Offender, 1977, p. 30). Clearly this did not happen.

The National Advisory Committee identified many of the same concerns regarding the Prison for Women that had been identified in previous reports: women were housed too far from their homes, release planning was problematic, the physical building was unsuitable, the needs of French-speaking women were not being met, and protection was inadequate for those who were viewed as being "less criminally sophisticated" than other inhabitants of the prison (Canada, National Advisory Committee on the Female Offender, 1977, p. 19). The Clark report outlined two approaches that could be followed to "decentralize" the incarceration of federally sentenced women. The first plan was similar to the one proposed by the Ouimet report (Canadian Committee on Corrections, 1969) in which the federal government would remain jurisdictionally responsible for the women who had been sentenced to federal time, but women who did not require a high-security setting could be incarcerated in provincial institutions through the purchase of services from provincial facilities. This plan also recommended the establishment of regional secure facilities for women who required a more secure setting. Conversely, provincial governments could purchase services from the federal government for those provincially sentenced women who required a more secure facility. The second plan involved the provincial governments assuming responsibility for all women incarcerated in their respective areas, irrespective of the length of incarceration. The National Advisory Committee Report (Canada, National Advisory Committee on the Female Offender, 1977) outlined the pros and cons associated with both plans. Of particular note, yet again, a report was recommending the closure of the Prison for Women, a step that would not occur for decades.

The Clark report was evaluated by the Advisory Council on the Status of Women in the fall of 1977 (Rosen, 1977). In this evaluation, the Clark report was criticized for taking a "soft-line approach" and not presenting much original content (Rosen, 1977, p. 41). According to Rosen, the Clark report did "more harm than good" because by recommending the closure of P4W, the future of the facility remained uncertain, making it more difficult to attract both new staff and the funding needed for capital projects (p. 42). As a result of the recommendation to close, the prison would, in effect, be placed in a state of inertia with respect to future development (Rosen, 1977).

That same year, a report to Parliament was made by the Subcommittee on the Penitentiary System in Canada (Canada, Subcommittee on the Penitentiary System in Canada, 1977). In the report's section on female inmates, the authors noted that female inmates experienced "outright discrimination" in the lack of "recreation, programs, basic facilities and space" available to them (p. 134). The authors further pointed out that from their examination of the kinds of offences most often committed by women and women's institutional behaviour, women clearly did not need to be incarcerated in what amounted to an "1835-style of maximum security institution" (p. 134). It is in this report that we find the much referenced description of the Prison for Women as "unfit for bears, much less women" (p. 135). The report to Parliament summed up the Prison for Women in Kingston as being "obsolete in every respect—in design, in programs and in the handling of the people sent there" (p. 135).

In 1978, a joint committee was struck to study the various alternatives for housing women who had been sentenced to federal time (Canada, Joint Committee to Study Alternatives, 1978). The committee consisted of representatives from the Elizabeth Fry Society, both federal and provincial corrections, and the Prison for Women Citizen's Advisory Committee. The joint committee considered options identified in previous reports and options they saw as potentially feasible. Interestingly, the joint committee was in favour of at least one secure, centrally located facility for women. Although the committee referenced the importance of maximizing exchange of service agreements with provincial corrections and making optimal use of community-based facilities, the support for continuing to have a central facility was counter to the recommendations of previous reports (the Archambault, Ouimet, and Clark reports, for example).

In 1978, the Needham report further evaluated the plans that had been proposed in the Clark report (Canada, National Planning Committee, 1978). The Clark report's plan 2 (the provincial takeover of federally incarcerated women) was not supported by Needham because of the lack of unanimity from the provinces (Canada, National Planning Committee, 1978). If one province did not agree with being responsible for housing federally sentenced women, then the plan could not work. The Clark report's plan 1 involved building regional facilities for those women who required a secure setting and transferring (to provincial facilities) those women who did not require a secure setting. However, the recommendations of the Needham report included the need for, at minimum, one regional facility in the East and one in the West. In addition, an emphasis was placed on using community-based residences for the women (Canada, National Planning Committee, 1978). Although the Needham report did support regionalization, it did not comment on the feasibility of establishing secure facilities in all regions across Canada. The authors of the report clearly stated that evaluation of financial considerations needed further study. As in previous reports, and echoed in the Needham report, was the recommendation that P4W be closed (Canada, National Planning Committee, 1978).

Creating Choices

The mandate of the Task Force on Federally Sentenced Women (TFFSW) was to assess the correctional management of women sentenced to federal prison in Canada, from the beginning of their sentences to the date of their warrants' expiry. Included in the mandate was the need to develop a strategic plan to guide and direct this process while respecting the needs specific to this group of women (Canada, Task Force on Federally Sentenced Women [TFFSW], 1990). In an innovative fashion, the TFFSW was actually co-chaired by the Correctional Service of Canada (CSC) and the Canadian Association of Elizabeth Fry Societies, who took a women-centred approach to their work. The members of the TFFSW were thus able to gain considerable insight because the experience of women was valued throughout the process of the investigation.

As was the case in numerous previous reports, the TFFSW, in its report *Creating Choices*, found that the needs of federally sentenced women were not being met. The report noted that the building itself was inadequate, the women were being incarcerated in an over-secure setting, the available programming was poor, the women were geographically isolated from their families, and the needs of francophone and Indigenous women were not being met (Canada, TFFSW, 1990). The TFFSW recommended the Kingston Prison for Women be closed and the women be moved to five regional facilities to be operated across Canada by the Correctional Service of Canada. In addition,

healing lodge
A facility designed to meet the needs of Indigenous offenders by offering services and programs that reflect Indigenous culture, beliefs, and traditions.

the report recommended a **healing lodge** be built in the Prairies to meet the unique needs of Indigenous women who were sentenced federally, by offering services and programs that reflect Indigenous culture, beliefs, and traditions.

Five principles were emphasized to guide the CSC in implementing change: empowerment, meaningful and responsible choices, respect and dignity, supportive environment, and shared responsibility (Canada, TFFSW, 1990). Hannah-Moffat (2001) was critical of the manner in which the "CSC's cooption of the feminist politics of difference and empowerment" occurred in relation to the implementation of the TFFSW report (p. 161).[1] By embracing these five principles, the CSC hoped to move closer to what had been described as a community-based ideal able to recognize the importance of, and be sensitive to, the diversity in Canadian communities. The Arbour inquiry (Canada, Commission of Inquiry, 1996) noted that on the heels of *Creating Choices* (Canada, TFFSW, 1990), and while the plans for the new regional facilities (including the hiring of staff) were under way, the CSC, and particularly the Prison for Women, came under public scrutiny for the regressive manner with which some women were treated as a result of what was to become known as the April 22nd incident.

The April 22nd Incident at the Prison for Women

In the early evening of April 22, 1994, an incident occurred outside the hospital area at the Prison for Women while some of the B range inmates were waiting for their medication. This area was controlled by four correctional officers. According to official accounts, two inmates approached the barrier, and one demanded her medication in an aggressive and loud manner. After what appeared to be a signal from one of the inmates, the group of six inmates jumped the officers. Threatening statements were reportedly made by inmates toward the correctional staff: "Give me the scissors so I can stick her" and "Grab the telephone cord. We'll string the bitch up, right here" (Canada, Commission of Inquiry, 1996, p. 33). The incident lasted only a few minutes.

segregation unit
An area of a prison where inmates are kept separate from the rest of the prison population.

As part of the correctional response to control the situation, a number of the inmates were maced by the correctional supervisor. All inmates involved were placed in the **segregation unit,** an area of the prison where inmates are kept separate from the rest of the prison population. Five of the six inmates eventually plead guilty to various charges, including attempted prison breach, assault, threat to cause bodily harm, and possession of a weapon for a purpose dangerous to the public peace. The correctional officers directly involved in the incident were negatively affected in a variety of ways. One officer was off work for a year and eventually left P4W. Another was off for three months and later left the prison. One did return to work immediately following the incident, but transferred to another institution when it became too difficult to continue working at P4W. A fourth officer attempted to return to work, but could not. She eventually left the Correctional Service of Canada. Interestingly, this officer had a bachelor's degree in criminology and women's studies, had previous correctional work experience, and had sought out employment with the Correctional Service of Canada so that she could work at P4W (Canada, Commission of Inquiry, 1996). Additional officers and staff and inmates who were not directly involved in the incident were also negatively affected by a heightened sense of fear and distrust that was a direct result of the unpredictable nature of the incident.

Over the course of four days (April 22 to April 26) in the segregation unit, times of unrest were interspersed between periods of calm. The inmates were reportedly verbally abusive to staff, and their instances of "acting out" included the throwing of such items as food, water, juice, and urine. The unrest in the segregation unit was not limited to the women who had been directly involved in the incident. Inmates already in segregation also engaged in problematic behaviour, and inmates not directly involved in the incident were reportedly involved in a slashing, a suicide attempt, and an attempted hostage taking (Canada, Commission of Inquiry, 1996).

On the evening of April 26, Mary Cassidy, the warden of P4W, called in a male Institutional Emergency Response Team (IERT) from Kingston Penitentiary to perform cell extractions in the segregation unit. The warden wanted the women to be "restrained, stripped, gowned, the cells stripped and the women returned to their cells" (Canada, Commission of Inquiry, 1996, p. 74). The IERT entered the segregation area and proceeded to remove the women from the cells. The procedure was videotaped by a member of the IERT (see Box 1.1).

BOX 1.1

Cell Extraction by the Institutional Emergency Response Team

The following is a description from the Arbour inquiry (Canada, Commission of Inquiry, 1996) of the all-male Institutional Emergency Response Team performing the first cell extraction in the segregation unit at the Prison for Women:

> Prior to the video being turned on, the IERT marched into the Segregation Unit in standard formation, approached Joey Twins' cell and banged on the bars of her cell with the shield. She immediately did as she was ordered, and when the video begins she is lying face down in her cell surrounded by IERT members who are holding her down. An officer now identified as a female member of the Prison for Women staff, cuts off Ms. Twins' clothing … while IERT members hold her down … Ms. Twins' hands are cuffed behind her back and her legs shackled. She is marched backwards out of her cell naked, and led to the corner of the range. There she is held against the wall with the clear plastic shield, with her back against the wall … Some IERT members stand around her while the IPSO [institutional preventive security officer], Mr. Waller, and maintenance men from

> the prison enter the Segregation Unit to begin stripping Ms. Twins' cell. The corner where Ms. Twins is standing is visible to anyone in the unit or standing in the doorway … While she is still being held in the corner, a paper gown is brought to Ms. Twins and tied around her neck. The effect is something like that of a bib. The paper gown neither covers her, nor provides warmth. Upon her return to the cell, an IERT member begins the extremely lengthy process of attempting to apply a body belt in substitution of her handcuffs, during which procedure her gown comes off. A body belt is a form of restraint equipment which, as the name implies, consists of a locked chain around the inmate's waist to which are attached locked cuffs attaching wrists to the locked belt, more or less at the side of the body … Finally, this lengthy procedure is completed and she is left lying on the floor of her cell in restraints (body belt and leg irons) and with a small paper gown.

Source: Canada, Commission of Inquiry into Certain Events at the Prison for Women in Kingston. (1996). *Commission of inquiry into certain events at the Prison for Women in Kingston* (the Arbour inquiry). Ottawa: Public Works and Government Services of Canada, p. 76. Used with permission.

▶ WHAT DO YOU THINK?

What do you think about the cell extraction at P4W in 1994? Do you think the inmates' rights were violated? If so, in what way were they violated?

Link to Arbour report: www.caefs.ca/wp-content/uploads/2013/05/Arbour_Report.pdf

Brief clip of a cell extraction from the 1994 incident at P4W: https://www.youtube.com/watch?v=Uz5l2AdUYa8

On April 27, most of the women consented to a body cavity search. It was their understanding that after giving their consent for this intrusive procedure, they would receive a cigarette and a shower. As Madame Justice Arbour noted, "the absence of a culture respectful of individual rights is perhaps nowhere more disturbing than on this issue" (Canada, Commission of Inquiry, 1996, p. 96).

The days following the cell extractions have been described as a time during which the women in the segregation unit were being denied so-called privileges that many of us would consider necessities. The women went without wearing anything but a paper gown until halfway through the day on April 27. They were without mattresses until May 10. They were not given the opportunity to shower regularly, their phone calls were restricted, and their initial requests for reading and writing materials were denied (Canada, Commission of Inquiry, 1996). The confinement of the women in segregation continued for many months (between seven-and-a-half and nine months). During this period, some women were transferred to the Regional Treatment Centre in the Kingston Penitentiary. Two of the women who had been transferred launched **habeas corpus**[2] applications, requesting an order by a judge instructing the detaining authority (usually the police) to produce the detainee in a court of law so that the judge can determine whether the individual is being lawfully detained or should be set free. Eventually all of the women were returned to the Prison for Women (Canada, Commission of Inquiry, 1996).

If it were not for the airing of sections of the IERT videotape on CBC's *the fifth estate* on February 21, 1995, the Canadian public likely would not have heard about the April 22nd incident and its aftermath to the extent that it did. Interestingly, the Solicitor General of Canada announced the call for an independent inquiry into the matter on the same day that *the fifth estate* aired its program, after he tabled the special report from the correctional investigator in the House of Commons. The commission of inquiry was appointed on April 10, 1995, by the governor general in council.

habeas corpus
An order by a judge instructing a detaining authority (usually the police) to produce the detainee in a court of law so that the judge can determine whether the individual is being lawfully detained or should be set free.

Commission of Inquiry into Certain Events at the Prison for Women in Kingston (the Arbour Inquiry)

Late in the spring of 1995, a commission of inquiry (the Arbour inquiry) was undertaken to investigate not the details of the incident that occurred outside the hospital on the evening on April 22 but the correctional response to that incident during the days, weeks, and months that followed.

Eight groups were granted standing for the first phase of the commission of inquiry[3] and more than 100 people were interviewed by the staff of investigators. During the second phase of the inquiry, round-table discussions were held on topics of particular importance to federally sentenced women, such as cross-gender staffing, Indigenous federally sentenced women, managing violence, and programming and treatment needs. Prior to the round-table discussions, various women's prisons were visited, and policy consultations were carried out with established academics and researchers who specialized in the area of women's imprisonment (Canada, Commission of Inquiry, 1996).

The Arbour inquiry report was clear in its criticism of the Correctional Service of Canada, which was described as adhering to a "deplorable defensive culture" (Canada, Commission of Inquiry, 1996, p. 176). The CSC approach was "to deny error, defend against criticism, and to react without a proper investigation of the truth" (p. 175). In conclusion, the commission of inquiry found a "disturbing lack of commitment to the ideals of justice on the part of the Correctional Service" and the need for increased judicial supervision with respect to how the CSC managed segregation and the grievance process (p. 197). In an overall sense, the Arbour inquiry report can be viewed as critical in the history of women's corrections. It serves as a scathing reminder of the injustices that are possible and of the importance for all of those employed in the criminal justice system to follow the rule of law when carrying out their duties.

► WHAT DO YOU THINK?

Why do you think it took so long to close the Prison for Women? What influence, if any, do you think the airing of the cell extractions on the fifth estate had on the closure? Can you think of any arguments in favour or against establishing one central maximum security institution for women, while maintaining regional facilities for minimum and medium security women?

Regional Facilities

As a result of the Arbour inquiry's strong criticism of the CSC for some of its operations that did not respect the rule of law (Canada, Commission of Inquiry, 1996), the CSC mission statement was amended to include the rule of law:

> The Correctional Service of Canada (CSC), as part of the criminal justice system and respecting the rule of law, contributes to public safety by actively encouraging and assisting offenders to become law-abiding citizens, while exercising reasonable, safe, secure and humane control. (CSC, 2012, ¶ 1)

By the early to mid-1990s, planning was under way to build the regional facilities and the healing lodge. The final locations of the regional facilities differed from the original recommendations of the TFFSW working group (Hayman, 2006). The new regional facilities[4] eventually included Grand Valley Institution for Women in Kitchener, Ontario; Nova Institution for Women in Truro, Nova Scotia; Joliette Institution in Joliette, Quebec; Edmonton Institution for Women in Edmonton, Alberta; and the Okimaw Ohci Healing Lodge in Maple Creek, Saskatchewan.

All the new regional facilities included cottage-style accommodations for the women, where each woman could have her own room. Communal kitchens, laundry areas, bathrooms, living rooms, and dining rooms were included in the plans for the cottages. The idea was to make the new prisons seem closer to the norms of community living (Hayman, 2006). An important feature of the new regional facilities was no permanent guard post in the living units. The guards, now called primary workers, patrolled the living units periodically throughout their shifts. Now, however, all multi-level facilities that accommodate maximum security offenders have a secure unit that does not operate like the cottages and has security personnel present at all times.

Federally sentenced women from the west coast of Canada were able to remain in British Columbia under an exchange of service agreement between the CSC and the province of British Columbia. The women were able to serve their sentences at the provincially run facility for women, the Burnaby Correctional Centre for Women (BCCW). Early in 2002, the BCCW was planned for closure, and the federal government was forced to investigate alternative locations to incarcerate federally sentenced women in British Columbia (CSC, 2013). The government decided to redesign the Sumas Community Correctional Centre and rename it the Fraser Valley Institution (FVI). Like other federal facilities for women, FVI consists of cottage-style living units and a secure unit for women classified as requiring maximum security needs.

Institutional profiles for the federally sentenced women's facilities across Canada are available on the website for the Correctional Service of Canada (2013). According to the website, all facilities, with the exception of the healing lodge, are considered multi-level facilities that accommodate women classified as minimum, medium, or maximum security offenders. The Okimaw Ohci Healing Lodge (OOHL) is classified as a minimum/medium security facility with a capacity of 44 beds. The Buffalo Sage Wellness House in Edmonton houses women classified as minimum security. See Table 1.3 for statistics of the inmate populations and a brief overview of these facilities.

static security
The reliance on physical security measures (cameras, fencing, and alarms, for example) to control the inmate population of a prison.

The *Creating Choices* report was vague regarding how the principles of change could actually be implemented in the new regional facilities (Hayden, 2006). The report stressed the need for "dynamic" security, as opposed to **"static" security**. That is, the preferable mode of security should not rely on physical security features (cameras, fences, alarms, for example) to control the inmate population of a prison, but instead

Table 1.3   Comparison of Canadian Facilities for Federally Sentenced Women

Institution	Year opened	Average Count (Jan.–July 2016)* by Security Level of Housing			Population Average Count Jan.–July, 2016*	Maximum capacity[†]
		Minimum	Minimum or Medium	Maximum		
Fraser Valley Institution	2004	13	60	10	83	112
Edmonton Institution for Women	1995	35	103	20	158	167
Okimaw Ohci Healing Lodge	1995	–	47	–	47	44
Grand Valley Institution for Women	1997	35	139	15	189	171
Joliette Institution for Women	1997	–	100	13	113	115
Nova Institution for Women	1995	8	54	10	72	81
Buffalo Sage Wellness House	2011	15	–	–	15	16[‡]
Regional Psychiatric Centre (Prairies)	1978	–	–	–	15	204[§]
TOTAL		106	503	68	692	690

*Source: Data obtained through an *Access to Information Act* request by D.S. Tavcer (July 20, 2016). Note that it was not possible in all cases to determine separate counts for minimum and medium security inmates. If the maximum capacity estimates on the CSC website are correct, then one can assume that most of the institutions are near maximum capacity.

[†]Source: Correctional Service of Canada. (2013). Institutional profiles. Retrieved from www.csc-scc.gc.ca/institutions/index-eng.shtml.

[‡]Source: Correctional Service of Canada. (2016). Correctional Service Canada healing lodges. Retrieved from www.csc-scc.gc.ca/aboriginal/002003-2000-eng.shtml.

[§] Note: RPC houses males and females. Capacity not included in total as number of women's beds unknown.

should be more interactive and driven through the relationships established between staff and the incarcerated women. The *Creating Choices* report also noted a discernible tendency to avoid acknowledging that women could be violent. Although the report suggested that approximately 5 percent of women might need a more secure setting, the report was not forthright in suggesting how a more secure setting could be implemented. The authors of the *Creating Choices* report characterized the majority of federal female offenders as "high needs" in terms of the interventions they would require and "low risk" in terms of their security status.

The CSC sought to address some of the recommendations of the *Creating Choices* report though various interventions, including those considered core programs. The primary thrust of these programs is usually for offenders to address their perceived inadequacies through the acquisition of a skill set. The treatment or intervention is more often than not cognitive-behavioural in nature. In this way, the woman is seen to be making "responsible choices" in an effort to take part in her own rehabilitation.

The various strategies employed by the CSC in the treatment of women offenders have been subjected to numerous criticisms (Hannah-Moffat & Shaw, 2000; Maidment, 2006; Pollack & Kendall, 2005). Others have pointed out that although the 2004 Program Strategy for Women Offenders clings to the notion of the voluntary aspect of the interventions and the need for informed consent, in reality, neither is likely (Hayman, 2006). A core program is identified as an area that a woman "should" address while incarcerated, even if she does not agree. In practice, an incarcerated woman is faced with only the appearance of choice. She can choose not to participate in a core program that has been included (possibly against her wishes) in her correctional plan; however, the parole board might take great interest in her decision not to participate and interpret the woman's rejection negatively.

Some have pointed out how the TFFSW report effectively "glossed over the difficult issues" (Hayman, 2006, p. 241). The language used in the *Creating Choices* report was such that the fact that they were actually talking about imprisonment was almost lost to the rhetoric (Hayman, 2006). By focusing on the language of victimization, the TFFSW essentially constructed an "image of the homogeneous federally sentenced woman" (Hayman, 2006, p. 241). As such, the federally incarcerated female became "idealized" so that all future plans, as put forth in *Creating Choices*, would "fit" this idealized fiction. For this reason, the new regional facilities were destined to be designed to accommodate the low-risk offender, in a cottage-style environment where correctional staff patrolled the living units, but were not stationed there. As Hayman (2006) pointed out, the approach taken by the TFFSW "inadvertently set federally sentenced women up for failure once they transferred to the new prisons" (p. 242). Because the women were diverse and did not fit the ideal image set up for them in the *Creating Choices* report, they, not surprisingly, did not fit into the new prisons.

Both the Edmonton and Nova institutions experienced incidents soon after they were opened; in both cases, the finger of blame was squarely pointed at the inmates. Hayman (2006) questioned this blame because to appreciate the reactions of the women to the new institutions, one must fully understand how the language used in the TFFSW report failed to identify the women as "prisoners," which had an effect on the women. Hayman (2006) contended that it was this "linguistic obfuscation" that "obscured the reality of their situation" (p. 242). In addition, Hayman holds the CSC to blame because the authorities allowed the Edmonton prison to be opened prior to its physical completion and transferred a disproportionately large number of maximum security women to an enhanced unit that could not adequately house them.

Crime Statistics and Women Offenders

Each summer, the Canadian Centre for Justice Statistics publishes Canadian crime statistics for the previous year. In 2014, the national crime rate decreased by 3 percent from the previous year, dropping to its lowest rate since 1969 (Statistics Canada, 2015). Although the crime rate has been in decline since the early 1990s, the Canadian criminal justice system continues to grow: in 2009, federal expenditures for the protection of persons and property topped $28 billion (Statistics Canada, 2011).

Women make up a very small percentage of those who come into conflict with the law. When considering the population of federal offenders in Canada, approximately 7 percent are female (Reitano, 2016). Prior to 1997, estimates ranged between 2 and 3 percent (Statistics Canada, 2007a). Interestingly, the jump in the percentage of women's admissions seems to have coincided with the opening of the regional facilities for women. Some may speculate that the increase in federal sentences for women (as a proportion of all those sentenced to federal time) may be reflective of judges' perceptions that the new regional facilities for women offered improved rehabilitative services from what had been available at the Prison for Women. Thus, when judges had the option for either a federal or a provincial (or territorial) sentence, they may have leaned toward a federal sentence.

Similar to the statistics for federally sentenced women, relatively few women have been sentenced provincially or territorially compared with their male counterparts. About 15 percent of overall admissions to provincial/territorial corrections are women (Reitano, 2016). The percentage of women being sentenced provincially has been increasing since 1978 (when data were first available), from approximately 5 percent in 1978 to 15 percent in 2015 (Reitano, 2016; Statistics Canada, 2007b). Although the data have not always shown linear growth year to year, the overall trend shows a steady increase in the percentage of women incarcerated provincially and territorially. The most recent statistics for 2015 indicate that 20 percent of those under community supervision were women, 11 percent of those in provincial and territorial custody were women, and 13 percent of those on remand[5] were women (Reitano, 2016).

As will be discussed in Chapter 2, crime is predominantly a male endeavour. The statistics on those who attend Canada's adult courts can yield information regarding the kinds of offences that women are accused of committing. About a third (32 percent) of women who appear before the courts in Canada are there for property offences, just under a quarter (22 percent) are there for crimes against the person, and one fifth (20 percent) are there to face charges related to the administration of justice (Hotten Mahoney, 2011).

Women as Offenders

In Part II of this text you will be introduced to the case of Renée Acoby, one of just a handful of women ever to have been declared a dangerous offender. In the chapters that follow you will read about Canadian female offenders and learn more about their backgrounds, and the factors that may have contributed to their criminalization. In addition, a separate chapter on female youth will focus on the nature and extent of youth offending, a history of how young female offenders have been treated by the justice system, and the challenges that are unique to youth offenders. In Chapter 5 on violent women offenders, you will learn what the latest research tells us about women who commit violent crimes like homicide and sexual assault. This section will conclude with an analysis of correctional assessment and treatment approaches, and the focus toward community reintegration.

Women as Victims

A case study of Ashley Smith, who tragically died while incarcerated at Grand Valley Institution for Women, begins Part III of the book. As you will see in the chapters that comprise this part, criminalized women in Canada represent some of the most marginalized members of our society. Incarcerated women experience much higher rates of mental disorder than are found in the general population. A high proportion of these women experienced abuse as children and adults, and have been victims of violence. Many share extensive histories of alcohol and substance abuse, limited education, and few marketable employment skills. For visible minority women (including Indigenous women) who are criminalized, their experiences of racism are often compounded with the classism and sexism faced by most women who have come in conflict with the law. After reading Chapter 9 you should have a better understanding of the legacy that colonialism has had on generations of Indigenous people, and how this has likely contributed to the overrepresentation of Indigenous women in Canadian jails and prisons today. The chapter on prostitution and murdered and missing women of Canada should also generate some questions in your mind as to how and why Canadian society has been so slow to react to this very real crisis.

Women as Workers

As you will see in the final section of the textbook, women are employed in all aspects of the criminal justice system. More women are police officers today than at any previous point in history. The number of women entering law schools equals or in some cases even exceeds the number of men. Women are employed in jobs in probation and parole, provincial/territorial corrections, and federal corrections. Some women have risen to positions of leadership and power within these various organizations, are involved in high-level policy decision-making, and will undoubtedly contribute to shaping the future of the criminal justice system in Canada. However, while progress has been made, it is important to remember that women's representation in the different fields is by no means equivalent to that of males. While women, as a group, have made great strides in policing, the courts, and corrections, many hurdles still exist to their receiving the same opportunities to excel as men do. In Part IV of the text you will read about how beliefs about gender roles and various job models interact to slot women into the "less important" jobs in an organization based on misguided stereotypes about what women's commitment to their jobs entail. You will learn why more women than men leave the law profession, and how women's career development and career paths in the legal fields differ from those of men, with fewer women lawyers achieving the partnership rank, working in more marginal positions, or working in the public sector. After reading these final chapters you will be well acquainted with the stereotypes and "role traps" that face women who work in the field of corrections and how women face higher levels of work–home conflict. While women have come a long way since first being permitted to attend law school, don a police uniform, or carry a skeleton key, there are still organizational barriers in the field and sexist attitudes among those working in the criminal justice system that must be overcome if women are ever to truly attain parity with men in this domain.

SUMMARY

The Canadian criminal justice system consists of three broad agencies: the police, the courts, and the correctional system. A person who comes into conflict with the law will likely interact with individuals from each of these interconnected bodies. Historically, criminalized women (and men for that matter) have not always been treated with respect by the justice system in Canada. The early history of corrections in Canada is replete with examples of abuses endured by those deemed to be criminal. The plight of criminalized women in Canada has been compounded by the tendency of correctional services (both federal and provincial) to treat women as an afterthought. Not until recently have attention and resources been directed toward correctional services for women.

Over the years, the majority of commissions studying the state of women's corrections have recommended the closure of Canada's infamous P4W. The closing of P4W and the completion of the regional facilities for women (as suggested in *Creating Choices*) was no doubt hastened by the scathing condemnations of the CSC made in the Arbour inquiry report. Although the new prisons may be aesthetically more pleasing than P4W, they are not without their critics (Hannah-Moffat & Shaw, 2000; Hayman, 2006; Pollack & Kendall, 2005).

Part I of the text will serve as an overview of the Canadian criminal justice system. In Part II the reader will be introduced to Canadian female offenders, including youth and violent offenders. As a group, women offenders tend to compose one of the most marginalized groups in society. An examination of correctional assessment and treatment will provide the reader with an appreciation of the challenges that exist in achieving community reintegration of women offenders. Victimization and the criminalization of women will be the focus of Part III, including chapters that delve into women and children as victims of crime, mental health, Indigenous women, and prostitution and murdered and missing women in Canada. The final section of the text tackles topics related to women's employment in the criminal justice system. Chapters in Part IV focus on women in policing, the courts, and the correctional systems. Upon finishing the text, the reader will be left with an appreciation of how women's experiences in the Canadian criminal justice context are unique and worth examining.

NOTES

1. For a comprehensive history of women's penal governance in Canada, see *Punishment in Disguise: Penal Governance and Federal Imprisonment of Women in Canada* (Hannah-Moffat, 2001).
2. "The writ of *habeas corpus* is available to any subject detained or imprisoned, not to hear and determine the case upon the evidence, but to immediately and in a summary way test

the validity of his detention or imprisonment" (Dukelow, 2002, p. 195). The rules pertaining to said applications can be found in the *Criminal Code* of Canada.

3. (1) The Canadian Association of Elizabeth Fry Societies; (2) the Citizens' Advisory Committee; (3) the correctional investigator; (4) the Correctional Service of Canada and the commissioner of corrections; (5) some members of the IERT; (6) the Inmate Committee; (7) some of the inmates involved in the incidents; and (8) the Public Service Alliance of Canada and the Union of Solicitor General Employees.

4. In March 2004, the Fraser Valley Institution for Women became the sixth regional federal institution for women to be opened in Canada.

5. Being on remand refers to being held in detention while awaiting an appearance in court.

DISCUSSION QUESTIONS

1. Outline the three broad agencies in the criminal justice system in Canada. What is the function of each, and how do they relate to one another?

2. What are the advantages of having a number of regional federal correctional institutions for women? What are the disadvantages? Are there any advantages to having just one federal correctional facility for women in Canada?

3. Why do you think so few women, relative to men, are convicted of committing crimes in Canada?

ADDITIONAL RESOURCES

Videos and Films

Dale, H., & Cole, J. (1981). *P4W* [Documentary]. Canada: Spectrum Films.

Fifth estate. Video File (Nov. 26, 2010). *Interview: Renee Acoby*. Retrieved from www.cbc.ca/fifth/blog/interview-renee-acoby.

Prouty, D. (1996). *First Nation Blue* (documentary). Canada: NFB.

Websites

Canadian Association of Elizabeth Fry Societies: www.caefs.ca

Correctional Service of Canada: www.csc-scc.gc.ca

Canada, Department of Justice: www.justice.gc.ca

REFERENCES

Canada, Commission Appointed to Inquire into and Report upon the Conduct, Economy, Discipline, and Management of the Provincial Penitentiary. (1849). *First report of the commissioners appointed to inquire into and report upon the conduct, economy, discipline, and management of the provincial penitentiary* (the Brown commission report). Montreal: Rollo Campbell.

Canada, Commission of Inquiry into Certain Events at the Prison for Women in Kingston. (1996). *Commission of Inquiry into Certain Events at the Prison for Women in Kingston* (the Arbour inquiry). Ottawa: Public Works and Government Services Canada.

Canada, Commission on the State and Management of the Female Prison at the Kingston Penitentiary. (1921). *Report on the state and management of the female prison at the Kingston Penitentiary* (the Nickle report). Ottawa: King's Printer.

Canada, Committee Appointed to Advise upon the Revision of the Penitentiary Regulations and the Amendment of the Penitentiary Act. (1921). *Report of the committee appointed by the Rt. Hon. C.J. Doherty, Minister of Justice, to advise upon the revision of the penitentiary regulations and the amendment of the Penitentiary Act* (the Biggar report). Ottawa: King's Printer.

Canada, Committee Appointed to Inquire into the Principles and Procedures Followed in the Remission Service of the Department of Justice of Canada. (1956). *Report of a committee appointed to inquire into the principles and procedures followed in the remission service of the Department of Justice of Canada* (the Fauteux report). Ottawa: Queen's Printer.

Canada, Department of Justice. (2017). Canada's court system. Retrieved from www.justice.gc.ca/eng/csj-sjc/ccs-ajc.

Canada, Department of Justice. (1947). *Report of General R.B. Gibson: A commissioner appointed under Order in Council P/C/ 1313, regarding the penitentiary system of Canada*. Ottawa: King's Printer.

Canada, Directors of the Penitentiaries. (1870). *First annual report of the directors of penitentiaries for the year 1868*. Ottawa: King's Printer.

Canada, Joint Committee to Study Alternatives for the Housing of the Federal Female Offender. (1978). *Report of the Joint Committee to Study Alternatives for the Housing of the Federal Female Offender* (the Chinnery report). Ottawa: Ministry of the Solicitor General.

Canada, National Advisory Committee on the Female Offender. (1977). *Report of the National Advisory Committee on the Female Offender* (the Clark report). Ottawa: Ministry of the Solicitor General.

Canada, National Planning Committee on the Female Offender. (1978). *Report of the National Planning Committee on the Female Offender* (the Needham report). Ottawa: Solicitor General Canada.

Canada, Royal Commission on Penitentiaries. (1914). *Report of the Royal Commission on Penitentiaries* (the MacDonell report). Ottawa: King's Printer.

Canada, Royal Commission to Investigate the Penal System in Canada. (1938). *Report of the Royal Commission to Investigate the Penal System of Canada* (the Archambault report). Ottawa: King's Printer.

Canada, Subcommittee on the Penitentiary System in Canada. (1977). *Report to Parliament by the subcommittee on the penitentiary system in Canada* (the MacGuigan report). Ottawa: Minister of Supply and Services Canada.

Canada, Task Force on Federally Sentenced Women. (1990). *Creating choices: Report of the Task Force on Federally Sentenced Women*. Ottawa: Department of the Solicitor General.

Canadian Committee on Corrections. (1969). *Report of the Canadian Committee on Corrections* (the Ouimet report). Ottawa: Queen's Printer.

Canadian Criminology and Corrections Association. (1968). *Brief on the woman offender: An official statement of policy*. Ottawa: Canadian Corrections Association.

Constitution Act, 1867 (UK), 30 & 31 Vict, c 3. Retrieved from http://laws-lois.justice.gc.ca/eng/Const/page-1.html.

Correctional Service of Canada. (1990). *The history of federal-provincial exchange of service agreements*. Ottawa: Eden Communications.

Correctional Service of Canada. (2008). The closing of the Prison for Women in Kingston July 6, 2000: Message from the Deputy Commissioner for Women, Correctional Service of Canada. Retrieved from www.csc-scc.gc.ca/text/pblct/brochurep4w/pre3-eng.shtml.

Correctional Service of Canada. (2012). Our mission. Retrieved from www.csc-scc.gc.ca/about-us/index-eng.shtml.

Correctional Service of Canada. (2013). Institutional profiles. Retrieved from www.csc-scc.gc.ca/text/region/inst-profil-eng.shtml.

Correctional Service of Canada. (2016). Correctional Service Canada healing lodges. Retrieved from www.csc-scc.gc.ca/aboriginal/002003-2000-eng.shtml.

Criminal Code, RSC 1985, c C-46.

Dukelow, D. (2002). *Dictionary of Canadian law* (3rd ed.). Toronto: Carswell.

Goff, C. (2008). *Criminal justice in Canada*. Toronto: Nelson Canada.

Hannah-Moffat, K. (2001). *Punishment in disguise: Penal governance and federal imprisonment of women in Canada*. Toronto: University of Toronto Press.

Hannah-Moffat, K., & Shaw, M. (2000). *An ideal prison? Critical essays on women's imprisonment in Canada*. Halifax: Fernwood Publishing.

Hayman, S. (2006). *Imprisoning our sisters: The new federal women's prisons in Canada*. Montreal & Kingston: McGill-Queen's University Press.

Hotton Mahoney, T. (2011). *Women and the criminal justice system*. Statistics Canada, no. 89-503-X. Retrieved from www.statcan.gc.ca/pub/89-503-x/2010001/article/11416-eng.pdf.

Maidment, M. (2006). "We're not all that criminal": Getting beyond the pathologizing and individualizing of women's crime. *Women and Therapy, 29*(3/4), 35–56.

Mazowita, B., & Greenland, J. (2016). Police resources in Canada. *Juristat, 36*(1), 1–22.

Pollack, S., & Kendall, K. (2005). Taming the shrew: Regulating prisoners through women-centred mental health programming. *Critical Criminology, 13*, 71–87.

Public Safety Canada. (2016). First Nations policing program. Retrieved from https://www.publicsafety.gc.ca/cnt/cntrng-crm/plcng/brgnl-plcng/index-en.aspx.

Reitano, J. (2006). *Police resources in Canada.* Ottawa: Canadian Centre for Justice Statistics.

Reitano, J. (2016). Adult correctional services, 2014/15. *Juristat, 36*(1), 1–16. Retrieved from www.statcan.gc.ca/pub/85-002-x/2016001/article/14318-eng.pdf.

Rosen, E. (1977). *An evaluation of the report of the national advisory committee on the female offender.* Ottawa: Advisory Council on the Status of Women.

Royal Canadian Mounted Police. (2017). Organization of the RCMP. Retrieved from www.rcmp-grc.gc.ca/about-ausujet/organi-eng.htm.

Strange, C. (1985). The criminal and fallen of their sex: The establishment of Canada's first women's prison, 1874–1901. *Canadian Journal of Women and the Law, 1,* 79–92.

Statistics Canada. (2007a). *Adult correctional services, admissions to provincial, territorial and federal programs, annual* [CANSIM table 251-0001]. Retrieved from http://www.statcan.gc.ca/tables-tableaux/sum-som/l01/cst01/legal30a-eng.htm.

Statistics Canada. (2007b). *Adult correctional services, admissions to provincial and territorial programs, annual* [CANSIM table 251-0002]. Archived at http://www.statcan.gc.ca.

Statistics Canada. (2011). *Federal government revenue and expenditures.* Retrieved from www.statcan.gc.ca/tables-tableaux/sum-som/l01/cst01/govt49b-eng.htm.

Statistics Canada. (2015). *Police reported crime statistics, 2014.* Retrieved from www.statcan.gc.ca/daily-quotidien/150722/dq150722a-eng.htm.

Supreme Court Act, RSC 1985, c S-26.

Wiebe, R., & Johnson, Y. (1998). *Stolen life: The journey of a Cree woman.* Toronto: Vintage Canada.

Female Crime: Theoretical Perspectives

Introduction

Every day in Canada and elsewhere, men are involved in campaigns such as the **White Ribbon Campaign,** which is led by men urging other men to help reduce the alarming rates of male-to-female victimization described in Chapter 7 (DeKeseredy, 2012). But despite any good deeds, crime—from genocide to terrorism, from crimes committed behind closed doors to on the streets—is essentially the product of men (DeKeseredy & Schwartz, 2005). Men "have a virtual monopoly" on the commission of crimes (DeKeseredy, 2011; Messerschmidt, 1997), and particularly crimes against women. Regardless of whether we discuss women offenders or women victims or women who work in the criminal justice professions, we must grasp the various theoretical underpinnings that drive and encourage such criminal (and non-criminal) behaviours.

We have yet to hear of a woman committing mass murder like the ones at Oregon's Umpqua College on October 1, 2015; the University of Alberta on June 15, 2012; Virginia Polytechnic Institute and State University on April 16, 2007; and Dawson College in Montreal on September 13, 2006 ("Montreal Gunman," 2006). Sometimes these mass killings are motivated by revenge (for bullying), by untreated mental illness, or by a hatred of women. On December 6, 1989, Marc Lépine killed 14 female engineering students at the École Polytechnique, an engineering school affiliated with the Université de Montréal. [1] His intent was to target women, as was evident during the shooting when he shouted, "I'm here to fight against feminism!" (Krajicek, 2014).

Of course there are women who commit crimes too, including violent crimes such as sexual assault and homicide, but such female offenders are few. And although fascinating, notorious female offenders such as Karla Homolka[2] and Aileen Wuornos should not detract our focus from the realities of the majority. Box 2.1 discusses the portrayal of Aileen Wuornos in the movie *Monster*.

Misogyny and Feminism

Women throughout time have endured a lower position in society. That position has shifted and taken various forms over the decades, but generally, women are reminded on a daily basis that their worth is considered less than a man's. This can be seen in the unequal distribution of labour, in the lower pay for the same work, and in the violence and objectification that appears in advertisements and media. Add differences of colour or sexual orientation, and we see even greater levels of discrimination and victimization (Sinha, 2013).

Misogyny is a word of Greek origin and is defined as a hatred of or hostility toward women. Although a noun, this term is the philosophical underpinnings of many subtle and overt acts of violence against women. Such acts can be criminal or also coercive and subliminal in politics, the work environment, and advertising, which can perpetuate a cycle of violence and victimization that often leads to women becoming offenders.

White Ribbon Campaign
A campaign founded in 1991 by a group of men seeking to end violence against women, in response to the 1989 massacre at Montreal's École Polytechnique. The White Ribbon Campaign now operates in more than 55 countries.

misogyny
A word of Greek origin that is defined as a hatred of or hostility toward women.

BOX 2.1

The Portrayal of Aileen Wuornos as a Monster

Monster is the title of a popular 2003 Hollywood movie based loosely on the life of female serial killer Aileen Wuornos. Charlize Theron won the Academy Award for Best Actress for her portrayal of Wuornos as a "masculine premeditating killer" of seven men in the late 1980s and early 1990s (Chesney-Lind & Eliason, 2006).

Regarding the movie *Monster*, Chesney-Lind and Eliason observe,

> The film used several strategies to masculinize the character of Lee Wuornos. She is dressed in men's clothing, she is depicted as physically larger and dominates her petite, more feminine partner ... Christina Ricci, who in no way physically resembles her real-life partner, Tyria Moore. Wuornos is depicted as the sole provider and the one who controls physical contact in the relationship. Placing the film's killing spree entirely within a nine-month time frame beginning with the initiation of her intimate relationship with a woman implies that her lesbian relationship rather than her appalling life circumstances (of abuse and exploitation) up to that point in her life, were to blame for her murders. Even the title suggests that to be lesbian and to be violent casts one into a non-human role. For a movie that is supposedly sympathetic to the horribly abused Wuornos, to name the film *Monster* is to perpetuate myths about the woman.[3] (Chesney-Lind and Eliason, 2006, p. 37)

See Figure 2.1 for an illustration of the relationship between misogyny, feminism, and misandry.

As described in Chapter 3, contrary to what the media may say, the Homolka murder case is not a typical example of female violence. Nor do we see a major surge in female youth violence such as that described in Garbarino's (2006) controversial book *See Jane Hit*, or in such quotes as this one by Ford (1998): "Bad girls: Girls are moving into the world of violence that once belonged to boys" (as cited in Chesney-Lind & Pasko, 2013b).[4] Note too, that, in the United States, females account for only 12 percent of all

FIGURE 2.1   Misogyny, Feminisim, and Misandry

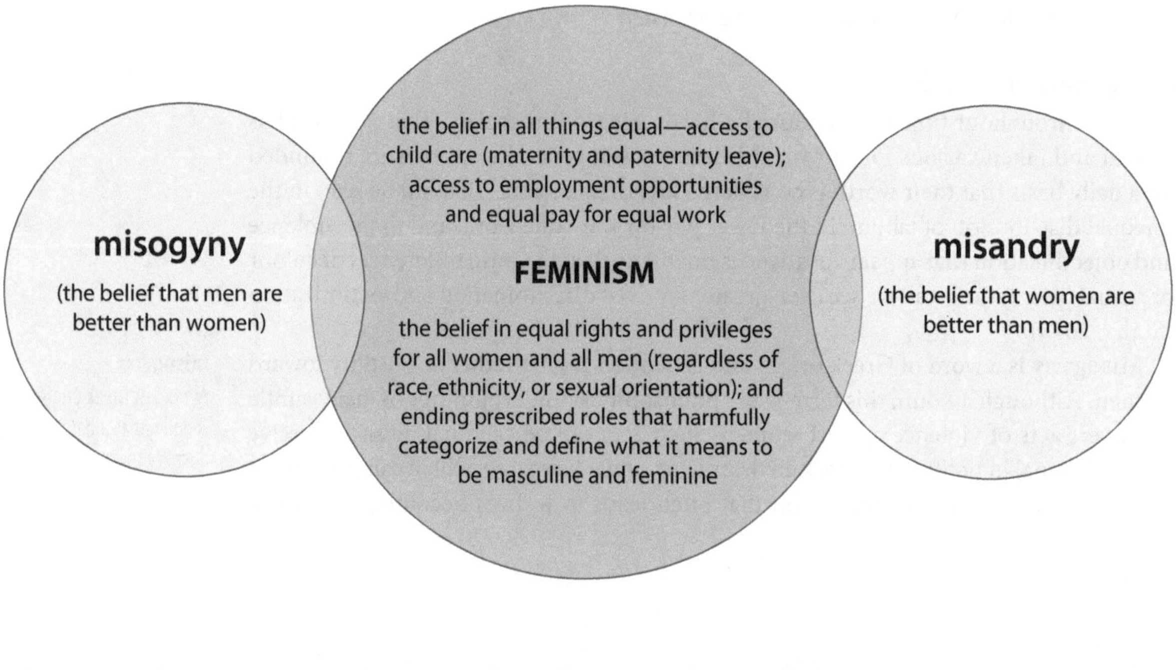

misogyny
(the belief that men are better than women)

FEMINISM
the belief in all things equal—access to child care (maternity and paternity leave); access to employment opportunities and equal pay for equal work

the belief in equal rights and privileges for all women and all men (regardless of race, ethnicity, or sexual orientation); and ending prescribed roles that harmfully categorize and define what it means to be masculine and feminine

misandry
(the belief that women are better than men)

serial killers (Hickey, 2012). Furthermore, no reliable study has found that men and women are equally likely to sexually abuse children, and the words of Holly Johnson (1987), from 20 years ago, still hold true in Canada today: "The number of women who are charged with *Criminal Code* offences amounts to [only] thousands each year" (p. 23). Most of those offences are for non-violent crimes (Statistics Canada, 2016b; Reitano, 2016).

This chapter will not repeat those data. Instead, our main objective is to review the most widely read and cited theories of female crime. There are many theories that attempt to explain the causes and consequences of criminal behaviour, and most of those theories historically included women as an afterthought. Theories created by men that focus solely on men have commonly been applied to women (Belknap, 2014) without requisite forethought. In other words, most criminological theories are "alarmingly gender-blind" (Gelsthorpe & Morris, 1988; Messerschmidt, 1993).

Not until the streams of feminism found solid ground did we evolve in our questioning of causes and consequences of criminal behaviour. This began from the roots of feminism, which grew to acknowledge the intersectionality of race and class along with gender.

Feminism is defined broadly as (1) the belief that women and men are, and have been, treated differently by our society; (2) the belief that women have frequently and systemically been unable to participate fully in all social arenas and institutions; and (3) the desire to change that situation. Feminist theories support the creation of a "new" point of view about society, one that looks at economics, politics, and social status from the perspective that women are not inferior, and men are not "the norm."

Sadly, though, feminism has constantly been the target of backlash, resulting in a need for its adherents to defend their beliefs and positions. Feminism has found its way into contemporary pop culture, which seems to reach more viewers (see Box 2.2).

Today, there are many different feminist theories, some of which reside under the umbrella of criminology. A few such theories are presented in this chapter, with the goal that understanding the foundation of feminism will help you critically deconstruct the issues presented within this textbook—issues pertaining to women victims, women offenders, and women who work in criminal justice professions.

feminism
(1) The belief that women and men are, and have been, treated differently by our society; (2) the belief that women have frequently and systemically been unable to participate fully in all social arenas and institutions; and (3) the desire to change that situation.

BOX 2.2

Feminism in Pop Culture

Feminism: The notion that women can be housewives, but only because they choose to be, NOT because it is their role in society.

Feminism: Boys can play with Barbies, and girls can own [*sic*] at sports.

Feminism: When men and women do the same work, they deserve the same pay.

Feminism: Being a woman in no way affects your ability to be funny or intelligent, and attractiveness should not factor into either of those things.

Feminism: Because if you're not a feminist, you're sexist.

Source: Slaughenhaupt, B. (2015, July 14). Feminism in pop culture. Retrieved from https://www.theodysseyonline.com/feminism-pop-culture.

Prior to describing and evaluating what feminist theories offer, it is first necessary to answer the question "What is a theory?"

What Is a Theory?

Social scientific theories of crime are like opinions: most people have them (Lilly, Cullen, & Ball, 2014).[5] For example, of the 84 people murdered in Toronto in 2007, 42 of the victims had been shot ("Toronto Homicides in 2007," 2008), and because most of the victims were people of colour, many people, including journalists, have offered their own explanations of the high rate of homicide in Toronto's black community. Consider the controversial theory proposed by conservative *Toronto Sun* columnist Michael Coren (2007), discussed in Box 2.3. Of course, other reasons for such gun-related deaths were and continue to be offered. Nevertheless, most of these theories are grounded in personal experiences or what people see, hear, or read in the media (Cote, 2002; DeKeseredy, Ellis, & Alvi, 2005). On the other hand, through empirical exploration and applying statistical realities (versus opinions), theory construction is a complex process that is heavily grounded in scientific research. More specifically, following Curran and Renzetti's (2001) thinking, a theory is defined here as "A set of interconnected statements or propositions that explain how two or more events or factors are related to one another" (p. 2).

BOX 2.3

One Journalist's Theory of Crime

Another murder in a Canadian black community, this time the victim being 11 years old. And it took only moments for white liberal politicians to blame law-abiding handgun owners and, yes, the United States of America.

Handguns have to be banned, they cried, and American gun laws are too soft. This has to be a first. Canadian leftists blaming a murder in Toronto on President George W. Bush. Orders of Canada and CBC T-shirts all round.

Such drivel does not, however, explain how Norway, with one of the highest rates of gun ownership in the world, manages to have one of the lowest crime rates.

Or how Israel, a society where guns are extraordinarily common, has so few criminal shootings.

Or how Britain with some of the most stringent gun control laws in the world has a violent crime rate that is virtually out of control.

It's too late to play silly games any more. If handguns are the cause of all this we have to ask why there are so few shootings in, for example, the Dutch, Ukrainian, Irish, Portuguese, Korean, Hindu or African communities. Why, in fact, there are so few shootings in any community outside of the West Indian and specifically Jamaican.

Oh Lord, the man must be mad. Silence him, stop him, call in a Human Rights Commission before it's too late!

Yet there is nothing racist about seeking answers that might save the lives of young black men and much that is racist about refusing to ask basic questions for fear that politically correct credentials be damaged.

If our leaders were braver they might admit that matriarchy is a fundamental theme of Jamaican society and the levels of fatherless families in the country's urban centres are staggering. This culture has been transferred to Canada. Just as it has to other Jamaican diaspora communities, which experience similar rates of violent crime.

It might be comforting to see every young single mom as a saint who works three jobs and is devoted to her children, but positive caricatures are just as unhelpful as are negative ones.

There are such mothers of course, but also young women who party late and work little. Who find themselves pregnant as teenagers and mothers of several children, perhaps from different fathers, by the time they are adults.

Such problems occur to various extents in all communities, but when the only male role model is the gangster on the street corner with the loud car, loud clothes and loud gun, the chances of leading a law-abiding life are minimal.

Made even harder by a dysfunctional obsession with disrespect.

A gesture or a harmless comment can indicate lack of respect and the need to shoot. Just last week in London, England, three young black men shot a doorman point blank in the face three times because he politely asked them not to smoke. Hard to believe that this was the result of oppression, racism and lack of government programs. Especially as the victim was himself black.

Poverty? Spare me. It is deeply insulting to assume that the poor are criminals.

Also ridiculous to assume that there is genuine, crippling poverty in a country with free education, health care and subsidized housing.

If we care we will halt the platitudes and try to help. No more patronizing blather, no more false scapegoats. If we care we will risk being called names. If we care.

Source: Coren, M. (2007, July 28). End the blather. *Toronto Sun*. Retrieved from www.torontosun.com. Reprinted by permission of Sun Media Corporation.

► WHAT DO YOU THINK?

Where is the scientific evidence that supports Michael Coren's "theory"? Although a learned journalist, does he hold any academic credentials in the study of crime? Are his points based on his opinion or do they have merit, and if so, what empirical evidence can you find to support them?

Many people view social scientific theories as academic products of "impractical mental gymnastics" (Akers, 1997, p. 1), "philosophy or logic that has little relevance for real-world situations" (Miller, Schreck, & Tewksbury, 2006, p. 5), or as "fanciful ideas that have little to do with what truly motivates people" (Akers, 1997, p. 1). Whether we like it or not, facts and data do not speak for themselves; they must be interpreted (Curran & Renzetti, 2001) and tested so that we can remove subjectivity (and opinion) from its conclusions.

If you don't test a theory, then it is just an opinion (Miller et al., 2006). Certainly, evaluating the strength of a theory entails a more complex process than what has been briefly described here. Still, as you will discover from reading this chapter and other relevant materials, some theories have more positives than negatives, and vice versa. Moreover, every theory described in this book and other criminology texts has limitations. Crime has no "pat explanation"; what we have, then, are "bad, good, and better theories" (Curran & Renzetti, 2001, p. 5).

In addition to serving as conceptual tools that help us make sense of data, theories are practical. For example, if you want solutions to problems, such as those examined in this text, you must first identify their causes. In fact, almost every policy or strategy developed to prevent or control crime is derived from some theory or theories (Akers, 1997; DeKeseredy et al., 2005). Even though some policies currently in place have been derived from what international criminologists have viewed as "bad" theories of crime, those examples are offered here and are generally referred to as early theories of female crime (Chesney-Lind & Shelden, 2014). In addition, contemporary and critical theories that are grounded in a feminist perspective are also presented. A feminist perspective in research, for example, is research that is committed to social equality based upon gender and also upon those who've been systemically disadvantaged due to ethnicity, race, sexual orientation, and/or poverty. Feminist research calls attention to possible sources of bias, it challenges our roots of knowledge, and it incorporates (and values) people with lived experience.[6]

Early Theories[7]

Lombroso and the Born Criminal

positivist school
One of the two major schools of criminology. Assumes the root causes of crime are from factors outside the control of the offender (such as biological or physiological issues).

Cesare Lombroso (1835–1909) was a **positivist criminologist**. Positivism assumes that human behaviour is determined and can be measured (Curran & Renzetti, 2001). Further, regardless of how many important progressive changes have occurred in contemporary North American society (the *Canadian Charter of Rights and Freedoms*, for example), racist, sexist, and classist visions of females in conflict with the law persist today. Lombroso played a major role in setting the stage for such views (Belknap, 2014) centuries ago.

Lombroso and William Ferrero (1895) published one of the first attempts to explain female crime in the book *The Female Offender* (Hahn Rafter & Gibson, 2004). For example, as widely read and cited feminist criminologist Meda Chesney-Lind (1999) points out in Box 2.4, this book heavily informs Canadian journalist Patricia Pearson's (1997) controversial analysis of violent women. Positivists such as Lombroso were (and in many ways still are) concerned with drawing our attention to the innate characteristics of criminals rather than their behaviours (Steffensmeier & Broidy, 2001).

BOX 2.4

Lombroso's Influence in the Late 1990s

Much of what Pearson's work serves up ... is old hat. Consider that Lombroso spent a good part of his book, *The Female Offender*, combing through the sensationalistic crimes of violent women. Lombroso, though, spared no thought for the equity approach in violence; instead, he felt that "the female criminal is doubly exceptional, as a woman and as a criminal." Normal women, he argued, are kept on the path of virtue by "maternity, piety, weakness," which means that the "wickedness" of the female offender "must be enormous before it could triumph over so many obstacles" (Lombroso, 1958, pp. 151–152). Lombroso then presents a series of historic [*sic*] and contemporary vignettes of violent women engaged in chilling and brutal crimes. His examples include mothers who killed their children, women who killed spouses and lovers, women who killed their rivals, women who killed other family members, women who instigated and enticed others to kill, and women who killed for material gain.

Now consider Pearson's chapters which include discussions of women who abuse and kill children, women who assault their spouses and lovers, and women who kill with others and women who kill alone (including women serial killers). Pretty similar in my estimation. Also similar is the reliance on details (usually gruesome) of specific women's crimes.

Source: Chesney-Lind, M. (1999). [Review of the book *When she was bad: Violent women and the myth of innocence.*] *Women and Criminal Justice*, 10(4), 114–118.

Deemed the "father of positivist criminology," Lombroso was heavily influenced by Charles Darwin's evolutionary studies. Like Darwin, Lombroso believed the best way to study a scientific issue was to develop a research hypothesis, then go directly to the relevant subject to measure or observe.

Lombroso performed autopsies on violent criminals whose skulls, he thought, were more suited to an animal than to a human. From there, he developed a perspective that criminals were "biological throwbacks" or *atavistic*. In other words, he saw criminals as not as far along the evolutionary ladder as law-abiding human beings. For Lombroso, atavistic people shared a number of characteristics, such as chimpanzee-like ears, bumps on their heads, large jaws, and so on.

Lombroso and Ferrero argued that because many female offenders were very young, they showed fewer atavistic characteristics than male criminals. According to these theorists:

> Very often, too, in women, the [degenerate] type is disguised by youth with its absence of wrinkles and the plumpness which conceals the size of the jaw and cheek-bones, thus softening the masculine and savage features. Then when the hair is black and plentiful … and the eyes are bright, a not unpleasing appearance is presented. In short, let a female delinquent be young and we can overlook her degenerate type, and even regard her as beautiful; the sexual instinct misleading us here as it does in making us attribute to women more of the sensitiveness and passion than they really possess. And in the same way, when she is being tried on a criminal charge, we are inclined to excuse, as noble impulses of passion, an act arises from the most cynical calculations. (Lombroso & Ferrero, 1895, p. 97)

Lombroso and Ferrero (1895) maintained that women were much less likely to commit crimes than men because of their special biological traits, such as their "piety, maternity, and want of passion, sexual coldness, weakness and undeveloped intelligence" (p. 151). When a woman did commit a crime, however, she was viewed as a "monster," one whose "wickedness must have been enormous before it could triumph over so many obstacles" (p. 152).

Many social scientists, especially feminists, agree with Gavigan's (1983) assertion that it "seems almost beyond absurd" that Lombroso's theory "should have ever been given credence" (p. 77), but remember the context of 1895. Lombroso was a "man of his times," and his perspective is a reflection of "malestream resistances to the suffragist movement and 19th century feminism" (Faith, 1993, p. 44) and a lack of scientific and theoretical exploration. Lombroso and Fererro made extravagant claims without providing strong empirical support (Boritch, 1997). Their analysis also dismisses the influence of broader social, political, economic, and cultural determinants of crime (Smart, 1976). Despite these flaws, as Chesney-Lind and Shelden (2014) point out, Lombroso's work "actually set the tone for much of the later work on female delinquency and crime" (p. 56).

Contemporary academics such as Belinda Morrissey (2003) and journalists such as Pearson (1997) are not the only people influenced by Lombroso and Ferrero's (1895) perspective on female offenders. For example, if your knowledge of female crime is based only on watching US movies, you would probably conclude that women in conflict with the law are masculinized monsters, lesbian villains, incarcerated teenage predators, or pathological killer beauties (DeKeseredy, 2000; DeKeseredy & Schwartz, 1996; Faith, 1993; Holmlund, 1994). Think about the portrayal of female criminals in such popular movies as *Single White Female*, *Basic Instinct*, *Fatal Attraction*, *The Hunger*, and *The Hand That Rocks the Cradle*. Think about the portrayal of villains in Disney movies such as *The Little Mermaid*, *Snow White*, *Sleeping Beauty*, and *Tangled*. The female villains are deranged and disfigured somehow, and the heroines are pious and gentle.

Consider how women are depicted in advertisements and commercials today. The dichotomy of "right" versus "wrong" is evident everywhere in society and even more

male privilege
The experience of subtle and overt advantages, as well as the absence of subtle and overt discrimination, in daily life simply by virtue of being male.

evident in the privileged space that men are allowed to fill versus women's spaces. Based on Peggy McIntosh's article on white privilege, **male privilege** is the experience of subtle and overt advantages, as well as the absence of subtle and overt discrimination, in daily life simply by virtue of being male. This can reveal itself in micro- and macro-level environments, political arenas, and institutions.

There are different standards in place for how we describe (and judge) male versus female behaviour. Even in the sports arena, women are criticized for their choices, questioned on their appearance, and demonized if they do not conform to outdated gender roles.

Pollak and the Masked Nature of Female Crime

Otto Pollak's *The Criminality of Women* (1950) and his co-edited collection of readings, *Family Dynamics and Female Sexual Delinquency* (Pollak & Friedman, 1969), were heavily influenced by the positivistic approach of Lombroso and Ferrero's *The Female Offender* (1895), despite it being published more than 50 years earlier. Pollak developed what Ellis and DeKeseredy (1996) refer to as a *dual-focus theory* of female crime, in which he focuses on both the biological causes of female crime and the causes of the reactions to female offences.

Pollak (1950) asserts that biological factors cause females to commit crimes as frequently as males; however, female crimes are more likely to involve sex, or cunning and deceit, or both and therefore are less visible or less likely to be reported. Pollak's key point is that women are better than men at hiding their offences (Belknap, 2014), which explains why many of their crimes have never attracted the agents of social control. Pollak associated women's ability to deceive criminal justice officials with the passive role they traditionally play during sexual intercourse. At the same time, official crime statistics (such as court and sentencing data) show that much female crime is masked by greater leniency and chivalry (that is, women are sentenced less severely because they are women). This chivalry is rooted in the social construction of women as passive, dependent, and requiring the protection of men, which in turn dictates that we must give them lighter sentences. It is also difficult for women to be thought of as anything other than fitting within the socially constructed box of conformity as maternal, compassionate, and emotional.

> Not enough attention has been paid to the physiological fact that man must achieve an erection in order to perform the sex act and will not be able to hide his failure. His lack of positive emotion in the sexual sphere must become overt to the partner and pretense of sexual response is impossible for him, if it is lacking. Woman's body, however, permits such a pretense to a certain degree and lack of orgasm does not prevent her ability to participate in the sex act. (Pollak, 1950, p. 138)

According to Pollak (1950), "It cannot be denied that this basic physiological difference may well have a great influence on the degree of confidence which the two sexes have in the possible concealment and thus on their character pattern in this respect" (p. 10). Concealment and deceit are learned during childhood, at a time when "natural aggressions are inhibited and forced into concealed channels" (p. 11).

By now you may be either laughing or saying to yourself, "Unbelievable that people believed such crap!" Well, not surprisingly, like Lombroso and Ferraro's (1895) offering,

Pollak's theory also lacks empirical support (Ellis & DeKeseredy, 1996). Further, his account does not recognize that women's traditionally passive role during sexual relations may be culturally, not biologically, determined (that is, they are told and required to be docile). Another point to consider is that instead of hiding orgasms, women may not be experiencing them due to their partners' insensitivity to certain sexual acts that give the women pleasure (Belknap, 2014), none of which is considered in Pollak's work.

Pollak (and Lombroso and Ferraro by default) are also criticized for ignoring the structural gender hierarchy in their respective societies, and its function as a possible source of male–female differences in crime and its control. This theory assumes that the inferior status of women is biologically determined and ignores the so-called dark side of chivalry, according to which women offenders are treated more harshly (by police and society) because they have stepped outside of their cultural box of expectations. This mistreatment is even more evident with women of colour (Barak, Leighton, & Flavin, 2010; DeKeseredy, 2000; Potter, 2015). Pollak's key point is that women are better than men at hiding their offences (Belknap, 2007), which explains why many of their crimes have never attracted the agents of social control. Pollak associated women's ability to deceive criminal justice officials with the passive role they traditionally play during sexual intercourse.

Cohen, Strain Theory, and Anomie Theory

Courses in criminology and criminal justice will expose you to many theories, some of which ignore or trivialize female crime. Many criminologists once thought women were naturally inhibited from committing crime. Consider the words of Albert Cohen (1955) in his widely read and cited book, *Delinquent Boys*:

> My skin has nothing of the quality of down or silk, there is nothing limpid or flute-like about my voice. I am a total loss with needle and thread, my posture and carriage are wholly lacking in grace. These imperfections cause me no distress—if anything, they are gratifying—because I conceive myself to be a man and want people to recognize me as a full-fledged, unequivocal representative of my sex. My wife, on the other hand, is not greatly embarrassed by her inability to tinker with or talk about the internal organs of a car, by her modest attainments in arithmetic or by her inability to lift heavy objects. Indeed, I am reliably informed that many women—I do not suggest that my wife is among them—often affect ignorance, frailty and emotional sustainability because to do so otherwise would be out of keeping with a reputation for indubitable femininity. In short, people do not simply want to excel; they want to excel as a man or as a woman. … Even when they adopt behaviour which is considered disreputable by conventional standards, the tendency is to be disreputable in ways that are characteristically masculine and feminine. (pp. 137–138)

Cohen's perspective exemplifies what is commonly labelled **strain theory** by Robert K. Merton (1938), which in turn was built upon the work of Émile Durkheim's **anomie** theory. As Hackler (1994) notes, "A long-standing deficiency of most strain theories is their neglect of the gender issue" (p. 198)—meaning, they neglect to incorporate the conditions, positions, and power of women relative to their societal status. To address this lack, Freda Adler (1975) and Rita Simon (1975) published important books that are outgrowths of strain perspectives. Here, and in many other sources, their theoretical contributions are referred to as women's liberation/emancipation theories of female crime.

strain theory
A criminological view that an individual's social setting generates certain goals and expectations. The failure of individuals to achieve these goals, and thus the inability to achieve the social treatment they expect, results in strain and creates alienation and negative relationships with others. When others are seen as blocking the means to achieve their goals, some alienated individuals resort to criminal behaviour.

anomie
A term used to describe societal conditions that negatively impact people. It emphasizes the importance of societal norms in regulating a person's goals. Durkheim's writings on this topic outline how social transformations (alienation and economic depression, for example) may stimulate anomic societal conditions (leading one to commit crime or opt out of participating in society).

Contemporary Feminist Theories[8]

Historically and in the current political atmosphere, termed by journalist Susan Faludi (1991) as "the backlash," a substantial number of people mock feminist researchers, practitioners, and activists (DeKeseredy & Dragiewicz, 2007). Heavily influenced by the media and by some religious groups and conservative politicians, these critics equate feminism with hating men, not shaving one's legs, going braless, being gay or lesbian, and advocating a pro-choice stance. Of course, some feminists fit into one or more of these categories; however, many men and women are feminists. In fact, the second author of this chapter is a feminist man,[9] who is united with other feminists by a deep desire to eliminate all forms of gender inequality, several of which are described in other parts of this book. Moreover, as Claire Renzetti (1993) correctly points out, the goal of feminist scholars is "not to push men out so as to pull women in, but rather to gender the study of crime and criminal justice" (p. 234). Like Kathleen Daly and Meda Chesney-Lind (1988) and other feminist scholars (for example, Maidment, 2006; Renzetti, 2013), we do not equate gender with sex. Instead, following Edwin Schur (1984), we refer to gender as "the sociocultural and psychological shaping, patterning, and evaluating of male and female behavior" (p. 10).

Because feminism takes many forms, painting all feminists with the same brush can be misleading. Renzetti (2013) for example, contends that at least 12 variations of feminist criminological theory exist, with major debates within each. For this chapter, we offer Kathleen Daly and Meda Chesney-Lind's (1988) definition, which refers to feminism as a "set of theories about women's oppression and a set of strategies for change" (p. 502). Their elements of feminism make it distinct from other perspectives occasionally referred to as "malestream," because the latter theories omit and/or misrepresent both gender and women's experiences (Messerschmidt, 1993):

- Gender is not a biological fact but a complex social, historical, and cultural product produced and defined by the society in which we live. Gender is related to, but not simply derived from, biological sex difference and reproductive capacities but more so the expected and prescribed roles one must adhere to for inclusion and acceptance.
- Gender and gender relations order social life and social institutions in fundamental ways.
- Gender relations and constructs of masculinity and femininity are not symmetrical but are based on an organizing principle of men's superiority to, and social and political dominance over, women.
- Systems of knowledge reflect men's view of the natural and social world; the production of knowledge is gendered.
- Women should be at the centre of intellectual inquiry, not peripheral, invisible, or appendages to men. (Daly & Chesney-Lind, 1988, p. 504)

Further, feminist scholars attempt to address how the intersection of race, class, and gender shape both women's involvement in rule-breaking activities and societal reactions to their appearance or behaviour (Carrington, 2015; Potter, 2015). I should note, however, the contention of some scholars that a feminist criminology does not exist, because neither feminism nor criminology is a monolithic enterprise. In other words, scholars use different feminist perspectives to explain a variety of criminological problems (Renzetti, 2013), such as those discussed throughout this text.

Feminist theorists and researchers have had a major impact on criminal justice policy (DeKeseredy, 2011; Lilly et al., 2014), such as the changes in our *Criminal Code* regarding sexual assault. This offence was originally called rape and limited to certain acts, and male husbands were exempt from the purview of the law for raping their wives. It wasn't until 1983 that changes were made so that any male or female could be charged with sexual assault (among other things). Still, because feminist work calls into question conservative "male-centred" ways of understanding crime and social control, it is constantly challenged and often ridiculed by conservative students, practitioners, and academics "who incorrectly" reduce feminist criticisms of gender-blind theories and research to "an attack on the sex of the researcher" (Flavin, 2004, p. 36). It is quite common to experience such a backlash from those who have traditionally held positions of power and privilege in society, but who are now being forced to re-examine that position.

Again, at least a dozen feminist criminological theories exist, each of which takes a distinct approach to understanding gender issues, asks different questions, and offers different theories of crime and the control of crime. In the sections that follow, we will limit the description of feminist contributions to the four major perspectives most frequently outlined in the feminist literature on criminology. Neither reality nor scholars fit neatly into slots. Writings by most feminist authors may easily bridge two or three perspectives, or may not easily fit any of them at all. Still, these categories are the ones most frequently identified by leading experts in the field. We begin by describing elements of liberal feminism.

Women's Liberation/Emancipation Theories

As one of the most widely recognized theories in North America, liberation theory stresses the need for equality *with* men. It purports that, to achieve inclusion, women must work within the established system (as opposed to dismantling it). Liberal feminists contend that women are discriminated against based on their sex; consequently, they are denied access to the same political, financial, career, and personal opportunities as men (Messerschmidt, 1993). For example, in 2007, only 22 percent of Prime Minister Stephen Harper's 32-member cabinet was composed of women. In 2015, when Justin Trudeau became prime minister, he purposely appointed his cabinet to include 50 percent women (as well as other visible and non-visible minority groups). This, however, was met with skepticism and many people challenged the value and competence of those women—despite the fact that in the many years prior to this, when the cabinet was made up mostly of men, no one challenged or questioned the competence of their inclusion.

The problem of gender inequality can be solved by clearing the way for "women's rapid integration into what has been the world of men" (Ehrenreich & English, 1978, p. 19) and by eliminating sexist stereotypes promoted by gender-role socialization in domestic settings, educational contexts, the media, and the government (Messerschmidt, 1993).

Among the several criminologists who have used liberal feminist theory to explain crime, perhaps the most famous are Freda Adler (1975) and Rita Simon (1975). Although the women's crime wave they described has never happened (Chesney-Lind & Pasko, 2013a; Gora, 1982; Steffensmeier & Steffensmeier, 1980), their perspectives are very popular among journalists. Further, although women are not becoming more violent, societal reactions to their behaviours have become more punitive, especially in the United States. For example, the public is now more likely to report violent females, the police are more likely to arrest them, the criminal justice system is more likely to prosecute them, and judges and juries are more likely to convict them (Renzetti, 2013). Furthermore, society reinforces the belief that women who challenge the traditional patriarchal gender-role structure (by committing crimes) are "unruly women" and therefore worthy of whatever punishment is issued by the justice system (Faith, 1993; Messerschmidt, 1986).

Liberal feminists stress the need for equal rights *with men*. This theory highlights that there is inequality of opportunities between men and women and it encourages women to become more competitive and assertive in meeting their own needs within and outside of the workforce.

For Adler and Simon, the female nature does not inhibit crime. Instead, it is because women lack opportunities to break the law that their involvement in crime is lessened. Adler and Simon believe that if given such opportunities, they would act (criminally) just like men. Adler (1975) and Simon (1975) are among the "first wave of women" of their generation to conduct criminological research and to help legitimize serious research on female crime and punishment (Faith, 1993; Renzetti, 2013).

Adler (1975, p. 16) analyzed US Federal Bureau of Investigation (FBI) arrest statistics and found that between 1960 and 1972,

- the number of women arrested for robbery increased by 277 percent, whereas the male rate rose 169 percent;
- the female embezzlement arrest rate increased 280 percent compared with a 50 percent increase for men;
- the female larceny arrest rate rose by 303 percent compared with an 82 percent increase for men; and
- the number of women arrested for burglary increased by 168 percent, whereas the male rate rose by 63 percent.

What caused the increases in female crime rates? Could it be the result of increased policing strategies to detect and apprehend criminal behaviour? Adler argued that although the women's liberation movement had opened up new roles for women in the military, education, business, and politics, it also opened up new roles for women in crime, which had historically been dominated by men.

Girls are not exempt from Adler's liberation/emancipation thesis. She argued (in the 1970s) that the women's movement seems to be "having a twofold influence on juvenile crimes" (1975, p. 95). As she put it,

> Girls are involved in more drinking, stealing, gang activity, and fighting—behavior in keeping with their adoption of male roles and in keeping with their escape from the confines of female constructed roles. The departure from the safety of traditional female roles and the testing of uncertain alternative roles coincide with turmoil of adolescence creating criminogenic risk factors, which are bound to create an increase in crime. These considerations help explain the fact that between 1960 and 1972 national arrests for major crimes show a jump for boys of 82 percent—for girls, 306 percent. (Adler, 1975, p. 95)

What Adler (1975) refers to as the "shady aspect of liberation" (p. 13) is also a major part of Simon's (1975) theory. However, Simon departs from Adler by arguing that the increase in female crime is limited mainly to property offences and that violent female crime has decreased. Moreover, Simon (1975) attributes the decrease in female violence to feminism, which makes women "feel more liberated physically, emotionally, and legally" and decreases their frustration and anger (p. 40). Consequently, women's desire to kill the male objects of their anger or frustration on whom they are dependent (lovers, husbands, and cohabiting partners, for example) declined (Simon, 1975, p. 40). Simon also predicted that female emancipation would contribute to an increase in female white-collar crime for the following reasons:

> As women become more liberated from hearth and home and become involved in full-time jobs, they are more likely to engage in the types of crime for which their occupations provide them with the greatest opportunities (banking, financial management, corporate roles, for example). Furthermore … as a function of both expanded consciousness, as well as occupational opportunities, women's participation role and involvement in crime are expected to *change* and *increase*. (Simon, 1975, p. 1, emphasis in original)

Simon's opportunities theory of female crime is described in Figure 2.2.

As Curran and Renzetti (2001) remind us, the liberation or emancipation theories described here should be commended for forcing "a contemporary reassessment of the relationship between sex and participation in criminal activity" (p. 126). However, these perspectives remain problematic.

First, police statistics are not accurate indicators of the extent of crimes committed because they tell us only the number of offences that have been brought to police attention; many illicit activities never come to their attention. Second, the number of females arrested in Adler's (1975) sample was so low that a small rise translated into major changes in overall percentage terms (Chesney-Lind & Shelden, 2014). When comparing male and female arrest rates, Adler (1975) did not control for the absolute base numbers from which the rates of increase were calculated. If, hypothetically, the base number of Canadian women who committed homicide was two in 2007 and it rose to four in 2008,

FIGURE 2.2   Simon's Opportunities Model of Female Crime

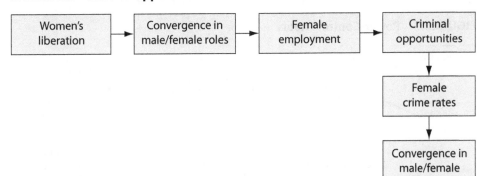

Source: DeKeseredy, W.S., Ellis, D., & Alvi, S. (2005). *Deviance and crime: Theory, research and policy.* Cincinnati: LexisNexis, p. 45.

one could argue that the female homicide rate rose by an alarming 100 percent; it doubled! On the other hand, if the base number of males who committed homicide in 2007 was 750 and rose to 1,000 in 2008, the increase in the male rate would appear to be markedly lower than the change to the female rate. As Curran and Renzetti (2001) point out, "if we look only at percent changes without taking into account these major absolute base differences, we end up with a very distorted picture of men's and women's involvement in crime" (p. 126).

Several other problems with the theories of Adler and Simon are widely cited;[10] however, their theories' popularity, at least in the minds of the general public, conservative politicians, and many journalists is undiminished (Chesney-Lind & Eliason, 2006; Chesney-Lind & Pasko, 2013a; DeKeseredy, 2000). Indeed, today, it is not unusual to read newspaper stories similar to the one that appeared on December 23, 1992, in the *Washington Post*: "Delinquent Girls Achieving a Violent Equality in DC" (Lewis, 1992). Here in Canada, the *Alberta Report* (McGovern, 1995) similarly argued, "Girls, it used to be said, were made of sugar and spice. Not anymore. The latest crop of teenage girls can be as violent, malicious and downright evil as the boys. In fact, they're leading the explosion in youth crime. It's an unexpected byproduct of the feminist push for equality" (p. 24).

Several academics have also recently recycled the work of Adler and Simon (Chesney-Lind & Shelden, 2014). Based on their analysis of New York City arrest data, Baskin, Sommers, and Fagan (1993) argued that "the growing drug markets and a marked disappearance of males" interact with other factors in poor inner-city communities "to create social and economic opportunity structures open to women's increasing participation in violent crime" (p. 406).

Power-Control Theory

Described in Figure 2.3 and often referred to as either a feminist or a social control perspective, the power-control theory developed by Hagan, Gillis, and Simpson (1987), and elaborated by Hagan in 1989, attempts to address where the "differences in the relative class positions of husbands and wives in the workplace make for gender variations in parental control and delinquent behavior of adolescents?" (p. 789). Although confined to a heteronormative construction of family, they argue that lower rates of female

FIGURE 2.3   Power-Control Theory

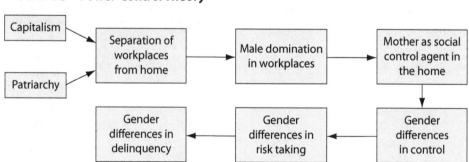

Source: DeKeseredy, W.S., Ellis, D., & Alvi, S. (2005). *Deviance and crime: Theory, research and policy*. Cincinnati: LexisNexis, p. 46.

delinquency are present in a family where the father is controlling, and that more equal male and female rates of delinquency are indicated when parental power is equalized.

Delinquency is, according to Hagan (1989), a type of risk-taking behaviour. It is fun, liberating, and gives youths the "chance to pursue publicly some of the pleasures that are symbolic of adult male status outside the family" (pp. 152–153). However, boys are more willing to take such risks (and are permitted by society to do so) than are girls, because boys are supervised less closely and punished less severely by their parents. Thus, the "taste for such risk-taking is channelled along sexually stratified lines" (p. 154) and responded to with the adage "boys will be boys."

Hagan et al. (1987) contend that parents' positions of power in the workplace are reproduced in the home and that affects the probability of their children committing delinquent acts. These theorists identify two general types of family structure based on parents' power in the workplace: patriarchal and egalitarian. Keep in mind that Hagan's theory is constrained within the heteronormative family structure.

Patriarchal Family Structure

The first type of family structure is **patriarchal**. This consists of a heterosexual union in which the husband works outside the home in a position of authority and a wife is delegated responsibility for keeping the house and socializing and controlling the children. Such families "socially reproduce daughters who focus their futures around domestic labour and consumption as contrasted with sons who are prepared for participation in direct production" (Hagan et al., 1987, p. 791). Patriarchy is not a single or simple concept; it is constructed out of various practices by various individuals and institutions through action or inaction that benefits men and disadvantages women (Code, 2000). It is a gendered system of social control that pervades all aspects of human existence, including politics, industry, the military, education, philosophy, art, literature, and civilization itself, particularly in North America, but evident everywhere in the world. This includes the "private" spheres of love, sexuality, marriage, and children (Bennett, 2006).

patriarchal structure
A heterosexual union in which the husband works outside the home in a position of authority and a wife is delegated responsibility for keeping the house and socializing and controlling the children.

Egalitarian Family Structure

The second type of family structure identified by Hagan et al., (1987) is egalitarian. Again confined within the heteronormative family structure, in egalitarian families, husbands and wives both work outside the home in positions of authority. An egalitarian family "socially reproduces daughters who are prepared along with sons to join the production sphere" (Hagan et al., 1987, p. 792). Further, both sons and daughters are inclined to engage in risk-taking activities, such as delinquency, and are punished in somewhat the same manner or level of severity.

Although some empirical evidence supports the power-control theory and its elaborated version (McCarthy, Hagan, & Woodward, 1999), this perspective has several key problems. For example, having a job does not necessarily mean that a woman has equal power at home. Although a growing number of men help around the house, most married women do all the cooking and cleaning for the house, are primarily responsible for child care, work outside of the home, and may even care for elderly parents or grandparents. And despite all of those jobs, they lack an equal decision-making power position (Alvi, DeKeseredy, & Ellis, 2000). Moreover, many women are psychologically, physically, and sexually abused by their husbands or cohabiting partners (DeKeseredy & Schwartz, 2013), which further undermines any perceived or real decision-making power.

In addition to neglecting the fact that a place in the paid marketplace does not automatically translate into power at home, Hagan and his colleagues ignore the fact that the power-control theory is a variation of the "women's liberation and emancipation leads to crime" premise. Of course, these theorists (Hagan et al., 1987; Hagen, 1989) do not explicitly state that women's liberation causes female crime, but they strongly suggest that the "mother's liberation" in joining the paid labour force causes daughters (and sons) to commit crimes. Despite these claims, statistics reveal the truth that even though there has been a major increase of women in the paid workforce over the past several decades, female delinquency has shown no corresponding increase (Chesney-Lind & Pasko, 2013a).

Socialist Feminism

Socialist feminism is a blending of some elements of Marxist and radical feminist theories. Marxist feminists view capitalism as the primary cause of both crime and male dominance over women, whereas radical feminists see male power and privilege (that is, patriarchy) as the root cause of all social relations, inequality, and crime (DeKeseredy & Schwartz, 1996; Renzetti, 2013). However, in socialist feminist analyses of crime and other social problems, neither class nor patriarchy is presumed to be dominant. Instead, class and gender relations are viewed as equally important, "inextricably intertwined," and "inseparable," interacting to determine the social order at any particular time in history (Jaggar, 1983; Maidment, 2006; Messerschmidt, 1986). Socialist feminists, such as Beirne and Messerschmidt (Messerschmidt, 1993; Beirne & Messerschmidt, 2014), argue that to understand class we must also recognize how it is structured by gender. And, conversely, that to understand gender requires an examination of how it is structured by class within society. Thus, socialist feminists assert that we are influenced by both class and gender relations.

One of the most important contributions to the development of a social feminist theory of crime was the publication of Messerschmidt's *Capitalism, Patriarchy, and Crime* (1986). Like other socialist feminist accounts, Messerschmidt's perspective treats class and gender as equally important, interacting factors that shape the types and seriousness of crime. He contends,

> It is the powerful (in both the gender and class spheres) who do most of the damage to society, not as is commonly supposed, the disadvantaged, poor, and subordinate. The interaction of gender and class creates positions of power and powerlessness in the gender/class hierarchy, resulting in different types and degrees of criminality and varying opportunities for engaging in them. Just as the powerful have more legitimate opportunities, so they have more illegitimate opportunities. (Messerschmidt, 1986, p. 42)

Women and girls are not major criminal threats to Canadian society. Thus, according to Messerschmidt's social feminist perspective on social control,

> The criminal justice system deals with females as it does with marginalized males: its task is to control nontraditional behavior. Publicizing and exaggerating women's involvement

in serious crime and linking it to the women's movement serves to delegitimize the general expansion of women into nontraditional roles in several ways. First, since criminal justice personnel are more likely today to label a female engaged in violence as criminal, female involvement in serious crime is exaggerated. Second, just as the state publicizes female involvement in criminality, it hides the criminality of *powerful males*. The overall contribution of women to serious crime is thereby magnified. Third, black and poor females in particular are publicized as increasingly dangerous. As with male offenders, racism and class bias in the criminal justice system results in more black and poor females being imprisoned than their white counterparts who have committed similar crimes. (Messerschmidt, 1986, p. 80, emphasis in original)

Messerschmidt's (1986) theory is directly relevant to the Canadian context. For example, as noted in subsequent chapters of this book and in other sources, Indigenous women are more likely than non-Indigenous women to be arrested and spend time in penal institutions for not paying fines. Canada's recorded population on January 1, 2016, was 36,048,500 (Statistics Canada, 2013, 2016a). New data from the National Household Survey (NHS) show that 1,400,685 people had an Indigenous identity in 2011, representing 4.3 percent of the total Canadian population. Indigenous people accounted for 3.8 percent of the population enumerated in the 2006 census, 3.3 percent in the 2001 census, and 2.8 percent in the 1996 census. However, they now account for 23.2 percent of the total inmate prison population. On any given day, there are approximately 3,500 Indigenous people in federal penitentiaries. Between 2001–2002 and 2011–2012, the incarcerated Indigenous population has increased by 37.3 percent, while the number of incarcerated Indigenous women has increased by 109 percent. Indigenous women offenders comprise 33 percent of the total inmate population under federal jurisdiction (Office of the Correctional Investigator, 2016).

Messerschmidt's theory attempted to improve on radical and Marxist feminism by simultaneously explaining class and gender differences in crime; however, his perspective has several limitations. Messerschmidt agrees that two views in particular are problematic. First, although Messerschmidt tried to develop a perspective in which class and gender were equally important, some reviewers, including Carol Smart (1987), argue that his theory did not achieve this goal because it "retained basic Marxist formulations" onto which he simply added gender (p. 328).

Marxism is a 19th-century political theory advanced by Karl Marx and Friedrich Engels suggesting that society is divided into economic classes. In any given era, one class is dominant and another is ascendant. Although Marxism has several variations, all Marxists believe that all social forces are ultimately economic in character and that all racial, social, and gender problems are ultimately reducible to fundamental economic issues. That is, social institutions, such as law, education, political structures, or our general beliefs, are in place because they essentially serve the interests of the dominant economic class (by keeping the powerful people rich).

A feminist perspective on this believes that we live in a society that has conditions that oppress people and block their movement toward a more dominant class. The belief is that lawmakers are biased (and sexist) since they are primarily (white) men wanting to keep their positions of power secure. It acknowledges a two-tiered society in which gender, class, and race are ignored and institutions perpetuate the oppression of these groups. Consider Figure 2.4.

Marxism
A 19th-century political theory advanced by Karl Marx and Friedrich Engels suggesting that society is divided into economic classes.

FIGURE 2.4 Equality Versus Equity

EXAMPLE 1

Equality

Everyone is given the same support. This may or may not provide individuals with equal access.

Equity

Different support is given to each individual to give them equal access.

Justice

The barrier to inequity is removed so that everyone has equal access without being given any support.

EXAMPLE 2

Three people want to go see a movie at the theatre: a child, a senior, and an adult. Regular admission costs are $5.00 for the child, $10.00 for the senior, and $15.00 for the adult. None of them have any money.

Equality

Each of the three people is given $10.00. The child and the senior can see the movie, but the adult cannot.

Equity

The child is given $5.00, the senior is given $10.00, and the adult is given $15.00 so they can all see the movie.

Justice

Admission to the movie is free on this evening, so they can all see the movie.

Applying a feminist lens to Marxist theory focuses in on our society's patriarchal nature, in which men have attained political and economic power over women and white men have attained that power over non-white men. A feminist theorist acknowledges this hierarchy and "is more likely to see patriarchy as the cause of the problem being examined, and to leave aside the question of the cause of patriarchy itself" (Schwartz & Slatin, 1984, p. 246).

Messerschmidt (1993, 2014) used these and other criticisms to develop a relatively new feminist theory of crime that emphasizes the relationship between masculinities and crime. It is to his *structured action theory* of corporate crime that we now turn, an account that builds on his earlier socialist feminist work.

Chapter 2 Female Crime: Theoretical Perspectives **51**

Structured Action Theory

Messerschmidt (2014) argues that "old-boy networks" play a key role in maintaining the gendered division of labour and perpetuating corporate crime. Such networks achieve this goal by selectively recruiting junior men who share members' norms, attitudes, values, and standards of conduct. If these young executives meet their senior counterparts' expectations (that is, if young men think and behave the same way as senior men), they are rewarded with money, authority, corporate control, and power; oftentimes this power and status is emitted over women and other unsuccessful men. Senior executives teach their recruits to act according to executive conceptions of masculinity. One of the most important practices that exemplifies these conceptions is the accumulation of financial profit, often through illegitimate means.

Corporate masculinity is distinct from those masculinities found on the street, on assembly lines, in the family, and elsewhere. For example, being a corporate "real man" entails "calculation, rationality as well as struggle for success, reward, and corporate recognition" (Messerschmidt, 1993, p. 136). Male executives compete with each other and measure masculinity according to their success in the business community. Corporate crime, then, is one technique of advancing the "gendered strategy of action" (DeKeseredy, Ellis, & Alvi, 2015, p. 192).

Corporations face many obstacles in their attempts to increase profits legitimately, such as uncertain and competitive markets, fluctuating sales, government regulations, and relations with unions (DeKeseredy & Schwartz, 2005, 2013). Messerschmidt (2014) asserts that these obstacles also threaten white corporate executive masculinity. Corporate crime, then, is a solution to both problems. That is, illegal and unethical practices are techniques of re-establishing or maintaining both masculinity and profit margins.

As Curran and Renzetti (2001) put it, "What about women?" (p. 224). Indeed, some readers may now ask, "How is structured action theory different from mainstream theories that focus only on women? This is a theory about men!" Although Messerschmidt's account is about men, it is a feminist perspective. To explain why so few women commit corporate crime, Messerschmidt seeks to understand the ways in which patriarchal forces shape crime, which is difficult to do by focusing only on women. Messerschmidt's account of corporate crime is one of the first to theorize the relationship between gender, class, and race/ethnicity.

So far, hypotheses based on Messerschmidt's structured action theory have not been tested. Ideally, scholars would do so by interviewing junior and senior corporate executives and studying those traits longitudinally.

Summary of Contemporary Feminist Theories

Feminist criminology is no longer in its infancy, and feminist theories have made many important contributions to the study of the problems and issues discussed throughout this book. Moreover, there is more than one feminist perspective on crime and more are being constructed to combine both macro- and micro-level factors, such as unemployment, globalization, deindustrialization, life events, stress, familial and societal patriarchy, and other factors (Renzetti, 2013).

Some criminologists (not surprisingly, male mainstream or conventional scholars) contend that it is "difficult to find direct empirical tests of feminist hypotheses" (Akers,

1997, p. 201). This difficulty, however, is not a problem for most feminist theorists, who do not want to develop accounts such Hagan et al.'s (1987) that make "global or grand theoretical statements" and generate hypotheses that are tested using "high-tech statistical analyses" (Daly & Chesney-Lind, 1988, p. 518). Rather, some feminist scholars test hypotheses derived from feminist theories of woman abuse. For example, the late Michael D. Smith (1990), a Canadian sociologist, gathered victimization survey data from 604 women in Toronto and tested the feminist hypothesis that wife beating results from abusive husbands' adherence to the ideology of familial patriarchy. Similarly, together with some colleagues in Canada and in the United States, DeKeseredy has tested several feminist hypotheses using data generated by surveys of several different populations (DeKeseredy, 2011; DeKeseredy & Schwartz, 2013).

Feminist theoretical work has also been critiqued by feminist scholars such as Miller (2003), who reminds us that "some of the most important critiques of feminist criminology have come from debates *among* feminists" (p. 22, emphasis in original). For example, the influence of class, race or ethnicity, and sexual orientation requires more attention (Carrington, 2015; Potter, 2015). Feminist theories could expand their attention to include white-collar and corporate crimes, as well as develop a sophisticated theory of women's aggression and violence that situates these behaviours in the context of patriarchy (Chesney-Lind & Eliason, 2006).

All theories have their limitations, and feminist perspectives are no exception; some theories are better than others, but all theories "have consequences" (Szasz, 1987). Attempts to address the criticisms raised here are already under way, and feminist theories of crime now play a key role in mapping the future of criminology and criminal justice.

SUMMARY

This chapter reviewed several theories of women's and girls' involvement in crime and victimization. You can now appreciate the variety of ways in which people could answer the question, "Why did she commit that crime?"

Unfortunately, most Canadian crime control policies are not based on sound sociological perspectives that focus on the major factors propelling women and girls into crime. Certainly, ample evidence shows that "get tough" approaches do little, if anything, to prevent many females from coming into conflict with the law. As Susan Miller (1998) puts it, "reducing crime is about getting smart, not about getting tough" (p. xxiii). She makes a valid point. As noted by Walker (1998), "One of the major obstacles in the search for sensible crime policies is the fact that there are many bad ideas" (p. 5).

NOTES

1. This terrifying event prompted the creation of the White Ribbon Campaign, a movement initiated in October 1991 by the Men's Network for Change (MNC) in Toronto, Ottawa, London, Kingston, and Montreal (DeKeseredy, Schwartz, & Alvi, 2000; Luxton, 1993). MNC drafted a document stating that violence against women is a major social problem, male silence about violence against women is complicity, and men can be part of the solution (Sluser & Kaufman, 1992; DeKeseredy, Dragiewicz, & Dragiewicz, 2017). Every year since the massacre, cities across Canada hold space on December 6 to remember those who were murdered (DeKeseredy, 2012).

2. Karla Homolka served the full 12-year sentence she received for her part (along with her then husband Paul Bernardo) in the abductions, rapes, and murders of Ontario schoolgirls Kristen French and Leslie Mahaffy, and Homolka's sister Tammy, a quarter-century ago. She is now married with three children and goes by the name Leanne Bordelais.

3. Sadly, too, in death penalty cases in the United States, the more "manly" lesbians appear to juries, the more likely they are to be convicted and seen as unworthy of compassion (Streib, 1994).

4. See Chesney-Lind and Eliason (2006) and Chesney-Lind and Irwin (2008) for detailed critiques of media and popular constructions of girls, women, and violence.

5. This section includes revised sections of work published previously by DeKeseredy (2000) and DeKeseredy, Ellis, and Alvi (2015).

6. The term *lived experience* is used to describe the first-hand accounts and impressions of living as a member of a minority or oppressed group. For example, when women talk about what it's like to be female in a predominantly male geek community, they are describing their lived experiences (Renzetti, 2013).

7. This section includes modified sections of work published previously by DeKeseredy (2000).

8. This section includes revised sections of work published previously by DeKeseredy and Schwartz (1996).

9. See DeKeseredy (2007) for a biographical account of how I became a feminist man.

10. See Chesney-Lind and Shelden (2014) and DeKeseredy (2000) for more in-depth critiques of these perspectives.

DISCUSSION QUESTIONS

1. What is a theory and what is the practical value of a theory?
2. Why do most theories of crime ignore women and girls in conflict with the law?
3. What are the key strengths and limitations of any one of the feminist theories? Create a chart to itemize each theory's strengths and limitations (or criticisms).
4. How can a theory be applied? Consider each of the feminist theories presented in this chapter and think of one or two ways in which it is evidence in practice. For example, a liberal approach would be applied by having women within a business be included (along with men) in making the policies for health benefits or parental leave.

ADDITIONAL RESOURCES

Videos and Films

Grosch, A., Hall, S., Riley-Grant, M., & Schmid, A. (Executive Producers), & Jenkins, P. (Writer/Director). (2003). *Monster* [Motion picture]. United States: Media 8 Entertainment and New Market Films.

McNabb Connolly (Firm). (2006). *100 days of freedom* [Video]. Canada: Cooper Rock Pictures.

Studer, D. (Executive Producer), & Teskey, S. (Director). (1997). *Karla Homolka* [TV Series]. Canada: The fifth estate.

Websites

White Ribbon Campaign: www.whiteribbon.ca

Canadian Association of Elizabeth Fry Societies: www.caefs.ca

REFERENCES

Adler, F. (1975). *Sisters in crime: The rise of the new female criminal*. New York: McGraw-Hill.

Akers, R.L. (1997). *Criminological theories: Introduction and evaluation* (2nd ed.). Los Angeles: Roxbury.

Alvi, S., Schwartz, M.D., DeKeseredy, W.S., & Maume, M.O. (2001). Women's fear of crime in Canadian public housing. *Violence Against Women, 7*, 638–661.

Barak, G., Leighton, P., & Flavin, J. (2010). *Class, race, gender, and crime: The social realities of justice in America* (3rd ed.). New York: Roman & Littlefield.

Baskin, D., Sommers, I., & Fagan, J. (1993). The political economy of female violent street crime. *Fordham Urban Law Journal, 20*, 401–417.

Beirne, P., & Messerschmidt, J.W. (2014). *Criminology* (6th ed.). New York: Harcourt Brace.

Belknap, J. (2014). *The invisible woman: Gender, crime, and justice* (4th ed.). Belmont, CA: Wadsworth.

Bennett, K. (2006). Kitchen drama: Performances, patriarchy, and power dynamics in a Dorset farmhouse kitchen. *Gender, Place & Culture, 13*(2). Retrieved from http://dx.doi.org/10.1080/09663690600573775.

Boritch, H. (1997). *Fallen women: Female crime and criminal justice in Canada*. Toronto: Nelson.

Canadian Charter of Rights and Freedoms, Part I of the *Constitution Act, 1982*, being Schedule B to the *Canada Act 1982* (UK), 1982, c 11.

Carrington, K. (2015). *Feminism and global justice*. London: Routledge.

Chesney-Lind, M. (1999). [Review of the book *When she was bad: Violent women and the myth of innocence.*] *Women & Criminal Justice, 10*(4), 114–118.

Chesney-Lind, M., & Eliason, M. (2006). From invisible to incorrigible: The demonization of marginalized women and girls. *Crime, Media, and Culture, 2*, 29–47.

Chesney-Lind, M., & Irwin, K. (2008). *Beyond bad girls: Gender, violence and hype*. New York: Routledge.

Chesney-Lind, M., & Pasko, L. (2013a). *The female offender: Girls, women, and crime*. New York: Sage.

Chesney-Lind, M., & Pasko, L. (2013b). *Girls, women, and crime: Selected readings*. Thousand Oaks, CA: Sage.

Chesney-Lind, M., & Shelden, R. (2014). *Girls: Delinquency and juvenile justice* (4th ed.). Pacific Grove, CA: Brooks/Cole.

Code, L. (2000). Introduction. In L. Code, Ed. *Encyclopedia of Feminist Theories* (pp. xv–xxvi). London, United Kingdom: Routledge.

Cohen, A. (1955). *Delinquent boys: The culture of the gang*. New York: Free Press.

Coren, M. (2007, July 28). End the blather. *Toronto Sun*. Retrieved from www.torontosun.com.

Cote, S. (2002). Introduction. In S. Cote (Ed.), *Criminological theories: Bridging the past to the future* (pp. xiii–xxiv). Thousand Oaks, CA: Sage.

Criminal Code, RSC 1985, c C-46.

Curran, D.J., & Renzetti, C.M. (2001). *Theories of crime* (2nd ed.). Boston: Allyn & Bacon.

Daly, K., & Chesney-Lind, M. (1988). Feminism and criminology. *Justice Quarterly, 5*(4), 497–538.

DeKeseredy, D., Dragiewicz, M., & Dragiewicz, M.D. (2017). *Abusive endings: Separation and divorce violence against women*. Oakland, CA: University of California Press. DeKeseredy, W.S. (2000). *Women, crime and the Canadian criminal justice system*. Cincinnati: Anderson.

DeKeseredy, W.S. (2007). Changing my life, among others: Reflections on the life and work of a feminist man. In S.L. Miller (Ed.), *Criminal justice and diversity: Voices from the field* (pp. 127–145). Boston: Northeastern University Press.

DeKeseredy, W.S. (2011). *Contemporary critical criminology*. London: Routledge.

DeKeseredy, W.S. (2012). Ending woman abuse on Canadian university and community college campuses: The role of feminist men. In J.A. Laker (Ed.), *Canadian perspectives on men and masculinities: An interdisciplinary reader* (pp. 69–89). Toronto: Oxford University Press.

DeKeseredy, W.S., & Dragiewicz, M. (2007). Understanding the complexities of feminist perspectives on woman abuse: A commentary on Donald G. Dutton's *Rethinking domestic violence*. *Violence Against Women, 13*, 874–884.

DeKeseredy, W.S., Ellis, D., & Alvi, S. (2015). *Deviance and crime: Theory, research and policy* (3rd ed.). Cincinnati: LexisNexis.

DeKeseredy, W.S., & Schwartz, M.D. (1996). *Contemporary criminology*. Belmont, CA: Wadsworth.

DeKeseredy, W.S., & Schwartz, M.D. (2005). Masculinities and interpersonal violence. In M.S. Kimmel, J. Hearn, & R.W. Connell (Eds.), *Handbook of studies on men & masculinities* (pp. 353–366). Thousand Oaks, CA: Sage.

DeKeseredy, W.S., & Schwartz, M.D. (2013). *Male peer support and violence against women: The history and verification of a theory*. Boston, MA: Northeastern University Press.

DeKeseredy, W.S., Schwartz, M.D., & Alvi, S. (2000). The role of profeminist men in dealing with woman abuse on the Canadian college campus. *Violence Against Women, 6*, 918–935.

Ehrenreich, B., & English, B. (1978). *For her own good.* Garden City, NY: Anchor.

Ellis, D., & DeKeseredy, W.S. (1996). *The wrong stuff: An introduction to the sociological study of deviance* (2nd ed.). Toronto: Allyn & Bacon.

Faith, K. (1993). *Unruly women: The politics of confinement and resistance.* Vancouver: Press Gang.

Faludi, S. (1991). *Backlash: The undeclared war against American women.* New York: Crown.

Fekete, J. (1994). *Moral panic: Biopolitics rising.* Montreal: Robert Davies.

Flavin, J. (2004). Feminism for the mainstream criminologist: An invitation. In B. Raffeal Price & N.J. Sokoloff (Eds.), *The criminal justice system and women: Offenders, prisoners, victims, & workers* (pp. 31–50). New York: McGraw Hill.

Garbarino, J. (2006). *See Jane hit: Why girls are growing more violent and what we can do about it.* New York: Penguin Press.

Gavigan, S. (1983). Women's crime and feminist critiques. *Canadian Criminology Forum, 6,* 75–90.

Gelsthorpe, L., & Morris, A. (1988). Feminism and criminology in Britain. *British Journal of Criminology, 28,* 93–110.

Gora, J. (1982). *The new female criminal: Empirical reality or social myth.* New York: Praeger.

Hackler, J. (1994). *Crime and Canadian public policy.* Scarborough: Prentice-Hall.

Hagan, J. (1989). *Structural criminology.* New Brunswick, NJ: Rutgers University Press.

Hagan, J., Gillis, A., & Simpson, J. (1987). Class in the household: A power-control theory of gender and delinquency. *American Journal of Sociology, 92,* 788–816.

Hahn Rafter, N., & Gibson, M. (Trans.). (2004). *Criminal woman, the prostitute, and the normal woman* by Cesare Lombroso with Guglielmo Ferrero (1893). Durham, NC: Duke University Press.

Hickey, E. (2012). *Serial murderers and their victims* (6th ed.). Belmont, CA: Wadsworth.

Holmlund, C. (1994). A decade of deadly dolls: Hollywood and the woman killer. In H. Birch (Ed.), *Moving targets: Women, murder and representation* (pp. 127–151). Berkeley, CA: University of California Press.

Jaggar, A. (1983). *Feminist politics and human nature.* Totowa, NJ: Rowman & Littlefield.

Johnson, H. (1987). Getting the facts straight: A statistical overview. In E. Adelberg & C. Currie (Eds.), *Too few to count: Canadian women in conflict with the law* (pp. 23–46). Vancouver: Press Gang Publishers.

Krajicek, D.J. (2014). Rifle-toting madman slaughters 14 women at Montreal university in 1989. *Daily News.* Retrieved from www.nydailynews.com/news/crime/misogynist-behind-montreal-massacre-1989-article-1.1971238.

Lewis, N. (1992, December 23). Delinquent girls achieving a violent equity in DC. *Washington Post,* p. 1.

Lilly, J.R., Cullen, F.T., & Ball, R.A. (2014). *Criminological theory: Context and consequences* (6th ed.). Thousand Oaks, CA: Sage.

Lombroso, C. (1958). *The female offender.* New York: The Wisdom Library.

Lombroso, C., & Ferrero, W. (1895). *The female offender.* New York: Philosophical Library.

Luxton, M. (1993). Dreams and dilemmas: Feminist musings on "the man question." In T. Haddad (Ed.), *Men and masculinities* (pp. 347–374). Toronto: Canadian Scholars' Press.

Maidment, M.R. (2006). Transgressing boundaries: Feminist perspectives in criminology. In W.S. DeKeseredy & B. Perry (Eds.), *Advancing critical criminology: Theory and application* (pp. 43–62). Lanham, MD: Lexington Books.

McCarthy, B., Hagan, J., & Woodward, T.S. (1999). In the company of women: Structure and agency in a revised power-control theory of gender and delinquency. *Criminology, 37,* 761–788.

McGovern, C. (1995, July 31). You've come a long way, baby: Prodded by feminism, today's teenaged girls embrace antisocial male behaviour. *Alberta Report,* pp. 24–27.

Merton, R.K. (1938). Social structure and anomie. *American Sociological Review, 3,* 672–682.

Messerschmidt, J.W. (1986). *Capitalism, patriarchy, and crime: Toward a socialist feminist criminology.* Totowa, NJ: Roman & Littlefield.

Messerschmidt, J.W. (1993). *Masculinities and crime: Critique and reconceptualization.* Lanham, MD: Roman & Littlefield.

Messerschmidt, J.W. (1997). *Crime as structured action: Gender, race, class, and crime in the making.* Thousand Oaks, CA: Sage.

Messerschmidt, J.W. (2014). *Crime as structured action: Doing masculinity, race, class, sexuality, and crime* (2nd ed.). Lanham, MD: Rowman & Littlefield.

Miller, J.M. (2003). Feminist criminology. In M.D. Schwartz & S. Hatty (Eds.). (pp. 15–29). *Controversies in critical criminology.* Retrieved from https://webcat.mtroyal.ca/vwebv/holdingsInfo?bibId=209776.

Miller, J.M., Schreck, C.J., & Tewksbury, R. (2006). *Criminological theory: A brief introduction.* Boston: Allyn & Bacon.

Miller, S.L. (1998). Introduction. In S.L. Miller (Ed.), *Crime control and women: Feminist implications of criminal justice policy* (pp. x–xxiv). Thousand Oaks, CA: Sage.

Montreal gunman called himself "angel of death." (2006, September 14). *CBC News*. Retrieved from www.cbc.ca/news/canada/montreal-gunman-called-himself-angel-of-death-1.575133.

Morrissey, B. (2003). *When women kill: Questions about agency and subjectivity*. London: Routledge.

Office of the Correctional Investigator. (2016). Aboriginal issues. Retrieved from www.oci-bec.gc.ca/cnt/priorities-priorites/aboriginals-autochtones-eng.aspx.

Pearson, P. (1997). *When she was bad: Violent women and the myth of innocence*. Toronto: Random House.

Pollak, O. (1950). *The criminality of women*. New York, NY: Barnes.

Pollak, O., & Friedman, A.S. (Eds.). (1969). *Family dynamics and female delinquency*. Palo Alto, CA: Science and Behavior Books.

Potter, H. (2015). *Intersectionality and criminology: Disrupting and revolutionizing studies of crime*. London: Routledge.

Reitano, J. (2016, March 22). Adult correctional statistics in Canada, 2014/15. *Juristat*. Statistics Canada Catalogue no. 85-002-X, p. 1–5.

Renzetti, C.M. (1993). On the margins of the malestream (or, they *still* don't get it, do they?): Feminist analyses in criminal justice education. *Journal of Criminal Justice Education*, 4, 219–234.

Renzetti, C.M. (2013). *Feminist criminology*. New York, NY: Routledge.

Schur, E.M. (1984). *Labeling women deviant: Gender, stigma, and social control*. Philadelphia, PA: Temple University Press.

Schwartz, M.D., & Slatin, G. (1984). The law on marital rape: How do Marxism and feminism explain its presence? *ALSA Forum*, 8, 244–264.

Simon, R.J. (1975). *Women and crime*. Lexington, MA: Lexington Books.

Sinha, M. (2013, February 25). Measuring violence against women: Statistical trends. *Juristat*. Statistics Canada Catalogue no. 85-002-X, p. 122.

Sluser, R., & Kaufman, M. (1992). *The white ribbon campaign: Mobilizing men to take action*. Paper presented at the 17th National Conference on Men and Masculinity. Chicago, IL. Smart, C. (1976). *Women, crime and criminology: A feminist critique*. London: Routledge & Kegan Paul.

Smart, C. (1987). [Review of the book *Capitalism, patriarchy and crime*]. *Contemporary Crises*, 11, 327–329.

Smith, M.D. (1990). Patriarchal ideology and wife beating: A test of a feminist hypothesis. *Violence and Victims*, 5, 257–273.

Statistics Canada. (2013). Aboriginal peoples in Canada: First Nations people, Metis, and Inuit. Catalogue no. 99-011-X2011001. Retrieved from http://www12.statcan.gc.ca/nhs-enm/2011/as-sa/99-011-x/99-011-x2011001-eng.pdf.

Statistics Canada. (2016a). Table 051-0005—Estimates of population, Canada, provinces and territories, quarterly (persons), CANSIM (database). Retrieved from http://www5.statcan.gc.ca/cansim/a26?lang=eng&retrLang=eng&id=0510005&&pattern=&stByVal=1&p1=1&p2=31&tabMode=dataTable&csid=.

Statistics Canada. (2016b, March 22). Youth correctional statistics in Canada, 2014/15. *Juristat*. Statistics Canada Catalogue no. 85-002-X, pp. 1–4.

Steffensmeier, D.J., & Broidy, L. (2001). Explaining female offending. In C.M. Renzetti & L. Goodstein (Eds.), *Women, crime, and criminal justice: Original feminist readings* (pp. 111–134). Los Angeles: Roxbury.

Steffensmeier, D.J., & Steffensmeier, R.H. (1980). Trends in female delinquency: An examination of arrest, juvenile court, self-report, and field data. *Criminology*, 18, 62–85.

Streib, V. (1994). Death penalty for lesbians. *National Journal of Sexual Orientation Law*, 1, 40–52.

Szasz, T. (1987). *Insanity: The idea and its consequences*. New York: John Wiley.

Toronto homicides in 2007. (2008). *CBC News*. Retrieved from www.cs.toronto.edu/~arnold/290/09s/lectures/03/CBC%20News%20In%20Depth%20%20Toronto%20Homicides%20in%202007.htm.

Walker, S. (1998). *Sense and nonsense about crime and drugs: A policy guide* (4th ed.). Belmont, CA: Wadsworth.

PART II
Female Offenders in Canada

Renée Acoby: Dangerous Offender

Jane Barker

Renée Acoby

In March 2011, Renée Acoby was declared a dangerous offender (DO). She was only the third woman to be given this designation in Canada.[1] What began in 2000 as a 3-and-a-half-year sentence for drug trafficking and assault with a weapon ballooned into a 21-and-a-half-year sentence, and ultimately into an indeterminate sentence (Botsford Fraser, 2012; Pazzano, 2011). In January 2015, Renée lost her appeal to have the DO designation removed, and later that same year she was denied parole (Borden Colley, 2015; Paul, 2015).

Renée took part in hostage-takings in Canadian prisons. The last one was in 2005, when she and another inmate confined two staff members for four hours at Grand Valley Institution for Women (Pazzano, 2015). The victims were subjected to various tortures (e.g., tied to chairs, eyes covered, force-fed medications, burned, sliced with broken glass, threatened with death) (Botsford Fraser, 2012; Paul, 2015; Stone, 2011). After the conviction for this event, the DO designation was sought for Renée.

Renée Acoby has been described by psychiatrist Dr. Scott Woodside as a psychopath, and as having "antisocial personality disorder with narcissistic traits" (Paul, 2015, ¶ 6). At her DO hearing, it was suggested that she did not care about the victims in her hostage-takings, to which she callously responded "is there a requirement in CSC [the Correctional Service of Canada] for me to care about correctional officers? Is there? Because I don't recall reading anything like that" (Paul, 2015, ¶ 16).

Renée experienced some traumatic events in her life, which one could hypothesize are contributing factors in her criminal behaviour. When she was six months of age, her father murdered her mother and soon after, her grandfather committed suicide. She was raised by her grandmother, who she thought was her mother. It wasn't until she was 9 years old that she was told the truth, and by 12 years of age she was described as angry and defiant. She was placed several times in secure custody settings for a variety of offences (Botsford Fraser, 2012). In 2000, at the age of 21, she was sentenced to three and half years for drug trafficking and assault with a weapon (Botsford Fraser, 2012; Stone, 2011). Over the subsequent years, she accumulated more convictions while incarcerated, which resulted in her current DO sentence.

For many years, Renée was subjected to CSC's Management Protocol, which was established in 2003 as a strategy to deal with incarcerated women who were deemed too challenging to be managed in any other way. The protocol demanded that any movement of an inmate would necessitate three staff members as well as the use of physical restraints (handcuffs and/or leg irons, for example) (Sapers, 2009). The Management Protocol was divided into a series of stages or steps, with inmate movement and associations being tightly regulated. In order to move through the stages and ultimately be released from the strict security requirements, women had to adhere to standards of behaviour that were difficult if not impossible to meet. The vague language in the document meant that women had little idea as to what was required to "graduate" away from the protocol. In 2009, the correctional investigator expressed grave concerns about the punitive nature of the protocol, and expressed his view that it was counter to the guiding philosophy of *Creating Choices* (TFFSW, 1990). He recommended that the protocol be abandoned.

Kim Pate[2] described the Management Protocol as a "violation of the Charter, security of the person, and international human rights standards" (Botsford Fraser, 2012, p. 5). It wasn't until May 2011 that the Management Protocol was rescinded (Sapers, 2013) by the Correctional Service of Canada.

In the chapters that follow, women's experiences with violence, their treatment in the correctional system, as well as female youth offenders will be discussed. Keep the case of Renée Acoby in mind as you read these chapters and consider the following questions.

QUESTIONS TO CONSIDER

1. Use the *Criminal Code* to look up the requirements placed upon the Crown to designate someone a dangerous offender (s 753). Do you think that Renée should have been declared a dangerous offender?
2. Do you think that the federal system of corrections (CSC) contributed to her dangerous offender designation?
3. How could her story have unfolded differently given more resources before and/or during her incarceration?

NOTES

1. Marlene Moore was the first woman to be declared a dangerous offender. She committed suicide at P4W in 1988. Lisa Neve was the second, in 1994, but five years later the designation was overturned.
2. Kim Pate is executive director of the Canadian Association of Elizabeth Fry Societies and a recently appointed Canadian senator.

REFERENCES

Borden Colley, S. (2015, November 16). Woman involved in multiple prison hostage-takings denied parole. *The Chronicle Herald*. Retrieved from http://thechronicleherald.ca/novascotia/1322613-woman-involved-in-multiple-prison-hostage-takings-denied-parole.

Botsford Fraser, M. (2012, September 12). Life on the installment plan. *The Walrus*. Retrieved from http://thewalrus.ca/life-on-the-instalment-plan.

Paul, G. (2015, January 9). Psychopath who took hostages at Kitchener prison loses appeal. *Waterloo Region Record*. Retrieved from www.therecord.com/news-story/5251368-psychopath-who-took-hostages-at-kitchener-prison-loses-appeal.

Pazzano, S. (2011, March 16). Woman declared dangerous offender in Kitchener. *Toronto Sun*. Retrieved from www.torontosun.com/news/canada/2011/03/16/17644586.html.

Sapers, H. (2009). *Annual report of the Office of the Correctional Investigator: 2008–2009.* Retrieved from www.oci-bec.gc.ca/cnt/rpt/annrpt/annrpt20082009-eng.aspx?texthighlight =%22management+protocol%22+women.

Sapers, H. (2013). Risky business: An investigation of the treatment and management of chronic self-injury among federally sentenced women. Ottawa: Office of the Correctional Investigator. Retrieved from www.oci-bec.gc.ca/cnt/rpt/pdf/oth-aut/oth-aut20130930-eng.pdf.

Stone, L. (2011, October 14). Canada's only female dangerous offender. *Edmonton Journal.* Retrieved from http://globalnews.ca/news/166014/canadas-only-female-dangerous -offender.

Canadian Female Offenders

Introduction

I want to share a conversation that I had a number of years ago with my sister. For the record, she has given her consent for me to relate it now and in this form. My sister is in her late forties, is married, and lives with her partner (and two cats) in a fashionable neighbourhood in Toronto. She has three university degrees, is pursuing a fourth, and makes her living as a freelance journalist and academic. She "fits" quite nicely into society—she is hardworking, responsible, and, if pressed to be categorized as such, she would likely describe herself as middle class. Now that you have a mental picture of her, you may be surprised that she once asked me how she could get a pardon.

About 30 years ago, my sister was arrested, charged, and convicted of public mischief for participating in a demonstration in which a road was blocked (an act of civil disobedience) in Kingston. The Oka crisis, a showdown between the Canadian Army and a group of Mohawks, captured the attention of the world and highlighted the issue of Indigenous land rights in Canada. As a result of actively participating in a demonstration to stop traffic on a bridge, my sister spent the day in jail.

Nearly 20 years later, my sister decided to see whether she could get a pardon. Although she was proud that she had been a part of the protest and didn't personally care about the record, it was problematic because it kept cropping up whenever she needed a security check. This background is a prelude to the conversation we had.

My sister called to tell me that she was having trouble getting information. She had left messages for a specific police officer (who, she had been told, could help her), but the officer had not returned her calls. My sister expressed her surprise that the officer had not called. As a journalist, she is savvy when locating information and people, and her affable social skills afford her a rapport with the people she interviews, both in person and by phone. Her difficulty in making contact with this officer was particularly puzzling to her.

Without missing a beat, I said something to the effect of "Are you *really* surprised that he won't call you back? To him, you're a criminal." My sister was completely shocked. In that one sentence, I had reduced her to one very powerful label—a criminal. Although this was clearly not my intention, she was able to see why the officer had not called her: to him she was not worthy of the return call; she was one of "them," not one of "us."

---

* The author thanks Shahid Alvi for allowing portions of his chapter "Visible Minority Women as Offenders and Victims" from the first edition of this book to be included here. The author also extends her gratitude to Kate Barker for agreeing to share her experience with the justice system.

This example is a powerful one, especially because my sister is not a "typical" offender (if such a thing really exists). The criminal justice system, like other aspects of society, operates on the basis of categories. At the broadest level are the dichotomous extremes of law breaker and law abider. As an accused person moves through the system, more categories appear. Categories are attached to crimes: offences are against the person or against property. In sentencing, there is federal and provincial (or territorial) time, defined by whether a sentence is more or less than two years. In prisons, offenders are classified according to security level (minimum, medium, or maximum). Everywhere in the criminal justice system are categorizations of some sort. Although categories may serve to impose order to a social world, some problematic and worrying consequences are associated with operating in this manner.

As Comack (1996) has noted, "women in prison are in very many ways no different from the rest of us: they are daughters, sisters, girlfriends, wives and mothers, and they share many of the experiences of women collectively" (p. 20). A similar comment was also made by Hatch and Faith (1989), who observed that "women in conflict with the law have more in common with other women than they do with male prison inmates, in terms of their socio-economic situation, program, and treatment needs" (p. 454). There is very little utility gained by categorizing female offenders according to their crime. There are a number of problems with taking this approach as a starting point to understanding why women offend. Firstly, if only the most recent offence is used to categorize a woman, any information related to her history of offending is summarily discarded. According to Comack (1996), we need to recognize that crime categories are simply legal constructions that represent the official version of the woman's behaviour. In an attempt to impose order on an event, the official version is given credence by the law, and any competing version is silenced. Crime categories serve to create a binary opposition between those who break the law and those who abide by it—thus emphasizing the criminal woman as "the other" (Comack, 1996). The setting up of this kind of an "us" versus "them" dichotomy may then lead to a positivist approach in which criminologists, in an attempt to understand why women break the law, look for the presence of variables, either intrinsic or extrinsic (Comack, 1996).

Classifications of Crimes

Although relying solely on crime classifications to reduce women's crimes to some sort of categorization is clearly problematic, we need to understand and appreciate the kinds of crimes that women are committing and being accused of committing and then compare this information with the case for men. For this reason, the nature and frequency of female offending in Canada is explored.

Females make up just over half (50.4 percent) of Canada's population (Milan, 2015), but account for far less than half of those who come into conflict with the law. Statistics for 2014–2015 show that just under 5 percent of the federal inmate population is female, up from 2.9 percent just 10 years earlier, representing a 50-percent increase (Office of the Correctional Investigator [OCI], 2015). In 2004, men were more likely to face multiple charges, whereas women were not (Kong & AuCoin, 2008). Fifteen percent of women offenders in 2006 were classified as repeat offenders, up from only 10 percent who were classified as such in 1997, and women were more likely to be one-time offenders (Kong & AuCoin, 2008). In comparison with 30 percent of incarcerated men who had a previous federal sentence, incarcerated women were less likely to have one such sentence. Similarly, provincially and territorially sentenced women were less likely than provincially and territorially sentenced men to have had a previous provincial or territorial sentence.

As noted in Chapter 1, statistics from Canada's adult courts can provide some information regarding the kinds of offences that women are found guilty of committing. Below, data are presented according to the types of crimes committed, broadly categorized as crimes against the person, crimes against property, and administration of justice offences.

Crimes Against the Person

Just over 21 percent of those women whose cases were completed in adult court in 2008–2009 were there for crimes against the person (Hotton Mahony, 2011). Since 2005–2006, the percentage of women found guilty of crimes against the person has increased marginally. In 2014–2015, 13.45 percent of those found guilty of such crimes were women, compared to 11.6 percent in 2005–2006 (Statistics Canada, 2016). As can be seen in Figure 3.1, in this category of convictions, males are clearly represented at a disproportionately higher rate than women.

Crimes Against Property

Nearly a third (32 percent) of all women whose cases are completed in adult court are there for a crime against property (Hotton Mahoney, 2011) and about a fifth (21.05 percent) of those convicted of crimes against property are women (Statistics Canada, 2016). Figure 3.2 illustrates that when it comes to crimes that are financial in nature, we tend to see higher conviction rates for women, although even these rates are still far lower than those of males.

FIGURE 3.1   Percentage of Males and Females Convicted of Crimes Against the Person in Canada in 2014–2015*

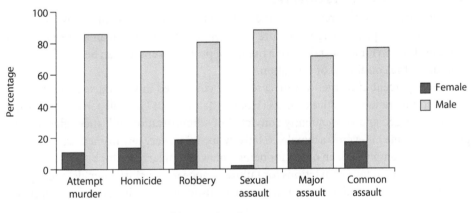

* Percentages do not add to 100 because sex is unknown in some instances.

Source: Statistics Canada. (2016). *Adult criminal courts, number of cases and charges by type of decision, annual* [CANSIM table 252-0053]. Retrieved from http://www5.statcan.gc.ca/cansim/a26?lang=eng&id=2520053.

FIGURE 3.2   Percentage of Males and Females Convicted of Crimes Against Property in Canada in 2014–2015*

* Percentages do not add to 100 because sex is unknown in some instances.

Source: Statistics Canada. (2016). *Adult criminal courts, number of cases and charges by type of decision, annual* [CANSIM table 252-0053]. Retrieved from http://www5.statcan.gc.ca/cansim/a26?lang=eng&id=2520053.

Of all convictions, the category of crimes against property shows the highest percentage of women who are found guilty. The categories of fraud and theft both approach the 30 percent level and have remained relatively stable since the early 1990s. Not surprisingly, a fairly small percentage of women are convicted in court on break and enter charges (although the percentage of women in this category has increased over time). Break and enter is considered one of the more violent of the crimes against property, because it involves a physical violation of a dwelling or place of work. Women are more likely to engage in the writing of bad cheques or credit card fraud (which results in a fraud charge) or shoplifting (which results in a theft charge) than breaking into a home or office.

Administration of Justice Offences

This category of offences refers to crimes related to the justice system and its administration. For example, a charge of failure to appear can be laid when an accused person does not show up for a court date, or a breach of probation charge can be laid for failure to abide by the conditions of probation.

Twenty percent of women whose cases were completed in the courts in 2008–2009 faced administration of justice charges (Hotton Mahony, 2011). Of all persons appearing in court charged and subsequently convicted of administration of justice offences, approximately one in seven is a female. Relatively speaking, very few women are convicted for failing to comply with an order, for being unlawfully at large, or for breaching probation. About one in four convictions for failure to appear is against a female, the highest rate of women convicted of an administration of justice offence (Statistics Canada, 2016).

Women's Offending

You now have an idea about the broad categories of offences (crimes against the person, property crimes, and violations against the administration of justice) that paint an overall picture of women's involvement in crime in Canada. However, this textbook would be remiss not to specifically mention those crimes that women are frequently associated with. By including this kind of a focus, we risk reinforcing the already negative stereotypes about women who come into conflict with the law. As will be noted later in this chapter, the public has a fascination with sensationalized media portrayals of female offenders. The media's distorted images of women in conflict with the law may then feed into these stereotypes. I do not want to perpetuate any caricatures of the female offender by including mention of specific sensationalized cases; instead, I hope to impart the need to acknowledge that women commit some types of crimes more often than others. Court statistics show that women's representation is highest in completed court cases of fraud (31 percent), prostitution (31 percent), and theft (30 percent) (Hotton Mahony, 2011). Although considerable debate has focused on whether some of these acts (prostitution and drug use, for example) should be criminalized, the fact remains that women in Canada are charged and convicted every day of engaging in drug- and prostitution-related activities. To ignore this reality would overlook an important facet of women's involvement with the criminal justice system in Canada.

Crimes Related to the Sex Trade

The sex trade has been called the oldest profession—and it can be found in most (some might assert all) communities across the country. It's also been called the oldest oppression by those who believe it is an exploitation of women. In 2013–2014, approximately 38 percent of those convicted of prostitution-related charges were women. Please see Chapter 10 for a thorough discussion and an in-depth analysis of prostitution and how the Canadian legal system has evolved in terms of its treatment of those who work in the sex trade.

Crimes Related to Illicit Drugs

Drug-related crimes in Canada include such offences as driving under the influence of illicit drugs and the possession, trafficking, and importation of such drugs. It is interesting to note that while the crime rate has declined in Canada since its peak in 1991, the rate of drug-related offences has increased dramatically (up 52 percent) since 1991 (Cotter, Greenland, & Karam, 2015). Most police-reported drug crimes (two out of every three) are related to cannabis, with cannabis possession accounting for more than half of these (Cotter et al., 2015). While rates of cannabis possession charges have decreased in recent years (down 15 percent in 2015 from 2014), rates of charges for possession of other controlled drugs and substances have increased by 17 percent for the same time period (Statistics Canada, 2016). Charges for trafficking offences in Canada also declined in 2015. In relative terms, few people are charged with importation or cultivation in Canada.

As is the case with other crimes, men significantly outnumber women in drug-related charges. In 2013, only 18 percent of those charged with drug-related offences were female. A larger proportion of women (29 percent) were charged with the import or export of drugs in 2013 than were charged with possession (17 percent) (Cotter et al., 2015). Although men clearly outnumber women in drug-related crimes, these offences represent some of the more common charges for which women are convicted, and for which they are sentenced to periods of incarceration (Finn, Trevethan, Carrière, & Kowalski, 1999). It has been noted that for many women who are involved in the drug trade, they are found in low-ranking, high-risk positions that often involve smuggling or transporting illicit substances (Cotter et al., 2015), a role, one can hypothesize, that is heavily influenced by economic necessity.

Theft and Fraud

The final category of women's offences to be discussed are crimes of theft and fraud. Men again outnumber women with respect to these offences. However, from a relative perspective, both theft and fraud are particularly favoured by women. About 37 percent of people charged with theft under $5,000 and 33 percent of those charged with fraud are women (Hotton Mahony, 2011). Historically, few women have been known to commit so-called masculine property crimes, such as break and enter or auto theft (Steffensmeier as cited in Hatch & Faith, 1989). This pattern has changed very little in the last 25 years, with women representing approximately 11 percent of all people charged with break and enter offences in 2009 (Hotton Mahony, 2011).

What kinds of thefts and frauds are women committing? Their crimes (such as passing of bad cheques, credit card fraud, and shoplifting) tend to centre on meeting the economic needs of themselves or their families. Hatch and Faith (1989) noted that, in 1987, women made up 44 percent of those charged with shoplifting items with a value of less than $1,000 and nearly one-third of those charged with theft greater than $1,000. In that same year, women made up approximately 27 percent of those charged with cheque and credit card fraud (Hatch & Faith, 1989).

Not all women who commit fraud are passing bad cheques or using credit cards fraudulently. As described in Box 3.1, later in this chapter, some women are charged with defrauding government agencies (such as welfare), a crime that can result in severe sanctioning. Research on women and fraud in Canada has been fairly scant. Atkinson (1998), in her study on neutralizations in male and female offenders, noted that female fraud offenders, as a group, were the most likely to accept neutralizations about fraudulent activities, suggesting that any interventions that sought to reduce neutralizations in offenders would likely be best suited to female (and not male) fraud offenders. For a more detailed account of Atkinson's (1998) study, the reader is referred to Chapter 6. In a more recent study completed in Israel, researchers found that female fraud offenders tended to be older than other female offenders and had the oldest average age (35 years) at the time of their first offence (Shechory, Perry, & Addad, 2011). They were described as "late onset" offenders who were found guilty of forgery, identity theft, and/ or the misappropriation of funds. By and large, this group had a limited amount of prior trauma in their lives, no past drug abuse, no previous criminal history, and no history of delinquent peers. As a group, they were better educated than most inmates, had more extensive employment histories, low levels of aggression, and high self-control (Shechory et al., 2011).

In their *Report to the Nations on Occupational Fraud and Abuse*, the Association of Certified Fraud Examiners (2016) noted that women were responsible for just under a third (31 percent) of all cases investigated worldwide. In Canada, women accounted for 35.4 percent of all cases that were investigated by this body. The median loss for frauds perpetrated by women worldwide was $100,000 (a figure quite a bit lower than the $187,000 median loss reported for male perpetrators of fraud) (Association of Certified Fraud Examiners, 2016).

► **WHAT DO YOU THINK?**

How do women's crimes relate to issues of economic disempowerment? What are the impacts of having a low level of education, few marketable skills, being underemployed or unemployed, and relying on inadequate social assistance? How might these factors impact on the criminalization of women?

What Do We Know About Visible Minority Female Offenders in Canada?

It has been noted that Indigenous women are greatly overrepresented in Canada's correctional system, relative to the total population of Indigenous people in Canada (see Chapter 9 for a thorough discussion of Indigenous female offenders). But what about other minorities? One Canadian scholar rightly claimed in 1999 that "there is, and there has been since Confederation, a disproportionate number of First Nations girls and females of colour in the justice system" (Reitsma-Street, 1999, p. 353). Despite academic and government recognition of the existence of racism within the criminal justice system and the potentially unique needs of minority women, little has been done in the way of systematic research on this issue since that time, nor has much progress been made to reduce racism within the criminal justice system; most efforts have been tokenistic or fruitless (Denney, Ellis, & Barn, 2006).

Recent estimates suggest that visible minorities[1] account for 18 percent of all federally sentenced Canadians. This is an increase of 40 percent over the previous five years (OCI, 2013a). It was pointed out that had it not been for increases in the numbers of Indigenous (722), black (598), and Asian (312) offenders from 2006 to 2011, there would have been no net growth in the offender population over this time period (OCI, 2012). As is the case with Indigenous peoples, blacks are overrepresented among correctional populations in Canada. Approximately 3 percent of the Canadian general population is black, but 9 percent of all federal inmates are black (OCI, 2012; OCI, 2013a). Blacks are one the fastest growing segments in corrections (OCI, 2012). It should be noted that compared to black men, there are relatively few black women in federal corrections. Only 4 percent of incarcerated black inmates are women, but these 55 women make up over 9 percent of all federally incarcerated women in Canada (OCI, 2013a).

Most of the black women (78 percent) are in custody at Grand Valley Institution in Kitchener, Ontario. While the number of black women in federal custody remained fairly consistent from 2000 to 2009, the number of black women who were federally incarcerated increased by 54 percent in 2010, and then by 28 percent by 2012 (OCI, 2013a). According to Lawrence and Williams (2006), some evidence indicates that black women in the United Kingdom, the United States, and Canada "receive prison sentences for importing drugs at rates greatly disproportionate to their populations ... and that drug-importation offences contribute significantly to the over-representation of black women in prisons" (p. 286). Support for this assertion can be seen in a recent report on the experiences of black inmates in the federal correctional system in Canada (OCI, 2013a). Over half (53 percent) of incarcerated black women are serving time for drug offences (OCI, 2013a). Interviews conducted by the OCI (2013a) with these women showed that many of them willingly carried drugs over the border because they were trying to get out of poverty. Others reported that they participated in the trafficking because of threats of violence aimed at their children or families. Many of these women face deportation at the conclusion of their sentences.

We need to pay closer attention to the ways in which intersecting social factors might explain offending patterns. For example, most women charged with theft have shoplifted items for themselves or their children, a finding that is not surprising, given that most of these women are poor. Recent reports indicate that 22 percent of racialized Canadians live in poverty (Canada, 2006), and although we have no data on the number of visible minority women who have been charged with shoplifting, we can reasonably assume that their situation is no different from that of their white counterparts. Similarly, welfare fraud is a direct outcome of both decreases in real income from welfare for many women and the increasing enthusiasm in some jurisdictions for charging and prosecuting women who commit welfare fraud (Addario, 2002). For many women charged with assault, their charges relate directly to their use of self-defence in cases of domestic violence, and the police practice of charging both men and women in these situations (Saunders, 1986). Visible minority women are not immune to being victimized by domestic violence, although the contours of their victimization may differ in important ways from those of non-minority women.

The types of offences that women commit are less violent than offences committed by men, and for visible minority females (like other women), their offences are related to women's subordinate economic and social status in Canadian society. Indeed, as one scholar points out, women's offending can be conceptualized as a form of economic survival tied to diminished opportunities and histories of personal victimization that reflect "the difficulty women have in extracting themselves from the relationships, addictions, and economic necessities which arise once they are immersed in 'street work'" (Gilfus, 2006, p. 13). Clearly, this link between criminalized behaviour and economic need has implications not only for prevention strategies that relate to the decriminalization and legalization of drugs such as marijuana and hashish (which would greatly reduce the criminalization of women and men) but also for the provision of adequate training, jobs, and social assistance for poor families and the ongoing struggle to eliminate violence against women.

Coping with Incarceration

By definition, any behaviour that a person employs to deal with a difficult situation, or a stressor, is a coping strategy. Just the nature of its purpose—to assist a person in coping with a stressor—makes it a coping strategy. Whether the strategy is functional (or dysfunctional) in the long run may remain to be seen. Note that the determination of whether an act is considered functional or dysfunctional can be considered to be a value judgment. A coping strategy used by one person in one situation could be deemed dysfunctional by an onlooker, and that same strategy used by another person could be considered functional.

For the purpose of exploring these concepts of coping as they relate to criminalized women, we can broadly categorize the strategies into those that are functional and those that are not. Some coping strategies may start out as functional (by definition, most begin this way) and become dysfunctional over time. The point is not to cast aspersions on any individual or group of people for their choices of coping strategies but to illustrate that some strategies may create additional problems in a person's life, which may then require additional coping. For example, whether a person uses heroin will not be debated with regard to whether its use is ethical or not, nor will it be the subject of a moralizing rant. That kind of opinion doesn't belong in a criminal justice text; however, this kind of drug use may be related to a criminal act that results in a conflict with the law, which *is* of import here, and as such, these types of coping strategies will be discussed.

Once a woman has arrived at a correctional facility, there is a lot to learn, a lot to get used to, and a lot to cope with. Many women in prison are mothers, and they are often the primary caregivers for their children (OCI, 2015). Among federally incarcerated women, 70 percent are mothers to children under 18 years of age (OCI, 2015). One of their biggest issues is the care of their children. Although some mothers are permitted to have their children with them in prison, the majority are not.[2] Issues arise pertaining to child custody and access. In some cases, the children of incarcerated women have been made wards of the court, effectively eliminating any future contact with their mothers. In other instances, mothers may worry about the safety of their children (Ferraro & Moe, 2003; Task Force on Federally Sentenced Women, 1990). If children themselves come into conflict with the law, mothers in prison may face a double dose of guilt for "not being there" for their child and for "setting a bad example." Although some might argue that incarcerated fathers face the same kinds of issues, in reality, for many of those incarcerated fathers, their partners in the community are and always have been the primary caregivers for the children (Ferraro & Moe, 2003).

Many women who are incarcerated face stressors related to the nature of the institution where they reside (Hayman, 2006). The policies and practices of any correctional facility may seem foreign to many, constituting stress on their own. For example, prisons offer very little privacy. Some might argue that prisons have *no* privacy, and that includes the violation of personal space experienced by many women. Part of the prison protocol may involve searches and pat-downs—having your possessions examined or having your body physically searched by correctional staff who have the authority to do so (Hayman, 2006). Inmates may be asked to give a urine sample or be strip-searched upon returning to the institution after being out on a pass. Freedom is limited in prison, where movement within the institution is constrained by rules and regulations regarding where an inmate can go and when an inmate can leave the living unit.

Lastly, consider the stressors associated with being forced to live with people you may not even choose to be friends with. First and foremost, many women have concerns about their safety in prison. The new regional facilities do not have security personnel in most of the living units 24 hours a day. Instead, the primary workers complete rounds, entering each living unit on a regular basis and at specified times to check that everyone is there and that all is as it should be. However, plenty of opportunities exist for women to be bullied or muscled by other offenders when the security staff is not present.

The daily stressors associated with prison life are varied, be they concerns about children, dealing with the lack of privacy, feeling physically constrained, worrying about personal safety, or tolerating the idiosyncrasies of those with whom one lives. These concerns all lead to increased stress in the lives of incarcerated women, and women might benefit from addressing these stressors with various kinds of coping strategies.

► **WHAT DO YOU THINK?**

Imagine that you have just been sentenced to a period of incarceration and you are on your way to a correctional facility. What is running through your mind? What kinds of concerns would you have about your living arrangements, your safety, and how you might be treated by the staff? Do you think the concerns you have would differ from the concerns that most women facing prison would have?

Coping with a History of Abuse

Comack (1996) noted that by identifying the ways in which criminalized women who had been abused in childhood resisted and coped with their experiences, it might be possible to uncover the strategies they used to take some kind of control over their current situations. She hypothesized that by taking control, the women were "developing particular survival skills" (p. 62) that helped the women cope with the consequences of being abused. The coping skills they developed included behaviours such as becoming sexually active, engaging in prostitution, and using drugs and/or alcohol. Comack also discussed some of the strategies women used to cope with abuse as an adult. Women's aggression was seen as being one such coping strategy. In addition, women who experienced domestic violence may have coped by contacting the police in hopes that some sort of intervention would occur or by attempting to obtain support from a shelter. She has made links between women's experiences of abuse and their subsequent violations of the law, emphasizing that "women's law violations become part of coping with, resisting and surviving experiences of abuse" (p. 83).

Comack (1996, 2005) examined how the concepts of coping, resisting, and surviving, as originally conceptualized by Kelly (1988, cited in Comack, 1996, 2005), allow for the exploration of the interrelatedness that may exist between women's histories of abuse and their criminal behaviours. In her analysis, Comack (2005) differentiates between these terms in the following manner:

- *Coping* refers to interpreting a woman's criminal behaviour in the context of how it enables her to deal with the past abuse and its possible long-term effects.
- *Resisting* refers to the law-breaking behaviour of some women, which can be interpreted as an attempt to resist the abuse that they are experiencing in the present.
- *Surviving* captures the very real position that some criminalized women find themselves in as they try to actively survive the dangers of their existence and in so doing illustrates how their abuse (current, or past, or both) is linked to their law-breaking behaviour.

By recounting some of the experiences of the 24 women she interviewed who were serving provincial sentences, Comack (2005) was able to show how the effects of abuse had permeated their lives, and how these threads of coping, resisting, and surviving abuse were woven through the women's lives and illustrated in their experiences of law-breaking behaviour.

Similar observations have been reported by Gilfus (1992, 2002). Gilfus (1992) proposed that for many of the 20 incarcerated women she interviewed across Canada, their use of criminal survival strategies was often the only viable option they could see to allow them to escape from the violence (physical and sexual) that permeated their lives. The women did not tend to characterize themselves as victims, but as survivors. In addition, they conceptualized their criminal actions—both their entry into criminal behaviour and their commitment to criminal behaviour—as being related to significant relationships in their lives. Gilfus (1992) noted that when it came to their criminal involvement, these women were not so much illustrating a "criminal career" as reflecting an "immersion in street crime" (p. 5). For them, the adoption of certain survival strategies that may involve criminal behaviour (which may seem like the only option available to some women) began the shift from being a victim to being an offender (Gilfus, 1992).

Some have suggested that for a woman who has been sexually abused as a child, certain aspects of a prison environment serve to constantly re-expose her to traumatic processes associated with prior abuse (Heney & Kristiansen, 1997). Using Finkelhor and Browne's (1985) conceptualization of these traumagenic dynamics, Heney and Kristiansen (1997) proposed that these dynamics of powerlessness, traumatic sexualization, stigmatization, and betrayal are all manifest, in one form or another, in the prison environment.

Traumatic sexualization refers to the way in which a child's sexuality is shaped (by the abuse) in a way that is developmentally inappropriate and dysfunctional in an interpersonal sense (Finkelhor & Browne, 1985). In prison, this dynamic is replicated in instances of institutionalized assaults, such as pat-downs, frisks, strip searches, and, in some cases, internal searches[3] (Heney & Kristiansen, 1997). Powerlessness, which was thought to be the most fundamental of the dynamics underlying child abuse, consists of the inherent power differential between the child victim of abuse and the abuser (Finkelhor & Browne, 1985). In prison, this dynamic of powerlessness is found in the structure of a correctional facility. The primary workers, warden, teachers, and case management officers—realistically, *everyone* who works or volunteers in a prison—are in a position of power over those who are incarcerated. Survivors of trauma may react to their sense of powerlessness by trying to control events in their environment, but this reaction is more of an illusion of control that ultimately contributes to their further feelings of powerlessness (Heney & Kristiansen, 1997).

The traumagenic dynamic of betrayal—that is, the experience of being betrayed by one's abuser or by those to whom disclosure of abuse has been made but who fail to do anything to intervene—is also re-experienced by women in prison. According to Heney and Kristiansen (1997), many incarcerated women feel betrayed by a society that didn't help them as children, which is the same society that later charged, convicted, sentenced, and imprisoned them, and is therefore seen to have become their persecutor.

Lastly, the dynamic of stigmatization refers to all of those negative messages conveyed to the victim of abuse by the abuser, and the experience of isolation that many face. These same messages are experienced by women in prison—that society views them as being different, abnormal, or in some way to be feared (Heney & Kristiansen, 1997). Women who are incarcerated must face many challenges while in prison, and for those women with an abuse history, the traumatic dynamics that might surface in the prison environment give them that much more to cope with.

Different Types of Coping Strategies

As already noted, people use many different kinds of coping strategies to deal with stressful events in their lives. Although many criminalized women use positive ways in which to cope with stressors, the focus of this section is on those strategies that are dysfunctional in nature. Such strategies include self-injury, suicide, and alcohol and drug use and abuse. This list is not an exhaustive inventory of strategies, but consists of those behaviours that are most often discussed in the literature.

Self-Injury

Self-injurious behaviour is not a new phenomenon. It has been studied in both forensic and non-forensic samples of women. The correctional investigator noted that a quarter of the female offender population has a history of self-injury (OCI, 2012). Self-injury can include many behaviours such as hanging, cutting, scratching, reopening wounds, head banging, biting, swallowing non-food items (such as glass), and inserting objects into the skin. Self-injurious behaviour should be considered a mental health issue and should not be treated as a matter of security (Heney, 1990; Sapers, 2010). However, the OCI has documented cases where CSC has shown an overreliance on the use of seclusion, inappropriate monitoring of restraints, limited access to services for women who have very complex mental health needs including self-injury, and inadequate resources to meet the needs of those with such complex mental health needs (OCI, 2012; OCI, 2013b; Sapers, 2011). In his most recent annual report (2014–2015), the correctional investigator described the following case:

> Over a period of eight months, there were ten documented incidents of self-injury including head-banging, cutting of arms and wrists and auto-asphyxiation, often resulting in the use of physical restraints. On a number of occasions, often after self-injuring with a ligature, she was transferred to an all-male Regional Treatment Centre so she could be monitored given the lack of 24 hour healthcare coverage at her parent institution. Placing a woman with a history of sexual abuse in an all-male institution is unacceptable, contravenes international standards and is not compliant with CSC policy. Additional funds were requested from CSC Regional Headquarters so that 24 hour healthcare coverage could be provided, however this request was denied. (OCI, 2015, p. 53)

In a recent examination of the treatment and management of self-injurious behaviour in federal corrections, it was noted that in one year (2012–2013) there were 901 recorded incidents of self-injury by 264 inmates in prisons in Canada. While only 14 percent of the offenders were female, they accounted for nearly 36 percent of the reported instances of self-injury (OCI, 2013b). Among the women, those who were identified as Indigenous accounted for about 45 percent of the self-injurious incidents. Seventeen offenders (like the woman described above) were deemed to be chronic or repetitive self-injurers and nine of these inmates were women (OCI, 2013b). This statistic is even more startling in light of the fact that women make up about 5 percent of the entire federal custodial population, but they account for over half of the chronic self-injurers in prisons across Canada (OCI, 2013b; OCI, 2015).

In a historical review of the scholarship on self-injurious behaviour in women, Shaw (2002) noted that published studies from the turn of the 19th century to the present tended to focus on middle-class, white women in England and North America. According to Shaw (2002), over this time period, self-injurious behaviour garnered four distinct shifts in attention: "1) varying degrees of clinical interest in and numbers of publications on self-injury, 2) changing conceptualizations of self-injury, 3) changing treatment approaches on self-injury, and 4) changing characterizations of women who self-injure" (p. 191).

In her feminist analysis, Shaw (2002) noted that women who self-injure do so to take control and to objectify their bodies, which helps them to alleviate symptoms of psychological distress they might be experiencing. Shaw points out the societal hypocrisy that exists because it is okay for society to objectify women's bodies, but if a woman objectifies her own body (through the act of self-injury), such an act is not "culturally sanctioned" (p. 206). Further, engaging in self-injury "is to make oneself ugly in this culture and to violate sacred beauty standards for women" (p. 206), an act not well tolerated by society.

Shaw (2002) summarized the major contemporary developments in terms of how self-injury has been conceptualized. She noted that the first development viewed self-injury as a "syndrome of impulse regulation" (p. 198) in which the self-injury itself was regarded as an addictive behaviour. In this approach, the contribution of environmental factors is minimized and emphasis is placed on the individual—the woman is unable to resist her own self-destructive impulses (Shaw, 2002). As a result of an increase in research that focused on childhood abuse, the second contemporary conceptualization emerged, that of self-injury as a coping strategy. Self-injury was seen as a way that "trauma survivors attempt to manage feelings of powerlessness, dissociation, intrusive memories, compulsions to re-enact the trauma and punish the body, and bodily alienation" (Shaw, 2002, p. 199). The most recent contemporary conceptualization involves neurological research that supports the view that the act of self-injury is accompanied by specific physiological antecedents and consequences that reinforce the act and contribute to the continuation of the behaviour, thus making the cessation of self-injury difficult to attain (Shaw, 2002). As Shaw points out, although the contemporary conceptualizations differ, some common threads run through each, and therefore more than one model is often considered. Most authors generally accept that "self-injury is a response to symptoms of psychological distress such as dissociation, feelings of helplessness and anxiety" and that "the act provides relief and a sense of control" (Shaw, 2002, p. 199).

An example of Shaw's (2002) second contemporary conceptualization can be seen in Jan Heney's (1990) *Report on Self-Injurious Behaviour in the Kingston Prison for Women* submitted to the CSC. Heney worked from a model of self-injury that characterized the behaviour as "a coping strategy that manifests itself as a result of childhood abuse (usually sexual)" (p. 4). According to Heney, the abused child is able to reconcile the abuse through a mechanism of self-blame. If the child is able to blame herself, then she may believe that she actually has some control over the situation and thus will be able to stop the abuse from occurring. Over time, the self-blame and the continued abuse reinforce the notion that "bad things do and will happen" (Heney, 1990, p. 4). Thus, when faced with this sense of inevitability with respect to the occurrence of bad things in the future, anxiety may abound. Heney postulated that "self-injury is an attempt to control the extent and timing of the anticipated pain which is seen as inevitable" (p. 4). Following the pain (attained through self-injury), anxiety is immediately lessened. So, in this sense, the reduced anxiety can be viewed as an "adaptive and resourceful behaviour" (Heney, 1990, p. 4). Heney conceptualized this process in a schematic representation (see Figure 3.3). Others have also conceptualized self-injury among prisoners as a coping strategy (Heney & Kristiansen, 1997; Pollack & Brezina, 2006).

In her detailed report, Heney (1990) outlined the extent of the problem at P4W; described the current institutional response to self-injury, injury reduction, and suicide identification; and drew her conclusions, including recommending some directions for the future. Nearly 60 percent of the inmates interviewed by Heney reported they had engaged in self-injurious behaviour at some point in their lives. The majority (92 percent) of these women indicated that the method they had used was slashing.[4] Other types of self-injurious behaviour included "headbanging, starvation, burning and/or tattooing" (Heney, 1990, p. 8). Of those women who reported self-injurious behaviour, 73 percent also reported a history of childhood abuse (Heney, 1990).

FIGURE 3.3   Self-Injurious Behaviour as a Coping Strategy

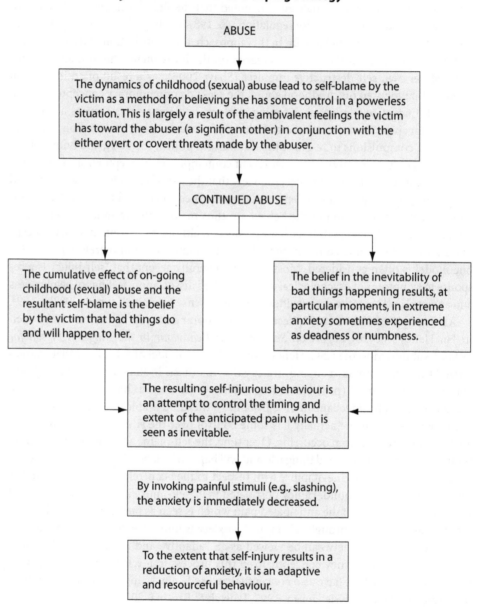

Source: Heney, J. (1990). Report on self-injurious behaviour in the Kingston Prison for Women. Ottawa: Correctional Service of Canada, p. 5.

Heney (1990) also indicated that outbreaks of self-injury tended to coincide with periods of extreme tension in the prison. According to the inmates interviewed, the tension that existed in the prison was most often caused by changes in prison policy, the attitudes of certain staff members toward the women, and instances of mass punishment.[5] Situational factors were most often identified by inmates as triggers for self-injurious behaviour. Almost half of the women indicated that their urge to self-injure was strongest in situations where they experienced feelings of helplessness and powerlessness. Approximately 7 percent of women interviewed indicated that the urge to self-injure arose when they were experiencing isolation.

At the time the report was written, the institutional policy for self-injury advised taking the woman to health care (or the community hospital) and then to segregation until a psychologist could assess her. In addition, an appearance was required before the Segregation Review Board, which met twice a week. Heney (1990) pointed out that according to this policy, a woman who self-injured might be kept in segregation for a number of days. In some cases, women were transferred to the regional treatment centre as a result of extreme self-injury. In her recommendations, Heney (1990) asserted that it be recognized that "self-injurious behaviour is a mental health issue as opposed to a security issue" (p. 14). Heney was clear in her view that segregation was not an appropriate response to self-injury, because of the isolation experienced by the woman and the perception that she was being punished for her behaviour. According to Heney, the use of segregation in these instances was more likely to increase, not decrease, any suicide potential. She suggested that in cases of self-injury, an assessment should be made by a professional trained in these issues (psychiatrist, psychologist, nurse, or physician). In those cases where a woman was not deemed to be able to function in the prison population because of high suicide potential, Heney (1990) suggested that she be kept in the health care area of the prison. Alternatively, if this option was not viable, she recommended the woman be transferred to another health care facility until she could be stabilized and returned to the prison population.

Despite the closure of the Prison for Women (P4W) and the opening of the regional facilities, self-injury remains an issue of concern with respect to women who are incarcerated federally in Canada. Prison policy regarding self-injury has been criticized (Hannah-Moffat, 2006; Kilty, 2006), and the question has been raised about whether, with respect to self-injury, prisons can develop "gender-sensitive, or 'gender-responsive' prison policies at all" (Bosworth, 2006, p. 157). Kilty (2006) asserted that the Correctional Service of Canada policy, as it relates to self-injury, is problematic, in particular that "women who self-injure are still routinely disciplined for their behaviour in Federal Canadian prisons through admittance to administrative segregation" (p. 161). By placing a self-injurious woman in administrative segregation for monitoring, the CSC is effectively increasing the woman's risk to self-injure because of the punitive and isolating nature of segregation (Kilty, 2006). Further, Kilty maintained that "self-injuring prisoners are being inappropriately constructed as risks to the institution" by the CSC (p. 162).

This assertion was echoed by Hannah-Moffat (2006) in response to Kilty's article. In her reaction essay, Hannah-Moffat noted that although self-injurious behaviour is not scored as a risk factor in the third-generation risk assessment measures, it is included as a consideration. In addition, Hannah-Moffat asserts that self-injurious behaviour is now being viewed by the CSC as a behaviour that is difficult to manage and a symptom of a mental health issue, instead of being viewed primarily as a coping strategy. According to Hannah-Moffat,[6] as an identified need, self-injurious behaviour will be targeted for treatment by programs such as dialectical behaviour therapy (DBT).[7] In her discussion of this issue, Hannah-Moffat raises the question of how the risk/need paradigm used in corrections is able to deal with those self-injurious women identified as having a need for treatment, but who do not embrace, for whatever reason, the treatment that is offered.

Thomas, Leaf, Kazmierczak,[8] and Stone (2006) have suggested that prison policy needs to recognize the role prison culture plays in self-injurious behaviour (SIB) because "viewing inmate difficulties in terms of a 'coping deficit' provides a policy guideline that, although recognizing the need to focus on the individual mental health of prisoners who self-injure, shifts attention to the broader context in which SIB occurs" (p. 197). In this conceptualization, Thomas et al. view self-injury as a symptom both of the state of a person's mental health and "of the pathology of prisons" (p. 197). Thomas et al. also suggest that policy-makers need to ensure that punitive segregation is used "only as a last resort" (p. 197).

Every CSC institution must have procedures in place to ensure that any suicide attempts or self-injurious behaviours are appropriately handled and that staff are educated and aware of the official policy with respect to both self-injury and suicide attempts. The CSC's official policy on suicide and self-injury may be found in Commissioner's Directive (CD) 843. While CD 843 does outline procedures for screening for suicide risk, CD 843 makes no distinction between monitoring for *suicidal* behaviour and monitoring for *self-injurious* behaviour; the term *suicide/self-injury watch* is used to denote the isolation of an inmate who is thought to be in imminent danger from either suicide or self-injurious behaviour (CSC, 2017). Although these two behaviours may be virtually indistinguishable from the point of view of an observer, the *intent* of each, from the perspective of the inmate, is very different.

Suicide

Research has suggested that a link may exist between self-injury and suicide attempts. In an examination of suicides over a ten-year period in the CSC, it was reported that 58 percent of those who committed suicide had some history of psychological problems, 60 percent had previously tried to kill themselves, more than a third had engaged in self-injury, and 85 percent had a history of substance abuse problems (CSC, 2012, cited in OCI, 2015). One American study found that women offenders who self-injured were 26 times more likely to attempt suicide than women offenders with no history of self-injury (Roe-Sepowitz, 2007).

Individuals in federal prison are more at risk to kill themselves than to be murdered (Larivière, 1997). The most likely method of suicide in federal institutions is by hanging, and suicide attempts occur disproportionally more often in physically isolated cells (e.g., segregation) (OCI, 2014). Suicide rates for prison populations are about seven times higher than for the general population (OCI, 2015). On average, there are ten suicides in federal corrections each year, accounting for approximately 20 percent of all deaths in custody (OCI, 2014).

Directives for prison staff specify that all inmates must be screened for suicidal ideation within the first 24 hours of being admitted to an institution, when placed in administrative segregation (whether voluntarily or for disciplinary reasons), and when staff have reason to believe an inmate is at risk for suicide. Whenever possible, a mental health professional is expected to assess the inmate, and assign him or her to a suicide watch level.

The question of *why* some incarcerated Canadian women attempt suicide remains to be fully addressed. Some research from Britain suggests that women in prison who attempt suicide but survive the attempt may have exhibited certain vulnerabilities before their incarceration, such as a history of self-harm, previous suicidal attempts, mental illness, sexual abuse, or sexual assault (Borrill, Snow, Medlicott, Teers, & Paton, 2005). According to this qualitative study, most of the women were able to identify specific triggers for their suicide attempt, many of which were situational[9] (Borrill et al., 2005). Similar vulnerabilities were identified in women who attempted suicide or self-injury in a quantitative study of nearly 3,000 incarcerated women in California and the United Kingdom (Kruttschnitt & Vuolo, 2007). The authors of this study reported an overlap in the predictors identified for self-injury and suicide attempt: prior self-injury, youthfulness, and current or prior mental health problems. The authors also report some evidence to suggest that "the prison regime in which particular prisons operate exerts a significant impact on mental health" (p. 138). Some would argue that sweeping correctional reforms are needed in Canada to prevent any more women from killing themselves in prison. Clearly, additional research is needed to more fully explore why some women attempt and commit suicide in Canadian jails and prisons, in the hopes that in the future, deaths, such as that of Ashley Smith (see the case study in Part III), can be prevented.

Alcohol and Drug Abuse

As will be seen in Chapter 7, the large percentage of women in the criminal justice system with problems associated with drug or alcohol use is well documented in the literature. Although some crimes are directly related to illegal substances by definition (for example, importing and trafficking offences), other crimes are more indirectly linked in some way to drugs or alcohol. Approximately 40 to 50 percent of crimes committed by a Canadian sample of male and female offenders could be attributed to drug and/or alcohol use (Pernanen, Cousineau, Brochu, & Sun, 2002). We assume that most of these crimes were not offences specific to possession, cultivation, importing, or trafficking in drugs because these crimes make up a relatively small percentage of all admissions to custody in Canada (Beattie, 2006). Compared with non-substance-abusing women, federally sentenced women who had a substance abuse problem were younger, began committing crimes at an earlier age, had more adult court experience and more previous escape attempts or convictions for being unlawfully at large, and were more likely to have been sent to segregation for disciplinary reasons (Dowden & Blanchette, 1999). Substance abusers were also more likely to be classified as higher need or higher risk than the non-substance-abusing women.

In terms of needs domains, women with substance abuse problems exhibited (other than the obvious area of substance abuse) significantly more needs with respect to the domains of associates, attitudes, employment, and marital/family (Dowden & Blanchette, 1999). Because of the number of domains in which substance-abusing women were identified as having more needs, their substance use might have served as a coping mechanism for other areas of their life. Alternatively, the relationship could be multi-directional: substance abuse may serve as a coping strategy *and* be a source of stress for other domain areas.

Some criminalized women have themselves made a link between their criminal behaviour and their use/abuse of alcohol or drugs (Buchanan et al., 2011; Comack, 1996; Furlong & Grant, 2006; Gilfus, 1992). Associations between victimization and drug and alcohol abuse in criminalized groups of women have also been noted in the literature (Gilfus, 2002; McClellan, Farabee, & Crouch, 1997). In addition to linking childhood abuse with later criminal behaviour, some researchers have hypothesized that increased rates of intimate partner victimization may be related to women's involvement in substance use and other illegal behaviours. In a study of provincially incarcerated women in Canada, women identified four catalysts for their use of alcohol and drugs, including family relationships (being introduced to the substance by a key male figure in their life), peer influence, experiencing loss, and internal or self-motivations (Buchanan et al., 2011).

Substance abuse may serve as a coping strategy for everyday stressors, whether they are related to prior trauma, street life, or to an abusive relationship (Gilfus, 2002). In an attempt to dull the pain associated with prior victimization, people may choose to use substances as a way of self-medicating (Buchanan et al., 2011; Comack, 1996; McClellan et al., 1997), or as a way of increasing their perception of power or control (Buchanan et al., 2011). Having less emotional support and more negative coping behaviours was found to be associated with more regular use of a specific drug[10] (El-Bassel et al., 1996). Although the temporal nature of the relationship was not able to be examined, the association between heavier drug use, poor coping, and less social support was supported (El-Bassel et al., 1996). Criminalized women may be no different from many others in society who choose to self-medicate to deal with stress, a coping strategy that may be considered functional; however, when the consequences of a criminalized woman abusing drugs or alcohol are evaluated, their behaviour may be viewed as considerably more dysfunctional.

The CSC has recognized that a high level of substance abuse problems is found among women offenders incarcerated federally in Canada and that many incarcerated women are survivors of past trauma (Furlong & Grant, 2006). High levels of previous trauma among samples of women offenders are well documented in the literature (Johnson & Lynch, 2013; Martin, McKenzie, Eljdupovic, & Colman, 2015; Moloney, van den Bergh, & Moller, 2009). Reductions in recidivism have been observed in women offenders who have completed substance abuse programming, compared with those who did not partake in such treatment (Dowden & Blanchette, 1999, 2002). The CSC has implemented the Women Offender Substance Abuse Program (WOSAP), which was designed as an intervention to meet an offender's substance abuse needs for the duration of her sentence (Furlong & Grant, 2006). The WOSAP program is thought to assist women by teaching them "coping strategies to deal with negative emotions associated with their trauma" (Furlong & Grant, 2006, p. 47). In an evaluation of the program, the researchers noted that the majority of women who participated in the intensive therapeutic treatment indicated that they had used substances as a way to cope. After program completion, the women showed significant improvements in their ability to cope as measured by the coping behaviour inventory. In this same evaluation, the majority (91 percent) of the women reported they were under the influence of drugs or alcohol when they committed their offence. Of those who had used drugs, almost three-quarters of the women believed their crime to be directly related to their involvement with drugs, and nearly half of those who had used alcohol came to a similar conclusion.

Although the use of illicit drugs or the use of prescription drugs for a purpose other than they were intended is not legal in Canada, the use of alcohol is.[11] If a criminalized woman decides to use alcohol as a means to cope with a stressor in her life, then she may face some dire consequences. If she drinks while incarcerated and is caught, she will be sanctioned in some manner: she may receive institutional charges, her security classification may be reviewed and increased, and she may be transferred to a more secure living unit or even another correctional facility. If her parole stipulations state that she must not drink, and she drinks while out on parole, then she risks having her parole suspended or terminated. These consequences are very serious for a behaviour that many others in society engage in daily.

Challenges to the Implementation of *Creating Choices*

As noted in Chapter 1, the mandate of the Task Force on Federally Sentenced Women (TFFSW) was to assess the correctional management of women sentenced to federal prison in Canada, from the beginning of their sentences to their date of warrant expiry. Included in the mandate was the need to develop a strategic plan to guide and direct this process in a way that was respectful of the needs specific to these women (TFFSW, 1990). The CSC faced some clear difficulties when it came to the operation of the new regional facilities for women. The TFFSW's (1990) report, *Creating Choices*, and the implementation of its recommendations were met with a number of criticisms (Hannah-Moffat, 2000). As Hannah-Moffat noted in 1995,

> Perhaps one of the most profound difficulties is that feminists have failed to adequately define the meaning and criteria of woman centeredness. The implementation of the task force's recommendations and the definition of woman centered have been left to Corrections Canada with little external (feminist) input. (p. 141)

When the new regional facilities were opened, they were not able to accommodate the needs of maximum security women. A chasm had developed between the ideal as illustrated in *Creating Choices* and the real as experienced by the Correctional Service of Canada in its attempt to operationalize the principles (that is, empowerment, meaningful and responsible choices, respect and dignity, supportive environment, responsibility) in the report. This failure to consider the pragmatics involved in implementing a woman-centred philosophy while balancing the systemic demands inherent in managing violent offenders was glaring. As Shaw (1999) pointed out,

> It is unfortunate that the model of the women-centred prison developed in *Creating Choices* failed to take account of the fact that women can be perpetrators of violence as well as victims. The failure to confront the issue of women's use of violence other than as a response to continued partner violence is not restricted to the Task Force alone, but has been characteristic of feminist accounts of women and violence within criminology more generally. (p. 258)

Other aspects of *Creating Choices* have also met with criticism (Pollack, 2000). In the section of the report entitled "Principle 2: Meaningful and Responsible Choices," the TFFSW, in explaining why this principle is important, notes that for many women their dependence on the state, on men, and on drugs and alcohol has meant that they have not had the kinds of opportunities or, in some cases, the ability to make sound choices in their lives. Pollack (2000) takes issue with this conceptualization of criminalized women as being dependent. She eloquently challenges the "discourse of dependency" that permeates the *Creating Choices* document, asserting that the authors of the report adopted "liberal notions of dependency which, through the use of a psychological discourse, constructs women's lawbreaking as a result of individual personality characteristics that render them 'dependent'" (p. 72). Dependency is then pathologized for the women. Pollack goes on to point out the classed, gendered, and racialized nature of dependency. In particular, her observations gleaned from interviews with Caribbean-Canadian women in prison were in stark contrast to the notions of dependency as described in *Creating Choices*. She noted that very few of the women she interviewed resembled the dependent women described by the TFFSW. The women interviewed by Pollack emphasized their wish to be self-sufficient, educated, and able to provide for their families. An undercurrent of "independence" was noted; however, it was ultimately undermined by societal factors (poor wages, difficulties with social services and other government agencies, systemic racism, and gender inequality, for example) that culminated in situations in which the women found it exceedingly difficult to attain or retain their independence (Pollack, 2000).

Although the voices of Indigenous women were certainly one focus of the TFFSW, a similar statement cannot be made regarding Caribbean-Canadian women. The voices of these women remained conspicuously silent in that document, but Pollack (2000) has provided a vehicle through which those absent voices can be heard. You might wonder how criminalized women who believe they have issues with dependency might react to Pollack's (2000) views. As has been noted previously, the majority of women who eventually come into conflict with the law share some common ground (financial stress, lack of education, unemployment, few marketable skills) that may be directly or indirectly related to a dependency—on the state, on a man, or on crime—to make ends meet. For women who have identified their dependency issues as having affected their lives, denying them their belief can be problematic. This area clearly warrants further inquiry. To my knowledge, however, no published responses (by members of the TFFSW) have addressed Pollack's (2000) criticisms of the *Creating Choices* document and the "discourse of dependency" she identifies.

recidivism
The repetition of a criminal behaviour by an individual who has already been convicted and punished for a previous offence. Because recidivism can be viewed as a measure of rehabilitative failure, it is also a measure of the effectiveness of rehabilitation programs and deterrents.

Research has examined the Level of Service Inventory—Revised: Self Report (LSI-R:SR), a questionnaire that estimates the risk of a person's likelihood of reoffending. Within samples of federally sentenced women, black women's scores on the LSI-R:SR were lower than those of white and Indigenous women, indicative of a lower risk for **recidivism** (Folsom & Atkinson, 2007). The majority of the black women in this study were serving their first federal sentence for drug-related crimes—in particular, importing and trafficking (Folsom & Atkinson, 2007). Perhaps what Pollack (2000) identifies as "independency" is a factor that also differentiates this particular sample of federally incarcerated women from the larger population of women serving federal time. Clearly, more research is needed to examine these issues in more depth.

Watchdog Groups

The Office of the Correctional Investigator

The Office of the Correctional Investigator (OCI) serves as an ombudsperson for federal offenders. The mandate of the OCI is specified in Part III of the *Corrections and Conditional Release Act*, which outlines the main function of the OCI to investigate and bring resolution to complaints from individual offenders (OCI, 2013c). In addition, the OCI has a responsibility to review the policies and procedures of the CSC that relate to individual complaints of offenders, in the hopes that specific areas of concern are identified in a timely manner and subsequently addressed (OCI, 2013c). In addition, special reports may be produced between annual reports, should any situation warrant immediate attention. For example, the Arbour inquiry was precipitated by a submission to the solicitor general of a special OCI report regarding issues related to the April 22 incident at P4W (Commission of Inquiry into Certain Events, 1996), and a report entitled "A Preventable Death" explored the death of Ashley Smith at Grand Valley Institution (Sapers, 2008).

Female offenders who wish to file a complaint can call a toll-free number to speak with a representative from the OCI during business hours, or a message can be left if they are calling outside of business hours. An offender may report a complaint on behalf of another offender, or a friend or family member can make a report to the OCI if they have a written release from the offender to do so. The OCI encourages inmates to submit their concerns in writing. The coordinator for federally sentenced women's issues visits the prisons regularly.

Citizens' Advisory Committees

First established in the mid-1960s, the Citizens' Advisory Committees (CACs) were formed to allow members of the public to contribute to the quality of the various programs and services offered to federally incarcerated people. CACs are now mandatory for all federal penitentiaries. Their mission is the protection of society through their interaction with CSC staff, the public, and offenders themselves. The CACs provide the CSC with both advice and recommendations concerning issues that pertain to correctional institutions. Each CAC functions as a liaison with the community in which a particular prison resides.

There are 90 CACs in operation across Canada, composed of approximately 400 people of varying demographic backgrounds. CAC members are appointed (by a representative of the CSC) and serve a two-year term on the committee (Correctional Service of Canada, 2014).

Canadian Association of Elizabeth Fry Societies (CAEFS)

The namesake of the Canadian Association of Elizabeth Fry Societies (CAEFS), Elizabeth Fry, was a Quaker prison reformer from England who sought to improve the conditions of people who were incarcerated in the early 19th century. Her tireless campaign to improve the lot of women and children incarcerated in London's Newgate Prison led to far-reaching prison reforms (Canadian Association of Elizabeth Fry Societies [CAEFS], 2015b). According to the CAEFS website (www.caefs.ca), Canada's first Elizabeth Fry Society was established in 1939 in Vancouver, but CAEFS was not incorporated as a non-profit voluntary organization until 1978.

women don't belong in cages

80% of imprisoned women are inside for poverty related offences.

90% of Aboriginal and 82% of all women in prison are survivors of incest, rape or physical assault.

The number of women in prison increased 200% in the past 15 years.

prisons are the real crime

A poster from the Canadian Association of Elizabeth Fry Societies

Used with the express permission of Association of Elizabeth Fry Societies (CAEFS).

decarceration
The opposite of incarceration. The decarceration movement strives to remove people from prisons. The Elizabeth Fry societies in Canada are proponents of decarceration.

All member societies must follow three guiding principles in their day-to-day operations. The first principle highlights the role that the CAEFS holds with respect to the development of policies and positions that affect women and the importance to act on those issues that are common to women. The second principle emphasizes the rights of women to have access equal to that of men to participate in programs and opportunities within the Canadian justice system "without fear of prejudice or discrimination on the basis of such factors as sex, race, disability, sexual orientation, age, religion and freedom of conscience, social or economic condition" (CAEFS, 2015c ¶ 2). The third principle espouses that "women who are criminalized should not be imprisoned" and that CAEFS will make every effort to prevent women from being incarcerated; in cases in which women are incarcerated, CAEFS will work to enable their earliest possible reintegration into the community (CAEFS, 2015c ¶ 3).

The goals of CAEFS include the desire to promote and increase the public's awareness of what is referred to as the "**decarceration**" of women. A second, related goal is to decrease the number of women who are criminalized and incarcerated across Canada. A third goal involves improving criminalized and incarcerated women's access to community-based, publicly funded health, social service, and educational resources. Lastly, CAEFS wants to encourage the Elizabeth Fry Societies and other women's organizations to work together to tackle issues of oppression, such as racism and poverty (CAEFS, 2015a).

The Media Image of Female Offenders in Canada

The media is a powerful tool that can shape our perceptions. Take a look at some recently made entertainment series (e.g., *Orange Is the New Black*, *Wentworth*), and you will see how women in prison are portrayed.

In my class on women and crime I routinely, at the beginning of the term, ask the students to name a female offender in Canada. Most of them can come up with only one name: Karla Homolka. They sometimes come up with the names of Americans, such as Aileen Wuornos or Andrea Yates—infamous women whose cases have been highly publicized in newspapers, magazines, television, and even the movies. Others might even include Martha Stewart in their response (although her case was considerably different from the kinds of women offenders usually in the media's focus).

Common to all the above-named women is that their lives have been sensationalized in the media, and as a result, their images have shaped our collective perception of what a female offender is. The reality is that most Canadian female offenders have not committed a heinous crime. They don't fit with the sensationalized images portrayed in the media. Canadian criminalized women are unlikely to become repeat offenders, and those who do reoffend tend not to escalate in terms of the severity of their crimes (Kong & AuCoin, 2008). A woman like Kimberly Rogers exemplifies, more often than not, the real picture of the female offender in Canada (see Box 3.1). When Kimberly Rogers died, she was receiving $520 a month in welfare, from which $52 was clawed back (a collection for an overpayment), leaving her with a total of $468 a month. After she paid

BOX 3.1

Two Fraud Cases: Conrad Black and Kimberly Rogers

A $102-million corporate theft vs. $13,500 in unauthorized welfare benefits—which one will pay the greater penalty? Conrad Black[12] and his business partner, David Radler, were charged with civil fraud by the US Securities and Exchange Commission. The Commission alleged that the pair stole US$85 million ($102 million Canadian) from the shareholders of Hollinger International Inc. "Black and Radler abused their control of a public company and treated it as their personal piggy bank," SEC Enforcement Director Stephen Cutler said when announcing the charges.

The Sudbury Welfare Case

Kimberly Rogers was a 40-year-old woman sentenced to house arrest for collecting $13,500 (US$11,200) in social assistance benefits while attending school on a student loan. "[She] had been prescribed medication for a range of health issues that prevented her from working" and was receiving standard Ontario welfare benefits of $520 per month, while paying $450 per month in rent. From 1996 to 1999, she also received a total of $49,000 in student loans from the Ontario Student Assistance Program to study social services at Cambrian College. When Rogers first began her studies, receiving both welfare and student loans was legal, and even encouraged as a strategy to help welfare recipients return to the workforce—but the practice was banned in 1996 by the Progressive Conservative government as part of its welfare reform legislation. Pregnant at the time she was caught, she was confined to her stifling apartment during a record-setting heat wave. "Rogers lived in desperate poverty," the *Toronto Star* reported. She was sentenced to six months of house arrest,

permitted to leave the house for medical, religious, or shopping reasons only on Wednesday mornings, and for a maximum of three hours. She was also ordered to repay the full amount of her overpayment. Ontario Works suspended her welfare benefits for three months, leaving Rogers with no income to pay her rent, buy food or medication, or even pay her fine. She died in 2001 by suicide from a drug overdose. "An inquest into her death revealed a glaring discrepancy between the government's view of 'welfare bums' and the reality of life on welfare in Ontario. … The [inquest] jury saw through the stereotypes and made 14 recommendations aimed at preventing future deaths in similar circumstances."

Silence and Inaction

The Liberal government of Premier Dalton McGuinty (2003–2013), who replaced Conservative Premiers Mike Harris (1995–2002) and Ernie Eves (2002–2003), did not implement all recommendations. McGuinty implemented a 3 per cent increase in welfare rates, to be followed by an annual cost of living increase, and eliminated the lifetime suspension of benefits.

Interesting to note is that those former premiers, who are now out of power and in many cases enjoying public pensions that make welfare benefits pale by comparison, have been silent about the crimes of Conrad Black. Those were left to American authorities.

Source: National Union of Public and General Employees. (2003). Two fraud cases: Conrad Black and Kimberly Rogers. Retrieved from http://archive.is/DLOGC. Reprinted by permission of NUPGE.

her rent of $450, only $18 remained ("Activists Push for Welfare Changes," 2003). How anyone could survive on this paltry amount of money is difficult to fathom.

Compare the case of Kimberly Rogers, and the general public's awareness of it, with the case of Karla Homolka. Many of you have probably heard of Karla Homolka, but perhaps not so many of you are familiar with the case of Kimberly Rogers. The case of Karla Homolka, perhaps "one of the most hated female killers in the world" (Morrissey, 2001, p. 83), was covered extensively on television, in the print media, and in film (Burton et al., 2006). In addition to these traditional media outlets, the Internet has spawned a new realm in which she can be vilified. If you Google the name "Karla Homolka," you will find 299,000 hits.[13] According to Morrissey (2001), around the time of Homolka's release from prison, the Internet site "Karla Homolka Death Pool: When the Game Is Over, We All Win" was launched to take bets on the date of her death (p. 83). This particular site was removed from the Internet, but as Morrissey pointed out, other websites focused on when and how Homolka would die (although the websites claimed they neither condoned nor promoted any sort of violence toward Homolka).

Most Canadians would agree that Karla Homolka has the dubious distinction of being Canada's most infamous female offender of the latter half of the 20th century (and someone to whom the media have afforded considerable attention). Nearly 25 years after her conviction, the media continues to report on Homolka. In 2012, an investigative journalist, Paula Todd, decided to look for her. Todd tracked Homolka to a Caribbean island where she found her living with her husband and three children. Todd documented her quest in an ebook entitled *Finding Karla*. More recently, in 2016, it was reported that Homolka was "living a soccer-mom's existence in Chateauguay, Quebec" and the media was once again focused on her and her children (Gatehouse, 2016). It seems likely that the media attention given to this case will continue to shape the perceptions of Canadians regarding women offenders in general.

▶ WHAT DO YOU THINK?

How are women offenders portrayed in popular culture? What books, movies, or television shows can you think of that include depictions of incarcerated women? What are the stereotypes that are portrayed? How do these portrayals differ from reality?

SUMMARY

Recall Comack's (1996) point made at the beginning of this chapter: that women who find themselves in conflict with the law are often no different from any other women; they all share the collective experience of being female in our society. However, these wives, partners, mothers, daughters, sisters, aunts, and cousins are different from non-criminalized women in one respect: they have shared the experience of being in conflict with the law and of facing the justice system up close and in person from "the other side." This distinction between "us" and "them" is fashioned from our desire (conscious or not) to categorize our world into neat packages of what is good and what is bad. The danger inherent in this categorization is obvious: to reduce a person to one label, to the label of criminal, serves the interest of no one.

We all must cope with life's stressors, and women who are criminalized are no different from anyone else in this regard. Some turn to strategies that have worked for them in the past but that are ultimately problematic for them, both now and in the long term. Drinking and drug use, self-injury, and attempts at suicide have been identified as some of these negative coping strategies. Positive or negative, functional or dysfunctional, good or bad, whichever coping strategy a woman chooses, she will select something that she has learned can offer her at least some short-term relief from the current stress that she is experiencing.

Many women in prison have experienced poverty, physical abuse, sexual abuse, substance abuse, and economic marginalization; and the majority are mothers, many of whom are lone parents. Visible minority women also live with the day-to-day experiences and consequences of the many facets of racism. Women's pathways to and out of crime cannot be understood without first understanding the ways in which race, class, and gender intersect to shape their experiences. There is no stereotypical female offender. However, few would argue that societal issues, such as classism, sexism, and racism, have not had an impact on who becomes criminalized in Canada. Generally, it is a subset of women who are the most negatively affected by these "isms" in our society who come to know the inside of a jail cell.

NOTES

1. According to the Canadian *Employment Equity Act*, the term *visible minorities* applies to "persons, other than Aboriginal people, who are non-Caucasian in race or non-white in colour."

2. The Correctional Service of Canada has a mother–child program that allows for some women to keep their children, usually newborns, with them in their living unit. Women must be screened for this program, and very few women participate in this program at any one time. See the section "Institutional Mother–Child Program" in Chapter 6 for more details.

3. Internal searches are carried out when a woman is suspected of concealing contraband in a body orifice. This kind of search can only be conducted with the woman's consent, and by a medical doctor.

4. *Slashing* refers to the intentional cutting of one's own body as a way to self-injure.

5. Heney (1990) noted that one instance of mass punishment was the cancellation of a dance in December 1988, as a result of alcohol being found in a cell.

6. Hannah-Moffat noted that she came to this conclusion after examining the CSC's 2004 program strategy for women and the CSC's protocols in place for the secure prison units.

7. For a description of DBT, see the section "Dialectical Behaviour Therapy" in Chapter 8.

8. On February 14, 2008, co-author Steve Kazmierczak went on a shooting rampage, killing himself and five other students at Northern Illinois University in DeKalb, Illinois (Davey, 2008).

9. The triggering events included "bullying, bereavement, an upsetting visit or telephone call, missed medication, or hearing voices or flashbacks which urged them to kill themselves" (Borrill et al., 2005, p. 67).

10. The specific drug in this study was crack cocaine.

11. Legal ages for drinking alcohol vary from province to province. In Ontario, the legal age for drinking alcohol is 19 years of age.

12. Conrad Black was found guilty in the United States of three counts of mail fraud and one count of obstruction of justice. He was sentenced to six and a half years' imprisonment, fined US$125,000, and ordered to forfeit US$6.1 million. On appeal his sentence was reduced to 42 months. Today he writes for the *National Post*. A pregnant Kimberly Rogers died by suicide from a drug overdose in 2001 and was found several days after she had died.

13. The term *Karla Homolka* was entered into the Google search engine by the author at approximately 9:30 a.m. on June 24, 2016; approximately 299,000 hits were obtained.

DISCUSSION QUESTIONS

1. Describe the data available from courts and correctional institutions in Canada. How are these data useful in identifying patterns of women's criminal behaviour?

2. Discuss the crimes that women are most often convicted of. What factors explain why women commit these crimes?

3. According to Hatch and Faith (1989), "women in conflict with the law have more in common with other women than they do with male prison inmates." Does this statement ring true today? Discuss.

4. What are some of the stereotypes that you can think of about women offenders? How do you think these stereotypes were formed? How would you suggest that public attitude/stereotypes towards women offenders be changed?

ADDITIONAL RESOURCES

Videos and Films

Cadieux, M. (Producer). (2003). *Sentenced to Life* [Motion Picture]. Canada: NFB.

Kohan, J., Friedman, L., Hess, S., & Herrmann, T. (Executive Producers). *Orange is the New Black* [Television Series]. New York: Netflix.

Perrier, P. (Director). (2007). *Cracked not broken* [Documentary]. Canada: Open Door Company.

Zammit, S. (Producer). (2005). *Life Inside Out* [Motion Picture]. Canada: NFB.

Websites

Correctional Service of Canada: www.csc-scc.gc.ca

Statistics Canada: www.statcan.ca

REFERENCES

Activists push for welfare changes. (2003, December 18). *North Bay Nugget*, p. A6.

Addario, L. (2002). *Six degrees from liberation: Legal needs of women in criminal and other matters*. Ottawa: Research and Statistics Division, Department of Justice Canada.

Association of Certified Fraud Examiners. (2016). *Report to the nations on occupational fraud and abuse: 2016 global fraud study*. Retrieved from https://s3-us-west-2 .amazonaws.com/acfepublic/2016-report-to-the -nations.pdf.

Atkinson, J. (1998). *Neutralizations among male and female fraud offenders*. Unpublished doctoral dissertation, Queen's University, Kingston, Canada: Theses Canada Portal, AMICUS No. 20673725.

Beattie, K. (2006). Adult correctional services in Canada, 2004/2005. *Juristat*, *26*(5), 1–33.

Borrill, J., Snow, L., Medlicott, D., Teers, R., & Paton, J. (2005). Learning from "near misses": Interviews with women who survived an incident of severe self-harm in prison. *The Howard Journal*, *44*, 57–69.

Bosworth, M. (2006). Self-harm in women's prisons [editorial introduction]. *Criminology and Public Policy*, *5*, 157–160.

Buchanan, M., Murphy, K., Smith Martin, M., Korchinski, M., Buxton., J., Granger-Brown, A., … Elwood Martin, R. (2011). Understanding incarcerated women's perspectives on substance use: Catalysts, reasons for use, consequences, and desire for change. *Journal of Offender Rehabilitation*, *50*, 81–100. doi: 10.1080/10509672.2011.546232

Burton, D., Goulding, R., Keskemety, R., McIntire, P., Miller, S., Perry, M., et al., (Producers), & Bender, J., Rosen, M., Rosen, B., & Sellers, M. (Writers). (2006). *Karla* [Motion picture]. United States: Quantum Entertainment & True Crime Investments LLC.

Canada (2006). *Snapshot of racialized poverty in Canada*. Retrieved from https://www.canada.ca/en/employment -social-development/programs/communities/reports/ poverty-profile-snapshot.html.

Canadian Association of Elizabeth Fry Societies. (2015a). Goals. Retrieved from www.caefs.ca/about-us/goals.

Canadian Association of Elizabeth Fry Societies. (2015b). Origin. Retrieved from www.caefs.ca/about-us/origin.

Canadian Association of Elizabeth Fry Societies. (2015c). Principles. Retrieved from www.caefs.ca/about-us/ principles.

Comack, E. (1996). *Women in trouble*. Winnipeg: Fernwood Publishing.

Comack, E. (2005). Coping, resisting, and surviving: Connecting women's law violations to the histories of abuse. In L.F. Alarid & P. Cromwell (Eds.), *In her own words: Women offenders' views on crime and victimization* (pp. 33–43). Los Angeles, CA: Roxbury.

Commission of Inquiry into Certain Events at the Prison for Women in Kingston. (1996). *Commission of Inquiry into Certain Events at the Prison for Women in Kingston (the Arbour inquiry)*. Ottawa: Public Works and Government Services Canada.

Correctional Service of Canada (2014). 2011–2012 Citizen advisory committees annual report. Retrieved from www.csc-scc.gc.ca/cac/003002-2002-eng.shtml.

Correctional Service of Canada (2017). *Commissioner's Directive 843: Management of inmate self-injurious and suicidal behavior*. Ottawa: Author. Retrieved from http://www.csc-scc.gc.ca/acts-and-regulations/843-cd -eng.shtml.

Corrections and Conditional Release Act, SC 1992, c 20.

Cotter, A., Greenland, J., & Karam, M. (2015). Drug-related offences in Canada, 2013. *Juristat*, *35*(1), Retrieved from

www.statcan.gc.ca/pub/85-002-x/2015001/article/14201
-eng.pdf.

Criminal Code, RSC 1985, c C-46.

Davey, M. (2008, February 16). Gunman showed few hints
of trouble. *New York Times*, p. A1. Retrieved from
www.nytimes.com/2008/02/16/us/16gunman.html.

Denney, D., Ellis, T., & Barn, R. (2006). Race, diversity and
criminal justice in Canada: A view from the UK.
Internet Journal of Criminology. Retrieved from https://
researchportal.port.ac.uk/portal/files/234698/Denney,
Ellis&_Barn_-_Race,_Diversity_and_Criminal
_Justice_in_Canada.pdf.

Dowden, C., & Blanchette, K. (1999). *An investigation into
the characteristics of substance-abusing women offenders:
Risk, need and post-release outcome* (Research Report
R-81). Ottawa: Correctional Service of Canada.

Dowden, C., & Blanchette, K. (2002). An evaluation of the
effectiveness of substance abuse programming for
female offenders. *International Journal of Offender
Therapy and Comparative Criminology, 46*, 220–230.

El-Bassel, N., Gilbert, L., Schilling, R., Ivanoff, A., Borne,
D., & Safyer, S. (1996). Correlates of crack abuse among
drug abusing incarcerated women: Psychological
trauma, social support, and coping behavior. *American
Journal of Drug and Alcohol Abuse, 22*, 41–57.

Employment Equity Act, SC 1995, c 44.

Ferraro, K., & Moe, A. (2003). The impact of mothering on
criminal offending. In L.F. Alarid & P. Cromwell (Eds.),
*In her own words: Women offenders' views on crime and
victimization* (pp. 79–92). Los Angeles, CA: Roxbury.

Finkelhor, D., & Browne, A. (1985). The traumatic impact
of child sexual abuse: A conceptualization. *The
American Journal of Orthopsychiatry, 55*, 530–541.

Finn, A., Trevethan, S., Carrière, G., & Kowalski, M. (1999).
Female inmates, Aboriginal inmates, and inmates serving
life sentences: A one day snapshot. *Juristat, 19*(5), 1–14.

Folsom, J., & Atkinson, J. (2007). The generalizability of the
LSI-R and the CAT to the prediction of recidivism in
female offenders. *Criminal Justice & Behavior, 34*(8),
1044–1056.

Furlong, A., & Grant, B.A. (2006). Women offender substance abuse programming: Interim results. *Forum on
Corrections Research, 18*(1), 45–48.

Gatehouse, J. (2016, April 29). Why Karla Homolka's children will pay for her crimes. *Maclean's*. Retrieved from
www.macleans.ca/culture/books/karla-homolkas
-children-will-pay-for-her-crimes.

Gilfus, M. (1992). From victims to survivors to offenders:
Women's routes of entry and immersion into street crime.
In L.F. Alarid & Cromwell (Eds.), *In her own words:*

Women offenders' views on crime and victimization
(pp. 5–14). Los Angeles, CA: Roxbury.

Gilfus, M. (2002). *Women's experiences of abuse as a risk
factor for incarceration*. Harrisburg, PA: VAWnet, a project of the National Resource Center on Domestic
Violence/Pennsylvania Coalition Against Domestic
Violence. Retrieved from www.vawnet.org.

Gilfus, M. (2006). From victims to survivors to offenders.
In L. Alrarid & P. Cromwell (Eds.), *In her own words:
Women offenders' views on crime and victimization*
(pp. 5–14). Los Angeles: Roxbury.

Hannah-Moffat, K. (1995). Feminine fortresses: Woman-
centered prisons? *The Prison Journal, 75*(2), 135–164.

Hannah-Moffat, K. (2000). Re-forming the prison:
Rethinking our ideals. In K. Hannah-Moffat & M. Shaw
(Eds.), *An ideal prison? Critical essays of women's impris-
onment in Canada* (pp. 30–40). Halifax: Fernwood
Publishing.

Hannah-Moffat, K. (2006). Pandora's box: Risk/need and
gender-responsive corrections. *Criminology and Public
Policy, 5*, 183–192.

Hatch, A., & Faith, K. (1989). The female offender in
Canada: A statistical profile. *Canadian Journal of
Women and the Law, 3*, 432–456.

Hayman, S. (2006). *Imprisoning our sisters: The new federal
women's prisons in Canada*. Montreal & Kingston:
McGill-Queen's University Press.

Heney, J. (1990). *Report on self-injurious behaviour in the
Kingston Prison for Women*. Ottawa: Correctional
Service of Canada.

Heney, J., & Kristiansen, C. (1997). An analysis of the
impact of prison on women survivors of childhood sexual abuse. *Women and Therapy, 20*(4), 29–44.

Hotton Mahony, T. (2011). *Women and the criminal justice
system*. Statistics Canada. Retrieved from www.statcan
.gc.ca/pub/89-503-x/2010001/article/11416-eng.pdf.

Johnson, K.A., & Lynch, S.M. (2013). Predictors of maladaptive coping in incarcerated women who are
survivors of childhood sexual abuse. *Journal of Family
Violence, 28*(1), 43–52.

Kilty, J. (2006). Under the barred umbrella: Is there room
for a women-centered self-injury policy in Canadian
corrections? *Criminology and Public Policy, 5*, 161–182.

Kong, R., & AuCoin, K. (2008). Female offenders in
Canada. *Juristat, 28*(1), 1–23.

Kruttschnitt, C., & Vuolo, M. (2007). The cultural context
of women prisoners' mental health. *Punishment and
Society, 9*, 115–150.

Larivière, M. (1997). *The Correctional Service of Canada
1996–1997 retrospective report on inmate suicides*.

Ottawa: Correctional Service of Canada. Retrieved from https://www.publicsafety.gc.ca/lbrr/archives/hv%206545.6%20l37%201996-97-eng.pdf.

Lawrence, S., & Williams, T. (2006). Swallowed up: Drug couriers at the borders of Canadian sentencing. *University of Toronto Law Journal, 56*, 285–332.

Martin, M.S., McKenzie, K., Eljdupovic, G., & Colman, I. (2015). Risk of violence by inmates with childhood trauma and mental health needs. *Law and Human Behavior, 39*(6), 614–623.

McClellan, D., Farabee, D., & Crouch, B. (1997). Early victimization, drug use, and criminality: A comparison of male and female prisoners. *Criminal Justice and Behavior, 24*(4), 455–476.

Milan, A. (2015). *Women in Canada: A gender-based statistical report*. Statistics Canada. Retrieved from www.statcan.gc.ca/pub/89-503-x/2015001/article/14152-eng.pdf.

Moloney, K.P., van den Bergh, B.J., & Moller, L.F. (2009). Women in prison: The central issues of gender characteristics and trauma history. *Public Health, 123*(6), 426–430.

Morrissey, B. (2001). "Dealing with the devil": Karla Homolka and the absence of feminist criticism. In A. Burfoot & S. Lord (Eds.), *Killing women: The visual culture of gender and violence*. Waterloo: Wilfrid Laurier University Press.

National Union of Public and General Employees. (2003). Two fraud cases: Conrad Black and Kimberly Rogers. Retrieved from http://archive.is/DLOGC.

Office of the Correctional Investigator. (2012). *Annual Report: 2011/12*. Retrieved from www.oci-bec.gc.ca/cnt/rpt/pdf/annrpt/annrpt20112012-eng.pdf.

Office of the Correctional Investigator. (2013a). *A case study of diversity in corrections: The black inmate experience in federal penitentiaries*. Retrieved from www.oci-bec.gc.ca/cnt/rpt/pdf/oth-aut/oth-aut20131126-eng.pdf.

Office of the Correctional Investigator. (2013b). *Risky business: An investigation of the treatment and management of chronic self-injury among federal sentenced women*. Retrieved from www.oci-bec.gc.ca/cnt/rpt/pdf/oth-aut/oth-aut20130930-eng.pdf.

Office of the Correctional Investigator. (2013c). Roles and responsibilities. Retrieved from www.oci-bec.gc.ca/cnt/roles-eng.aspx.

Office of the Correctional Investigator. (2014). *A three-year review of federal inmate suicides* (2011–2014). Retrieved from www.oci-bec.gc.ca/cnt/rpt/pdf/oth-aut/oth-aut20140910-eng.pdf?texthighlight=suicide.

Office of the Correctional Investigator. (2015). *Annual Report: 2014/15*. Retrieved from www.oci-bec.gc.ca/cnt/rpt/pdf/annrpt/annrpt20142015-eng.pdf.

Pernanen, K., Cousineau, M., Brochu, S., & Sun, F. (2002). *Proportions of crimes associated with alcohol and other drugs in Canada*. Ottawa: Canadian Centre on Substance Abuse. Retrieved from www.ccsa.ca/Resource%20Library/ccsa-009105-2002.pdf.

Pollack, S. (2000). Dependency discourse as social control. In K. Hannah-Moffat & M. Shaw (Eds.), *An ideal prison? Critical essays of women's imprisonment in Canada* (pp. 72–81). Halifax: Fernwood Publishing.

Pollack, S., & Brezina, K. (2006). Negotiating contradictions: Sexual abuse counseling with imprisoned women. *Women and Therapy, 29*(3–4), 117–133.

Reitsma-Street, M. (1999). Justice for Canadian girls: A 1990s update. *Canadian Journal of Criminology, 31*, 335–364.

Roe-Sepowitz, D. (2007). Characteristics and predictors of self-mutilation: A study of incarcerated women. *Criminal Behaviour and Mental Health, 17*, 312–321.

Sapers, H. (2008). *A preventable death*. Retrieved from www.oci-bec.gc.ca/cnt/rpt/pdf/oth-aut/oth-aut20080620-eng.pdf.

Sapers, H. (2010). Annual report of the Office of the Correctional Investigator 2009–2010. Ottawa: Office of the Correctional Investigator. Retrieved from http://www.oci-bec.gc.ca/cnt/rpt/pdf/annrpt/annrpt20092010-eng.pdf.

Saunders, D.G. (1986). When battered women use violence: Husband-abuse or self-defense? *Violence and Victims, 1*(1), 47–60.

Shaw, M. (1999). "Knowledge without acknowledgement": Violent women, the prison and the cottage. *Howard Journal, 38*(3), 252–266.

Shaw, N. (2002). Shifting conversations on girls' and women's self-injury: An analysis of the clinical literature in historical context. *Feminism and Psychology, 12*, 191–219.

Shechory, M., Perry, G., & Addad, M. (2011). Pathways to women's crime: Differences among women convicted of drug, violence and fraud offenses. *The Journal of Social Psychology, 151*(4), 399–416.

Statistics Canada (2016). *Adult criminal courts, number of cases and charges by type of decision, annual* [CANSIM table 252-0053]. Retrieved from http://www5.statcan.gc.ca/cansim/a26?lang=eng&id=2520053.

Task Force on Federally Sentenced Women. (1990). *Creating choices: Report of the Task Force on Federally Sentenced Women*. Ottawa: Department of the Solicitor General.

Thomas, J., Leaf, M., Kazmierczak, S., & Stone, J. (2006). Self-injury in correctional settings: "Pathology" of prisons or of prisoners? *Criminology and Public Policy, 5*, 193–202.

Female Youth in Conflict with the Law

Introduction

According to the Canadian Centre for Justice Statistics, the overall rate of male youth offending is approximately three times that of young females, and the overall patterns and nature of female youth offending are consistently different from those of young males (Allen & Superle, 2016; Fitzgerald, 2003; Kong & AuCoin, 2008). Moreover, although females comprise approximately one-fifth of all young offenders charged by police, since the mid-1980s, more females have been charged with violent offences; however, as we will see, this trend has more to do with the perception that young women are becoming more violent, not the reality (DeKeseredy, 2000; Department of Justice Canada, 2005).

Because young males are more likely to offend than young females, more research and criminal justice attention has been paid to male youth offending. Deeply entrenched cultural expectations regarding girls' and boys' behaviours have played a significant role in limiting what we know about female youth offending (Corrado, Odgers, & Cohen, 2000). It is well known, for example, that social norms regarding normal behaviour for boys differ from those that girls are expected to conform to. Girls are expected to be less aggressive, and are socialized to be so, whereas aggressive or confrontational behaviours in young males are normalized as "boys being boys." Thus, when young females come into conflict with the law, they are often seen as more deviant than males because they are presumed to be acting outside of the roles transmitted to them and reproduced by socialization processes (Chesney-Lind & Okamoto, 2001). Moreover, in criminology, female offending has historically been seen as a minor subset of male offending, not as a phenomenon that needs to be theorized in its own right as different from male crime (Belknap & Holsinger, 2006; Chesney-Lind, 2006).

My approach in this chapter is to provide a *contextualized* discussion of female youth offenders. In other words, my contention is that we cannot understand young female offenders (or offenders in general) unless we understand the contours and consequences of the many different ways in which people interact with their social, economic, and political environments. Furthermore, unless we take a serious interest in the ways that factors such as social class, ethnicity, and gender serve to condition and set limits on young people's behaviour, it is impossible to fully appreciate the nature of youth offending and to therefore provide appropriate criminal justice or other responses to offending.

In this chapter, we will briefly review the history of criminal justice responses to young offenders, examine the extent and contours of female youth offending in Canada, and consider the current criminal justice response to offending. We will begin by examining what we know historically about youth in conflict with the law.

A Brief History of the Criminal Justice Response to Female and Male Offending[1]

Although very little is known about juvenile offending during the pioneer settlement era in Canada, much less is known about girl offending. Most historical commentaries in Canada in this time frame (and even later) focus on youth under the homogeneous category of *children*, comprising both males and females, with cursory attention paid to the differences between male and female offending.

▶ WHAT DO YOU THINK?

How should we define children and youth? To what extent are these categories arbitrary?

This focus is not surprising, given that scholarly efforts to render female delinquency visible have occurred only relatively recently (Chesney-Lind, 2001). We do know, however, that most transgressions committed by young males and females during the pioneer settlement era were relatively minor. According to Carrigan (1998), the bulk of wrongdoing consisted of "violations of local ordinances, nuisance offences, vandalism, petty theft, and breaches of the moral laws" (p. 25). Although boys were more likely to offend than girls, certain offences, such as prostitution, abortion, and infanticide, were more likely to be committed by girls.

At this point in Canada's history, young people were viewed as miniature adults. Working-class children toiled alongside adults and were expected to demonstrate the same sense of morality and duty as adults. Not surprisingly, when children were convicted of a crime, they were subject to the same set of laws and often the same dispositions, including incarceration alongside grown-ups.

Legislation focused specifically on youth in Canada began with the passing in 1857 of *An Act for the More Speedy Trial and Punishment of Juvenile Offenders*. This Act was designed to accelerate trial processes and to reduce the possibility of juvenile delinquents serving long jail sentences prior to trial. Juvenile delinquents were defined as offenders under the age of 16, and their sentencing consisted of imprisonment in a common jail or confinement in a correctional house, either with or without hard labour, for no longer than three months, or a fine not to exceed five pounds. The accused could also be ordered to restore stolen property or pay the equivalent compensation (Gagnon, 1984, pp. 21–22).

During the mid-1900s, a shift in the Canadian economy from an agricultural to an industrial base triggered new demands for industrial labourers, which in turn was fuelled by the arrival of immigrant children from Europe. Many of these poor and neglected children were labelled as tramps and drifters with emotional and moral problems, and they were often singled out as those responsible for the bulk of what was considered youth crime (Alvi, 2000; Carrigan, 1998). Furthermore, the so-called failures were seen by authorities as emanating from the failure of parents and families to adequately socialize and control their children. Gradually, the alleged malfunctioning of families stimulated a trend toward the use of other social institutions to control and discipline young people. Compulsory schooling began to be seen as the mechanism by which children could be trained for the new demands of the industrial economy and could be controlled and socialized to behave appropriately (Barrett & McIntosh, 1982).

In the justice system, a new doctrine of *parens patriae* emerged, encouraging the idea that children in conflict with the law required the state to act as a "kindly parent" that would take on the responsibilities of the "failed family" (Bala, 1997). Continuing assumptions were that lower-class families and their children were primarily to blame for youth deviance, and that youth who had failed to comply with the law were to be held to a set of middle-class standards emphasizing proper care and nurturance, love, discipline, and education so that they could rise above their station in life. Coupled with this development was the sense that modern societies needed to soften their response to youth crime, a view championed notably by the child-saving movement (Platt, 1977). A new legal approach to youth offending was thought to be necessary; in 1908, Parliament passed the *Juvenile Delinquents Act* (JDA).

Briefly, section 38 of the JDA instructed judges to treat the child offender as a "misdirected and misguided" individual (not a criminal) who required appropriate "aid, encouragement, help and assistance." In addition to focusing on proper judicial process, the Act represented a social welfare approach to youth in conflict with the law, emphasizing the best interests of the child. Despite this new philosophy, however, children over the age of 14 could still be transferred to adult court at the discretion of the juvenile court judge if they had been accused of serious crimes such as murder or treason.

Sentencing under the JDA consisted of a range of dispositions, including a fine not to exceed $25, probation, placement in a foster home or in Children's Aid, or commitment to an industrial school (see Alvi, 2000 for a detailed discussion).

Although the JDA was a positive development because it focused on children's needs, not on bad children, problems with the legislation persisted. The idea of "the best interests of the child" could be interpreted in very different ways by judges and police, and a great deal of arbitrariness was evident across provinces with respect to age limits, legal representation, and sentencing. Due process was inconsistently applied across jurisdictions, and considerable class and gender bias had been built into the Act. For instance, immigrant and working-class children tended to receive harsher sentences compared with their middle-class counterparts, who were often released to their parents. In addition, girls, but not boys, could be arrested for the nebulous offence of "sexual immorality," a status offence usually applied to socially disadvantaged girls (Bala, 1997). Indeed, in this era, most criminal justice practitioners equated young female criminality with sexual delinquency and with women's increasing emancipation through access to work, wider contact with men, and wider opportunities for personal expression (Tanner, 1996, p. 191). Convicted female youth were more likely to be in custody, were subject to longer stays than males for similar offences, and were provided with little education other than training for domestic duties (Reitsma-Street, 1993; West, 1984). Despite these and other problems with the Act, for 75 years the JDA continued to provide the legal framework within which young offenders would be tried and sentenced.

In the 1950s and 1960s, in the context of tremendous social and cultural changes in Canada and elsewhere, shifting perceptions about the role of youth in society stimulated debate over the utility of the JDA. The passing, in 1982, of the *Canadian Charter of Rights and Freedoms* guaranteed Canadians a range of legal rights, such as equal treatment before the law, the right to legal counsel, and the right not to be subjected to cruel or unusual punishment. Many policy-makers then realized that the JDA would probably not withstand legal challenges under the Charter (Hylton, 1994). In 1965, a federal committee tasked with studying the problem of the legal response to juvenile crime concluded that the legislation needed to be changed, and in 1984, the *Young Offenders Act* (YOA) was passed into law (see Box 4.1).

For the first time in Canadian history, federal legislation (that is, the YOA) reflected the idea that juvenile justice should embody a balance between the rights of society (to protection from crime) and the rights of the individual (to fair, equitable, and consistent justice). The Act emphasized personal responsibility, but did not abrogate parents of their responsibilities for proper supervision, control, and socialization of children. Importantly, the YOA also stepped away from the notion of young offenders as misguided children and toward the idea that young offenders are, indeed, special kinds of criminals.

A special section of the Act (section 4) addressed "Alternative Measures," a set of principles maintaining that, whenever possible, youth should be diverted from the

---

BOX 4.1

The Central Principles of the Young Offenders Act as Outlined in Section 3

3(1) It is hereby recognized and declared that

(a) crime prevention is essential to the long-term protection of society and requires addressing the underlying causes of crime by young persons and developing multi-disciplinary approaches to identifying and effectively responding to children and young persons at risk of committing offending behaviour in the future;

(a.1) while young persons should not in all instances be held accountable in the same manner or suffer the same consequences for their behaviour as adults, young persons who commit offences should nonetheless bear responsibility for their contraventions;

(b) society must, although it has the responsibility to take reasonable measures to prevent criminal conduct by young persons, be afforded the necessary protection from illegal behaviour;

(c) young persons who commit offences require supervision, discipline and control, but, because of their state of dependency and level of development and maturity, they also have special needs and require guidance and assistance;

(c.1) the protection of society, which is a primary objective of the criminal law applicable to youth, is best served by rehabilitation, wherever possible, of young persons who commit offences, and rehabilitation is best achieved by addressing the needs and circumstances of a young person that are relevant to the young person's offending behaviour;

(d) where it is not inconsistent with the protection of society, taking no measures or taking measures other than judicial proceedings under this Act should be considered for dealing with young persons who have committed offences;

(e) young persons have rights and freedoms in their own right, including those stated in the *Canadian Charter of Rights and Freedoms* or in the *Canadian Bill of Rights*, and in particular a right to be heard in the course of, and to participate in, the processes that lead to decisions that affect them, and young persons should have special guarantees of their rights and freedoms;

(f) in the application of this Act, the rights and freedoms of young persons include a right to the least possible interference with freedom that is consistent with the protection of society, having regard to the needs of young persons and the interests of their families;

(g) young persons have the right, in every instance where they have rights or freedoms that may be affected by this Act, to be informed as to what those rights and freedoms are; and

(h) parents have responsibility for the care and supervision of their children, and, for that reason, young persons should be removed from parental supervision either partly or entirely only when measures that provide for continuing parental supervision are inappropriate.

Source: *Young Offenders Act*, RSC 1985, c. Y-1.

criminal justice system because of its stigmatizing effects. Those deemed eligible to participate in Alternative Measures might be encouraged to reconcile with their victims or to provide restitution, an apology, or service to the community. Wardell (1986) argues that although Alternative Measures looked like a good idea on paper, more likely the government saw them as a way to reduce the cost of youth justice because the responsibility for the transgressing youth would fall to his or her community not the criminal justice system. Moreover, only about 20 percent of cases were dealt with via alternative methods, and some evidence suggests that Indigenous and minority youth tended to be excluded from participation (Canadian Centre for Justice Statistics, 1994; Church Council on Justice and Corrections, 1996; Pleasant-Jette, 1993).

The federal government (Department of Justice Canada, 2005) pointed to three main concerns with the YOA:

> First, not enough was being done to prevent troubled youth from entering a life of crime. Second, the system needed to improve the way it dealt with the most serious, violent youth: not just in terms of sentencing but also in ensuring that these youth were provided with the intensive, long-term rehabilitation that is in their and society's interest. Third, the system relied too heavily on custody as a response to the vast majority of non-violent youth when alternative, community-based approaches could do a better job of instilling social values such as responsibility and accountability, helping to right wrongs and ensuring that valuable resources are targeted where they are most needed. (p. 1)

Although the YOA was optimistically seen as a way of fixing the problems inherent in the JDA, its existence was relatively short-lived. By the late 1990s, dissatisfaction with the YOA had already resulted in numerous calls for reform. Essentially, those emphasizing the role of social issues (such as poverty, abuse, gender and class discrimination, to name a few) in the etiology of youth crime saw the YOA as a prime example of the gradual slide in Canadian society toward a law and order mentality, coupled with the decontextualization of criminal behaviour.

▶ WHAT DO YOU THINK?

To what extent is youth crime an "event?" Or is it a process?

Although the term *law and order* has a **prima facie** inherent appeal, the content of the modern law and order efforts warrants scrutiny. In this respect, and as I have emphasized elsewhere, the modern approach to law and order essentially involves placing the emphasis for youth crime on young people's individual failings, thereby removing from analysis the role of social risks and protective factors. Moreover, modern law and order ideology assumes that we can do very little to prevent youth crime (or adult crime for that matter), and the focus, therefore, must be on managing the problem **post hoc**.

Thus, the *Young Offenders Act* was essentially a tool and administrative framework for managing young offenders, not a tool for addressing crime prevention (McGuire, 1997). Moreover, in a social environment in which the media (despite stable crime rates) happily constructed fake waves of youth crime (Sprott, 1996) and concomitant public fear about being victimized by youth superpredators, many stakeholders felt that the

prima facie
On the face of things.

post hoc
After the fact.

YOA was too soft on young offenders and that renewed calls for more stringent law and order would soon follow.

In 2003, the new and current Act governing youth crime—the *Youth Criminal Justice Act* (YCJA)—became law. The new Act, instead of being a completely different approach to the adjudication and treatment of youth offending is, I would argue, merely a continuation and indeed an intensification of the ideology of managing risky children and does not deal meaningfully with the social conditions that foster criminal behaviour. The YCJA represents the political desire to be all things to all people because it attempts to protect the public, while stating that rehabilitation, reintegration, and alternatives to incarceration of offenders should also be of paramount concern (Barber & Doob, 2004; Doob & Cesaroni, 2004; Hartnagel, 2004; Varma & Marinos, 2000). And, although alternatives to incarceration as codified in the "Extrajudicial Measures" section of the YCJA (formerly "Alternative Measures" under the YOA) may seem progressive, it is still too early to tell whether these alternatives have been implemented equitably across ethnic, class, and gender lines and whether they will have their intended effect. Indeed, as some writers have argued, it may be more accurate to see the so-called progressive elements of the YCJA as part of a "responsibilization" strategy, in which young people in conflict with the law must choose to cooperate and partner with communities to successfully reintegrate themselves into society (Garland, 2000; Mann, Senn, Girard, & Ackbar, 2007). Such a strategy, then, tends to place the onus for change squarely on the shoulders of individual youth, while glossing over or completely overlooking the social forces and conditions that generate crime.

The YCJA explicitly declares that the objectives of the youth justice system are to *prevent* crime, rehabilitate and reintegrate offenders, and hold young offenders accountable for their actions by enforcing meaningful consequences, while simultaneously understanding that young people lack the maturity of adults and that a youth's rights should be respected (Department of Justice Canada, 2007). Thus, the underlying principle of the YCJA can be captured in the phrase (used first in the United Kingdom) "tough on crime, tough on the causes of crime."

The extent to which real efforts are being made to deal meaningfully with the social causes of youth criminality remains to be seen. Recent political statements seem to indicate that in the near future more emphasis will be on strengthening the criminal justice system's response to youth crime, than on fortifying families, children, and the social conditions in which they live (see Box 4.2), despite the difficulties associated with neighbourhood disorganization and government recognition that the most serious young offenders come from disrupted homes characterized by violence, physical and sexual abuse, poverty, substance abuse, attachment disorders, and poor housing. Furthermore, despite political promises nearly 20 years ago to eliminate child poverty by the year 2000, today nearly one in five Canadian children lives in poverty (Campaign 2000, 2016), youth suicide rates have risen (BC Partners for Mental Health and Addictions Information, 2006), and good evidence suggests that a large majority of incarcerated youth suffer from mental health problems (Gretton & Clift, 2011; Odgers, Burnette, Chauhan, Moretti, & Reppucci, 2005).

This brief history of youth crime legislation points to a gradual shift from welfare models of youth criminal justice, in which young people's social and economic needs are rightly seen as the primary focus in dealing with youth criminality, toward a law

BOX 4.2

Tory Bill Proposes Violent Youth Be Tried as Adults

If the Conservative government has its way, more young offenders would be tried as adults ...

The government introduced their Crime Bill by starting off with proposed changes to the Youth Criminal Justice Act.

These are the key proponents of their proposal:

- Tougher sentences
- Allowing for pretrial detention
- Allow courts to consider deterrence and denunciation as objectives of youth sentences

Justice Minister Rob Nicholson said young offenders need to be held accountable when they commit violent crimes.

"These amendments to the Youth Criminal Justice Act are intended to help hold young lawbreakers accountable to their victims and their community, and instill within them a sense of responsibility for their delinquent or criminal behaviour," he said.

The minister also said the new legislation would be tougher on bail conditions for repeat offenders or youth accused of committing violent crimes.

Nicholson also said there will be a more comprehensive review of the Youth Criminal Justice Act next year.

Critics were hesitant to applaud the move.

Yvon Godin, the NDP whip, called the move "smoke and mirrors" on CTV's *Mike Duffy Live*.

"If a youth is dangerous to the people, the judge already has that power. This bill won't change anything," he told the show's host Mike Duffy Monday.

However, Jay Hill, the Conservative Party whip, said a recent commission in Nova Scotia found that law officials feel like they do not have enough power when it comes to young offenders.

"In the opinion of the inquiry, judges do not have sufficient power to ensure proper detention of a violent youth if he does pose a threat to others," he told Duffy.

Liberal whip Karen Redman said the party agrees the Act needs to be re-examined but that they would want to study the Conservative proposal further.

"We certainly do agree that repeat violent offenders need to be looked at," she said.

"A lot of these recommendations seem to be consistent with the report that came out of Nova Scotia," she continued. "We've said all along we're very supportive of that but we do want to make sure that the principles of the Youth Criminal Justice bill are not undermined."

Source: Tory bill proposes violent youth be tried as adults. (2007, November 19). *CTV.ca News*. Retrieved from www.ctvnews.ca. Reprinted by permission of CTVglobemedia.

and order approach that focuses on individual traits, behaviours, and responsibilities, not on social factors. This shift has been conditioned by changing perceptions of what it means to be a young person in Canadian society, and only very recently by what it means to be a young *female* in our society.

Readers may have noticed that no attempts were made within the first two legislative frameworks to acknowledge and address how gender (or ethnicity and class) shapes both the level and content of youth crime. In contrast, as Mann and her colleagues (2007) point out, the YCJA *does* mandate that criminal justice practitioners respect gender and other differences. In light of this apparent acknowledgment of the gendered nature of youth offending, let us now turn to data on the extent and nature of young women's and girls' offending in Canada compared with their male counterparts.

The Extent and Nature of Female Offending

When confronted with statistical data on particular phenomena, a good tenet of social science methodology is to ask the question "compared with what or whom?" This section provides data on the extent and nature of young female offending, but will also compare these data with data on their male counterparts. The central reason for this approach is to first highlight similarities and differences between male and female young offenders and then to point to social and policy implications for the youth criminal justice system.

The problems associated with understanding crime by using official sources of data are legion and well known. Briefly, official statistics of crime, which emanate primarily from the police and the courts, represent police or court activity, not an accurate measure of criminal acts and do not provide much detailed information on the nature of the criminal acts themselves (Alvi, 2000). Also, official crime statistics will vary greatly depending on the willingness of the public to actually report criminal victimization, on the ways in which law enforcement is practised, and on changes in legislation (Canadian Centre for Justice Statistics, 1997; Carrington & Moyer, 1994).

Consider, for example, what has happened with respect to bullying in Canadian schools, which in previous eras was considered to be a fight or disagreement but is now often interpreted as an incident of assault warranting police intervention (DeKeseredy, 2000). Consider too that cyberbullying has become a key concern in modern society, though we know little about its antecedents and we are not even certain how to define it (see Alvi, Downing, & Cesaroni, 2015). Similarly, problems occur with the accuracy and quality of official statistics because police apprehend individuals but do not always charge them with crimes. Indeed, according to Statistics Canada (Silver, 2007), police laid fewer formal charges against youth in 2006 compared with the years prior to implementation of the YCJA, with the exception of violent crimes, for which almost 75 percent of youth who were apprehended were formally charged.

Another problem, particularly important in relation to offending by young women, is the critical role played by the media in inflating and sensationalizing female crime. For example, although it has been well established that males are primarily responsible for the vast majority of violent crime, the media sometimes misrepresent the nature and extent of female violence, for example, by making claims that such violence has "increased by 200 percent from last year," despite the raw counts of (for example) one female who committed homicide last year, compared with three this year. Although the reported percentage increase of 200 percent in this example is mathematically correct, the misleading impression is that of a massive increase in female youth homicides, a reaction that can and often does fuel fear and hysteria among the general public, policy-makers, and others, which is simply unwarranted (Artz, Nicholson, & Rodriguez, 2005; Schissel, 1997). Feminist criminologists have now developed a large body of work locating the motives for such hysteria in women's historical and contemporary inequality with men, gender stereotyping, and racism, thereby placing female youth and adult crime in its proper context and drawing attention to the ways in which media routinely sensationalize and misrepresent female youth crime despite the vast disparity in numbers compared with their male counterparts. Thus, the fact remains that data on female youth crime should be scrutinized and interpreted carefully.

For an understanding of the nature and extent of most crimes, victimization and self-report studies of crime are widely acknowledged to be more accurate than data from official sources (Macdonald, 2002). Although few in number, and for the most part confined to studies of particular jurisdictions, victimization and self-report surveys of youth criminality across Canada show clearly that females commit different kinds of crimes than males, less frequently than males, and for different motives.

The International Youth Survey is the Canadian portion of the International Self-Reported Delinquency Study, which collected data from Europe, the United States, and Canada. The 2006 Canadian study, conducted with 3,200 young people in grades 7 to 9, found that of the boys surveyed, twice as many had committed violent acts (30 percent) compared with girls (15 percent), and boys were marginally more likely (30 percent) to report committing property offences than girls (26 percent) (Savoie, 2007). This general pattern of findings has been replicated numerous times.

Table 4.1 presents some results of a national sample survey of Canadian youth aged 12 to 15 years, focusing on self-reported delinquency and victimization. Drawing on a sample of youth from the National Longitudinal Survey of Children and Youth (NLSCY), young people were asked to report how often they had engaged in a range of property-related offences in the past year, such as stealing something from school, damaging property, fencing stolen goods, breaking into a vehicle to steal, stealing a vehicle, or setting fire to something on purpose. They were also asked to state how many times they had participated in violent delinquency, which included fighting causing physical injuries, carrying a stick or club as a weapon, carrying a knife as a weapon, fighting with a weapon, threatening someone for money or property, or carrying a gun for defence.

As can be seen from Table 4.1, nearly one-third of male youth reported committing both property-related and violent delinquency, whereas far fewer females (one in five, and one in ten, respectively) reported committing the same acts. Further, and as criminological research findings have shown for a very long time, males were only about one-and-a-half times more likely than females to engage in property offences, but nearly three times more likely to commit violent acts.

Other victimization studies corroborate the patterns shown in Table 4.1. For example, a study of Alberta school youth between grades 7 and 12 found that more than one-third (36.4 percent) of males reported engaging in a moderate number (three to seven) to a high number (more than eight) of tincidents of delinquency in the past year, compared with less than one-third (29.8 percent) of females (Gomes, Bertrand, Paetsch, & Hornick, 2003). When these figures were further examined for differences between males and females in relation to the *types* of crime they reported committing, the authors found that 13.2 percent of males reported engaging in property-related delinquency more than four times in the past year, compared with 7.8 percent of females. As expected, twice

Table 4.1   Self-Reported Delinquent Acts Committed by Males and Females Aged Between 12 and 15 Years, 1998–99

	Males	Females	Male-to-Female Ratio
	Percent		
Total property-related delinquency	29.3	19.1	1.6:1
Total violent delinquency	29.2	10.1	2.9:1

Source: Adapted from Fitzgerald, R. (2003). *An examination of sex differences in delinquency* (Report no. 85-561-MIE). Ottawa: Minister of Industry, p. 11.

as many males (12 percent) as females reported engaging in violence-related delinquency over the past year.

Both of these studies also tapped into male and female youths' experiences of victimization at the hands of other youth. Here, females in the NLSCY study reported a mean victimization score of 0.57, on a scale in which 0 indicated no victimization and 12 indicated frequent victimization. Conversely, the males in the study reported a mean score of 1.18 on the same scale. As the authors of this study note, however, the NLSCY questions on victimization were non-specific, meaning the questions did not distinguish between types of victimization. Thus, although young women are much more likely than young men to be the victims of crimes such as rape or sexual assault, young men are more likely to report being injured in the context of assaults or robbery (Loeber, Kalb, & Huizinga, 2001).

Authors of a more recent victimization and self-report study of high school and street youth in Toronto found important gender differences in deviant activities (Tanner & Wortley, 2002). Table 4.2 presents self-report data from this study on lifetime offending for male and female high school students and street youth.

As shown in Table 4.2, the differences in rates of offending between males and females are again entirely expected, given the results of prior studies. Notably, however, significant differences are shown in the rates reported by street youth (male and female) compared with high school students. The gender differences within street youth persist

Table 4.2   Percentages of High School Students and Street Youth Reporting Selected Non-Violent and Violent Offences at Some Time in Their Life, by Sex

	Non-Violent Offences			
	High school students		Street youth	
	Females	Males	Females	Males
Break and enter	4.4	14.4	44.0	57.3
Auto theft	1.9	8.2	27.6	44.2
Bike theft	3.8	21.0	26.7	56.9
Selling of illegal drugs	8.1	19.0	62.9	66.4
Vandalism/property damage	31.0	51.9	61.2	58.4
Major theft (over $50)	10.9	23.6	55.2	68.2
	Violent Offences			
Carrying a weapon in public	3.3	13.7	37.6	48.4
Robbery/extortion	0.6	5.5	20.7	31.1
Assault with intent to cause serious harm	1.2	6.0	23.5	27.8
Sexual assault	0.0	1.2	0.9	3.3

Source: Adapted from Tanner, J., & Wortley, S. (2002). *The Toronto youth crime and victimization survey*. Toronto: Centre of Criminology, University of Toronto, pp. 116, 127.

(with the exception of vandalism or property damage), and street youth reported engaging in criminal offences to a greater extent than high school students. This finding suggests that the *social context* and conditions within which young males and females live play a significant role in the nature and level of their offending. Indeed, as Tanner and Wortley (2002) point out:

> The traditional gender gap in offending is, however, significantly diminished among street youth … This finding suggests that the conditions of the street may have a much greater impact on overall deviance than the social conditions imposed by one's gender. (p. 110)

Thus, these data and data from numerous other studies provide ample evidence pointing both to girls' lower likelihood of committing violent and non-violent offences and to how this likelihood changes when males and females encounter different social circumstances. However, although these data provide useful insights into the nature of female offending, another important question needs to be posed regarding *trends* in male and female offending in Canada. Put differently, is female youth crime on the rise, as many people seem to believe? Before answering this question, let us consider the problem of confidence in the reliability of data on youth crime. Doob and Cesaroni (2004) address the matter this way:

> We do not have definitive information about how much crime there is in a community, let alone how much youth crime. It follows that we do not have any definitive evidence as to whether youth crime has increased, decreased, or stayed the same in the past few years. (p. 118)

Despite the problem of less than perfect data, some conclusions about the nature of youth crime can be determined from official statistics on court appearances, which provide one measure of young people's involvement with the criminal justice system. By focusing on homicide statistics, we reduce the possibility of underestimating because homicide is a crime that is almost always reported. As Meloff and Silverman (1992) note, the vast majority of homicides committed by young people between 1961 and 1983 were perpetrated by boys (89 percent) as compared with girls (11 percent).

Data from the 1980s until the most recent period for which statistics are available paint a similar picture. As Figure 4.1 suggests, overall, the trends for both males and females who were accused of homicide over the past 30 years have essentially remained stable. Despite variations from year to year (particularly for males), these data do not support the claim of an "overall pattern in the number of young offenders charged with homicide offences" (Doob & Cesaroni, 2004, p. 126). One pattern we are already familiar with is obvious; namely, young males are far more likely to be accused of homicide than young females. Moreover, as noted earlier, the small *number* of females charged with homicide means that when a difference exists in the rate of homicides from one year to the next, reporting the *percentage* increase will overdramatize the reality of homicide perpetrated by females.

Figure 4.1 presents only raw counts of charges, not rates. Because rates account for changes in population, they are important if we are to gain accurate understandings of any real increase in crime rates for young offenders. Accordingly, Figure 4.2 presents data on charge rates for young female and male offenders (from official data) between 1996 and 2002. From these data we can see that charges on both violent and property

FIGURE 4.1   Male and Female Youth Aged 12 to 17 Accused of Homicide in Canada, 1974–2005

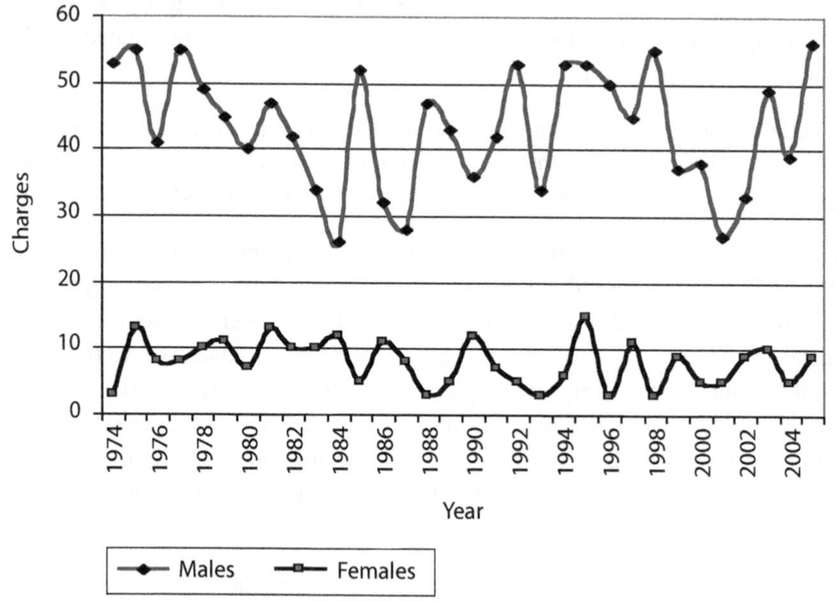

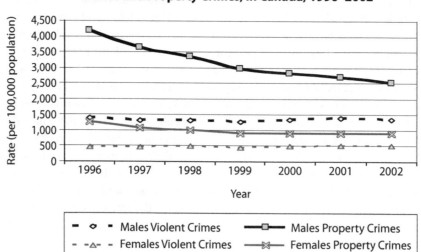

Source: Statistics Canada. (2007b). *Homicide survey, victims and persons accused of homicide, by age group and sex, Canada* [CANSIM table 253-0003]. Available from http://www5.statcan.gc.ca/cansim/a26?lang=eng&id =2530003.

FIGURE 4.2   Male and Female Youth Aged 12 to 17 Charged with Violent Crimes and Property Crimes, in Canada, 1996–2002

Source: Adapted from Statistics Canada. (2007a). *Adults and youths charged, by sex and offence category, Canada, provinces and territories, annual* [CANSIM table 109-5009]. Available from http://www5.statcan.gc.ca/cansim/ a26?lang=eng&retrLang=eng&id=1095009.

offences for female young offenders have essentially remained stable, whereas for young males, charges for property offences have decreased and charges for violent offences have remained stable. Some controversy surrounds the proper interpretation of these data.

Although the data suggest that rates of violent crime committed by young females have not increased (see, for example, Dell & Boe, 1998), others argue that girls (and boys) are committing more serious offences than in the past (see Box 4.3). As noted earlier, this perception derives in part from the great deal of media attention accorded to the alleged increase in girls' use of violence and aggression, buttressed by sensational (but nevertheless tragic) cases such as that of Reena Virk (see Box 4.4). The issue is further complicated because, in Canada, *charges* for violent offences filed against female youth have increased, although many scholars have argued that this increase in charge rates reflects bias in the justice system in which girls are increasingly being charged for minor offences at higher rates than boys (Chesney-Lind & Shelden, 1992; DeKeseredy, 2000; Sprott & Doob, 2003). Doob and Cesaroni (2004) support this theory:

> Boys ... are being brought to court at a lower rate now than they had been and, as a result, can be seen as making girls look relatively worse.... Girls are not involved in as much violence as are boys, and when they are, they are disproportionately likely to be involved in *less serious* forms of violence. (p. 135; emphasis added)

BOX 4.3

Viciousness of Youth Attacks Increases While Numbers Remain Static

The memories came rushing back for Len Libin with the news of a fatal attack on a Grade 11 student walking home from a game of pickup basketball last week.

Three years ago, Libin's son, then a 17-year-old athlete and bright student, was beaten into a coma in a random attack by two teenagers and an adult.

The victims of such attacks, says the senior Libin, "so often seem to be just good kids that you hear about that haven't really created problems and just for some reason, I don't know why, are picked."

Joel Libin survived and, despite having to go through extensive rehabilitation, has done "remarkably well," says his father.

The 17-year-old killed last week was not so fortunate.

He was buried Friday, a week after he and three Filipino friends walked past a group of Indo-Canadian teenagers who allegedly called out racial slurs.

There was a chase and the victim, apparently the slowest in the group, was caught and beaten with a blunt object. He died hours later in hospital.

The sheer viciousness of seemingly random attacks by teenagers seems to be increasing, say youth crime experts, although they maintain the actual number of youth murders has remained static.

"What strikes me as a researcher is what I say is an apparent increase in the brutality," says Ray Corrado, a criminologist at Simon Fraser University.

Sibylle Artz, an expert in youth violence at the University of Victoria, agrees.

"That seems to be a consensus among many people who deal with the youth directly," she says.

"They all tell the same story, that they have this experience of this being more brutal, more extreme," says Artz.

"When an attack is perpetrated, it doesn't stop when somebody's down."

The Vancouver teen's death comes on the heels of a Toronto 12-year-old's slaying, allegedly by three teenagers, who were charged with first-degree murder. The victim's brother is one of the accused.

In another high-profile case, three Alberta teenagers were sentenced last month to spend 60 days in custody for spiking a slushie with a toxic chemical and serving it to a fellow student.

The motive appears to have been a dislike for the victim, whom the girls suspected of hacking into one of their computers and erasing the hard drive.

Stranger killings are far more rare, says Corrado. Police aren't aware of any prior relationship between the Vancouver victim and his alleged attackers.

One of the more controversial aspects of the Filipino youth's killing is the suggestion that race was a contributing factor.

Police have hesitated to say the attack was racially motivated, although they acknowledge racial taunts were called out by members of the Indo-Canadian group before [the] Filipino teenager and his friends were chased.

The principal of the victim's school said last week she didn't view the attack as a racial incident.

"I think it was a violent incident," said Jennifer Palmer of Charles Tupper secondary school. "I think the people who perpetrated it may have behaved that way to any group of kids walking down the street."

In a narrow sense, the killing may have been racially motivated, says Corrado.

"The larger question is, would it have happened with another group of young people there that were even (Indo-Canadian)," he says, suggesting the answer would be "yes."

"The violence is what they are looking for; the particular target, they are not."

Regardless of motivation, Corrado and Artz said the number of youth killings in Canada has stayed at roughly the same level—40 to 50 a year—for the last few decades.

"While the acts are horrific, there is very little indication that youth murder has gone up," says Corrado.

"Canada's youth are still quantitatively relatively nonviolent, definitely compared to the United States," he says. "We're not a society where we need to be in constant fear of young people."

The criminologist could only speculate when asked for an explanation as to why [the] brutality of random acts seems to be increasing.

"I've argued it might reflect the cultural norms of the last 15, 20 years, where video games and movies and music, even television, portray a level of violence that is really extraordinary," says Corrado.

Artz agrees. "I believe that having the imagery constantly in front of them, (communicating) that it's fine to use weapons, clubs, action-hero type behaviours.

"We are normalizing the use of violence in our efforts to sell goods."

Source: Yearwood-Lee, E. (2003, December 7). Viciousness of youth attacks increases while numbers remain static. *Canadian Press*. Available at http://www.thefreeradical.ca/research/violentCrimeStatsCanada.html. Reprinted by permission of The Canadian Press.

BOX 4.4

Accused in Virk Case Goes on Trial for Third Time

More than seven years after a burning cigarette was extinguished on her 14-year-old daughter's face, her beaten body tossed in a river to drown, Reena Virk's mother testified again Monday at the trial of the young woman accused of killing her.

Kelly Ellard, 22, has been tried twice previously for second-degree murder in Virk's death.

Suman Virk spat the words out again as she was asked to describe the last few hours she spent with her daughter.

The girl was troubled, in and out of foster homes, but that night she was just like a regular kid. Running to the store with her younger brother and sister to get candy. Watching TV with the family.

Virk said her daughter's name is forever associated with murder.

"I don't think anybody will ever forget the horrific details of this murder," she said outside the courthouse. "I think the name Reena Virk will always bring back the horrors of Nov. 14th, (1997), no matter when and where it's mentioned."

That was the night, Virk said, that Reena, an awkward girl with few friends, got a phone call from a girl she met at a group home. A bunch of kids were hanging out at a local school and after much hesitation, Reena decided to go meet them. She didn't know many of them.

The crowd of 14-, 15- and 16-year-olds were getting rowdy, drinking, smoking pot in a field and shattering a window at the school.

Crown prosecutor Catherine Murray said witnesses will testify that a group of eight girls went under the Craigflower Bridge with Reena and began beating her.

"You will hear that Reena was punched and kicked repeatedly. You'll hear she was then left sitting in the mud at the bottom of the stairs, slumped over, injured, crying and bleeding from the face."

Murray alleged that Reena pulled herself up the stairs and managed to make it across the bridge and that Kelly Ellard, and the key witness against her, Warren Glowatski, followed.

"Three people crossed the Craigflower Bridge that night, only two came back," Murray said.

Glowatski is serving time for his role in Virk's death.

Murray said Glowatski will testify that Ellard forced Virk to take off her jacket and her shoes. Glowatski will say that the two began to punch and kick the injured girl, Murray said, and that each grabbed one of Reena's legs.

Glowatski stopped as Ellard pulled Reena into the water, Murray said.

Reena Virk's body was pulled out of the Gorge waterway a week later.

During that week, Murray said, witnesses will testify that Ellard bragged at school about what she had done to Reena.

"Kelly Ellard told them she killed Reena. We say that the things Kelly Ellard told people reveal a knowledge only a murderer, the murderer, would have."

Ellard's lawyer, Peter Wilson, asked the jurors if they had ever been the subject of a nasty rumour, and how awful it felt.

"Have you ever noticed how rumours almost seem to fuel themselves? They build up such steam that they can't be stopped," he said.

"Most of the people involved were young. That means they were impressionable, as we all were. As the witnesses testify, take note of the difference between real evidence and recollection."

The trial is expected to last three weeks.

Source: Accused in Virk case goes on trial for 3rd time. (2005, February 22). *CTV.ca News*. Retrieved from http://www.ctvnews.ca. Reprinted by permission of The Canadian Press.

In the International Youth Survey mentioned earlier, about half of the delinquent girls and boys reported that they started committing delinquent acts before the age of 12 (Savoie, 2007, p. 5). Thus, regarding the onset of delinquent behaviour, little difference separates girls from boys. However, males and females have distinct differences in terms of the pathways they take toward criminal behaviour. For example, the few young females who engage in violent behaviour tend to have been the victims themselves of sexual discrimination and physical, psychological, or emotional victimization, and these experiences are often related to the kinds of offences they commit (Belknap & Holsinger, 2006; Katz, 2000; Mallicoat, 2007).

Put differently, young females' social and emotional experiences are different in many ways from those of young males, and understanding these differences is essential in helping us to comprehend the clear gender gap in offending (Holsinger, 2000; Sharp, Brewster, & Love, 2005). Although male young offenders suffer what Belknap and Holsinger (2006) refer to as "alarmingly high" levels of physical, emotional, and verbal abuse (p. 65) and in many cases have suffered traumatic experiences with parents or guardians, most studies demonstrate that female young offenders have experienced much higher levels of such abuse, and the effects of such abuses in childhood are stronger predictors of future delinquency for girls than for boys (American Bar Association & National Bar Association, 2001; English, Widom, & Brandford, 2001; Makarios, 2007). Moreover, these experiences are also more commonly found in the lives of young males and females who come from economically and socially disadvantaged backgrounds (Jacob, 2006; Steffensmeier & Haynie, 2000).

Thus, as we have seen from data presented in this section, girls are less likely to commit offences for the vast majority of criminal offence categories, and they are more likely to have experienced a range of problems in their lives that are well known to be associated with crime and delinquency. In the following section, we examine the nature of Canadian criminal justice responses to girls in trouble with the law and relate these responses to the realities of girls' life experiences.

The Criminal Justice Response to Female Youth Crime

Despite overwhelming evidence of the different developmental needs and social experiences of girls and boys, the criminal justice system response to youth female offending in Canada has, for the most part, been less than adequate. One of the primary reasons for the gap between the realities of girls' lives and criminal justice responses to their offending likely lies once again in our society's deeply ingrained attitudes toward the proper roles and behaviours of women.

To illustrate this claim, consider that researchers have long known that girls tend to be punished more often than boys for minor crimes and for breaching court orders, thereby prompting these scholars to argue that girls are kept in custody "for their own protection"—in other words, so they will not get into further trouble associated with the pull of drugs, boyfriends, peers, and street life (Corrado et al., 2000). But another way of looking at this phenomenon is in terms of the deep paternalism that it reflects. As Artz and her colleagues (2005) note, some good evidence corroborates the notion that girls are still being handed sentences that reflect the ethos to "protect them as much as possible." However, because the YCJA prohibits incarceration of young people for child protection, social welfare, or mental health needs, future research is needed to determine the extent to which this provision has been successful in decreasing youth custody for females (Mann et al., 2007).

Derived from youth court data, Table 4.3 provides an overview of the types of sentences handed down to young female and male offenders in the year 2000 (the last year such data were available). The data suggest that females are slightly less likely to receive a custodial sentence (open or secure custody, for example) than males. Females are also correspondingly more likely to receive probation, community service sentences, or alternative sentences. For the most part, these slight differences probably reflect the relatively more minor nature of offences committed by girls (Bell, 2002). Further, according to Statistics Canada, the top three offences committed by female and male youth who reoffend are the same crimes—theft, common assault, and offences against the administration of justice (Thomas, Hurley, & Grimes, 2002). However, female youth are less likely than male youth to be recidivists or to have prior convictions (Sanders, 2000).

In addition, responses to criminality differ *within* the category of young female offenders. For example, race plays a role in the sentencing response to young females. In 2004–2005, although Indigenous youth made up 7 percent of the Canadian population, they comprised 44 percent of the young females admitted to the correctional system, and nearly one-third of the females admitted to open custody (Calverley, 2007; Canadian Centre for Justice Statistics, 2016). Although evidence suggests racism plays a role in the clearly disproportional representation of Indigenous girls in some forms of custody, readers should note that Indigenous families (and the children of recent immigrant and "racialized" families) are some of the poorest in Canada (Campaign 2000, 2016). Thus, some inherent quality of the individual associated with the concept of race is not at issue here. Instead, racism creates barriers to adequate education and employment,

Table 4.3   Types of Dispositions in Canadian Youth Courts, as a Percentage of Total Dispositions, by Sex, 2000

	Males		Females	
	Number	**Percent**	**Number**	**Percent**
Total dispositions	48,144		11,897	
Secure custody	8,914	18.52%	1,544	12.98%
Detention for treatment	—	0.00%	—	0.00%
Open custody	8,620	17.90%	1,731	14.55%
Probation	22,600	46.94%	6,453	54.24%
Fine	2,940	6.11%	562	4.72%
Compensation	160	0.33%	20	0.17%
Pay purchaser	15	0.03%	2	0.02%
Compensation in kind	189	0.39%	22	0.18%
Community service	2,946	6.12%	960	8.07%
Restitution	30	0.06%	5	0.04%
Prohibition, seizure, forfeiture	120	0.25%	28	0.24%
Conditional discharge	98	0.20%	42	0.35%
Absolute discharge	782	1.62%	262	2.20%
Other dispositions (includes other sentences, such as essays, apologies, and counselling programs)	730	1.52%	266	2.24%

Source: Adapted from Statistics Canada. (2007c). *Number of cases heard in youth courts, by most significant disposition, age and sex of the accused, annual data based on the fiscal year* [CANSIM table 252-0009].

which lead to poverty and forms of discrimination, which in turn are strongly associated with youth crime (Alvi, 2002; Pearcy, 1991).

The Canadian justice system does not track the ethno-racial background of offenders (except for Indigenous offenders) for fear that such reporting may fuel discriminatory attitudes among the general public, create moral panics, or reproduce the false perception that race is a valid concept.[2] Consequently, we do not know with any certainty whether other visible minority girls are treated in discriminatory ways within the criminal justice system.

As we can see from Table 4.4, between 1997 and 2005, the likelihood (for both males and females) of being released from closed or open custody has been in steady decline. In addition, as we might expect with the introduction of the YCJA, the number of youth sentenced to community services (including all services in which youth would be supervised in the community, such as probation, the community portion of a custody and supervision order, deferred custody, and restitution and community service orders) has

Table 4.4 Number of Youth Custody and Community Services (YCCS) Releases from Canadian Correctional Services, by Sex, 1997–2005

Year	Males			Females		
	Total secure custody	Total open custody	Total community sentences	Total secure custody	Total open custody	Total community sentences
1997–98	6,005	5,743	—	1,073	1,295	—
1998–99	5,027	5,550	—	1,043	1,273	—
1999–2000	4,392	5,234	—	900	1,128	—
2000–1	4,319	5,362	—	887	1,183	—
2001–2	4,790	5,196	—	995	1,328	—
2002–3	2,664	2,732	—	508	557	—
2003–4	2,059	2,667	19,929	354	558	5,588
2004–5	1,765	2,221	22,383	280	505	6,752

Source: Adapted from Statistics Canada. (2007d). *Youth custody and community services (YCCS), releases from correctional services, by sex and length of time served, annual* [CANSIM table 251-0015]. Available from http://www5.statcan.gc.ca/cansim/a26?lang=eng&id=2510015.

seen a corresponding increase since 2003. It is too early to tell whether this trend toward decarceration will continue and whether sufficient resources are in place to service the increased community supervision orders within communities in some jurisdictions (Carrington & Shulenberg, 2005).

Female youth who are sentenced to closed or open custody face numerous challenges because few programs are specifically geared to the needs of young female offenders (Pate, 2008). Moreover, as seen in the quotation below, the experiences of some young female incarcerated offenders can be both extremely traumatic and dangerous. As the Canadian Association of Elizabeth Fry Societies (2008) points out:

> To make matters worse, young women usually end up being jailed in mixed youth centres. This results in many incidents of sexual harassment and rape, most of which go unreported. When we conducted research on young women in custody we found two rather shocking results. First, we discovered that many young women do not define what they experience as sexual harassment or rape. Instead, they talk about it as being flirting or fooling around, or their "turn in the closet." Secondly, for those who do identify what they experience as sexual harassment or rape, most claim that they would not report such assaults. (Institutional Abuse Issues, ¶ 5)

As a prelude to assessing the effectiveness of current strategies designed to deal with female young offenders, let us examine the data, presented in Table 4.5, from a study conducted with 500 incarcerated serious or violent young offenders in British Columbia.

These data point clearly not only to the importance of the roles played by a range of social problems in contributing to youth crime in general but also to the critical roles of race, class, and gender relations. Although both Indigenous and non-Indigenous

Table 4.5 Percentages of Family Dysfunction Reported in a Sample of 500 Indigenous and Non-Indigenous Male and Female Youth Incarcerated for Serious or Violent Offences

	Indigenous Males	Indigenous Females	Non-Indigenous Males	Non-Indigenous Females
Alcoholism	85.9%	88.2%	70.6%	45.3%
Drug abuse	73.8%	73.5%	57.1%	55.3%
Victim of physical abuse	53.3%	75.0%	44.5%	55.4%
Victim of sexual abuse	19.3%	57.6%	17.3%	33.8%
Mental disorder	16.1%	29.4%	21.8%	32.0%
Criminal record	78.1%	70.6%	66.9%	69.3%
Foster care	68.9%	81.8%	30.8%	32.9%

Source: Corrado, R.R., & Cohen, I.M. (2002). A needs profile of serious and/or violent Aboriginal youth in prison. *Forum on Corrections Research, 14.* Retrieved from http://www.csc-scc.gc.ca/research/forum/e143/e143g-eng.shtml.

offenders in this sample reported experiencing high levels of family dysfunction prior to being incarcerated, the experiences of Indigenous youth differ in many respects from those of their non-Indigenous counterparts. Indeed, alcoholism, drug abuse, physical and sexual assault, and being placed in foster care are all reported with greater frequency by Indigenous youth than non-Indigenous youth. Especially important given the focus of this chapter, however, is the comparison between non-Indigenous and Indigenous females. According to these data, Indigenous females are far more likely to report having lived with foster care families or in families where alcoholism, drug abuse, and sexual and physical abuse were widely prevalent.

Once again, an important conclusion is that a recognition and understanding of gender differences are undoubtedly important in creating effective treatment responses for juvenile offenders because in many respects female youth needs are clearly different from male youth needs. And, in many ways, being an Indigenous youth is a further complication. Thus, the *interrelationship* between race and gender (and other factors) should be considered when dealing with female young offenders. As scholars, we should also be mindful of the insights that might be gained by intersectional perspectives on people's lives. Briefly, intersectionality urges us to consider how multiple types of oppression (such as race, class, and gender) intersect in time and space to produce and condition people's experiences of social, political, and cultural difference (see Crenshaw, 1995) What then, are the implications of these realities, for policy, research, and programming?

The core intention of the YCJA is to deal with the causes of crime (such as poverty, racism, and social exclusion) while simultaneously imposing meaningful consequences on young offenders (Department of Justice Canada, 2005). Currently, however, the balance of the Canadian criminal justice system's response to youth in conflict with the law seems to be tilted in favour of a risk management strategy, not the social correlates of criminal offending.

Briefly, the risk management approach assumes that the central task of criminal justice agencies is to efficiently manage away the risk these offenders pose to the general public, increasingly through the use of risk assessment tools, of which some scholars have been quite critical (see, for example, Pate, 2006). Thus, by focusing attention on the attributes of the offender and emphasizing an actuarial approach, risk management strategies are prone to diverting attention from the social, economic, and political forces that shape and condition young people's lives.

It is easy and important to legislate that gender differences should be taken into account in the youth criminal justice process. It is also straightforward to write into law a concern for understanding the ways in which the socio-economic milieu conditions the lives of young people. It is quite another thing, however, to use that legislation to drive real change at the social level. Poverty, for example, is associated with housing problems, parental stress, the inability to learn, and street crime, all of which are still a reality in Canada, as are sexism, violence against women and girls, bullying, and mental illness. Young people's use of antidepressant drugs rose significantly in the 1990s, their use of illegal drugs has not decreased, and suicide is still the second-leading cause of death for young people in Canada (BC Partners for Mental Health and Addictions Information, 2006; Boyce, 2004; Skinner & McFaull, 2012). These and other *precursors* of youth crime must be the target of any real effort to reduce the problem. And in tackling these precursors, it is critical that policy-makers, criminal justice practitioners, and other stakeholders understand and take gender seriously.

SUMMARY

This chapter has examined the history of youth criminal justice law in Canada, from its early incarnation as gender-blind legislation to its recognition, on paper at least, of the importance of recognizing gender differences in offending. The chapter has also provided data and commentary on persistent and important differences in the nature and extent of offending patterns between young females and males.

Key points for the reader are that young females offend at a far lower rate than males, and the kinds of offences they commit are less serious on the whole than those committed by males. Moreover, although many aspects of the social backgrounds that condition these young people's lives are similar, females have unique experiences, particularly in relation to physical and sexual abuse. The chapter concludes by suggesting that these unique experiences and the ways in which race, class, and gender intersect and play out in young women's lives deserve attention at the levels of both policy and practice.

NOTES

1. Portions of this section contain revised material that was previously published by Alvi (2000).
2. For more on the issue of collecting data on race and ethnicity in the criminal justice system, see the debate in the *Canadian Journal of Criminology*, 1994, volume 36, number 2.

DISCUSSION QUESTIONS

1. Given the theories of female crime proposed in this book, and based on your reading of this chapter, which theory or theories best explain female youth crime?
2. If you were in charge of reducing female offending among Canadian youth, what kinds of social programs would you emphasize or create?
3. Over the past decade, visible minorities' immigration to Canada has increased substantially and all projections suggest that this trend will continue. Focusing specifically on young females, what are the implications of this trend for the Canadian justice system?

ADDITIONAL RESOURCES

Suggested Readings

Youth and Violence Fact Sheet, Public Health Agency of Canada, www.phac-aspc.gc.ca/sfv-avf/index-eng.php

Website

Canadian Association of Elizabeth Fry Societies: http://www.caefs.ca

REFERENCES

Accused in Virk case goes on trial for 3rd time. (2005, February 22). *CTV.ca News*. Retrieved from www.ctvnews.ca.

Allen, M.K., & Superle, T. (2016). Youth crime in Canada, 2014. *Juristat*, 1.

Alvi, S. (2000). *Youth and the Canadian criminal justice system*. Cincinnati: Anderson Press.

Alvi, S. (2002). A criminal justice history of children and youth in Canada. In B. Schissel & C. Brooks (Eds.), *Marginality and condemnation: An introduction to critical criminology in Canada* (pp. 193–209). Toronto: Fernwood.

Alvi, S., Downing, S., & Cesaroni, C. (2015). The self and the "selfie": Cyber-bullying theory and the structure of late modernity. In S.R. Maxwell & S.L. Blair (Eds.), *Contemporary perspectives in family research*. Volume 9: *Violence and crime in the family: Patterns, causes and consequences* (pp. 383–406). Bingley, UK: Emerald Group Publishing.

American Bar Association, & National Bar Association. (2001). *Justice by gender: The lack of appropriate prevention, diversion and treatment alternatives for girls in the justice system*. Washington, DC: Author.

Artz, S., Nicholson, D., & Rodriguez, C. (2005). Understanding girls' delinquency: Looking beyond their behaviour. In K. Campbell (Ed.), *Understanding youth justice in Canada* (pp. 289–312). Toronto: Pearson.

Bala, N. (1997). *Young offenders law*. Concord, ON: Irwin Law.

Barber, J., & Doob, A.N. (2004). An analysis of public support for severity and proportionality in the sentencing of youthful offenders. *Canadian Journal of Criminology and Criminal Justice*, 46, 327–328.

Barrett, M., & McIntosh, M. (1982). *The anti-social family*. London: Verso.

BC Partners for Mental Health and Addictions Information. (2006). *Suicide: Follow the warning signs*. Vancouver: Author.

Belknap, J., & Holsinger, K. (2006). The gendered nature of risk factors for delinquency. *Feminist Criminology*, 1, 48–71.

Bell, S. (2002). *Young offenders and juvenile justice: A century after the fact* (2nd ed.). Toronto: ITP Nelson.

Boyce, W. (2004). *Young people in Canada: Their health and well-being*. Ottawa: Health Canada.

Calverley, D. (2007). *Youth custody and community services in Canada, 2004/2005* (Report no. 85-002-XIE2007002). Ottawa: Canadian Centre for Justice Statistics.

Campaign 2000. (2016). *A road map to eradicate child and family poverty*. Toronto: Author.

Canadian Association of Elizabeth Fry Societies. (2008). *Labelling young women as violent: Vilification of the most vulnerable*. Retrieved from http://www.caefs.ca/wp-content/uploads/2013/05/Labelling-Young-Women-as-Violent-Vilification-of-the-most-vulnerable.pdf.

Canadian Centre for Justice Statistics. (1994). *A review of the alternative measures survey, 1991–92*. Ottawa: Statistics Canada.

Canadian Centre for Justice Statistics. (1997). Justice data fact finder [Monograph]. *Juristat, 16*(9).

Canadian Centre for Justice Statistics. (2016). Youth correctional statistics in Canada, 2014/2015. (Catalogue no. 85-002-X.) *Juristat,* 13.

Canadian Charter of Rights and Freedoms, Part I of the *Constitution Act, 1982,* being Schedule B to the *Canada Act 1982* (UK), c 11.

Carrigan, D.O. (1998). *Juvenile delinquency in Canada: A history.* Concord, ON: Irwin.

Carrington, P., & Moyer, S. (1994). Trends in youth crime and police response, pre- and post-YOA. *Canadian Journal of Criminology, 36,* 1–28.

Carrington, P.J., & Shulenberg, J. (2005). *The impact of the Youth Criminal Justice Act on police charging practices with young persons: A preliminary statistical assessment.* Ottawa: Department of Justice Canada.

Chesney-Lind, M. (2001). "Out of sight, out of mind": Girls in the juvenile justice system. In C. Renzetti & L. Goodstein (Eds.), *Women, crime and criminal justice: Original feminist readings* (pp. 27–43). Los Angeles: Roxbury Publishing.

Chesney-Lind, M. (2006). Patriarchy, crime and justice: Feminist criminology in an era of backlash. *Feminist Criminology, 1,* 6–26.

Chesney-Lind, M., & Okamoto, S.K. (2001). Gender matters: Patterns in girls' delinquency and gender responsive programming. *Journal of Forensic Psychology Practice, 1,* 1–28.

Chesney-Lind, M., & Shelden, M. (1992). *Girls, delinquency and juvenile justice.* Belmont, CA: Brooks/Cole.

Church Council on Justice and Corrections. (1996). *Satisfying justice: A compendium of initiatives, programs and legislative measures.* Ottawa: Author.

Corrado, R., Odgers, C., & Cohen, I. (2000). The incarceration of female young offenders: Protection for whom? *Canadian Journal of Criminology, 42,* 189–207.

Corrado, R.R., & Cohen, I.M. (2002). A needs profile of serious and/or violent Aboriginal youth in prison. *Forum on Corrections Research,* 14. Retrieved from www.csc-scc .gc.ca/text/pblct/forum/e143/e143g-eng.shtml.

Crenshaw, K. (1995). Mapping the margins: Intersectionality, identity politics, and violence against women of color. In K. Crenshaw, N. Gotanda, G. Peller, & K. Thomas (Eds.), *Critical race theory: The key writings that formed the movement* (pp. 357–383). New York: The New Press

DeKeseredy, W.S. (2000). *Women, crime and the Canadian criminal justice system.* Cincinnati, OH: Anderson.

Dell, C., & Boe, R. (1998). *Female young offenders in Canada* (rev. ed.). Ottawa: Correctional Services of Canada, Research Branch.

Department of Justice Canada. (2005). *A strategy for the renewal of youth justice.* Ottawa: Author.

Department of Justice Canada. (2007). Canada's new government announces a plan to strengthen the Youth Criminal Justice Act. Retrieved from http://www .collectionscanada.gc.ca/webarchives/20071116051025/ http://canada.justice.gc.ca/en/news/nr/2007/doc_32155 .html.

Doob, A.N., & Cesaroni, C. (2004). *Responding to youth crime in Canada.* Toronto: University of Toronto Press.

English, D., Widom, C.S., & Brandford, C. (2001). *Childhood victimization and delinquency, adult criminality, and violent criminal behavior: A replication and extension* (Report no. NCJ 192291). Washington, DC: National Institute of Justice.

Fitzgerald, R. (2003). *An examination of sex differences in delinquency* (Rep. no. 85-561-MIE). Ottawa: Minister of Industry.

Gagnon, D. (1984). *History of the law for juvenile delinquents* (Government working paper no. 1984-56.) Ottawa: Ministry of the Solicitor General of Canada.

Garland, D. (2000). The culture of high crime societies: Some preconditions of recent "law and order" policies. *British Journal of Criminology, 40,* 347–375.

Gomes, J.T., Bertrand, L.E., Paetsch, J.J., & Hornick, J.P. (2003). Self-reported delinquency among Alberta's youth: Findings from a survey of 2,001 junior and senior high school students. *Adolescence, 38,* 75–91.

Gretton, H.M., & Clift, R.J. (2011). The mental health needs of incarcerated youth in British Columbia, Canada. *International Journal of Law and Psychiatry, 34*(2), 109–115.

Hartnagel, T. (2004). The rhetoric of youth justice in Canada. *Criminal Justice, 4,* 355–374.

Holsinger, K. (2000). Feminist perspectives on female offending: Examining real girls' lives. *Women and Criminal Justice, 12,* 23–51.

Hylton, J.H. (1994). Get tough or get smart? Options for Canada's youth justice system in the twenty-first century. *Canadian Journal of Criminology, 36,* 229–246.

Jacob, J.C. (2006). Male and female youth crime in Canadian communities: Assessing the applicability of social disorganization theory. *Canadian Journal of Criminology and Criminal Justice, 48*(1), 31–60.

Katz, R.S. (2000). Explaining girls' and women's crime and desistance in the context of their victimization experiences: A developmental test of revised strain theory and the life course perspective. *Violence Against Women, 6,* 633–660.

Kong, R., & AuCoin, K. (2008). Female offenders in Canada. *Juristat, 28*(1), 1–22.

Loeber, R., Kalb, L., & Huizinga, D. (2001). *Juvenile delinquency and serious victimization.* Washington, DC: Department of Justice, Office of Justice Programs, Office of Juvenile Justice and Delinquency Prevention.

Macdonald, Z. (2002). Official crime statistics: Their use and interpretation. *Economic Journal, 112,* F85–F106.

Makarios, M.D. (2007). Race, abuse and female criminal violence. *Feminist Criminology, 2,* 100–116.

Mallicoat, S. (2007). Gendered justice: Attributional differences between males and females in the juvenile courts. *Feminist Criminology, 2,* 4–30.

Mann, R.M., Senn, C.Y., Girard, A., & Ackbar, S. (2007). Community-based interventions for at-risk youth in Ontario under Canada's Youth Criminal Justice Act: A case study of a "runaway" girl. *Canadian Journal of Criminology and Criminal Justice, 49,* 37.

McGuire, M. (1997). C.19: An Act to Amend the Young Offenders Act and the Criminal Code—"Getting tougher?"(Canada). *Canadian Journal of Criminology, 39,* 185–214.

Meloff, W., & Silverman, R.A. (1992). Canadian kids who kill. *Canadian Journal of Criminology, 34,* 15–34.

Odgers, C., Burnette, M., Chauhan, P., Moretti, M., & Reppucci, N.D. (2005). Misdiagnosing the problem: Mental health profiles of incarcerated juveniles. *Canadian Child and Adolescent Psychiatry Review, 14,* 26–29.

Pate, K. (2006). *The risky business of risk assessment.* Ottawa: Canadian Association of Elizabeth Fry Societies.

Pate, K. (2008). Why do we think young women are committing more violent offences? Retrieved from http://www.caefs.ca/wp-content/uploads/2013/05/Why -Do-We-Think-Young-Women-Are-Committing-More -Violent-Offences.pdf.

Pearcy, P. (1991). *Youth/criminal gangs in British Columbia.* Victoria, BC: Ministry of the Solicitor General.

Platt, A. (1977). *The child savers: The invention of delinquency.* Chicago: University of Chicago Press.

Pleasant-Jette, C.M. (1993). Creating a climate of confidence: Providing services within Aboriginal communities. In *National Round Table on Economic Issues and Resources (Royal Commission on Aboriginal Issues).* Ottawa: The commission.

Reitsma-Street, M. (1993). Canadian youth court charges and dispositions for females before and after implementation of the Young Offenders Act. *Canadian Journal of Criminology, 35,* 437–458.

Sanders, T. (2000). *Sentencing of young offenders in Canada, 1998/99.* Ottawa: Canadian Centre for Justice Statistics.

Savoie, J. (2007). *Youth self-reported delinquency, Toronto, 2006.* Ottawa: Statistics Canada.

Schissel, B. (1997). *Blaming children: Youth crime, moral panics and the politics of hate.* Halifax: Fernwood Publishing.

Sharp, S., Brewster, D.R., & Love, S.R. (2005). Disentangling strain, personal attributes, affective response and deviance: A gendered analysis. *Deviant Behavior, 26,* 122–157.

Skinner, & McFaull, S. (2012). Suicide among children and adolescents in Canada: Trends and sex differences, 1980–2008. *Canadian Medical Association Journal, 184*(9), 1029–1033

Silver, W. (2007). *Crime statistics in Canada, 2006* (Report no. 85-002-XIE). Ottawa: Ministry of Industry.

Sprott, J. (1996). Understanding public views of youth crime and the youth justice system. *Canadian Journal of Criminology, 38,* 271–290.

Sprott, J.B., & Doob, A.N. (2003). It's all in the denominator: Trends in the processing of girls in Canada's youth courts. *Canadian Journal of Criminology and Criminal Justice, 45,* 73–80.

Statistics Canada. (2007a). *Adults and youths charged, by sex and offence category, Canada, provinces and territories, annual* [CANSIM table 109-5009]. Available from http://www5.statcan.gc.ca/cansim/a26?lang=eng &retrLang=eng&id=1095009.

Statistics Canada. (2007b). *Homicide survey, victims and persons accused of homicide, by age group and sex, Canada* [CANSIM table 253-0003]. Available from http://www5.statcan.gc.ca/cansim/a26?lang=eng&id =2530003.

Statistics Canada. (2007c). *Number of cases heard in youth courts, by most significant disposition, age and sex of the accused, annual data based on the fiscal year* [CANSIM table 252-0009].

Statistics Canada. (2007d). *Youth custody and community services (YCCS), releases from correctional services, by sex and length of time served, annual* [CANSIM table 251-0015]. Available from http://www5.statcan.gc.ca/cansim/ a26?lang=eng&id=2510015.

Steffensmeier, D., & Haynie, D.L. (2000). Gender, structural disadvantage, and urban crime: Do macrosocial variables also explain female offending rates? *Criminology, 38,* 403–439.

Tanner, J. (1996). *Teenage troubles: Youth and deviance in Canada*. Scarborough, ON: Nelson.

Tanner, J., & Wortley, S. (2002). *The Toronto youth crime and victimization survey*. Toronto: Centre of Criminology, University of Toronto.

Thomas, M., Hurley, H., & Grimes, C. (2002). Pilot analysis of recidivism among convicted youth and young adults, 1999/00. *Juristat, 22*(9), 1–19.

Tory bill proposes violent youth be tried as adults. (2007, November 19). *CTV.ca News*. Retrieved from http://www.ctvnews.ca.

Varma, K.N., & Marinos, V. (2000). How do we best respond to the problem of youth crime? In J. Roberts (Ed.), *Criminal justice in Canada: A reader* (pp. 221–232). Toronto: Harcourt Brace.

Wardell, B. (1986). The Young Offenders Act: A report card 1984–1986. In D. Currie (Ed.), *The administration of -justice* (pp. 128–158). Saskatoon: Social Research Unit, University of Saskatchewan.

West, W.G. (1984). *Young offenders and the state: A Canadian perspective on delinquency*. Toronto: Butterworths.

Yearwood-Lee, E. (2003, December 7). Viciousness of youth attacks increases while numbers remain static. *Canadian Press*. Available from http://www.thefreeradical.ca/research/violentCrimeStatsCanada.html.

Young Offenders Act, RSC 1985, c Y-1.

Youth Criminal Justice Act, SC 2002, c 1.

Violent Women Offenders

Introduction

One of the most consistent findings in the study of female criminality is that women commit far fewer crimes than men, and even more so when only violent offences are considered. Hence, while women are responsible for approximately 23 percent of all criminal offences, they are responsible for only approximately 14 percent of the officially recorded violent offences in Canada (Statistics Canada, 2016a). Although various theories have been proposed to explain violence by women, more research is still needed to satisfactorily explain why women commit fewer violent crimes than men. Nevertheless, violence perpetrated by women is increasingly studied, and theoretical postulations about gender similarities and differences in the etiology of violence are increasingly supported by a growing body of empirical verifications. In turn, these studies provide an empirical basis for the development of differential assessment and treatment practices for women who have engaged in violent behaviour. As we will see, however, much remains to be known, and accurate assessments and effective treatment of violent behaviour among women await further empirical verifications.

This chapter reviews our current understanding of violent offending by women. Specifically, it will cover prevalence, offending characteristics, and, where relevant, assessment and treatment practices. Violent offending encompasses a number of offences, including assaults, homicides, and sexual offences. Because of theoretical and empirical differences in these different types of offending behaviour, this chapter examines women who engage in non-sexual violence (general violence, intimate partner violence, and homicides) separately from those who engage in sexual violence (all crimes with a sexual component but excluding prostitution and related offences).

Women Who Offend Violently: Prevalence

One of the most consistent findings over the years is that women commit far fewer violent crimes than men. Rates of officially recorded violence by women increased tremendously (in comparison with earlier base rates) from the early 1980s until the mid-2000s and have now levelled off. It is unclear why rates increased so dramatically until the mid-2000s. Pollock and Davis (2005) have speculated that this increase actually reflects changes in arrest decisions by the police (for example, changes in criminal justice system policy dictating that anyone who has engaged in intimate partner violence must be charged and the recognition that women engage in sexually assaultive behaviour), and not an actual increase in violence by women. Hence, current rates would be a much more accurate reflection of actual violent offending by women. This explanation awaits empirical validation.

In Canada, the rate of women charged for a violent offence[1] almost quadrupled between 1981 and 2001 to reach approximately 150 women charged for a violent crime per 100,000 women in the population (Public Safety and Emergency Preparedness Canada, 2008). This rate was stable until 2008 and has since slightly decreased (Statistics Canada, 2016a). In contrast, although the rate of men charged with violent offences peaked in 1993 at 930 males per 100,000 males in the population, it then steadily decreased to reach approximately 800 men per 100,000. A 2011 Canadian report concluded that the rate of men charged with a violent crime had declined by 32 percent, while the rate of women had increased by 34 percent (Brennan, 2012). At first glance, this conclusion suggests that violence by women has increased tremendously in recent years, but a closer examination reveals that despite this increase, the base rate of violence by women continues to be low. For example, in 2011, men were responsible for more than 80 percent of all violent crimes in Canada (Brennan, 2012).

BOX 5.1

The Emancipation Postulate

The stable or slightly decreasing rate of female violent offending is particularly interesting because the increase in violence by women previously led to a general conclusion that women were becoming more violent, mostly as a result of the liberation of women (see Pollock & Davis, 2005). The assumption was that women were not violent in the past because of their socialization and their traditional roles as nurturers, and that as women gained more societal opportunities for equality, they also became "equal opportunists" in criminal behaviour (Adler, 1975). In essence, by becoming "liberated," women were allowed to engage in previously unheard-of behaviour, such as violence. Pollock and Davis (2005) insist that this premise is a fallacy that has created more myths about women; although women are universally less violent than men, a small percentage of violent crimes have always been committed by women. However, should the emancipation postulate be correct, given that the rate of women charged of violent crimes has levelled off (based on official records), could this mean that progress in women's rights has stopped or even regressed?

General Violence

Research on violence by women typically includes assaults and robberies, whereas intimate partner violence and homicides are treated as separate issues. Although robberies are considered violent offences by Canadian federal law (Department of Justice Canada, 1992), these crimes do not always involve interpersonal violence and will not be considered in this chapter. From 2010 to 2015, women were found guilty of 16 to 18 percent of all assaults (common and aggravated) committed in Canada (Statistics Canada, 2016a).

Characteristics of Violent Women and their Offences

Women who commit violent offences tend to be in their mid-thirties or younger and most of them have at least one child (Rettinger & Andrews, 2010; Robitaille & Cortoni, 2014). These women tend to have witnessed much violence in their homes of origin and, compared to non-violent female offenders and male violent offenders, are more likely to have been victims of physical or sexual violence (see Chesney-Lind & Pasko, 2013). Not surprisingly, due to their frequent victimization histories, these women also tend to demonstrate more mental health problems compared to women from the general population (Fazel, Sjöstedt, Grann, & Langström, 2010).

Research supports the notion that at least a subset of female violent offenders has characteristics similar to those of male violent offenders. In their examination of hostility among female offenders, Verona and Carbonell (2000) found that repeat female violent offenders were more anti-social, had lower inhibitions against acting out violently, and made more use of instrumental violence during the commission of crimes than non-violent women and women who killed. These characteristics are highly similar to those of male offenders who chronically under-regulate their emotions, suggesting that factors related to violence in some women may be gender-neutral as opposed to gender-informed. The term *gender-neutral* refers to characteristics that are linked to the criminal behaviour and are equally applicable to men and women. The term *gender-informed* refers to factors unique to women offenders or that operate differently for women. For example, negative emotionality, particularly sadness and anger, seems to play a more prevalent role in female violence (Murdoch, Vess, & Ward, 2012). Although some authors argue that gender-neutral factors do not exist (e.g., Hannah-Moffat, 1999), research increasingly suggests that some factors do relate to violent behaviour regardless of gender. For example, there is strong evidence that poor self-control is a similar precursor of violence in men and women (Alarid, Burton, & Cullen, 2000; Blackwell, 2000).

Individual characteristics alone, however, are not sufficient to explain violent offending among women. An understanding of violence also needs to include a consideration of situational factors. Unemployment, low socio-economic status, poverty, and lack of access to educational and vocational opportunities all contribute to female violence (Pollock, Mullings, & Crouch, 2006; Salisbury & Van Voorhis, 2009). These characteristics are also found in the male offender population but appear to operate differently for women. According to Bottos (2008), various social factors such as a lack of educational and vocational opportunities, which appear to contribute to women's violence, come from differential societal opportunities afforded to men versus women.

The context in which women offend violently is consistently found to be of importance in the understanding of their violence. In particular, it is well documented that violence by women is most often related to interpersonal conflicts. For example, Sommers and Baskin (1993) interviewed and examined the file information of 65 women who had been arrested for a violent street crime. Their study showed that the interaction between the victim and the offender, and sometimes the verbal interaction with a third party, were fundamental to the women's assaults. Hirschinger et al. (2003) further reported that more than three-quarters of the cases of violence by women they studied ($n = 167$) were in fact mutual, which makes it difficult to qualify who is the victim and who is the offender. Mullins and Miller (2008), in their detailed analyses of the violent offences of three women, found that their violence was the result of a long-lasting complex and nuanced relational process with an important continuity and discontinuity of events during which both the victim and the offender were at play. Within this context, the offender's behaviour was often found to be a direct response to some behaviour on the part of the victim, such as the victim becoming belligerent toward the offender. Finally, studies consistently report that women's violence tends not to be planned, and that substance abuse is frequently involved when violence occurs (Weizmann-Henelius, Putkonen, Naukarinen, & Eronen, 2009).

Although it is well established that cognitions that support violence are associated with men's violent behaviour, there has been surprisingly little research on the cognitions of violent women. In her study of the offence process among 24 women convicted of a violent offence, St-Hilaire (2012) found, similar to Sommers and Baskin (1993), that in problematic situations, many of these women mistakenly attributed blame to others and perceived their violence as an appropriate response to the situation. Violent offenders' cognitive schemas bias would also prime them to interpret others' behaviour as hostile and to respond aggressively (Sestir & Bartholow, 2007). Although much more research is needed to better understand how these cognitive schemas develop in women, for at least some of the female offenders, hostile cognitions would likely be linked to their negative life experiences such as physical victimization.

To provide a better understanding of the association between cognitions and violence, research has focused on the cognitive schemas, referred to as *implicit theories*, which support men's violence (Polaschek, Calvert, & Gannon, 2008). Implicit theories are defined as underlying and interconnected beliefs that influence conscious thoughts and their related behaviours (Ward, 2000). To examine the nature of the implicit theories that support violent offending among *women*, Robitaille and Cortoni (2014) analyzed the cognitions of 17 women convicted of violent offences and found both similarities and differences between their implicit theories and those of male violent offenders (see Polaschek et al., 2008). First, two gender-neutral implicit theories were identified: (1) violence is normal, and (2) I lose control. These implicit theories indicate that some women believe violent behaviour is common and normative—a belief they attributed to the violent environment they were emerged in since their childhood, and that they engaged in violence because they lose control over their behaviour.

Second, the study identified four implicit theories among the violent women that have not been found among men: (1) I am not violent; (2) life was too hard on me; (3) I need to protect myself and others; and (4) those who act unfairly deserve to be beaten. The women who held the "I am not violent" implicit theory did not, or would not, recognize their violence, describing themselves instead as kind and nurturing individuals. Interestingly, most of the women in the study held the "Life was too hard on me" implicit theory. These women reported that they perceived their lives as too difficult, and believed that their negative life experiences had led to a build-up of negative feelings which they repressed until it was expressed through violence. The women who exhibited the "I need to protect myself and others" and the "Those who act unfairly deserve to be beaten" implicit theories explained that their violent behaviour emerged as soon as they, or someone they knew, were in danger (or even threatened of danger), or whenever violence was needed to obtain others' respect or to regain their own self-respect. Some of these women viewed themselves as saviours or protectors of weaker others. They reported that it was their duty to intervene—violently—to help others, and perceived themselves as heroes. This first-ever study on the cognitive schemas of violent women demonstrated both similarities and differences in the cognitive mechanisms related to female and male violent offending. Further research is yet needed to confirm these findings in independent samples of women offenders.

The Offence Process in General Violent Offending

The offence process that leads to general violent offending among women has only recently been the subject of systematic research. The main advantages of an offending process model are that it provides information on the proximal and distal elements that led to the offending, as well as on the underlying dynamics of these elements, to better understand how and why a woman acts violently. These models usually consider the offender's developmental experiences, the temporal period (three or six months, for example) preceding the offence, the events at the time of the offence, and the post-offence period. To date, there have been few studies that examined the offence process of violent women. Chambers, Ward, Eccleston, and Brown (2011) tested a model previously developed for assaultive men, the pathways model of assault, on a sample of 17 women convicted of an assault in New Zealand. Their results indicated that while 9 out of the 17 women's offence pathways could be fitted into the existing male pathways, in the 8 remaining cases, there were elements of the women's offence pathways that could not be accounted for by the male model. Instead of attempting to fit women's offence process into an existing male model, Murdoch, Vess, and Ward (2010, 2012) proposed the descriptive model of women violent offenders, which was developed from women offenders' data ($n = 19$) also in New Zealand. The Murdoch et al. model presents *background variables* (violent lifestyle, victimization, familial characteristics), the *pre-offence build-up* (offence trigger such as anger or jealousy, powerlessness, or defensiveness, which leads to either a desire for a redress of harm or procurement of goods), *offence variables* (context, victims, emotions), and *post-offence variables* (blaming others or self, arrest), and shows the importance of developmental experiences in emotional and behavioural dysregulation, which is common to all female violent offenders.

Interestingly, while this work was going on in New Zealand, St-Hilaire (2012) was concurrently examining the offence process of 24 women incarcerated in the Quebec correctional system who had been convicted of violent offences (excluding intimate, sexual, and homicidal violence). She found, similar to Murdoch et al. (2012), that the difficulties experienced by women from childhood to adulthood have a long-lasting impact on violent behaviour. These difficulties, called early vulnerability factors, are described in the first phase of her model and include psychological, physical, and sexual victimization; witnessing violence; conflictual environment at home; and parents with poor parental skills. The exposure to these factors later influenced the adoption of either a marginal or criminal lifestyle. These women had poor social support, and demonstrated a lack of effective coping strategies.

The second phase of the model describes the pre-offence buildup as months to weeks before the offence, and the acute phase as days to minutes before the offence. The pre-offence buildup encompasses an accumulation of negative events and the use of inadequate strategies to face those events. The acute phase represents the moments that immediately precede the violent behaviour. The women in the study reported that during this period, they either felt they were on the verge of violence or they had blacked out and were unable to remember what had happened. Substance use, conflicts, or dramatic events such as the removal of children tend to take place in this phase. The third phase involves the occurrence of the offence itself. This phase is divided into two different profiles, depending on the type of violence: instrumental (act) versus expressive (react). Women who followed an instrumental path more often acted within a criminal context, and were driven by monetary or other gains (drugs, for example), or by the desire to be more respected by their entourage. These women reported being generally thrilled or excited by their violence in these contexts. Women who followed an expressive path reacted emotionally to an interaction with the victim during which they felt threatened, bullied, or attacked. In many cases, the offender had attempted various non-violent strategies to stop the conflict before she acted violently, but ended up losing control. The final phase of the model focuses on the period following the violence. In this phase, women faced consequences of their behaviour, mostly negative (prison, removal of children, low self-esteem, or remorse, for example), although some were also positive (monetary gain, reputation, feeling accepted). It is also during this phase that women engaged in much post-offence rationalization to justify their offending behaviour, including minimizing their responsibility for the offence and blaming external factors such as alcohol or drug use, lack of sleep, or even the victims themselves.

While there were some similarities between the St-Hilaire and Murdoch et al. models, St-Hilaire was the first to identify that some women do purposefully engage in instrumental violence. Hence, the offence variables included in her model allowed the distinction of expressive and utilitarian violence, which may actually occur jointly. Another difference was that the post-offence phase in the St-Hilaire model also included the various impacts of the violent act on the participant's life, and identified that these extend over longer periods than had been identified by Murdoch et al. (2012). While both the St-Hilaire and Murdoch et al. models provided much-needed new knowledge, more systematic studies are still needed to fully understand the offending process of female violent offenders.

Intimate Partner Violence

Although the use of violence by women toward their intimate partners has been recognized since the mid-1980s (Swan & Snow, 2003), intimate partner violence perpetrated by women is still not well understood and debates about its prevalence and causes are ongoing. One major debate is about the issue of gender symmetry in intimate partner violence. Population-based research consistently shows that women engage in as much intimate partner violence as men, and that an equal number of women and men are victims of such violence (Archer, 2000; Dutton, 2012; Kimmel, 2002). For example, in Canada, the latest self-reported data reveal that 4 percent of Canadian women and 4 percent of Canadian men engage in intimate partner violence (Statistics Canada, 2016b).

Despite this reported gender equivalency in rates of intimate partner violence, women nevertheless continue to incur much more severe injuries than men when they are victims of such violence (Archer, 2000; Statistics Canada, 2016b). This gender difference in severity of injury is, it is argued, a clear indication that intimate partner violence should not be viewed as symmetric (see Straus, 2011). Much research supports this position. Specifically, crime victimization studies consistently find that serious intimate partner violence (that is, the type that escalates in severity over time) is primarily perpetrated by males (Kimmel, 2002), and that women are more susceptible than men to suffer from post-traumatic stress in relation to their victimization (Statistics Canada, 2016b). For example, while as many Canadian men as women reported having been victims of intimate partner violence in 2014, women were twice as likely to have suffered more severe violence (34 percent versus 16 percent for men), such as having been sexually abused, beaten, strangled, or threatened with a gun or a knife (Statistics Canada, 2016b). Similarly, in his international dating violence study, Straus (2008) analyzed self-reported experiences of intimate partner violence of 13,601 university students in 32 nations. He found that almost one-third of the students, male and female, physically assaulted a dating partner in the previous 12 months, and that the most frequent pattern of violence was bidirectional (that is, both partners were violent). Dominance by one partner, which is associated with an increased probability of more severe violence, was, however, mainly perpetuated by men, while women reported self-defence as the main reason for assaulting a partner.

Such results demonstrate the importance of considering not only the physical but also the psychological consequences of such violence. Indeed, studies often measure only the frequency of intimate partner violent acts, mostly using the Conflict Tactic Scale (CTS) developed by Straus (1990). Since these studies consider all acts of violence such as throwing an object, pushing, slapping, punching, or using an object to hit the other person as equivalent, it is not surprising that they have consistently shown that women engage in at least as many, if not more, violent acts as their male partners (Kimmel, 2002). Hence, although the CTS has proven helpful in research designed to understand intimate partner violence, it has been widely criticized for treating all acts of violence as equal, regardless of their severity, as well as failing to take into account the context in which the violence was perpetrated (Kimmel, 2002). For example, it would be of importance to assess whether only the woman committed intimate partner violence or if both partners were involved. In their study of women arrested alone and dual (both partners) arrestees, Muftié, Bouffard, and Bouffard (2007) showed that when the woman was the only arrestee, the man was more likely to be physically injured while in dual arrestees, the woman was more likely to be physically injured. Focusing only on the physical acts themselves, as opposed to the context in which these acts take place, and failing to consider coercive control and intimidation, would obscure important information about the differences between male and female perpetrators of intimate partner violence (Dasgupta, 2002).

In addition, a few rare studies investigated why in population-based research reports men are much more often victims of intimate partner violence perpetrated by women than indicated by official records. It is likely that the generally less severe physical consequences of intimate violence by women, and the fear of prejudice or judgment explain this disparity between self-reported and official rates of men's victimization at the hand of their female partner. Johnson (1995) proposed that population-based surveys reflect situational couple violence, more commonly committed by women, while arrestees and health or shelter studies capture instead incidents of more severe violence, termed "intimate terrorism," which is almost exclusively perpetrated by men. Ansara and Hindin (2010) showed that women and men victims of intimate partner violence ($n = 1231$) seek more help from formal institutions, such as health professionals or police, as the severity of the violence increases. Ansara and Hindin (2010) also suggested that the lower rates of officially recorded intimate partner violence reported by male victims might be explained by the availability of fewer services for men compared to women. In another study comprising 372 men victims of intimate partner violence in the Netherlands, Drijber, Reijnders, and Ceelen (2013) found that the most important reason for men not to report the abuse is the belief the police would not take any action.

▶ WHAT DO YOU THINK?

Do you believe that all forms of intimate partner violence are perceived the same way by police officers and health professionals whether perpetrated by women or men? Do you know any services available for women victims of intimate partner violence in your area? What about services for men?

Johnson (1995, 2010) established the most cited typology of intimate violence in which he categorized male and female intimate violence into four different types. The first type, *intimate terrorism*, is typified by severe and frequent violence that escalates over time. This type is the most commonly known and the most severe; it is associated with battered woman syndrome and is almost exclusively committed by males. In fact, studies that report data on female intimate terrorists usually show levels of severity of violence among women that are considerably lower than that of men (Johnson, 2010). The second type, *common couple violence*, considered the most frequent type of violence between intimate partners, is typically related to a need to control a specific situation as opposed to a generalized need for control of the other person. This type of violence is most commonly initiated by either partner in response to a situational conflict and does not tend to escalate. The third type, *violent resistance*, is violence committed as a direct response, self-defence or otherwise, to violence. This category primarily comprises women who engage in violence in response to male intimate terrorism (Miller, 2005). The final type, *mutual violent control*, the least common, describes relationships in which both partners engage in violence for generalized control of the other person and of the relationship.

Most research shows that women typically tend to exhibit either common couple violence or a violent resistance pattern of intimate partner violence. For example, in her review of the literature, Dasgupta (2002) found that women list self-defence as a frequent motivation for their violent behaviour toward their partner (see also Miller & Meloy, 2006; Swan & Snow, 2002, 2003). She also found that intimate partner violence by women is often triggered by actual abuse or perceived threats to their children or loved ones. Similarly, Stuart et al. (2006) reported that self-defence, poor emotion regulation, provocation by the partner, and retaliation for past abuse were the most common reasons for intimate partner violence by women. Additionally, women who were victims of more severe violence almost exclusively listed self-defence as a reason for using violence against a partner. Other studies, however, have failed to find sex differences in reasons or motives for intimate partner violence (e.g., Shorey, Meltzer & Cornelius, 2010). Overall, the balance of the studies suggest that failing to consider the context leads to an incomplete understanding of intimate partner violence by women, with the result that assessment and treatment services may not appropriately target the relevant contributing elements.

Women Who Kill

In Canada, adult women are responsible for about 13 percent of all homicides (Mulligan & Miladinovic, 2015). This proportion has not changed much over the last three decades and is similar to rates recorded in other countries. Indigenous women are charged with a homicide offence 23 times more often than non-Indigenous Canadian women (Mulligan & Miladinovic, 2015). As with other violent crimes committed by women, research consistently shows that the victims of women who kill tend to be people they know, mainly their intimate partner or ex-intimate partner. In Canada in 2014, 93 percent of all homicides by women were committed against people they knew. Statistics from other countries also show that very few of all homicides by women are committed against strangers (Kirkwood, 2003). In contrast, approximately 25 percent of all homicides committed by men are against strangers (Greenfeld & Snell, 1999). Victims of women tend to be acquaintances, intimate partners, or other family members. In a multi-country study that grouped estimates of homicide rates committed by men and women in 66 countries, Stöckl et al. (2013) found that 38.6 percent of the victims of homicides perpetrated by women were an intimate partner, which is six times higher than that found for male homicides (6.3 percent).

Interestingly, like male offenders, women tend to kill men, not other women. In her US study of 136 women convicted of homicides in Detroit, Goetting (1988) found that 88 percent of the victims were males. Similar results were also present in a Canadian study which found that 74 percent of the victims of homicides committed by women were males (Hoffman, Lavigne, & Dickie, 1998). Finally, women who kill are less likely to have an offending history (Hoffman et al., 1998; Putkonen, Weizmann-henelius, Lindberg, Rovamo, & Häkkänen-Nyholm, 2011), indicating that, as with other types of violence, gender-informed contexts likely play a role in why women kill.

The Nature of Homicides by Women

Studies on women's homicide generally report four types of homicide: spousal homicide, child homicide, homicides related to other types of offences such as assault or robbery, and "others." Spousal homicides include murder of an actual or past intimate partner. Child homicides are typically committed against the woman's own child or a child in her care. Homicides related to other offences involve situations in which the homicide was the result, but not the intent, of another crime (robbery, for example). Finally, while the category of "others" varies according to studies, it typically includes homicides committed in self-defence or those committed against a stranger.

In a test of this categorization, Hoffman et al. (1998) analyzed 181 cases of female offenders serving a Canadian federal sentence for homicide. Of these women, approximately 50 percent were serving a sentence for second-degree murder or its equivalent. Forty percent had been convicted of manslaughter, and the remaining 10 percent were serving a sentence for first-degree murder. Interestingly, 27 percent of all women had committed the homicides in the company of a co-offender, and 16 percent of the women in the study, although convicted for homicide, had not actually killed anyone: they had been convicted for their role as a conspirator or accomplice, typically during the commission of a robbery in which the co-offender killed the victim. In their study, Hoffman et al. (1998) found that the largest category of homicides by women consisted of theft/assault/robbery homicides (28 percent), followed by spousal homicide (25 percent), child homicide (14.5 percent), and self-defence homicide (6 percent).

An Australian review of all homicides committed by women in the state of Victoria between 1985 and 1995 focused on the circumstances in which women killed (Kirkwood, 2003) and found similar results, although the proportion of women who had killed their partner was much higher: of the 86 women included in the study, 40 percent had killed a partner or ex-partner. Kirkwood (2003) established that approximately one-third of those homicides occurred as a spontaneous response to an assault by the spouse. Another third of those women demonstrated a long history of victimization by their spouse. The data showed that these women had reached a point where they believed they had no escape from the violence and constantly feared they would be killed. These women were the most likely to plan and conceal their killing. This phenomenon, known as battered woman syndrome, has been recognized in Canada as a legitimate defence for homicide (Greenspan & Rosenberg, 2007). The remaining one-third of women killed their partners for reasons other than violence, such as in response to the man's threat to take the children. In contrast to male spousal homicides, Kirkwood (2003) found no cases in which the woman had killed her spouse for such reasons as jealousy or as part of the woman's pattern of abuse and control of her partner.

Of the women in Kirkwood's (2003) study, 19 percent had killed a child. Central to these killings were problems and pressures associated with mothering, and some of these women had either attempted suicide or committed suicide after killing their children. Overall, this group was comprised of women who believed they could not fulfill their own and others' expectations of themselves as mothers. In all cases, these women struggled with poverty, difficulties with partners, social and cultural isolation, and/or mental illness. These findings are consistent with research showing that women who commit infanticide (the killing of an infant, usually one's own child) typically have social and economic stresses, a history of abuse, unsupportive partners, and difficulties caring for the child (Friedman, Horwitz, & Resnick, 2005). Very few studies include women who committed neonaticide (the murder of one's own newborn child during the first 24 hours of life) as this is generally viewed as a different offence.

The final group in Kirkwood's study consisted of women who killed non-intimate individuals. Although some women killed other extended family members, the majority had killed friends, acquaintances, neighbours, or other known individuals. Only a few of these homicides involved strangers, and in all those cases the women had acted with a co-offender. The majority of homicides of non-intimate individuals were the result of interpersonal conflicts that arose over such issues as sexual jealousy, arguments or insults, or previous assaults. Some offences took place during the commission of other criminal acts, such as prostitution or robbery. Most women in this category were younger than the women in the other two groups, had a history of substance abuse, and lived in a criminal subculture that condoned violence to resolve problems and to survive. Within this context, these women had been both victims and perpetrators of violence. These women were as likely to kill other women as they were to kill men.

Why Do Women Kill?

Historically, it was believed that most women killed mostly because of mental illness or other psychopathology (Goetting, 1988; Ogle, Maier-Katkin, & Bernard, 1995). While this appears to be true for some offenders, studies indicate that it is not the case for every woman. In their Canadian study, Hoffman et al. (1998) found that approximately 33 percent of the women presented with mental health concerns, including 8 percent had been diagnosed with schizophrenia. In Canada, women who kill while actively psychotic would typically be found not criminally responsible for their crimes on account of mental disorder (Greenspan & Rosenberg, 2007). These women would have therefore been diverted to the mental health system as opposed to the prison system and would not have been part of the study. Hoffman et al. found that depression was the most common mental health concern among the women in the study. Their study also showed that two-thirds of the women had a history of substance abuse, which is recurrently found in studies on women's homicide (Putkonen et al., 2011).

Putkonen et al. (2011) explored gender differences in the psycho-social history of 91 women and 91 men convicted of homicide between 1995 and 2004 in Finland. They found that women had more often received prior mental health treatment and were more likely to have had a history of suicidal behaviour than men (Putkonen et al., 2011). Flynn, Abel, While, Mehta, and Shaw (2011), in their UK study of 4,572 homicide offenders of whom 10 percent were women, found differential rates of mental health problems when different types of homicides were considered. Specifically, significantly more women than men who killed their child had a lifetime history of mental health problems (68 percent versus 28 percent), while more men than women who killed their spouse had a history of mental health problems (33 percent versus 19 percent). Furthermore, Putkonen et al. (2011) showed that although both women and men had experienced adversity in childhood, more women had witnessed or experienced family violence. These results are consistent with the idea that a comprehensive theory of homicides by women needs to incorporate individual, situational, and structural variables (Ogle et al., 1995).

The Assessment and Treatment of Violent Women

The goals of a specialized assessment of violent women offenders are to determine the likelihood of violent reoffending and to ascertain areas for therapeutic intervention to reduce that risk. Correctional services generally use either structured clinical judgment or actuarial tools to assess risk of reoffending. To date, while validated risk assessment tools for male offenders have been developed, very few studies have focused on the development and validation of women-specific risk assessment tools (Blanchette & Brown, 2006; Van Voorhis, Salisbury, Wright, & Bauman, 2008).

The Level of Service Inventory—Revised (LSI-R; Andrews & Bonta, 1995) is a widely used scale designed to appraise recidivism risk, identify criminogenic needs for intervention, and inform recommendation for treatment among men and women. Specifically, the LSI-R assesses covariates of criminal conduct, known as the "Central Eight " (criminal history; anti-social attitudes; anti-social associates; anti-social personality traits; education and employment; family and marital relationships; leisure and recreation; and substance abuse). It has been suggested that the LSI-R has predictive validity for men but not for women (Reisig, Holfreter, & Morash, 2006), although several studies contradict this assumption (see the meta-analyses by Olver, Stockdale, & Wormith, 2014; Smith, Cullen, & Latessa, 2009; Yang, Wong, & Coid, 2010).

Olver et al. (2014) conducted a meta-analysis on the predictive validity of the LSI-R for men and women. Their analysis included 137,931 offenders, of which almost 27,000 were women, the largest sample of women included in a study on risk assessment tools conducted to date. The mean length of follow-up was 26.4 months. The findings on gender and the LSI-R were twofold. First, the authors found that men generally scored higher than women on the total scale, and also higher on the prior offences, criminal associates, leisure/recreation, substance abuse, anti-social pattern, and attitudes components. In contrast, women scored higher on the education/employment, family/marital, financial, accommodations, and personal/emotional components. Differences were, however, small in magnitude in both cases. Second, they found that LSI-R total scores predicted general and violent recidivism for both men and women, but the prediction of general recidivism was slightly better for women. This finding is similar to that of Smith et al. (2009) who also found that the LSI-R validly predicted general recidivism among 14,000 women. Analyzing the predictive power of each component of the LSI-R, Olver et al. (2014) found that the Big Four (criminal history, anti-social attitudes, anti-social associates, and anti-social personality traits) strongly predicted recidivism for both genders but that differences in prediction were also present. Specifically, the lack of education and/or employment more strongly predicted men's violent recidivism, while substance abuse and personal/emotional predicted women's general recidivism. The number of studies that examined women's violent recidivism separately was too small to conclude on the matter.

Overall, findings from the Olver et al. (2014) meta-analysis are consistent with the idea that some risk and needs are gender-neutral while others are gender-informed. This suggests that some factors might be of more importance for women in comparison with men, and vice versa. Further, although gender-neutral risk assessment instruments such as the LSI-R do predict general recidivism among women, there is evidence that the LSI-R over-predicts risk among women. Specifically, Andrews et al. (2012) found that both men and women who scored in the high-risk category of the LSI-R had actual equivalent high rates of recidivism. When moderate- or low-risk categories were considered, however, the findings showed that the actual recidivism rates of women were much lower than those of men with identical scores on the scale. This indicates that while the scale itself is predictive of recidivism among women, its calibration (the level of risk associated with each score of the scale) needs to be revisited for women.

Besides calibration problems, research has also established that the inclusion of gender-responsive factors such as parental stress, family support, and anger/hostility improved the predictive validity of gender-neutral risk assessment schemes such as the LSI-R. For example, Van Voorhis et al., (2008) developed the Women's Supplemental Risk/Needs Assessment, which is comprised of both gender-neutral and gender-informed factors. Their primary validation of this tool was conducted on 1,613 women and showed that both types of factors have predictive validity, but that the inclusion of the gender-informed factors improved the prediction of recidivism for women. Other research has also uncovered gender-relevant issues that merit consideration for inclusion in risk assessment tools for female offenders. Benda (2005) found that family factors such as prosocial family support and the presence of children are predictors of positive community reintegration for female but not male offenders. Finally, Andrews et al. (2012) found a stronger relationship between substance abuse and recidivism among women than among men, which suggests that this factor has some level of gender-specificity.

Besides the risk of recidivism, the assessment needs to identify areas that would benefit from therapeutic interventions. Blanchette and Brown (2006) suggest that, similar to other women offenders, all areas of functioning of the woman convicted of violent offences be examined to determine her strengths and the areas that require work. Given the consistent finding that most violence committed by women involves some type of interpersonal relationship, relationship issues and interpersonal problem-solving skills are likely central areas to target in treatment. In contrast to men, women tend to be in more need of extensive appropriate supportive social networks, which are an important part of their ability to deal with stress (Rumgay, 2004). Consequently, treatment should be based on a relational model that provides these women with previously lacking healthy connections with others and healthy supportive social networks. As explained by Covington and Bloom (2006), a relational model entails the recognition that women's psychological needs are best met when they add meaningful connections with others in their lives rather than simply separate themselves from problematic relationships. This model is based on developmental psychological research which shows that while all humans seek both connection with and differentiation from others, women need more connections while men require more differentiation (Gilligan, 1982).

Other areas that have likely contributed to a woman's violent behaviour and would likely benefit from intervention are attitudes and beliefs that supported her decision to engage in violence, emotional management (particularly anger management), and coping strategies (Ogle et al., 1995; Verona & Carbonell, 2000). Some other factors that need addressing are those more consistently related to general recidivism in women, such as the presence of anti-social attitudes and having criminal associates. Although these factors have not been necessarily linked to violent offending in all women, a subset of violent women would likely exhibit difficulties in these areas. In addition, based on the findings of the various types of violent behaviours committed by women, different approaches may be warranted according to individual crime differences. For example, the cognitive schemas of a battered woman who killed her partner because she feared for her life would likely be very different from those of an intoxicated woman who killed an acquaintance with whom she had a quarrel. Although cognitive interventions would be indicated in both cases, the focus of the interventions would be very different.

The assessment and treatment of domestic abusers would, by necessity, involve an examination of the context in which the violence took place. Although men and women predominantly use intimate partner violence in different contexts and for different motives, female perpetrators of intimate partner violence have typically been required to engage in therapeutic interventions based on male models of violence. These models are most likely inadequate for these women and ineffective in addressing their treatment needs. An examination of the full context that led to the intimate partner violence would help to establish the pattern of this violence and the elements that contributed to the woman's behaviour. Tailored interventions could then be developed to address these elements.

Few studies exist that have examined the best treatment approaches for women who have committed homicide. Besides the treatment issues discussed above, women who have killed may need additional interventions to address some of the unique aspects of their crimes. In addition, the context of a woman's relationship with her victim may be particularly significant (Kirkwood, 2003). For example, many of these women may present characteristics of battered woman syndrome, necessitating treatment for their victimization. Not all women who have killed their partner have been battered, however, demonstrating the importance of carrying out a comprehensive assessment of the elements that led to the homicide. Women who have killed their children may present with characteristics of powerlessness, alienation from others, and an inability to effectively deal with life's pressures (Friedman et al., 2005; Kirkwood, 2003). Treatment in these cases would include the development of self-esteem, effective coping strategies, and positive healthy relationships.

Finally, most violent women will need additional help to rebuild their lives in a manner that removes the need for violent offending. As with all female offenders, these women may require support to improve their general community functioning, with a particular focus on their ability to develop and maintain a more stable lifestyle with less dependence on others. Some women may have particular problems in the area of mental health, requiring additional specifically designed intensive intervention, such as dialectical behaviour therapy (Linehan, 1993). Areas such as education, employment, and recreational activities may also require additional services outside of treatment. Consequently, part of treatment will be to help these women develop and access appropriate networks and services.

Women Who Sexually Offend

Sexual offending by women is not a phenomenon new to the 21st century. Saradjian (2010) traced back to 1857 the first formal writings on child sexual abuse committed by a female offender, and recent data indicate that 12 percent of sexual offenders are women (Cortoni, Babchishin, & Rat, 2016). What is new, perhaps, is the increased societal and professional recognition that women can and do engage of their own accord in sexually offending behaviour. This recognition contrasts with early writings such as those of Mathis (1972), who thought that it was unthinkable for a woman to engage in sexual contact with a child and that even if she did, "What harm could be done without a penis?" (p. 54). In fact, it is now established that victims of female sexual offenders suffer the same traumatic effects as victims of male sexual offenders, including depression, rage, substance abuse, self-injury, suicidal ideation, problematic relationships, and difficulties with sexuality (Denov, 2004). In addition, for too many victims of women, the traumatic effect of the sexual abuse is compounded by the fact that many mental health professionals disbelieve them when they disclose their sexual victimization at the hand of a woman (Hetherton, 1999), particularly when the offender is the victim's mother (Denov, 2004).

According to Denov (2004), there has been a lack of attention to the issue of sexual offending by women as a result of socio-cultural views that describe women as nurturing, protecting, non-aggressive, and most importantly non-sexual. Within these views, the acknowledgment that women might willingly choose to sexually abuse children creates cognitive dissonance that is often resolved by reframing this abuse as, for example, misguided attempts at intimacy (Denov, 2004; Hetherton, 1999). To accept that some women willingly and purposefully engage in sexually offending behaviour against children or adults requires that stereotypical perceptions about sexual offending by women be challenged. First, many professionals minimize the nature of sexual offending by women, believing that it is less serious than that of men (Denov, 2001). The reality is that women engage in the same range of sexually offending behaviour as men, the majority of which are directed at underage victims. Their sexually offending acts include exposing one's genitals, fondling, oral contact, penetration (vaginal, anal), and the use of objects, all of which can be perpetrated on the victim or by the victim on the offender (Johansson-Love & Fremouw, 2006; Peter, 2009; Pflugradt & Allen, 2012). Online child sexual abuse images, including videos (R. Shilling, Interpol, personal communication, June 29, 2013) are also produced by women (Elliot & Ashfield, 2011).

Second, while the existence of sexual offending by women is undisputed, debates regarding its prevalence continue. Various studies are cited as proof of an extreme under-reporting of sexual offending by women in contrast to official rates. For example, Allen (1991) surveyed 75 males and 65 females convicted of sexual offences against children and found that 36 percent of the male offenders and 72 percent of the female offenders had been sexually abused as children. Of those, 45 percent of the males and 6 percent of the females reported that their sexual abuser had been female. As another example, in their study on the prevalence of child abuse, Finkelhor, Hotaling, Lewis, and Smith (1990) interviewed 1,145 men and 1,481 women via telephone. They found that 16 percent of the men and 27 percent of the women had been sexually abused as a child. While the majority had been victimized by a man, 17 percent of the victimized men and 1 percent of the victimized women reported a female perpetrator. Unfortunately, other than the Finkelhor et al. (1990) study, prevalence studies on female sexual offenders mostly use convenience samples, a practice that yields sample-specific instead of population-wide estimates.

In efforts to provide more systematic information about the prevalence of female sexual offenders, Cortoni and her colleagues (Cortoni et al., 2016; Cortoni & Hanson, 2005; Cortoni, Hanson, & Coache, 2009) estimated the proportion of sexual offenders who are women from two general sources of information. The first source was official police or court reports that detailed the gender of the offender. The second source was victimization surveys. The 2005 and 2009 studies included data from five countries, and both official and victimization data showed that women constituted approximately 5 percent of all sexual offenders. Data for these studies, however, dated as far back as 1984 and may not have reflected the increased recognition by society and the criminal justice system of the problem of sexual offending by women (Ford, 2006). To address this problem, as well as other statistical issues, Cortoni et al. (2016) conducted an updated, meta-analytic review of the prevalence of female sexual offending, defined as the proportion of sexual offenders who are female, based on official reports and victimization surveys using 17 samples from 12 countries. The results revealed very different results from the earlier studies. When only official data were examined, the findings showed that females constituted only 2 percent of all reported sexual offenders. In contrast, the prevalence rates based on self-reported victimization surveys was about six times higher than the official rates (that is, 12 percent—see Cortoni et al., 2016). Further, the prevalence of females among sexual offenders was about 2 percentage points higher in the juvenile samples than in the adult samples. This latter finding is consistent with the general offender literature, which consistently shows a higher ratio of female to male offenders among juveniles when compared to adult offenders. For example, in Canada in 2009, girls were responsible for 28 percent of all juvenile offences reported to the police, while women were responsible for 22 percent of all adult offences (Hotton Mahoney, 2011).

Who Are Female Sexual Offenders?

Research shows that female sexual offenders tend to come from families with low or middle socio-economic status, generally have few educational or vocational qualifications, and are significantly less financially secure than their male counterparts (Cortoni & Gannon, 2016). While early work suggested female sexual offenders suffer from particularly high rates of mental health problems, later studies showed their rates are similar to those of violent (non-sexual) female offenders (Fazel et al., 2010), which is likely related to their history of victimization. Although all female offenders (sexual or not) have much higher rates of poly-victimization (physical, sexual, and/or emotional victimization) both in childhood and adulthood than non-offenders (Blanchette & Brown, 2006), particularly high rates of poly-victimization are found among female sexual offenders, typically ranging from 50 to 80 percent (e.g., Gannon, Rose, & Ward, 2008; Levenson, Willis, & Prescott, 2015). Further, female sexual offenders tend to have particularly severe victimization histories that include more extensive and intrusive sexual victimization and multiple perpetrators (Johansson-Love & Fremouw, 2006).

Many researchers have focused on establishing typologies of female sexual offenders in an effort to explain why they offend. Based on either qualitative (e.g., Mathews, Matthews, & Speltz, 1989) or quantitative data (e.g., Sandler & Freeman, 2007; Vandiver &

Kercher, 2004), typological work has established three general categories of female sexual offenders: those who offend against adolescent victims (typically males); those who offend against adults (typically other women); and those who exclusively offend against children of either sex. Within each group, women may be solo offenders (commit their sexual offence on their own), or commit their sexual offences in company of others (co-offending). Research shows that approximately 35 percent of all female sexual offenders commit their offence with a co-offender who is most frequently their romantic partner (Williams & Bierie, 2015).

Not considered to be sexual offenders are women who knowingly allow someone else access to a child for sexual purposes (for example, a mother is aware that the father is sexually offending against the children but fails to intervene; a woman facilitates sexual access to a child/teenager for financial gains). The literature sometimes refers to these women as "passive" sexual offenders. Some jurisdictions may also consider women with such offences as sexual offenders, hence requiring them to undergo standard sexual offender treatment. Such designations presuppose that the factors that underlie a woman's motivations to allow sexual access/not intervene in child sexual abuse situations are identical to those that motivate a woman to engage in actual sexual offending behaviour. While, to our knowledge, no research has systematically investigated women who failed to intervene in sexual abuse situations, there are indications that women convicted of providing sexual access to youth for financial gains (that is, prostitution-related offences) are generally more anti-social and more akin to female non-sexual offenders than women who have committed contact or pornography-related sexual offences on a child (Cortoni, Sandler, & Freeman, 2015; Sandler & Freeman, 2009). For these women, the underage youth appears to be a commodity to be used for financial gains (Cortoni, Sandler, & Freeman, 2015).

The Offence Process of Female Sexual Offenders

Although typologies help to describe female sexual offenders, they cannot be used to draw conclusions about either the factors that led to the sexually offending behaviour or the risk for further sexual offending. In contrast, offence process models provide detailed descriptions of the elements that combine to lead to the offending behaviour. These models are typically generated from the offence narratives of offenders themselves using inductive qualitative analysis, and they describe not only how and why the offence process unfolds but also specific patterns of sexual offending.

There have been a number of attempts at establishing the offence process of female sexual offenders based on patterns of contextual, behavioural, cognitive, and affective events that facilitate and maintain female sexual offending (DeCou, Cole, Rowland, Kaplan, & Lynch, 2015; Desfachelles & Cortoni, 2014; Gannon et al., 2008). These studies show that female sexual offending, like male sexual offending, takes place within the context of a negative life pattern that consists of negative styles of thinking, unhealthy emotional and sexual regulation, and unproductive or counterproductive coping strategies that eventually lead to the sexually offending behaviour.

Female sexual offenders' personal histories and life circumstances are remarkably similar across studies. These women have problematic personal histories that consist of relationship problems; victimization histories and associated mental health issues; and major life stressors related to work, financial, or health problems, and legal difficulties.

These factors set the stage for problems with substance abuse, poor boundaries in the child–adult relationship, and a "one thing leads to another" passive mode of being. Various combinations of these elements set up the conditions for three different gender-informed pathways to offending.

One pathway, called *directed* or *co-offending*, describes women who co-offend with their male partner. Co-offending processes involve abuse by the partner, wishing to please the partner, giving in to demands, social isolation of the woman, or using the children as bargaining chips for personal or financial gains (DeCou et al., 2015; Desfachelles & Cortoni, 2014; Gannon et al., 2008). The offending couples tend to have particularly unconventional sexual lives that include activities such as frequenting swingers' clubs; engaging in sexual relations with strangers or the spouse's friends, or in public places; and frequently viewing pornography, often in the presence of the children (Desfachelles & Cortoni, 2014). In this pathway, the sexual offending behaviour is not an isolated incident; it tends to repeats itself over numerous occasions, sometimes over a long period of time.

The second pathway, called *implicit-disorganized* or *solo*, refers to an offence process that involves women establishing a relationship with the victim in efforts to meet their own interpersonal and emotional needs (DeCou et al., 2015; Gannon et al., 2008). Within this context, victims tend to be viewed as adult-like and as having engaged in a consensual and reciprocal relationship. In this pathway, the woman adjusts circumstances to increase the physical and emotional contact with the victim (Gannon et al, 2008). For example, she may establish a pattern of adult-like relational behaviours with a young victim such as discussing intimate sexual details of her life. Alcohol is frequently present in this offending process, co-offending tends to be absent, and while victims can be of any age, they tend to be children or adolescents.

The third pathway, called *explicit-approach*, describes a process in which women explicitly planned their sexual offences with specific goals in mind such as sexual gratification, intimacy with the victim, revenge and humiliation, or financial reward. The latter goals usually refer to those women who sexually exploit a youth for financial gains such as those found in prostitution-related offending. The women in this pathway tend to experience positive affect such as excitement or satisfaction in relation to their offences and exhibit cognitions congruent with those emotional states, such as thoughts of revenge or anticipated financial gains. Both solo and co-offending are found in this pathway although in cases of co-offending, the women always offend under their own volition (Gannon et al., 2008). Generally, the women in this pathway tend to demonstrate the most anti-social features, such as a history of non-sexual offending and attitudes supportive of criminal activity.

Assessment of Female Sexual Offenders

One major task for professionals within the criminal justice system is the evaluation of risk of recidivism (that is, the likelihood offenders will do it again) among individuals who have been detected and sanctioned for their offending behaviour. There are a number of instruments validated for the assessment of risk of sexual recidivism among adult and juvenile *males* adjudicated for sexual offences (see Craig, Beech, & Cortoni, 2013, and Hempel, Buck, Cima, & Van Marle, 2013, for a review). In contrast, there is no instrument validated to assess risk of sexual recidivism among adult or juvenile *female* sexual offenders. In absence of such tools, some evaluators use male-based instruments to assess risk of sexual recidivism among female sexual offenders. This is a serious mistake for two reasons. First, the rates of sexual recidivism among women greatly differ from those of males. In their meta-analysis of the recidivism rates of 2,490 female sexual offenders with an average follow-up time of 6.5 years, Cortoni, Hanson and Coache (2010) found that 20 percent of these women had recidivated with a new crime of any type; 6 percent had committed a new violent (including sexual) offence; and only 1.5 percent had committed a new sexual offence. In contrast, the sexual recidivism rate of male sexual offenders is 13.5 percent over 5 years (Hanson & Morton-Bourgon, 2005). As risk assessment tools are calibrated for the recidivism rates of men, they will yield estimates of risk that are much too high for women. Second, the items contained in the male risk assessment tools have not been found to predict sexual recidivism among women. As such, not only would the tools over-predict risk in female sexual offenders, they would do so on the basis of items that are not valid for women.

Since the male-based tools are invalid for women, the evaluator needs to decide which factors may be related to a specific woman's increased risk of sexual recidivism and, on the basis of the presence and strength of these factors, how likely she will be to commit a new sexual offence. Because of their extremely low sexual recidivism rates, the likelihood of a false positive prediction of recidivism among women will be very high. False positive prediction occurs when it is predicted that an individual will reoffend, but he or she does not. To reduce this possibility, the recidivism risk factors clinically judged to be relevant in a given female sexual offender must be sufficiently present—in fact, quite blatant (for example, she tells you she will do it again; see Cortoni et al., 2010)—in order to make a determination of high risk for sexual recidivism among women.

Because women are much more likely to reoffend with a non-sexual offence than with a new sexual offence, their assessment should generally focus on their risk of general recidivism (Cortoni, & Gannon, 2016). There exists a large body of literature that examined the factors related to general recidivism among women (see Blanchette & Brown, 2006, for a review) and there is reason to believe that these factors are also relevant for the prediction of non-sexual recidivism among female sexual offenders. These factors could be referred to as gender-neutral as they equally predict general recidivism among male and female offenders (Andrews & Bonta, 2010). Specifically, the number of prior convictions for any type of offence (misdemeanors, drugs, violence) is related to non-sexual general or violent recidivism among female sexual offenders. In addition, just like with males, being at a younger age (under 30) was related to non-sexual recidivism among these women (Sandler & Freeman, 2009).

Treatment

It could be argued that, given their low sexual recidivism rates, there is no need to provide sexual offender-specific treatment to women. Correctional interventions, however, should aim at reducing all likelihood of future recidivism, not just some specific types of reoffending. As such, female sexual offenders should be provided with the opportunity to engage in a comprehensive treatment approach that targets all areas of their functioning in order to address their general likelihood of criminal recidivism—not just sexual reoffending. As discussed earlier in this chapter, there are a variety of motivations for sexual offending behaviour among women; these would require elucidation during treatment. Generally, the goals of treatment should be to address the factors related to the offending behaviour in a manner that is responsive to the gender of the offender (Cortoni, 2016). As such, as part of the treatment process, the needs that were fulfilled by the sexually offending behaviour should be identified, and alternate positive ways to meet those needs should be developed. Regardless of the combination of issues that may be present for a specific woman, it is highly likely that treatment will need to focus on the five broad areas in which female sexual offenders demonstrate difficulties: (1) cognitive processes, (2) emotional processes, (3) intimacy and relationship issues, (4) sexual dynamics, and (5) psycho-social functioning.

Cognitive processes refer to the cognitions that support a generally negative lifestyle as well as sexual offending. Not surprisingly, women, like men, minimize and justify their sexually offending behaviour. The underlying motivations for this denial and minimization are likely to be highly similar to those of males, such as shame or wanting to share responsibility with others. In terms of general offence-supportive cognitions, research indicates that female offenders, like males, believe that males are specifically entitled to sexually offend. In contrast to males, they do not tend to view themselves as sexually entitled, nor do they view all children as sexual beings, but they do tend to view men as dangerous (see Gannon & Alleyne, 2013, for a review).

Emotional processes refers to the difficulties many female sexual offenders have in regulating their emotional states. This is often due to their victimization histories. Within this context, and not surprisingly, intimacy and relationship issues are particularly problematic among female sexual offenders. Among male sexual offenders, problems in relationships tend to manifest themselves through some form of emotional identification with children, instability in current intimate relationships, hostility toward women, general social rejection/loneliness, and a general lack of concern for others (Hanson, Harris, Scott, & Helmus, 2007). In contrast, female sexual offenders tend to lack boundaries and to engage in various unhealthy relationships. Many of them also exhibit patterns of relationships characterized by abuse and excessive dependence on others, typically the men in their lives (Eldridge & Saradjian, 2000; Gannon et al., 2008). In addition, they tend to lack practical and emotional support from family and friends (Gannon et al., 2008).

Female sexual offenders also need to address sexual boundaries issues and, if present, deviant sexual interests. It is important to note that it is still unclear whether the deviant sexual preferences of female sexual offenders are similar to those of males (Abel & Osborn, 2000). It is also unclear what etiological role deviant sexual interests and arousal may play in female sexual offending given that women's general sexual arousal patterns are different from those of men (Chivers, Rieger, Latty, & Bailey, 2004; Suschinsky, Lalumière, & Chivers, 2009). What is clear, however, is that while sexual gratification plays a role for some female sexual offenders, a desire for intimacy—rather than a sexual desire—with either a victim or a co-offender is often at the source of the offending (DeCou et al., 2015; Gannon et al., 2008).

Finally, like all female offenders, women who sexually offend typically require much extensive support to improve their general functioning and to manage stress (Rumgay, 2004). Treatment should address the interrelationships among these factors as well as help the woman develop a self-management plan that includes goals for a healthier life. This approach recognizes that the sexual offending behaviour cannot be treated in isolation from the rest of the woman's life, ensures that all areas of functioning are targeted, and allows for flexibility to tailor the treatment according to each woman's individual treatment needs (Cortoni, 2016).

SUMMARY

This chapter reviewed the prevalence of violent offending by females, their individual and environmental characteristics, the theories to explain their behaviour, and the assessment and treatment of these women. Female violent offenders can be divided into two general categories: women who engage in general violence and women who engage in sexual violence. General violence includes assaults, intimate partner violence, and homicides. Sexual violence includes all crimes with a sexual component, excluding crimes related to prostitution. Generally, female offenders have much lower rates of any types of offending than males and tend to recidivate at much lower rates than males. These lower rates are particularly true of female sexual offenders. Ongoing research is focused on understanding why women engage in violence; much remains to be known.

Although some women share some of the same characteristics as male offenders, some important differences arise, among others, from studies on their offending process. These differences must be taken into account when assessing and treating women offenders. Specifically, the context in which the offences took place in interaction with the factors contributing to women's criminal behaviour must be addressed. Women's lives and their societal experiences differ from those of men, and their experiences will influence both their criminal behaviour and their rehabilitation. Although some women present prototypical anti-social features related to their violence, others commit their offences in response to stressors they have failed to effectively manage. The violent female offender's cognitive and emotional issues and her general community functioning must therefore be taken into account when assessing her needs and planning her treatment program.

NOTE

1. In these statistics, violent offences include homicide, attempted murder, assault, robbery, abduction, and sexual offences (Public Safety and Emergency Preparedness Canada, 2008).

DISCUSSION QUESTIONS

1. Although women commit fewer violent offences than men, the consequences of violent offences committed by women are non-negligible. Given that the context of female offending is of particular importance in understanding how women become violent offenders, what might be appropriate societal responses to prevent their criminality?
2. Some authors argue that determining a woman's risk of recidivism based on a male view of offending is inappropriate (Hannah-Moffat, 1999, for example). Considering that women have lower base rates of violence, including sexual violence, should we be concerned about assessing the risk of reoffending among female violent offenders?
3. Current treatment approaches for female violent offenders are based on limited theoretical and empirical knowledge of the factors that lead to violent offending. These treatment approaches are general in that all female offenders, violent or not, are offered similar programs that mainly target self-management and reintegration strategies. How could the

consideration of gender-neutral and gender-informed factors improve this treatment? How would such factors manifest themselves among female violent offenders?

ADDITIONAL RESOURCES

Suggested Readings

Chesney-Lind, M., & Pasko, L., (2013). *The female offender* (3rd ed.). Thousand Oaks, CA: Sage.

Cortoni, F. (2017). *Female sexual offenders: A handbook for assessment, treatment and management*. Brandon, VT: Safer Society Press.

van Wormer, K. (2010). *Working with female offenders: A gender-sensitive approach*. Hoboken, NJ: John Wiley & Sons.

Videos and Films

Mushkeg Productions (Producer), & Low Horn, C. (Director). (2014). *It was a woman: Surviving female sexual abuse* [Motion Picture]. Available at http://www.itwasawoman.com/IWAW_en.

Websites

Public Safety Canada: www.ps-sp.gc.ca

Correctional Service of Canada: http://www.csc-scc.gc.ca

Statistics Canada—CANSIM tables: http://www5.statcan.gc.ca/cansim/

REFERENCES

Abel, G.G., & Osborn, C. (2000). The paraphilias. In M.C. Gelder, J.J. Lopez-Ibor & N.C. Andreasen (Eds.), *New Oxford Textbook of Psychiatry* (pp. 897–913). Oxford, UK: Oxford University Press.

Adler, F. (1975). *Sisters in crime: The rise of the new female criminal*. New York: McGraw-Hill.

Alarid, L.F., Burton, V.S., & Cullen, F.T. (2000). Gender and crime among felony offenders: Assessing the generality of social control and differential association theories. *Journal of Research in Crime and Delinquency, 37*(2), 171–199.

Allen, C.M. (1991). *Women and men who sexually abuse children: A comparative analysis*. Orwell, VT: Safer Society Press.

Andrews, D.A., & Bonta, J. (1995). *Level of Service Inventory–Revised*. Toronto: Multi-Health Systems.

Andrews, D.A., & Bonta, J. (2010). *The psychology of criminal conduct* (5th ed.). Cincinnati, OH: Anderson.

Andrews, D.A., Guzzo, L., Raynor, P., Rowe, R.C., Rettinger, J., Brews, A., & Wormith, S. (2012). Are the major risk/need factors predictive of both female and male reoffending?: A test with the eight domains of the level of service/case management inventory. *International Journal of Offender Therapy and Comparative Criminology, 56*, 113–133.

Ansara, D.L., & Hindin, M.J. (2010). Formal and informal help-seeking associated with women's and men's experiences of intimate partner violence in Canada. *Social Science and Medicine, 70*(7), 1011–1018.

Archer, J. (2000). Sex differences in aggression between heterosexual partners: A meta-analytic review. *Psychological Bulletin, 126*, 651–680.

Benda, B.B. (2005). Gender differences in life-course theory of recidivism: A survival analysis. *International Journal of Offender Therapy and Comparative Criminology, 49*(3), 325–342.

Blackwell, B.S. (2000). Perceived sanction threats, gender, and crime: A test and elaboration of power-control theory. *Criminology, 38*(2), 439–488.

Blanchette, K., & Brown, S.L. (2006). *The assessment and treatment of women offenders: An integrated perspective*. Chichester, UK: John Wiley & Sons.

Bottos, S. (2008). *Women and violence: Theory, risk, and treatment implications* (Research Report R-198). Ottawa: Correctional Service of Canada.

Brennan, S. (2012). Police-reported crime statistics in Canada, 2011. *Juristat, 85*(2) 1–40.

Chambers, J.C., Ward, T., Eccleston, L., & Brown, M. (2011). Representation of female offender types within the pathways model of assault. *International Journal of Offender Therapy and Comparative Criminology, 55*(6), 925–948.

Chesney-Lind, M., & Pasko, L. (2013). *The female offender: Girls, women and crime* (3rd ed.). Thousand Oaks, CA: Sage.

Chivers, M.L., Rieger, G., Latty, E., & Bailey, J.M. (2004). A sex difference in the specificity of sexual arousal. *Psychological Science, 15,* 736–744.

Cortoni, F. (2016). Treatment of female sexual offenders. In L.E. Marshall & W.L. Marshall (Eds.), *The Wiley Handbook on the theories, assessment & treatment of sexual offending: Volume 3* (pp. 1265–1283). Chichester, UK: Wiley-Blackwell.

Cortoni, F., Babchishin, K.M., & Rat, C. (2016). The proportion of sexual offenders who are female is higher than thought: A meta-analysis. *Criminal Justice and Behavior, 44*(2), 145–162.

Cortoni, F., & Gannon, T.A. (2016). The assessment of female sexual offenders. In L. Craig & M. Rettenberger (Eds), *The Wiley Handbook on the theories, assessment & treatment of sexual offending: Volume 2* (pp. 1017–1036). Chichester, UK: Wiley-Blackwell.

Cortoni, F., & Hanson, R.K. (2005). *A review of the recidivism rates of adult female sexual offenders* (Research Report R-169). Ottawa: Correctional Service of Canada.

Cortoni, F., Hanson, R.K., & Coache, M.E. (2009). Les délinquantes sexuelles : prévalence et récidive. *Revue internationale de criminologie et de police technique et scientifique, LXII,* 319–336.

Cortoni, F., Hanson, R.K., & Coache, M.E. (2010). The recidivism rates of female sexual offenders are low: A meta-analysis. *Sexual Abuse: A Journal of Research and Treatment, 22,* 387–401.

Cortoni, F., Sandler, J.C., & Freeman, N.J. (2015). Are females convicted of promoting prostitution of a minor like females convicted of traditional sexual offenses? A brief research report. *Sexual Abuse: A Journal of Research & Treatment, 27,* 324–334.

Covington, S.S., & Bloom, B.E. (2006). Gender-responsive treatment and services in correctional settings. *Women & Therapy, 29,* 9–33.

Craig, L., Beech, A.R. & Cortoni, F. (2013). What works in assessing risk in sexual and violent offenders. In L.A. Craig, L. Dixon, & T.A. Gannon (Eds.) *What works in offender rehabilitation: An evidence based approach to assessment and treatment* (pp. 94–114). Chicester, UK: Wiley-Blackwell.

Dasgupta, S.D. (2002). A framework for understanding women's use of nonlethal violence in intimate heterosexual relationships. *Violence Against Women, 8,* 1364–1389.

DeCou, C.R, Cole, T.T., Rowland, S.E., Kaplan, S.P., & Lynch, S.M. (2015). An ecological process model of female sex offending: The role of victimization, psychological distress, and life stressors. *Sexual Abuse: A Journal of Research and Treatment, 27,* 302–323.

Denov, M.S. (2004). The long-term effects of child sexual abuse by female perpetrators: A qualitative study of male and female victims. *Journal of Interpersonal Violence, 19,* 1137–1156.

Department of Justice Canada. (1992). *Corrections and Conditional Release Act.* Ottawa: Government of Canada.

Desfachelles, M., & Cortoni, F. (2014, October). *Female sexual co-offenders: Life-course trajectories and offense process.* Paper presented at the 33rd Annual Research and Treatment Conference of the Association for the Treatment of Sexual Abusers, San Diego, CA.

Drijber, B.C., Reijnders, U.J., & Ceelen, M. (2013). Male victims of domestic violence. *Journal of Family Violence, 28*(2), 173–178.

Dutton, D.G. (2012). The case against the role of gender in intimate partner violence. *Aggression and Violent Behavior, 17*(1), 99–104.

Eldridge, H., & Saradjian, J. (2000). Replacing the function of abusive behaviors for the offender: Remaking relapse prevention in working with women who sexually abuse children. In D.R. Laws, S.M. Hudson, & T. Ward (Eds.), *Remaking relapse prevention with sex offenders: A sourcebook* (pp. 402–426). Thousand Oaks, CA: Sage.

Elliott, I.A., & Ashfield, S. (2011). The use of online technology in the modus operandi of female sex offenders. *Journal of Sexual Aggression, 17*(1), 92–104.

Fazel, S., Sjöstedt, G., Grann, M., & Langström, N. (2010). Sexual offending in women and psychiatric disorder: A national case-control study. *Archives of Sexual Behavior, 39,* 161–167.

Finkelhor, D., Hotaling, G., Lewis, I.A., & Smith, C. (1990). Sexual abuse in a national survey of adult men and women: Prevalence characteristics, and risk factors. *Child Abuse & Neglect, 14,* 19–28.

Flynn, S., Abel, K. M., While, D., Mehta, H., & Shaw, J. (2011). Mental illness, gender and homicide: A population-based descriptive study. *Psychiatry Research, 185*(3), 368–375.

Ford, H. (2006). *Women who sexually abuse children.* Chichester, UK: John Wiley & Sons.

Friedman, S.H., Horwitz, S.M., & Resnick, P.J. (2005). Child murder by mothers: a critical analysis of the current state of knowledge and a research agenda. *American Journal of Psychiatry, 162*(9), 1578–1587.

Gannon, T.A., & Alleyne, E.K.A. (2013). Female sexual abusers' cognition. *Trauma, Violence, and Abuse, 14*, 67–79.

Gannon, T.A., Rose, M.R., & Ward, T. (2008). A descriptive model of the offense process for female sexual offenders. *Sexual Abuse: A Journal of Research & Treatment, 20*, 352–374.

Gilligan, C. (1982). *In a different voice: Psychological theory and women's development*. Cambridge, MA: Harvard University Press.

Goetting, A. (1988). Patterns of homicide among women. *Journal of Interpersonal Violence, 3*(1), 3–19.

Greenfeld, L.A., & Snell, T L. (1999). *Women offenders*. Washington, DC: US Department of Justice, Office of Justice Programs, Bureau of Justice Statistics.

Greenspan, E.L., & Rosenberg, M. (2007). *Martin's annual Criminal Code*. Aurora, ON: Canada Law Book.

Hannah-Moffat, K. (1999). Moral agents or actuarial subject: Risk and Canadian women's imprisonment. *Theoretical Criminology, 3*, 71–94.

Hanson, R.K., Harris, A.J.R., Scott, T.L., & Helmus, T. (2007). *Assessing the risk of sexual offenders on community supervision: The Dynamic Supervision Project*. (User Report No. 2007-05). Ottawa: Corrections Research, Public Safety Canada. Retrieved from https://www.publicsafety.gc.ca/cnt/rsrcs/pblctns/ssssng-rsk-sxl-ffndrs/index-en.aspx.

Hanson, R.K., & Morton-Bourgon, K.E. (2005). The characteristics of persistent sexual offenders: A meta-analysis of recidivism studies. *Journal of Consulting and Clinical Psychology, 73*, 1154–1163.

Hempel, I., Buck, N., Cima, M., & Van Marle, H. (2013). Review of risk assessment instruments for juvenile sex offenders: What is next? *International Journal of Offender Therapy and Comparative Criminology, 57*, 208–228.

Hetherton, J. (1999). The idealization of women: Its role in the minimization of child sexual abuse by females. *Child Abuse & Neglect, 23*, 161–174.

Hirschinger, N.B., Grisso, J.A., Wallace, D.B., McCollum, K.F., Schwarz, D.F., Sammel, M.D., … Anderson, E. (2003). A Case-Control Study of Female-to-Female Nonintimate Violence in an Urban Area. *American Journal of Public Health, 93*(7), 1098–1103.

Hoffman, L.E., Lavigne, B., & Dickie, I. (1998). *Women convicted of homicide serving a federal sentence: An exploratory study*. Ottawa: Correctional Service of Canada.

Hotton Mahony, T. (2011). *Women and the criminal justice system* (No. 89-503-X). Ottawa: Statistics Canada. Retrieved from www.statcan.gc.ca/pub/89-503-x/2010001/article/11416-eng.htm.

Johansson-Love, J., & Fremouw, W. (2006). A critique of the female sexual perpetrator research. *Aggression and Violent Behavior, 11*, 12–26.

Johnson, M.P. (1995). Patriarchal terrorism and common couple violence: Two forms of violence against women. *Journal of Marriage and the Family, 57*, 283–294.

Johnson, M.P. (2010). *A typology of domestic violence: Intimate terrorism, violent resistance, and situational couple violence*. Boston: University Press of New England.

Kimmel, M.S. (2002). "Gender symmetry" in domestic violence: A substantive and methodological research review. *Violence Against Women, 8*(11), 1332–1363.

Kirkwood, D. (2003). Female perpetrated homicide in Victoria between 1985 and 1995. *Australian and New Zealand Journal of Criminology, 36*, 152–172.

Levenson, J.S., Willis, G.M., & Prescott, D.S. (2015). Adverse childhood experiences in the lives of female sex offenders. *Sexual Abuse: A Journal of Research and Treatment, 27*(3), 258–283.

Linehan, M.M. (1993). *Cognitive behavioral therapy for borderline personality disorder*. New York: Guilford Press.

Mathews, R., Matthews, J., & Speltz, K. (1989). *Female sexual offenders: An exploratory study*. Orwell, VT: Safer Society Press.

Mathis, J.L. (1972). *Clear thinking about sexual deviation*. Chicago: Nelson Hall.

Miller, S.L. (2005). *Victims as offenders: The paradox of women's violence in relationships*. New Brunswick, NJ: Rutgers University Press.

Miller, S.L., & Meloy, M.L. (2006). Women's use of force: Voices of women arrested for domestic violence. *Violence Against Women, 12*, 89–115.

Muftié, L.R., Bouffard, J.A., & Bouffard, A.L. (2007). An exploratory study of women arrested for intimate partner violence: violent women or violent resistance. *Journal of Interpersonal Violence, 22*(6), 753–774.

Mulligan, L., & Miladinovic, Z. (2015). Homicide in Canada, 2014. *Juristat, 34*(1), 1–8.

Mullins, C.W., & Miller, J. (2008). Temporal, situational and interactional features of women's violent conflicts. *The Australian and New Zealand Journal of Criminology, 41*(1), 36–62.

Murdoch, S., Vess, J., & Ward, T. (2010). Descriptive model of the offence process of women violent offenders: Distal background variables. *Psychiatry, Psychology and Law, 17*(3), 368–384.

Murdoch, S., Vess, J., & Ward, T. (2012). A descriptive model of female violent offenders. *Psychiatry, Psychology and Law, 19*(3), 412–426.

Ogle, R.S., Maier-Katkin, D., & Bernard, T.J. (1995). A theory of homicidal behavior among women. *Criminology, 33,* 174–193.

Olver, M.E., Stockdale, K.C., & Wormith, J.S. (2014). Thirty years of research on the level of service scales: A meta-analytic examination of predictive accuracy and sources of variability. *Psychological Assessment, 26*(1), 156–176.

Peter, T. (2009). Exploring taboos: Comparing male and female perpetrated child sexual abuse. *Journal of Interpersonal Violence, 24,* 1111–1128.

Pflugradt, D.M., & Allen, B.P. (2012). A grounded theory analysis of sexual sadism in females. *Journal of Sexual Aggression, 18,* 325–337.

Polaschek, D.L.L., Calvert S.W., & Ganon, T.A. (2008). Linking violent thinking implicit theory-based research with violent offenders. *Journal of Interpersonal Violence, 24*(1), 75–96.

Pollock, J.M., & Davis, S. (2005). The Continuing Myth of the Violent Female Offender. *Criminal Justice Review, 30*(1), 5–29.

Pollock, J.M., Mullings, J., & Crouch, B. (2006). Violent women: Findings from the Texas women inmates study. *Women and Criminal Justice, 13,* 69–97.

Public Safety and Emergency Preparedness Canada. (2008). *Corrections and conditional release statistical overview: Annual report 2008.* Ottawa: Minister of Public Safety.

Putkonen, H., Weizmann-henelius, G., Lindberg, N., Rovamo, T., & Häkkänen-Nyholm, H. (2011). Gender differences in homicide offenders' criminal career, substance abuse and mental health care: A nationwide register-based study of Finnish homicide offenders 1995–2004. *Criminal Behaviour and Mental Health, 21,* 51–62.

Reisig, M.D., Holtfreter, K., & Morash, M. (2006). Assessing recidivism risk across female pathways to crime. *Justice Quarterly, 23*(3), 384–405.

Rettinger, L.J., & Andrews, D.A. (2010). General risk and need, gender specificity, and the recidivism of female offenders. *Criminal Justice and Behavior, 37*(1), 29–46.

Robitaille, M.-P., & Cortoni, F. (2014). La pensée des femmes violentes?: Les théories implicites liées au comportement violent. *Canadian Journal of Behavioural Science/Revue Canadienne Des Sciences Du Comportement, 46*(2), 175–184.

Rumgay, J. (2004). Living with paradox: Community supervision of women offenders. In G. McIvor (Ed.), *Women who offend* (pp. 99–125). London: Jessica Kingsley.

Salisbury, E.J., & Van Voorhis, P.V. (2009). Gendered pathways: A quantitative investigation of women probationers' paths to incarceration. *Criminal Justice and Behavior, 36*(6), 541–566.

Sandler, J.C., & Freeman, N.J. (2007). Typology of female sex offenders: A test of Vandiver and Kercher. *Sexual Abuse: A Journal of Research and Treatment, 19,* 73–89.

Sandler, J.C., & Freeman, N J. (2009). Female sex offender recidivism: A large-scale empirical analysis. *Sexual Abuse: A Journal of Research and Treatment, 21,* 455–473.

Saradjian, J. (2010). Understanding the prevalence of female-perpetrated sexual abuse and the impact of that abuse on victims. In T.A. Gannon, & F. Cortoni (Ed.), *Female sexual offenders: Theory, assessment, and treatment* (pp. 9–30). Chichester, UK: Wiley-Blackwell.

Sestir, M.A., & Bartholow, B.D. (2007). Theoretical explanations of aggression and violence. In T.A. Gannon, T. Ward, A.R. Beech, & D. Fisher (Eds.), *Aggressive offenders' cognition: Theory, research, and practice* (pp. 157–178). Chichester, UK: John Wiley & Sons.

Shorey, R.C., Meltzer, C., & Cornelius, T.L. (2010). Motivations for self-defensive aggression in dating relationships. *Violence and Victims, 25*(5), 662–676.

Smith, P., Cullen, F.T., & Latessa, E.J. (2009). Can 14,737 women be wrong? A meta-analysis of the LSI-R and recidivism for female offenders. *Criminology & Public Policy, 8*(1), 183–208.

Sommers, I., & Baskin, D.R. (1993). The situational context of violent female offending. *Journal of Research in Crime and Delinquency, 30,* 136–162.

St-Hilaire. G. (2012). *Le processus de passage à l'acte violent chez les femmes (The offense process among violent women).* Unpublished Master's thesis. Université de Montréal.

Statistics Canada. (2016a). *Adult criminal courts, number of cases and charges by type of decision, annual* [CANSIM table 252-0053]. Retrieved from http://www5.statcan .gc.ca/cansim/a26?lang=eng&id=2520053.

Statistics Canada. (2016b). Family violence in Canada: A statistical profile, 2014. *Juristat, 85,* 1–77.

Stöckl, H., Devries, K., Rotstein, A., Abrahams, N., Campbell, J., Watts, C., & Moreno, C.G. (2013). The global prevalence of intimate partner homicide: A systematic review. *The Lancet, 382,* 859–865.

Straus, M.A. (1990). Measuring intrafamily conflict and violence: The Conflict Tactic (CT) Scale. In M.A. Straus & R.J. Gelles (Eds.), *Physical violence in American families* (pp. 29–47). New Brunswick, NJ: Transaction Books.

Straus, M.A. (2008). Dominance and symmetry in partner violence by male and female university students in

32 nations. *Children and Youth Services Review, 30*(3), 252–275.

Straus, M.A. (2011). Gender symmetry and mutuality in perpetration of clinical-level partner violence: Empirical evidence and implications for prevention and treatment. *Aggression and Violent Behavior, 16*(4), 279–288.

Stuart, G.L., Moore, T.M., Gordon, K.C., Hellmuth, J.C., Ramsey, S.E., & Kahler, C.W. (2006). Reasons for intimate partner violence perpetration among arrested women. *Violence Against Women, 12*, 609–621.

Suschinsky, K.D., Lalumière, M.L., & Chivers, M.L. (2009). Sex differences in patterns of genital sexual arousal: Measurement artifacts or true phenomena? *Archives of Sexual Behavior, 38*, 559–573.

Swan, S.C., & Snow, D.L. (2002). A typology of women's use of violence in intimate relationships. *Violence Against Women, 8*, 286–319.

Swan, S.C., & Snow, D.L. (2003). Behavioral and psychological differences among abused women who use violence in intimate relationships. *Violence Against Women, 9*(1), 75–109.

Van Voorhis, P., Salisbury, E., Wright, E., & Bauman, A. (2008). *Achieving accurate pictures of risk and identifying gender responsive needs: Two new assessments for women offenders.* Washington, D.C.: National Institute of Corrections, United States Department of Justice.

Vandiver, D.M., & Kercher, G. (2004). Offender and victim characteristics of registered female sex offenders in Texas: A proposed typology of female sexual offenders. *Sexual Abuse: A Journal of Research and Treatment, 16*, 121–137.

Verona, E., & Carbonell, J.L. (2000). Female violence and personality: Evidence for a pattern of overcontrolled hostility among one-time violent female offenders. *Criminal Justice and Behavior, 27*, 176–195.

Ward, T. (2000). Sexual offenders' cognitive distortions as implicit theories. *Aggression and Violent Behavior, 5*(5), 491–507

Weizmann-Henelius, G., Putkonen, H., Naukarinen, H., & Eronen, M. (2009). Intoxication and violent women. *Archives of Women's Mental Health, 12*, 15–25.

Williams, K.S., & Bierie, D.M. (2015). An incident-based comparison of female and male sexual offenders. *Sexual Abuse: A Journal of Research and Treatment, 27*, 235–257.

Yang, M., Wong, S.C.P., & Coid, J. (2010). The efficacy of violence prediction: A meta-analytic comparison of nine risk assessment tools. *Psychological Bulletin, 136*(5), 740–767.

Correctional Assessment and Treatment: Toward Community Reintegration

Introduction

In this chapter, we examine the theory and research that form the basis of effective correctional practice. Canada is a world leader in this area, having developed a model that emphasizes the importance of accurately assessing an offender's risk, identifying appropriate treatment needs, and providing effective treatment specifically suited to each offender.

Assessment is central to this model, and therefore it is important to understand how assessments are carried out: the type of information used, how it is collected, and how it is combined to help decision-makers. After an initial assessment has been completed, an offender is placed into a correctional unit according to their security level and personal needs and offered treatment services. To be effective, treatment must be responsive to an offender's needs and personal characteristics.

To promote successful community reintegration, preparatory programs are offered to women before they leave prison. These programs are followed by support and supervision when the woman is living in the community.

Throughout this chapter, we consider how assessment and treatment practices suit women in particular. Being "too few to count" (Adelburg & Currie, 1987) has meant that female offenders have less often been the focus of correctional research than male offenders. As a result, some of the assessment measures and treatment programs currently in use were developed for male offenders and then adapted to female offenders. In the last decade, we have seen the implementation of gender-specific assessments and treatment services. These are the result of an increase in new studies focused on female offenders.

Assessment

Psychological assessments are carried out to provide decision-makers and treatment providers with information at different points in the criminal justice system. In the court system, assessments are used to determine whether an accused is fit to stand trial and to help judges make sentencing decisions. In the correctional system, assessments are carried out to determine inmates' security levels, their treatment needs, and their risk of reoffending.

Assessment, therefore, is the foundation of effective correctional treatment as first articulated by Andrews and his colleagues (Andrews, Bonta, & Hoge, 1990). These Canadian researchers outlined a model that guides the assessment and treatment of offenders. Made up of three principles—risk, needs, and responsivity—this model has informed correctional practice throughout the world and continues to play a central role in our understanding of effective correctional practice (Blanchette & Brown, 2006; Gendreau, French, & Gionet, 2004; Rettinger & Andrews, 2010; Ward, Mesler, & Yates, 2007).

The Risk-Need-Responsivity (RNR) Model

The Risk Principle (Matching Level of Service to Risk)

According to the risk principle, we should begin by estimating, as accurately as possible, an offender's likelihood to reoffend. After this risk is known, offenders should be provided with services according to their level of risk: higher-risk offenders should be given more intense services and lower-risk offenders, less intense or no services (Bonta & Andrews, 2007).

To determine risk, and thus the level of service required, Andrews and his colleagues developed the Level of Service Inventory (LSI), a measure of offender needs across ten domains: (1) criminal history, (2) employment/education, (3) financial, (4) family/marital, (5) accommodation, (6) leisure/recreation, (7) companions, (8) alcohol/drug problems, (9) emotional/personal, and (10) attitudes. The LSI was designed to assist with the decisions of how to implement the least restrictive amount of supervision and how to identify dynamic areas of risk and need that could be addressed by programming to reduce risk (Andrews & Bonta, 1995). This assessment tool has been used with female offenders and will be discussed in more detail later in the chapter.

The Needs Principle (Assessing Criminogenic Needs to Target in Treatment)

The needs principle focuses on assessing offenders' criminogenic needs. These needs are directly related to offenders' criminal behaviour and include anti-social attitudes, anger control, substance abuse, and, in men, deviant sexual interest. According to this principle, non-criminogenic needs, such as childhood sexual abuse, low self-esteem, eating disorders, and poor health, although potentially important areas for clinical treatment, should not be the focus and priority within the correctional setting if they are not related to offending.

criminogenic need
A factor or behaviour that is related to criminal behaviour or recidivism.

As outlined in Box 6.1, researchers have identified eight major areas of **criminogenic need** that apply to male and female offenders, four that are strongly associated with recidivism and four others that moderately predict reoffence. Although offenders of both sexes have been found to share similar criminogenic needs (Andrews et al., 2012; Dowden & Andrews, 1999; Rettinger & Andrews, 2010), some researchers have suggested that their level of importance and the way in which they relate to offending may vary. For example, substance abuse and personal/emotional needs seem more predictive of female reoffending than male (Oliver, Stockdale, & Wormith, 2014). Furthermore, additional criminogenic needs may be unique to female offenders (Atkinson, 1998; Blanchette, 2001).

Efforts have been made to create gender-specific assessment tools identifying and measuring needs such as parental stress, low self-esteem, trauma history, and poverty (Van Voorhis, Wright, Salisbury, & Baumann, 2010). Despite being more prevalent among women, these factors have yet to be proven to predict recidivism better than Andrews and Bonta's original Central Eight. It is important, therefore, to differentiate between factors to which women are more often exposed and those which are directly related to their offending.

The differentiation between criminogenic and non-criminogenic needs is controversial and it is especially relevant for women in the criminal justice system because women are generally more likely to seek help than men. Therefore, establishing clearly which treatment targets relate to criminogenic needs and which to general well-being will help to ensure that offenders are not prevented from obtaining privileges, such as early release, due to either their willingness to seek help for their non-criminogenic needs or the severity of their mental health problems. Just as we should not deny parole to an offender with an unresolved heart condition, women should not be kept incarcerated due to their non-criminogenic problems. However, differentiating between criminogenic and non-criminogenic needs is not always easy in the area of mental health. For example, imagine that a woman is struggling with the effects of child sexual abuse. Is it fair to tie her level of risk to her progress in dealing with her anxiety or self-injury?

▶ WHAT DO YOU THINK?

Should a woman who admits to drinking four glasses of wine per day and who commits a large bank fraud over several years while maintaining an otherwise excellent work record as a loans officer be required to deal with her problem drinking to gain release?

What would you want to know before you decide whether her drinking is a criminogenic or non-criminogenic treatment need?

These questions need to be asked because female offenders demonstrate more mental health symptoms than male offenders (Brown, Hirdes, & Fries, 2015) and are more likely to seek treatment for a variety of issues while incarcerated. Despite this, they should not necessarily be required to resolve all of their issues to gain release or increased privileges. The challenge then is to identify those factors that are related to a specific woman's risk of reoffending (her criminogenic needs) and those related to her general well-being (her non-criminogenic needs).

Unfortunately, determining the cause of any individual's criminal behaviour can be difficult. Furthermore, as noted in Chapter 2, theories of criminal behaviour are not well developed for women because they are much less frequently involved in criminal activity than men. This difference in criminal activity by sex increases with offence severity; thus, women who commit serious offences, or who offend chronically, are more atypical of their sex than male offenders are of theirs. As a result, in attempts to explain their atypical behaviour, mental health needs (depression, post-traumatic stress, and anxiety, for example) are likely to be identified as contributing factors. For male offenders, who are more typical of their sex and who are less likely to discuss emotional problems (Howerton et al., 2007), attitudes, substance abuse, and meaningful work are more frequently identified as relevant treatment goals.

Notwithstanding these observations, it is important to note that mental health needs can occasionally be criminogenic. For example, experiencing psychological distress, regardless of the circumstances of the original crime, may increase an offender's risk for relapse, which will be discussed further when we turn to dynamic risk assessment.

The Responsivity Principle (Matching Treatment to Clients' Characteristics)

This principle promotes the use of evidence-based treatments matched to an offender's personality, strengths, learning style, motivation, and abilities. Evidence-based treatments are those that have been found to be effective, at least in comparison with no treatment, in a number of scientific studies. Cognitive behavioural interventions are often recommended because they have shown the most promise to date across both male and female offender populations (Andrews & Bonta, 2006; Gehring, Van Voorhis, & Bell, 2010; Tripodi, Bledsoe, Kim, & Bender, 2011). The most effective treatment should be used, and it should be tailored to the offender, male or female, Indigenous or non-Indigenous, well-educated or not. Advocates of gender-responsive treatment argue that programs for female offenders must be holistic, taking into account women's broader context in society, the importance of their interpersonal relationships, and their trauma histories (Gobeil, Blanchette, & Stewart, 2016; Tam & Derkzen, 2014; Wright, Van Voorhis, Salisbury, & Bauman, 2012; Zakaria, Allenby, Derkzen, & Jones, 2013). These responsivity issues will be discussed in detail later in the chapter.

Before we examine how the risk-need-responsivity model is applied to specific types of assessment, we will look at how decision-makers gather information about an offender and how they make their decisions.

Sources of Information Used in Decision-Making

Although correctional services and community programs vary considerably in the psychological measures (if any) they use in assessment, some assessment domains and sources of information are commonly used. Information about an offender can be gathered from the woman herself (self-report), from institutional records and from those who know her (collateral sources), from institutional records, and from psychological tests (Atkinson, 1995).

Self-Report Information

Information from the offender can be obtained from structured self-report questionnaires and interviews. Questionnaires are not psychological tests that assess underlying personality constructs or intelligence but are methods of systematically gathering self-report information about certain areas (such as assertiveness or depression) and providing norms for comparing groups of women. Some assessors prefer to collect this information in a face-to-face interview. Interviews allow the assessor to tailor questions to the individual offender and to probe further when comments are voiced that imply pro-criminal sentiments or cognitive distortions. Despite the number and type of assessment tools available, interviews are considered an important component of any offender assessment. Interviews should be structured and systematic to increase efficiency and to reduce the likelihood that significant information will be overlooked.

Institutional Records and Collateral Sources

In addition to gathering information directly from the offender herself, decision-makers need to corroborate the offender's account whenever possible. Corroboration is commonly achieved through review of institutional records, but when internal files are incomplete or inaccurate, corroboration can involve interviewing collateral sources, such as family and employers, and reviewing police reports, victim impact statements, and previous assessment and treatment reports. Although these tasks take time, especially when some reports are not readily available to the assessor, corroboration of the offender's self-report is essential prior to estimating an offender's risk of recidivism.

Psychological Tests

The third source of information commonly used to assess risk comes from psychological testing. Psychological tests measure underlying constructs, such as intelligence or personality, and often include validity scales to identify purposeful faking or misunderstanding of the questions because of mental illness or lack of motivation. Psychological tests are less transparent than questionnaires or inventories and may therefore yield less-biased information. Unfortunately, in the absence of a commonly agreed upon theory of female offending, assessors may have difficulty determining which tests to use and the weights to assign to the scores.

Types of Decision-Making (Clinical Judgment versus Actuarial Assessment)

Regardless of whether an assessor relies on an interview, a questionnaire, or a psychological test, the assessment is more accurate and therefore more useful when it is structured and based on actuarial information (Blanchette & Taylor, 2004; Harris, Rice, Quinsey, & Cormier, 2015). In the past few decades, much work has been carried out to improve the way in which we assess offenders, and risk assessment has improved the most.

Clinical judgment alone is no longer an acceptable basis for decision-making in most correctional services. Responsible correctional practice requires that psychologists use valid instruments designed for a specific purpose and shown to be reliable when applied properly. In correctional services, however, the lack of validated assessment tools for women led to a heavy reliance on clinical judgment for many years. Due to the fact that actuarial, or statistical, methods have now been shown to work with female offenders, the Canadian correctional service encourages their use in risk assessment.

When it comes to predicting the likelihood that an offender will reoffend, correctional managers, lawyers, and the public have difficulty believing that expert opinion and clinical judgment are not as accurate as structured actuarial measures. Indeed, in a classic study, Quinsey and Ambtman (1979) demonstrated that experts such as forensic psychiatrists did not fare any better than high school teachers when it came to predicting reoffending based on file information. The experts' opinions were weakened by focusing on the current offence and institutional behaviours that reflect mental health problems, instead of focusing on risk-related characteristics. This finding has been supported in subsequent research (Aegisdottir et al., 2006).

What exactly is actuarial prediction, and how do we know that it is better than clinical judgment? We will begin by describing the two types of decision-making.

Clinical Judgment

Clinical judgments are opinions rendered by those working with offenders, such as parole officers, prison staff, and professionals (such as psychologists and psychiatrists), using informal, unstructured methods. Clinical judgment does not rely on pre-established guidelines regarding the information to consider, the sources to use, and how to combine different types of information. As such, the judgment varies from professional to professional and perhaps also within professionals over time. When asked, most professionals

clinical judgment
A predominantly qualitative decision made by a corrections professional regarding the recidivism risk posed by an offender.

will provide a set of implicit guidelines that they use to make their decisions. Unfortunately, they do not always follow their own guidelines and can be biased by irrelevant factors, as demonstrated in the study of forensic psychiatrists and high school teachers described above.

Actuarial Assessment

In contrast, actuarial decisions are based on the measurement and combination of clearly defined types of information. This statistical approach (Harris et al., 2015) is highly structured and objective and has proven to be more accurate than clinical judgment (Aegisdottir et al., 2006; Grove & Meehl, 1996). Assessors collect information from files and/or from the offender herself and weigh this information according to a predetermined mathematical formula. The answer is then tallied, and the result is an estimate of the offender's probability of reoffending within a given period of time, usually three, seven, or ten years. The information used in actuarial instruments has been shown to best predict general and violent reoffending. Most instruments have converged on a similar set of items, which are related to the criminogenic factors discussed earlier (see Box 6.1).

BOX 6.1

Criminogenic Needs

The *needs principle* highlights the difference between offender needs that are related to recidivism and those that are not. Needs that are associated with recidivism are known as *criminogenic* needs, and these needs must be targeted in treatment to reduce recidivism. Eight areas of criminogenic need apply to both male and female offenders:

The "Central Eight" Criminogenic Needs

1. Anti-social behaviour: having committed many crimes
2. Anti-social personality pattern: impulsive, daring, egocentric, lacking in empathy and remorse
3. Anti-social attitudes: holding values, beliefs, and rationalizations that support engaging in criminal activity
4. Anti-social associates: associating with people who approve of criminal behaviour and therefore provide social support for it
5. Education/employment: history of poor performance at school and/or work, not satisfied with school/work
6. Family/marital: poor parenting and marital relationships
7. Leisure/recreation: lacking involvement in pro-social hobbies or sports
8. Substance abuse: abuse of alcohol and/or drugs

Source: Andrews, D.A., Bonta, J., & Wormith, S. (2006). The recent past and near future of risk and/or need assessment. *Crime & Delinquency, 52*, 7–27.

Many researchers have examined the accuracy of clinical judgment versus actuarial assessment. The conclusion in the scientific literature is clear: actuarial prediction, although not perfect, is significantly more accurate than clinical judgment, including structured clinical judgement (Aegisdottir et al., 2006; Hilton & Simmons, 2001). Unfortunately, despite decades of research, some professionals continue to replace or override actuarial predictions with their own opinion.

▶ WHAT DO YOU THINK?

Given the scientific evidence demonstrating the superiority of actuarial or statistical risk assessment methods, should these be mandatory in the Canadian correctional system? Under what circumstances might the use of clinical judgment be acceptable?

Assessment for Classification

Classification assessments are necessary for effective correctional treatment. Classification involves grouping people according to their similarities or differences. In corrections, offenders are grouped by security level (maximum, medium, or minimum), compatibility (ability to get along with other inmates), and treatment needs (substance abuse, emotion regulation, etc.). If carried out properly, classification aids in the effective and fair management of offenders. As Blanchette and Brown (2006) point out, classification guides the management of offender behaviour because it assists correctional staff in determining the kinds of privileges (often associated with security level) that may be safely made available to different groups of offenders as they progress through their sentences.

After an offender has been sentenced to serve time in either a federal prison or a provincial correctional centre, she is assessed by correctional staff to determine her security level and thus the most appropriate placement in her home region.

Placement decisions must take several factors into consideration:

- Public safety. Is the offender a high, medium, or low risk to escape? If she escapes, is she likely to reoffend violently?
- The smooth running of the institution. Will the offender integrate well into the general inmate population? Are there any offenders (such as a co-accused) or groups of offenders (such as a gang or ethnic group) with whom she is not compatible? If so, for her safety and the smooth running of the institution, she may be placed in a different institution or, in extreme cases, such as for those who have testified against others or committed certain sexual offences, in administrative segregation.
- The least restrictive environment for the offender. Although public safety needs to be ensured and certain offenders need to be kept separated, women should not be housed in more restrictive environments than necessary. Prison itself is restrictive enough without having an inmate's liberty further curtailed by unnecessary placement in maximum security or segregation.

Classification assessments are usually carried out by correctional staff, such as case managers, who complete a thorough file review and then interview an offender soon after her arrival in a new institution. They collect information on known criminogenic factors such as criminal history, including age of first arrest and conviction, escape attempts, length of present sentence, nature of offence, substance abuse history, accomplices, and gang memberships. This information is then weighed and combined quantitatively in a predetermined manner to obtain a total score that indicates the offender's required minimum level of security (the actuarial approach). Classification assessments are carried out periodically throughout an offender's stay in an institution with the goal of reducing security levels as the offender demonstrates more pro-social attitudes and behaviours until she is ready for release to a halfway house or the community.

cascading
The process of placing offenders in progressively lower security facilities as they respond positively to rehabilitative programs and near their release date. Although cascading is frequently desirable, it is not always possible.

The process of gradually reducing security, called **cascading**, ideally takes place prior to an offender's release. (For an illustration of cascading, see Box 6.2.) Offenders without a history of escape, who comply with their correctional program by attending their programs and avoiding institutional misconduct are eventually reclassified at a lower security level and eligible to move to less secure environments with more privileges. Doing this gradually over a period of time allows institutional staff to observe how the offender copes with fewer restrictions while still providing the support and supervision that she needs. In ideal circumstances, an offender should have been living in minimum security with passes to the community for some time before her release. In Canada,

---

BOX 6.2

An Example of Cascading

Admission to new institution	→	Assessment for classification purposes

↓

Placement in *maximum security* due to history of escape risk and substance abuse

3-month case management review	→	Reclassification interview

↓

Security level is dropped to *medium* due to pro-social behaviour within the institution, such as good job performance, lack of institutional charges, and active participation in treatment. The offender shows no evidence of substance use based on random urinalysis testing.

6-month case management review	→	Reclassification interview

↓

Security level is dropped to *minimum* despite a recent institutional charge of disobeying a direct order. This act was considered a minor charge; job performance and treatment plan compliance (random urinalysis testing and substance abuse treatment) remained satisfactory.

↓

Release to halfway house in the community for further supervision

men's institutions are classified by security level, whereas for women all institutions are multi-level except the Healing Lodge, which only serves minimum and medium security level classifications. Multi-level institutions allow women to stay in the same regional institution, close to their families, despite their security classification changing.

The Correctional Service of Canada, which has committed to using gender-informed classification tools, has developed the Security Reclassification Scale for Women (SRSW) (Blanchette & Taylor, 2004). The SRSW was based on known risk factors for female offenders and risk factors identified through consultation both with researchers who have developed other classification measures and with those who work most closely with female offenders. The researchers began with 176 items and whittled these down to nine items that best predicted institutional conduct using an actuarial approach (see Box 6.3). The final version of the SRSW was carefully evaluated in a three-year field test, and again after two years of use, and was found to be reliable and valid for Indigenous and non-Indigenous female offenders alike (Blanchette & Taylor, 2005; Gobeil & Blanchette, 2007).

BOX 6.3

Security Reclassification Scale for Women (SRSW)

1. Correctional plan: program motivation
2. Maintains regular positive family contact
3. Number of convictions for serious disciplinary offences *during the review period*
4. Number of recorded incidents *during the review period*
5. History of escape or unlawfully at large from work release, temporary absences, or community supervision
6. Pay level *during the review period*
7. Number of times offender was placed in involuntary segregation for being a danger to others or the institution *during the review period*
8. Total number of successful escorted temporary absences *during the review period*
9. Custody rating scale incident history

Source: Blanchette, K., & Taylor, K. (2005). *Development and field test of a gender-informed security reclassification scale for women offenders* (Research Report R-167). Ottawa: Correctional Service of Canada.

The SRSW is scored by a case manager who works closely with the offender, using information from institutional files and staff reports. The SRSW has a 30-point scoring range: higher scores represent a higher assessed risk and thus a higher security rating. Review periods are normally every six months.

When compared with the previous method of using structured clinical judgment to make classification decisions, this new scale resulted in fewer placements to maximum security and more placements to minimum security, thus improving the correctional service's ability to meet their mandate to keep offenders in the least restrictive environment possible while ensuring public safety. The SRSW was also found to be significantly more predictive of institutional misconduct than its predecessor (Blanchette & Taylor, 2005; Gobeil & Blanchette, 2007). In sum, this new actuarial measure is more accurate and more liberal than the CSC's earlier measure, which relied more on clinical judgment.

Assessment for Release Decision-Making

Psychologists are frequently called on to make risk assessments for parole boards to use in release decision-making. Because these assessments often carry a lot of weight, psychologists working with female offenders need to choose appropriate instruments and methods for determining risk.

▶ WHAT DO YOU THINK?

Psychologists perform different tasks in correctional services. They provide psychological treatment to offenders and they also conduct risk assessments for the parole board. Do you think it is appropriate for a psychologist to complete a risk assessment for the parole board on an offender whom she has been seeing in treatment? Why or why not?

Applying Actuarial Risk Assessment to Female Offenders

The science of predicting criminal recidivism has improved dramatically in the past few decades. Few correctional services rely solely on unstructured clinical judgment. Several actuarial instruments are used to predict the risk of an offender committing a new offence of any kind, and of *his*[1] committing a new violent and/or sexual offence, in particular. These instruments tend to predict criminal recidivism quite well when applied to men of various ages and races, and even when used for men diagnosed with a personality or other mental disorder (for a comprehensive review of the actuarial prediction of anti-social behaviour, see Harris et al., 2015).

As we have seen across the correctional landscape, many of the instruments originally developed for men and validated using male samples have now been tested to determine their suitability for women (Folsom & Atkinson, 2007; Rettinger & Andrews, 2010). In addition, some researchers have been working to adapt or develop new instruments specifically for women (de Vogel, de Vries Robbé, van Kalmthout, & Place, 2012; Van Voorhis et al., 2010). The research on these "gender-responsive" instruments is mixed and they do not currently fare as well as the traditional RNR instruments, such as the LSI, when it comes to predicting general and violent recidivism.

Women comprise a much smaller proportion of the inmate population, making up just 7 percent of federal offender admissions, 16 percent of provincial/territorial offenders (Reitano, 2017), and approximately 7 percent of state and federal offenders in the United States (Carson & Anderson, 2016). These small percentages likely explain why the validation and development of actuarial instruments for women lags behind that of men.

Therefore, correctional agencies need to work together to develop and test actuarial instruments. With such a small number of females incarcerated in any one jurisdiction in any given year, large-scale studies need to be conducted across several years to gather enough data to determine which factors should be included and in what combination for different types of women. These efforts can benefit from the large body of research on risk appraisal carried out with male offenders because the correlates of crime are, *in general*, similar across genders.

Sex Differences in the Correlates of Crime

Are the correlates of crime similar for adult male and female offenders? Feminist research-ers theorize that women have different pathways into crime (Daly, 1994); that they are more likely to have victimization histories (Leschied, 2011) and subsequently have higher rates of drug dependence (Fazel, Bains, & Doll, 2006), self-harm, and mental illness (Benda, 2005; Brown & Motiuk, 2005). They are also more likely to have childcare re-sponsibilities and be socially and economically marginalized (Holtfreter, Reisig, & Morash, 2004). Alone or in combination, these factors are believed to bring them into conflict with the law along a gendered pathway. According to this theory, assessment tools based on male theories of crime (the Central Eight criminogenic needs) are not valid when applied to women.

To address this issue, Andrews and his colleagues (2012) examined how well the Level of Service/Case Management Inventory (LS/CMI) and its Youth Version (YLS/CMI) predicted the recidivism rates of women and men, girls and boys. They looked back at five large studies of male and female offenders and computed the degree to which LS/CMI subscale scores (the Central Eight) predicted reoffence rates. If this instrument and the Central Eight are gender-neutral, then they should predict recidivism for both sexes. If women's pathways to crime are different than men's and our assessment of their risk to reoffend must include gender-specific factors such as poverty, trauma history, and parental stress, for example, then we would not expect the LS/CMI to predict female recidivism.

Across all of the samples studied, the scores for all eight needs areas predicted reof-fending for both men and women, girls and boys, and only one, substance abuse, performed significantly differently. Substance abuse score was a much stronger predic-tor of recidivism among females than males.

Overall, the Central Eight needs predicted the recidivism of females better than males. These rather surprising findings suggest that this instrument is equally, or more, valid for predicting recidivism among female offenders than it is for male offenders.

Despite the general effectiveness of the Central Eight in predicting reoffence, there are offender subgroups whose reoffending is harder to predict. One such group are female fraud offenders. Among fraud offenders, there is evidence of sex differences in the use of **neutralizations**, or "rationalizations after the fact" (see Box 6.4).

neutralization
An offender's rationalization that seeks to mitigate the effects of a crime. For example, a fraud offender passing bad cheques might tell herself that the money from the cheques was used to buy groceries to feed her children. In her mind, the damage from the fraud is mitigated by the good from the groceries.

BOX 6.4

Neutralization Theory

Fraud offenders appear to endorse the dominant moral code of society (they agree that crime is wrong and also which crimes are the most serious), but seem to use neutralizations or rationalizations to excuse their illegal behaviour. For example, a fraud offender might tell her-self that the money she is stealing from her bank is necessary for her to provide properly for her two young daughters, thereby neutralizing the "wrongness" of the act and allowing her to continue.

Atkinson (1998), who had observed female fraud of-fenders frequently using neutralizations in her clinical work, decided to test neutralization theory. Groups of male and female offenders, half of whom were convicted of fraud offences and half of whom had other types of con-victions, were asked to rate the seriousness of a variety of crimes and immoral acts. Their ratings were compared with those of male and female community volunteers. As predicted by neutralization theory, participants in all six groups closely agreed with each other on the seriousness of various crimes and immoral acts. The dominant moral code was endorsed by offenders and non-offenders alike. The next step was to test whether offenders, especially fraud offenders, were more likely to accept neutralizations as explanations for crimes and whether there were sex differences.

All six groups were asked to complete a neutralization scale that described a number of crimes and asked participants to choose an appropriate disposition or sentence for the offender. Further information about the offence, the victim, or the offender was then provided, and participants were asked to reassess their original sentence. For example, a bank robber might be initially sentenced to five years in prison, but upon learning that the bank robber was crazed with grief due to the death of his child, some participants reduced the sentence by a few years. Likewise, if a man convicted of theft was assigned 18 months, but the thief was later described as a middle-aged school principal with no criminal record who was "a pillar of the community," some participants

reduced his sentence to a $10,000 fine and community service. The degree to which participants reduced sentences as a result of different types of neutralizations was measured and compared.

The neutralization prediction was confirmed for women but not for men. Female fraud offenders neutralized more than male fraud offenders; that is, they believed more than their male counterparts that sentences should be reduced because of extenuating circumstances. Female fraud offenders also neutralized more often than female non-fraud offenders and female non-offenders. Among the men, all groups neutralized to the same degree. This finding suggests that correlates of crime are not always the same for men and women. In this case, neutralization may be a criminogenic factor for female fraud offenders but not for their male counterparts. Thus, treatments targeting neutralizations may be uniquely suited to female fraud offenders.

Source: Atkinson, J.L. (1998). *Neutralizations among male and female fraud offenders*. Doctoral dissertation, Queen's University, Kingston, ON.

Assessing Changes in Risk Level

Actuarial instruments combine known risk factors to produce an estimate of the likelihood that an individual offender will reoffend in general (commit any type of crime) or reoffend violently. The risk factors included are almost always static or unchangeable items, such as sex, criminal history, and childhood problems. The use of static or historical factors means that an offender's risk can never go down, only up. That is, if a woman accumulates further offences, her criminal history score will increase, but she can do nothing to improve the score based on her past.

In theory, intervention services are intended to reduce an offender's risk. To determine whether such services *do* reduce an offender's risk, and which types of services reduce risk the best, a measure of dynamic risk is needed. Dynamic risk predictors are changeable factors and can be divided into stable factors (personality disorders and deviant sexual preferences, for example) and acute factors (those that are rapidly changing, such as negative moods and intoxication) (Hanson & Harris, 2000).

If a measure were to be based on dynamic factors, especially those that could be changed through intervention, such as drug use or employment, then we could monitor an offender's changing risk status over time; when she took steps to lower her risk, by avoiding drugs and criminal peers, for example, her risk score would decrease. During periods of difficulty (when unemployed, depressed, or using drugs), her dynamic risk score would increase, reflecting an increase in risk. If such dynamic risk assessments were possible, parole officers could monitor a woman's progress more accurately and provide appropriate services (including a possible return to incarceration) as needed.

Although an actuarial assessment tool based on dynamic factors alone would be ideal, and some have been developed for males (Hanson & Harris, 2000; Quinsey, Coleman,

Jones, & Altrows, 1997), to date, none has been shown to compare to the predictive accuracy of the more static measures. To test the predictive utility of a dynamic measure, research must show that changes in risk level (the total score) are associated with changes in recidivism. Unfortunately, this type of research is still in its infancy. As a result, psychologists usually employ a measure of static risk to determine an offender's long-term likelihood of reoffending and then note what steps, if any, she is taking to reduce that risk. In the end, therefore, a scientifically proven methodology with reasonably good accuracy (an actuarial assessment) is used to anchor an offender's risk level, and then clinical judgment is applied to determine how that risk can be modified.

In summary, actuarial measures perform quite well, and much better than clinical judgment, at predicting the long-term recidivism risk for male offenders. These measures also appear promising when applied to female offenders. The drawback is that actuarial measures are unable to detect changes in risk levels. Thus, they cannot aid in the prediction of *when* an offender is at risk of reoffending; to accomplish this type of prediction, researchers are working on actuarial models based on dynamic, or changeable, factors.

Treatment

Why should prisons be concerned with treatment? Aren't offenders in prison as punishment for committing a crime? Isn't it enough that they are given a "time out" from society? Isn't being in prison enough of a deterrent not to offend again? If not, what else is needed? These issues have been debated throughout the history of imprisonment. This section examines these and other issues surrounding treatment for female offenders.

Why Treatment?

Criminal justice sanctions have many purposes, including punishment for the crime committed, protection of society from criminal activity, deterrence of the person from committing another crime, and rehabilitation of the offender. Rehabilitation requires some type of intervention to help offenders to avoid future criminal activity.

In recent years, much rhetoric has circulated on "getting tough" on crime. This sentiment has translated into harsher sentences and more intermediate sanctions, such as intensive supervision of offenders in the community, boot camps, and electronic monitoring. The effects of these types of punishments on recidivism were examined by Smith, Goggin, and Gendreau (2002) in a meta-analysis (that is, by combining the findings of a group of studies for statistical analysis). These researchers synthesized the results of 117 studies that had examined the effects of various criminal justice punishments on recidivism in male and female, youth and adult offenders. The results indicated that criminal justice punishments had no effect on recidivism. Offenders who received prison sentences were more likely to reoffend than those given community sanctions, and offenders with longer sentences were slightly more likely to reoffend than those with shorter sentences. The effects were the same for women as for men. This finding has been echoed by other researchers (Lipsey 2009; Lowencamp, Latessa, & Smith, 2006) who conclude that custody, control, and deterrence (the "getting tough" approach to crime) does not reduce recidivism. Instead, high-quality therapeutic programs delivered to moderate and high-risk offenders are more effective at reducing crime.

Thus, imprisonment on its own is not enough to help offenders avoid further criminal activity. Treatment is required to assist offenders to make the changes in their lives that will support them remaining crime-free. This may be especially true for women who have a higher incidence of substance use and mental health problems.

Types of Treatment

The correctional system uses two main types of treatment: interventions that focus on criminogenic needs and interventions that address non-criminogenic needs, such as self-esteem or past history of abuse. Female offenders have access to both types of treatments. Although a wide range of programs are available within the provincial correctional systems, most female offenders within these systems are serving very short sentences and therefore cannot take part in lengthy treatment programs. Thus, the focus of this section is on those programs that are available to federally incarcerated women because these programs tend to be lengthier and several have been the focus of systematic evaluation.

Correctional Treatment Programs

Most correctional treatment programs are based on Andrews and Bonta's (2006) risk, needs, and responsivity principles. As described at the beginning of the chapter, according to the risk principle, treatment services need to match the offender's risk level. That is, offenders who are at a high risk to reoffend should receive the highest intensity treatments (that is, longer programs, more hours per week of treatment, etc.), whereas offenders at low risk should receive few or no therapeutic services.

The needs principle highlights the difference between offender needs that are related to recidivism and those that are not. The needs associated with recidivism, known as criminogenic needs, are the needs that are targeted in treatment to reduce recidivism.

The assessment process, as already discussed, identifies specific problems in the offender's life that led to her offending. These specific problems or criminogenic needs are the focus of correctional treatment programs.

The responsivity principle has two parts:

1. the *general responsivity principle*, which states that social learning and cognitive-behavioural strategies, which have been shown to be the most powerful interventions for change, should be used (see Box 6.5 for more details on cognitive-behaviour therapy); and
2. the *specific responsivity principle*, which refers to delivering treatment in a way suited to the offender's learning style or ability.

Treatment must be matched to the client, which may involve adapting materials to the appropriate literacy level, cultural background, or gender. In terms of gender, some of the responsivity factors for female offenders are the importance of relationships, including the therapeutic relationship, in women's lives, and differences in communication style (Blanchette & Brown, 2006). Women, for example, tend to communicate with more body language than men and to speak less and interrupt less in mixed groups.

In terms of the general responsivity principle, social learning refers to the acquisition of beliefs, attitudes, and behaviours from other people. Criminal behaviour, for example, may be learned from family, friends, or associates whom we value. These people may teach the skills for committing crime and reinforce an involvement in crime.

> **BOX 6.5**
>
> ### Cognitive-Behaviour Therapy
>
> Cognitive therapy focuses on the client's thoughts and teaches her to challenge or refute negative or self-defeating thoughts, such as "no one likes me" or "I will never be able to quit smoking." This therapy also helps clients to examine the origin of their thoughts and evaluate their reasonableness. For example, if a friend walks by Kristen in the hall at school and doesn't say hello, Kristen might think that her friend is angry with her and that she is not speaking to her. This situation could make Kristen feel angry with her friend, which in turn could interfere with their friendship. A cognitive therapist would challenge this conclusion and have Kristen seek other possible explanations, such as "maybe my friend was preoccupied and didn't see me, or perhaps she wasn't feeling well." In this way, Kristen would learn not to make assumptions without checking them out. If one of these alternative explanations turns out to be the case, instead of feeling angry, Kristen might feel empathy or concern for her friend.

Cognitive-behavioural treatments have long been used by psychologists to treat a variety of problems, including depression (Beck, Rush, Shaw, & Emery, 1979), anxiety (Burns, 1999), and personality problems (Linehan, 1993). The cognitive part of the treatment refers to how we think and, specifically, how we think about the problem, whether it is applied to depression, anxiety, or some other problematic behaviour. The theory behind cognitive therapy is that by changing the way we think about a situation, we can change how we feel about it. In the example of this approach in Box 6.5, the student attributed her friend's behaviour to anger, which made her feel angry. When she changed how she was thinking about the situation (perhaps her friend wasn't angry), her feelings about it also changed (from anger to concern).

▶ WHAT DO YOU THINK?

While cognitive-behavioural therapy has been proven effective in research studies, it may not work well for certain individuals. What type or types of offenders might not respond well to cognitive-behavioural therapy?

In contrast to cognitive therapy, which focuses on thoughts, behaviour therapy focuses on concrete behavioural change. Clients keep records of their behaviour, set specific behavioural goals with their therapist, and evaluate their progress regularly. An example is a treatment for heavy drinking in which the goal may be to reduce the consumption of alcohol (Dimeff, Baer, Kivlahan, & Marlatt, 1999). The client records the number of drinks consumed per week, sets a goal of reducing her consumption, and monitors her drinking. Specific behavioural strategies to meet the goal include allowing more time between drinks, alternating alcoholic drinks with non-alcoholic drinks, or switching from stronger to weaker alcoholic drinks (from hard liquor to beer, for example).

Together, social learning and cognitive-behavioural techniques are the most effective interventions for criminal behaviour (Andrews & Bonta, 2006). With these techniques, people can gain better control over their thoughts and feelings and make behavioural changes in their lives.

In addition to using evidence-based therapies, the responsivity principle directs us to adapt interventions to specific offenders' characteristics, including gender. All principles of effective correctional treatment have largely been developed on male offenders and later adapted for female offenders. How well do they apply to female offenders? Dowden and Andrews (1999) conducted a meta-analytic review of treatment outcome studies involving female offenders. They found that those programs that adhered to the basic tenets of effective correctional treatment were the most effective in reducing recidivism. That is, programs that targeted higher-risk offenders, focused predominantly on criminogenic needs, and used cognitive-behavioural and social learning treatment strategies resulted in stronger treatment effects. Note that some of the most common needs that are targeted for female offenders (self-esteem and past victimization) were not included in any of the studies examined (Dowden & Andrews, 1999). Therefore, the authors concluded that "it remains unclear as to whether these are criminogenic or noncriminogenic needs for female offenders" (p. 449). It is also worth noting that most of the studies in the meta-analysis were based on young female offenders (Blanchette & Brown, 2006). Adult female offenders may vary in some important ways from young female offenders.

Blanchette and Brown (2006) have thoroughly reviewed evidence from a wide variety of sources for treatment effectiveness with female offenders. Included in their review were programs based on the risk-need-responsivity principle and those based on other principles, such as feminist and relational theory.

Feminist therapy focuses on the societal, cultural, and political causes of, and solutions to, issues presented by clients. This theory is sensitive to inequality in society, particularly gender inequality, and the role that it plays in women's psychological distress. Feminist therapy focuses on the client's strengths and on a collaborative relationship between the client and therapist.

According to relational theory, connecting with other human beings is necessary for healthy development. This theory defines healthy relationships as those based on empathy, empowerment, and mutuality.

Blanchette and Brown (2006) conclude that, to date, little solid evidence supports the effectiveness of treatments that are *not* based on the risk-need-responsivity principle. However, they also see other treatment approaches—such as feminist therapy and relational therapy—as being consistent with the risk-need-responsivity principle. Feminist therapy's focus on the client's strengths and a collaborative relationship is not contrary to the risk-need-responsivity principle. In terms of relational theory, a high-quality relationship is one of the conditions of effective correctional programs: "A high-quality relationship creates a setting in which modeling and reinforcement can more easily take place. Important to such a relationship is an open, flexible, and enthusiastic style wherein people feel free to express their opinions, feelings, and experiences" (Andrews & Bonta, 2006, p. 354). It is more likely that the high-quality relationship is a necessary condition for therapeutic change but never a sufficient condition on its own.

As a result of their review, Blanchette and Brown (2006) concluded that gender should be viewed as a general, not a specific, responsivity factor. A specific responsivity factor would deliver treatment in a way that is suited to an individual's learning style. However, because women have many commonalities, gender should be considered a general responsivity factor. Blanchette and Brown (2006) have reformulated the general responsivity principle for female offenders as follows:

A gender-informed responsivity principle states that in general, optimal treatment response will be achieved when treatment providers deliver structured behavioural interventions [grounded in feminist philosophies and social learning theory] in an empathic and empowering manner [a strength-based model] while simultaneously adopting a firm but fair approach. (p. 126)

Note that the reformulated general responsivity principle for female offenders incorporates feminist theory and assigns equal weight to women's strengths and risks in the rehabilitation process.

Principles for Treatment of Female Offenders

All programs for federal female offenders must be offered within a women-centred perspective to ensure recognition of women's social realities and the context of their lives. *Creating Choices*, a report by the Task Force on Federally Sentenced Women (Canada, Task Force on Federally Sentenced Women, 1990) outlined five principles for the treatment of female offenders:

1. Empowerment: The lack of power women feel to control their own lives and the low levels of self-esteem felt by them represent a primary need of female offenders. Empowerment is the process by which women gain insight into their situation, identify their strengths, and are supported and challenged to take positive action to gain control of their lives.
2. Meaningful and responsible choices: Female offenders need to be made aware of the resources available to them and the consequences of their decisions so they can make informed decisions. When women are able to make such decisions, they develop a sense of control over their lives, which ultimately leads to an improvement of self-esteem and self-worth.
3. Respect and dignity: Respect is essential between correctional staff and female offenders. A person treated with respect and dignity is likely to gain self-respect and to respond to others in a similar fashion.
4. Supportive environment: A positive environment can foster personal development and promote physical and psychological health. A supportive environment ensures equality of services in a respectful atmosphere while allowing for meaningful and responsible choices to be generated.
5. Shared responsibility: All levels of government, correctional services, businesses, voluntary and private sector organizations, and the community have a responsibility to help develop, implement, monitor, and evaluate programming services for federally sentenced women.

Core Correctional Programs

The principles outlined in *Creating Choices* have been used to guide the development of core programming for female offenders. Initially, programs were organized by specific criminogenic need, such as substance use, reasoning, anger and emotions management, and sex offending (Correctional Service of Canada, 2008b).

In 2010, following a review of women's programming, the correctional service moved to a model that grouped programs by level of intensity, not type of need. There are now four programs that lie on a continuum of increasing intensity and are designed to address the complexity of women's needs. The amount of programming needed by an individual offender is determined by her level of risk, with higher intensity programs being delivered to higher risk women. A culturally relevant version of this program is available for Indigenous offenders.

Upon admission to a federal institution, all women participate in a low intensity, 12-week Engagement Program. It serves as a foundation for the higher intensity programs. Women who are assessed as being at higher risk continue on to the Moderate and perhaps the High Intensity Program. Once a woman has completed her prescribed programming, she is eligible for a final 12-week program to help her maintain positive change (see Table 6.1).

Table 6.1   Female Offender Continuum of Care

Program	Risk Level	Program Targets
Engagement Program (WEP) 12 group sessions	Delivered to all women admitted to a federal institution (low, medium, and high risk).	Motivation for change, social skills in a group setting, identifying problematic behaviours, and learning about the self-management plan.
Moderate Intensity Program (MIP) 40 group sessions	For those assessed as moderate to high risk who have completed the WEP.	Pro-criminal attitudes and associates, relationships, self-awareness, and managing emotions.
High Intensity Program (HIP) 52 sessions	For those assessed as high risk who have completed the MIP.	Consequential thinking, decision making, self-management and emotional regulation, healthy relationships, and conflict resolution.
Self-Management Program 12 group sessions	For program completers in the institution and for those on release in the community.	Effective communication skills, processing change, and effective goal-setting. Provides women with the support needed to maintain positive change.
Sex Offender Program 59 group + 7 individual sessions	For women who have offended sexually. May be taken with MIP.	Identification and intervention to address the factors that have contributed to the woman's offence.

Source: Correctional Service of Canada. (2014). Correctional programs. Retrieved from http://www.csc-scc.gc.ca/correctional-process/002001-2001-eng.shtml#s2.

Clearly grounded in the RNR principles (matching treatment to risk level and using cognitive-behavioural approaches), this program follows cognitive-behavioural principles and empowers women by teaching them to identify their problem behaviours and intervene to moderate or replace them with more adaptive behaviours.

Evaluated by Harris, Thompson, and Derkzen in 2015, women who completed these programs, along with their facilitators or groups leaders, were more likely to report improved skills, attitudes, motivation, and knowledge of program content. Unfortunately, these same women who completed their required programs did not have a lower return to custody rate than women who dropped out of their treatment or did not attend at all. This suggests that ongoing work is needed to refine these programs.

► **WHAT DO YOU THINK?**
Should correctional treatment be mandatory (required for release) for offenders? Why or why not?

Indigenous Offenders

In Canada, federally sentenced Indigenous female offenders have access to a correctional institution that has been designed as a healing lodge. In recognition of the importance of nature in Indigenous healing and culture, this institution is located in a rural area surrounded by woodland. The focus is on the safety of the female offenders, staff, and the public while encouraging healing, wellness, and a safe return to the community. Indigenous culture and spirituality are an integral part of the life at the lodge. Elders are onsite all day to lead prayers, healing ceremonies, and talking circles. All programs are presented in a manner that is culturally- and gender-sensitive, which addresses the responsivity factor for Indigenous female offenders. The main programs offered at the healing lodge are the same as those offered at other women's facilities.

Indigenous Female Offender Correctional Program

CSC has worked with Indigenous communities, Elders, and Indigenous advisory boards to develop and deliver culturally relevant programs for Indigenous offenders. These programs recognize the social realities and context of the lives of Indigenous offenders and are designed to ensure that Indigenous offenders' needs are met in terms of culture, tradition, and spirituality.

Programs Addressing Non-Criminogenic Needs

Female offenders often have other needs that may not fit into the area defined as criminogenic. Some of these needs are mental health, education, employment, parenting, and social programs.

Mental Health

Assessment and treatment for serious mental disorders is covered in Chapter 8. One area of mental health treatment that may be provided for any female offender is that of counselling for abuse and trauma.

Abuse and Trauma

Because of the high rate of victimization in the lives of female offenders (Bonta, Pang, & Wallace-Capretta, 1995; Heney, 1990; Shaw, 1994), treatment programs for women often address past experiences of abuse (Correctional Service of Canada, 2008b). These programs include an educational component that aims to increase awareness of trauma and abuse issues, such as the different forms of abuse and the context in which they occur. The programs also help women to build resources in the community and to know where to go for help. More intensive work is also provided on issues such as healthy relationships and coping strategies.

In general, a history of past victimization is not predictive of an increased risk for reoffending (Bonta et al., 1995), which is why it is not a criminogenic need. Past victimization may be viewed as a responsivity factor because emotional distress from the abuse may interfere with the woman's ability to benefit from treatment for her crimi-nogenic needs. If she is very anxious, angry, or frequently injuring herself as a direct result of abuse, dealing with the abuse will allow her to reap more benefit from core treatment programs for her criminogenic needs.

In some specific cases, victimization may be directly related to a woman's offence, thereby making it a criminogenic need. For example, a woman might overreact to something a man says or does by responding violently. The man's behaviour may have evoked memories of past abuse and led to her inappropriate response. Thus, the issue of past abuse may blur the line between criminogenic and non-criminogenic needs for female offenders.

Some scholars, however, would take issue with this conceptualization of the effects of past victimization on criminal behaviour in women, arguing that such an approach ignores or minimizes the effects of the socio-economic background of female offenders (Hannah-Moffat, 2006; Pollack, 2005). Whereas the risk-need-responsivity approach places responsibility for problematic behaviours on the woman herself, feminist scholars like Hannah-Moffat (2006) and Pollack (2005) emphasize the importance of socio-economic and gender issues, such as sexism, in shaping the behaviours of female offenders. For example, self-injurious behaviour may be seen as a rational response to an oppressive and abusive life situation because it provides emotional relief and a sense of control over a life that is controlled by others. These feminist-oriented authors have much to add to our understanding of female offenders. Yet a more individualistic ap-proach is needed when one is faced with a woman in immediate need of assistance.

Education and Employment Programs

Several education and employment programs are available to female offenders based on the belief that they will be useful for successful reintegration into the community. For example, a lack of skills to earn a legitimate income may contribute to a woman's decision to seek illegal means to support herself, such as drug trafficking or prostitution. Improving her education or learning new job skills may provide a woman with the means of earning a legitimate income and avoiding crime. Although education and employment needs may not be directly associated with offending, upgrading in these areas has been found to reduce the likelihood that a woman will have her parole revoked (Wilton & Stewart, 2015). In addition, newly released women identified employment in particular as a "protective" factor, in that being employed helped them establish and maintain a pro-social lifestyle (Gobeil, 2008).

Social Programs

Institutional Mother-Child Program

Two-thirds of incarcerated women are mothers of children under five years of age (Cor-rectional Service of Canada, 2008a). The aim of the Mother-Child Program is "to foster positive relationships between federally incarcerated women and their children by provid-ing a supportive environment that promotes stability and continuity for the mother-child relationship" (Correctional Service of Canada, 2016). The pre-eminent consideration for participation in the program is the best interests of the child, including the child's safety, security, and physical, emotional, and spiritual well-being. The major components of the program are full-time, onsite residency of children up to the age of four with their mother and part-time residency (weekends and holidays) of children up to the age of 12 with their mother. Both mother and child live in a house that is shared with several other female offenders who may or may not have children with them. Those offenders who do not have children are carefully screened prior to being placed in such a house to ensure that no one with a history of violence against children could reside there. All mothers must complete a parenting skills program and meet other criteria (such as being of minimum or medium security classification) prior to being allowed to live with their children. Unfortunately, the number of women who are deemed eligible to take part in this program is small (Brennan, 2014).

Spirituality

All facilities have chaplains available, who can provide pastoral care directly to female offenders or arrange for care in a wide variety of faiths. Volunteers from various faith communities provide support to female offenders both while incarcerated and on their release into the community.

Leisure, Recreation, Arts, and Crafts

Leisure and recreational facilities are available within the correctional system. Some sites offer specialized programs, such as a horticultural program, where women learn about growing and caring for plants, and a canine program, where women learn to care for and train dogs. A leisure skills program can help women to understand the role that leisure plays in society and the importance of leisure as part of a balanced lifestyle. Because leisure activities can contribute to personal development and to a sense of well-being, women are taught how to reach their leisure goals by effective planning for leisure, overcoming obstacles, and using creative ways to take part in low-cost activities.

Social Integration Program for Women

The goal of this program is to provide women with the knowledge and skills needed to make a successful transition from the institution to the community. The program is made up of several independent modules and women can attend the modules relevant to their situation. The content is based on areas that were found to be problematic for female offenders, such as money management and finding a job. To reduce the stress associated with community re-entry, stressful life situations, such as finding affordable housing, making new friends, and re-establishing family ties, are also addressed. At the end of the program, it is hoped that the women will be better equipped to return to the community.

Community Reintegration

Because the transition from institutional life to community life is believed to be a key factor in the successful reintegration of offenders, correctional services strive to provide a continuum of care. As described above, the Correctional Service of Canada provides female offenders with services such as the Self-Management Program, which may begin either in the institution or in the community, as well as the Social Integration Program for Women.

To ensure the most successful reintegration possible, adequate planning is needed prior to release, supported by appropriate supervision and programming upon release. Ideally, planning should begin long before an offender is eligible for release and include an assessment of ongoing treatment needs and an audit of available resources (accommodation, family and friend support, job opportunities, for example) and potential obstacles (such as associates and type of work).

The challenge is determining which of these needs areas most closely relates to recidivism and therefore provides the most important target for ongoing intervention. A burgeoning body of research has examined the predictive validity of community functioning in general, and specific factors, such as health, finances, and accommodation, which may relate to recidivism among female offenders. Although a generic rating of community functioning has not proven to be closely associated with recidivism among women (Brown & Motiuk, 2005; Gates, Dowden, & Brown, 1998; Greiner, Law, & Brown, 2015), some specific areas, especially employment and associates, hold promise. Of the Central Eight needs, changes in employment and associates are the best predictors of recidivism (Greiner et al., 2015).

A Correctional Service of Canada questionnaire originally developed for male offenders on release in the community has recently been applied to help predict which changes in a released female offender's circumstances best predict non-violent and violent recidivism. The Community Integration Scale (CIS) has proven to be effective in predicting both non-violent and violent recidivism among female offenders in the community (Dowden, Serin, & Blanchette, 2001; Law, 2004). The CIS domains most predictive of recidivism among female offenders were, again, employment and associates.

Gobeil (2008) surveyed a small sample of women who had been back in the community for one to five years. These women rated the period right after release as the most difficult. This period is often spent in a halfway house away from one's family and home. Halfway houses have strict rules and drugs may be present. During this time, women are usually not yet employed or attending school. It is easy to see how these circumstances could place a woman at high risk for relapse. As time elapses and they gain full parole, they can return to their homes, partner, and children and often begin to work. The women surveyed identified two important ingredients for their success in the community. First, making a personal commitment to remain crime- and/or drug-free. Second, the quality of their relationships upon release. If they had a good relationship with their children, partner, and parole officer, they felt better able to remain crime-free during this high-risk period (Gobeil, 2008). In a similar study in the U.S., the most important factors for women's success upon release were the number of children and relationships (Benda, 2005).

Echoing these women's voices, several years later when Canadian parole officers were asked what might facilitate female offenders' successful integration into the community, they emphasized the importance of developing support networks before women are released, especially for women with children (Thompson, Lufty, Derkzen, & Bertrand, 2015). Employment and housing were also identified as pressing needs for women upon release.

Overall, this research indicates that relationships and employment stand out as the primary needs of women under community supervision. Particular attention to the needs of Indigenous female offenders is warranted because, compared to their non-Indigenous counterparts, they face significantly more challenges upon release (McConnell, Rubenfeld, Thompson, & Gobeil, 2014).

► WHAT DO YOU THINK?

Given that supportive relationships improve the success of female offenders returning to the community, what type of program could the CSC design to address this need?

Programming

To reduce recidivism, offenders may be encouraged or required by law to participate in programming upon release. Such programming can include educational upgrading, vocational training, substance abuse treatment, cognitive skills training, or other types of programming as deemed necessary by the case management team and endorsed by the parole authorities. Programs available to offenders in the community vary across jurisdiction but include those provided by the CSC and the Canadian Association of Elizabeth Fry Societies (CAEFS) and those available to all community members (for example, Alcoholics Anonymous, Narcotics Anonymous, and community mental health programs).

About half of all women under federal jurisdiction in Canada are on conditional release in the community. Despite this high percentage, because so few women are serving federal sentences at any one time and because they are so widely dispersed geographically, services specific to female offenders in any single community are rarely available. Thus, programming for female offenders in the community must be flexible and creative, often making use of non-correctional programs (Fortin, 2004).

Female offenders, like any newcomer to a city, must find a family physician and perhaps a psychologist or social worker in order to obtain ongoing treatment. If mental health treatment is one of an offender's release conditions, then the parole officer is responsible for ensuring that it is available.

Supervision

Supervision is the second component of effective reintegration. Although the priority is to protect the public by monitoring the behaviour of offenders to anticipate when they may relapse and commit a new crime, offenders also benefit by having a supportive supervisor close by to help them stay crime-free. Applying the risk-need-responsivity model, supervision services should be provided in relation to an offender's risk level. Thus, the highest-risk offenders receive the most intense supervision (placement in a halfway house and weekly check-ins with a parole officer, for example), and the lowest-risk offenders receive little or no supervision, perhaps monthly check-ins at the police station.

Supportive supervisors can help a woman identify when she is starting to slip and work with her to prevent a relapse. Risk factors might include a return to a dysfunctional relationship or an increasing association with drug users. By helping the woman to confront these behaviours, the parole officer can alert her to the need to apply what she has learned in treatment to avoid a return to anti-social behaviour and possibly to jail. In keeping with the risk-need-responsivity model, supervision should be responsive to the needs of offenders. Important considerations include the type and length of parole, gender, and Indigenous status. For example, to address gender responsivity issues in supervision, specially selected and trained female parole officer teams have been organized in Montreal and Toronto (Gagnon, 2004).

As noted in Chapter 3, the Canadian Association of Elizabeth Fry Societies (CAEFS) originated to support and advocate for women in conflict with the law. CAEFS plays a large role in supporting women upon release, operating halfway houses across the country, and providing supervision and programming to women on parole and probation.

SUMMARY

After an offender has been classified according to her level of risk, her treatment needs, and her compatibility, she is placed in a living unit in a prison or correctional facility, usually in a region closest to her home. Following assessment of her criminogenic and non-criminogenic needs, she and her case manager will agree on a treatment plan.

Treatment may consist of individual or group programming for her criminogenic needs; that is, those needs that, if treated, will result in a reduction in the probability of her reoffending. Other non-criminogenic needs, such as self-esteem or the effects of victimization, may also be addressed. At times, a blurring of these needs may occur; for example, the need to treat the effects of victimization may or may not be directly related to her pattern of offending. The importance of other areas of her life is not to be overlooked; for example, the need for employment, housing, parenting skills, and to be living with her young children. At all times, programs must be offered within a women-centred perspective that ensures women's social realities are recognized.

The offender will meet with her case manager at regular intervals to review her security level and treatment plan progress. If things are going well, she will be cascaded to a lower security level and granted passes to visit the community. When she is ready for parole, a psychologist will assess her risk using one of the actuarial instruments that have been validated for female offenders. Relying on her clinical judgment, the psychologist will then add her assessment of the dynamic factors by estimating the degree to which the static risk factors may have been reduced through correctional programming. The psychologist then offers her opinion about how to reduce this risk, often in consultation with the offender herself.

If the offender is deemed a manageable risk, she will be released on parole into a halfway house or to her home. She will be supervised by a parole officer and, if needed, attend programs offered by the CSC or those generally available in the community. Throughout this process, she will be supported by members of the Canadian Association of Elizabeth Fry Societies.

The Correctional Service of Canada, which has responsibility for federal offenders (those serving sentences of two years or more), has demonstrated its commitment to evidence-based and gender-responsive practice. CSC conducts frequent reviews of its assessment tools and correctional programs and incorporates the findings of independent researchers into their practice.

NOTE

1. The initial development of actuarial instruments to predict risk focused entirely on male offenders.

DISCUSSION QUESTIONS

1. What is the purpose of offender classification?
2. What is meant by criminogenic and non-criminogenic risk factors?
3. What is the drawback of using static risk factors instead of dynamic risk factors in actuarial risk prediction?
4. Is the following statement true or false? Explain your answer. "There is no point in spending taxpayers' dollars on treating issues that are not related to a woman's offending."
5. What services are available to help women safely reintegrate into the community?

ADDITIONAL RESOURCES

Suggested Readings

Barrett, M.R., Allenby, K., & Taylor, K. (2010). *Twenty years later: Revisiting the task force on federally sentenced women* (Report No. R-222). Ottawa: Correctional Service Canada. Retrieved from http://www.csc-scc.gc.ca/research/005008-0222-01-eng.shtml.

Blanchette, K., & Brown, S.L. (2006). *The assessment and treatment of women offenders*. West Sussex, UK: John Wiley & Sons.

Bonta, J. (2002). The effects of punishment on recidivism. *Public Safety Canada Research Summary, 7*(3). Retrieved from www.publicsafety.gc.ca.

Films and Videos

CBC News Big Picture. (2014). *Inside Canada's prisons: Women behind bars*. (Documentary Three from 24:20 – 46:10). Retrieved from https://www.youtube.com/watch?v=1GbMsNap0_0.

Correctional Service of Canada. (2015). *Beyond the Fence: A virtual tour of a Canadian penitentiary* [Virtual tour]. Retrieved from http://www.csc-scc.gc.ca/csc-virtual-tour/index-eng.shtml.

Websites

Correctional Service of Canada Women's Corrections: www.csc-scc.gc.ca/women

Canadian Association of Elizabeth Fry Societies: www.caefs.ca

Public Safety Canada: www.publicsafety.gc.ca

REFERENCES

Adelburg, E., & Currie, C. (Eds.). (1987). *Too few to count: Canadian women in conflict with the law*. Vancouver: Press Gang.

Aegisdottir, S., White, M.J., Spengler, P.M., Maugherman, A.S., Anderson, L.A., Cook, R.S., ... Rush, J.D. (2006). The meta-analysis of clinical judgment project: Fifty-six years of accumulated research on clinical versus statistical prediction. *Counseling Psychologist, 34*, 341–382.

Andrews, D.A., & Bonta, J. (1995). *LSI-R: The level of service inventory—revised*. Toronto: Multi-Health Systems.

Andrews, D.A., & Bonta, J. (2006). *The psychology of criminal conduct* (4th ed.). Cincinnati, OH: Anderson.

Andrews, D.A., Bonta, J., & Hoge, R.D. (1990). Classification for effective rehabilitation: Rediscovering Psychology. *Criminal Justice and Behaviour, 17*, 19–52.

Andrews, D.A., Bonta, J., & Wormith, S. (2006). The recent past and near future of risk and/or need assessment. *Crime & Delinquency, 52*, 7–27.

Andrews, D.A, Guzzo, L., Raynor, P., Rowe, R.C., Rettinger, L.J., Brews, A., & Wormith, S. (2012). Are the major risk/need factors predictive of both female and male reoffending? A test with the eight domains of the level of service/case management inventory. *International Journal of Offender Therapy and Comparative Criminology, 56*(1) 113–133.

Atkinson, J.L. (1995). *The assessment of female sex offenders*. An unpublished, internal report prepared for the Correctional Service of Canada.

Atkinson, J.L. (1998). *Neutralizations among male and female fraud offenders*. Doctoral Dissertation, Queen's University, Kingston, Ontario.

Beck, A.T., Rush, A.J., Shaw, B., & Emery, G. (1979). *Cognitive therapy of depression*. New York: Wiley.

Benda, B.B. (2005). Gender differences in life-course theory of recidivism: A survival analysis. *International Journal of Offender Therapy and Comparative Criminology*, 49: 325–342.

Blanchette, K. (2001). Classifying female offenders for effective intervention: Application of the case-based principles of risk and need. *Forum on Corrections Research*, 14(1). Retrieved from http://www.csc-scc.gc.ca/text/pblct/forum/e141/141h_e.pdf.

Blanchette, K., & Brown, S.L. (2006). *The assessment and treatment of women offenders*. West Sussex, UK: John Wiley & Sons.

Blanchette, K., & Taylor, K. (2004). Development and validation of a security reclassification scale for women. *Forum on Corrections Research*, 16(1). Retrieved from http://www.csc-scc.gc.ca/research/r167-eng.shtml.

Blanchette, K., & Taylor, K. (2005). *Development and field test of a gender-informed security reclassification scale for women offenders* (Research Report R-167). Ottawa: Correctional Service of Canada.

Bonta, J., & Andrews, D.A. (2007). *Risk-need-responsivity model for offender assessment and rehabilitation* (User Report no. 2007-06). Ottawa: Public Safety Canada.

Bonta, J., Pang, B., & Wallace-Capretta, S. (1995). Predictor of recidivism among incarcerated female offenders. *The Prison Journal*, 75(3), 277–294.

Brennan, S. (2014). Canada's Mother-Child Program: Examining its emergence, usage and current state. *Canadian Graduate Journal of Sociology and Criminology*, 3(1), 11–33.

Brown, G.P., Hirdes, J.P., & Fries, B.E. (2015). Measuring the prevalence of current, severe symptoms of mental health problems in a Canadian correctional population: Implications for delivery of mental health services for inmates. *International Journal of Offender Therapy and Comparative Criminology*. 59(1), 27–50.

Brown, S.L., & Motiuk, L.L. (2005). *The Dynamic Factor Identification and Analysis (DFIA) component of the Offender Intake Assessment (OIA) process: A meta-analytic, psychometric and consultative review* (Research Report R-164). Ottawa: Research Branch, Correctional Service of Canada.

Burns, D.D. (1999). *The feeling good handbook* (Rev. ed.). New York: Plume/Penguin Books.

Canada, Task Force on Federally Sentenced Women. (1990). *Creating choices: Report of the task force on federally sentenced women*. Ottawa: Department of the Solicitor General.

Carson, E., & Anderson, E. (2016). *Bulletin: Prisoners in 2015*. U.S. Dept. of Justice Bureau of Justice Statistics. NCJ 2509229.

Correctional Service of Canada. (2008a). Women offender programs and issues. Study of the Mother-Child Program. Retrieved from http://www.csc-scc.gc.ca/publications/fsw/fsw24/fsw24e-eng.shtml.

Correctional Service of Canada. (2008b). Women offender programs and issues. Retrieved from http://www.csc-scc.gc.ca/publications/005007-5150-eng.shtml.

Correctional Service of Canada. (2014). Correctional programs. Retrieved from http://www.csc-scc.gc.ca/correctional-process/002001-2001-eng.shtml#s2.

Correctional Service of Canada. (2016). Commissioners Directive 768. Institutional Mother-Child Program. Retrieved from http://www.csc-scc.gc.ca/politiques-et-lois/768-cd-eng.shtml.

de Vogel, V., de Vries Robbé, M., van Kalmthout, W., & Place, C. (2012). Risk assessment of violent women; Development of the "Female Additional Manual" (FAM). *Tijdschr Psychiatr*, 54(4), 329–338.

Dimeff, L.A., Baer, J.S., Kivlahan, D.R., & Marlatt, G.A. (1999). *Brief alcohol screening and intervention for college students: A harm reduction approach*. New York: Guilford Press.

Dowden, C., & Andrews, D.A. (1999). What works for female offenders: A meta-analytic review. *Crime and Delinquency*, 45, 438–452.

Dowden, C., Serin, R., & Blanchette, K. (2001). *The application of the Community Intervention Scale to women offenders: Preliminary findings* (Research Report R-97). Ottawa: Research Branch, Correctional Service of Canada.

Fazel, S., Bains, P., & Doll, H. (2006). Substance abuse and dependence in prisoners: A systematic review. *Addiction*, 101, 181–191.

Folsom, J., & Atkinson, J.L. (2007). The generalizability of the LSI-R and the CAT to the prediction of recidivism in female offenders. *Criminal Justice and Behavior*, 34, 1044–1056.

Fortin, D. (2004). *Program strategy for women offenders*. Ottawa: Correctional Service of Canada.

Gagnon, R. (2004). Implementation of a supervision project for federally-sentenced women in Montreal. *Forum on Corrections Research*, 16(1), 13–14.

Gates, M., Dowden, C., & Brown, S.L. (1998). Community functioning. *Forum on Corrections Research*, 10(3), 35–37.

Gehring, K., Van Voorhis, P., & Bell, V. (2010). "What works" for female probationers? An evaluation of the Moving On program. *Women, Girls, and Criminal Justice*, 1, 6–10.

Gendreau, P., French, S., & Gionet, A. (2004). What works (what doesn't work): The principles of effective correctional treatment. *Journal of Community Corrections, 13,* 4–30.

Gobeil, R. (2008). *Staying out: Women's perceptions of challenges and protective factors in community reintegration* (Research Report R-201). Ottawa: Correctional Service Canada.

Gobeil, R., & Blanchette, K. (2007). Revalidation of a gender-informed security reclassification scale for women offenders. *Journal of Contemporary Criminal Justice, 23,* 296–309.

Gobeil, R., Blanchette, K., & Stewart, L. (2016). A meta-analytic review of correctional interventions for women offenders: Gender-neutral vs. gender-informed approaches. *Criminal Justice and Behavior, 43*(3), 301–322.

Greiner, L.E., Law, M.A., & Brown, S. (2015). Using dynamic factors to predict recidivism among women: A four-wave prospective study. *Criminal Justice and Behavior, 42*(5), 457–480.

Grove, W.M., & Meehl, P.E. (1996). Comparative efficiency of informal (subjective, impressionistic) and formal (mechanical, algorithmic) prediction procedures: The clinical–statistical controversy. *Psychology, Public Policy, and Law, 2,* 293–323.

Hannah-Moffat, K. (2006). Pandora's box: Risk/need and gender-responsive corrections. *Criminology and Public Policy, 5,* 183–192.

Hanson, R.K., & Harris, A.J.R. (2000). Where should we intervene? Dynamic predictors of sexual offense recidivism. *Criminal Justice and Behavior, 27,* 6–35.

Harris, A., Thompson, J., & Derkzen, D. (2015). *Assessment of Women Offender Correctional Programming (WOCP) outcomes* (Research Report R-374). Ottawa: Correctional Service of Canada.

Harris, G.T., Rice, M.E., Quinsey, V.L., & Cormier, C. (2015). *Violent offenders: Appraising and managing risk* (3rd ed.). Washington, DC: American Psychological Association.

Heney, J. (1990). *Report on self-injurious behaviour in the Kingston Prison for Women.* Ottawa: Correctional Service of Canada.

Hilton, N.Z., & Simmons, J.L. (2001). The influence of actuarial risk assessment in clinical judgments and tribunal decisions about mentally disordered offenders in maximum security. *Law and Human Behavior, 25,* 393–408.

Holtfreter, K., Reisig, M.D., & Morash, M. (2004). Poverty, state capital and recidivism among women offenders. *Criminology and Public Policy, 3,* 185–209.

Howerton, A., Byng, R., Campbell, J., Hess, D., Owens, C., & Aitken, P. (2007). Understanding help-seeking behaviour among male offenders: Qualitative interview study. *BMJ, 334,* 303–309.

Law, M. (2004). *A longitudinal follow-up of federally sentenced women in the community: Assessing the predictive validity of the dynamic characteristics of the Community Intervention Scale.* Unpublished doctoral dissertation, Carleton University, Ottawa.

Leschied, A.W. (2011). *The treatment of incarcerated mentally disordered women offenders: A synthesis of current research.* (Corrections Research: User Report). Ottawa: Public Safety Canada.

Linehan, M. (1993). *Cognitive-behavioral treatment of borderline personality disorder.* New York: Guilford Press.

Lipsey, M. (2009). The primary factors that characterize effective interventions with juvenile offenders: A meta-analytic overview. *Victims and Offenders, 4,* 124–147.

Lowenkamp, C.T., Latessa, E.J., & Smith, P. (2006). Does correctional program quality really matter? The impact of adhering to the principles of effective intervention. *Criminology and Public Policy, 5,* 201–220.

McConnell, A., Rubenfeld, S., Thompson. J., & Gobeil, R. (2014). *A profile of women under community supervision* (Research Report R-287). Ottawa: Correctional Service of Canada.

Oliver, M.E., Stockdale, K.C., & Wormith, J.S. (2014). Thirty years of research on the Level of Service scales: A meta-analytic examination of predictive accuracy and sources of variability. *Psychological Assessment, 26,* 156–176.

Pollack, S. (2005). Taming the shrew: Regulating prisoners through women-centered mental health programming. *Critical Criminology, 13,* 71–87.

Quinsey, V.L., & Ambtman, R. (1979). Variables affecting psychiatrists' and teachers' assessments of the dangerousness of mentally ill offenders. *Journal of Consulting and Clinical Psychology, 47,* 353–362.

Quinsey, V.L., Coleman, G., Jones, B., & Altrows, I. (1997). Proximal antecedents of eloping and reoffending among supervised mentally disordered offenders. *Journal of Interpersonal Violence, 12,* 794–813.

Reitano, J. (2017). Adult correctional statistics in Canada, 2015/2016. (Catalogue No. 85-002-X.) *Juristat.* Retrieved from http://www.statcan.gc.ca/pub/85-002-x/2017001/article/14700-eng.pdf.

Rettinger, L.J., & Andrews, D.A. (2010). General risk and need, gender specificity, and the recidivism of female offenders. *Criminal Justice and Behavior, 37*(1), 29–46.

Shaw, M. (1994). *Ontario women in conflict with the law: A survey of women in institutions and under community supervision in Ontario*. Toronto: Research Services, Strategic Policy and Planning Division, Ministry of the Solicitor General and Correctional Services.

Smith, P., Goggin, C., & Gendreau, P. (2002). *The effects of prison sentences and intermediate sanctions on recidivism: General effects and individual differences* (User Report 2002-01). Ottawa: Public Safety and Emergency Preparedness Canada.

Tam, K., & Derkzen, D. (2014). *Exposure to trauma among women offenders: A review of the literature* (Research Report R-333). Ottawa: Correctional Service of Canada.

Thompson, J., Lutfy, M., Derkzen, D., & Bertrand, M. (2015). *The needs of women offenders under community supervision* (Research Report R-338). Ottawa: Correctional Service of Canada.

Tripodi, S.J., Bledsoe, S.E., Kim, J.S., & Bender, K. (2011). Effects of correctional-based programs for female inmates: A systematic review. *Research on Social Work Practice, 21*(1), 15–31.

Van Voorhis, P., Wright, E.M., Salisbury, E.J., & Bauman, A. (2010). Women's risk factors and their contributions to existing risk/needs assessment: The current status of a gender-responsive supplement. *Criminal Justice and Behavior, 37*, 261–288.

Ward, T., Mesler, J., & Yates, P. (2007). Reconstructing the risk-need-responsivity model: A theoretical elaboration and evaluation. *Aggression and Violent Behavior, 12*, 208–228.

Wilton, G., & Stewart, L. (2015). *The additive effects of women offenders' revised participation in multiple correctional interventions* (Research Report R-369). Ottawa: Correctional Service of Canada.

Wright, E.M., Van Voorhis, P., Salisbury E.J., & Bauman, A. (2012). Gender-responsive lessons learned and policy implications for women in prison: A review. *Criminal Justice and Behavior, 39*(12), 1612–1632.

Zakaria, D., Allenby, K., Derkzen, D., & Jones, N. (2013). *Preliminary development of a dynamic risk assessment tool for women: An examination of gender neutral and gender specific variables* (Research Report R-280). Ottawa: Correctional Service of Canada.

PART III

Victimization and Criminalization

Ashley Smith

D. Scharie Tavcer

Coralee Smith, mother of Ashley Smith, 19, who choked herself to death in her segregation cell in 2007, speaks after testifying at an inquest into the tragedy in Toronto on Thursday, February 21, 2013. The family's lawyer, Julian Falconer, looks on.

The death of Ashley Smith while in the custody of the Correctional Service of Canada (CSC) is a stark reminder of the complex needs some female offenders have and corrections' inability to effectively deal with those issues.

Ashley Smith was a troubled 19-year-old young woman when she died in a segregation cell at the Grand Valley Institution for Women on October 19, 2007. Her legal troubles began at age 14 on a mischief charge for throwing crabapples at a mail carrier. From then onward she was moved 17 times, shuttled among 8 different prisons and treatment centres in less than a year, as officials tried to figure out how to manage her behaviour and treat her mental illness. She was not an easy inmate to manage. She verbally and physically assaulted correctional staff and she would regularly threaten suicide and strangle herself. When officers entered her cell, occasionally she would direct her rage at them.

> Whenever attempts to negotiate the removal of a ligature failed, staff would (on most occasions) enter Ms. Smith's cell and use force, as required, to remove it. This often involved the use of physical handling, inflammatory spray, or restraints. Ms. Smith was generally non-compliant with staff during these interventions … (grabbing, spitting, kicking, biting) occurred in circumstances when physical force was being applied against her by correctional staff [versus randomly at her own volition].

In 2007, she strangled herself while prison guards watched through the cell window, following the warden's orders not to enter the cell "if she's still breathing" (CHAIM Centre, 2015). The policy in Canada is to video-record all strip searches and use of force incidents. Three guards and one manager were charged and a wrongful death lawsuit was launched. The charges were eventually dropped, the lawsuit (with the Smith family) was settled, but a coroner's inquest happened in November and December 2012. Its mandate was to understand the factors leading to her death, in what way CSC was responsible, and how a similar situation can be avoided.

Correctional Investigator Howard Sapers also investigated the circumstances leading to her death. In his 2008 report, *A Preventable Death*, Mr. Sapers articulated the ways in which corrections officials violated the *Corrections and Conditional Release Act* in its care and treatment of Ashley Smith at the individual, institutional, regional, and national levels. His report revealed that Ms. Smith received virtually no treatment; a comprehensive treatment plan was never put into place despite almost daily contact with institutional psychologists; and attempts to obtain a full psychological assessment were thwarted, in part by the decision to constantly transfer Ms. Smith from one institution to another. Without a full and proper diagnosis, the correctional staff was working in the dark and most lacked any specialized mental health training. With time, Ms. Smith's self-injurious behaviours (primarily tying a ligature around her neck) became more frequent and increased in dangerousness. This, in turn, triggered even more security-focused responses from corrections, up until her death.

QUESTIONS TO CONSIDER

1. Read the Correctional Investigator's report and determine for yourself if things could have been done differently that day: http://www.oci-bec.gc.ca/cnt/rpt/oth-aut/oth-aut2008 0620info-eng.aspx.
2. Read the coroner's inquest: http://www.csc-scc.gc.ca/publications/005007-9009-eng.shtml. Do you think these recommendations are realistic and fair? Is anything missing?
3. Why is the Ashley Smith case important for correctional staff at all levels to review and study? Why is it important for post-secondary students to study?

REFERENCES

CHAIM Centre, University of Carleton. (2015). Prisons & mental health: Violence & truth-telling. Retrieved from https://carleton.ca/chaimcentre/2015/prisons-truth-telling/.

Correctional Service of Canada. (2013). Coroner's inquest touching the death of Ashley Smith. Verdict of Coroner's Jury—*The Coroners Act*—Province of Ontario. Retrieved from http://www.csc-scc.gc.ca/publications/005007-9009-eng.shtml.

Office of the Correctional Investigator. (2008). *A preventable death*. Retrieved from http://www .oci-bec.gc.ca/cnt/rpt/oth-aut/oth-aut20080620info-eng.aspx.

The legacy of Ashley Smith. (2013, February 15). *The National Post*. Retrieved from http://news .nationalpost.com/full-comment/national-post-editorial-board-the-legacy-of-ashley-smith.

Experiences of Female Offenders: The Intersection of Victimization and (re)Offending

Introduction

It has been said that we all begin as a *tabula rasa*—a blank slate upon which the experiences of our lives are then written. This concept may be useful to keep in mind as we explore in this chapter the kinds of experiences shared by many women who are in conflict with the law. Various types of childhood abuse (physical, sexual, emotional) and trauma, and both childhood and adult experiences of poverty, classism, racism, sexism, partner abuse, and victimization, are understood to negatively influence a woman's decision to engage in criminal behaviour. How people cope with these experiences is individualistic and is discussed further in Chapter 3. It must be emphasized that not *all* individuals who have had these experiences as children or adults go on to commit crime. And conversely, not every woman who has been in conflict with the law has been abused as a child, sexually assaulted, and/or lived in poverty. Although these experiences are shared by many women in prison, they are not shared by *all*. But for those women who are in the criminal justice system and who have had such negative experiences, the intersection of these elements is important to understand.

Many of the women and girls who come in conflict with the law have had adverse childhood experiences; they have been victims of physical, sexual, and/or emotional abuse, typically at the hands of an immediate family member. They may have run away, been homeless, been in foster care, and lived in poverty. Many have not finished high school, experience racism and/or sexism, and many have abusive relationships into adulthood. The research varies when it tries to seek a causal relationship between victimization and offending but no study, so far, has been able to prove a definitive causal link. But if we look at the women who are in our courts and prisons, it cannot be denied that most them have been victims (many times over) prior to their offending.

Comack and Balfour (2004) explored how violent women may be conceptualized as betraying their gender. Their behaviour and criminal acts do not easily fit into how society tends to think of violence. A woman who has committed a violent act may be seen to be an anomaly, because members of society (including the criminal justice system) tend to equate aggression with masculinity (Comack & Belfour, 2004). In this sense, a violent, aggressive woman fits neither the mental picture of a person who is usually aggressive, nor the concept of some preconceived notion of what it means to be a woman.

Women committing violent crime is explored in depth in Chapter 5, but the point to keep in mind as we progress through this chapter is that female offenders often tend to have also been victims in their childhood and adulthood, which intersects with other existing realities for them (race, ethnicity, poverty), resulting in a higher risk to engage in criminal behaviour, which is sometimes violent (such as killing an abusive partner).

Histories of Abuse—From Victim to Survivor to Offender

The fact that so many girls and women who find themselves in conflict with the law report histories of childhood abuse is well documented in many academic studies (Adelberg & Currie, 1993; Alarid & Cromwell, 2006; Browne, Miller, & Maguin, 1999; Chesney-Lind & Pasko, 2013; Chesney-Lind & Rodriguez, 1983; Comack, 2005; DeKeseredy, 2000; Heney & Kristiansen, 1997; Maeve, 2000; Mahony, 2011; Pollock, 2002; Radosh, 2002; Sapers, 2012; Sapers, 2013; Sinha, 2013; Sommers, 1995). Research confirms that adverse childhood experiences can lead to problems in adulthood. A strong correlation exists between adverse childhood experiences and adult addiction, violence, mental illness, and suicide. "[Seventy percent] of individuals in a detox program reported sexual and physical abuse histories" (Liebschutz et al., 2002, p. 126). We must not infer a cause–effect relationship; not all victims grow up to be offenders and not all offenders have had abusive histories. But there is a connection that is worth exploring and understanding.

And sadly, that connection begins in the homes of many children. Statistics Canada (2016b) reports that 80 percent of child and youth victims know their abuser, who is most likely to be a close family friend or a direct family member. A youth who is being abused may run away from home, struggle with addiction, take part in criminal activity, become homeless, attempt suicide, and/or become an abuser. And as an adult, they may continue to struggle with drugs, alcohol, depression, or other mental health issues, engage in criminal activity, and/or experience homelessness (Sheldon Kennedy Child Advocacy Centre, 2015), all of which can lead into the justice system.

In Alberta, the Sheldon Kennedy Child Advocacy Centre has a multidisciplinary approach to addressing childhood abuse. Their primary goal is to provide a coordinated and integrated response to child abuse by housing all relevant partners in one building (police, investigators, researchers, psychologists, clinicians, social workers, etc.). In 2014-15, the Centre assessed close to 1,500 infants, children, and youth, where 63 percent of those were females and sexual abuse was the most common type of abuse experienced (65 percent).

According to Statistics Canada's (2016a) police-reported data for 2013, 243.5 of every 100,000 children and youth were victims of family-related violence. As we know, family-related violence and sexual violence are two of the most under-reported offences. For various reasons, victims choose not to contact police—because of fear of retribution, not being believed, and more. Therefore, we must always consider the source of the statistic we are reading.

Physical assault was the most common type of family violence against children and youth (134.4 per 100,000 population), followed by sexual offences (73.9 per 100,000). While rates of physical assault against children and youth perpetrated by a family member were similar for males and females, rates of sexual assault against female children and youth were more than four times higher than their male counterparts.

Rates of family violence against children and youth in the territories tended to be higher than the provinces (Boyce, 2015). Nunavut had the highest rate of police-reported family violence (1,420.5 per 100,000 population), followed by the Northwest Territories (932.4), and Yukon (886.3). In the provinces, violence against children and youth were highest in Saskatchewan (461.4) and lowest in Ontario (161.8).

See Figure 7.1 for a variety of statistics about family violence in Canada in 2014.

As with most crimes, males were most often identified as the perpetrator of the violence against girls (79 percent). However, not all male perpetrators of violence against girls were adult men, as one-third (30 percent) of males accused were under the age of 18 years (Sinha, 2013).

- A child who suffers abuse may become violent, do poorly in school (they're 30 percent less likely to graduate from high school), and pull away from friends.
- A youth may run away from home, struggle with addiction, take part in criminal activity, become homeless (they're 26 times more likely to be homeless), attempt suicide, or even become an abuser.
- An adult may struggle with drugs, alcohol, depression, or other mental health issues, engage in criminal activity (they're twice as likely to be arrested), or experience homelessness.

In a 2007 prospective-cohorts design study, the intersection of race and gender with abuse history and crime was explored (Makarios, 2007). The study found support for abuse as a stronger predictor of violence for women, more so than for men, but no difference was found for abuse as a predictor across a variety of races. This work suggests that "although the effects of abuse may be specific between males and females, the effects of abuse within the female population [are] general" (Makarios, 2007, p. 111).

In comparison with the general population, the violence experienced in the lives of some incarcerated women has been described as both severe and pervasive (Blanchette & Brown, 2006; Browne et al., 1999). A relationship between childhood sexual abuse and later arrests for prostitution-related crimes has also been demonstrated (Bowen, 2013; Farley, 2005; Hughes, 2000; Raphael & Ellison, 2013; Widom & Ames, 1994), and others have postulated that a host of possible pathways to incarceration may stem from abusive experiences (Blanchette & Brown, 2006; Gilfus, 2002; Owen, Wells, & Pollock, 2017). These pathways, from victimization to incarceration, may include various processes that are seen to criminalize the efforts made to escape from childhood violence, or they may involve processes that serve to influence women's involvement in crime through their entrapment in violent relationships (Gilfus, 2002). In short, victimization can lead to offending and/or more victimization.

Conceptualizing Victims

When the term *crime victim* comes up during our daily conversations, it generally refers to a person harmed by a sexual assault, burglary, act of vandalism, or another form of interpersonal violence, such as homicide. The reality is that we all have been impacted by crime—either we have been a victim directly or we know someone who has been a victim. And for some women and girls, those victimization experiences seem to influence a direction toward criminal behaviour.

FIGURE 7.1 Family Violence in Canada, 2014

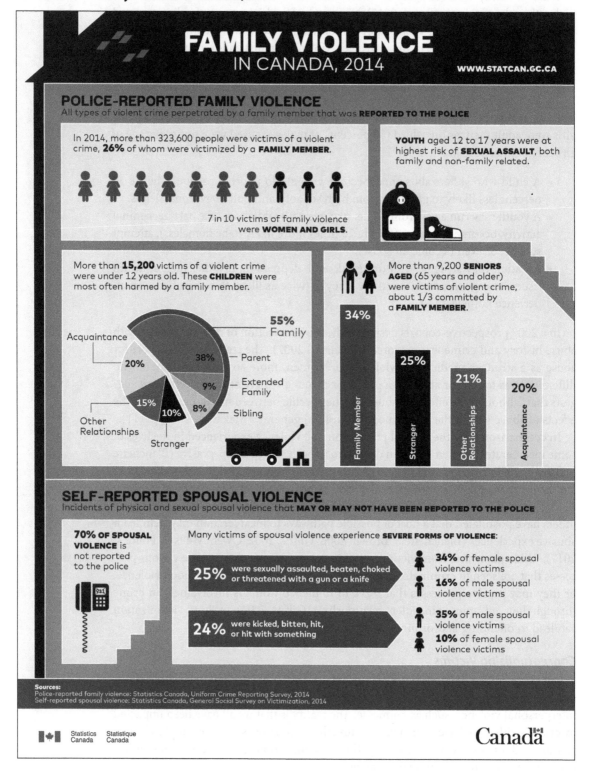

FAMILY VIOLENCE
IN CANADA, 2014

WWW.STATCAN.GC.CA

POLICE-REPORTED FAMILY VIOLENCE
All types of violent crime perpetrated by a family member that was **REPORTED TO THE POLICE**

In 2014, more than 323,600 people were victims of a violent crime, **26%** of whom were victimized by a **FAMILY MEMBER**.

7 in 10 victims of family violence were **WOMEN AND GIRLS**.

YOUTH aged 12 to 17 years were at highest risk of **SEXUAL ASSAULT**, both family and non-family related.

More than **15,200** victims of a violent crime were under 12 years old. These **CHILDREN** were most often harmed by a family member.

55% Family

Acquaintance
20%

38% — Parent

9% — Extended Family

15%

10%

8% — Sibling

Other Relationships

Stranger

More than 9,200 **SENIORS AGED** (65 years and older) were victims of violent crime, about 1/3 committed by a **FAMILY MEMBER**.

Family Member	Stranger	Other Relationships	Acquaintance
34%	25%	21%	20%

SELF-REPORTED SPOUSAL VIOLENCE
Incidents of physical and sexual spousal violence that **MAY OR MAY NOT HAVE BEEN REPORTED TO THE POLICE**

70% OF SPOUSAL VIOLENCE is not reported to the police

Many victims of spousal violence experience **SEVERE FORMS OF VIOLENCE**:

25% were sexually assaulted, beaten, choked or threatened with a gun or a knife

34% of female spousal violence victims

16% of male spousal violence victims

24% were kicked, bitten, hit, or hit with something

35% of male spousal violence victims

10% of female spousal violence victims

Sources:
Police-reported family violence: Statistics Canada, Uniform Crime Reporting Survey, 2014
Self-reported spousal violence: Statistics Canada, General Social Survey on Victimization, 2014

Statistics Canada   Statistique Canada

Canadä

Thirty years ago, Elias (1986) pointed out the importance of understanding how women conceptualize their own victimization, but we still seem to be hesitant to do so fully, even though numerous books and articles have documented the voices of incarcerated women relating their own accounts of their experiences of violence (Chesney-Lind & Rodriguez, 1983; Comack, 2005; Comack & Brickey, 2007; DeHart & Lynch, 2012; Gilfus, 1992; Maeve, 2000; Owen et al., 2017; Sered & Norton-Hawk, 2014; Sommers, 1995). This emphasis on asking women to describe how they conceptualize their violence in their own voice is a positive step toward understanding the intersection of why so many criminalized women have adverse victimization experiences.

Comack and Brickey (2007) noted a tendency to interpret women's violent behaviour in terms of three constructs that, as they point out, are different "yet not disconnected": women as "bad," "mad," or "victim" (p. 1). They were interested in identifying to what extent women who were criminalized identified with, or rejected, these constructs. They found that the women who were interviewed did, to varying extents, identify with these constructs. However, they did stress that "the women's experiences of violence—both their own and that which has been directed at them—have had a long-lasting impact on who they are" (p. 27). This sentiment echoes previous research with incarcerated women by Chesney-Lind & Rodriguez, 1983; Comack, 2005; Gilfus, 1992; Maeve, 2000; and Sommers, 1995.

Box 7.1 provides one controversial example of what Elias was talking about—the importance of listening to the women who live with these experiences. In September 2007, the Canadian government, led by Prime Minister Stephen Harper, eliminated funding to a national non-profit women's group that works to help end violence against women and other forms of female victimization across Canada. The National Association of Women and the Law (NAWL) vowed to use volunteers to keep up its efforts to combat violence against women, improve living conditions for those on low incomes, achieve pay equity, obtain funding for universal child care, and other causes. NAWL lost its funding despite a $13 billion federal budget surplus. The government slashed outlays for women's advocacy projects and eliminated the Court Challenges Program, which funded legal actions by rights advocates. The Tories said Status of Women Canada would no longer fund organizations pressing policy-makers to improve conditions for women. "The Harper government is trying to silence women's groups who speak out against its right-wing agenda," NAWL board member Pamela Cross said. "These are ideologically driven cuts that demonstrate a defective concept of women's equality and democracy" (Whittington, 2007).

This denunciation has far-reaching consequences. Not only does it convey the message that women's victimization (and resources to support them) is not a priority for government, it also reduces the venues toward which women (and their families) can find help. Such lack of support can have generational impacts, like what we see from descendants of the residential schools—individuals who aren't able to access support and treatment carry that trauma with them while they parent children who grow up in an environment that lacks necessary resources. By eliminating such supports, victims are "twice victimized"—first by violence and then by society's lack of social support.

BOX 7.1

Opposition MPs Denounced the Moves by the Harper Government

"Women are being silenced in Canada," Liberal MP Maria Minna (Beaches–East York) told the NAWL press conference. "How can we … say we are promoting rights for women in Afghanistan when our government is forcing women's organizations to close [in our own country]?"

New Democrat MP Irene Mathyssen said "the closure of NAWL will turn back the clock on women's equality in Canada."

NAWL, a non-profit legal reform organization set up in 1974, has, among other things, worked to strengthen laws dealing with rape, improve family law, and ensure women's equality was specifically included in the Charter of Rights. Cross said the group will continue by using volunteers, but that its effectiveness as a resource will be undercut by the closing of its office.

Heritage Minister José Verner told a news conference that NAWL might have some projects eligible for funding but that research and advocacy work would not qualify.

Source: Whittington, L. (2007, September 9). Women's group closes after losing its funding: Opposition MPs say Harper government "turning back clock." Toronto Star, p. AA12.

Related to what Elias stated above, entire categories of people sometimes (often if they are women) are not "allowed" to be crime victims. For example, one California police department stamped all reports of violent crimes against prostitutes as NHI—"No Human Involved"—and did not follow up on them (DeKeseredy & Schwartz, 2013). In Canada, it wasn't until Robert Pickton was arrested that people started asking why it took so long to investigate reports of missing women from Vancouver's Downtown Eastside. The Missing Women Commission of Inquiry (Oppal, 2012) was initiated to explain why and how the number of missing women accumulated, over two decades, without any investigative resolution. The Inquiry, which ended in 2013, revealed critical police failures and determined there existed a systemic bias and discrimination against Indigenous persons, prostitutes, and the drug-addicted homeless. Over a decade later, there is now a National Inquiry into the Missing and Murdered Indigenous Women and Girls of Canada. Apart from British Columbia, there are hundreds of cases of missing and murdered women that remain unsolved, with advocates asking if bias and discrimination has fuelled ignoring this reality. Further detail about this can be found in Chapter 10.

Experiences of Incarcerated Women

Gilfus (1992) used the life histories of women incarcerated in an American prison to illustrate the transition of some women "from victims to survivors to offenders" (p. 5). Two of the dominant themes that emerged in her analysis of the interviews were sexual abuse and incest and multiple types of abuse and neglect during childhood. One of the conclusions that she drew from this research was that prior violence was a strong factor in women's future criminalization. Moreover, Gilfus speculated that for some women, the strategies that they employed to survive such abuse represented the "beginning of a process of transition from victim to offender" (p. 12). Women in Canadian prisons report similar childhood realities.

In a survey of women who were under community supervision or in institutions in Ontario, Shaw (1994) found that 72 percent of the women indicated a history of physical abuse. In this same sample, nearly half (48 percent) reported having experienced sexual abuse. In total, more than three-quarters of the women surveyed reported a history of either physical or sexual abuse, and 70 percent indicated that they had experienced emotional abuse. Twenty years later, the statistics have not changed for the better. Across Canada, 85 percent of federally sentenced women have a history of physical abuse, while 68 percent have a history of sexual abuse (Sapers, 2012). This rate increases to 90 percent for Indigenous women (Canadian Human Rights Commission, 2003).

Comack (1996) has been quick to point out that there is a danger in looking at connections between abuse (or any other variable for that matter) and female offending, so as not to "pathologize" women's experiences without losing sight of the structural context in which they move (p. 82). The structural approach—to contextualize women's offending as a consequence of the kind of society (racist, capitalist, patriarchal) in which we live—allows for the focus of inquiry to shift from that of individual behaviour as an explanation of women's offending (Comack, 1996) to one on a macro-level (what is our society doing that permits violence against women and what is happening in our society that leads victimized women to crime?).

Irrespective of the role (or lack thereof) victimization plays in offending (and reoffending),[1] many women in our jails and prisons have high rates of victimization. This obliges questioning if we are to effectively manage and treat women and girl offenders.

Recidivism

Relative to men, women have lower rates of recidivism and pose far less risk to community safety. Only 2 percent of federally sentenced women are returned to prison for the commission of a new offence with less than 0.5 percent of them for a violent offence (Pollack, 2008). Most women whose parole is revoked are imprisoned for administrative breaches (versus committing another crime, let alone a violent crime) (Kong & AuCoin, 2008).

Regardless of the type of offences women commit (most commonly non-violent and/ or property offences), overall, they commit crime less so than men. The same is seen when we compare men and women and violent offences. For homicide, robbery, and assault, men on average commit four to five times the amount of violent offences than do women. For more information about recidivism, return to Chapter 6.

Female Youth

Because young males are more likely to offend than young females, more research and criminal justice attention has historically been paid to male youth offending. When young females come into conflict with the law, they are often seen as more deviant than males because they are presumed to be acting out against society's roles and expectations. Female offending has historically been a minor subset of male offending, not a phenomenon that needs to be theorized on its own. We argue that the unique characteristics of female youth and their (pervasive) childhood experiences warrants individualized theoretical and practical attention.

Girls are less likely to commit offences in a clear majority of criminal categories, but girls 15 to 18 years of age have higher levels of criminal activity (2,898/100,000) than adult women (631/100,000), although female youth crime is lower than their male counterparts (female youth: 2,147/100,000 versus male youth: 10,084/100,000). Since the late 1990s, the rates of custodial and open custodial sentences for both male and female youth has remained steady separately and in comparison to one another.

Indigenous Women and Girls

Indigenous females in Canada are proportionately more likely to experience physical and/or sexual abuse as a child than their male counterparts (14 percent versus 5 percent) and Indigenous people (9 percent) are proportionately more likely than non-Indigenous people (4 percent) to have been a victim of spousal violence (Mahony, 2011). The overall rate of violent victimization among Indigenous people was more than double that of non-Indigenous people in 2014 (163 incidents per 1,000 people versus 74 incidents per 1,000 people). Regardless of the type of violent offence (or youth versus adult statistics), rates of victimization are almost always higher for Indigenous people than for non-Indigenous people.

Indigenous females make up 4 percent of the total female population in Canada, but are disproportionately represented as youth and adults in our prisons. In 2009, female Indigenous youth accounted for 44 percent of admissions to open or secure custody, 34 percent of admissions to remand, and 31 percent of admissions or intakes to probation. The over-representation is greatest in the Yukon and Northwest Territories (100 percent), Saskatchewan (93 percent), and Manitoba (91 percent). Also in 2009, 35 percent of adult women (and 23 percent of men) admitted to sentenced custody identified as an Indigenous person. Indigenous adult women comprised more than 85 percent of admissions of provincial sentenced custody in Saskatchewan and Manitoba and just over half in Alberta, yet Indigenous adults represented only 11 percent, 12 percent, and 5 percent respectively of those provincial general populations (Mahony, 2011).

In 2014, one in four admissions (24 percent) to provincial/territorial corrections were of Indigenous persons; Indigenous adults accounted for 20 percent of admissions to federal corrections; and Indigenous females accounted for 36 percent of admissions to provincial/territorial custody, compared to 25 percent for male admissions (Statistics Canada, 2016a). For more information about this over-representation, see Chapter 9.

Violence Against Lesbian, Bisexual, and Transgender Women

Canada's governments have adopted various laws to protect its minority groups, such as provisions under article 718.2 of the *Criminal Code* calling for more severe sentences for hate-motivated crimes. People who self-identified as homosexual or bisexual in the 2013 General Social Survey (GSS) had the highest violent victimization rate at 207 incidents per 1,000 population, compared to 69 per 1,000 for heterosexuals (Perreault, 2015). However, police-reported data in 2013 reveal something different. Of all police-reported hate crimes, only 16 percent were those based on a hatred of someone's sexual orientation. The highest violent victimization was for hate crimes against someone's race or ethnicity (51 percent) (Allen, 2015).

What this illustrates is that hate crimes against minority groups do occur, but also that for certain types of violent crimes, people choose not to report their victimization to police. Perhaps this is out of fear, or from a perception that society and the criminal justice system are less concerned with women, and/or gay or trans women.

Factors That Impact Victimization and (re)Offending

The Correctional Service of Canada employs a variety of case management and assessment tools to assist offenders in developing effective treatment plans aimed at reducing their likelihood of reoffending once released. One of the goals is to identify and distinguish between an offender's criminogenic and non-criminogenic needs.

Criminogenic factors are those that increase or impact an offender's likelihood to commit crime. Such factors can be adverse childhood experiences, lack of education, lack of employability, addiction, and/or mental illness (see Chapter 6 for more detail). Some factors can be changed and are called dynamic factors (how I interact with society); whereas, those that we cannot change (e.g., the number of times I was arrested last year) are called static factors.

What we understand is that these criminogenic risk factors can also be considered experiences of victimization. In women and girls, they intersect and interact with each other in a way that makes it difficult to separate victim and offender. Women in our criminal justice system are most commonly a combination of both factors.

Racism and Discrimination

Issues pertaining to racism experienced by women who are Indigenous or another visible minority are covered in depth in Chapters 3 and 9. Therefore, the coverage of racism is cursory in this chapter. Gilfus (1992) reported that a common theme of racial violence emerged in her dialogues with incarcerated women. According to the Correctional Service of Canada's *Creating Choices* report, some of the Indigenous female inmates interviewed believed they had been targets of racism in the prison and experienced discrimination. Further, it was their perception that few staff were sensitive to their cultural practices and backgrounds (Bush-Baskette, 2004; Canada, TFFSW, 1990).

Pollock (2002) discussed how the construct of dependency has been used as a means of social control in and out of prisons. She noted that many of the Caribbean-Canadian women with whom she spoke reported that their criminal behaviour had occurred to avoid having to be dependent on anyone—including the state, an intimate partner, a friend, or a relative. Pollock noted that approximately 10 percent of women incarcerated federally were black and, as is the case with Indigenous women, black women were over-represented within the prison populations—provincially and federally (Canada, TFFSW, 1990).

Drug and Alcohol Abuse

The fact that a large percentage of women involved in the criminal justice system have had some association with drug or alcohol use is well documented (CAEFS, 2016; Canadian Centre on Substance Abuse & Pernanen, 2002; Lo, 2004; Owen et al., 2017; Sapers, 2013; Sered & Norton-Hawk, 2014). Rarely do we see incarcerated women whose histories do not involve substances.

A survey about drug and alcohol use was conducted (Lightfoot & Lambert, 1991, 1992) at the Kingston Prison for Women (which closed in 1995). A total of 80 women agreed to take part in this research:

- their mean age was 34 years;
- most were single;

- few reported having obtained education beyond high school;
- the majority (62 percent) had children;
- most reported that their work prior to incarceration had been unskilled labour;
- compared with male offenders, the women reported lower levels of alcohol dependence, as measured by the Alcohol Dependence Scale developed by H.A. Skinner (1982). Most of the women (72.5 percent) were classified as having low levels of dependence on alcohol as measured by the ADS (Lightfoot & Lambert, 1992).
- for most of the women, family problems predominated, followed by legal, work, and health problems;
- about two-thirds of the women reported drug use in the six months prior to the commission of their index offence (the offence that resulted in the current prison term);
- in comparison with male offenders, similar proportions of women were reporting substantial and severe levels of substance abuse problems, but more women scored as having "no problems" with drug use than did men. And nearly half of the sample of women stated that to quit using drugs, they would have needed some sort of professional intervention.

Decades later, drug and alcohol abuse remain issues for federally incarcerated women, but a myriad of other issues concurrently exist for women before and during their incarceration (Gobeil, 2009; Grant & Gileno, 2008, as cited in Matheson, Doherty, & Grant, 2009; OCI, 2016):

- more than half of all female offenders have identified a mental health issue compared to 26 percent of male offenders;
- more than 70 percent are mothers with children under age 18;
- 68 percent report being sexually abused and 86 percent physically abused prior to their incarceration;
- 52 percent are serving a sentence of between two to four years;
- a higher proportion of female offenders reported that they had completed high school or equivalent before incarceration (35 percent) compared to men (25 percent);
- 80 percent of female offenders in Canadian federal institutions have substance abuse problems.

Many readers would likely not take issue with the statement that the abuse of alcohol and/or drugs can have devastating effects on the individuals involved, on their friends, families, peers, and communities, and on society as a whole. Drug-related charges are only one way in which illegal substances are directly related to criminal behaviour. Being in possession of a small amount of a controlled substance is, in and of itself, a crime known as possession (*Controlled Drugs and Substances Act*, s. 4), and affects a minority of all those who are charged with drug-related crimes. It is important to note that many court cases deal with charges related to cannabis—more than half of all completed drug-related cases in adult criminal court in each province, with the exception of British Columbia (32 percent). In total, 85 percent of accused persons in completed drug-related adult court cases were male, and for both males and females, the type of drug most frequently involved varied by age: cannabis-related cases for male youth (79 percent) and female youth (66 percent of such cases) (Statistics Canada, 2013).

As our country moves toward legalizing possession of small amounts of cannabis (the *Cannabis Act* currently before Parliament), it will be interesting to study its effect on drug charges and convictions across the provinces.

Links between victimization and substance abuse in criminalized women have also been widely noted (Cotter, Greenland, & Karam, 2015; Owen et al., 2017; Sered & Norton-Hawk, 2014), and some suggest that increased rates of intimate partner violence may also be related to women's involvement with substances and other illegal behaviours (Browne et al., 1999).

James (2004, as cited in DeHart & Lynch, 2012) reported findings based on personal interviews with nearly 7,000 jail inmates in 2002. Female inmates reported higher rates of both physical (45 percent) and sexual abuse (36 percent) than male inmates (11 percent and 4 percent, respectively), and about 10 percent of women and 1 percent of men had experienced both types of abuse. For men, the majority of abusers were parents or guardians, while for women, the majority were relationship partners (James, 2004, as cited in DeHart & Lynch, 2012).

Others have suggested that substance abuse may serve as a coping strategy for those who face struggles associated with street life or an abusive relationship (Flores, 2016; Gilfus, 2002). Comack (1996) notes that "most of the women I spoke with reported that they had problems with drugs and/or alcohol" and that for a number of women, they were able to make some direct link between their substance use and their conflicts with the law (p. 119). In a related observation, for some women, it was among that drug subculture at school that they "found their first feeling of acceptance and belonging" (Gilfus, 1992, p. 8).

In addition, the conceptualization of "women as victims" may be problematic because it has been thought to mirror the same kinds of "us" versus "them" dimensions that have plagued the criminal justice system, such as those of law abider/law breaker and victim/offender (Comack, 1999). The following quote succinctly illustrates the major problem with supporting such dualistic thinking: "So long as women are recognized only as victims and not as active agents, there is little need to embrace or integrate feminist analyses into the criminological agenda" (Comack, 1999, p. 165). Although acknowledging how a history of victimization may affect the lives of criminalized women is necessary, "putting all of one's eggs in one basket" is dangerous when attempting to understand a complexly determined outcome, such as that of becoming criminalized.

Others have pointed to the systemic way in which the concept of victim has been twisted to fit the agenda of those who serve to benefit from pathologizing and individualizing crimes of women (Maidment, 2006). Maidment challenges the way in which women's crime is conceptualized by the Canadian criminal justice system, and more specifically, the prison system. In her analysis, Maidment clearly illustrates how the language that is seen to dominate "the system" serves to both pathologize women's involvement in crime and, at the same time, individualize it so that it can then be "treated" by those employed within that same system. She stresses that this practice occurs in the absence of any kind of meaningful contextual analysis, which is a serious flaw in the current system. Maidment (2006) clearly emphasizes a need for those involved in the academic study of criminalized women

to reverse our preoccupation with privileged accounts of knowledge which guide our research and policy agendas and focus our attention to seeing the world from the perspective
of those with first-person knowledge of the racist, classist, heterosexist, and gendered ways
in which our societal institutions operate. It is the thinking of those with a vested interest in
promulgating an individualistic and pathological approach to treating those on the margins
which is most urgently in need of correction. (p. 53)

Although Maidment (2006) has very clearly identified issues related to what she has
termed the *individualization* and *pathologization* of women by the current system,
women in the criminal justice system remain in need of assistance to reduce the probability that they will come into conflict with the law again. As discussed by Jill Atkinson in
Chapter 6, the assessment and treatment of criminalized women in Canada is an area
that has received some significant attention in recent years (Blanchette & Brown, 2006).

Poverty and Financial Stress

Prior to a discussion about the impact that financial stress may or may not have on the
lives of criminalized women, the reader should be aware of some staggering statistics
related to poverty in general.

In Canada, one in seven (or 4.9 million) people live in poverty and almost one in
four women live at or below the poverty line, as measured by the low income cut-offs
(LICOs) used by Statistics Canada (Lochhead & Scott, 2000). Approximately 2.5 million
women (23 percent of women over age 15) were living in poverty during 1993 or 1994
(Lochhead & Scott, 2000). Two decades later, 21 percent of single mothers live in poverty
(compared to 7 percent of single fathers) with an average income of $42,300, or 70 per-
cent of the average $60,400 income of male lone-parent families. In 2010, women aged
25 to 54 earned an average of $52,500 (versus $70,700 by men) (Williams, 2010), accounting for about 72 cents for every dollar earned by a man (Canada Without Poverty,
2017; Morissette, Picot, & Lu, 2013; Moyser, 2017).

About 606,000 children lived in low-income families in 2008, unchanged from 2007
but 29 percent fewer than in 2003; in addition, 36 percent of all children (about 218,000)
living in low-income families lived in a lone-parent family headed by a woman (Williams,
2010).

Although being poor is not a prerequisite for criminal behaviour, and certainly not
all people living in poverty commit crime, we cannot ignore the strain that poverty puts
on people under certain circumstances. To draw a link between conditions of economic
strife and criminal behaviour makes intuitive sense, especially for certain types of
crimes, such as theft, fraud, and prostitution-related offences, and it can be seen in men
as well as women. Marital status also plays a role in risk of victimization and offending
(DeKeseredy, Dragiewicz, & Schwartz, 2017; DeKeseredy & Schwartz, 2013), including
that certain cultures also subscribe to antiquated notions of gender roles. The man's role
as the economic provider is not only part of many women's expectations, but is still
fundamental to most men's self-identity (Adams & Coltrane, 2008; Conway, 2001;
DeKeseredy & Schwartz, 2013; Edin, 2000). And when that gender norm is not met,
we know that women whose male partners suffer from job instability are three times
as likely to be victims of intimate violence, a situation that worsens when the couple
lives in a financially disadvantaged neighbourhood (DeKeseredy, Alvi, Schwartz, &
Tomaszewski, 2003; Edin, 2000; Elias, 1986; Fox & Benson, 2006).

DeKeseredy et al.'s (2003) *Quality of Neighbourhood Life Survey* was administered to residents of six public housing estates in the west end of a metropolitan centre in eastern Ontario. Approximately 19 percent of the women stated that they had been physically assaulted by intimate partners in the year before the study. This figure is much higher than uncovered by the US National Violence Against Women Survey that revealed only 1.3 percent of women reported they had been physically assaulted by intimate partners (Tjaden & Thoenes, 2000). One could easily dismiss the discrepancy by arguing that these two surveys used different methods and thus obtained different results. Nevertheless, Renzetti and Maier's (2002) New Jersey study provides further support for the assertion that public housing women are at higher risk than their more affluent counterparts (Venkatesh, 2003): 50 percent of the women they interviewed reported victimization. As Holzman, Hyatt, and Dempster (2001) remind us, "demographic, economic, and geographic factors associated with high incidence of violent victimization of women appear to find a nexus in public housing" (p. 665).

Canadian research has also illustrated the importance of economics in the choices of crimes. Pollack (2000) has emphasized the experiences of the incarcerated Caribbean-Canadian women she interviewed, and suggested that their "lawbreaking is often an attempt to avoid dependency and to provide for the various family members who are in fact *dependent upon them* [emphasis in original]" (p. 75). Most of the women she interviewed were convicted of crimes (shoplifting, drug importation, drug trafficking, frauds) that are, more often than not, economically motivated. Many of the women were very clear in drawing a causal relationship between financial strain and their criminal behaviour, since their income did not come close to what was needed to support themselves and their families. The following quote from R.J., one of the women Pollack (2000) interviewed, speaks volumes:

> So all the Black women I know are in this institution, they're here for financial gain. None of us are suffering from the norm of being a drug addict or being sexually molested by our father … We're in here purely for financial gain. We don't fit the stereotype of the "normal" inmate that's in here. We're here for *financial gain*. (p. 76; emphasis in original)

Education and Economics

There is also a link between education and employment and crime: the higher a woman's education, the higher the likelihood that she will be employed (Moyser, 2017; Statistics Canada, 2003). But what if her income (74 percent of a male's income) is not sufficient to support her and her family?

A study in 2006 demonstrated that three-quarters of women who had a university degree were employed in a paid position; 59 percent employment for women with a high school diploma; and 38 percent employment for women with some high school education (Statistics Canada, 2003). By 2015, higher levels of educational attainment matter more for women's employment than they do for men's: 69.3 percent for women with a high school diploma compared to 83.1 percent for those with a university degree; 81.9 percent for men with a high school diploma and 89.9 percent for those with a university degree (Moyser, 2017). Imprisoned women also have much lower employment rates than incarcerated men: in 1996, 80 percent of the women serving time in a federal facility were unemployed at the time of admission, compared to 54 percent of men (CAEFS, 2016).

High educational attainment does not translate into a guarantee that a woman will not be poor (or victimized or abused), but certain protective factors are found to be associated with having an education, albeit of less influence today than perhaps in the past (Lochhead & Scott, 2000).

Offenders in general have lower levels of education than individuals in the general population. In 1993/94, 70 percent of newly admitted federal offenders tested below the grade 8 literacy equivalency while more than four in five new inmates (86 percent) scored below grade 10 (Boe, 1998). In 1998/99, approximately one-third (35 percent) of female inmates in provincial-territorial facilities had a grade 9 education or less, and about half of female federal inmates (48 percent) had a grade 9 education or less. By 2006, 44 percent of all offenders who were 25 years or older at the time of admission had never completed high school (versus 21 percent of those of similar age in the general population) (Kong & AuCoin, 2008; Statistics Canada, 2012).

Relationship Violence

Our society has become a place where it is routine to ask why do women stay in an abusive relationship instead of asking why do men abuse women. Our culture perpetuates blame and shame directed at victims, more than it criticizes how childhood abuse leads us to problems in adulthood.

There are many reasons, unique to each woman and circumstance, that explain why women stay in abusive relationships. Let us not forget the prevalence and frequency of the fact that many young children (boys and girls) experience abuse or witness violence growing up that basically educates them that solving problems with violence is common and normal, even in love relationships.

For adult women in abusive relationships, it is not easy to pack up and walk away, with or without kids.

Even at young ages, boys can develop strong masculinist and pro-abuse attitudes, as they are heavily influenced by the ideology of familial patriarchy, which is a key determinant of various types of woman abuse within various types of intimate relationships (DeKeseredy & Schwartz, 2013).

▶ WHAT DO YOU THINK?

What behaviours are considered typically female and typically male? In what ways has society taught us that it's "natural" for men to be more physical and to express their emotions differently from women? (Think back to when you were in primary school.)

In 2011, intimate partners, including spouses and dating partners, were the most common perpetrators of violence against women (45 percent), followed by acquaintances or friends (27 percent), strangers (16 percent), and non-spousal family members (12 percent). In contrast, in violent crimes against men, intimate partners were the least common perpetrators (12 percent) versus strangers and friends or acquaintances, who were the most common (39 percent and 40 percent, respectively) (Sinha, 2013, p. 14).

Menard (2001) is one of many feminist scholars who assert that the physical abuse of women occurs "in all demographic and social groups, cutting across age, race, ethnicity, sexual orientation, and economic circumstances" (p. 708, as cited in DeKeseredy

& Schwartz, 2013). Although her contention is factually true, assault is not spread equally among these groups (Burczycka, 2016; DeKeseredy & Schwartz, 2013; Sokoloff & Dupont, 2005). Some women are at higher risk than are others—such as those married or cohabitating, those with drug/alcohol addiction, those who are poor, uneducated, or homeless—as noted above.

There are also different rates of relationship violence among the provinces and territories, and even among cities. In 2013, the national average was 252.9 per 100,000 population. Ontario (166.9 per 100,000 population), Prince Edward Island (196.3), British Columbia (231.2), and Nova Scotia (235.4) recorded the lowest rates of police-reported family violence. In contrast, Saskatchewan (489.4 per 100,000 population) and Manitoba (375.8) recorded the highest rates of the provinces. The rates in the territories were even higher: Northwest Territories was 2,020.2 per 100,000, Nunavut was 2,768.7 per 100,000, and Yukon recorded a rate of 903.9 per 100,000 population (Statistics Canada, 2016a, p. 8).

Among cities, Ottawa–Gatineau recorded the highest rate (327.9 per 100,000) of police-reported family violence in 2013, followed by Saguenay (314.3), Québec City (291.4), Montréal (281.5), and Trois-Rivières (276). The lowest rates of family violence were reported in Guelph (129.8), St. Catharines–Niagara (132), and London (134). In comparison, the national rate among cities stood at 196.5 per 100,000 (Statistics Canada, 2015, pp. 17–18). See Figure 7.2 for data about domestic conflict in Calgary.

► **WHAT DO YOU THINK?**

What would make it difficult for you to quickly leave your current living situation—even if it is a happy one? What things might make it even more difficult or complicated for a woman to leave an abusive relationship (e.g., pets, kids, rental lease, etc.)?

Models of Relationship Violence

A variety of models have been put forth by researchers to help understand the causes of relationship violence. Walker's (1979) influential work on the cycle of violence experienced by battered women explained it as occurring in three predictable phases. It begins with a period of tension-building (can be hours, days, or weeks in length), during which time the woman senses that a battering incident is imminent. The specific act of violence constitutes the second phase and is immediately followed by the final phase, which is commonly referred to as the "honeymoon phase," characterized with calm and loving gestures, gifts, and promises. Although this model was used by practitioners for years, it is highly debated among many researchers.

Another model to understanding relationship violence is the Duluth Model. Widely accepted by researchers and practitioners, the Duluth Model can be characterized as a gender-based cognitive–behavioural approach to counselling and/or educating men who are mandated by the courts to domestic violence treatment programs. The curriculum exposes the multitude of behaviours in what is referred to as the "Power and Control Wheel" (see Figure 7.3). It attempts to challenge the denial or minimization associated with abusive behaviour that is particularly prevalent among court-ordered

FIGURE 7.2 Calgary Police Service Infographic About Domestic Conflict

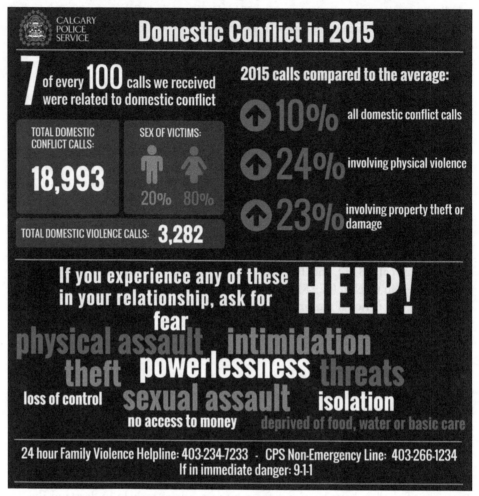

men (Gondolf, 2007) by itemizing the vast array of means and methods used to exert power and control over another.

Marital Status

Canadians in general perceive family and household settings as "havens in a hostile world" (Lasch, 1977, p. 564 as cited in DeKeseredy, 2010); whereas in fact, the most dangerous place (according to statistics) for a heterosexual woman is in the home she shares with her male partner. Absolutely there are stranger attacks and unknown predatory offenders who commit violence against women, but that reality is fractional. What US sociologists Richard Gelles and Murray Straus stated 20 years ago still holds true for Canadian (and American) women and girls today: "You are more likely to be physically assaulted, beaten, and killed in your own home at the hands of a loved one than anyplace else, or by anyone else in society" (p. 18, as cited in DeKeseredy, 2010). Many people find this statement hard to believe or they choose not to believe it; after all, we prefer to "stay out of my neighbour's business" and to "keep family issues within the

FIGURE 7.3   The Power and Control Wheel

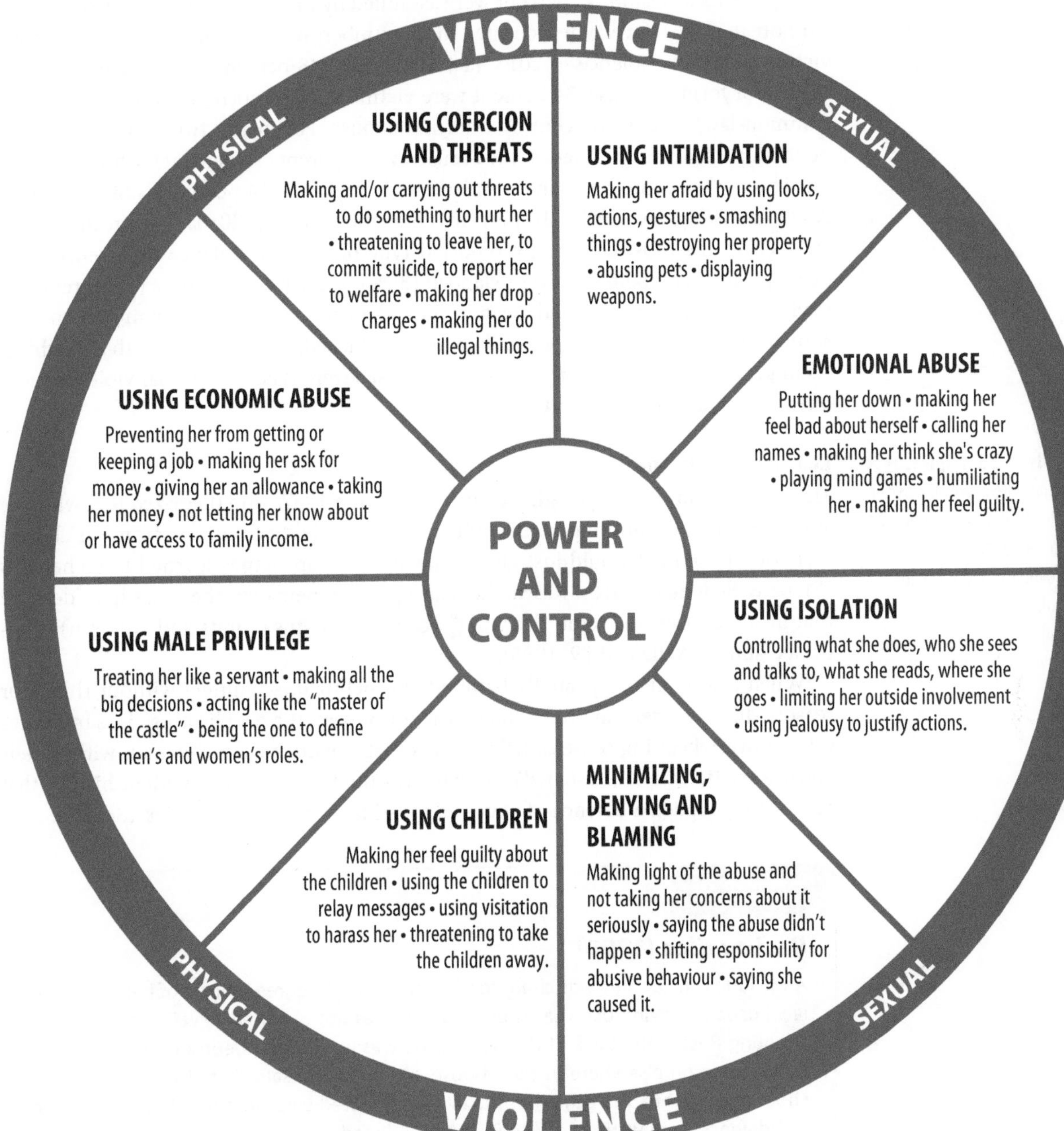

VIOLENCE

PHYSICAL

SEXUAL

USING COERCION AND THREATS

Making and/or carrying out threats to do something to hurt her • threatening to leave her, to commit suicide, to report her to welfare • making her drop charges • making her do illegal things.

USING INTIMIDATION

Making her afraid by using looks, actions, gestures • smashing things • destroying her property • abusing pets • displaying weapons.

USING ECONOMIC ABUSE

Preventing her from getting or keeping a job • making her ask for money • giving her an allowance • taking her money • not letting her know about or have access to family income.

EMOTIONAL ABUSE

Putting her down • making her feel bad about herself • calling her names • making her think she's crazy • playing mind games • humiliating her • making her feel guilty.

POWER AND CONTROL

USING MALE PRIVILEGE

Treating her like a servant • making all the big decisions • acting like the "master of the castle" • being the one to define men's and women's roles.

USING ISOLATION

Controlling what she does, who she sees and talks to, what she reads, where she goes • limiting her outside involvement • using jealousy to justify actions.

USING CHILDREN

Making her feel guilty about the children • using the children to relay messages • using visitation to harass her • threatening to take the children away.

MINIMIZING, DENYING AND BLAMING

Making light of the abuse and not taking her concerns about it seriously • saying the abuse didn't happen • shifting responsibility for abusive behaviour • saying she caused it.

PHYSICAL

SEXUAL

VIOLENCE

family." This culture of silence perpetuates family violence as a social problem and prevents people from seeking help.

Separated and divorced women are more at risk of violence than married women (DeKeseredy et al., 2017). Women tell us that "they were never more frightened than in the days, weeks, or months after they moved out" (Stark, 2007, p. 116, as cited in DeKeseredy, 2013). The 2004 Canadian General Social Survey (GSS) data showed that, among women with a former husband or male cohabiting partner who had been violent during the relationship, 49 percent were assaulted by their ex-partners after separation (Mihorean, 2005). Over a decade later, those numbers have not changed much. Among victims of family violence in 2013, just under half (48 percent) were victimized by a current or former spouse: 34 percent were victimized by a current spouse (married or common-law), and 14 percent by a former spouse. For nearly two in ten victims of police-reported family violence, the accused was a parent (17 percent), while for about one in ten, the accused was an extended family member (14 percent), sibling (11 percent), or his/her own child (10 percent) (Statistics Canada, 2016a). According to the 2014 GSS, "the most commonly-reported type of spousal violence experienced was being pushed, grabbed, shoved or slapped (35%). A quarter of victims (25%) reported having been sexually assaulted, beaten, choked, or threatened with a gun or a knife. A similar proportion (24%) reported having been kicked, bit, hit, or hit with something. As in previous years, women reported the most severe types of spousal violence more often than men" (Burczcka, 2016, p. 3).

Learned Helplessness

learned helplessness
A mental state in which a person accepts that nothing they do can control or stop the painful situation(s) and subsequently become unable or unwilling to avoid those painful encounters even if they are "escapable."

This is a concept that was originated by Seligman in 1967, who theorized that when an animal learns that nothing it did influenced their ability to escape from an abusive scenario, the animal would just give up trying to escape—they learned to be helpless (Maier & Seligman, 2016). Researchers and practitioners over the years have debated that in some cases, the same "learning" occurs in victims (adults and children) of repeated abuse (Walker, 1979, 1995).

When a woman is repeatedly battered and belittled, seemingly without rhyme or reason, she no longer can predict how to avoid/prevent the next beating. This translates into an overwhelming sense of helplessness that constrains some women within their abusive relationships. *R v Lavallee* (1990) was the first case in Canadian history that successfully argued a defence of abuse as a justifiable excuse to murder. (See Box 7.2.)

BOX 7.2

R v Lavallee (1990)

Angelique Lyn Lavallee was charged with the second-degree murder of her common-law husband, Kevin Rust. That she killed Rust was not disputed. Lavallee admitted to shooting Rust in the back of the head as he was leaving her bedroom to return to a party going on elsewhere in their house, although she said that she was aiming to shoot over his head to scare him. What was debated was whether Lavallee acted in self-defence from years of abuse Rust had inflicted upon her (Sheehy, 2000, p. 198).

Shaffer (1997) raised concerns that the Supreme Court's decision could have negative repercussions for women. Originally labelled battered woman syndrome, the view that battered women had some sort of a syndrome (i.e., disease) could perpetuate a stereotype of how an abused woman should act and look like. And more specifically for women of colour, Tang (2003) asserts that women who don't fit the mould of a passive and helpless victim run the risk of not having their claims of self-defence heard fairly.

Following the *Lavallee* decision, the Canadian Association of Elizabeth Fry Societies lobbied for four years to convince the federal Minister of Justice to have an *en bloc* review of cases in which women had been convicted of killing their partners, both before and after the *Lavallee* decision (Sheehy, 2000). Ninety-eight women applied to have their cases included in the self-defence review by Judge Ratushny. Because of the exclusion criteria used, only 14 women were interviewed for the review, and in the end, only seven were given some sort of recommendation of relief (Sheehy, 2000). The result was that "no women were released from prison because of the SDR [self-defence review]" (Sheehy, 2000, p. 198).

Women's Emergency Shelters

Hundreds of millions of dollars are spent to operate Canada's shelters (Taylor-Butts, 2007) and yet the numbers of abused women and children serviced continues to grow. In 2005-06, approximately 75,000 women and children used a shelter (Taylor-Butts, 2007). In 2009/2010, 593 shelters provided a combined total of 11,461 beds, 757 more beds than in 2007/2008 (Canadian Network of Women's Shelters & Transition Houses, 2015). In 2013/2014, 120,000 women and children used a shelter across Canada (Beattie & Hutchins, 2015).

There are fewer services provided by shelters that exclusively serve villages and rural communities, and 58 percent of shelters indicate that they require additional and/or improved services to meet client needs (e.g., child care, outreach, affordable housing, and housing resources, etc.).

Without a safe place to go to, many women end up homeless, couch surf among friends or family, or stay in the abusive home. Limited resources, especially in rural areas, end up as factors that impact women's victimization risk—sometimes staying (in an abusive relationship) is the only option, especially if society continues to blame her for the abuse in the first place.

Sexual Violence

Sexual assault is defined as violating the sexual integrity of an individual and includes behaviours from touching and groping through to forced intercourse (s. 265, *Criminal Code*). Rape laws in Canada were revised in 1986, which broadened the scope of the definition and expanded rape into three categories, depending on the severity of the incident (ss. 271–273). More specifically, level 1 sexual assault criminalizes assault of a sexual nature that violates the sexual integrity of a person. Sexual assault with a weapon or causing bodily harm (level 2) criminalizes sexual assault that involves a weapon, bodily harm, or threats to cause bodily harm to a person. Lastly, aggravated sexual assault (level 3) criminalizes sexual assault that wounds, maims, disfigures, or endangers the life of another person (Boyce, 2015).

In 2014, there were 20,700 sexual assaults reported to police, the majority (98 percent) of which were classified as level 1 sexual assault. Police-reported sexual assaults decreased in almost all provinces and territories between 2013 and 2014, except for Yukon (+6 percent) and Saskatchewan (+4 percent).

It is important to note that this number is not a true representation of sexual assault in Canada, because (1) many people do not report their victimization to police; and

(2) these statistics represent only those incidents which were reported to police. Self-reported victimization data confirm those points in that 88 percent of sexual assaults experienced by Canadians aged 15 years and older are *not* brought to the attention of police (Perreault, 2015).

In addition to the expanded categories, two other key changes in the law were made. The definition now included the fact that men as well as women can be victims (and perpetrators) of sexual assault, and it removed the exemption given to husbands. Where once the law implied that husbands could not be charged with sexual assault against their wives, today our laws permit police to lay charges against anyone regardless of their marital status, age, sexual orientation, or gender.

Also important to understand is the legal definition of consent. The age of consent in Canada is 16—which means that anyone under that age cannot legally consent to sexual relations. Rest assured that our country does not seek to criminalize teenagers who are having sex with each other, but the difference in ages between partners and whether one is in a position of authority over the other are important elements:

- If a child is under age 12 they cannot consent, in any form, to sexual activity;
- If a child is 12-13 years of age, they can consent to sexual activity with another person who is no more than 2 years older;
- If a child is 14-15 years of age, they can consent to sexual activity with another person who is no more than 5 years older;
- Once age 16 and older, you can consent to sexual activity with any person of any age if that person is not in a position of authority (e.g., teacher, coach, employer, etc.).

Furthermore:

- A person who has diminished mental capacity is considered legally *unable* to consent to sexual acts regardless of their age (e.g., a person with Down syndrome or a senior who has dementia);
- A person who is intoxicated or otherwise impaired is legally *unable* to consent to sexual acts; and
- A person who is unconscious is legally *unable* to consent to sexual acts.

For consent to be valid by law, it must be verbal, ongoing, and voluntary.

- Verbal consent means that an audible "yes" must be communicated to signal consent; the absence of "no" does not equate with consent.
- Ongoing consent means that at any time a person may change his/her mind about sexual activity; they have a right to do so and ignoring or devaluing their change of mind and continuing to engage in sex acts constitutes sexual assault.
- Voluntary consent means that a person must not be coerced or pressured or threatened (or perceive coercion, pressure, or threats) when giving their consent. For example, if I am 15 and my hockey coach is 29 and he engages in sexual behaviour with me, I may feel pressured to participate because he's my coach and he's in charge of my hockey career.

In our *Criminal Code*, the three sections of sexual assault each have sentencing parameters. Mandatory minimums are only imposed under certain conditions (see Table 7.1).

Table 7.1   Minimum and Maximum Dispositions for Sexual Assault

Level of Sexual Assault	Minimum Disposition	Maximum Disposition	Exceptions
Level I Sexual assault s. 271	**Summary** Fine, probation, house arrest, community service No minimum jail **Indictable** Fine, probation, house arrest, community service No minimum jail	18 months 10 years	Mandatory minimum jail sentences exist: If the victim's age is below 16;
Level II Sexual assault with a weapon or threat s. 272	**Indictable** No minimum jail	14 years	If a firearm was used; If the accused is part of organized crime;
Level III Aggravated sexual assault s. 273	**Indictable** 4 years minimum	Life	If the accused is a repeat offender

Source: D. Scharie Tavcer

We cannot help but question the message this may send to victims, potential victims, and perpetrators.

Facts and Figures

In most GSS cycles on victimization, men and women show relatively similar rates for all violent victimization, but women have always reported higher rates of sexual victimization. According to the 2004 GSS, there were about 512,000 incidents of sexual assault, representing a rate of 1,977 incidents per 100,000 population aged 15 and older. Given that most sexual assaults go unreported, police-reported sexual assault counts are lower: 24,200 sexual offences recorded in 2007 (Brennan & Taylor-Butts, 2008). Ten years later, in 2014, women recorded a higher rate for all violent victimization (85 incidents per 1,000 women) than men (67 per 1,000) (Perreault, 2015). This finding is primarily due to the fact that the sexual assault rate—a crime in which the majority of victims are women—remained stable over the past decade, while the rates for robbery and physical assault—in which the majority of victims are men—dropped significantly since 2004.

Girls (under age 18) were more frequently the victims of a sexual offence than boys. In 2012, four of every five (81 percent) child victims of a sexual offence were female (Cotter & Beaupré, 2014).

Rape Prevention

Educational and prevention campaigns typically focus on women and their responsibility to avoid sexual assault (versus campaigns directed at men to avoid sexually assaulting someone). This culture of blame and shame is argued to perpetuate violence against women, to excuse male behaviour, and to foster an environment of silence. Victims do not report out of fear of not being believed, being re-victimized within the criminal justice system, and being shamed for failing to prevent the assault.

Despite massive education efforts, many men remain unaware of how the fear of male violence affects women daily. Consider the exercise presented in Box 7.3.

BOX 7.3

Class Exercise: Raising Awareness Between Men and Women

In your group of friends, ask males and females to describe the techniques they use to prevent themselves from being raped. For men, most don't say anything except maybe something like, "Avoid going to prison." Then make note of the way women describe their avoidance strategies. A completely different picture emerges. A long list of responses can be written, including such things as avoiding night classes, not walking alone at night, carrying whistles and alarms, calling the campus foot patrol for escorts to the bus or a car, avoiding certain types of clothing, not drinking too much, not flirting too much, being sure your drink isn't spiked, being sure to party with a female friend so you each can look out for each other, and a host of other preventive measures.

Source: Katz, J. (2006). *The macho paradox: Why some men hurt women and how all men can help.* Naperville, IL: Sourcebooks.

An exercise like the one in Box 7.3 can go on for an hour or longer and it quickly shows that many women are not alone in their worries. Women are concerned about their safety and their routine activities are heavily governed by a well-founded fear of being sexually assaulted. It's as if we live in a society where it is assumed that women will be sexually assaulted at some point, so we better find ways to protect ourselves! It also illustrates the reality that women are conditioned to be responsible for their own rapes. Almost all the prevention and education efforts have inundated women, whereas no such efforts are directed at men who may rape.

College and University

Many women's lives do not become safer when they enter university or college. Students in post-secondary schools are at a higher risk of various types of violence—both men and women. But for women that violence is often sexual assault.

Canadian Association of College and University Student Services (CACUSS) conducts a regular study on student health. It has the largest data set of post-secondary student health behaviours: 43,000 students from 41 Canadian institutions respond to the National College Health Assessment (NCHA) survey, now the NCHA-II. Perhaps your college/university participated too? As with any survey tool, we must be cognizant of the fact that such studies greatly underestimate the extent of violence.

The Spring 2016 study (CACUSS, 2016) asked students if, during 2015, they had experienced different types of abuse. The results of the survey are shown in Table 7.2

As you can see from the NCHA-II data, in most of the categories, a larger percentage of women experienced some form of violence during their post-secondary careers.

Attitudes about dating are also an indication of our culture's acceptance of violence. In a small study (182 respondents) conducted at an Alberta university, male students were asked if they could distinguish between dating advice taken from conventional magazines and quotes from convicted rapists (Tavcer, 2015). The purpose was to contribute to the existing literature about young men's attitudes toward women and sex,

Table 7.2   Percentage of Male and Female Respondents Who Self-Reported Types of Abuse

Type of Abuse	Male %	Female %	Total %
A physical fight	9.4	3.3	5.2
A physical assault (not sexual assault)	4.4	3.7	4.0
A verbal threat	25.9	19.9	22.0
Sexual touching without their consent	4.3	13.1	10.7
Sexual penetration attempt without their consent	1.0	4.6	3.6
Sexual penetration without their consent	0.5	2.5	2.0
Stalking	2.8	8.2	6.7
An emotionally abusive intimate relationship	7.4	11.6	10.5
A physically abusive intimate relationship	2.0	2.1	2.1
A sexually abusive intimate relationship	1.1	2.7	2.3

Source: Healthy Campus Alberta (n.d.). NCHA-II Spring 2016 Canadian Reference Group. Retrieved May 17, 2017 from http://healthycampusalberta.ca/ncha/.

and employed a partial replication of the work conducted in the United Kingdom (UK) by Horvath, Hegarty, Tyler, and Mansfield (2011).

Horvath et al.'s (2011) work examined whether young men could distinguish between statements made within "lads' magazines" to those of convicted rapists. In many countries today, we find considerable discussion of what is often called the sexualization or pornification of the public sphere—the notion that the advertising world is influenced by the pornography industry and in the depictions of sexuality that prevail in this commercial field (Angelone, Mitchell, & Grossi, 2015), and which largely remain unquestioned (Krebs, Lindquist, Warner, Fisher, & Martin, 2007). Participants in the UK study attributed slightly fewer quotes to lads' magazines than to convicted rapists. They guessed correctly only 56.1 percent of the time when they attributed a quote to lads' magazines and only 55.4 percent of the time when they attributed a quote to a convicted rapist.

In the Alberta study, similar results were found. Can you figure out who said it?

"A woman may like anal sex because it makes her feel incredibly naughty and she likes feeling like a dirty slut. If this is the case you can try all sorts of humiliating acts to help live out her filthy fantasy."[2]	
Said by a convicted rapist	52.9%
Stated in a men's magazine	47.1%

"There's a certain way you can tell that a woman wants to have sex. The way they dress, they flaunt themselves."[3]	
Said by a convicted rapist	58.8%
Stated in a men's magazine	41.2%

Rape Culture

Another factor known to impact violence are rape myths. The development of the Illinois Rape Acceptance Scale (IRAS) by Lonsway & Fitzgerald (1995) expanded Burt's (1980) Cultural Myths and Supports for Rape scale. Both works assess how cultural myths and stereotypes support sexual violence. The Alberta study also replicated this work (Tavcer, 2015).

rape culture
A set of beliefs that encourages male sexual aggression and supports violence against women in the form of words, jokes, advertising, media, objectification, and gendered norms.

Rape culture is a term to describe a cultural milieu in which sexual violence is supported (Abbey, McAulson, & Thomson-Ross, 1998; Burgess, 2007; DeKeseredy & Schwartz, 2016; Malamuth & Sockloskie, 1991). One examination of core cultural beliefs and attitudes about rape was first termed "rape myths" in Burt's (1980) classic article. Burt defined such myths as "prejudicial, stereotyped, or false beliefs about rape, rape victims, and rapists" (Burt, 1980, p. 217).

In the sample of male students from one Alberta university, approximately 75 percent of respondents "completely agree, somewhat agree, and neutral/don't know" in response to the question: "Women who are caught cheating on their boyfriends/husbands/partners sometimes claim it was rape because they don't want to admit the truth" (Tavcer, 2015). Additionally, 25 percent of respondents believed a woman is responsible for her victimization if she's drunk or if she wears "slutty" clothes. Twenty percent of respondents believed that men rape because of a strong biological desire for sex; because if they're drunk, they are acting unintentionally.

Although this study was one sample within one university in Canada, it does illustrate the fact that unsettling beliefs in young men continue to exist. And that more work needs to be done to focus education and prevention efforts toward men and boys.

SUMMARY

Most Canadians agree about the seriousness of physical and sexual assault. And despite the backlash, statistical evidence proves that the violence continues. Regardless of one's political or academic leanings, the statistics cannot be ignored. From childhood into adulthood, girls and women are at risk to experience many different forms of violent victimization. And unfortunately, those numbers have not significantly changed over the past decades.

Furthermore, because of such abusive histories, many women commit crimes (of various sorts) and become offenders in our various justice systems and can be victimized again because of their offender status. The intertwining of childhood and adult victimization with adulthood offending and reoffending are connected. By taking a whole life perspective (Belknap, 2010), we can appreciate the impact that various experiences may have had on a woman's life trajectory, whether that path intersects with aspects of the criminal justice system or not. We must be cognizant that the uniqueness of individuals is not lost when we search for commonalities to better understand why some women become offenders and others do not. And although many criminalized women share certain life experiences, we must be mindful that a person's experiences do not define the individual. All that being said, a common thread among us all exists. Although it might be simplistic to assume there is one answer to the question of why women commit crimes, that shouldn't mean that it isn't worth asking the questions.

NOTES

1. Reoffending is also called *recidivism*—the notion that certain factors have influenced or caused an individual to commit crime once again, even after being sanctioned or jailed.
2. "Stated in a men's magazine" is the correct answer.
3. "Said by a convicted rapist" is the correct answer.

DISCUSSION QUESTIONS

1. The focus on criminalized women's histories of abuse is sometimes referred to as "the abuse excuse." Such a defence has been applauded by some and criticized by others. What are its strengths and weaknesses?
2. What kinds of social and economic factors may be linked to the criminalization of women?
3. In the federal correctional system, women with a low level of education are encouraged to improve their educational level while incarcerated. Why does the correctional service place such an emphasis on educational attainment?
4. Describe the data available from courts and correctional institutions in Canada. How are these data useful in identifying patterns of women's criminal behaviour? Is anything missing?
5. Why do you think Canadians worry more about (and educate their kids about) "stranger danger" than they do about family violence?
6. What training or education or law is needed that would truly stop violence against women and girls?

ADDITIONAL RESOURCES

Suggested Readings

Prison for women: The Arbour Inqury. Retrieved from http://www.caefs.ca/resources/issues -and-position-papers/prison-for-women-arbour-inquiry/.

The Canadian Encyclopedia, Prison for women closes, (about P4W). Retrieved from http://www.thecanadianencyclopedia.ca/en/article/prison-for-women-closes/.

Films and Videos

Dick, K., (Writer/Director). (2015). *The hunting ground* [Documentary]. Retrieved from http://www.imdb.com/title/tt4185572/.

Lazarus, M., & Wunderlich, R. (Directors). (1994). *Defending our lives* [Film]. Cambridge Documentary Films.

Ministry of Community Safety and Correctional Services. *Ashley Smith inquest* (2013) [Video]. Retrieved from http://www.cbc.ca/news/canada/ashley-smith-jurors-watch-video-showing -her-death-1.1364650.

O'Connor, E.T. (Producer), & Smith, M. (Director). (1994). *The ultimate response: Trouble at P4W Kingston* [Documentary]. Canada: CBC The Fifth Estate. Retrieved from https://curio .ca/en/video/the-ultimate-response-4162/.

Websites

Canadian Association of Elizabeth Fry Societies: www.caefs.ca

It's On US: http://www.itsonus.org

National Association of Women and the Law (NAWL): www.nawl.ca

National Sexual Violence Resource Center: http://www.nsvrc.org

Title IX: Know your IX: www.knowyourix.org/college-resources/title-ix/

Groups That Encourage Men to Help End Sexual Assault

A Call to Men: www.acalltomen.org
Men Against Violence Against Women: www.mavaw.org
Men Can Stop Rape: www.mencanstoprape.org
MenEngage Alliance: www.menengage.org
Mentors in Violence Prevention: www.mvpnational.org
White Ribbon Campaign: www.whiteribbon.ca

REFERENCES

Abbey, A., McAulson, P., & Thomson-Ross, L. (1998). Sexual assault perpetration by college men: The role of alcohol, misperception of sexual intent, and sexual beliefs and experiences. *Journal of Social and Clinical Psychology, 17*(2), 167–195.

Adams, M., & Coltrane, S. (2008). *Gender and families* (2nd ed.). Lanham, MD: Rowman & Littlefield.

Adelberg, E., & Currie, C. (1993). *In conflict with the law: Women and the Canadian justice system*. Vancouver: Press Gang.

Alarid, L., & Cromwell, P. (2006). *In her own words: Women offenders' views on crime and victimization*. Los Angeles: Roxbury.

Allen, M. (2015). Police-reported hate crime in Canada, 2013. (Catalogue no. 85-002-X). Centre for Justice Statistics, Ottawa: Statistics Canada.

Angelone, D., Mitchell, D., & Grossi, L. (2015). Men's perceptions of an acquaintance rape: The role of relationship length, victim resistance, and gender role attitudes. *Journal of Interpersonal Violence, 30*(13), 2278–2303.

Beattie, S., & Hutchins, H. (2015). *Sheltering*. Retrieved from http://www.statcan.gc.ca/pub/85-002-x/2015001/article/14207-eng.htm.

Belknap, J. (2010). Rape: Too hard to report and too easy to discredit victims. *Violence Against Women, 16*(12), 1335–1344.

Blanchette, K., & Brown, S. (2006). *The assessment and treatment of women offenders: An integrative perspective*. University of Leicester, UK: John Wiley & Sons.

Boe, R. (1998). *A two-year follow-up of federal offenders who participated in the Adult Basic Education (ABE) Program*. (Research Report R-60). Ottawa: Correctional Service of Canada.

Bowen, R.R. (2013). *The walk among us: Sex work exiting, re-entry, and duality*. Master of Arts thesis for School of Criminology, SFU.

Boyce, J. (2015). *Police-reported crime statistics in Canada, 2014*. Statistics Canada. Ottawa: Statistics Canada.

Brennan, S., & Taylor-Butts, A. (2008). *Sexual assault in Canada 2004 and 2007*. Statistics Canada, Canadian Centre for Justice Statistics Profile Series. Ottawa: Statistics Canada.

Browne, A., Miller, B., & Maguin, E. (1999). Prevalence and severity of lifetime physical and sexual victimization among incarcerated women. *International Journal of Law and Psychiatry, 22*, 301–322.

Burczycka, M. (2016). Family violence in Canada: A statistical profile, 2014. *Juristat, 36*(1). Statistics Canada. Ottawa: Canada.

Burgess, G. (2007). Assessment of rape-supportive attitudes and beliefs in college men: Development, reliability, and validity of the rape attitudes and beliefs scale. *Journal of Interpersonal Violence, 22*(8), 973–993.

Burt, M.R. (1980). Cultural myths and supports for rape. *Journal of Personality and Social Psychology, 38*(2), 217–230.

Bush-Baskette, S. (2004). The war on drugs as a war against Black women. In M. Chesney-Lind & L. Pasko (Eds.), *Girls, women, and crime: Selected readings* (pp. 185–194). Thousand Oaks, CA: Sage.

Canada, Task Force on Federally Sentenced Women (TFFSW). (1990). *Creating choices: Report of the task force on federally sentenced women*. Ottawa: Department of the Solicitor General.

Canada Without Poverty (2017). *Basic statistics about poverty in Canada*. Retrieved from http://www.cwp-csp.ca.

Canadian Association of College and University Student Services (CACUSS). (2016, September 7). *Canadian student health data 2016*. Retrieved November 20, 2016, from Canadian Reference Group: Executive Summary: http://www.cacuss.ca/health_data.htm.

Canadian Association of Elizabeth Fry Societies (CAEFS) (2016). *Fact sheets*. Retrieved from http://www.caefs.ca/resources/fact-sheets-in-pdf/.

Canadian Centre on Substance Abuse, & Pernanen, K. (2002). *Proportions of crimes associated with alcohol and other drugs in Canada*. Ottawa: Canadian Centre on Substance Abuse.

Canadian Human Rights Commission (2003). *Protecting their rights: A systematic review of human rights in correctional services for federally sentenced women.* Retrieved from http://www.chrc-ccdp.ca/sites/default/files/fswen.pdf.

Canadian Network of Women's Shelters & Transition Houses. (2015). *Factsheets.* Retrieved from ENDAW: http://endvaw.ca/resources/factsheets/.

Chesney-Lind, M., & Pasko, L. (2013). *The female offender: Girls, women, and crime* (3rd ed.). Thousand Oaks, CA: Sage.

Chesney-Lind, M., & Rodriguez, N. (1983). Women under lock and key: A view from the inside. *The Prison Journal, 63,* 47–65.

Comack, E. (1996). *Women in trouble.* Black Point, NS: Fernwood.

Comack, E. (1999). New possibilities for a feminism "in" criminology? From dualism to diversity. *Canadian Journal of Criminology, 41,* 161–170.

Comack, E. (2005). Coping, resisting, and surviving: Connecting women's law violations to the histories of abuse. In L.F. Alarid & P. Cromwell (Eds.), *In her own words: Women offenders' views on crime and victimization* (pp. 33–43). Los Angeles: Roxbury.

Comack, E., & Balfour, G. (2004). *The power to criminalize.* Halifax, NS: Fernwood.

Comack, E., & Brickey, S. (2007). Constituting the violence of criminalized women. *Canadian Journal of Criminology and Criminal Justice, 49,* 1–36.

Controlled Drugs and Substances Act (1996). SC 1996, c 19.

Conway, J.F. (2001). *The Canadian family in crisis* (4th ed.). Toronto: Lorimer.

Cotter, A., & Beaupré, P. (2014). *Police-reported sexual offences against children and youth in Canada, 2012.* Statistics Canada, Canadian Centre for Justice Statistics. Ottawa: Statistics Canada.

Cotter, A., Greenland, J., & Karam, M. (2015). Drug-related offences in Canada, 2013. *Juristat, 35*(1).

Criminal Code, RSC 1985, c C-46.

DeHart, D., & Lynch, S.M. (2012). Gendered pathways to crime: The relationship between victimization and offending. In C.M. Renzetti, S.L. Miller, & A.R. Gover (Eds.), *Routledge international handbook of crime and gender studies* (Vol. 1, pp. 120–138). London, UK: Taylor & Francis.

DeKeseredy, W.S. (2000). *Women, crime and the Canadian criminal justice system.* Cincinnati, OH: Anderson.

DeKeseredy, W.S. (2010). The hidden violent victimization of women. In S.G. Shoham, P. Knepper, & M. Kett (Eds.), *International handbook of victimology* (pp. 559–585). CRC Press.

DeKeseredy, W.S. (2013). Separation/divorce sexual assault. In L.M. McOrmond-Plummer, P. Easteal, & J.Y. Levy-Peck (Eds), *Intimate partner sexual violence* (pp. 65–76). London, UK: Jessica Kingsley Publishers.

DeKeseredy, W.S., Alvi, S., Schwartz, M.D., & Tomaszewski, E.A. (2003). *Under siege: Poverty and crime in a public housing community.* Lanham, MD: Lexington Books.

DeKeseredy, W.S., Dragiewicz, M., & Schwartz, M.D. (2017). *Abusive endings: Separation and divorce violence against women.* Los Angeles: University of California Press.

DeKeseredy, W.S., & Schwartz, M.D. (2013). *Male peer support & violence against women: The history & verification of a theory.* Boston: Northeastern University Press.

DeKeseredy, W.S., & Schwartz, M.D. (2016). Thinking sociologically about image-based sexual abuse: The contribution of male peer support theory. *Sexualization, Media, & Society.* DOI: 10.1177/2374623816684692/.

Edin, K. (2000). What do low-income single mothers say about marriage? *Social Problems, 47,* 112–133.

Elias, R. (1986). *The politics of victimization: Victimology and human rights.* New York: Oxford University Press.

Farley, M. (2005). Prostitution harms women even if indoors: Reply to Weltzer. *Violence Against Women 11,* 950–964. DOI: 10.1177/1077801205276987.

Flores, J. (2016). *Caught up: Girls, surveillance, and wraparound incarceration.* Oakland, CA: University of California Press.

Fox, G.L., & Benson, M.L. (2006). Household and neighbourhood contexts of intimate partner violence. *Public Health Reports, 121*(4), 419–427.

Gilfus, M. (1992). From victims to survivors to offenders: Women's routes of entry and immersion into street crime. In L.F. Alarid & P. Cromwell (Eds.), *In her own words: Women offenders' views on crime and victimization* (pp. 5–14). Los Angeles, CA: Roxbury.

Gilfus, M.E. (2002). *Women's experiences of abuse as a risk factor for incarceration.* Harrisburg, PA: VAWnet, a project of the National Resource Center on Domestic Violence/Pennsylvania Coalition Against Domestic Violence.

Gobeil, R. (2009). *Profile of federally sentenced women drug offenders.* Correctional Service of Canada. Retrieved from http://www.csc-scc.gc.ca/research/r204-eng.shtml.

Gondolf, E.W. (2007). Theoretical and research support for the Duluth Model: A reply to Dutton and Corvo. *Aggression and Violent Behavior, 12,* 644–657.

Grant, B. & Gileno, J. (2008). *The changing federal offender population.* Ottawa: Correctional Service of Canada.

Healthy Campus Alberta (n.d.). NCHA-II Spring 2016 Canadian Reference Group. Retrieved May 17, 2017 from http://healthycampusalberta.ca/ncha/.

Heney, J., & Kristiansen, C. (1997). An analysis of the impact of prison on women survivors of childhood sexual abuse. *Women & Therapy, 20,* 29–44.

Holzman, H.R., Hyatt, R.A., & Dempster, J.M. (2001). Patterns of aggravated assault in public housing: Mapping the nexus of offense, place, gender, and race. *Violence Against Women, 7,* 662–684.

Horvath, M.A., Hegarty, P., Tyler, S., & Mansfield, S. (2011). "Lights on at the end of the party": Are lads' mags mainstreaming dangerous sexism? *British Journal of Psychology, 103*(4). DOI: 10.1111/j.2044-8295.2011.02086.x.

Hughes, D. (2000). The "Natasha Trade": The transnational shadow market of trafficking in women. *Journal of International Affairs, 53*(2), 625–651.

Katz, J. (2006). *The macho paradox: Why some men hurt women and how all men can help.* Naperville, IL: Sourcebooks.

Kong, R. &. AuCoin, K. (2008). Female offenders in Canada. *Jursitat, 28*(1), 1–23.

Krebs, C., Lindquist, C., Warner, T., Fisher, B., & Martin, S. (2007). *The campus sexual assault study.* National Institute of Justice, Department of Justice USA. Washington: USA.

Liebschutz J., Savetsky, J.B., Saitz, R., Horton, N.J., Lloyd-Travaglini, C., & Samet, J.H. (2002). The relationship between sexual and physical abuse and substance consequences. *Journal of Substance Abuse Treatment, 22*(3), 121–130.

Lightfoot, L., & Lambert, L. (1991). *Substance abuse treatment needs of federally sentenced women* (Technical Report #1). Ottawa: Correctional Service of Canada.

Lightfoot, L., & Lambert, L. (1992). *Substance abuse treatment needs of federally sentenced women* (Technical Report #2). Ottawa: Correctional Service of Canada.

Lo, C. (2004). Sociodemographic factors, drug abuse, and other crimes: How they vary among male and female arrestees. *Journal of Criminal Justice, 32,* 399–409.

Lochhead, C., & Scott, K. (2000). *The dynamics of women's poverty in Canada.* Ottawa: Status of Women Canada.

Lonsway, K.A., & Fitzgerald, L.F. (1995). Attitudinal antecedents of rape myth acceptance: A theoretical and empirical reexamination. *Journal of Personality and Social Psychology, 68*(4), 704–711.

Maeve, M. (2000). Speaking unavoidable truths: Understanding early childhood sexual and physical violence among women in prison. *Issues in Mental Health Nursing, 21,* 473–498.

Mahony, T. H. (2011). Women and the criminal justice system. No. 89-503-X. Retrieved from http://www.statcan.gc.ca/pub/89-503-x/2010001/article/11416-eng.pdf.

Maidment, M. (2006). "We're not all that criminal": Getting beyond the pathologizing and individualizing of women's crime. *Women and Therapy, 29*(3/4), 35–56.

Maier, S.F., & Seligman, M.E. (2016). Learned helplessness at fifty: Insights from neuroscience. *Psychological Review, 123*(4), 349–367.

Makarios, M. (2007). Race, abuse and female criminal violence. *Feminist Criminology, 2,* 100–116.

Malamuth, N., & Sockloskie, R. (1991). Characteristics of aggressors against women: Testing a model using a national sample of college students. *Journal of Consulting and Clinical Psychology, 59*(5), 670–681.

Matheson, F.I., Doherty, S., & Grant, B.A. (2009). *Women offender substance abuse programming & community reintegration.* Correctional Service of Canada. Retrieved from http://www.csc-scc.gc.ca/research/092/r202-eng.pdf.

Mihorean, K. (2005). *Trends in self-reported spousal violence.* In Family Violence in Canada: A statistical profile. Ottawa: Statistics Canada.

Morissette, R., Picot, G., & Lu, Y. (2013). *The evolution of Canadian wages over the last three decades.* Social Analysis Division, Statistics Canada. (Catalogue no. 11F0019M—No. 347). Retrieved from http://www.statcan.gc.ca/pub/11f0019m/11f0019m2013347-eng.pdf.

Moyser, M. (2017). *Women and paid work.* (Catalogue no. 89-503-X). Statistics Canada. Retrieved from http://www.statcan.gc.ca/pub/89-503-x/2015001/article/14694-eng.pdf.

Office of the Correctional Investigator (OCI). (2016). *Annual report.* Retrieved from http://www.oci-bec.gc.ca/cnt/rpt/annrpt/annrpt20152016-eng.aspx.

Oppal, W. T. (2012). *Forsaken: The report of the missing women commission of inquiry.* Retrieved from http://www.missingwomeninquiry.ca/obtain-report/.

Owen, B., Wells, J., & Pollock, J. (2017). *In search of safety: Confronting inequality in women's imprisonment.* Oakland, CA: University of California Press.

Perreault, S. (2015). Criminal victimization in Canada, *Juristat, 35*(1). Statistics Canada. Ottawa: Canada.

Pollack, S. (2000). Dependency discourse as social control. In K. Hannah-Moffat & M. Shaw (Eds.), *An ideal prison? Critical essays on women's imprisonment in Canada* (pp. 72–81). Halifax: Fernwood Publishing.

Pollack, S. (2008). *Locked in, locked out: Imprisoning women in the shrinking and punitive welfare state* (pp. 5–6) Waterloo, ON: Wilfrid Laurier University. Retrieved from http://efryottawa.com/documents/Lockedin Lockedout-SPollockresearchreport.pdf.

Pollock, J. (2002). *Women, prison and crime.* Belmont, CA: Wadsworth.

R v Lavallee (1990). [1990] 1 SCR 852.

Radosh, P. (2002). Reflections of women's crime and mothers in prison: A peacemaking approach. *Crime and Delinquency, 48*, 300–315.

Raphael, J., & Ellison, M.C. (2013). Prostitution: The gendered crime. In C.M. Renzetti, S.L. Miller, & A.R. Gover (Eds.), *Routledge international handbook of crime and gender studies* (pp. 141–157). London: Routledge.

Renzetti, C.M., & Maier, S.L. (2002). "Private" crime in public housing: Fear of crime and violent victimization among women public housing residents. *Women's Health and Urban Life, 1*, 46–65.

Sapers, H. (2012). *Annual report of the office of the Correctional Investigator 2011–2012 to the Minister of Public Safety and the Government of Canada.* Retrieved from http://www.oci-bec.gc.ca/cnt/rpt/pdf/annrpt/annrpt20112012-eng.pdf.

Sapers, H. (2013). *Annual report of the office of the Correctional Investigator 2012–2013 to the Minister of Public Safety and the Government of Canada.* Retrieved from http://www.oci-bec.gc.ca/cnt/rpt/annrpt/annrpt20122013-eng.aspx#sVI.

Sered, S.S., & Norton-Hawk, M. (2014). *Can't catch a break: Gender, jail, drugs, and the limits of personal responsibility.* Oakland, CA: University of California Press.

Shaffer, M. (1997). The battered woman syndrome revisited: Some complicating thoughts five years after R. v. Lavallee. *University of Toronto Law Journal, 47*, 1–33.

Shaw, M. (1994). *Ontario women in conflict with the law: A survey of women in institutions and under community supervision in Ontario.* Ottawa: Research Services, Strategic Policy and Planning Division, Ministry of the Solicitor General and Correctional Services.

Sheehy, E. (2000). Review of the self-defence review. *Canadian Journal of Women and the Law, 12*, 198–234.

Sheldon Kennedy Child Advocacy Centre. (2015). One critical issue. One integrated response: Report the community 2015-2018. Retrieved from https://d3n8a8pro7vhmx.cloudfront.net/skcac/pages/430/attachments/original/1448571167/SKCAC_COMMUNITY_REPORT_2015-web.pdf?1448571167.

Sinha, M. (2013). Measuring violence against women: Statistical trends. Canadian Centre for Justice Statistics. *Juristat.* Retrieved March 30, 2017 from http://www.statcan.gc.ca/pub/85-002-x/2013001/article/11766-eng.pdf.

Skinner, H.A. (1982). Alcohol Dependence Scale. Toronto: University of Toronto. Retrieved from http://www.emcdda.europa.eu/html.cfm/index3583EN.html.

Sokoloff, N.J., & DuPont, I. (2005). Domestic violence at the intersections of race, class, and gender: Challenges and contributions to understanding violence against marginalized women in diverse communities. *Violence Against Women, 11*(1), 38–64.

Sommers, E. (1995). *Voices from within: Women who have broken the law.* Toronto: University of Toronto Press.

Statistics Canada. (2003). *Women and men in Canada: A statistical glance, 2003.* Ottawa: Status of Women Canada.

Statistics Canada. (2012). *Population 15 years and over by highest certificate, diploma or degree, by age groups (2006 Census).* Summary Table Based on 2006 Census of Population. Retrieved from http://www.statcan.gc.ca/tables-tableaux/sum-som/l01/cst01/educ43a-eng.htm.

Statistics Canada. (2013). Table 252-0012. Youth custody and community services (YCSS), admissions to correctional services, by sex and Aboriginal identity, annual, CANSIM (database) (Accessed January 31, 2017).

Statistics Canada. (2016a). *Family violence in Canada: A statistical profile, 2013.* Canadian Centre for Justice Statistics. Retrieved from http://www.statcan.gc.ca/pub/85-002-x/2016001/article/14303-eng.pdf.

Statistics Canada. (2016b). *Family violence in Canada*, 2014 [Infographic]. Retrieved from http://www.statcan.gc.ca/pub/11-627-m/11-627-m2016001-eng.htm.

Tang, K. (2003). Battered woman syndrome testimony in Canada: Its development and lingering issues. *International Journal of Offender Therapy and Comparative Criminology, 47*, 618–629.

Tavcer, S. (2015). *Pornification: A study into young men's attitudes and beliefs toward dating, sex, and sexual assault.* Mount Royal University Institutional Repository. Retrieved from http://hdl.handle.net/11205/256.

Taylor-Butts, A. (2007). Canada's shelters for abused women, 2005/2006. *Juristat, 27*(4), 1–19.

Tjaden, P., & Thoenes, N. (2000). *Full report of the prevalence, incidence, and consequences of violence against women: Findings from the national violence against women survey.* Centers for Disease Control and Prevention. Retrieved from https://www.ncjrs.gov/pdffiles1/nij/183781.pdf.

Venkatesh, S. (2003). The state in public housing research. *Criminology & Public Policy, 3*, 53-56.

Walker, L. (1979). *The battered woman.* New York: Harper & Row.

Walker, L. (1995). The transmogrification of a feminist foremother. *Women & Therapy, 17*, 517–529.

Whittington, L. (2007, September 9). Women's group closes after losing its funding: Opposition MPs say Harper government "turning back clock." *Toronto Star*, p. AA12.

Widom, C., & Ames, A. (1994). Criminal consequences of childhood sexual victimization. *Child Abuse and Neglect, 18*, 303–318.

Williams, C. (2010). *Economic well-being of women in Canada.* Ottawa: Statistics Canada.

Women Offenders and Mental Health

Introduction

Mental health problems create special challenges for women offenders and for those who work with them. Such problems can complicate many aspects of their lives, including how they cope with the prison system and how they integrate back into the community. Of course, the majority of women with mental health problems do not come into conflict with the law, and many women in prison do not suffer from a mental illness. However, because some women with mental disorders do end up in prison—an environment that is not designed for them—their situation requires special attention.

Perhaps the best way to understand mental illness is to first look at what it is not—that is, mental health. The World Health Organization (2014) defines mental health as:

> a state of well-being in which every individual realizes his or her own potential, can cope with the normal stresses of life, can work productively and fruitfully, and is able to make a contribution to his or her community.

On the other hand, mental illnesses are health problems that can affect thinking, mood, and behaviour or some combination of these. They are usually associated with personal distress and can interfere with functioning in many areas of life such as family, education, or employment.

Mental illness is a term that encompasses all mental disorders. The *Diagnostic and Statistical Manual of Mental Disorders*, Fifth Edition, referred to as the *DSM-5* (American Psychiatric Association [APA], 2013), has established a system for classifying mental disorders. It defines a mental disorder as follows:

> A mental disorder is a syndrome characterized by clinically significant disturbance in an individual's cognition, emotion regulation, or behavior that reflects a dysfunction in the psychological, biological, or developmental processes underlying mental functioning. Mental disorders are usually associated with significant distress or disability in social, occupational, or other important activities. An expectable or culturally approved response to a common stressor or loss, such as the death of a loved one, is not a mental disorder. Socially deviant behavior (e.g., political, religious, or sexual) and conflicts that are primarily between the individual and society are not mental disorders unless the deviance or conflict results from a dysfunction in the individual, as described above. (p. 20)

The classification system is designed to simplify the assessment and treatment of people displaying unusual behaviours due to mental illness. For example, someone who is constantly preoccupied with recurring thoughts and the need to carry out rituals (such as constantly checking to see if the stove is turned off) may be diagnosed with an obsessive-compulsive disorder. This common language makes it easier for mental health professionals to understand and assist the person.

The *DSM-5* provides diagnostic criteria, which are mainly a list of specific symptoms and other conditions required for a diagnosis such as the age of the person or how long they have had the symptoms. It also provides detailed descriptions of the disorders. It is organized largely in terms of when the disorder might develop along the lifespan. Disorders that are diagnosed early in life such as intellectual disabilities or autism spectrum disorder are near the beginning, whereas cognitive disorders that are due to impairments of later life such as Alzheimer's disease are near the end.

How does a woman with a mental disorder end up in the prison system? See Box 8.1 for a brief summary of the routes that may be taken by a woman with a mental disorder suspected of breaking the law.

BOX 8.1

Mental Health Facility or Prison?

When a woman with a mental disorder comes to the attention of the criminal justice system, she faces several decision points at which she may be directed to either the criminal justice system or the mental health system.

Police Contact

The first point of contact is with the police. This would happen in a case where the woman's behaviour potentially involved some kind of illegal activity. At this stage, a decision is made whether or not to charge the woman. The police must also decide whether the woman's behaviour suggests that she is suffering from a mental disorder to the extent that she should be apprehended, taken to a judge, and ordered to a hospital for a psychiatric assessment. This procedure is authorized by provincial and territorial mental health legislation. Following the assessment, if the physician determines that the woman meets the strict criteria, as detailed in the province's mental health act, for an involuntary admission, then she is deemed "certifiable" and admitted for a longer period of assessment or treatment. Usually the criteria for this is that she is a danger to herself or others or is incapable of caring for herself.

Appearing Before Court

If the woman is charged with an offence under the *Criminal Code*, the judge may remand the woman to custody, place her on bail, or remand her to a psychiatric hospital for an assessment, usually for up to 30 days.

Fit or Unfit to Stand Trial

The outcome of the assessment will determine whether the woman is fit to stand trial. The woman will be found unfit to stand trial if, due to a mental disorder, she is unable to conduct a defence. This judgment is made when the accused cannot understand the nature and the object of the proceedings, cannot understand the consequences of the proceedings, or cannot communicate with counsel (is unable to discuss her case rationally with a lawyer).

Not Guilty, Guilty, or Not Criminally Responsible on Account of Mental Disorder (NCRMD)

A woman found not guilty is free to go without any conditions. If the woman is found guilty, the judge can exercise several sentencing options, ranging from fining the woman to sending her to prison. If the woman is found not criminally responsible on account of mental disorder (NCRMD), the judge again has several options from which to choose: an absolute discharge because the accused is judged not to be a threat to public safety; a discharge to the community with conditions, usually for some type of treatment; or sending the person to a forensic psychiatric unit where a release decision is made by a review board of lawyers, psychiatrists, and laypersons.

Therefore, to be diverted from the criminal justice system to the mental health system, a woman with a mental disorder whose behaviour has attracted the attention of the law must meet strict criteria. A diagnosis of a mental disorder is not sufficient: she must also meet specific criteria throughout the process. A woman with a mental disorder who has committed an offence could conceivably understand the proceedings of the court and instruct her lawyer that an NCRMD defence not be presented. Note that an NCRMD defence is often brought forward in court by the defending lawyer. If the accused woman is charged with a relatively minor offence, the defence may not seek an NCRMD disposition, fearing that more time may be served on an indefinite term in a psychiatric hospital than with a short prison sentence.

Source: Gray, J.E., Shone, M.A., & Liddle, P.F. (2008). *Canadian mental health law and policy*, 2nd ed. Toronto: Butterworths.

The Prevalence and Nature of Mental Disorders Among Offenders

Prevalence refers to the number or proportion of cases of any disorder in a population at any given time. In this section, the following questions will be addressed: What types of mental disorders are found among offenders? What are the current rates of mental disorders among offenders? Are the rates different for male and female offenders? Are the rates changing? Do the rates of offenders with mental disorders differ from those in the community?

The first attempt to document mental disorders among female federal offenders took place in 1989, at what was, at that time, the only federal institution for women in Canada—the Prison for Women (Blanchette & Motiuk, 1996). Male offenders had been surveyed in 1988, thereby providing an opportunity for direct comparison of various mental disorders between the groups. All participants were administered a structured diagnostic interview aimed at determining whether they had ever had a psychiatric diagnosis during their lifetime. The results showed that, as compared with male offenders, the women had much higher rates of all types of mental disorders except for anxiety and anti-social personality disorder (which is characterized by irresponsibility, recklessness, impulsiveness, and little regard for the needs of others or for the law). Women offenders also had higher rates of alcohol and drug dependency than the men.

More recently, male and female offenders were assessed once again with a structured interview in order to determine how many of them met the criteria for mental disorders, either currently or over their lifetime (Beaudette, Power, & Stewart, 2015; Derkzen, Barker, McMillan, & Stewart, 2016). The results of these studies can be seen in the first two columns of Table 8.1. Note that a high proportion of both male (73.0 percent) and female offenders (79.2 percent) met the criteria for at least one mental disorder. Alcohol or substance abuse was the most frequent problem for all offenders, with the rate of abuse being much higher among the women. The women offenders also had high rates (even higher than the men) on personality (anti-social and borderline), anxiety, and mood disorders.

High rates of mental disorders among offenders, especially women, have been a consistent finding by whatever method has been used to assess them. For example, when processing offenders on admission to the federal correctional system, it was found that 30.1 percent of the women and 14.5 percent of the men had previously been hospitalized for psychiatric reasons (Public Safety Canada, 2008). In a study designed to obtain a better understanding of the mental health needs of federal women offenders,

Derkzen, Booth, McConnell, and Taylor (2013) found high rates of mental disorders among their sample. Over their lifetimes, 94 percent of the women offenders had experienced symptoms that could have possibly led to a mental health diagnosis, and the vast majority of them (85.2 percent) may have met the criteria for more than one disorder. Looking at the lifetime prevalence of a disorder is bound to yield higher rates than examining that of a current one; however, the pattern is similar to previous results. The women had high rates of depression, anxiety, and anti-social personality disorder. Substance abuse, including alcohol, was extremely high, with 80 percent of the sample reporting this problem at some point in their lives.

In addition to the disorders already mentioned, a disproportionate number of women offenders have been found to be of below-average intellectual abilities, including some with intellectual disabilities. Intellectual disability is defined by the *DSM-5* (APA, 2013) as "a disorder with onset during the developmental period that includes both intellectual and adaptive functioning deficits in conceptual, social, and practical domains" (p. 33). That means that the person has difficulties with such things as reasoning, problem solving, planning, academic learning, and so on. Between 1.3 and 3.9 percent of males and 0.7 to 6.5 percent of females in federal prisons are estimated to meet the criteria for intellectual disability ("A health care needs assessment," 2004). These numbers are higher than the 1 percent estimate in the general population (APA, 2013).

Table 8.1   Prevalence of Current Mental Disorders Among Several Samples

	% Female Offenders[a]	% Male Offenders[b]	% Female Community Sample	% Male Community Sample
Psychotic disorders	4.6	3.3	0.7[d]	0.5[d]
Mood disorder	22.1	16.9	5.8[c]	3.6[c]
Anxiety disorders	54.2	29.5	3.2[c]	2.0[c]
Borderline personality disorder (lifetime only)	33.3	15.9		
Anti-social personality (lifetime only)	49.4	44.1	0.8[d]	6.5[d]
Alcohol/substance abuse	76.0	49.6	2.5[c]	6.4[c]
Any disorder	79.2	73.0		

NOTE: The percentages do not add up to 100 percent because some offenders have more than one diagnosis.

[a] Source: Derkzen, D., Barker, J., McMillan, K., & Stewart, L. (2016). *Rates of current mental disorders among women offenders in custody in CSC*. Ottawa: Research Branch, Correctional Service of Canada.
[b] Source: Beaudette, J., Power, J., & Stewart, L. (2015). *National prevalence of mental disorders among incoming federally-sentenced men offenders*. (Research Report No. R-357). Ottawa: Research Branch, Correctional Service of Canada.
[c] Source: Pearson, C., Janz, T., & Ali, J. (2013). *Mental and substance abuse disorders in Canada*. Statistics Canada, Catalogue no. 82-624x. Retrieved from http://www.statcan.gc.ca/pub/82-624-x/2013001/article/11855-eng.htm.
[d] Source: Bland, R.C., Orn, H., & Newman, S.C. (1988). Lifetime prevalence of psychiatric disorders in Edmonton. *Acta Psychiatrica Scandinavica, 77* (Suppl. 338), 24–32.

Less information is available on the mental health status of provincial and territorial offenders. These offenders are generally serving shorter sentences because they have usually committed offences that are less serious than those of federal offenders. The mental health of provincially sentenced women in Ontario was one of the issues examined by Shaw (1994) in her survey of female offenders living in institutions or in the community under supervision. Of the women interviewed, 80 percent of those in institutions and 67 percent of those in the community reported suffering from at least one mental health problem. Of all women surveyed, depression (51 percent) and anxiety (40 percent) were cited most often. Physical and sexual abuse were common among the sample, with 72 percent reporting having been physically abused and 48 percent having been sexually abused.

Finn, Trevethan, Carrière, and Kowalski (1999) conducted a profile of women offenders who were housed in Canadian federal, provincial, and territorial facilities in 1996. Data on the provincial and territorial offenders indicated that women offenders had more mental health needs than their male counterparts. Substance abuse and emotional problems were, once again, ranked higher for the women than the men. Thus, provincial and territorial female offenders have higher rates of mental illnesses than men, similar to their federal counterparts.

Although the reasons for the gender difference are uncertain, evidence suggests that the high rate of exposure to violence, particularly sexual violence, in the lives of girls and women may have contributed to their mental health problems (Tam & Derkzen, 2014). In a Canadian study by Bonta, Pang, and Wallace-Capretta (1995), 61 percent of female offenders reported having been physically abused and 54 percent reported having been sexually abused. Note that among the Canadian population in general, Sinha (2013) found that rates of violence are higher among Indigenous women than non-Indigenous women. The authors of an American study of women offenders with substance abuse problems found that the women offenders had more extensive histories of victimization than male offenders with substance abuse problems (Messina, Grella, Burdon, & Prendergast, 2007). Not only did the women experience a higher rate of abuse than men but the abuse lasted over a longer period of their lives—from childhood into their teens and adulthood.

The high rate of abuse among women offenders may lead to coping strategies that result in their being diagnosed with a mental disorder (Heney, 1990). Women who have been abused often continue to experience strong feelings of emotional distress and are motivated to seek relief. However, some of the methods that they choose—for example, substance abuse and self-injury—offer only short-term relief and create new problems.

Childhood abuse may also lead to mental health problems in adulthood. For example, symptoms of borderline personality disorder, such as difficulties with trusting people and with regulating one's emotions, may have their roots in childhood abuse. Abused girls have had their trust violated, often repeatedly, and usually by adults they knew and trusted. Their ability to develop and maintain emotionally stable relationships is compromised by this experience. See Box 8.2 for further information on borderline personality disorder.

BOX 8.2

Borderline Personality Disorder

The term *borderline personality disorder* was first coined in the early part of the 20th century, when psychopathology was viewed as being on a continuum from "normal" to "neurotic" to "psychotic." People with severe emotional problems who did not fit into the neurotic or psychotic categories were labelled *borderline* to indicate that they fell between these two categories. The term has since come to refer to a particular personality structure with distinctive features.

According to *DSM-5* (APA, 2013), people with a diagnosis of borderline personality disorder go through life making frantic efforts to avoid real or imagined abandonment. They are overly sensitive to any possible indication of abandonment and react strongly with fear or anger—for example, when someone arrives unexpectedly late or leaves early. They often start intense relationships and idealize new friends or therapists. However, at the first sign that the new person is not there for them, they devalue the person and feel abandoned, leading to a drop in mood and a negative self-image. People with borderline personality disorder often have a history of childhood abuse, neglect, or early parental loss. These early traumatic experiences have likely contributed to the development of this disorder.

Another way of looking at the symptoms of this disorder is to categorize them into five areas:

1. Emotional dysregulation, characterized by emotional instability and problems with anger
2. Interpersonal dysregulation, characterized by unstable relationships and efforts to avoid loss
3. Behavioural dysregulation, characterized by suicide threats and self-damaging behaviours, including substance abuse
4. Cognitive dysregulation, characterized by disturbances in thinking
5. Self-dysfunction, characterized by unstable self-image and chronic feelings of emptiness.

Source: American Psychiatric Association. (2013). *Diagnostic and statistical manual of mental disorders* (5th ed.). Arlington, VA: Author; Linehan, M.M. (1993). *Cognitive-behavioral treatment of borderline personality disorder*. New York: Guilford Press.

▶ WHAT DO YOU THINK?

Is there any justification for housing women with mental disorders in prison? What kinds of challenges are likely to be faced by women with mental disorders in prison? What kinds of challenges are faced by those who work with these women?

Co-Occurring Disorders

Thus far, we have examined only individual diagnoses; however, in reality, most offenders with mental health problems are diagnosed with more than one disorder. The most common second disorder among women offenders is a substance abuse disorder. A study that included both male and female offenders in Canada and the United States found that, as a group, offenders with drug or alcohol problems were more likely than others to have suffered from traumatic stress, to be depressed, or to have an anti-social or borderline personality disorder (Ruiz, Douglas, Edens, Nikolova, & Lilienfeld, 2012). When they compared results between the genders, they found that the women had higher rates than the men on traumatic stress, depression, and borderline personality disorder. Men were more likely to have an anti-social personality disorder.

As compared with male offenders, women offenders more often have more than one diagnosis and their disorders are often related to past histories of trauma such as physical or sexual abuse. Among a sample of Canadian women offenders, all of the women who had a dependency to some type of substance, also had at least one other diagnosis (Derkzen et al., 2013). It may be that women who are dealing with trauma and the subsequent mental health issues may turn to substances as a coping mechanism that ultimately creates more problems for them. Thus, the assessment and treatment of women offenders with mental disorders are complicated by the multiple mental health and substance abuse problems faced by these women.

Women with mental health disorders have historically been treated differently from their male counterparts. Box 8.3 looks at the grim life that faced "criminal lunatic" women in the 19th century.

BOX 8.3

Asylums for Women

Women offenders with mental disorders ("criminal lunatics") were the first offenders in Canada to be admitted into an early forensic mental health system—that is, an "asylum for criminal lunatics" as opposed to the penitentiary. Previously, criminals, "the insane," and debtors were all held in prison. In the late 1800s, criminals and those considered insane were separated into two new facilities: the Kingston Penitentiary in Kingston and the Provincial Lunatic Asylum in Toronto. However, "criminal lunatics" posed a problem. They did not fit into either facility. They also posed a philosophical problem: if they were insane, then they were not responsible for their behaviour, but being convicted for an offence implied that they were responsible. This dilemma persists to some extent today.

In 1855, a temporary lunatic asylum was opened within the Kingston Penitentiary for male offenders. A decision was made not to house the women among these men and therefore they were kept at the Provincial Lunatic Asylum in Toronto. In 1857, the women were sent to what was to become the Rockwood Asylum in Kingston, a lunatic asylum that was still in the planning stages. Because the asylum had not yet been built when the women arrived, they were accommodated in the horse

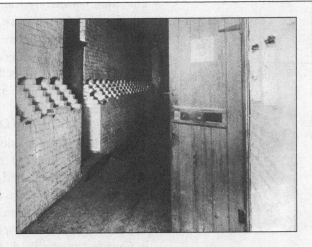

stables for the next 11 years—three years after the asylum had been opened to accommodate male offenders from the penitentiary. The women lived in 3-metre by 1.5-metre cells that were illuminated only by the light that shone through the bars of their peepholes. The cells had thick wooden doors with slots where food was pushed through. As can be imagined, these women had very limited human contact.

Source: Kendall, K. (1999). Criminal lunatic women in 19th century Canada. *Forum on Corrections Research, 11*(3), 46–49.

Rates of Mental Disorders in the Community

Few thorough epidemiological studies report the rates of mental disorders in the Canadian community. As part of a larger survey on health in Canada, Statistics Canada included questions designed to diagnosis six mental health disorders (Pearson, Janz, & Ali, 2013). For the men and women surveyed, the rates of mood disorders, anxiety disorders, and alcohol and drug abuse were much lower than those of the prison samples (see Table 8.1). When the rates of these disorders are compared between the community and prison samples by gender, the largest discrepancy is seen between the offender and community women in their abuse of alcohol or drugs (76.0 percent versus 2.5 percent, respectively). Also note that the women offenders had higher rates of alcohol/substance abuse than the male offenders, contrary to the trend in the community sample.

An older Canadian study followed a protocol similar to that used in the studies on offenders previously discussed—that is, they used a structured interview to assess mental health disorders among a community sample (Bland et al., 1988). When their results for psychotic disorders and anti-social personality disorders are compared with the offender samples, it can be seen that the offenders are much more likely to be diagnosed with these disorders than people in the community (see Table 8.1). This pattern holds true for both male and female offenders.

Borderline personality disorder was not assessed in the community studies discussed above. The *DSM-5* reports that its rate in the general population varies from 1.6 percent to 5.9 percent and that 75 percent of the people diagnosed with it are female (APA, 2013). Judging by these rates, borderline personality disorder is another mental disorder that is more common among offenders than in the general population. As noted in Table 8.1, it is diagnosed in women offenders at almost twice the rate of male offenders.

Changing Rates of Mental Disorders in Prison Populations

As early as the 1930s, a relationship was noted between the size of the populations in the mental health system and in the criminal justice systems. Penrose's law states that the population size of prisons and psychiatric hospitals are inversely related: that is, as one goes up, the other goes down (Webster & Hucker, 2007). Although this description is probably an oversimplification, some association seems to exist between the populations of prisons and psychiatric hospitals, with some people moving between the two systems.

In Canada, the psychiatric hospital population has been reduced over the past two decades, which has led to an increase in the numbers of offenders with mental health problems entering the criminal justice system (Webster & Hucker, 2007). People who previously would likely have been hospitalized for behaviours inappropriate or unacceptable to society are now living in the community or on the street and are more likely to come into contact with police because of their behaviour. The Canadian Mental Health Association has stated that "Canadian prisons have replaced former psychiatric hospitals" (Canada, Senate Standing Committee on Social Affairs, Science and Technology, 2004, p. 98).

It is not surprising, then, that the proportion of people with mental health problems entering the criminal justice system appears to be on the rise. Within the federal correctional system, between 1997 and 2002, the proportion of offenders (male and female) who were assessed as having mental health problems on admission increased significantly (Boe & Vuong, 2002). This trend is continuing. The rate of women offenders with a mental health diagnosis entering the federal correctional system has more than doubled—from 13 percent in the fiscal year of 1996–1997 to 29 percent in the year 2008–2009 (Correctional Service of Canada, 2009).

Women Offenders with Mental Disorders

Women offenders with mental health problems are a varied group. The most common problems they experience are personality disorders and alcohol and drug abuse (see Table 8.1). Diane Charron has had problems in both areas (see Box 8.4). She suffered a particularly difficult childhood that undoubtedly played a role in shaping the person she became. As an adult, she had tremendous difficulty managing her emotions and often felt sad or angry. At times, she felt hopeless. She frequently self-injured by cutting her arms, and she also attempted suicide. From prison, she speaks openly about her distress in a documentary film about her life (Ménard, Turgeon, & Cadieux, 2003).

BOX 8.4

Diane Charron

Diane Charron was 19 years old when she participated in the stabbing death of a man. Her co-accused was a 43-year-old man who initiated an assault on the victim out of revenge, but it was Diane who dealt the fatal blows with a knife. Diane, who was under the influence of drugs at the time, agreed to participate because it seemed like an opportunity to get revenge for all of the bad things that had happened to her in her life. The two men were ex-criminals who she believed would get into a fight but she did not expect it to lead to death. As a result of this incident, her co-accused received a six-year sentence while she was sentenced to life.

Up to this point Diane had lived a very difficult life. At the age of 18 months, she was placed in a foster home where she was neglected and frequently beaten. In her early teens, she was placed in a much better foster home where she was well treated, but by this time she was quite damaged emotionally. As a result, she was often truant, started using drugs, and ran away from home. She was placed in a group home for a while, but again she ran away. At the age of 15, she was raped.

In her late teens, she was living on her own, drinking heavily, and using drugs. She was also in and out of the local psychiatric hospital. She tended to hang around with older men, one of whom became her co-accused. Her situation was clearly unstable, if not chaotic.

Once in prison, Diane became very depressed and attempted suicide. She also frequently cut her arms for relief from her emotional torment. She would rather experience physical pain than emotional pain. She felt remorse for what she had done, writing to her second foster mother, "I should be dead. I took someone's life. I shouldn't live." After a few years in prison, she was admitted to a psychiatric hospital, where she was treated for several years. However, on her return to prison, her mental health problems worsened again. She was diagnosed with borderline personality disorder and frequently felt depressed and self-injurious. Eventually, she was again admitted to a psychiatric hospital, where she once again showed much improvement.

In Diane's case, the severity of her mental health problems has resulted in her remaining in prison much longer than someone else with a similar sentence and probably much longer than was intended. At 10 years past her parole eligibility date, she had never appeared before the Parole Board. The fragile state of her mental health made it more complicated for her to prepare for such an appearance. Also, she sabotaged any attempts for conditional release. When such opportunities were within reach, she became highly self-injurious or threatened staff, although she did not carry out these threats. For Diane, her lifelong struggle with mental health problems stemming from her abusive childhood has led to her offence and complicated her return to society.

Note that Diane did finally get released, and in 2011, after spending three years at a halfway house run by the Elizabeth Fry Society, she moved into a supervised apartment for people with mental health problems (Société Elizabeth Fry du Québec, 2011).

Source: Ménard, J. (Producer), Turgeon. J. (Producer), & Cadieux, M. (Writer/Director). (2003). *Sentenced to life* [Motion picture]. Canada: National Film Board.

Another example of a personality disorder in a woman offender can be seen in Box 8.5. In this case, the offender was older than most typical offenders and did not have a criminal background. She was married and the mother of a young child at the time of her offence. Therefore, she had managed to live in society well into adulthood. At the time of her offence, however, she was experiencing a great deal of stress. Her emotional instability and impulsiveness affected the choices she made to deal with her stress.

BOX 8.5

Lisa Samberg

Lisa Samberg was 40 years old when she fed her 16-month-old daughter 30 crushed sleeping pills mixed with apple sauce and then suffocated the baby with a plastic bag over her head while she slept. Then Lisa tried to take her own life by overdosing on pills, slashing her wrists, and suffocating herself. However, she survived and was charged with the death of her child.

During the trial, it came to light that Lisa had mental health problems and severe stressors in her life. She was, however, able to understand the consequences of her actions and to understand the court proceedings, so she was capable of facing her charge. She had been diagnosed with borderline personality disorder, her husband had threatened to serve her with divorce papers on her 40th birthday, and she was losing her apartment. She

also felt betrayed by her parents, who were helping her ex-husband.

Her lawyer argued that she should be found not criminally responsible on account of mental disorder. He suggested that the weight of so many stressors caused her to snap. Lisa honestly believed she was doing the right thing when she decided to kill her daughter. Lisa wrote in a suicide letter that she considered killing only herself but decided to kill the baby to save her from a dead mother and a bad father. She wanted the baby to have a chance of a stable family in the afterlife.

Lisa Samberg was convicted of manslaughter and sentenced to two years in a halfway house where she could receive treatment.

Source: *R v Samberg*, 2003 CanLII 68782 (Qc CS).

Women offenders suffering from mental disorders such as schizophrenia are less common than women offenders with other mental health problems, such as personality disorders. Women who have schizophrenia may hear voices that tell them to commit a crime. These voices can be very powerful and are referred to as "command hallucinations." When experiencing these hallucinations, the people feel compelled to obey the voices, which can order them to steal, assault, or kill someone, leading to serious offences.

Depression and anxiety are often seen among women offenders and may have pre-existed the offence or developed in prison. The impact of dealing with one's crime and coping with a prison sentence can lead to low moods, anxieties, and feelings of worthlessness and hopelessness.

Because so many women offenders have been victims of physical and/or sexual abuse, post-traumatic stress disorder is not uncommon among them. These women may have intrusive thoughts about the incidents or flashbacks to the incidents and are easily provoked to anger. Substance abuse is a common problem for women with another mental disorder—adding to the complications and challenges in their lives.

When assessing the mental health of women offenders, it is important to consider the background and environment in which these women have grown up and have lived in as adults. They may have experienced sexism and violence that have had a strong negative impact on their lives and have led to behaviours that have come to be labelled as criminal or pathological. The role that such labelling plays in the development and current status of their mental health should not be underestimated. Some authors would even argue against any such labelling of women offenders because it focuses the social problem of women offenders onto the individual women, whereas the root of the problem is the sexism, racism, classism, and violence that they have experienced (Kendall, 2000). In this analysis, solutions to the problem of women offenders need to be targeted at a societal level and not an individual one.

The Relation of Mental Health Status to Offending

In popular culture, people with mental illnesses are commonly depicted as being dangerous. They act in ways that are strange and unpredictable and provide fodder for sensational books and movies. But are they really more dangerous than others?

What we know about this area is unclear because there are many factors that complicate the interpretation of the research. In general, however, most studies that compare the rate of offending of people with mental illnesses with that of the general public find a higher rate of criminal activity among those with mental illnesses (Choe, Teplin, & Abram, 2008). Hodgins (1998), for example, found that both men and women who had been hospitalized with a diagnosis of a major mental disorder had more likely been convicted of a crime than people who had never been admitted to a psychiatric hospital. The difference in the proportion of offending between the hospitalized group and the non-hospitalized group was even larger for convictions of violent offences.

What role does mental illness play in offending? One factor that frequently appears in the literature is the abuse of alcohol or drugs in the criminal behaviour of people with mental illnesses (Steadman et al., 1998; Wallace, Mullen, & Burgess, 2004). Steadman et al. (1998), for example, found that substance abuse was the main factor in predicting violent behaviour in discharged psychiatric patients. They stated that "there was no significant difference between the prevalence of violence by patients without symptoms of substance abuse and the prevalence of violence by others living in the same neighborhoods who were also without symptoms of substance abuse" (p. 393). Does this mean that people with mental illnesses are at no higher risk for violence than anyone else in the community? No. The patients in this study were twice as likely to abuse substances when they were first discharged from the hospital as the community sample (Torrey, Stanley, Monahan, & Steadman, 2008). These authors also noted that alcohol and drug abuse among the patients raised their risk of violence more than it did for the community sample. Substance abuse is thus an important factor in violent and criminal behaviour in people with mental illnesses.

A second factor that may have an impact on criminal behaviour in people with mental illnesses is whether they are compliant with their mental health treatment. Discharged patients who regularly attended their treatment sessions in the community were found to engage in less violent behaviour than those who did not (Steadman et al., 1998; Torrey et al., 2008).

What about *women* with mental illnesses? Hodgins (1998) noted that "mental disorders were associated with a greater increase in the risk of criminality and violence among women" (p. S31). Why? It is likely that substance abuse once again plays a role. As already noted, there is a very high rate of substance abuse among women offenders, especially those with mental health problems.

Not all mental disorders have the same level of risk for criminal activity. Even within a certain diagnosis, the level of risk for offending can change. For example, schizophrenia is associated with an increased risk of offending (Bloom & Wilson, 2000; Wallace et al., 2004). Not all people with schizophrenia are violent; only a minority are. But among this small minority, a relationship has been found between aggression and the appearance of psychotic symptoms; that is, when the psychotic symptoms were active, the person with schizophrenia was more likely to become violent (Bloom & Wilson, 2000). Also, people with schizophrenia who were not taking their medication and who were using alcohol or drugs were at increased risk of engaging in violent crime (Bloom & Wilson, 2000).

Mood disorders have a complex association with criminal activity. The main symptom of depression is a low mood. Other symptoms are a loss of concentration, a lowering of self-worth, a pessimistic view of the future, and thoughts of suicide or self-harm (APA, 2013). When people are depressed, they often do not have the energy or inclination to become involved with crime. The exceptions are people who are depressed enough to not care about their life, because they can be dangerous to others. For example, in "suicide by cop," or victim-precipitated homicide, depressed people have been known to become aggressive toward police officers in the hope that the officers will kill them.

Manic episodes, on the other hand, involve a prolonged higher mood or irritable mood and include symptoms such as grandiosity, insomnia, and increased motor activity. People in a manic state are prone to taking risks that may bring them into conflict with the criminal justice system.

One could speculate that people with mental health problems may be targeted for arrest by police because of police bias toward the mentally ill, but the limited research in this area has not borne this out. A Canadian study did not find that police officers held any more negative views toward people with mental illnesses than the general public (Cotton, 2004). An American study found no evidence of bias against people with mental illnesses in the arrest pattern of officers in the five police departments that they examined (Engel & Silver, 2001).

However, there remains widespread concern that police officers are more likely to use force in encounters with people with mental illnesses (Toronto Police, 2014). Police services in Canada have been concerned with the issue of interactions between officers and people with mental illnesses for many years. As a result, they have tackled the issue on several fronts—by developing training programs for all officers; by creating special teams of officers with more intensive training to handle these types of interactions; by having a mental health worker attend calls with them; and by fostering improved relationships with the mental health system (Cotton & Coleman, 2017). Psychologists and other mental health professionals have worked along with the police on these initiatives. Currently, police services continue to examine and evolve their strategy for dealing with people with mental illnesses (Cotton & Coleman, 2017).

▶ WHAT DO YOU THINK?

How should police officers respond to situations where someone with a mental health problem is behaving in a manner that could lead to harm to themselves or others? What specific steps should they take?

Recidivism Rates of Offenders with Mental Disorders

How do the reoffence or recidivism rates of offenders with mental disorders in general, and women in particular, compare with the reoffence or recidivism rates of other offenders? As already noted, in comparison with low-risk populations (that is, the community), people with mental disorders have a higher rate of involvement with crime. When we compare offenders with mental disorders with other offenders, however, the story changes. Bonta, Law, and Hanson (1998) examined the predictors of reoffending for offenders with mental disorders and other offenders. In their study, they reviewed the research of many previous studies, which comprised both male and female offenders. Compared with other offenders, offenders with mental disorders were found to be less likely to reoffend in general or to reoffend violently. Severe mental disorders, such as schizophrenia, were inversely related to general and violent recidivism, whereas mood disorders, such as depression, showed no relationship with reoffending. Also, the researchers noted that the predictors of reoffending for offenders with mental disorders were the same as the predictors for other offenders (criminal history and early onset of criminality, for example). The person's clinical diagnosis was not shown to be a predictor of their reoffending.

One reason why no relationship was found between some severe mental disorders and offending is the transient nature of mental illness. Although hallucinations and delusions may trigger criminal behaviour in the short run, they have no predictive utility in the long run (Bonta et al., 1998). After the acute symptoms of the illness have abated, either on their own or with treatment, the psychopathology that was supportive of criminal behaviour may have disappeared.

Although offenders with mental disorders are at less risk to reoffend, people working in the criminal justice system and the general public view them as more dangerous than other offenders. Offenders with mental disorders are not released from prison as early as other offenders and tend to serve more of their sentences before release (Porporino & Motiuk, 1995; Villeneuve & Quinsey, 1995). After their release from prison, offenders with mental disorders are returned to custody more often than other offenders, not for having committed a new offence, but for having violated a condition of their supervision, such as drinking or using drugs (Porporino & Motiuk, 1995). Other offenders are most often returned only after committing a new crime. Porporino and Motiuk (1995) note that a bias appears to be working against offenders with mental disorders; they are handled more cautiously despite being less likely to reoffend than other offenders in the sample.

What about women offenders with mental disorders? One study compared the rate of recidivism for women offenders with mental disorders to that for women offenders without such disorders (Blanchette & Motiuk, 1996). These researchers found no difference in the recidivism rates between these two groups: both groups committed new offences at the same rate. The women with mental disorders were, however, more often returned to custody for violating the conditions of their release, just as in the mixed sample previously discussed. One important difference between this sample and the previous one is that the women offenders with mental disorders were not matched with the other women offenders for criminal history. The women offenders with mental disorders had more prior violent offences on their record, suggesting that they may have been at higher risk than the other women. This finding may explain why their recidivism rate was not lower than that of women offenders without mental disorders, as was found in the mixed sample previously discussed. If a less risky sample of offenders with mental disorders had been used, they may have recidivated at a lower rate than the women offenders without mental disorders, just as was found in the mixed sample.

In terms of determining predictors of recidivism, Blanchette and Motiuk (1996) found that, similar to the findings in the mixed sample, the same predictors that work for other populations are relevant for women with mental disorders (for example, criminal history and early onset of criminality).

The Assessment of Offenders with Mental Disorders

The process of assessing offenders for mental health problems is very similar to that in any other setting. The main approaches to assessing mental disorders are brief screening interviews, in-depth interviews, structured interviews, paper and pencil tests, and behavioural observations. Each approach has strengths and weaknesses, and sometimes more than one method is used to maximize the collection of relevant information. A brief discussion of each approach follows.

Mental Health Screening

Canadian federal and provincial correctional facilities have committed to implementing a screening process for all offenders entering their systems (Correctional Service of Canada, 2012a). A trained staff member conducts a brief screening of each offender upon arrival at a correctional facility. The screening consists of a series of questions designed to assess the probability that the person may have a mental disorder. The results of this screening will determine whether further assessment is warranted.

Interviews

The most commonly used method of assessing mental disorders is for the clinician to interview the person. Typically, a psycho-social interview is used to examine many facets of the person's life. The clinician must first rule out the possibility that any current mental health problems are caused by a physical problem or by alcohol or drug use, so questions are asked pertaining to these two areas. Often an interview will begin with background information from childhood. Early childhood illnesses, injuries, and physical, sexual, or emotional abuse may be relevant to the current problems experienced by the person. For example, childhood sexual abuse may lead to low self-esteem and depression or to substance abuse. Lingering symptoms of post-traumatic stress disorder may also persist into adulthood.

A thorough history will be taken of the present symptoms that brought the client to the clinician. The clinician needs to determine when these symptoms started, what was going on in the person's life at that time, and the seriousness of the symptoms in terms of their impact on the person's life. For example, are they able to do the things that they normally do? Are the symptoms keeping them from doing things that they usually enjoy?

When completing a psycho-social history on a woman, a family history would be included. Information such as the makeup of the family in which the woman was raised and some details of her childhood and adolescence would be gathered. Another important area of family functioning is the extent of support that the person receives from family members. Families can range from being extremely helpful to being non-existent to being just another stressor in the person's life. It is important for the clinician to know what role the family plays in the person's life and whether family members are available to provide assistance if necessary.

Other areas that may be discussed in the interview are employment, finances, and social and recreational activities. These areas may be strengths or assets in a person's life or further stressors that need to be dealt with. For example, if a woman is well educated and has a good job, these assets will help to offset stressors in other areas of her life. If, however, the woman has little education, unstable employment, and few financial resources, then these may be additional stressors with which she needs help.

The outcome of all of this provides the clinician with a thorough history and detailed information about the present concerns and the resources available to assist the woman. The clinician will then be able to determine whether significant mental health problems are present and to develop a plan to work on any identified problem areas.

One shortcoming of the interview process is the issue of the reliability of the information gathered. A person, especially during times of acute episodes of a disorder, may be unwilling or unable to provide enough information to contribute to an accurate assessment. For this reason, information is typically also collected from external sources, such as official records from hospitals or schools or from interviews with other family members.

Structured Interviews

Structured interviews are more formal types of interviews where the questions have been set in advance. These interviews are geared toward a specific goal, such as making a diagnosis. One example is the Diagnostic Interview Schedule, which was used in the research on assessing the prevalence of mental disorders in federal offenders discussed earlier in this chapter (Blanchette & Motiuk, 1996). The answers provided by the participants determine whether a diagnosis is to be made and the nature of that diagnosis.

Another commonly used structured interview is the Structured Clinical Interview for the *DSM-5*, also referred to as the SCID (First, Williams, Karg, & Spitzer, 2016). The SCID provides a systematic method of assessing the symptoms that make up the *DSM-5* criteria for the various mental disorders. As an example, a question that asks about hearing voices that others cannot hear addresses auditory hallucinations, which is one of the criteria for the diagnosis of schizophrenia. Other questions ask about moods, anxieties, and alcohol use. This structured interview then aids the clinician in making a diagnosis.

Paper and Pencil Tests

Paper and pencil tests are widely used to assess all types of mental health problems. They have the advantages of being simple to administer, objective to score, and time-efficient, requiring little of the clinician's time. The results of the tests can be compared with other people's scores, thereby assisting the clinician with the diagnostic process. For example, if the woman's scores are similar to those of people who have been diagnosed with depression, then she is likely also depressed.

A variety of well-developed, standardized, comprehensive tests are available, such as the Personality Assessment Inventory (Morey, 2003), and the Millon Clinical Multiaxial Inventory–III (Millon, 2006). These tests comprise questions related to symptoms associated with a wide range of mental disorders. The results of these tests will help determine whether a woman is experiencing symptoms severe enough to require treatment.

Other paper and pencil tests are much smaller in scale and aim to assess only one particular problem area. One example is the Beck Depression Inventory (Beck, Ward, Mendelson, Mock, & Erbaugh, 1961). This is a 21-item self-report scale that has been in use for decades. Extensive research has found this test to be a reliable measure of depression. The questions cover all symptoms of depression, such as feeling sad, feeling pessimistic, having suicidal thoughts, and problems with eating, sleeping, and lack of energy. This test takes only about 10 minutes to administer, so it is a quick and reliable screening tool for depression and possible suicide risk.

Because of the extent of abuse in the lives of women offenders, the long-term, negative traumatic effects of abuse are an area worthy of thorough assessment. One test designed for this purpose is the Trauma Symptom Inventory, developed by Briere, Elliot, Harris, and Cotman (1995). This test comprises 100 questions pertaining to trauma symptoms, such as depression, anger/irritability, anxiety, and intrusive experiences. People with histories of physical or sexual abuse score high on this test and would need further assessment and treatment.

Behavioural Observations

Another type of assessment is that of simply observing people and recording how they respond to various situations. Incarceration provides extensive opportunities for observing how a woman might interact with others, her communication style, and her activities. Such observations are a useful part of an assessment. Specific published scales of behavioural assessment may be used or the clinician may develop a scale tailored to the woman being assessed. For example, to determine whether a woman has difficulty controlling her emotions, such as anger, a checklist of her interactions with others could be devised. Staff who work closely with the woman, and the woman herself, could note any angry outbursts and the events that may have provoked them. In this way, relevant treatment targets can be identified.

One area in which direct observation is particularly important is the assessment of suicide potential. A woman may choose not to tell anyone that she is considering suicide. Observant staff, however, may notice changes in her behaviour, such as keeping to herself more than usual or not interacting with her usual friends or not engaging in her normal activities. Sudden changes in any areas of a woman's activities may alert staff to inquire further about her current mental state.

The object of assessment, then, is to identify and clarify problems that people are experiencing. The results of a thorough assessment will guide the direction that treatment will take. For example, if a woman is feeling low in mood, she could be clinically depressed or she might be feeling low as part of a pattern of unstable emotions that indicate borderline personality disorder. For each of these problems, a very different treatment approach would be used. Therefore, the clinician needs to be able to fully understand the nature of the presenting problems, a process that is best achieved by a thorough assessment.

The Treatment of Offenders with Mental Disorders

The gold standard for treating offenders in general is the application of the risk-need-responsivity principles of Andrews and Bonta (2006). The *risk principle* states that criminal behaviour can be predicted and treatment services need to be matched to the risk level of the offender; that is, an offender of higher risk would need extensive treatment, whereas a low-risk offender would need little or no intervention. The *needs principle* states that, for treatment to be effective in lowering the risk of recidivism, it must target the needs of the offender that are directly related to reoffending (that is, the criminogenic needs—the needs related to the predictors of recidivism—such as criminal attitudes). The *responsivity principle* has two facets: (1) the *general responsivity principle* states that social learning and cognitive-behavioural strategies, which have been shown to be the most powerful interventions for change, should be used; and (2) the *specific responsivity principle* states that treatment should be delivered in a way that is suited to the offender's learning style or ability. For example, an offender who is of low intelligence would need services geared to her level of understanding.

Although most of the research on these principles has involved males or mixed samples of offenders, one study examined the effectiveness of the risk principle on women offenders in Ohio (Lovins, 2007). Women who had completed an intensive treatment program were compared with those who had not. The level of risk of these women was also examined. The researchers found that the high-risk women who completed treatment were half as likely to reoffend as those who had received no treatment. Low-risk women in intensive treatment were three times more likely to reoffend than those without treatment. The author did not speculate on why the low-risk women failed to benefit from treatment. It is possible that, because these women were already of low risk, there was little room for improvement. However, this supposition does not account for why their risk level increased, as opposed to staying the same.

Most of the treatment programs that address offenders' criminogenic needs have been developed and validated on male offenders because the vast majority of offenders are male. Also, there is a huge overlap between the needs of male and female offenders—for example, substance abuse and the lack of education and employment (Hollin & Palmer, 2006). When the effectiveness on women offenders of programs developed for men was examined, it was found that they were at least as effective for the women as they were for men (Gobeil, Blanchette, & Stewart, 2016).

What about the effectiveness of programs designed especially for women? Although the needs of men and women may be similar, the routes that they took to acquiring those needs may be different and may therefore require different approaches to treatment. Women offenders are more likely to suffer from a mental disorder and to have parenting stress and a history of trauma. Gender-informed programs include these factors in their design as well as considering a more woman-centred theoretical approach drawing from feminism and focusing on the woman's strengths rather than deficiencies. When gender-informed programs were evaluated, they were found to be even more significantly associated with reductions in recidivism than other programs (Gobeil et al., 2016). This more woman-centred approach could be considered a responsivity issue, whereby the treatment program has been adapted to the learning style of the woman offender.

Because women with mental disorders have such a high rate of substance abuse, it is worthwhile to examine the evidence for the effectiveness of substance abuse treatment programs for women offenders. In a review of such programs in several countries, it was found that the most successful programs, in terms of reduction of recidivism, were intensive programs such as residential therapeutic communities, particularly those with a follow-up component to support the women on release to the community (Stewart & Gobeil, 2015). See Box 8.6 for a description of a therapeutic community.

BOX 8.6

Therapeutic Community

A therapeutic community is a highly structured residential treatment program, usually for dealing with substance abuse problems. In the majority of communities, there are several phases that the client must pass through to successfully complete the program. This whole process can last from six months to a year, depending largely on the severity of the problem and the client's response to treatment. Well-defined criteria, such as full participation in all aspects of the program and total abstinence from alcohol and drugs, must be met in order to advance to the next phase of a program. Because all of the participants live together, there is a great emphasis on peer support and accountability.

Therapeutic communities take a holistic approach and are highly intensive, involving all facets of the client's life. Individual and group counselling is provided to address social skills, problem solving, anger management, education, employment, and any other issues that could again lead to the misuse of substances. Typically, the client's strengths are also identified and built upon. Once the program is completed, many therapeutic communities provide an after-care component in order to support the client through the difficult process of re-entry into the community.

In Canada, the Correctional Service of Canada's substance abuse treatment program for women offenders was evaluated by Matheson, Doherty, and Grant (2009). They compared the rates of recidivism of participants who completed the whole program with those who completed only the introductory component (which was primarily educational) and/or the relapse prevention part of the program. What they found was that the women who completed the whole program, which included an intensive treatment component, returned to prison less often than those who only completed the introductory and/or relapse prevention parts of the program—however, only marginally so and not at a significantly lower rate. Only when the women who completed the whole program also participated in the community relapse prevention and maintenance part of the program were huge gains obtained. This result highlights the importance of the continuity of treatment for women offenders as they transition back into the community, where they may face their old triggers for substance abuse.

Women Offenders with Mental Disorders

Women offenders with mental disorders often have many of the same treatment needs as other offenders—needs for assistance with employment, finances, and pro-criminal attitudes, for example. However, they often have additional mental health needs that require attention first before they can focus on treatment programs for their criminogenic needs. In other cases, the mental disorder may be the criminogenic need itself. This would be the case where hallucinations or delusions led directly to the crime.

Types of Treatment

In general, offenders with serious mental disorders are treated similarly to people in the community. Offenders have access to mental health professionals, including psychiatrists who can prescribe medication to target symptoms of their illnesses. For example, a depressed offender would have her low mood targeted for treatment, whereas the treatment for a schizophrenic offender would focus on her hallucinations or delusions.

In addition, psychological treatments such as cognitive-behavioural therapy may be used. This therapy can help change some thinking patterns, including such thoughts as "I am worthless," which sustain a depressed mood. By challenging the accuracy of this thought—for example, by examining the evidence for or against the statement—the patient is encouraged to change this thought to a more useful one, such as "I am a worthwhile person." Such a change in thinking can affect the woman's outlook and allow for positive changes in her life.

Within the Canadian federal correctional service, an overall mental health strategy has been developed for women offenders (Laishes, 2002). The goal of the strategy is "to develop and maintain a continuum of care that addresses the varied mental health needs of women offenders in order to maximize well-being and to promote effective reintegration" (Laishes, 2002, p. 10). The strategy notes that offenders are legally entitled to treatment for mental disorders regardless of its impact on recidivism and that this treatment must meet community standards

Since then, a new mental health strategy has been implemented for all offenders—both male and female (Correctional Service of Canada, 2012b). This strategy also emphasizes the importance of a continuum of mental health care. Mental health services must be available for offenders from admission (mental health screening), throughout incarceration, and up to and including release to the community. Many of the principles of this strategy reflect those of the women's mental health strategy (Laishes, 2002), although specific aspects have been updated as programs and services have changed over the years. Both documents have provided structure and guidance to staff in dealing with offenders with mental disorders at all stages of their sentence.

One of the outcomes of the mental health strategy for women offenders (Laishes, 2002) was the development of specific structured living units for women with mental health problems within the regular federal women's institutions (Sly & Taylor, 2005). Women with minimum or medium security classifications are admitted voluntarily to these residential settings. The units provide 24-hour support and staff supervision in a therapeutic environment, thereby allowing for more intensive treatment than in the regular institutional setting. The therapeutic approach adopted by these units is dialectical behaviour therapy (Linehan, 1993).

Dialectical Behaviour Therapy

Dialectical behaviour therapy (DBT) is a variant of cognitive-behaviour therapy that was designed specifically to treat people diagnosed with borderline personality disorder (Linehan, 1993). People with borderline personality disorder have difficulty regulating their emotions and have very unstable relationships due to their tendency to initially idealize people and then to become angry and disappointed in them for minor or misperceived slights. They have negative feelings about themselves and often engage in self-damaging behaviours, such as self-injury, suicide attempts, and substance abuse.

The term *dialectic* refers to a logical examination of ideas, often through questions and answers, to determine their validity. Dialectics form the basis of the approach of this type of therapy; that is, the client's beliefs are examined logically and challenged appropriately. A hallmark of DBT is its "reconciliation of opposites in a continual process of synthesis" (Linehan, 1993, p. 19). One example is the acceptance of clients just as they are, while at the same time trying to teach them to change.

DBT has several main or core strategies, such as validating the woman's responses by acknowledging, for example, that her responses make sense in her current life. Other core strategies include skills training and problem solving. Skills training is conducted in a group format, whereas individual psychotherapy sessions help women to integrate the new skills into their daily lives. The goals of the treatment, in the short run, are for the women to gain insight into their behaviours and to learn how to control their emotions and behaviours. In the long run, the goal is to move the women "toward more balanced and integrative responses to life situations" (Linehan, 1993, p. 124). Thus, through the acquisition of skills such as emotional control and problem solving, the woman will be more effective in her responses and will have an increased quality of life. See Box 8.7 for a description of how people learn to regulate their emotions.

BOX 8.7

Emotion Regulation Skills

People with borderline personality disorder experience strong and unstable emotions. They often feel angry, frustrated, depressed, and anxious. These strong emotions can lead to problematic behaviours, such as self-harm or substance abuse, which may be attempts to find relief from these emotions. Emotional regulation, then, is a very important component of treatment for borderline personality disorder.

The first step in learning to regulate emotions is to identify the emotion that is being experienced. Clients are taught how to pay attention and be mindful of what they are experiencing and to describe their emotional states. They learn how to increase their tolerance of distressing emotions and to use strategies to reduce negative emotions and to increase positive ones.

An example of this process is an exercise whereby the client learns to describe the feeling of sadness using many different terms, such as despair, grief, unhappiness, and so on. Next, the client examines events that may have prompted the state of sadness, such as not getting something that she wanted or being separated from a loved one. The client's beliefs behind the precipitating event are then interpreted; for example, perhaps she is sad after not getting something that she wanted because she believes she will not get what she wants or needs in life. Perhaps she is sad about being separated from someone she loves because she believes that the separation will last for a long time or forever. These beliefs can be examined and confronted in order to ascertain their validity. Lastly, positive experiences need to be built into the clients' lives. They learn how to focus on doing more pleasant things that bring them happiness. In this way, by learning how to manage negative emotional states and increasing the number of positive ones, they are better equipped to control their emotions and lead a more self-directed, satisfying life.

Source: Linehan, M.M. (1993). *Cognitive-behavioral treatment of borderline personality disorder.* New York: Guilford Press.

The effectiveness of the DBT program was evaluated by Blanchette, Flight, Verbrugge, Gobeil, and Taylor (2011). This thorough study examined the results of a number of paper and pencil tests of the offenders' mental health symptoms before and after the program. The level of the offenders' functioning within the facility was also assessed, as well as how many offenders returned to custody after release. What they found was that the women improved greatly on a wide variety of measures of psychological symptoms. Assessments by the women themselves, as well as by the staff, found that the women offenders felt less anxious and depressed after participating in the program. These women also obtained higher scores on measures of self-control, including their ability to manage their emotions. Maladaptive coping skills such as confrontation and avoidance of problems were used less often. After participating in the program, the women also showed a reduction in involvement with institutional incidents, including self-injury. In terms of their recidivism rates, the study found that their rate of return to prison for a new offence was much lower than for other offenders. However, their return to prison for any reason, such as violating a condition of their release or for a new of-fence, was higher. This phenomenon has been noted in previous studies (Blanchette & Motiuk, 1996; Porporino & Motiuk, 1995), resulting in much speculation over the cause. One possibility is that these women are treated differently—for example, with more caution than other women offenders. However, more work needs to be done to uncover the reason with any certainty.

SUMMARY

As compared with community samples, offenders—both male and female—exhibit higher rates of mental disorders. The greatest discrepancy between the offender and community samples is seen in the offenders' abuse of alcohol and/or drugs relative to people in the community. This difference is greatest for the women, where the women offenders' rate of abuse is 30 times that of community women. The rate of alcohol/substance abuse among women offenders is also higher than that of male offenders. Women offenders are more often diagnosed with other mental disorders than are male offenders, especially with a borderline personality disorder, anxiety, or a mood disorder.

One area of significance in the histories of women offenders is that of physical and sexual abuse. Compared with women in the community, women offenders have ex-perienced both types of abuse at a much higher rate. Compared with male offenders, women offenders not only have a higher rate of abuse but also have experienced more severe abuse over a longer period of time.

The abuse that many women offenders have experienced as children and adults contributes to the emotional difficulties they face while incarcerated. They are dealing with issues of betrayal and abandonment and the emotional pain of past histories of physical and sexual abuse. These experiences are not easily overcome, and they may lead to lasting difficulties with moods, self-image, and emotional control. The mental health symptoms that women offenders subsequently exhibit, such as self-injury and substance abuse, may be coping strategies they engage in to find relief.

A smaller group of women suffer from problems such as schizophrenia and intel-lectual disabilities, which are more likely due to their own physiological or biological makeup. For a number of reasons, these women have fallen into the criminal justice system instead of the mental health system.

Compared with other women, women with mental illnesses have a higher rate of involvement in criminal activity. Substance abuse, however, plays a key role in their violent or criminal behaviour. Compared with other women offenders, women offend-ers with mental illnesses are at no higher risk to reoffend.

Women offenders with mental health problems pose many challenges for the criminal justice system. The adoption of a national mental health strategy for all prov-inces and territories and for the federal correctional system is a positive step toward addressing these challenges. A process of ongoing review and implementation of improved assessment and treatment approaches is key. In this manner, the needs of women offenders with mental health problems can best be met, both while the women are incarcerated and while they integrate back into society.

DISCUSSION QUESTIONS

1. According to Sinha (2013), Canadian women are more often the victims of violence than men, but only by 5 percent. Recent research has found that the figure has gone up to 20 percent (Statistics Canada, 2015). However, the nature of their victimization is very different. Women are more often the victims of sexual assault and by someone they know, often an intimate partner, whereas men are more often victims of physical assault by a stranger, friend, or acquaintance. How could this different pattern of victimization contribute to the difference seen in the mental health of men and women offenders?

2. If the only treatment programs available for women offenders were designed for male offenders, do you think that women should be expected to participate in them? Why or why not?

3. You are asked for your opinion about a woman offender who is creating problems in the institution. She is often upset—for example, yelling at staff or crying and slashing herself. Several therapists have tried to help her to understand her problems with the hope that this understanding will lead to changes in her behaviour. However, she keeps "firing" them for not being there for her—that is, for not always being able to see her immediately and not always agreeing with her. What do you think may be going on with her? What possible approach within the prison system might be helpful for her?

4. What are the most important factors that would help a woman offender with a mental disorder remain in the community after her release from prison?

ADDITIONAL RESOURCES

Suggested Readings

Blanchette, K., & Brown, S.L. (2006). *The assessment and treatment of women offenders*. West Sussex, UK: John Wiley & Sons.

Mental health strategy for corrections in Canada: A federal-provincial-territorial partnership. Retrieved from www.csc-scc.gc.ca/health/092/MH-strategy-eng.pdf.

Websites

Canadian Mental Health Association: www.cmha.ca

Mental Health Commission of Canada: www.mentalhealthcommission.ca

REFERENCES

American Psychiatric Association. (2013). *Diagnostic and statistical manual of mental disorders* (5th ed.). Arlington, VA: Author.

Andrews, D.A., & Bonta, J. (2006). *The psychology of criminal conduct* (4th ed.). Cincinnati: LexisNexis/Anderson.

Beaudette, J., Power, J., & Stewart, L. (2015). *National prevalence of mental disorders among incoming federally-sentenced men offenders*. (Research report no. R-357). Ottawa: Research Branch, Correctional Service Canada.

Beck, A.T., Ward, C.H., Mendelson, M., Mock, J., & Erbaugh, J. (1961). An inventory for measuring depression. *Archives of General Psychiatry, 4*, 561–571.

Blanchette, K., Flight, J., Verbrugge, P., Gobeil, R., & Taylor, K. (2011). *Dialectical behavior therapy within a women's structured living environment* (User report no. 2011, R-241). Ottawa: Research Branch, Correctional Service of Canada.

Blanchette, K., & Motiuk, L. (1996). *Female offenders with and without major mental health problems: A comparative investigation* (Research report no. R-6). Ottawa: Research Branch, Correctional Service of Canada.

Bland, R.C., Orn, H., & Newman, S.C. (1988). Lifetime prevalence of psychiatric disorders in Edmonton. *Acta Psychiatrica Scandinavica, 77* (Suppl. 338), 24–32.

Bloom, J., & Wilson, W.H. (2000). Offenders with schizophrenia. In S. Hodgins & R. Müller-Isberner (Eds.), *Violence, crime and mentally disordered offenders: Concepts and methods for effective treatment and prevention* (pp. 113–130). West Sussex, UK: John Wiley & Sons.

Boe, R., & Vuong, B. (2002). Mental health trends among federal inmates. *Forum on Corrections Research, 14*(2), 6–9.

Bonta, J., Law, M., & Hanson, K. (1998). The prediction of criminal and violent recidivism among mentally disordered offenders: A meta-analysis. *Psychological Bulletin, 123*(2), 123–142.

Bonta, J., Pang, B., & Wallace-Capretta, S. (1995). Predictors of recidivism among incarcerated female offenders. *The Prison Journal, 75*, 277–294.

Briere, J., Elliot, D., Harris, K., & Cotman, A. (1995). Trauma symptom inventory: Psychometrics and association with childhood and adult victimization in clinical samples. *Journal of Interpersonal Violence, 104*, 387–401.

Canada, Standing Senate Committee on Social Affairs, Science and Technology. (2004). *Mental health, mental illness and addiction: Overview of policies and programs in Canada* (Interim report). Ottawa: Author.

Choe, J.Y., Teplin, L.A., & Abram, K.M. (2008). Perpetration of violence, violent victimization, and severe mental illness: Balancing public health concerns. *Psychiatric Services, 59*, 153–164.

Correctional Service of Canada. (2009). *The changing federal offender population*. Retrieved from http://www.csc-scc.gc.ca/research/sr-2009-eng.shtml.

Correctional Service of Canada. (2012a). *Mental health strategy for corrections in Canada*. Retrieved from www.csc-scc.gc.ca/health/092/MH-strategy-eng.pdf.

Correctional Service of Canada. (2012b). *Towards a continuum of care: Correctional Service Canada mental health strategy*. Retrieved from www.csc-scc.gc.ca/002/006/002006-2000-eng.shtml.

Cotton, D. (2004). The attitudes of Canadian police officers toward the mentally ill. *International Journal of Law and Psychiatry, 27*, 135–146.

Cotton, D. & Coleman, T. (2017). The evolution of police interactions with people with mental health problems: The third generation (strategic) approach. In C. Mitchell & E. Dorian, (Eds.), *Police psychology and its growing impact on modern law enforcement: Advances in psychology, mental health, and behavioral studies* (pp. 252–273). Hershey, PA: IGI Global.

Criminal Code, RSC 1985, c C-46.

Derkzen, D., Barker, J., McMillan, K., & Stewart, L. (2016). *Rates of current mental disorders among women offenders in custody in CSC*. Ottawa: Research Branch, Correctional Service of Canada.

Derkzen, D., Booth, L., McConnell, A., & Taylor, K. (2013). Mental health needs of federal female offenders. *Psychological Services, 10*(1), 24–36.

Engel, R.S., & Silver, E. (2001). Policing mentally disordered suspects: A reexamination of the criminalization hypothesis. *Criminology, 39*, 225–252.

Finn, A., Trevethan, S., Carrière, G., & Kowalski, M. (1999). Female inmates, Aboriginal inmates and inmates serving life sentences: A one day snapshot. *Juristat, 19*(5), 1–14.

First, M.B., Williams, J.B., Karg, R.S. & Spitzer, R.L. (2016). *Structured clinical interview for DSM-5 disorders (SCID-5CV)*. Washington, DC: American Psychiatric Press.

Gobeil, R., Blanchette, K., & Stewart, L. (2016). A meta-analytic review of correctional interventions for women offenders: Gender-neutral versus gender-informed approaches. *Criminal Justice and Behavior, 43*(3), 301–322.

Gray, J.E., Shone, M.A., & Liddle, P.F. (2008). *Canadian mental health law and policy* (2nd ed.). Toronto: Butterworths.

A health care needs assessment of federal inmates in Canada. (2004). *Canadian Journal of Public Health, 95* (Suppl. 1), S1–S63.

Heney, J. (1990). *Report on self-injurious behaviour in the Kingston Prison for Women*. Ottawa: Correctional Service of Canada.

Hodgins, S. (1998). Epidemiological investigations of the associations between major mental disorders and crime: Methodological limitations and validity of conclusions. *Social Psychiatry & Psychiatric Epidemiology, 33*, S29–S37.

Hollin, C.R., & Palmer, E.J. (2006). Criminogenic need and women offenders: A critique of the literature. *Legal and Criminological Psychology, 11*, 179–195.

Kendall, K. (1999). Criminal lunatic women in 19th century Canada. *Forum on Corrections Research, 11*(3), 46–49.

Kendall, K. (2000). Psy-ence Fiction: Inventing the mentally-disordered female prisoner. In K. Hannah-Moffat & M. Shaw (Eds.), *An ideal prison? Critical essays of women's imprisonment in Canada* (pp. 83–93). Halifax: Fernwood.

Laishes, J. (2002). *The 2002 mental health strategy for women offenders*. Ottawa: Correctional Service of Canada.

Linehan, M.M. (1993). *Cognitive-behavioral treatment of borderline personality disorder*. New York: Guilford Press.

Lovins, L. (2007, June). *Application of the risk principle to female offenders*. Poster presentation at the Canadian Psychological Association Conference, Ottawa.

Matheson, F.I., Doherty, S., & Grant, B.A. (2009), *Women offender substance abuse programming & community reintegration* (Report R-202). Ottawa: Correctional Service of Canada,. Retrieved from www.csc-scc.gc.ca/research/r202-eng.shtml.

Ménard, J. (Producer), Turgeon, J. (Producer), & Cadieux, M. (Writer/Director). (2003). *Sentenced to life* [Motion picture]. Canada: National Film Board.

Messina, N., Grella, C., Burdon, W., & Prendergast, M. (2007). Childhood adverse events and current drug-dependent prisoners. *Criminal Justice and Behavior, 3*(4), 1385–1401.

Millon, T. (2006). *Millon Clinical Multiaxial Inventory–III (MCMI–III) manual* (3rd ed.). Minneapolis, MN: Pearson Assessments.

Morey, L. (2003). *Essentials of PAI assessment.* Hoboken, NJ: John Wiley & Sons.

Pearson, C., Janz, T., & Ali, J. (2013). *Mental and substance abuse disorders in Canada.* Statistics Canada, Catalogue no. 82-624x. Retrieved from http://www.statcan.gc.ca/pub/82-624-x/2013001/article/11855-eng.htm.

Porporino, F., & Motiuk, L.L. (1995). The prison careers of mentally disordered offenders. *International Journal of Law and Psychiatry, 18,* 29–44.

Public Safety Canada. (2008). *Corrections and conditional release overview: An annual report 2008.* Catalogue no. PS1-3/2008E. Ottawa: Public Works and Government Services Canada.

R v Samberg, 2003 QC CS 68782.

Ruiz, M.A., Douglas, K.S., Edens, J.F., Nikolova, N.L., & Lilienfeld, S.O. (2012). Co-occurring mental health and substance use problems in offenders: implications for risk assessment. *Psychological Assessment, 24*(1), 77–87.

Shaw, M. (1994). *Ontario women in conflict with the law: A survey of women in institutions and under community supervision.* Ontario: Ministry of the Solicitor General and Correctional Service of Canada.

Sinha, M. (Ed.). (2013). Measuring violence against women: Statistical trends. *Juristat.* Statistics Canada, Catalogue no. 85-002-X, p. 122. Retrieved from http://www.statcan.gc.ca/pub/85-002-x/2013001/article/11766-eng.htm.

Sly, A., & Taylor, K. (2005). *Evaluation of psychosocial rehabilitation within the women's structured living environments* (User report no. 2005, R-163). Ottawa: Research Branch, Correctional Service of Canada.

Société Elizabeth Fry du Québec. (2011, November). *Report of the Société Elizabeth Fry du Québec to the General Assembly of CAEFS.* Retrieved from www.elizabethfry.ca/cms_docs/241/QC_rapport_CAEFS_nov_2011.docx.

Statistics Canada. (2015). Criminal victimization in Canada, 2014. *Juristat.* Retrieved from www.statcan.gc.ca/pub/85-002-x/2015001/article/14241-eng.htm.

Steadman, H.J., Mulvey, E.P., Monahan, J., Robbins, P.C., Appelbaum, P.S., Grisso, T., … Silver, E. (1998). Violence by people discharged from acute psychiatric inpatient facilities and by others in the same neighborhoods. *Archives of General Psychiatry, 55,* 393–401.

Stewart, L., & Gobeil, R. (2015). Correctional interventions for women offenders: A rapid evidence assessment. *Journal of Criminological Research, Policy and Practice, 1*(3), 116–130.

Tam, K., & Derkzen, D. (2014). *Exposure to trauma among women offenders: A review of the literature.* (User report no. 2014, R-333). Ottawa: Research Branch, Correctional Service of Canada.

Toronto Police. (2014). *Police encounters with people in crisis: An independent review conducted by the Honourable Frank Iacobbucci for Chief of Police William Blair, Toronto Police Services.* Retrieved from https://www.torontopolice.on.ca/publications/files/reports/police_encounters_with_people_in_crisis_2014.pdf.

Torrey, E.F., Stanley, J., Monahan, J., & Steadman, H.J. (2008). The MacArthur violence risk assessment: Two views ten years after its initial publication. *Psychiatric Services, 59,* 147–152.

Villeneuve, D.B., & Quinsey, V.L. (1995). Predictors of general and violent recidivism among mentally disordered inmates. *Criminal Justice and Behavior, 22,* 397–410.

Wallace, C., Mullen, P.E., & Burgess, P. (2004). Criminal offending in schizophrenia over a 25-year period marked by deinstitutionalization and increasing prevalence of comorbid substance use disorders. *American Journal of Psychiatry, 161,* 716–727.

Webster, C.D., & Hucker, S. (2007). *Violence risk: Assessment and management.* Toronto: John Wiley & Sons.

World Health Organization. (2014). *Mental health: A state of well-being.* Retrieved from www.who.int/features/factfiles/mental_health/en.

CHAPTER 9 / BRENDA M. RESTOULE* (WAUB-ZHE-KWENS; EAGLE CLAN)

Indigenous Women and the Criminal Justice System

Introduction

The criminal justice system in Canada was originally developed for the needs of white men, resulting in assessments, services, and programs that are not gender- or culture-specific. When applied to female offenders it has resulted in ill-equipped services that largely ignored female-specific risk factors and health needs. For Indigenous women, this means that their culture-specific needs have also gone ignored. The Correctional Service of Canada (CSC) has a number of directives to ensure gender- and culture-specific programming more adequately meets the needs of its changing offender profile.

After numerous challenges and reports such as *Creating Choices* (Canada, Task Force on Federally Sentenced Women [TFFSW], 1990) and the report by the Arbour Inquiry (Canada, Commission of Inquiry into Certain Events, 1996), CSC has acknowledged programming must better address the unique needs and risk factors of women, including Indigenous women. To date, the correctional system continues to strive to meet many of these recommendations. Indigenous women are a unique group who experience racism, discrimination, and marginalization within the Canadian criminal justice system despite the numerous reports calling for significant changes to CSC.

As a group, Indigenous people[1] generally experience racism, discrimination, and marginalization from the Canadian population. They experience significant social and health problems that exacerbate their marginalized status in society. Indigenous communities face numerous social and economic disadvantages, including poverty and unemployment, low educational attainment, lack of clean drinking water, poor sewage systems, poor housing conditions, high rates of suicide and accidental deaths, high incidence of poor health conditions (chronic and infectious diseases), high rates of addictions (to alcohol, drugs, and other substances), high rates of trauma and mental health problems, disproportionate numbers of children in the child welfare system, and all forms of violence.

The correctional system in Canada continues to inadequately address the unique needs and risk factors of Indigenous women, in part due to policies that group Indigenous women either under the general category of women or Indigenous (grouping them with men), thereby ignoring the need to develop programs, services, and assessment

* Special acknowledgment is given to Alexandra Gault for assisting in gathering statistics and literature to support the revisions in this chapter. Chi-miigwech!

tools that adequately meet *both* gender- and culture-specific needs of Indigenous women. Consequently, Indigenous female offenders and national organizations, such as the Native Women's Association of Canada, claim that Canada's correctional system is discriminatory and racist toward Indigenous women.

Indigenous People and Colonialism in Canada

The 2011 census identified 4.3 percent of the Canadian population as Indigenous.[2] A breakdown of this percentage shows that 60.8 percent of all Indigenous people in Canada identify as First Nation (2.6 percent of the Canadian population), 32.3 percent as Métis (1.4 percent of the Canadian population), while 4.2 percent identify as Inuit (0.2 percent of the Canadian population). The percentage of Indigenous people in Canada has increased 20.1 percent since the 2006 census and they continue to be the fastest growing population in Canada.

The Indigenous population is much younger (median age of 28 years) than the Canadian population (median age of 41 years), and seniors comprise a smaller percentage (5.9 percent) compared to the Canadian population (14.2 percent). Many posit that the greatest reason for the significant disproportion in ages between the Indigenous and non-Indigenous population is the relatively poor health and social conditions of Indigenous people, resulting in a shorter lifespan. It is the conditions in which Indigenous people live that have their basis in colonialism, which continues to negatively impact their lives, making it the single largest risk factor for Indigenous people to become involved in the criminal justice system.

Colonialism can be defined as the systematic oppression of a people through a variety of assimilationist measures that are intended to eradicate the peoples and/or their sense of individual and cultural identity.[3] In Canada, colonialism began with the arrival of the European settlers and has taken many forms, from the establishment of treaties, to defining who an Indigenous person is, to controlling Indigenous movements and livelihoods, to the banning of cultural practices and traditional languages, to the institution of residential schools, to name a few.

Colonialist practices as they pertain to Indigenous people continue today in Canada, with the continued existence of policies and governmental laws that are carried out by government departments and organizations that fail to comprehend the colonialist nature of their practices. These practices are far subtler today, but still notable in such arenas as a separate health care system, inadequate funding formulas for programs and services, inadequate responses to the effects of the residential school system, lack of education on Indigenous people's history and their contributions in Canada, lack of acknowledgment of Indigenous rights and sovereignty, and the continued marginalization of Indigenous people in Canada.[4]

Colonialism continues to affect Indigenous people in their daily lives through both overt and subtle racism and lack of culturally safe and appropriate programming and services. The commissioners of Manitoba's Public Inquiry into the Administration of Justice and Indigenous People discussed the complexities and impact of the colonial relationship that exists between Indigenous people and the government:

> Cultural oppression, social inequality, the loss of self-government and systemic discrimination, which are the legacy of the Canadian government's treatment of Indigenous people,

are intertwined and interdependent factors, and in very few cases is it possible to draw a simple and direct correlation between any of them and the events which lead an individual Indigenous person to commit a crime or to become incarcerated. We believe that the overall weight of the evidence makes it clear that these factors are crucial in explaining the reasons why Indigenous people are over-represented in … jails. (Manitoba, Public Inquiry, 1991, p. 86)

Trauma is a common backdrop in the lives of Indigenous people; the result of colonization and assimilation policies and practices imposed on Indigenous people, such as the Indian residential schools (IRS), the "Sixties Scoop," and the *Indian Act*, to name those most recognizable. It is well documented that all of these have led to the loss of land, language, culture, and identity, which are directly tied to the intergenerational consequences of poor health and social and economic conditions that Indigenous people and their communities continue to face today. Colonialism has contributed to Indigenous risk factors, including involvement in the criminal justice system (National Parole Board, 2004).

The oppressive nature of the *Indian Act* has particularly impeded the health and well-being of Indigenous women who have often been subjected to discriminatory laws meant to strip them of their connection to land, community, family, and culture. In some cases, these laws have forced them to leave their family and community (i.e., loss of Indian status), while in other cases they have been forced to flee for their safety (i.e., domestic violence and lack of women shelters), while in other cases poor social conditions and lack of opportunities have caused them to leave (i.e., poverty). Indigenous women often find themselves in urban centres where they continue to experience many of the same social and economic challenges while now also facing isolation, dislocation, racism, and systemic discrimination. By the time Indigenous women end up in the justice system, they have faced a multitude of social injustices that result in significantly higher needs to be addressed to improve their well-being and ultimately lead to successful reintegration into society and community.

Racism, sexism, and discrimination of Indigenous women is a dangerous reality in Canadian society. Indigenous women are more likely to be victims of violence, to die as a result of violence, to be the victim of domestic violence, and are more often the victims of the most severe forms of spousal violence, and the victims of sexual assault (Wesley, 2012). These statistics highlight the current crisis of Indigenous women in Canadian society that has led to the significant overrepresentation of murdered and missing Indigenous women and girls. Please see Chapter 10 for a more thorough examination of this crisis and its impact on Indigenous women in corrections.

The impact of colonialism on Indigenous women has resulted in serious and long-standing consequences that continue to beleaguer contemporary Indigenous women to this day. Traditional roles as keepers of family and community, language, and culture have been lost and replaced with negative stereotypes that encourage the view of Indigenous women as unequal, worthless, and unintelligent, thereby not requiring respect from those around them, both in their community and in society at large. Many argue that the high rates of violence against women and children in Indigenous communities are a direct result of colonialism, which forever changed the way women and children were viewed by men. Understanding colonialism as the foundation for the many social ills and the discrimination experienced by Indigenous women must be the cornerstone to comprehending what is needed for Indigenous women to reclaim their role in the community and society. As noted by an Indigenous parolee:

> The critical difference is racism. We are born to it and spend our lives facing it. Racism lies at the root of our life experiences. The effect is violence, violence against us, and in turn our own violence. The solution is healing; healing through traditional ceremonies, support, understanding and the compassion that will empower Indigenous women to the betterment of ourselves, our families and our communities. (Indigenous parolee, cited in Canada, TFFSW, 1990, p. 9)

▶ WHAT DO YOU THINK?

Does colonialism link to poor social determinants of health or criminality for Indigenous women? Could it apply to both?

Indigenous People and the Justice System

I am particularly concerned with silencing along the lines of race (more appropriately culture) ... It merely reflects that my voice is the voice of a Mohawk woman ... It is only through my culture that my women's identity is shaped. It is the teachings of my people that demand we speak from our own personal experiences.

> Montour-Angus, 1996, cited in *The lived experience of discrimination: Aboriginal women who are federally sentenced* (Montour-Angus, 2002, p. 33).

Indigenous people are the largest and fastest-growing population in the correctional system, and their disproportionate growth could have serious implications for Indigenous people and the criminal justice system for many years to come. Because 28 percent of Indigenous people are under the age of 14, forecasters predict a significant increase in the youth and young adult population within the next decade. This growth is especially salient considering that those under the age of 35 are seen as being most at risk for criminal activity, according to the National Parole Board (2004). In fact, Wesley (2012) already notes an alarming upward trend between 2000 and 2010: a 90 percent increase in the number of Indigenous women who are federally incarcerated. The face of Indigenous offenders is also getting younger, with a mean age of 27 years. Information supports the notion that the negative social factors experienced by Indigenous people place this group at higher risk of becoming and remaining involved in the criminal justice system. Based on the 2014–2015 correctional investigator's report (Office of the Correctional Investigator of Canada, 2015), Indigenous people account for 24.4 percent of the overall federal inmate population: 68 percent First Nation, 26.5 percent Métis, and 5.5 percent Inuit. According to the OCI 2007 report, the best estimate of the overall incarceration rate for Indigenous people in Canada is 1,024 per 100,000 adults compared with 117 per 100,000 incarcerated adults in the non-Aboriginal population (OCI, 2007, p. 20).

In the 2015 report by the OCI, they report that Indigenous offenders have some startling outcomes; they are more often classified as higher risk and higher needs, overrepresented in segregation and maximum security populations, disproportionately involved in use of force interventions and prison self-injury, released later in their sentence, and more likely to return to custody.

Indigenous people are challenged with navigating the criminal justice system, making the likelihood of incarceration much higher. The conflicts Indigenous people face with the police and the court system often result in greater likelihood of being sentenced. Box 9.1 summarizes the difficulties Indigenous people face in the Canadian criminal justice system.

BOX 9.1

Indigenous People and the Criminal Justice System

According to a report by the Canadian Criminal Justice Association, Indigenous people experience the following problems with respect to the criminal justice system:

- more likely to be denied bail
- more time spent in pretrial detention
- more likely to be charged with multiple offences, and often for crimes against the system
- more likely not to have legal representation at court proceedings
- Indigenous clients, especially in northern communities, where the court party flies in the day of the hearing, spend less time with their lawyers
- because court schedules in remote areas are poorly planned, judges may have a limited time to spend in the community

- more than twice as likely to be incarcerated than non-Indigenous offenders
- Indigenous Elders, who are spiritual leaders, are not given the same status as prison priests or chaplains in all institutions
- Indigenous people often plead guilty because they are intimidated by the court and simply want to get the proceedings over with
- offences are often related to violence (usually against another Indigenous person and/or a family member), social disorder, crimes against the system, or petty crimes
- at least half of all offences are alcohol-related

Source: Canadian Criminal Justice Association. (2000). Aboriginal peoples and the criminal justice system: Part IV—Aboriginal peoples and the justice system [Special issue]. *Bulletin.* Retrieved from http://caid.ca/CCJA .APCJS2000.pdf.

Often, many of the problems experienced by Indigenous people in the criminal justice system may be exacerbated by language barriers. The criminal justice system has failed to provide written and digital media in Indigenous languages to improve navigation through the court process (CCJA, 2000). Translation services are often less than adequate to meet legal standards, and Indigenous-speaking persons are disallowed from sitting as jurors. According to the Royal Commission on Aboriginal Peoples (Canada, RCAP, 1996):

> It appears that they have little understanding of their legal rights, of court procedures, or of resources such as legal aid and most Indian people enter guilty pleas because they do not really understand the concept of legal guilt and innocence, or because they are fearful of exercising their rights. In remote areas, the Aboriginal people appear confused about the functions of the court, particularly where the Royal Canadian Mounted Police officers also act as Crown Prosecutors, or where the magistrates travel about in police aircrafts. (p. 167)

Compared to their non-Indigenous counterparts, Indigenous offenders have numerous challenges:

- younger
- poorer
- more likely to be incarcerated for a violent offence
- higher needs related to employment and education

- more extensive involvement with the youth criminal justice system
- higher incidence of health problems
- more likely to have abused drugs and alcohol at an earlier age
- more likely to have been physically abused
- report parental absence or neglect more frequently
- more likely to have been involved in the child welfare system
- gang affiliated

Indian residential school impacts (self or family member) are a common factor that is an experience without parallel for non-Indigenous offenders.

The divergence between Indigenous and Euro-Canadian values have also added to the disproportionate number of Indigenous people in the criminal justice system. Core Indigenous values, such as a desire for community harmony, avoidance of confrontational and adversarial positions, preservation of relationships, and reluctance to show emotions, often create a dissonance with the goals of the criminal justice system. Oftentimes, Indigenous people choose to plead guilty to a crime to restore harmony to the community and preserve relationships; they are much less concerned with the issue of guilt and punishment. Ross (1992) also reports that many of these traditional Indigenous values lead those involved in the court process (such as lawyers, judges, and psychiatrists) to falsely label Indigenous people as unresponsive, uncommunicative, uncooperative, and lacking remorse. Table 9.1 highlights the conflict that exists between Indigenous and Western-based justice values (CCJA, 2000).

In an attempt to alleviate the conflict that exists between the Indigenous understanding of justice and the Western-based meaning of justice, in 1994, the Canadian government introduced the *Corrections and Conditional Release Act* (CCRA). Section 4(h) of the Act states that correctional policies, programs, and practices shall "respect gender, ethnic, cultural and linguistic differences and be responsive to the special needs of women and Aboriginal peoples," and sections 79 to 84 explicitly discuss the needs of Indigenous offenders (Morin, 1999). The CCRA's ability to reduce the disproportionate number of Indigenous people in the criminal justice system will be discussed later in this chapter.

Indigenous Women in the Correctional System

If my little brother had died in a big city in Ontario rather than on a reserve in Saskatchewan I know I would have been allowed to go to his funeral.

Indigenous prisoner at Prison for Women, cited in *Creating Choices* (Canada, TFFSW, 1990, p. 6).

Indigenous women are disproportionately represented in the correctional system in Canada, provincially and federally: in 2015, they represented 35.5 percent of the federal women's population with similar overall representation in women's provincial and territorial institutions. Statistics indicate that the greatest overrepresentation for Indigenous women occurs in the Prairie region where the majority of federally sentenced Indigenous women are located (McIvor & Johnson, 2003).

The National Parole Board (2004) has observed increases in Indigenous overrepresentation in correctional institutions every year since 1998-99, which supports data collected by Statistics Canada. Projections by CSC for 2017 indicate higher numbers of

Table 9.1 Comparison Between Western and Traditional Indigenous Justice Values

	Western Justice	Traditional Indigenous Justice
Justice system	**Adversarial**	**Non-confrontational**
Guilt	• European concept of guilty/not guilty	• No concept of guilty/not guilty
Pleading guilty	• The accused has the right against self-incrimination. Thus, it is not seen as dishonest to plead not guilty when one has actually committed the offence.	• It is dishonest to plead not guilty if one has committed the crime. • (Indigenous values of honesty and non-interference)
Testifying	• As part of the process, witnesses testify in front of the accused.	• Reluctance to testify • (Indigenous values of being non-confrontational and preserving relationships)
Truth	• Expectation to tell the "whole truth"	• It is impossible to know the "whole truth" in any situation.
Witnesses	• Only certain people are called to testify in relation to specific subjects.	• Everyone is free to give their say. • Witnesses do not want to appear adversarial and often make every attempt to give answers that please counsel, thus often changing their testimony.
Eye contact	• Maintaining eye contact conveys that one is being truthful.	• In some Indigenous cultures, maintaining eye contact with a person of authority is a sign of disrespect.
Verdict	• Accused is expected to show, during proceedings and upon a verdict of guilt, remorse and a desire for rehabilitation.	• Accused must accept what comes to him/her without a show of emotion.
Incarceration/probation	• Means of punishing/rehabilitating offender	• Completely absolves Indigenous offender of responsibility of restitution to victim
Function of justice	• Ensure conformity, punish deviant behaviour, and protect society	• Heal the offender • Restore peace and harmony to the community • Reconcile the offender with victim/family that has been wronged • Punishment is not the objective.

Source: Canadian Criminal Justice Association. (2000). Aboriginal peoples and the criminal justice system [Special issue]. *Bulletin*, pp. 26–27. Retrieved from http://caid.ca/CCJA.APCJS2000.pdf.

new admissions in the Indigenous population, particularly in the west and the north. Reports investigating Indigenous people in the correctional system note the greatest increase has occurred with Indigenous women, with a staggering 131 percent increase between 1998 and 2008 (Canadian Human Rights Commission, 2003; Correctional Service of Canada [CSC], 2000; Mann, 2009). The Public Inquiry into the Administration of Justice and Indigenous People (Manitoba, Public Inquiry, 1991) attempted to explain the high proportion of Indigenous offenders:

> Why in a society where justice is supposed to be blind, are the inmates of our prisons selected so overwhelmingly from a single ethnic group? Two answers suggest themselves immediately; either Aboriginal people commit a disproportionate number of crimes, or

they are the victims of a discriminatory justice system. We believe that both answers are correct, but not in the simplistic sense that some people might interpret them. We do not believe, for instance, that there is anything about Aboriginal people or culture that predisposes them to criminal behaviour. Instead, we believe that the causes of Aboriginal criminal behaviour are rooted in a long history of discrimination and social inequality that has impoverished Aboriginal people and consigned them to the margins of … society. (p. 85)

Indigenous female offenders are significantly younger, with a median age on admission of 29 versus 33 years for their non-Indigenous counterparts, with 49.4 percent of all Indigenous female offenders under the age of 30 (Mann, 2009). Over two-thirds were identified as having high needs for personal/emotional orientation, substance use, and employment—needs that remained unchanged at the time of release. A high proportion of Indigenous women access programming; however, the average wait for these programs is 238–264 days. These long wait times are a result of Indigenous women receiving higher classification levels, where maximum security classification levels result in less access to programming. In 2007, 45 percent of Indigenous women were classified as maximum security, 44 percent medium security, and only 18 percent minimum security. Box 9.2 includes a profile of Indigenous female offenders.

BOX 9.2

Indigenous Women's Profile in CSC

- younger
- single
- incarcerated for serious offences
- low level of education
- low employment levels
- more extensive criminal history including youth convictions, previous adult convictions (provincial and/or federal), and previous community supervisions
- history of past breaches and failures to comply with conditional release terms and/or community sanctions (low reintegration level)
- assessed as high need for programming

Source: Wesley, M. (2012). *Marginalized: The Aboriginal women's experience in federal corrections.* Retrieved from https://www.publicsafety.gc.ca/cnt/rsrcs/pblctns/mrgnlzd/mrgnlzd-eng.pdf.

Indigenous women report greater levels of physical and sexual abuse, which translates to displaying a greater number of trauma-related symptoms. Many have stories of exposure to all types of violence and racism, and they reported dealing with the traumatic memories of abuse by attempting suicide, abusing substances and prescription drugs, and engaging in self-harm in attempts to reduce the tension and anger they felt (Dell & Boe, 2000). According to the *Creating Choices* report (Canada, TFFSW, 1990), Indigenous drug-abusing female offenders were addicted to substances for longer periods than their non-Indigenous counterparts, usually for 10 to 25 years.

The high mental health needs of Indigenous female offenders has translated into high usage rates of mental health programs (76 percent), addictions programs (60 percent), and personal counselling (27 percent) in the correctional system. Although these numbers are promising, concerns have been raised by Mann (2009) that the current mental health services offered through CSC are often individualized and don't take into account the historical, contextual, and complex trauma that Indigenous female offenders have been victim to throughout their lifetimes. Without attention to the complex mental health needs of Indigenous female offenders, the risk of reoffending remains high as risk factors are not adequately addressed.

> … I definitely think that being as Aboriginal women, we definitely need to have programs directly regarding our spirituality, our culture, and our traditions and the beliefs that we carry with us.
>
> Unnamed Indigenous woman quoted in *Needs assessment of federal Aboriginal women offenders* (Bell, Trevethan, & Allegri, 2004).

Under the *Corrections and Conditional Release Act* (CCRA), sections 77 and 80 provide the directive that CSC must provide gender-specific programming and must be relevant to Indigenous culture. CSC has recognized the need to address self-injury, a coping strategy that is widely witnessed among female offenders. Reports such as *Creating Choices* have identified the importance of addressing self-injury using a strong mental health approach. Unfortunately, in the OCI report, self-injury is on the rise and is particularly high for Indigenous female offenders (17 times more likely than non-Indigenous female offenders); the current practice to address this is to increase security classification, because it is defined as a risk to security. When security level for a woman increases, it has impacts on her programming and limits her human interaction; in many cases the woman is placed in segregation. The OCI also notes that the unnecessary use of force actually increases the level of emotional distress for the woman and leads to further deterioration in the female offender's mental health. This holds particular concern for Indigenous female offenders, who are layered with issues of systemic and institutional racism and discrimination that likely has serious implications for their mental health and well-being.

On the tenth anniversary of the Arbour Inquiry, the Canadian Association of Elizabeth Fry Societies found that Indigenous women had a higher likelihood of being segregated more frequently and for longer periods of time than all other female offenders (McIvor & Johnson, 2003), with almost half of all segregation admissions in 2013–2014 being Indigenous women (OCI, 2015). The rates of violence and inmate assaults involving Indigenous women have doubled, while use of force (against an offender) incidents have tripled in the last ten years (OCI, 2015). The response by CSC was to create a management protocol meant to manage high-needs/high-risk female offenders that could be considered a "super maximum designation." The protocol was applied to "… female inmates after involvement in an incident that has either caused serious harm to others or may have jeopardized other persons and she is deemed to be unmanageable in the regular maximum security population" (Wesley, 2012). This protocol was applied almost exclusively to high-needs/high-risk Indigenous women offenders. Wesley reports that in 2009, four of the five women under this protocol were Indigenous, and by 2011, all four women under this protocol were Indigenous. Those who were handled by this protocol were highly controlled in their interactions and movements, including use of constraints. The OCI has been highly critical of this protocol, identifying the very negative impacts it could have on the mental and emotional well-being of those managed under this protocol, since these women experience excessive isolation and deprivation of human contact. Indigenous women are particularly vulnerable to the deleterious effects of segregation and research suggests that extended periods of isolation can trigger an onset of mental illness (Wesley, 2012). Recommendations since 2009 by the OCI and the Women Offender Sector have called for the management protocol to be abolished, and after a review of the strategy it was eliminated in 2013. Following the 2007 death of Ashley Smith, a young Indigenous woman[5] with a history of self-injury and mental health problems who was placed in segregation over the long term as a way to manage her presumably high-risk behaviours, it is critically important for CSC to design a system to support healing from intergenerational trauma for Indigenous women.

There is clear indication that Indigenous women who end up in the correctional system arrive with higher needs across many social determinants of health. The behaviours they exhibit, such as violence toward self or others, are a direct result of their mental health needs and the level of trauma they have experienced in their lives. Under the management protocol, Indigenous women were extremely restricted and were unable to access any programming, including cultural programming, that could help them to improve their mental and emotional well-being. Clinical practice highlights that the best way to address these needs is to use a trauma-informed approach that supports a woman in a caring, supportive network, that builds on strengths and teaches skills in and for Indigenous women, and that is grounded in their cultural knowledge and practices. Unfortunately, the use of segregation (and the now defunct management protocol) directly contravenes the evidence by applying a punitive approach that has strong inferences of being colonial and racist in its application.

▶ WHAT DO YOU THINK?

If trauma-informed care approaches are understood as the best evidence for supporting those with a history of trauma, does CSC have the appropriate resources to support Indigenous women with significant mental health needs that are a result of personal and intergenerational trauma?

Indigenous women experience disproportionately high levels of high-risk behaviours while incarcerated. In a position paper written on behalf of the Native Women's Association of Canada, McIvor and Johnson (2003) reported that federally sentenced Indigenous women commit disproportionately more violent crimes prior to and during their federal incarceration, thereby leading to longer federal sentences. They also reported that federally sentenced Indigenous women were found to have completed suicide at a disproportionately high rate while incarcerated. The hopelessness experienced by Indigenous women during incarceration can be felt in the words of an Indigenous parolee: "When I went to prison I lost everything I ever had, not just the material things, but all the relationships I ever had in my life" (Canada, TFFSW, 1990, p. 7).

Indigenous women also experience more challenges in leaving the correctional system. For example, federally sentenced Indigenous women were less successful on conditional release than any other group of female offenders and were found to have the lowest rate for being granted either day or full parole. Not surprisingly, federally sentenced Indigenous women were more likely to be incarcerated than to be on conditional release.

Statistics from 2000 indicate that Indigenous women were less successful in completing their conditional release, resulting in their return to prison. Thus, they remain incarcerated for longer periods of time than non-Indigenous women. In 2000, CSC reported they were making efforts to increase the number of Indigenous women in the community through conditional release programs.

However, the challenges remain ten years later for incarcerated Indigenous women; Wesley (2012) reports that in 2010 over 75 percent of Indigenous female offenders remain incarcerated until their statutory release date, 10 percent higher than non-Indigenous female offenders. An additional 33.42 percent are detained past their statutory release date. Overall, Indigenous female offenders continue to be granted day and full parole less often.

Challenges Faced by Indigenous Female Offenders in Corrections

Indigenous women who become involved in the justice system almost immediately become vulnerable to the racist, sexist, and discriminatory practices embedded within the justice system. National Indigenous and women's organizations all point to systemic issues as a primary cause of the overrepresentation of Indigenous women in the criminal justice system. The systemic factors that increase the likelihood that an Indigenous woman will become involved in the court system include overpolicing, overcharging, insensitive and uninformed legal professionals and sentencing and structural barriers in the courts (Montour-Angus, 2002).

In his book *Dancing with a Ghost*, Rupert Ross (1992), a Crown attorney, discusses the lack of cultural awareness training the legal profession receives to equip them to comprehend Indigenous values and their world view. According to Ross, without a sound knowledge and an understanding of an Indigenous world view, adequately representing the individual and making appropriate recommendations on sentencing are nearly impossible. Ross espouses that learning about the Indigenous world view must be embedded in understanding the historical oppression and discrimination faced by Indigenous people, which continues to this day for many Indigenous people and communities.

Once admitted to prison, all women undergo an offender intake assessment (OIA) to determine the woman's risk and security classification and to identify programming needs. The OIA, introduced in 1994 and initially developed for men, is also used to "predict how well she … will integrate into the community upon release if identified needs are not adequately addressed" (Dell & Boe, 2000, p. 3). Wesley (2012) notes:

> the scale fails to take into account any cultural or gender specific issues, as such Aboriginal women are at a double disadvantage on the basis of race and gender. Aboriginal women are pre-disposed to a higher classification due to a number of systemic and historical factors which contribute to their life circumstances and experiences. (p. 24)

The scale also does not take into account the collective colonial experiences of Indigenous women, which likely impacts their criminogenic factors. In Wesley's report (2012), she quotes Dr. Montour:

These risk scales are all individualized instruments. This must be seen as a significant and central problem for applying these instruments to Aboriginal people (male or female). This individualizing of risk absolutely fails to take into account the impact of colonial oppression on the lives of Aboriginal men and women. Equally, the colonial oppression has not only had a devastating impact on individuals but concurrently on our communities and nations. This impact cannot be artificially pulled apart as the impact on the individual and the impact on the community are interconnected. (p. 25)

Dell and Boe (2000) examined the information collected as part of OIAs for federally sentenced female offenders and identified that Indigenous women were rated as a higher risk for reoffending (42 percent) than Caucasian women (29 percent). Indigenous women were less likely to be rated as either a moderate or low risk for reoffending. This information remained consistent in 2007, when Indigenous women accounted for 45 percent of all women in the maximum security population, 44 percent of all women classified as medium security, and 18 percent of all women classified as minimum security (Wesley, 2012).

Predictably the situation is more acute for Native women. They often receive more restrictive security classifications despite the fact that their offence or past institutional behaviour is comparable to that of a non-Native who is classified as low security risk. The Native woman is punished further when her participation in Native Sisterhood meetings is not recognized as serving a rehabilitative function by those assessing her eligibility for early release. Security classification is, therefore, an incident of racial discrimination. (Women's Legal Education and Action Fund, 1989, p. 3)

Indigenous women's overrepresentation in the high-risk category is usually a result of more (violent) criminal offences and longer sentences. Dell and Boe (2000) note that 85 percent of Indigenous women had previous involvement in the adult court system, compared with 58 percent of the overall offender population. Further, federally sentenced Indigenous women were almost four times more likely to have had a previous admission to the federal correctional system. Similar youth statistics reveal that 65 percent of Indigenous youth female offenders and only 19 percent of Caucasian female youth offenders had previous involvement in youth court.

Statistics such as these reveal that the assessment measure has a strong discriminatory bias against Indigenous women. Further, Wesley (2012) argues that when the risk management criteria are applied to Indigenous communities this tool, which has a middle-class bias, fails to take into consideration the experiences of Indigenous women and obscures the results negatively when they enter the correctional system. The application of the tool has also been critiqued by Hannah-Moffat and Shaw (2001), who report a subjective bias to the tool, and when used with Indigenous female offenders, cite embedded racism within the tool.

CSC has acknowledged more research is needed on the effectiveness of the OIA tool for predicting risk and assessing needs for all female offenders (Dell & Boe, 2000). The Canadian Human Rights Commission (2003) has stated that the tool has no validity for women or Indigenous offenders. At the time of the OCI report, CSC was conducting a pilot project for a new tool that would be more culturally and gender sensitive. However, by 2011, reports on the newly developed tool were dismally similar to the outcomes of the OIA (Wesley, 2012). CSC appears to have no plans to redesign the new tool to reduce the discriminatory bias that exists, leaving the author to believe that CSC has reverted to dealing with the overclassification through the "reclassification methods," which are conducted every six months for Indigenous women. This system has failed to create any changes in the disproportionate numbers of Indigenous women in the correctional system or those who are classified as high risk.

The lack of a culture- and gender-specific needs/risk assessment at the time of incarceration creates further challenges for Indigenous women in accessing culturally appropriate programming.

> It is racism, past in our memories and present in our surroundings that negates non-native attempts to reconstruct our lives. Existing programs cannot reach us, cannot surmount the barriers of mistrust that racism has built. Physicians, psychiatrists and psychologists are typically White and male. How can we be healed by those who symbolize the worst experiences of our past? (Indigenous parolee, cited in Canada, TFFSW, 1990, p. 9)

Montour-Angus (2002) and others have argued that CSC has continually failed to meaningfully take into consideration how colonialism affects service delivery for federally sentenced Indigenous women. This includes the lack of legitimacy extended to Indigenous knowledge and healing practices as part of the rehabilitative component in the correctional plan. The absence of understanding in the protocols of cultural services negatively impacts Indigenous programming offered in the correctional system. The inadequacy of CSC programming does not support Indigenous women to gain a sense of their individual and cultural identity, which is important to healing.

Federally sentenced Indigenous women report that the Canadian criminal justice system has been unsympathetic to their needs and suffering. In fact, many have provided examples of having been the target of racism and discrimination throughout the court process and in the correctional system because no one understood the Indigenous cultural values, traditions, or ceremonies, all important facets in regaining a sense of empowerment that supports healing. Montour-Angus (2002) also argues that referring to Indigenous correctional programming as "Aboriginal issues" inappropriately denotes Indigenous people's realities as a problem that is akin to victim blaming, another form of perpetuating discrimination against Indigenous people. The *Creating Choices* report also acknowledged the impact of colonialism on Indigenous women in the justice system, pointing out that it has created a climate of distrust, where Indigenous women view the system as one that sets rules to govern them without acknowledging their unique needs and realities. As described by Patricia Montour-Angus (2002):

> Not only can we not separate the Aboriginal and the woman, it is important to understand we also share a common Aboriginal history. That common history is the history of racism, oppression, genocide, and ethnocide. It is one further way in which we are distinct. This shared history impacts on Aboriginal federally sentenced women in two ways. First, as the racism of prisons or the criminal justice system has largely been ignored or vanished, the situation of Aboriginal women as participants in Canadian society cannot be understood by prison administrators or correctional bureaucrats. It is these individuals who have historically controlled the administration of criminal justice. This has left Aboriginal federally sentenced women in an impossible situation. The people who hold the key to their release, they cannot trust. This lack of trust is not the sole responsibility or failure of individuals (prisoners or correctional employees) but a systemic failure to address racism. (p. 7)

The temptation to perceive the multiple layers of discrimination perpetuated by colonialism and experienced by Indigenous women in the criminal justice system as either additive or cumulative should be resisted. Taking either stance would suggest that the multiple layers of discrimination are separate from each other; however, these layers of discrimination should be considered interdependent, overlapping, and intersectional. Intersectional discrimination, a relatively new legal term, is defined as "intersectional oppression that arises out of the combination of various oppressions which, together, produce something unique and distinct from any one form of discrimination standing alone" and is a distinct experience for Indigenous women (Montour-Angus, 2002, p. 34). Therefore, intersectional discrimination is experienced distinctly *only if* one is an Indigenous woman.

An excellent example of intersectional discrimination is the labelling of Indigenous women as violent. Compared with male violence, Indigenous women's crimes do not stand out as excessive. However, when compared with non-Indigenous women's crimes, they do stand out, which has resulted in Indigenous women's overrepresentation in maximum security classification. However, a further argument suggests that the discrimination experienced by Indigenous women in the justice system may be more likely referred to as compound discrimination. Compound discrimination is a form of "double-whammy" discrimination an Indigenous woman experiences because she is *both* Indigenous and a woman. Using these definitions, one can decipher that Indigenous women have experienced colonialism (due to being Indigenous) and paternalism (due to being female)—a double whammy in the criminal justice system. Therefore, when Indigenous women's needs are embedded in women's needs or Indigenous needs, no true comprehension is possible of the distinct challenges that are faced by Indigenous women in the correctional system. In the words of an Indigenous woman parolee:

> To be a woman and to be *seen* as violent is to be especially marked in the eyes of the administration of the prisons where women do time, and in the eyes of the staff who guard them. In a prison with a male population, our crimes would stand out much less. Among women we [Indigenous women] do not fit the stereotypes, and we are automatically feared, and labelled as in need of special handling. The label violent begets a self-perpetuating and destructive cycle for [Indigenous] women within prisons. (Indigenous parolee, cited in Canada, TFFSW, 1990, p. 12)

► WHAT DO YOU THINK?

Do Indigenous women face more discrimination than any other group in the justice system?

The Gladue Decision and Its Potential

The Supreme Court of Canada has, in fact, recognized the colonialist nature of the law in dealing with Indigenous women. In 1995, Jamie Tanis Gladue was found guilty of murdering her common-law husband while intoxicated and was sentenced to federal incarceration. She appealed the sentencing decision, stating that the court had not considered distinct issues that affect Indigenous people. In a landmark decision in 1999, the Supreme Court of Canada stated that when determining sentencing, the court system must take into consideration the colonialist actions against Indigenous people in comprehending why they engage in criminal behaviour. This landmark decision, known as the *Gladue* decision, has demanded that the court system examine culture- and gender-specific issues to learn who the offender is as a person and not base a determination solely on the nature of her offence.

Current circumstances indicate that the court system is still ill-equipped to enforce the principles of *Gladue* due to lack of knowledge about *Gladue* as well as the unique culture- and gender-specific issues for Indigenous women. Without this information, justice workers are ill-prepared and lack knowledge of the kinds of information that must be examined and considered in preparing for sentencing and release planning. Since the landmark decision of *Gladue*, the justice system is still attempting to determine how to interpret and implement the *Gladue* principles to address the colonial impacts on Indigenous people. As noted by Sugar and Fox (1990):

> Our understanding of law, of courts, of police, of the judicial system, and of prisons are all set by lifetimes defined by racism. Racism is not simply set by the overt experiences of racism, though most of us have known this direct hatred, have been called "dirty Indians" in school, or in foster homes, or by police or guards, or have seen the differences in the way we are treated and have known this was no accident. Racism is much more extensive than this. Culturally, economically, and as Peoples we have been oppressed and pushed aside by Whites. We were sent to live on reserves which denied us a livelihood, controlled us with rules that we did not set, and made us dependent on services we could not provide for ourselves. (pp. 9–10)

CSC has a directive in place that *Gladue* principles must be considered when assessing security classification and placement of Indigenous offenders. The fact that Indigenous women are still overclassified or have not received more opportunities for conditional placement/release would suggest that *Gladue* principles are not being applied. The ability to apply *Gladue* principles requires a culturally competent workforce, including knowledge to apply *Gladue*. Wesley (2012) reports that staff received training on *Gladue* in the winter of 2011 even though the *Gladue* decision was handed down 12 years prior! Mann (2009) is highly critical of CSC's lack of adequate staff training on the application of *Gladue* in the areas of assessing need and risk. Similarly, the Parole Board of Canada is also obligated to apply the principles of *Gladue* when considering an Indigenous person for parole application. Once again, the workforce demonstrates low competency in applying the principles due largely to lack of adequate training. Parole board members were only trained on this in 2011 and according to Mann (2009), the level of training was minimal and inadequate. By law, *Gladue* reports are to be prepared for parole hearings, but those responsible for this task have limited training and understanding of *Gladue* principles. This has led to differences in the application of *Gladue* with some officers applying the principles, others not, while even more apply them inappropriately (Mann, 2009).

▶ WHAT DO YOU THINK?

This chapter highlights information that suggests *Gladue* has not been fully embraced within the justice system. What might be some reasons for this? If there is concern about the applicability of *Gladue*, should it be applied to all Indigenous women regardless of their connection to Indigenous community, language, or culture?

The Ever-Changing Face of Indigenous Corrections

We have often said that the women inside have the understanding to help themselves, that all that is required is the right kind of resources, support, and help. The money spent on studies would be much better spent on family visits, on culturally appropriate help, on reducing our powerlessness to heal ourselves. But the reality is that prison conditions grow worse. We cry out for a meaningful healing process that will have real impact on our lives, but the objectives and implementation of this healing process must be premised on our need to heal and walk in balance.

> Fox and Sugar, cited in *The lived experience of discrimination: Aboriginal women who are federally sentenced* (Montour-Angus, 2002, p. 1).

Creating Choices and the Arbour Inquiry formed the catalyst for recommending sweeping changes in women's corrections, acknowledging the current system was developed by, for, and with male needs in mind, which has limited applicability for federally sentenced women. The two documents highlight women's unique needs and criminogenic factors that require specialized programming to support their reintegration into society. These documents also highlighted that within federally sentenced women, Indigenous women are a distinct group whose needs are multi-layered. The *Corrections and Conditional Release Act*, released in 1994, was meant to address the recommendations made in the two documents by considering the unique needs of Indigenous people and women. The CCRA states that correctional policies, programs, and practices shall "respect gender, ethnic, cultural and linguistic differences and be responsive to the special needs of women and aboriginal peoples." Sections 79 to 84 address the needs of Indigenous offenders, including programs, spiritual leaders and Elders, parole plans, and any other aspect that would address Indigenous offenders' distinct needs.

The following is a review of some of the major changes that were implemented and a critical analysis of the success of these changes for Indigenous women in the correctional system.

Okimaw Ohci Healing Lodge

Healing for Aboriginal women means the opportunity, through Aboriginal teachings, programs, spirituality and culture, to recover from histories of abuse, regain a sense of self-worth, gain skills and rebuild families. Through healing, Aboriginal women are able to change or release negative behaviours such as addictions and criminal behaviour. Delving deep into issues allows for an intensive healing experience, which improves their ability to re-establish themselves in their community.

> Okimaw Ohci Healing Lodge Operational Plan, 2004, cited in *The ten-year status report on women's corrections, 1996–2006* (CSC, 2006, p. 22).

One of the most significant recommendations from *Creating Choices* (Canada, TFFSW, 1990) was to abolish the old Prison for Women (P4W) at Kingston, Ontario, in favour of regional facilities that would bring women closer to their homes and their families. This recommendation included the specific mention of the need for a regional facility that was premised on Indigenous values and philosophies to support Indigenous women's healing. The intent of the regional facilities was also based on a feminist perspective that recognized federally sentenced women had lower risk factors than men and did not require the same level of security.

Five regional facilities were opened across the country, including the Okimaw Ohci Healing Lodge (OOHL) in 1995. This 30-bed facility with single and family residential units (to accommodate children) was developed with, by, and for Indigenous women, with significant contributions made by the Nekaneet First Nation, Saskatchewan, which is home to OOHL.

The operational plan and facility design focused on the importance of nature in Indigenous culture, the need for privacy in healing, community interactions, and Indigenous-specific intervention strategies (CSC, 2006). As envisioned in *Creating Choices*, the planning of OOHL included CSC representatives, Indigenous community partners, and Elders who

Okimaw Ohci Healing Lodge (OOHL) in Nekaneet First Nation, Saskatchewan

together identified a plan for staffing, training, and program development. The opening of OOHL was meant to ameliorate past concerns of cultural isolation for federally sentenced Indigenous women. OOHL's Indigenous-specific programming addressed past concerns, including the need for more female staff of Indigenous descent who understood Indigenous healing practices, and greater access to Elders and cultural ceremonies or practices.

Perhaps the biggest criticism of OOHL remains the issue of security classification. Indigenous women are required to be classified as medium or minimum security to be accepted to OOHL. As previously mentioned, Indigenous women continue to remain overrepresented in higher security classifications. Despite numerous calls to permit all Indigenous women, regardless of their classification, to attend OOHL, such change has been staunchly refused by the CSC. The denial is based on the CSC's assertion that Indigenous women who are classified as maximum security present too great a risk and need to be able to meet the demands and expectations of OOHL. Many authors (McIvor & Johnson, 2003; Montour-Angus, 2002) discount CSC's reasons as discriminatory and colonial, with the end result that not all Indigenous women are able to take advantage of the unique programming offered at OOHL. To counter criticisms, CSC has implemented measures such as a healing lodge readiness assessment, a healing readiness commitment form, and a "champion" for the lodge in each regional facility. These measures are an attempt to support Indigenous women's desires both to attend OOHL and to reduce their security classification so they can be considered for a transfer. Information is not available to adequately assess whether these measures have promising results.

Although OOHL offers Indigenous-specific programming, its status as the only facility of its kind in Canada for Indigenous women creates many barriers and challenges. Its placement was a wise decision, based on the overrepresentation of Indigenous women from the Prairie region; however, women from other parts of the country who are interested in accessing Indigenous-specific programming are not always eager to leave their home region and be away from their families. The programming offered at OOHL is based on the teachings and philosophy of the tribes/nations located on the Prairies. This approach has implications for Indigenous women from non-Prairie areas because such programming does not adequately meet the philosophy, world view, and cultural practices of Nations from eastern Canada, the Pacific region, Inuit, or Métis people. Repeated recommendations by the Correctional Investigator of Canada (2006–2014) to consider a similar facility in eastern Canada has not been acted upon by CSC at this time. Therefore, OOHL does not meet all of the cultural needs of Indigenous women from different Indigenous groups, which means that some Indigenous women continue to experience cultural isolation while incarcerated.

Questions have been raised about how well the new regional facilities have ameliorated geographical isolation for federally sentenced women (Montour-Angus, 2002). During the operation of P4W, all women offenders and their families received financial compensation for family visits and phone calls home because of the significant geographical distances that many of them faced. After the establishment of the regional facilities, this compensation was abolished under the premise that women would now be closer to home. However, some federally sentenced women remain hundreds of miles from their homes, and if their families are poor (as is often the case for Indigenous women), the likelihood of regular contact with them is low. This isolation from families is particularly relevant if an Indigenous woman chooses to transfer to OOHL from outside of the Prairie region. Because Indigenous women in this situation may be thousands of miles away from home, and their families may not have the financial means to attend the facility, these women continue to experience geographical isolation from their families.

Another unforeseen consequence of the new facilities has been the reduced profile of the Native Sisterhood, an active group of Indigenous women at P4W who supported each other in their healing and their experiences of incarceration, while ensuring that the rights, needs, and challenges of federally sentenced Indigenous women remained visible. The unity demonstrated through Native Sisterhood no longer is present because of the low numbers of Indigenous women in some institutions (e.g., Quebec). The deterioration of the Native Sisterhood has likely resulted in less sharing, less support, and less activism to highlight the needs of federally sentenced Indigenous women and increase feelings of empowerment for Indigenous women. As stated by one former offender:

> Because of the Native Sisterhood I finally knew the meaning of spirituality. I learned how to pray in a sweat and with sweetgrass. I learned the meaning of the Eagle feather and colours. With that I was even more proud of who I was in my identity. (Indigenous ex-prisoner, cited in Canada, TFFSW, 1990, p. 10)

Cultural Needs and Challenges Faced in the Correctional System

Native women believed that their behaviour was misinterpreted by white staff, and that this led to the prescribing of drugs. Several Native women talked about what an alien environment prison was compared to the familiarity of life in Native communities. The way Native women chose to respond to this was to become quiet and observe how things were conducted. These women said that their behavioural reaction, one of quietness, was misinterpreted by the prison psychologist as a type of suppression of their anger and bitterness ... believed that because the prison did not know how to relate to Native Americans they then wanted to control them.

From *The lived experience of discrimination: Aboriginal women who are federally sentenced.* (Montour-Angus, 2002, p. 25).

Since the release of *Creating Choices* in 1990, a major shift has occurred in the recognition of Indigenous people's rights to have access to Indigenous spirituality and ceremonies on a regular basis. The commissioner's directives, as outlined in Morin (1999), highlight the policy objectives related to ceremonies, spiritual practices, healing initiatives, recognition of spiritual Elders, and the Native liaison program. Although the most intensive Indigenous programming is located at OOHL, CSC asserts that Indigenous women in other regional facilities have access to spiritual Elders, Indigenous ceremonies and practices, and Indigenous-specific programming (such as Aboriginal Pathways, Spirit of a Warrior, and Circles of Change). During interviews with Indigenous women at the Edmonton Institution for Women, where a large Indigenous population is incarcerated, the following comment was made:

> A lot of women I find use the Elder as a resource, meet with her quite regularly. As far as programming goes, I was really, really shocked to see that there was nothing here, absolutely nothing Indigenous based in the lines of programming. (Montour-Angus, 2002, p. 19)

Unfortunately, these programs are not always available in all regional facilities, due once again to low numbers of Indigenous women in these facilities who would access these programs. This situation creates a barrier for Indigenous women to receive culturally appropriate programming in their home region, particularly if it requires they seek a transfer to OOHL. Although Indigenous women are given the opportunity to participate in Indigenous-specific programming, they are also required to complete core programming (even at OOHL), which CSC asserts is relevant for all federally sentenced individuals, regardless of gender or race. Because core programming is based on the needs identified in the OIA tool (which has been brought into question for its lack of gender- and culture-specific relevance), the core programming may also be irrelevant across genders and cultures.

New programming from 2011, developed by a national trainer, is intended to be more holistic, designed around the medicine wheel, and supported by an Elder, and includes three different programs: an Indigenous women's Engagement Program, a Moderate Intensity Program, and a High Intensity Program. Benefits for Indigenous women or improvements in reducing rates of overclassification and increasing conditional releases have not yet been reported. An interesting consideration and caution about the Indigenous programming should however be taken into account; these programs are not developed from the perspective of Indigenous knowledge as evidence, since there is still a reliance on CSC to use mainstream knowledge within these programs, almost as though Indigenous practices and teachings are "not enough" to fulfill the goal of healing Indigenous women. Another caution about the program noted by the author is use of the medicine wheel as a common tool for all Indigenous female offenders when there is ample evidence and reports that remind us of the unique differences in language, beliefs, and practices of Indigenous nations across this country. Simply stated, the medicine wheel does not have applicability for all Indigenous female offenders. What is known is that these programs are not equally available in all women's institutions, based on low numbers of Indigenous female offenders, staff turnover, and restriction in eligibility. In some cases, such as the Mother-Child Program, significant program changes were made, which has led to less women finding the program applicable or useful, thereby reducing its utilization rates considerably. Core elements to this program meant to increase the women's sense of safety, connection to her family, and support of healthy relationships—all necessary to well-being from an Indigenous perspective as well as important to reducing risk—were effectively removed, rendering it ineffective in meeting its goal.

CSC has also introduced a Pathways Unit in a few women's institutions, where the ultimate goal is to support Indigenous women to heal using primarily cultural programming that is inclusive of access to Elders and cultural practices/ceremonies. It is a promising initiative but may still face challenges to be realized in institutions where numbers of Indigenous women are low. To expand on the use of culturally appropriate facilities, CSC, under section 81, has opened the Buffalo Sage Wellness House in Edmonton in the last few years as a community residential facility for women under a medium or minimum security classification and planning for conditional release. It is posited that the Pathways Unit is meant to be an alternative to the Okimaw Ohci Healing Lodge if women wish to stay in their region and not move far away from their family or their cultural territory and teachings. No reports were available at this time to evaluate its successes.

The frustration around programming is often exacerbated by concerns expressed by federally sentenced Indigenous women that the staff delivering these programs are often non-Indigenous. Indigenous women report that having correctional officers deliver core programs creates a conflict of interest: Indigenous women have reported that programs have been withheld from them as a form of punishment and to force conformity to the rules of the facilities. These disciplinary measures, as reported by Morin (1999), lead to tension between staff and inmates, uncooperative behaviour by the female inmates, and negative perceptions by the staff. Such measures have further detrimental long-term effects on the Indigenous woman because of the delay in accessing and completing programming required for their correctional plan. These delays then result in some Indigenous women being incarcerated until their statutory release date, creating greater likelihood of reoffending because of fewer identified supports available further into a conditional release program. Another general concern is staff's lack of personal or practical experience to teach the skills necessary to support healing (Montour-Angus, 2002). Added to this is the concern that non-Indigenous staff have a limited understanding of Indigenous realities, which may render them ignorant or unsympathetic to the suffering experienced by federally sentenced Indigenous women.

Fortunately the management protocol (also known as the super maximum security classification) has been eliminated because it was observed that Indigenous women under the protocol did not have access to core and Indigenous-specific programming, which made it difficult for these women to reduce their risk and to be removed from management protocol. Wesley (2012) and Mann (2009) both reported these women had poor access to Native liaison services, cultural ceremonies, and Elder involvement, and staff had less respect for these initiatives or their positive impact on Indigenous women. The high ratio of male officers assigned to those under the defunct management protocol may have increased feelings of distress that threatened the mental health of Indigenous female offenders, particularly when there is a real or perceived belief in lack of safety for the woman (Mann, 2009).

Montour-Angus (2002) asserts that changes have been made within the regional facilities that were unintended by the recommendations of *Creating Choices* in 1990. She reports that security has been intensified to include fences, razor wire, repeated strip searching, and the use of security cameras—measures that are commonly found in a maximum security institution. The new challenges posed by the CSC's attempt to provide feminist perspectives to the correctional system, while maintaining many of the existing (male-dominated) facets of the correctional system, continue to result in a system that is less than adequate in its responsiveness to the needs of Indigenous women. Cultural needs are an important part of programming and are sometimes seen as a secondary component for Indigenous women. Therefore, the security classification of a woman appears to shape her experience while incarcerated because it determines the kind of facility she will be housed in. The quality of an Indigenous woman's classification and the experience she has are marked more by her security classification than a man's because Indigenous women are denied the benefits (that is, the cottage-like accommodations in a medium security facility) intended for incarcerated women. Once again, investigation reveals that Indigenous women continue to experience cultural isolation during their period of incarceration regardless of CSC's attempts to ameliorate these concerns (Mann, 2009).

Has the CCRA Created Meaningful Change?

Morin (1999) conducted a study with Indigenous women to learn whether *Creating Choices* had positively affected their lives since its introduction in 1990. Her work identified that maximum security Indigenous women continued to experience discrimination despite government policies and programs to combat discrimination. See Box 9.3 for a list of concerns identified by these women. From this list, it is obvious that the changes recommended by *Creating Choices* (Canada, TFFSW, 1990) and the Arbour Inquiry (Canada, Commission of Inquiry into Certain Events, 1996) are not being made adequately or in a timely and gender- and culturally-appropriate manner.

BOX 9.3

Federally Sentenced Indigenous Women's Perspective

- 100 percent identified the need for more contact with Elders. Elder counselling should be made available on a full-time basis. Elder interventions should also be available when disagreements arise, which should be recognized in the correctional plan.
- 76 percent indicated security levels are not explained to them. In order for the Indigenous women to work on lowering their security level, reason for changes in security levels must be explained, and the correctional plan's relation to increases or decreases in security level must be deciphered.
- 100 percent stated Indigenous ceremonies need to be recognized as part of the correctional plan for their healing effects.

- 100 percent stated programs facilitated by staff do not work but create animosity and anger among female inmates.
- 58 percent stated Indigenous culture needs to be treated with respect. Some women reported that time limits have been placed on the ceremonies and that protocols for ceremonies were not followed by staff.
- 100 percent reported a lack of communication between management, the primary worker, and the woman. When problems occur, the Indigenous women are often blamed for being manipulative. This displacement of authority is viewed as oppressive.
- 76 percent stated that CSC needs to ensure that core programs are available in all institutions. Completion of core programs is mandatory in the correctional plan to lower security levels, but these programs are not available in some institutions.
- 76 percent stated that their application to the Okimaw Ohci Healing Lodge was not even considered or processed.
- 88 percent stated they had taken steps to reduce their security levels but were not supported by staff for various reasons.
- 76 percent stated that CSC needs to hire more Indigenous staff who practise their culture and are not judgmental.
- 76 percent indicated they had controlled their behaviour and had requested programs but staff did not respond to their needs to provide the programs.

Source: Morin, S. (1999). *Federally sentenced Aboriginal women in maximum security: What happened to the promises of "Creating choices"?* Ottawa: Correctional Service of Canada.

Sections 81 to 84 of the *Corrections and Conditional Release Act* grant authority for the CSC to facilitate and fund capacity-building initiatives in Indigenous communities that would result in successful reintegration of Indigenous people into their communities. In order for these initiatives to work, federally sentenced Indigenous women need to know their rights and privileges under the CCRA. The Native Women's Association of Canada (McIvor & Johnson, 2003) report that CSC has failed to adequately educate federally sentenced Indigenous women about their options for decarceration, including the possibility of serving their sentence in a community-based setting. CSC also needs to identify, develop, and refine community initiatives that are willing and able to accept custodial care for an Indigenous woman serving a prison sentence.

At the time of the release of the correctional investigator's report (Correctional Investigator Canada, 2006) and the simultaneous release of the CSC's *Ten-Year Status Report on Women's Corrections* (CSC, 2006), very few (if any) community initiatives were in place to support an Indigenous woman serving her time in an Indigenous community setting (Montour-Angus, 2002). Both reports highlighted that CSC's Indigenous Initiatives Branch was in the process of developing regional and national action plans to address these shortcomings. One such action plan has resulted in a conditional release planning kit that is disbursed throughout CSC, to all the regional facilities and to Indigenous communities to provide a comprehensive guide to release options.

The Native Women's Association of Canada report (McIvor & Johnson, 2003) expressed a concern with the feasibility of the CSC implementing section 84 of the CCRA. In the report, the association identifies current budget constraints within CSC that led to the denial of transfers under this section of the Act. The association also reported that CSC determines the viability of an Indigenous community to provide the necessary care and support for an Indigenous woman during incarceration or parole supervision. This authority creates concerns because CSC has not demonstrated its own internal viability in recognizing, acknowledging, developing, or offering cultural programs that are adequate and sufficient to meet the needs of federally sentenced Indigenous women. Therefore, the Native Women's Association of Canada provides a valid concern about the implication of CSC making such determinations because CSC may not positively support innovative and culturally valid Indigenous community initiatives that are willing to support Indigenous women in their reintegration plans. Ultimately, it highlights the ongoing colonial bias of CSC to make decisions about Indigenous people and communities without the cultural foundation to do so.

CSC has also developed nine full-time positions across the country to create links between Indigenous offenders (male and female) and Indigenous communities. These positions, Indigenous community development officers (ACDOs), are expected to increase Indigenous "community interest in participating in the correctional process and to initiate section 84 release planning" (CSC, 2006, p. 24). Although these measures are a step in the right direction, they are more than ten years overdue for Indigenous people involved in the correctional system.

Other measures have been implemented to assist in reducing the disproportionate number of Indigenous people in the correctional system. The Parole Board has implemented a panel review with an Indigenous cultural advisor as an alternative hearing approach that is more sensitive to the unique needs of Indigenous offenders. The hearing is based on Indigenous values, including holding the hearing in a circle, using cultural ceremonies (prayers and smudges, for example), and inviting the participation of the affected parties. The board members are also briefed on Indigenous culture, traditions, and experiences, including information specific to the tribe or culture of the offender. Statistics from the Parole Board (2004) indicate both an increased use of alternative hearings and higher rates of Indigenous offenders being granted all forms of conditional release over a five-year period (60 percent increase in day parole and 25 percent for full parole). Unfortunately, the ability to sustain this program has been difficult and the promising statistics have faded away, as Mann (2009) notes that fewer Indigenous offenders request this process and there are fewer Elders available to provide it.

Mann's (2009) report for the OCI is aptly called *Good Intentions, Disappointing Results*, as there has been some positive movement in better meeting the needs of Indigenous women but the outcomes have not been remarkable. Some of the highlights of Mann's report are shown in Box 9.4.

Finally, in 1991, the federal government introduced the First Nations policing policy to allow for "access to police services that were professional, effective, culturally appropriate and accountable to the communities they serve" (CCJA, 2000, p. 31). This policy is an important step in making the criminal justice system more responsive to the cultural needs of Indigenous people. Benefits that have been identified include the following:

- A decrease in the number of arrests
- Less tension when an Indigenous police officer is involved
- The combination of police training and an officer's knowledge of and commitment to the community

BOX 9.4

Highlights of the Report *Good Intentions, Disappointing Results*

- CSC has few strategies and policies in place to ensure Indigenous programming is consistently available.
- Few accountability measures such as evaluation and data to demonstrate they are narrowing the gap.
- CSC has not demonstrated the capability to effectively engage Elders or recruit competent, knowledgeable staff for the culture-specific programming, which leads to continued inconsistencies in availability of the programs.
- Lack of an Indigenous gang strategy.
- Assessment tools remain culturally inappropriate and irrelevant to the realities of Indigenous women that have ramifications during their sentences.
- Application of *Gladue* principles in classification, reclassification, and segregation are not apparent.

- Limited use of legislated approaches to improving Indigenous offenders' reintegration.
- Inconsistent and shortage of Indigenous programming contributes to delayed parole.
- A Northern strategy that would apply to Inuit has not been realized after three years of consultations.
- Healing Lodges are not accessible, well-used, well-defined, or well-monitored and are without clear directives, all taking away from anticipated positive benefits.

Source: Mann, M. (2009). *Good intentions, disappointing results: A progress report on federal Aboriginal corrections.* Office of the Correctional Investigator. Retrieved from http://www.oci-bec.gc.ca/cnt/rpt/pdf/oth-aut/oth-aut20091113-eng.pdf.

However, problems also plague this initiative—mainly issues related to poor or inadequate funding that leads to high attrition rates because of low salaries and the pressures afforded to Indigenous police officers who carry a dual role of policing (generally a profession with much distrust in the community) and being a family member and community member (CCJA, 2000).

▶ **WHAT DO YOU THINK?**

Has CSC done enough to support healing for Indigenous women? Consider what you know of any new information from research, programs, and documents that support the need to consider other forms of "evidence." Should CSC use Indigenous knowledge and culture as a foundation to all Indigenous programming?

SUMMARY

Indigenous women are disproportionately represented in the criminal justice system in Canada, and population statistics suggest this trend will continue. Their overrepresentation is multi-causal: social and economic disadvantages, opposing values of justice, discrimination and racism, lack of gender- and culture-relevant assessment tools, lack of culturally-relevant programming, and colonialism. In the last 20 years, significant documents, government policies, and court decisions have identified ways to combat the negative implications of colonialism that incarcerated Indigenous women continue to deal with on a daily basis.

Although the intent of these documents, policies, and decisions is valuable and significant, only a limited impact has been realized on reducing the number of Indigenous women in the criminal justice system. Some promising initiatives can be expanded to improve the status of incarcerated Indigenous women; for example, the measures used to develop and implement the opening of Okimaw Ohci Healing Lodge. However, careful consideration must be given to the need for Indigenous involvement, participation, and ownership if such initiatives are to succeed. It will also be critical for the justice system to acknowledge Indigenous knowledge as valid evidence that highlights the need for culture as a foundational component of all programming in order to realize healing and reduce rates of Indigenous people in the justice system.

Until the justice system is prepared to recognize, acknowledge, and address the imbedded colonialism within the system, only limited gains can be expected in improving the status of Indigenous women in the criminal justice system. The reader is directed to The Truth and Reconciliation Commission of Canada's Calls to Action. There are 17 calls to action specific to justice; the majority of these (#30–40, 42) are directed at specific action to reduce overrepresentation of Indigenous people in the justice system. These Calls to Action support a way forward.

NOTES

1. The term *Indigenous people* refers to those internationally defined as having a set of specific rights based on their historical ties to a particular territory, and their cultural or historical distinctiveness from other populations that are often politically dominant.
2. The term *Indigenous* is the constitutional term that refers to First Nations, Inuit, and Métis people in Canada.
3. For a more complete discussion of the definition and impact of colonialism, see Montour-Angus (1999) and Stevenson (1999).
4. For more information on the impact of colonialism on Indigenous people in Canada please review the Calls to Action for the Truth and Reconciliation Commission (2015).

   The reader is referred to the First Nations Mental Wellness Continuum Framework (2015) for a discussion on culture as a foundation to wellness. Further opportunities to consider wellness from a holistic perspective that considers the Indigenous social determinants of health can be found within this model.
5. There are conflicting reports about Ashley Smith's heritage, but she has been taken up as an important example of the problems with current prison practices, especially for vulnerable populations like Indigenous women.

DISCUSSION QUESTIONS

1. Discuss how the needs of Indigenous women are unfairly recognized by the criminal justice system.
2. Colonialism plays a significant role in the reality of Indigenous women's lives prior to, during, and after incarceration. Identify historical and present-day colonialist acts and describe their impact on Indigenous women.
3. Examine how the *Gladue* decision, the *Corrections and Conditional Release Act*, *Creating Choices*, and the Arbour Inquiry attempt to ameliorate colonial consequences that result in discriminatory treatment of Indigenous women in the criminal justice system.
4. Okimaw Ohci Healing Lodge is a direct result of recommendations made by *Creating Choices*. Discuss the advantages and disadvantages of regional facilities such as Okimaw Ohci in improving the lives of federally sentenced Indigenous women.

ADDITIONAL RESOURCES

Suggested Readings

Canada, Royal Commission on Aboriginal Peoples. (1996). *Report of the Royal Commission on Aboriginal Peoples: Vol. 3. Gathering strength.* Ottawa: Indian and Northern Affairs Canada.

Covert, K. (2015). *Statistics in context: Aboriginals in Canada's prisons.* CBA National. Retrieved from http://www.nationalmagazine.ca/Blog/June-2015/Statistics-in-context -Aboriginals-in-Canada-s-pris.aspx.

Kunic, D., & Varis, D.D. (2009). *The Aboriginal Offender Substance Abuse Program (AOSAP): Examining the effects of successful completion on post-release outcomes.* Ottawa: Correctional Service of Canada.

Ross, R. (1996). *Returning to the teachings: Exploring Indigenous justice.* Toronto: Penguin Books.

Solomon, A. (1994). *Eating bitterness: A vision beyond prison walls.* Toronto: NC Press.

Welniak, N. (2010). *The outcome of a recommendation pertaining to federally sentenced Aboriginal women.* Retrieved from http://dtpr.lib.athabascau.ca/action/viewdtrdesc.php ?cpk=0&id=44203.

Wesley-Esquimaux, C.C. & Smolewski, M. (2004). Historic trauma and Aboriginal healing. Ottawa: Aboriginal Healing Foundation.

Films and Videos

Macdonald, N. (2016, February 18). Canada's prisons are the "new residential schools" [Video file]. *Maclean's.* Retrieved from http://www.macleans.ca/news/canada/canadas-prisons -are-the-new-residential-schools/.

Rennie, S. (2014, December 2). Huge increase in number of Aboriginal women in Canadian prisons [Video file]. The Canadian Press. Retrieved from https://www.thestar.com/news/ canada/2014/12/02/huge_increase_in_number_of_aboriginal_women_in_canadian _prisons.html.

Websites

Aboriginal Legal Services of Toronto: www.aboriginallegal.ca
Canadian Association of Elizabeth Fry Societies: www.caefs.ca/
Indigenous and Northern Affairs Canada: www.aadnc-aandc.gc.ca
Native Women's Association of Canada: www.nwac.ca
The Truth and Reconciliation Commission of Canada: www.trc.ca

REFERENCES

Bell, A., Trevethan, S., and Allegri, N. (2004). *Needs assessment of federal Aboriginal women offenders.* Correctional Services Canada Research Reports. Retrieved from http://www.csc-scc.gc.ca/research/r156-eng.shtml.

Canada, Commission of Inquiry into Certain Events at the Prison for Women in Kingston. (1996). *Commission of inquiry into certain events at the Prison for Women in Kingston* (the Arbour Inquiry). Ottawa: Public Works and Government Services of Canada.

Canada, Task Force on Federally Sentenced Women. (1990). *Creating choices: Report of the task force on federally sentenced women.* Ottawa: Department of the Solicitor General.

Canadian Criminal Justice Association. (2000). Aboriginal peoples and the criminal justice system [Special issue]. *Bulletin.* Retrieved from http://caid.ca/CCJA .APCJS2000.pdf.

Canadian Human Rights Commission. (2003). *Protecting their rights: A systemic review of human rights in correctional services for federally sentenced women.* Retrieved from http://www.chrc-ccdp.ca/sites/default/files/ fswen.pdf.

Correctional Investigator of Canada. (2006). *Annual report of the Office of the Correctional Investigator 2005–2006.* Ottawa: Ministry of Public Works and Government Services Canada.

Correctional Service of Canada. (2000). *Statistical overview: Women offenders sector*. Ottawa: Author.

Correctional Service of Canada. (2006). *The ten-year status report on women's corrections, 1996–2006*. Ottawa: Author.

Correctional Service of Canada. (2013). *Demographic overview of Aboriginal people in Canada and Aboriginal offenders in federal corrections*. Retrieved from http://www.csc-scc.gc.ca/aboriginal/002003-1008-eng.shtml.

Correctional Service of Canada. (2016). *Correctional Services Canada Healing Lodges*. Retrieved from http://www.csc-scc.gc.ca/aboriginal/002003-2000-eng.shtml.

Corrections and Conditional Release Act, SC 1992, c 20.

Dell, A. & Boe, R. (2000). *An examination of Indigenous and Caucasian women offender risk and needs factors* (Research Report R-94). Ottawa: Correctional Service of Canada.

Hannah-Moffatt, K. & Shaw, M. (2001). *Taking risks: Incorporating gender and culture into the classification and assessment of federally sentenced women in Canada*. Ottawa: Status of Women Canada.

Manitoba, Public Inquiry into the Administration of Justice and Indigenous People. (1991). *Report of the Indigenous justice inquiry of Manitoba: The justice system and Indigenous people* (vol. 1). Winnipeg: Queen's Printer.

Mann, M. (2009). *Good intentions, disappointing results: A progress report on federal Aboriginal corrections*. Office of the Correctional Investigator. Retrieved from http://www.oci-bec.gc.ca/cnt/rpt/pdf/oth-aut/oth-aut20091113-eng.pdf.

McIvor, E. & Johnson, E. (2003). Detailed position of the Native Women's Association of Canada on the complaint regarding the discriminatory treatment of federally sentenced women by the Government of Canada: Filed by the Canadian Association of Elizabeth Fry Societies. Retrieved from http://www.caefs.ca/wp-content/uploads/2013/05/nwac_submission.pdf.

Montour-Angus, P. (1999). Considering colonialism and oppression: Indigenous women, justice and the "theory" of decolonization. *Native Studies Review, 12*, 63–94.

Montour-Angus, P. (2002). *The lived experience of discrimination: Aboriginal women who are federally sentenced*. Ottawa: Canadian Association of Elizabeth Fry Societies.

Morin, S. (1999). *Federally sentenced Aboriginal women in maximum security: What happened to the promises of "Creating Choices"?* Ottawa: Correctional Service of Canada.

National Parole Board. (2000). *Special study on federal female offenders from 1995/96 to 1999/00*. Ottawa: Performance Measurement Division, National Parole Board.

National Parole Board. (2004). *Performance monitoring report, 2003–2004*. Ottawa: Performance Measurement Division, National Parole Board.

Office of the Correctional Investigator (OCI). (2007). *Annual report, 2006–2007*. Retrieved from http://www.oci-bec.gc.ca/cnt/rpt/pdf/annrpt/annrpt20062007-eng.pdf.

Office of the Correctional Investigator (OCI). (2015). *Annual report, 2014–2015*. Retrieved from http://www.oci-bec.gc.ca/cnt/rpt/annrpt/annrpt20142015-eng.aspx#s8.

Public Safety Canada. (2015). *2015 Corrections and conditional release statistical overview*. Retrieved from https://www.publicsafety.gc.ca/cnt/rsrcs/pblctns/ccrso-2015/index-en.aspx#d4.

Ross, R. (1992). *Dancing with a ghost: Exploring Indian reality*. Markham: Reed Books Canada.

Statistics Canada. (2011). *Aboriginal peoples in Canada: First Nations People, Métis and Inuit*. Retrieved from http://www12.statcan.gc.ca/nhs-enm/2011/as-sa/99-011-x/99-011-x2011001-eng.cfm.

Stevenson, W. (1999). Colonialism and First Nations women in Canada. In E. Dua & A. Robertson (Eds.), *Scratching the surface: Canada and anti-racist feminist thought* (pp. 49–80). Toronto: Women's Press.

Sugar, F. & Fox, L. (1990). *Survey of federally sentenced women in the community*. Ottawa: Task Force on Federally Sentenced Women.

Wesley, M., LL.B. (2012). *Marginalized: The Aboriginal women's experience in federal corrections*. Retrieved from https://www.publicsafety.gc.ca/cnt/rsrcs/pblctns/mrgnlzd/mrgnlzd-eng.pdf.

Women's Legal Education and Action Fund (LEAF). (1989). Report to the court challenges program on case development regarding unequal treatment of federally imprisoned women. Toronto: Author.

Prostitution and Missing and Murdered Women and Girls in Canada

Introduction

"Prostitution is not the oldest profession; it is the oldest oppression."

Nicholas Kristof

If ever there was a topic most debated, it is prostitution. Beliefs about it vary greatly, from one end of the spectrum to the other, and they vary within provinces and across countries. In Canada, each province has the autonomy to administer the federal law and justice system how it sees fit, which is often driven by the ruling political party at the time. And furthermore, you may find that within one province, the various municipal and/or provincial policing agencies have different mandates when it comes to enforcing prostitution laws and choosing subjects to target. All of this adds to the complexity of supporting "the best" idea to address prostitution.

Prostitution involves two specific and symbolic domains of society—sexual relations and economics—and since these domains are highly gendered, the female prostitute or sex worker has long represented a troubling figure, disrupting what are traditionally deemed to be natural gender binaries (males should be active whereas females should be passive; economics is in the public domain whereas sexual relations is relegated to the private arena). Often simultaneously viewed as an inevitable feature of all human societies, prostitution is held to meet the supposedly powerful and biologically given sexual impulses of men. Thus it is sometimes described as a "necessary evil" and considered to protect the virtue of "good" girls and women by "soaking up" excess male sexual urges which would otherwise lead to rape and marital breakdown (O'Connell-Davidson, 2007).

Take what you will from such dichotomies, there remain a variety of ideas and positions about prostitution and this chapter will introduce you to some of the ideas that currently consume the literature. What is presented here is overly succinct but the intent is to provide you with factual information so that you may contribute to the recurring and robust debate.

What Is Prostitution?

The term *prostitution* is popularly used to refer to the trade of sexual services for payment in cash or similar (O'Connell-Davidson, 2007). Often sex is traded for money but also for things like food and shelter, drugs, or commodities, such as rent or debt repayment. Others (Musto, Jackson, & Shi, 2015) apply an intersectional lens to a definition:

Prostitution is a gendered, sexualized, and racialized labor system, one that typically involves the exchange of sexual services for money, goods, or other benefits. Sex work encompasses different types of intimate arrangements that blur the boundaries between erotic, emotional, and economic labor. Sex work is also part of an industry and commercial market that is global in reach and diverse in its spatial, legal, and occupational organization. (p. 279)

In previous editions of the *Criminal Code of Canada* there existed definitions and offences of prostitution (see Box 10.1). On a global level, the United Nations has defined prostitution and sexual exploitation under its trafficking and migration protocols (see Box 10.2). After *R v Bedford* (2013; discussed below), the rewriting of those laws removed the term *prostitution* and clarified some of the offence categories. Prostitution, the exchange of sex for money, has always been legal in Canada (as long as parties are adults and no one is coerced or forced). But the *Criminal Code* prohibits virtually every other activity related to prostitution in almost every conceivable public or private place (Betteridge & Csete, 2016).

BOX 10.1

Definitions and Offences of Prostitution Before *R v Bedford*

- Section 210 of the *Criminal Code* made it illegal to keep a place for the purpose of prostitution (known as a common bawdy house), or to be found in such a place.
- Section 211 made it illegal to transport a person to a common bawdy house.
- Section 212 prohibited enticing, encouraging, or forcing a person to engage in prostitution (procuring), and living on the avails of prostitution.
- Section 213 made it illegal to communicate in a public place or stop a person or vehicle for the purposes of engaging in prostitution. *Public place* is defined broadly, to include any place to which the public has a right of access and includes motor vehicles.

BOX 10.2

The United Nations Convention

The Protocol to Prevent, Suppress and Punish Trafficking in Persons, especially Women and Children, which supplements the United Nations Convention against Transnational Organized Crime states that:

(a) "Trafficking in persons" shall mean the recruitment, transportation, transfer, harbouring or receipt of persons, by means of the threat or use of force or other forms of coercion, of abduction, of fraud, of deception, of the abuse of power or of a position of vulnerability or of the giving or receiving of payments or benefits to achieve the consent of a person having control over another person, for the purpose of exploitation. Exploitation shall include, at a minimum, the exploitation of the prostitution of others or other forms of sexual exploitation, forced labour or services, slavery or practices similar to slavery, servitude or the removal of organs;

(b) The consent of a victim of trafficking in persons to the intended exploitation set forth in subparagraph (a) of this article shall be irrelevant where any of the means set forth in subparagraph (a) have been used.

Source: United Nations Treaty Collection. (2017). Chapter XVIII Penal Matters 12 a: *A protocol to prevent, suppress and punish trafficking in persons, especially women and children, supplementing the United Nations convention against transnational organized crime*. (2000, November 15). New York: United Nations, *Treaty Series*, vol. 2237, p. 319; Doc. A/55/383.

Canada's *Criminal Code* defines trafficking in section 279.01(1) as:

Every person who recruits, transports, transfers, receives, holds, conceals or harbours a person, or exercises control, direction or influence over the movements of a person, for the purpose of exploiting them or facilitating their exploitation is guilty of an indictable offence and liable

(a) to imprisonment for life and to a minimum punishment of imprisonment for a term of five years if they kidnap, commit an aggravated assault or aggravated sexual assault against, or cause death to, the victim during the commission of the offence; or

(b) to imprisonment for a term of not more than 14 years and to a minimum punishment of imprisonment for a term of four years in any other case.

R v Bedford

The case was initiated in 2007 by three Ontario sex workers, Terri Jean Bedford, Amy Lebovitch, and Valerie Scott, who asked the court to strike down the three sections of the *Criminal Code* because they violate sex workers' constitutional right to security of the person guaranteed under the *Charter of Rights and Freedoms*. Their point was that the contradictory and convoluted laws made sex work dangerous and did not permit it to be a recognized form of labour; they argued for a change to the laws.

In 2013, the Supreme Court of Canada ruled that three sections, section 210 (keeping or being found in a bawdy house), section 212(1)(j) (living on the avails of prostitution), and section 213(1)(c) (communicating in public for the purpose of prostitution), violate the section 7 right to security of the person protected by the *Canadian Charter of Rights and Freedoms*. All three laws have been struck down. The court stated:

The prohibitions at issue do not merely impose conditions on how prostitutes operate. They go a critical step further, by imposing dangerous conditions on prostitution; they prevent people engaged in a risky—but legal—activity from taking steps to protect themselves from the risk. (para. 60)

What this means is that because it is (was) illegal to engage in sex work in a public place (communicating...) and it is (was) illegal to be in a brothel or similar establishment (keeping or found in a common bawdy house), sex workers were forced into the dark alleys and other unsavoury corners of society where they were easily preyed upon and forced into debt servitude (pimps and organized crime) because it was illegal for sex workers to earn a living from sex work (living on the avails...), which was in fact a legal enterprise (Betteridge & Csete, 2016).

The sections from the Charter that applied to the challenge of prostitution laws were:

- Section 1 permits the government to justify a law or action that otherwise violates a Charter right, if it meets certain conditions.
- Section 2(b) guarantees everyone freedom of expression.
- Section 2(d) guarantees everyone freedom of association.
- Section 7 protects everyone from violations of "life, liberty and security of the person," except where the violation is "in accordance with the principles of fundamental justice."
- Section 15 guarantees everyone equality before and under the law, and equal protection and benefit of the law.

In June 2014, the federal government (under Stephen Harper) tabled new legislation (Bill C-36) in response to the Supreme Court ruling. Bill C-36, the *Protection of Communities and Exploited Persons Act*, which came into force on December 6, 2014 (Government of Canada, 2015). The legislation criminalized the purchase of sexual services from any person, thereby making prostitution illegal in Canada for the first time. The Act emulated a version of the "Nordic Model," first implemented in Sweden in 1999, which treats all prostitution as exploitation of primarily women and girls and aims to reduce its incidence by focusing on penalizing the purchasers of sexual services and those who benefit financially from the prostitution of others (such as pimps and organized crime; Rotenberg, 2016).

To date, Alberta is the only province in Canada with legislation that provides police and children and family services with the tools to apprehend kids engaging in prostitution or at risk of engaging in it. Enacted in 1999, the *Protection of Children Involved in Prostitution Act* (PChiP), gives authorities the right to place kids (age 18 and under) in protective safe houses where they receive medical and psychological care, education, detox (if needed), and other supports to be able to stop sexual exploitation (Government of Alberta, 2010). In 2007, this Act was revised and it is now known as the *Protection of Sexually Exploited Children Act* (PSECA, 2014). One of the major changes was an increase to the age limit for services. Other countries have adopted novel approaches to addressing prostitution or sexual exploitation (see Box 10.3).

BOX 10.3

Prostitution and Exploitation Acts Around the World

- The Nordic Model—officially known as the *Swedish Sex Purchase Act* (1999)—makes paying for sex a crime but selling sex is not.
- In 2001, Germany instituted laws that mandated sex workers be treated like workers in any other industry, which allows them to sue for better wages and have full access to health insurance, pensions, and other benefits.
- In the Netherlands, prostitution is considered a profession like any other, according to the law and by society in general. Legislation in 2001 was enacted that allows sex workers the right to claim for hygienic working conditions, security at the workplace, and to pay income tax. "Forced" prostitution and procuring minors remain illegal.
- In 2003, New Zealand passed a law to decriminalize prostitution—sex work is no longer considered a crime.

What Statistics Tell Us About Prostitution

Any reported statistics about the prevalence of prostitution and/or arrest and charges laid against violators of prostitution laws need to be taken with a grain of salt. Since it is typically an underground or hidden industry, it is difficult to count the numbers of people involved in prostitution (the sellers or the buyers). Only when police conduct stings or sweeps will that city be able to report on numbers of those arrested; that in itself is limited to only those caught. And each police service may prioritize stings and sweeps differently (youth versus adults), thereby collecting different data than their counterparts in another city or province.

All of that being said, in 2016, the Canadian Centre for Justice Statistics released a report that included collated prostitution data (gathered from police services across Canada) for the first time since the 1990s. Rotenberg (2016) reported that between 2009 and 2014 (a period prior to *R v Bedford*, 2013), there were 16,879 prostitution incidents (communicating or attempting to communicate with a person for the purpose of engaging in or obtaining sexual services) reported by police, which represents less than 0.1 percent of all crimes reported during the same period.

Changes in prostitution legislation have a direct influence on police-reported prostitution crimes (see Figure 10.1 for more detail). For instance, in 1985, an offence prohibiting communicating in public places for the purposes of purchasing or selling sexual services was enacted (Bill C-49). A large increase in police-reported prostitution incidents under the communicating offence was noted following the implementation of Bill C-49. When new prostitution legislation (Bill C-36) was implemented in 2014, a decline in the rate of police-reported prostitution offences, largely attributed to communicating offences, was evident (Rotenberg, 2016). In 2014, the rates of prostitution offences also varied across the provinces (see Figure 10.2) and cities (see Figure 10.3).

Close to half (43 percent) of persons arrested for a prostitution-related offence between 2009 and 2014 were female, compared with less than one quarter (23 percent) of persons accused of any other type of offence overall during the same time period. Females accused of prostitution were much younger than the men who purchased (or tried to purchase) sexual services (median age of 31 versus 42), and repeat contact with police was more frequent among female accused (27 percent) compared with male accused (3 percent). And between 2008/2009 and 2013/2014, 30 percent of prostitution cases processed in criminal courts resulted in a guilty verdict; this was much lower than for criminal court cases in general (64 percent).

FIGURE 10.1   Trends in the Rate of Prostitution Offences Between 1962 and 2014

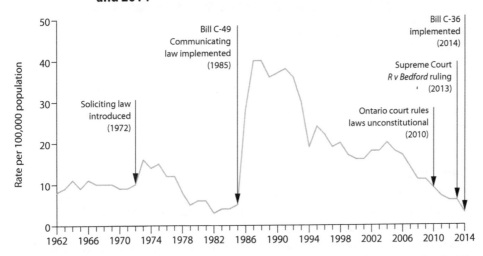

Note: Rates are calculated on the basis of 100,000 population. Populations are based upon July 1st estimates from Statistics Canada, Demography Division.

Source: Rotenberg, C. (2016). Prostitution offences in Canada: Statistical trends (Chart 1). Catalogue no. 85-002-X. Statistics Canada *Juristat*, *36*(1), 4.

FIGURE 10.2   2014 Rates of Police-Reported Prostition Offences by Province

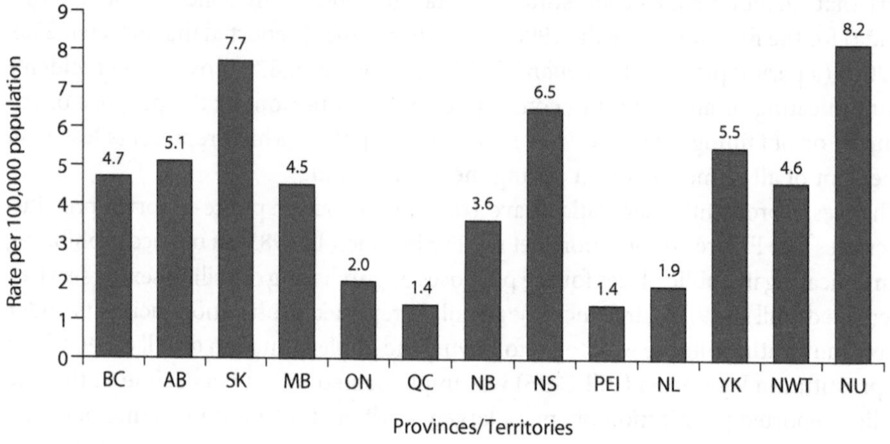

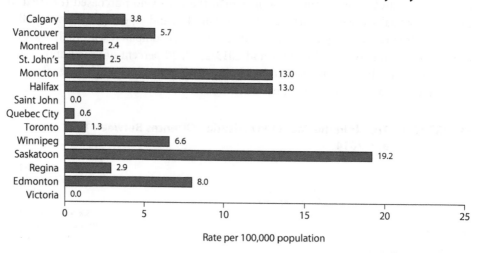

Source: Rotenberg, C. (2016). Prostitution offences in Canada: Statistical trends (Table 1). Catalogue no. 85-002-X. Statistics Canada *Juristat, 36*(1), 21.

FIGURE 10.3   2014 Rates of Police-Reported Prostition Offences by City

Source: Rotenberg, C. (2016, p. 22). Prostitution offences in Canada: Statistical trends (Table 2). Catalogue no. 85-002-X. Statistics Canada *Juristat, 36*(1), 22.

Adults Versus Children

First and foremost, we must acknowledge that Canada does not consider children to be prostitutes; we consider children to be exploited. Our laws and cultural compass do not permit children under the age of 16 to consent to sexual interactions.

Section 150.1(1) through (6) inclusive in our *Criminal Code* articulates consent to sex:

- Children age 16 and under cannot consent to sex;
- If there is a relationship of trust or authority, and/or dependency between the complainant and accused, then it is considered sexual assault;

- If the complainant is between the ages of 12 and 14 and accused is less than two years older, then it is NOT considered sexual assault;
- If the complainant is between 14 and 16 and accused is less than five years older and they are married, then it is NOT considered sexual assault.

Prostitution Versus Sex Trafficking

Sex trafficking and sex work do not exist in a vacuum; both are embedded in broader socio-economic processes that uniquely disadvantage women (Williams, 2011). An interconnected global economy, labour migration by both sexes, violence, and cultural norms have increasingly pushed women into migration (and prostitution) as a survival strategy. The traffic in women is inseparable from gender inequality, migration, cultural mores, and poverty, which impact everyone, regardless of their gender, class, race, or national origin (Williams, 2011). The defining characteristics of sex trafficking in international protocols and national legislation rests upon the premise that some variation of "force," "fraud," and/or "coercion" must have taken place. Focusing on sex trafficking specifically as a migration issue reveals the xenophobia, sexism, and institutionalized disregard for the poor that underlies much of contemporary discourse on the subject. Sex trafficking and institutional responses to it are social processes supported both directly and indirectly by the complicity of societies (Dewey, 2008).

▶ WHAT DO YOU THINK?

Consider whether sex trafficking occurs across borders or within countries. What does sex trafficking look like in your city/province? If a person is trafficked by people who are not associated with a criminal organization, does it still constitute trafficking? Discuss your opinion.

What Are Prostitution's Causes and Contributing Factors?

Depending on your position along the continuum of prostitution discussed below, your belief in its causes may differ. But what we can claim with empirical evidence is that when we ask men and women who used to work in the sex industry, the majority have had negative, harmful, and destructive experiences prior to entering prostitution as well as while working in prostitution. Some of those causes and contributing factors are presented here. By no means is this list exhaustive, but rather an introduction to those most harmful.

Adverse Childhood Experiences

Survival sex work involves exchanging sex for money to meet basic substance needs such as food and shelter. Oftentimes it is young people or teens who have run away from their homes or groups homes because of abuse, neglect, and/or violence. Now on the streets, they face finding ways in which to survive. The average age of entry into prostitution (sexual exploitation) in Canada is 14 (McIntyre, 2005; McIntyre, 2010); that means that on average, the adults who we see today engaged in prostitution conducted their first transaction around age 14. McIntyre has been researching prostitution and sexual exploitation from the experiences of workers and clients. Of the men and women who were reinterviewed for *Strolling Away* (McIntyre, 2005), 100 percent had a background of sexual and physical abuse prior to their involvement in prostitution and while working, and 81 percent had a background of involvement with child welfare.

Addiction

Data from drug and alcohol treatment programs also point to triggering factors in childhood. In one study, 72 percent of adults reported physical and/or sexual violence histories, and of those, 75 percent of cases occurred during childhood (Liebshutz, Savestky, Saitz, Horton, Lloyd-Travaglini, & Samet, 2012).

Drugs and alcohol are also used to lure youth into prostitution. They are used as a means of coping while working in prostitution, or to support an addiction, all of which pushes and pulls people (youth and adults) into the cause–effect cycle of prostitution (McIntyre, 2005; McIntyre, 2010).

Mental Illness

More prevalent in women than men, experiencing sexual and physical abuse as a child often leads to mental illnesses, such as depression, personality disorders, self-harm, and self-medicating, which in turn can lead to addiction and chronic mental illness. The cause–effect cycle continues—being vulnerable, ill, or addicted can lead to prostitution and being involved in prostitution can lead to coping with drugs and alcohol. Further-more, suicide rates are also correlated with childhood adverse experiences and sexual exploitation.

In 2013, the national rate of suicide in Canada was 10.5 per 100,000 (Statistics Canada, 2017a). By province/territory, Nunavut had the highest rate of suicide in 2013 at 119 per 100,000 and Ontario had the lowest at 8.4 per 100,000.

Poverty

Marginalization is the social process by which individuals and groups are relegated to the fringe of society. It is closely tied to the concepts of social exclusion and social dis-advantage, which in turn systematically block people from rights, opportunities, and resources that are normally available in a society. Marginalization is closely related to vulnerability to predation, and creates the climate in which people living on the street and/or engaged in prostitution are often ignored or forgotten. Poverty can push people into committing crimes as well as engaging in prostitution as a means of survival. That in turn can position people within the cause–effect cycle of prostitution, addiction, vio-lence, and mental illness noted above. High levels of unemployment (poverty), violence, and addiction force many into prostitution (Bruckert & Parent, 2004).

The Prostitution Debate

Goldstein (2006) offers that the debate and discourse about prostitution often lobby around two socially constructed images. On one end, there is the image of "… the in-nocent victim, to be protected and relocated," while on the other end there is the image of the prostitute as "an affront to public morality and hygiene to be controlled and contained" (Kantola & Squires, 2004, p. 80). In the first image, a victimization lens, it is sexual violence that is the result of an unequal distribution of power between men and women in society, and women are then portrayed as victims of sexual domination (Outshoorn, 2004). It is the idea of the fallen woman who has been led down a path of moral destruction; the woman appears to lack any free choice and is simply responding to negative societal forces. This then requires intervention and protection, and if there is a victim, then there must be a perpetrator. The focus shifts to that perpetrator as the way to handle the issue, such as a change in legislation in Sweden by making it illegal to purchase sex (a.k.a., Johns or "dates") and illegal to force someone to engage in prostitution (a.k.a., pimps or "boyfriends").

The other image is classified as "public nuisance discourse." These ideas are most often created and perpetuated through the media, particularly in Canada (Van Brunschot, Sydie, & Krull, 1999). An intense concentration on street workers in the media can be attributed to two key factors: (1) visibility; and (2) the link of prostitution to crime and disease. Prostitutes are most often characterized by what they are *not* instead of what they are. They are described by the norms and values (created by others in society) that they violate. They are defined by the problems they create for other people (condoms on the street, proximity to businesses) rather than by the problems that they themselves face (coercion, poverty, addiction). "It [is] the visible evidence of deviant bodies and deviant sexuality that [is] the issue" (Van Brunschot et al., 1999, p. 267); in other words, the proof of the sex trade is oftentimes more offensive to community members than the actual exchange of sex that is occurring (Van Brunschot et al., 1999).

Canada's laws were inherited from the British monarchy. Historically, the aim of the law was to deal with the public nuisance created by street workers and brothels or bawdy houses (Goff, 2016). The law today is still intended to keep prostitution out of sight (Lowman, 2005), which has led to further alienation and vulnerability (by forcing sex workers underground). Scambler (1997) points to the fact that "it is the street worker … who attracts the attention of politicians, the police, and other agencies of moral regulation and surveillance," while "off street or indoor workers are inconspicuous to the point of invisibility" (p. 105). Street-level sex workers are not targeted because they are viewed as more or less guilty than indoor sex workers. The key difference is visibility. Indoor workers do not affect property values or contribute to perceived crime and disease in a community. The strongest voice in public nuisance discourse comes from a community level—those who argue that they are directly impacted by the sex trade. The problem is constructed as a restricted issue for those individuals who live or work in the area. Prostitution is often viewed as a "necessary evil," as long as it takes place in another area (Van Brunschot et al., 1999). This **NIMBY (not in my backyard)** type of mentality is reflective of the visibility issue. People want the problem out of their area and do not give much thought to where the problem goes, just that it is removed from their "backyard."

Repeated evidence demonstrates that the root causes of prostitution are of no interest to community members. The issues of highest importance are community aesthetics and property values. Residents believe that prostitution creates a very poor environmental and social impression. The neighbourhood also experiences heightened fear for the safety of women and children (Kantola & Squires, 2004). This serves to reinforce traditional patriarchal views, where men are strong and women and children are in need of protection. Women who are involved in prostitution are therefore doubly deviant in that they not only violate the law but also a gendered prescription of sexuality. Kantola and Squires (2004) point out that in prostitution "[t]he debate is underpinned

NIMBY (not in my backyard) A belief that change in one's neighbourhood will deteriorate the property value of homes and businesses.

by a strong notion of respectable female sexuality which excludes the idea of commercial sex" (p. 81). And the news media is able to constantly reinforce the same stereotypes (Hallgrimsdottir, Philips, & Benoit, 2006) by using a stereotypical image of the drug-addicted prostitute bringing disease and crime into a neighbourhood. Noteworthy is that next to no attention is paid to the purchasers of sex (the "Johns"). Despite that official statistics reveal Johns come in all shapes, sizes, ages, races, and marital statuses, they are often ignored or kept hidden from NIMBY discussions. No one is demanding that these men (and it is primarily men) stop bringing disease, drugs, and money into communities seeking to buy sexual services.

The Continuum of Prostitution

Sociologists and criminologists (and other academics) have tried to develop and apply theoretical perspectives to explain sex work and the sex industry. No one theory fully encompasses the causes, consequences, and components within the sex industry, but many theories encapsulate valid points to consider and/or dispute (Scambler & Scambler, as cited in Scambler, 1997).

Socio-biological theories start from the proposition that differences between males and females can be explained by biology. And that sex work is believed to be a social imperative to accommodate the overpowering male sex drive, and therefore the sex industry is needed to serve that purpose.

Socio-pathological theories claim that female sex work is the result of some deep and underlying pathology or abnormal psyche in women that drives them to violate societal norms.

Feminist theories typically draw on the concept of patriarchy and that sex work is a result of men's domination and control over female bodies and sexuality. Patriachy also reinforces that women are sexual objects and it permits their violation at the hands of men.

While none of those theories entirely explains sex work or sexual exploitation fully and completely, they each have something to offer. Extended from those theories is the spectrum of ideology—how we think society should deal with prostitution. Figure 10.4 illustrates the continuum of prostitution.

FIGURE 10.4   The Continuum of Prostitution

Abolition   Criminalization   Decriminalization   Legalization

Abolition

Farley (2004) adamantly claims that regardless of whether prostitution is legal or illegal or decriminalized or regulated, violence and harm are inherent. And psychological harm (as well as medical harm) often follows time spent in the sex industry. Many studies have documented that physical and sexual violence are part of the norm for any woman (or man) involved in sex work (Betteridge & Csete, 2016; Valera, Sawyer, & Schiraldi, 2001, as cited in Farley, 2004; MacKinnon, 2005).

Abolition assumes all sex work is abusive, victimizing, and enslaving. Abolitionists seek to eradicate prostitution entirely and refuse to accept the personal agency of sex workers. Ekberg (2004) advocates for the Swedish model, where prostitution is officially acknowledged as a form of male sexual violence against women and children, one of the cornerstones being that the root cause is men's demand for and use of women and girls for sexual exploitation. She goes on by claiming that all forms of legal or policy measures that legalize different prostitution activities (brothels, pimps, traffickers, brothel owners, and buyers) are seen as anathema to gender equality and the rights of women and girls to live lives free of exploitation and male violence.

The street-based sex worker is often the most vulnerable. They are ignored and alienated and have little to no choice in being selective of clients or ensuring their physical safety. Box 10.4 discusses the case of missing and murdered women from Vancouver's Downtown Eastside. The subject of missing and murdered women, sex workers, and the vulnerability of Indigenous women is discussed in more depth later in the chapter.

BOX 10.4

Vancouver's Missing and Murdered Women

Over 60 women went missing from the Vancouver Downtown Eastside (DTES) between the early 1980s and 2002. These women were the epitome of vulnerable, caught in a cycle of violence, distress, addiction, and/or mental illness. They were further marginalized by their involvement in the survival sex trade.

Although investigators found DNA remnants of over 50 women on his farm, Robert William "Willie" Pickton of Port Coquitlam was only charged with the murders of 26 of these women and convicted on just 6 counts in 2007.

On September 27, 2010, the Missing Women Commission of Inquiry was established to look into the conduct of the police investigations in this case. Commissioner Wally Oppal's 2012 final report found that "the missing and murdered women were forsaken twice: once by society at large and again by the police." The inquiry recognized that the intersection of existent laws, social norms and mores, and police culture all played an important role in shaping the relationship between the police and women in the DTES, and potentially affected whether or not (and how) the police investigations into the women's disappearances was handled (Oppal, 2012). As a result, years passed before attention was paid to finding the dozens of missing women.

Criminalization

To criminalize aspects of prostitution is to make it illegal to sell sex or purchase sex or both. Such an approach is grounded in the philosophy of abolition, where goals are to enforce a moral ethos that selling and buying sex is wrong, and that exploiting and forcing people into sex work should be punished. There are two approaches to criminalization:

1. The act of prostitution and all of its associated acts are illegal (China, Islamic republics, South Africa); or

2. The act of prostitution is not illegal, but all of its associated acts are illegal, such as soliciting, procuring, brothel-keeping, abetting brothel-keeping, living off sex work earnings, vagrancy, loitering, public nuisance (India, UK, Sweden, Canada).

Criminalization aims to prevent or eliminate certain actions from happening in society by making them illegal. Think about all of the many other laws in our *Criminal Code*—laws that articulate behaviours that are not acceptable in society and will result in punishment (murder, robbery, fraud, etc.). Criminalizing prostitution comes from that same place—that society acknowledges the inherent harm of prostitution and tries to prevent people from engaging in prostitution-related behaviours by making those behaviours against the law.

Decriminalization

Betteridge & Csete (2016) describe decriminalization as providing limited "zones of tolerance" (New Zealand, Australia, Sweden) that provide a balance between supporting sex workers (offering them means of exiting and/or harm-reduction support to keep them safe) and reducing or eliminating exploitation and forced prostitution. Evaluations of decriminalization conducted by the PIVOT Legal Society (2006) reveal that:

- When clients are directed away from street-level known areas of prostitution, sex workers go indoors (brothels, massage parlours, hotels, and the Internet) where it can be done more safely;
- Sex workers who are left on the streets face more violent clientele, more unsafe sex, with no time to assess the safety of clients; and
- There is no evidence that crimes associated with the sex industry (such as drug trafficking, theft, robbery) are impacted as a result of decriminalization.

The PIVOT Legal Society (2006) goes on to proclaim that criminalization of commercial and consensual sexual activity is not only unnecessary, it fosters and fuels violence. It undermines sex workers' access to justice, weakens their ability to maintain health, denies the protection of labour laws, limits their options, and takes away the right to sexual autonomy. Advocates of decriminalization (and legalization) go on to say that criminalizing sex work marginalizes and isolates workers. In New Zealand, where sex work was decriminalized in 2003, sex workers can receive customers in their own small, secure establishments, are empowered to oblige clients to use condoms, and can draw on labour laws to negotiate working conditions (Mensah & Bruckert, 2012).

Legalization

Legalization typically means that the entire industry of prostitution (and its various players, acts, and components) is legal and regulated by municipal and/or provincial governments (Betteridge & Csete, 2016). This would categorize prostitution as bona fide work, which must follow provincial and municipal workplace health and safety regulations, health care benefit requirements, conditions of licensing, and taxable income (such as in the Netherlands, and Nevada in the US). From this position, female (and male) sex workers do not consider themselves to be victims or exploited or as products of a patriarchal social structure. In the words of one such sex worker to her parents:

"You've known me for 28 years… I can sort of understand the [sic] up reasoning that makes Catherine MacKinnon and Andrea Dworkin look at me and tell me I'm being exploited whether I think so or not, but *you should know better.*" … What I've never understood is why my parents can't wrap their heads around the idea that sex work might be a healthy, positive choice for me, and why they haven't worked harder over the years to try. I understand why my parents are concerned for my safety. I'm concerned for my safety too, and have a better grasp on what I need to do to keep myself safe than they do. But understanding sex work on a conceptual level seems like something they could handle. Maybe they could read everything ever written by every sex workers' rights activist from Priscilla Alexander to Carol Leigh and still think that sex work is degrading towards women—towards me. I really don't think so. (Hustle, 2012)

Legalizing all aspects of prostitution comes from the old adage that "if you can't beat them, join them." Advocates believe that prostitution is inevitable and a byproduct of most all societies around the world; therefore, it only makes sense to legalize and regulate it. This way, governments can recoup some of the costs—instead of money going into the hands of pimps and traffickers, money would go into government coffers in the form of business licenses and property taxes. Furthermore, arguments in favour of legalization also claim that doing so would virtually eliminate the criminal elements and violence, and increase health, safety, and agency of men and women everywhere.

▶ WHAT DO YOU THINK?

Where do you sit on the continuum of prostitution? Are you pro-legalization or completely against prostitution and all its forms as the abolitionist?

Missing and Murdered Women and Girls of Canada

Every year in Canada, approximately 65,000 people are reported as missing to police. There is no one single authoritative list of missing and murdered women and girls for all of Canada. Lack of statistics feeds controversy and debate over the actual number of victims and the subsequent strategies needed to combat it. One calculation estimates between 600 and 1,000 women and girls are missing or have been murdered across Canada. The Royal Canadian Mounted Police (RCMP) (2014) have recorded incidents of homicides (men and women) and unresolved missing persons totalling 1,181 (164 missing and 1,017 homicide victims).

Public Safety and Emergency Preparedness Canada (2005), on the other hand, indicates that over 100,000 persons are reported missing annually, approximately 4,800 persons were still recorded missing after a year, and approximately 270 new cases of long-term missing persons are reported annually. As well, between 20 and 30 sets of human remains are found each year in Canada. British Columbia has historically had the highest number of missing persons within Canada. Reasons posited for this trend include the extensive coastline, large wilderness areas, and a large transient population due to mild weather conditions.

There are similarities across all female homicides in that they are perpetrated mostly by men, and the men know their victims (i.e., an acquaintance or a spouse) (Oppal, 2012). Advocates believe the RCMP figures underestimate the crisis because they do not include deaths unduly deemed not to be suspicious or disappearances that were never reported. Some believe the true number of killings and disappearances is closer to 4,000 annually (Baum, 2016). Many types of perpetrators have been brought to justice, such as Paul Bernardo and Karla Homolka in Ontario; Thomas Svekla, Joseph Laboucan, and Michael Briscoe in Alberta; Robert Pickton and Clifford Olsen in British Columbia, as well as many remaining unknown.

Statistics Canada has not historically gathered and analyzed information about missing persons because going missing is not a crime (whereas prostitution offences are recorded). In recognition of this paucity of information, efforts are underway (at the federal level) to build a national missing persons database, one that communicates between all federal, provincial, and municipal policing bodies and Statistics Canada.

An arm of the federal government, the National Centre for Missing Persons and Unidentified Remains (NCMPUR Operations) of the RCMP is Canada's national centre that assists law enforcement, medical examiners, and chief coroners with missing persons and unidentified remains investigations across the country. They define a missing person as:

> Anyone reported to police or by police as someone whose whereabouts are unknown, whatever the circumstances of their disappearance, and they are considered missing until located. A missing person under the age of 18 is classified as a missing child. In the case of a missing child, they are considered missing if they are no longer in the care or control of their legal guardian and have not been removed by law, and they are considered missing until returned to appropriate care and control. (Government of Canada, 2017)

Homicides of Sex Workers

For decades, sex workers and the sexually exploited, primarily women, have been disappearing and dying violently and at alarming rates. Between 1991 and 2014, Rotenberg (2016) reported that there were 294 recorded homicides of sex workers, where 34 percent of those homicides remained unsolved, a much greater proportion than for homicides that did not involve a sex worker victim (20 percent). It is important to note here that "recorded homicides of sex workers" relies on the offence file labelled as such—only if police identify the victim as a sex worker and only if a homicide is brought to police attention.

Project Eclipse, Canada's first investigative case conference, was organized by the RCMP in 1991 in Victoria to look into 26 unsolved homicides of women from Vancouver and Victoria between 1985 and 1991. More than half of the victims were believed to be engaged in the sex trade. The conference concluded that a single killer was not responsible for 26 homicides, but that several of the murders were linked. In 1998, the bodies of two women engaged in the sex trade were found in alleys in the DTES; these became known as the "Alley Murders." Three women from the DTES were found murdered in the mountains near Agassiz or Mission, BC; these became known as the "Valley Murders." And since the early 1970s, many women and girls have disappeared along the Yellowhead Highway 16 in northern BC, which runs between Prince Rupert and Prince George and has become known as the "Highway of Tears."

Missing and Murdered Indigenous Women

The Native Women's Association of Canada (NWAC) has documented that, over the past 30 years, more than 500 Indigenous women and girls have gone missing or have been found murdered in communities across Canada. In 2014, the overall homicide rate for Indigenous victims was six times higher than that of non-Indigenous people (Miladinovic & Mulligan, 2015). Between 1997 and 2014, there were 71 female sex worker victims of homicide who were identified as Indigenous, representing one in three (34 percent) of all female sex worker victims. This is more than double the proportion of Indigenous female homicide victims who were not sex workers (16 percent) (Rotenberg, 2016). RCMP-recorded incidents of Indigenous female homicides and unresolved missing Indigenous females between 1980 and 2012 is 1,181 missing and 1,017 homicide victims (RCMP, 2014). There are 225 unsolved cases of either missing or murdered Indigenous females, whose cause of disappearance was categorized at the time as "unknown" or "foul play suspected." The total indicates that Indigenous women are overrepresented among Canada's murdered and missing women.

Indigenous men also disappear and die violently, but the national inquiry is focusing solely on women and girls because of their overall disproportionate rate of victimization. A disproportionate number of the missing and murdered women are Indigenous: while three percent of BC's population consists of Indigenous women, they comprise approximately 33 percent of the missing and murdered women. Of the 33 women whose DNA was found on Pickton's farm, 12 were Indigenous. Indigenous women experience higher levels of violence, both in terms of incidence and severity, and are disproportionately represented in the number of missing and murdered women across Canada. And the RCMP (2014) also believe that Indigenous women are roughly seven times more likely to be slain by a serial killer than non-Indigenous women.

Shortly after the RCMP's 2014 report was published, 15-year-old Tina Fontaine's body was pulled from a Winnipeg river—a high-profile homicide case that reignited calls for a national inquiry (Baum, 2016). Every month and every year, another woman's body is found: 25-year-old Victoria Lynn Isabelle Levesque's body was found east of Calgary in 2017; in 2014, Loretta Saunders' body was found on the side of a New Brunswick highway; Cherisse Houle, age 17, was discovered murdered in 2009; and the incidents have no end in sight.

Intergenerational Trauma and the Vulnerability of Indigenous Women

Systemic and institutionalized racism, as well as the effects of historical violence, such as residential schools, the *Indian Act*, and other legacies of colonization have resulted in generations of violence in the daily lives of Indigenous women throughout Canada. There is much diversity among Indigenous women. Some are First Nations, others Métis or Inuit. Some live on reserves, and many more live off reserves, in towns and cities across Canada. The department of Aboriginal Affairs and Northern Development Canada (2006) reported that there were over 100,000 First Nations women aged 15 and over living on reserves. Furthermore, almost 330,000 Indigenous women lived off reserves: approximately 135,000 Métis women and approximately 16,000 Inuit women.

The 2012 Aboriginal Peoples Survey (Scott & Smith, 2015) reported that Canada was home to 859,970 First Nations people; 451,795 Métis; and 59,445 Inuit, with the rest reporting other two Aboriginal identities (26,485) or more than one Aboriginal identity (11,415). From 2006 to 2011, the First Nations population in Canada increased by 23 percent, while the Métis population rose by 16 percent, and the Inuit population by 18 percent. Of those who identified as First Nations in 2011, three-quarters (75 percent or 645,940) reported being a Treaty Indian or a Registered Indian as defined by the *Indian Act*. Over one-third (38% or 328,445) of all First Nations people (50% of First Nations people who were Treaty or Registered Indians, or 322,650 individuals) lived on a reserve.

Indigenous people (and women, in particular) are much more likely than non-Indigenous people to be victims of violent crime and spousal violence. Statistics Canada (2017b) reports that 24 percent of Indigenous women reported being victims of spousal violence in 2004, more than three times higher than the rate for non-Indigenous women (7 percent); and 40 percent of Indigenous people were the victims of childhood physical and/or sexual abuse, compared with 29 percent for non-Indigenous people.

Statistics Canada's report goes on to state that Indigenous women are also seven times more likely to be murdered than non-Indigenous women. Research conducted by the Native Women's Association of Canada informs that Indigenous women and girls are as likely to be killed by a stranger or an acquaintance as they are by an intimate partner—very different from the experiences of non-Indigenous women in Canada, whose homicide rates are often attributed to intimate partner violence.

While violence against Indigenous people has been the focus of social policy and research recently, their overrepresentation as victims or offenders in the justice system has been long standing. Various studies and reports have illustrated this elevated risk of victimization, such as those produced by the Native Women's Association of Canada, the Truth and Reconciliation Commission of Canada, the Royal Canadian Mounted Police, and Statistics Canada (Boyce, 2016, pp. 3–6). In 2014, the overall rate of violent victimization among Indigenous people was more than double that of non-Indigenous people (163 incidents per 1,000 people versus 74 incidents per 1,000 people). Regardless of the type of violent offence, rates of victimization were almost always higher for Indigenous people than for non-Indigenous people. Additionally, Indigenous people (9 percent) were more likely than non-Indigenous people (4 percent) to have been a victim of spousal violence in the past five years. Specifically, women (10 percent) were about three times as likely to report being a victim of spousal violence as non-Indigenous women (3 percent), and Indigenous men (8 percent) were twice as likely as their non-Indigenous counterparts (4 percent).

Such violence is intergenerational and has been normalized but not openly discussed—violence in many communities is chronic and endemic and is connected to the abuse suffered in residential schools. The link between loss of culture to intergenerational violence is recurrent. Residential school survivors re-entered their communities with physical and emotional scars that did not get treated; they were not parented properly, and in turn were not able to properly parent children of their own. The cycle of abuse, coping with drugs and alcohol, self-loathing, shame, and trauma was passed onward to the next generation. The long-term impact of these colonialist policies continues to be keenly seen and felt by the overrepresentation of Indigenous peoples in nearly every measured indicator of social and physical suffering in Canada and within the criminal justice system (Fry, 2011; Oppal, 2012).

National Inquiry into Missing and Murdered Indigenous Women and Girls

In response to calls for action from Indigenous families, communities, and organizations, as well as non-governmental and international organizations, the Government of Canada launched the National Inquiry into Missing and Murdered Indigenous Women and Girls in September 2016.

Indigenous organizations and leaders asserted that Canada was not doing all it could as a signatory to the United Nations Declaration on the Rights of Indigenous Peoples (United Nations General Assembly, 2007). Grand Chief Sheila North Wilson of northern Manitoba—who coined the social media hashtag #MMIW for missing and murdered Indigenous women—noted that it was women who organized the vigils and annual marches calling for an inquiry. Since her culture is matriarchal, taking care of the women also means taking care of families and communities (Baum, 2016).

The National Inquiry into Missing and Murdered Indigenous Women and Girls (MMIWG) is independent from the government and is composed of five commissioners from across the country. The commissioners' mandate is to examine and report on the systemic causes of all forms of violence against Indigenous women and girls in Canada by looking at patterns and underlying factors, including social, economic, and historical factors, and to examine institutional policies and practices. The mission is to learn the truth by honouring the lives and legacies of Indigenous women and girls. This encompasses three goals (Girls, 2016):

1. Finding the truth
2. Honouring the truth
3. Giving life to the truth as a path to healing

While the terms of reference do not specify the social ills that should be looked at, the following factors will undoubtedly be examined: the overrepresentation of Indigenous children in the child-welfare system, racism, sexism, inadequate on-reserve housing and education opportunities, poverty, addiction, sexual exploitation, domestic violence, and insufficient public transit (specifically along the "Highway of Tears" in northern British Columbia, where numerous women have died or disappeared in recent decades). The commissioners must make recommendations on "concrete and effective action that can be taken" as well as suggest ways to honour the victims. The commissioners and their staff can conduct hearings wherever they see fit, but their mandate says they should especially do so within Indigenous communities. The commissioners are authorized to establish regional and issue-specific advisory bodies comprising, among others, victims' relatives. They can take into consideration previous studies, including the Truth and Reconciliation report (2015), into the horrors experienced by Indigenous children in the residential school system and the Oppal Inquiry in British Columbia (Oppal, 2012), which examined police failures in investigating the disappearances of women slain by serial killer Robert Pickton.

The federal government also passed an order in council launching the inquiry under the *Inquiries Act*, which states that the MMIWG commissioners may issue subpoenas to compel testimony and documents. The inquiry's terms of reference preclude the commissioners from making findings of civil or criminal liability. Some of the most important and controversial areas of discussion—child welfare and policing, for example—fall outside federal jurisdiction. To overcome this and ensure that the inquiry is national and not just federal, the provinces and territories have agreed to pass companion orders in council. These orders will empower the commission to pursue matters of provincial and territorial jurisdiction.

The commissioners of the National Inquiry into MMIWG officially began work in September 2016. Their first report, an interim document setting out preliminary findings and recommendations, was to be submitted before November 1, 2017. The final report is due a year later. The MMIWG Inquiry must be understood within the provincial, national, and international phenomenon of the serial murder of women and, more specifically, targeted groups of women. The fact-finding mandate focuses on a specific group of female victims and the police response in a particular time and place, but it is connected to this broader phenomenon of critical dimensions. (See also Box 10.5.)

BOX 10.5

"Frustrated Families Vow to 'Blockade' Missing and Murdered Inquiry Hearings'"—CBC News

According to a CBC News report, "Some family members of missing and murdered Indigenous women and girls are vowing to blockade meetings of the national inquiry to protest what they call a disastrous start." The inquiry has cycled through three directors of communications in ten months, and has been plagued by complaints from family members about compressed timelines. The first interim report from the inquiry is due in November 2017, but one father of a murdered woman states that calls to the 1-800 number are not returned and emails go unanswered. Another parent of a murdered woman claims that Elders speaking their Indigenous languages are not understood by record keepers, and there is little respect paid to sacred instruments like the drum, fire ceremonies, and tobacco. Many feel that the inquiry has placed blame unfairly on families for cancelling scheduled meetings this summer rather than admit they were simply not prepared. Indigenous Affairs Minister Carolyn Bennett was able to hold pre-inquiry meetings throughout the country in a matter of months, but nearly a year after the launch of the national inquiry, things remain largely at a standstill. As of May 2017, the inquiry has spent approximately 10 percent of its $53-million budget. Marion Buller, the chief commissioner, admitted that mistakes had been made and that more needs to be done to regain the trust of family members. Concern from several families is that this report will be shelved like many others and the process feels like an adjudication or court instead of an Indigenous knowledge-based collaboration.

Sources: Tasker, J.P. & Zimonjic, P. (2017, May 19). MMIWG chief commissioner still has "hope" despite rocky start. CBC News; and Tasker, J.P. (2017, May 23). Frustrated families vow to "blockade" missing and murdered inquiry hearings. CBC News.

SUMMARY

Discussion and debate surrounding prostitution, sex work, sexual exploitation, and Indigenous women have circled within Canada for decades. Advocates, service providers, and academics have been pressuring governments to take action. Beginning in 2015, these issues are now on the desks of federal cabinet ministers coast to coast. This does not mean that the issues and problems are now solved. It will take years (perhaps even more than one generation) before substantive and prolonged change is weaved within our society's social and cultural fabric.

In the meantime, we can continue this important work together; we can keep the discussions flowing. Research is needed to inform practice and financial support is required for various bodies (police, the courts, social services, schools, etc.) in order to carry out recommendations and make significant change.

DISCUSSION QUESTIONS

1. If money was unlimited, where would you direct funding that would work to eliminate violence against women, eliminate racism and sexism against Indigenous women, and/or address sex work and sexual exploitation?
2. Compare and contrast countries—choose one country and compare its prostitution laws and policies against Canada's. What key differences or similarities emerge?
3. Why do you think it has taken the federal government this long to initiate an Inquiry into the Missing and Murdered Indigenous Women and Girls of Canada?
4. Review the Call to Action Report of the Truth and Reconciliation Commission and choose one of the calls to action within it. What practical things would be needed to implement those recommendations fully and completely?
5. Consider the causes and consequences of prostitution identified within this chapter. Which do you think has a stronger correlation than others?
6. Describe the data available from courts and correctional institutions in Canada. Discuss the crimes that women are most often convicted of and explain why negative attention is paid to prostitution offences, despite their low occurrence?

ADDITIONAL RESOURCES

Suggested Readings

The Aboriginal Multi-Media Society. (2016). The unsolved: Missing and murdered Indigenous women and girls. www.ammsa.com/content/missing-and-murdered-indigenous -women-and-girls.

Statistics Canada. (2017). *Women in Canada: A gender-based statistical report* (Catalogue no. 89-503-X). Retrieved from http://www5.statcan.gc.ca/olc-cel/olc.action?objId=89-503 -X&objType=2&lang=en&limit=0.

Truth and Reconciliation Commission of Canada. (2015). *Final report of the Truth and Reconciliation Commission of Canada*. www.trc.ca/websites/trcinstitution/index.php?p=890.

Films and Videos

Correctional Service of Canada. (2015). *Beyond the fence: A virtual tour of a Canadian penitentiary* [Virtual tour]. Retrieved from http://www.csc-scc.gc.ca/csc-virtual-tour/index-eng.shtml.

The Fifth Estate. (2010, January 8). *Out of control: the Ashley Smith case* [Video]. Retrieved from www.cbc.ca/fifth/episodes/2009-2010/out-of-control.

The Globe and Mail. (2014, June 5). *What Canada's new prostitution legislation means for sex workers* [Video]. Retrieved from www.theglobeandmail.com/news/news-video/video-what -canadas/article19018150/.

Websites

Canadian Occupational Safety: www.cos-mag.com/ohs-laws-regulations/32364-sex-workers -facing-increased-safety-risks/

RCMP Project Kare: http://www.rcmp-grc.gc.ca/ab/community-communaute/mis-dis/kare/ index-eng.htm

RCMP Joint Forces Operation: www.rcmp-grc.gc.ca/on/prog-serv

The National Centre for Missing Persons and Unidentified Remains (NCMPUR Operations): www.canadasmissing.ca

The Sixties Scoop: https://sixtiesscoopclaim.com

Truth and Reconciliation Commission of Canada: http://reconciliationcanada.ca/

REFERENCES

Aboriginal Affairs and Northern Development Canada. (2006). *Aboriginal women in Canada: A statistical profile from the 2006 census.* Retrieved from https://www.aadnc-aandc.gc.ca/DAM/DAM-INTER-HQ/STAGING/texte-text/ai_rs_pubs_ex_abwch_pdf_1333374752380_eng.pdf.

Baum, K.B. (2016, August 31). Nine things to know about the national inquiry into missing and murdered Indigenous women. *The Globe and Mail.*

Betteridge, G., & Csete, J. (2016). Criminalization of sex work: A human rights crisis in Canada and beyond. (pp. 1–46). Sexual Exploitation Working Group Conference, Edmonton.

Boyce, J. (2016). Victimization of Aboriginal people in Canada, 2014. Canadian Centre for Justice Statistics. (Catalogue no. 85-002-X.) Retrieved from http://www.statcan.gc.ca/pub/85-002-x/2016001/article/14631-eng.pdf.

Bruckert, C., & Parent, C. (2004). *Organized crime and human trafficking in Canada: Tracing perceptions and discourses.* Research and Evaluation Branch. Ottawa: Royal Canadian Mounted Police.

Canadian Charter of Rights and Freedoms, Part I of the *Constitution Act, 1982*, being Schedule B to the *Canada Act 1982* (UK), c 11.

Criminal Code, RSC 1985, c C-46.

Dewey, S. (2008). *Hollow bodies: Institutional responses to sex trafficking in Armenia, Bosnia, and India.* West Hartford, CT: Kumarian Press.

Ekberg, G. (2004). The Swedish law that prohibits the purchase of sexual services: Best practices for prevention of prostitution and trafficking in human beings. *Violence Against Women, 10*(10), 1187–1218.

Farley, M. (2004). Bad for the body, bad for the heart: Prostitution harms women even if legalized or decriminalized. *Violence Against Women, 10*(10), 1087–1125.

Fry, H. (2011). *Interim report—Call into the night: An overview of violence against Indigenous women.* Standing Committee on the Status of Women. Ottawa: Public Works and Government Services Canada.

Girls, N.I. (2016). *National inquiry into missing and murdered Indigenous women and girls.* Retrieved from National Inquiry into Missing and Murdered Indigenous Women and Girls: http://www.mmiwg-ffada.ca/en/.

Goff, C. (2016). *Criminal justice in Canada*, 7th ed. Toronto: Nelson.

Goldstein, S. (2006). *It's not one size fits all prostitution policy: An examination of the social constructions of prostitution and an examination of alternative models of prostitution.* Course work, School of Criminology, Simon Fraser University, Burnaby, BC.

Government of Alberta. (2010). *Protection of sexually exploited children and youth.* Edmonton: Government of Alberta.

Government of Canada. (2015). Prostitution criminal law reform: Bill C-36, the *Protection of Communities and Exploited Persons Act.* Retrieved from http://www.justice.gc.ca/eng/rp-pr/other-autre/c36fs_fi/.

Government of Canada. (2017). *Canada's missing.* Retrieved from http://www.canadasmissing.ca/index-eng.htm.

Hallgrimsdottir, H.K., Philips, R., & Benoit, C. (2006). Fallen women and rescued girls: Social stigma and media narrative of the sex industry in Victoria, B.C., from 1980 to 2005. *Canadian Review of Sociology and Anthropology 43*(3), 265–280.

Hustle, R. (2012, September 7). How to tell your parents you're a prostitute. Retrieved from http://jezebel.com/5941073/how-to-tell-your-parents-youre-a-prostitute.

Kantola, J., & Squires, J. (2004). Discourses surrounding prostitution policies in the UK. *European Journal of Women's Studies, 11*(1), 77–101.

Liebshutz, J., Savestky, J.B., Saitz, R., Horton, N.J., Lloyd-Travaglini, C., & Samet, J.H. (2012). The relationship between sexual and physical abuse and substance abuse consequences. *Journal of Substance Abuse Treatment 22*(3), 121–128.

Lowman, J. (2005). Submission to the Subcommittee on Solicitation Laws of the Standing Committee on Justice, Human Rights, Public Safety and Emergency Preparedness. Retrieved from http://mypage.uniserve.ca/~lowman/.

MacKinnon, C.A. (2005). *Women's lives, men's laws.* Cambridge, MA: Belknap Press of Harvard University Press.

McIntyre, S. (2005). *Strolling away.* Department of Justice Canada. Retrieved from http://host.jibc.ca/seytoolkit/pdfs/strolling away.pdf.

McIntyre, S. (2010). *Under the radar: The sexual exploitation of young men in western Canada.* Retrieved from http://www.humanservices.alberta.ca/documents/child-sexual-exploitation-under-the-radar-western-canada.pdf.

Mensah, M.N., & Bruckert, C. (2012). 10 reasons to fight for the decriminalization of sex work. Retrieved from http://maggiestoronto.ca/uploads/File/10reasons.pdf.

Miladinovic, Z., & Mulligan, L. (2015). *Homicide in Canada, 2014.* Canadian Centre for Justice Statistics. (Catalogue no. 85-002-X). Retrieved from http://www.statcan.gc.ca/pub/85-002-x/2015001/article/14244-eng.pdf.

Musto, J., Jackson, C.A., & Shi, E. (2015). Prostitution and sex work. In J.D. Wright (Ed.), *International encyclopedia of the social and behavioral sciences* (2nd ed., pp. 279–285). Amsterdam: Elsevier.

O'Connell-Davidson, J. (2007). Prostitution. In G. Ritzer (Ed.), *Blackwell encyclopedia of sociology.* Retrieved from Blackwell Reference Online doi:10.1111/b.9781405124331.2007.x.

Oppal, W.T. (2012). *Forsaken: The report of the missing women commission of inquiry.* British Columbia Commissioner. Vancouver: Government of British Columbia.

Outshoorn, J. (2004). Pragmatism in the polder: Changing prostitution policy in The Netherlands. *Journal of Contemporary European Studies, 12*(2), 165–176.

PIVOT Legal Society. (2006). *Beyond decriminalization: Sex work, human rights, and a new framework for law reform.* Vancouver: The Law Foundation of Canada.

Protection of Sexually Exploited Children Act (2014). Alberta Regulation 194/2007. Retrieved from https://www.canlii.org/en/ab/laws/regu/alta-reg-194-2007/latest/alta-reg-194-2007.html.

Public Safety and Emergency Preparedness Canada. (2005). *DNA Missing Persons Index (MPI), A public consultation paper.* Retrieved from http://z13.invisionfree.com/PorchlightCanada/ar/t2631.htm.

R v Bedford, 2013 SCC 72, [2013] 3 SCR 1101.

Rotenberg, C. (2016). Prostitution offences in Canada: Statistical trends. (Catalogue no. 85-002-X). Statistics Canada *Juristat, 36*(1).

Scambler, G. (1997). Conspicuous and inconspicuous sex work: The neglect of the ordinary and the mundane. In G. Scambler and A. Scambler (Eds.), *Rethinking prostitution: Purchasing sex in the 1990s.* (pp. 105–120). London: Routledge.

Scott, K.K., & Smith, K. (November 3, 2015). Aboriginal peoples: Face sheet for Canada. Catalogue no. 89-656-X2015001. Aboriginal Statistics Division, Statistics Canada. Retrieved from http://www.statcan.gc.ca/pub/89-656-x/89-656-x2015001-eng.pdf.

Statistics Canada. (2017a). *Deaths and mortality rate (age standardization using 1991 population), by selected grouped causes and sex, Canada, provinces and territories* (table). CANSIM (database).

Statistics Canada. (2017b). *Family violence in Canada: A statistical profile, 2015.* Retrieved from http://www.statcan.gc.ca/daily-quotidien/170216/dq170216b-eng.htm.

Tasker, J.P. (2017, May 23). Frustrated families vow to "blockade" missing and murdered inquiry hearings. CBC News. Retrieved from http://www.cbc.ca/news/politics/mmiwg-families-blockade-hearings-1.4127452.

Tasker, J.P. & Zimonjic, P. (2017, May 19). MMIWG chief commissioner still has "hope" despite rocky start. CBC News. Retrieved from http://www.cbc.ca/news/politics/mmiwg-media-avail-criticism-1.4124463.

United Nations General Assembly. (2007). *United Nations Declaration on the Rights of Indigenous Peoples*: *Resolution/adopted by the General Assembly, 2007, October 2, A/RES/61/295.* Retrieved from http://www.unhcr.org/refworld/docid/471355a82.html.

United Nations Treaty Collection. (2017). Chapter XVIII Penal Matters 12 a: *A protocol to prevent, suppress and punish trafficking in persons, especially women and children, supplementing the United Nations Convention against transnational organized crime.* (2000, November 15). New York: United Nations, *Treaty Series,* vol. 2237, p. 319; Doc. A/55/383.

Van Brunschot, E.G., Sydie, R.A., & Krull, C. (1999). Images of prostitution: The prostitute and the print media. *Women and Criminal Justice, 10*(4), 47–70.

Williams, K. (2011). Classroom discussion guide for Hollow Bodies: Institutional responses to sex trafficking in Armenia, Bosnia, and India. Retrieved from https://styluspub.presswarehouse.com/resrcs/other/156549265X_brochure.pdf.

PART IV
Women Working in the Canadian Criminal Justice System

Sexual Harassment in the RCMP

Jane Barker

Nearly five years after first going public in November 2011 with allegations of sexual harassment in the RCMP, Corporal Catherine Galliford was offered a settlement in a civil case against four RCMP officers, BC's minister of justice, and the attorney general of Canada. Galliford was diagnosed with PTSD, which she attributed to years of harassment in the RCMP. The details of the civil settlement were not made public. Following Galliford's public claim, a number of other women filed similar individual claims (Dufresne & Clancy, 2016), and two class action suits have been filed (Klein Lawyers, 2016; Quan, 2016). Current RCMP Commissioner Bob Paulson was appointed in 2011 and in 2016, he reported that one of the key challenges (for the RCMP) was "harassment litigation" (Quan, 2016, p. 9).

In one class action suit, Janet Merlo alleged that she endured "name-calling, sexist pranks, and requests for sexual favours" throughout her 19-year career in the RCMP (Bains, 2016, p. 17). Linda Davidson, a 27-year veteran of the RCMP, is the lead plaintiff in a similar proposed class action suit filed in 2015 (Quan, 2016). Like Galliford, Davidson suffers from PTSD and noted that it was not until her symptoms were somewhat manageable that she was able to file the lawsuit (Quan, 2016). Numerous instances of sexual harassment were alleged by Davidson, including male officers trying to kiss her, undress her, touch her breast, placing sex toys in her work area, and calling her derogatory names (Quan, 2016).

In 2012, the Senate directed the Standing Committee on National Security and Defence to investigate the issue of sexual harassment in the RCMP. Commissioner Paulson was a key witness and he did not deny the existence of sexual harassment in the RCMP, noting "there are, there have been, and sadly, there may well be other bona fide victims of sexual harassment in the RCMP" (MacKinnon, 2013). In 2013, the Senate's Standing Committee on National Security and Defence released its final report (including 15 recommendations) on its investigation of harassment in the RCMP (Lang & Dallaire, 2013).

On December 1, 2014, the *Enhancing the RCMP Accountability Act* came into force. This Act aimed to strengthen the review and complaints process and modernize the "discipline, grievance and human resource management processes for members" (*Enhancing Royal Canadian Mounted Police Accountability Act*, 2013, summary). As a way to monitor the RCMP's progress towards transforming its culture, they implemented a Gender and Respect Action Plan that set out clear milestones to be met (Public Safety Canada, 2014).

Criticisms have been levelled against the new Act, specifically that the timelines for hearing cases are vague and some have concerns that there may be instances where those on medical leave who have alleged harassment may find that their employment has been terminated under a clause that allows "the commissioner to fire officers for the 'promotion of economy or efficiency' within the force" (MacDonald & Gillis, 2015, p. 21). The RCMP has put more focus on recruiting women, promoting them, and introducing respectful workplace policies and practices (Quan, 2016). However, the policy changes made by the RCMP have not been without criticism and have been referred to by Galliford as "smoke and mirrors" (Bains, 2016).

In July 2016, former auditor general Sheila Fraser was appointed by Public Safety Minister Ralph Goodale as a special advisor to investigate harassment in the RCMP. Fraser's mandate will be to examine how the RCMP has dealt with issues of sexual harassment and to determine the risk of sexual violence in the organization, with the goal to ensuring a safe workplace for those employed by the RCMP (Crawford, 2016).

On October 6, 2016, Commissioner Paulson offered a public apology to both current and former female RCMP officers and employees who have suffered as a result of sexual harassment in the workplace. He announced a settlement to the two class action suits, and it was reported in the media that $100 million has been earmarked for compensation (Bronskill, 2016). In this unprecedented settlement, women who experienced sexual harassment while working for the RCMP will be eligible for between $10,000 to $220,000 (Perkel, 2017).

In the chapters that follow, women's experiences working in police services, community and custodial corrections, and the court sector will be explored. Keep in mind the issues of sexual harassment noted in these class action suits as you read these chapters, and consider the following questions.

QUESTIONS TO CONSIDER

1. How do you define sexual harassment and how does that differ from sexual assault?
2. Do you think that sexual harassment similar to that alleged in the RCMP could have happened in other police services in Canada? Why or why not?
3. Why do you think it took so long for these women to come forward with their allegations of sexual harassment?
4. If you were being sexually harassed at your place of work, would you report it? What might prevent you from coming forward with allegations of sexual harassment?

REFERENCES

Bains, C. (2016, May 3). BC Mountie says sexual harassment settlement still means RCMP needs policies. The Canadian Press. Retrieved from http://www.ctvnews.ca/canada/b-c-mountie-says-sexual-harassment-settlement-still-means-rcmp-needs-policies-1.2885800.

Bronskill, J. (2016, October 6). RCMP earmarks $100 million in compensation for sexual harassment against female Mounties. Global News. Retrieved from http://globalnews.ca/news/2986688/rcmp-to-settle-in-class-action-harassment-claims-from-former-mounties/.

Crawford, A. (2016, July 7). Sheila Fraser to advise government on RCMP's handling of harassment complaints. CBC News. Retrieved from http://www.cbc.ca/news/politics/rcmp-harassment-sheila-fraser-1.3668481.

Dufresne, M., & Clancy, N. (2016, May 3). RCMP settles sex harassment suit with Catherine Galliford. CBC News. Retrieved from http://www.cbc.ca/news/investigates/rcmp-settles-with-former-spokesperson-catherine-galliford-1.3562708.

Enhancing Royal Canadian Mounted Police Accountability Act, SC 2013, c 18.

Klein Lawyers, LLP. (2016). *RCMP class action*. Retrieved from http://www.callkleinlawyers.com/class-actions/current/rcmp/.

Lang, D., & Dallaire, R. (2013). *Conduct becoming: Why the Royal Canadian Mounted Police must transform its culture. Final report of the Standing Senate Committee on National Security and Defence*. Retrieved from http://www.parl.gc.ca/Content/SEN/Committee/411/secd/rep/rep14jun13-e.pdf.

MacDonald, N., & Gillis, C. (2015, February 27). Inside the RCMP's biggest crisis. *Maclean's*, 16–24. Retrieved from http://www.macleans.ca/society/inside-the-rcmps-biggest-crisis/.

MacKinnon, L. (2013, June 3). RCMP chief hits back at "outlandish" harassment claims. CBC News. Retrieved from http://www.cbc.ca/news/politics/rcmp-chief-hits-back-at-outlandish-harassment-claims-1.1358721.

Perkel, C. (2017, May 31). Landmark deal in RCMP sexual-harassment class action wins court approval. CBC News. Retrieved from http://www.cbc.ca/beta/news/canada/british-columbia/rcmp-sexual-harassment-class-action-1.4140138.

Public Safety Canada. (2014). *The Government of Canada's response to the Standing Senate Committee Report on Harassment in the RCMP*. Retrieved from http://www.marketwired.com/printer_friendly?id=1898840.

Quan, D. (2016, March 27). RCMP dogged by second class-action lawsuit alleging rampant sexual harassment. *Financial Post*. Retrieved from http://news.nationalpost.com/news/canada/rcmp-dogged-by-second-class-action-lawsuit-alleging-rampant-sexual-harassment.

Women Working in Policing

Introduction

According to Statistics Canada (2016), there were 68,700 sworn police officers in Canada in 2015. Women now make up slightly more than 20 percent of police officers (14,332 officers), up from only 10 percent in 1986, and from less than 1 percent in 1966 (Statistics Canada, 2006). Paralleling changes in female representation in other traditionally male-dominated occupations, Canadian policing is slowly inching toward equitable representation by women—though there are still significant barriers to the acceptance of females in police organizations (Bikos, 2016; Prenzler & Sinclair, 2013). The recent settlement of a $100-million-dollar class action sexual harassment lawsuit, based on sexual harassment of female RCMP officers dating back as far as 1974 (Bronskill, 2016), and the October 16, 2016 Ontario Human Rights Tribunal hearing involving claims of a "poisoned work environment" for female officers in the Toronto Police Service (Hasham, 2016) demonstrate that the culture of policing continues to be resistant to the acceptance of females. On January 31, 2016, veteran Calgary police officer Jen Magnus tearfully resigned before a meeting of the Calgary police commission, claiming she had been "bullied, sexually harassed, degraded, and chastised" by male officers and the Calgary police organization itself during her 14-year career as a Calgary police officer; she pointed to the failure of the police organization to speak up about the problem, and its failure to publicly release a 26-page 2013 audit of the police service that found evidence of a culture of "bullying, harassment, intimidation, and retaliation" as confirmation that the ongoing harassment and bullying of women officers is still not taken seriously, prompting her resignation (CBC News, 2017).

Women still account for the overwhelming majority of civilian positions (68 percent) in policing, and most female police officers (83 percent) are at the rank of constable. Only a small fraction (1.6 percent) of females hold senior rank positions in policing, and very few women are found in police specialty positions, like homicide, emergency response (e.g., "SWAT"), K-9 units, or forensics (Dodge, Valcore, & Klinger, 2010; Murphy, 2006; Statistics Canada, 2016). Without equitable representation of women across the various specializations and ranks within the police organization, the traditionally male "linear" model of police career progression results in few women being promoted into the most senior ranks, where they might have the most influence on changing and "role modelling" a more gender equitable and feminist-oriented police organization (Silvestri, Tong, & Brown, 2013). Many experts (Morash & Haarr, 2012; Rabe-Hemp, 2008; Riccucci, Van Ryzin, & Lavena, 2014; Schuck, 2014) argue that an increase in the number of female police officers, in particular at the most senior ranks, will lead to a shift in the priorities, policies, and practices pursued by police organizations in the 21st century that better reflects the principles of modern community policing (Archbold & Schulz, 2012; Government of Manitoba, 2014; Sims, Scarborough, & Ahmad, 2003).

▶ WHAT DO YOU THINK?

If a woman was appointed commissioner of the RCMP, would it make a difference in the way in which women officers are treated in the RCMP? Would it change the way RCMP policing is carried out? Why or why not?

The Early History of Policing in Canada

The early history of policing in Canada can be traced to 1651 and the appointment of the first police officers (actually, night watchmen) in Quebec City, in what was then the French colony of New France (Barnes, 1991; Kelly & Kelly, 1976). For the most part, however, the early colonists relied on the military to enforce order in the towns and rural areas or, if needed, they took matters into their own hands (Carrigan, 1991).

The fall of New France in 1759 ushered in a new era in the development of the colonies: English law and legal institutions were imposed,[1] and martial rule and order slowly gave way to civil law and order, at least in the towns. The American Revolution in 1776, and later the 1837 rebellions in both Upper and Lower Canada, coupled with growing levels of crime in the towns, further pressed home the need to establish law and order throughout the remaining English colonies in North America (Barnes, 1991). Although the *Parish and Town Officers Act* of 1793 had provided for the appointment of unpaid constables in each of the provincial districts in Upper Canada, the first paid, full-time police constables were not appointed until 1835, in Toronto, followed shortly thereafter by Kingston (in 1841), Hamilton (in 1846), Montreal (in 1853), and Halifax (in 1864), among others (Barnes, 1991; Schmalleger, MacAlister, & McKenna, 2004). The creation of Canada as a country in 1867 further stimulated the need for and establishment of police forces both in towns and cities (for example, in Victoria in 1873, in Winnipeg in 1874, and in Calgary in 1885) and nationally in the north and the west, in the form of the North-West Mounted Police in 1873 (Barnes, 1991; Griffiths, Whitelaw, & Parent, 1999; McKenna, 1998; Schmalleger et al., 2004).

Early Canadian policing in towns and cities was based on the English model of policing originated in 1829 by Sir Robert Peel (Ericson, 1982; McKenna, 1998). The North-West Mounted Police was modelled on the Royal Irish Constabulary (Seagrave, 1997), a paramilitary force designed (under Peel's influence) to maintain order in rural Ireland (Police Service of Northern Ireland, 2008).

Read about Canada's first (unofficial) female police officer in Box 11.1.

Women in Early Policing in Canada

Canada's first paid policewomen were hired in Vancouver and Edmonton in 1912, followed by similar hirings in Toronto in 1913 and in Montreal in 1915 (LeBeuf & McLean, 2004). Gender stereotyping characterized the duties of these early female police officers, relegating them mainly to the roles of social workers and guardians of public morality

BOX 11.1

Canada's First Female Police Officer

Rose Fortune (1774–1864) was Canada's first female police officer. Born into slavery in Virginia in 1774, her Empire Loyalist family emigrated to the Annapolis Valley in Nova Scotia when she was ten. Despite widespread discrimination against members of Nova Scotia's black community, Rose Fortune started two successful businesses, including a baggage delivery and a wake-up call service for passengers on ships at the seaport. As a result of her frequent trips to the seaport, Rose started monitoring activity on the docks, setting curfews, and reporting suspicious activities to authorities—effectively appointing herself as Canada's first, albeit unpaid, female police officer.

Source: *The Canadian encyclopedia*. Retrieved from http://www.thecanadianencyclopedia.ca/en/article/rose-fortune/.

Rose Fortune was Canada's first female police officer.

(LeBeuf & McLean, 2004; Lewis-Horne, 2002), which was reinforced by not issuing these early policewomen with uniforms or other police paraphernalia. In fact, police forces had been pushed by increasingly influential middle-class women's organizations (such as the Women's Christian Temperance Union) into hiring at least a few women officers on moral grounds to shield vulnerable children and women from the too-often drunken, disorderly, and corrupting behaviour of men (LeBeuf & McLean, 2004; Lewis-Horne, 2002).

The use of policewomen fell into decline during the 1920s, '30s, and '40s, a consequence of declining interest and support from women's organizations, resistance and/or lack of acceptance from male-dominated police forces, and rising unemployment rates among males (LeBeuf & McLean, 2004). At the same time, the rise of the "professional" (Kelling & Moore, 1998) or crime-control model of policing further contributed to the decline in hiring of female officers. This model's emphasis on a paramilitary command structure, reactive response, and strict adherence to the definition of the law conflicted with the perceived roles that women could serve in policing (LeBeuf & McLean, 2004).

Although the post-Second World War period (1945–1965) saw an increase in the representation of women among police officers (Lewis-Horne, 2002), still, by 1966, less than 1 percent of police officers in Canada were women. Not until the baby-boom generation (those born between 1946 and 1966) had matured into adulthood did traditionally male-dominated occupations, policing among them, take serious notice of the need to address the representation and role of women in these occupations (LeBeuf & McLean, 2004; Ranson, 2005). By the late 1960s, confronted by increasingly well-educated and career-oriented women, coupled with growing legal requirements to ensure equitable opportunities for employment of women in government agencies

(Frost, 1997; Goff, 2001), municipal police organizations began to creep toward equitable representation of women in policing (Statistics Canada, 2006). Still, among some of the largest police forces in the country, policing remained a "males only" preserve.

Better Late Than Never? Female Constables in the RCMP

From the time of its formation in 1873, women played an important, if largely unrecognized, role in the North-West Mounted Police as unpaid support staff or as occasional matrons and jailers, additional duties often carried out by the wives of Mounties, the so-called "second man" at remote, sparsely populated postings (Royal Canadian Mounted Police, 2016; Schmidt, 2011). In 1900, the force hired its first female special constable to assist with the care of female prisoners at the Whitehorse Detachment in the Northwest Territories, and by the time the North-West Mounted Police was officially renamed the Royal Canadian Mounted Police in February 1920, a growing number of women were employed as civilian and special constables in the force, including as fingerprint and lab technicians (Royal Canadian Mounted Police, 2016). Between 1922 and 1942, Dr. Francis McGill served as director of the Saskatchewan region forensic identification laboratory. Still, it was not until publication of the *Report of the Royal Commission on the Status of Women in Canada* in September 1970 that the RCMP was compelled to open its doors to the recruitment of female police constables:

> 478. The federal government also employs women in the Royal Canadian Mounted Police. Although uniformed women are now common in municipal police forces, the uniformed service of the Royal Canadian Mounted Police has remained strictly a male preserve. (Royal Commission on the Status of Women in Canada, 1970)

Recommendation #54 of the *Report* (Royal Commission on the Status of Women in Canada, 1970) therefore stated:

> 54. We recommend that enlistment in the Royal Canadian Mounted Police be open to women.

In September 1974, amid a barrage of national media coverage, the first troop of 32 RCMP female police officer trainees, Troop 17, arrived at the Depot training academy in Regina, Saskatchewan. According to Donna Burns, one of the 30 Troop 17 female constables to graduate to active duties in March 1975, public fascination with the new female RCMP constables meant that "You'd stop the police car at an intersection and people would be walking by and they'd be pointing" (Schmidt, 2011). On the other hand, Burns recalled, patrons at a fish and chip shop in Port Alberni, BC, stood by as she was assaulted and choked by a suspect she was trying to arrest, waiting and watching to see how she would handle herself. Later, at his court appearance, the suspect was asked by the presiding judge, "How dare you assault a member of the RCMP, let alone a female member?" (Schmidt, 2011).

Public attitudes toward acceptance of female RCMP constables were magnified within the RCMP organization. Ridicule and harassment of female constables by male RCMP members was common, and Burns herself was forced to fight off the unwanted sexual advances of a senior male officer while on a work-related trip out of town: upon their return to the detachment, she was intimidated into keeping quiet about the incident by the male officer, telling only her husband, a fellow RCMP constable (Schmidt, 2011).

Female Constables in Provincial Police Forces

Though municipal police forces had operated in towns and cities in Ontario since the early 1800s, by 1900 it was clear that the constables operating in villages and rural areas in the province, legacies of the *Parish and Town Officers Act* of 1793, operated with almost no training, equipment, or backup support. In an attempt to bring a semblance of consistency and order to the operations of these constables, the Ontario government by order in council established the Ontario Provincial Police (OPP) on October 13, 1909 (Higley, 1984). Like the federal RCMP, the OPP model was based on the Royal Irish Constabulary model of policing (Higley, 1984; Seagrave, 1997).

Like the RCMP, women civilians worked for the Ontario Provincial Police force in secretarial capacities since nearly the very beginning of the force. The first recorded official appointment of a female civilian, as secretary to the commissioner, took place in May 1921 (Higley, 1984). However, it was not until May 1974, only a few months before the RCMP also acted, that the first class of 15 female OPP constable recruits, class #90, began training at the Ontario Police College (Higley, 1984). Upon completion of training, the new female constables were posted to various detachments throughout Ontario and assumed the full range of constable duties (After 65 years, 1974).

A loosely combined municipal–rural police force for Quebec was established by Lord Durham in 1838. This force was formally named the Sûreté provinciale du Québec by Premier Maurice Duplessis in 1938, with the title shortened to Sûreté du Québec in 1968. Like the RCMP and the OPP, women played a role as secretaries and matrons until the first female Sûreté constable, Nicole Juteau, assumed active duties in 1975. By the end of the 1970s, there were about 20 female police officers in the Sûreté (Sûreté du Quebec, 2016).

▶ WHAT DO YOU THINK?

Why do you think it took so long for the RCMP, the OPP, and the Sûreté to accept female constables into their ranks? Is it true, as some argue, that policing by its very nature, especially with the potential for aggression and violence, is better suited to males? What does the research on this topic tell us—who makes a better police officer—a woman or a man?

Women in Non-Traditional Jobs

According to the traditional "gender model" explanation of job behaviour (Banihani, Lewis, & Syed, 2013; Feldberg & Glenn, 1979), women who enter non-traditional, male-dominated occupations are governed by their prior socialization to identify primarily with their family role as opposed to their job role. Jurik and Halemba (1984) summarize the main features of the gender model by noting that, compared with males:

> Female workers are (1) less involved in their work and less committed to their careers than men (Brim, 1958; Psathas, 1968), (2) disinterested in the intrinsic aspects of their work (Kuhler, 1963), (3) more concerned with friendships than organizational influence or other working conditions (Rossi, 1965), and (4) more willing to submit to bureaucratic subordination and less concerned with autonomy than men. (Simpson & Simpson, 1969, p. 551)

Conversely, according to this explanation, males are job-driven (Jurik & Halemba, 1984; Lee & Hayes James, 2007). Gender and gender-socialization processes are therefore key variables in explaining the attitudes, expectations, experiences, and career choices of females and males at work. Alternatively, Kanter's (1976, 1977) job model of occupational behaviour argues that attitudes, expectations, experiences, and career choices are more a function of one's location in the organization than a consequence of one's gender (Jurik & Halemba, 1984). According to this model, the jobs available to women in organizations are often lower-level positions and/or are jobs that are not perceived to lead to advancement or promotion (Kanter, 1977; South, Bonjean, Corder, & Markham, 1982).

In fact, definitions of gender roles (gender models) and the way in which we have organized how work is done (job models) derive from long-standing social-structural arrangements and cultural ideas that lead us to accept without question that so-called important jobs can only be done in one way to be considered professional and to remain competitive (Mirchandi, 1999; Prokos & Padavic, 2002). Consequently, women are slotted into the jobs they have, especially in male-dominated areas of work, based on the assumption that because they have a greater commitment to their family and domestic roles, their commitment to the job will be much less than a man's (Armstrong & Armstrong, 1990; Okhuysen, Lepak, Ashcraft, Labianca, Smith, & Steensma, 2013). As evidence of women's lesser degree of job commitment, male co-workers and employers often point to women's higher rates of workplace absenteeism, their interest in part-time positions and job-sharing arrangements, their requests for pregnancy-related accommodations and parental leaves, coupled with their higher rates of attrition (Bagilhole, 2002; Hadfield, 1995; Lassalle & Spokane, 1987; Lee & Hayes James, 2007). As justifications for hiring and promoting males over females, some traditionally male-dominated workplaces point to their need for full-time work continuity, availability for overtime work, and overall 100 percent commitment to the work (Collander & Woos, 1997; Legault & Chasserio, 2013).

BOX 11.2

Career Profile: One Female Police Detective

Some kids grow up knowing exactly what they want to do as an adult, while other people find themselves heading in a career path they never would have imagined as a child. For Detective Helen Bennison (not her real name), a career in policing was not something she ever thought about. Growing up as a youngster, she did not have any family members in policing and she did not see anyone who looked like her represented in her local police service.

While attending university to complete a three-year bachelor degree in social sciences, Bennison found herself drawn to many of the criminal justice courses. In the summer of her second year, she applied for a summer job as a cadet working in the Quarter Master Stores for a large police service, and even had a chance to go on a ride-along with a police emergency response team. Still, for Bennison, she didn't think about a career in policing—she didn't know any women who were police

officers. After graduating from university, Bennison got a well-paying job with a financial institution. But, after a few months in her job, she found herself wanting something else, and decided to find out more about policing—in particular, what kind of requirements there were to be hired as a police officer.

Never having had to prepare for the rigorous physical testing that is needed to meet the physical standards required of police officers, at first Bennison struggled to master the various techniques required. She found herself a personal trainer and before long felt she was ready to take the police constable selection test and pass it. In September 2006, with her certificate in hand, Bennison applied to only one police service. In December 2006, she was hired by that police service and sent off to complete the police recruit training course.

Bennison was posted to a busy division of a large police service. Being a police rookie is a demanding job—there is a lot to learn, and always a lot going on. Early on, Bennison experienced one of the hardships that female police officers must endure on the job—another officer made it his mission to harass her and make Helen's work life "hell." Before long, rumours spread and it seemed like none of the other officers would speak to Bennison, even on radio calls. She left work one day only to find that someone had "keyed" her car in the parking lot of the police station, leaving long scratches in the paint. Surely, if she kept her mouth shut and head down, the harassment would end soon. She put in for a transfer to another shift and, thankfully, another constable, who was aware of her situation, gave her a glowing recommendation, highlighting that she was a hard worker. For Bennison, the transfer made all the difference.

At her new division, Bennison had the opportunity to meet a female officer who was considered to be one of the best undercover officers in policing, and a leader in not only the province but in all of Canada. She encouraged Bennison to apply to the undercover program.

After completing a number of training courses specific to Undercover Techniques, Bennison was assigned to the Drug Squad, Street Enforcement Team. With no real-life experience with drugs or undercover work, on her second day on the team she was given $20 and told to make a drug "buy." Bennison went into a retail store officers suspected of actively dealing drugs and soon came out with her first buy of crack cocaine, surprising even herself! With a boost to her confidence, she went on to work with the drug squad for another three and a half years, while at the same time, she became part of joint forces operations with other police services, as well as carrying out intelligence work for other divisions in her own police service.

According to Bennison, before long she was "eating, sleeping, and living" undercover police work. Her work led to many prosecutions and convictions of criminals involved in drugs and other crimes. Sometimes she had to act as the girlfriend of a known drug user or of another undercover police officer, the "baby mamma," and sometimes as the friend of a user "scum bag." One day, Bennison got a call about an emergency undercover that needed to go down that same day. Another female undercover officer was in a jail cell with the target suspect, a female. Bennison was to play the role of a friend of the undercover officer in the cell, who had come to pick her up after she was released from jail. The undercover play worked perfectly—Bennison picked up both the undercover officer and her new cellmate "friend"—who soon disclosed to her newfound friends her part in a recent homicide. The information and evidence collected would later lead to three convictions in the homicide.

Undercover work is all consuming, and soon Bennison realized it was time to move on to other areas of policing, and to look to be promoted. After going back "on the road" as a patrol constable for a brief period, Bennison was promoted to the rank of sergeant in December 2015. Though it is customary in policing to complete a year on the road as a sergeant after promotion, she was quickly promoted to the Criminal Investigations Bureau (CIB) as detective in September 2016.

Bennison's current role as detective in CIB is a rewarding position. She supervises and investigates a wide range of criminal matters, dealing with victims, witnesses, and accused persons. With a wealth of experience and skill under her belt, she is an inspiration to women in policing—and testament, as in her own career, to how important a role model and mentor can be to the success of female police officers.

Source: Det. H. Bennison (personal interview conducted by Det. K. Woodbury, January 10, 2017).

For women, then, the availability of jobs per se and the availability of specific jobs within a workplace are a function of both (1) the long-standing cultural stereotypes about which role will inevitably be *more* important to women (the family/domestic role or the work/career role) and (2) the cultural belief that the employment of too many women in so-called important positions in the workplace organization will, consequently, negatively affect the professionalism and competitiveness of the organization (Lee & Hayes James, 2007; Ranson, 2005). Women entering non-traditional occupations can therefore expect to experience treatment based not on *who* they are, but rather on *what* they are believed to represent in terms of future job performance and commitment (Bagilhole, 2002; Legault & Chasserio, 2013).

Anker (1998) and Bolton and Muzio (2007) note that as female representation in male-dominated jobs increases, pressure to address *what* women are as workers in the workplace grows, such that the organization must, of necessity, address workplace issues that stem from the dual responsibility (the family/domestic role *and* the work/career role) that biologically and culturally has been defined for women. Significantly, research shows that women do not demonstrate lower levels of commitment to the workplace, nor are their career aspirations significantly different from those of men (Bagilhole, 2002; Jurik & Halemba, 1984; Phillips & Imhoff, 1997; Worden, 1993); instead, confronted by the dual role they must play in society, women are blocked from pursuing job and career goals in the same way that men are able to pursue them (McKinnon & Ahola-Sidaway, 1995; Metcalfe & Dick, 2002; Ranson, 2005). Consequently, as the proportion of women in non-traditional jobs grows, and as women's workplace needs and arrangements are addressed, changes in workplace organization and, eventually, workplace culture will occur, although these changes may be initially perceived as threatening to male co-workers and to the organization itself (Anker, 1998; Huffman, Cohen, & Pearlman, 2010; Ranson, 2005).

▶ WHAT DO YOU THINK?

Nearly 50 percent of the Canadian labour force is made up of women, and graduation rates from post-secondary education are higher for women than men. Given the changes that have happened in the makeup of the Canadian labour force in the past 15 years, why do you think occupations like policing appear to be so resistant to greater representation of women?

Between 1971 and 1981, the percentage of adult women in the Canadian labour force increased from 44 percent to more than 60 percent (Cooke-Reynolds & Zukewich, 2004). Significantly, much of the growth in women's participation occurred among married women and women with children (Cooke-Reynolds & Zukewich, 2004). As women's labour force participation rates increased, pressure to give women access to non-traditional (that is, male-dominated) jobs mounted, prompting Western governments at all levels to continue to implement a host of employment equity legislation and policies designed to address demands for equity in hiring (Busby, 2006; Fleming & Lafferty, 2003; LeBeuf & McLean, 2004; Potts, 1983). As discussed above, in the mid-1970s, the last of Canadian police forces, the RCMP, OPP, and Sûreté du Quebec, finally opened the doors to female police constables.

During the same time period, in response to growing concerns about rising crime rates, declining public support, and mistrust of the police (Lombardo & Lough, 2007), police forces in Canada and in other Western countries began to move away from the centralized, "tough guy, top down" law and order professional model of policing to a service-oriented, community policing model in an attempt to engage members of the public and their support in addressing an increasingly broad range of public disorder and crime (Gill, Weisburd, Telep, Vitter, & Bennett, 2014; Kelling & Moore, 1998). The shift in emphasis from "crime fighting" skills to community engagement skills paralleled public and political pressures to hire more female police officers in order to be more representative of and accountable to the communities being policed (Lombardo & Lough, 2007).

Career Profile: RCMP Sergeant Penny Hermann

After graduating in 1995 from Trent University with a degree in psychology and French, Penny Hermann wanted to do something with her life to help people, something that would make the world a better place. Penny was encouraged by a friend to check out policing as a possible career, and she went ahead and completed an application for the RCMP. After successfully completing the testing and selection process, on April 1, 1996, Hermann began the 28 weeks of rigorous recruit training at the Royal Canadian Mounted Police Academy, Depot Division, in Regina, Saskatchewan. Upon completing the Depot training program, the newly graduated RCMP police officer was posted to Morinville, Alberta, where she was assigned to general law enforcement duties.

As the "newbie" on the job, Hermann recognized quickly that she had a lot to learn about policing. It would take time for her to develop self-confidence in her abilities to do all of the aspects of the job. Still, her supervisors at the detachment noted her strong work ethic and her easy and approachable manner with people, which proved to be a big help in conducting investigations.

In 2003, with six years of RCMP policing experience under her belt, Hermann transferred back to her home town of Ottawa and was assigned to General Duty Protective Policing. Looking for opportunities to advance up the ranks, she transferred to Regina, Saskatchewan, in 2007 and was promoted to the rank of corporal. Her new role was at the RCMP Training Academy, where she started out as a team leader in applied sciences—but Hermann would soon start a new chapter in her career that would bring out a side of her unknown even to her family, when she became only the sixth female drill instructor in the history of the RCMP Depot academy. At only five-feet-four-inches tall, Penny did not fit the Hollywood image of a drill instructor—but then, in the RCMP, a drill instructor is not there to intimidate or to instill fear, but rather to use drill to endow cadets with a sense of organizational belonging, self-discipline, and teamwork. Her success as a drill instructor was highlighted in the 2015 edition of *Red Coat Diaries*.

While at Depot, Hermannn also developed a program called the "Silent Partner." To honour those police officers who have died in the line of duty, she researched the life of every fallen officer, even contacting family members to learn more. Each RCMP recruit is now given a

RCMP officer Penny Hermann.

card with the memory of a fallen officer to keep with them as their "silent partner," and to keep the memory of the fallen member alive. In recognition of the Silent Partner program, Hermann received a Commanding Officer's Certificate of Appreciation.

A natural transition from training cadets to recruiting potential cadets was Hermann's next career move. In 2011, she transferred to Milton, Ontario, where she took on the role of Proactive Recruiting Supervisor for the RCMP. Recruitment is an important job that can shape the future of a policing organization. In March 2015, Hermann was promoted to the rank of sergeant, as the non-commissioned officer in charge of media relations for RCMP "O" division.

Many proud moments are associated with Hermann's career in policing, including representing the RCMP in numerous Red Serge events, such as leading troops onto the football field for the Grey Cup in 2013, being a representative in Las Vegas for Tourism Saskatchewan, being the Troop Commander for Opening and Closing Ceremonies for both Pan Am and Parapan Am Games in 2015, and carrying the cup for the Ice Hockey World Championships in January 2015.

Performing her duties as media relations sergeant, Hermann continues to serve the RCMP proudly. Her current role includes liaising with partners, such as other police services, Canadian government agencies, and the media.

Source: RCMP Sgt. P. Hermann (personal interview conducted by Det. K. Woodbury, January 12, 2017).

Women's Work and the Future of Policing

The experience of women in policing in Canada generally conforms to the experience of women in other traditionally male-dominated jobs. Although women have been a part of Canadian policing for nearly 100 years, today only 21 percent of constables in Canada are women, and only 11 percent of non-commissioned officers and 6 percent of senior officers are female (Statistics Canada, 2016). Policing continues to have one of the lowest proportions of females of all the traditionally male-dominated occupations (Anker, 1998; Franklin, 2008), despite considerable evidence that females perform equally as well as males in carrying out the range of policing duties (Archbold & Schulz, 2012; Brown, 1998; Janzen, Muhajarine, & Kelly, 2007; Linden & Minch, 1984; Seagrave, 1997).

BOX 11.4

Career Profile: Staff Sergeant Laura Houliston

Laura Houliston first became interested in policing while studying social work at the University of Waterloo. In the social work program, she had an opportunity to complete a placement in youth probation and work alongside police officers. After completing her degree in social work, in 1995, Houliston joined the Ontario Provincial Police.

Houliston's first posting was to the Cochrane, Ontario, OPP detachment where she performed general law enforcement duties. After completing six years of her "duration posting" in Cochrane, she transferred to the Sudbury, Ontario, OPP detachment to accommodate her spouse's career move to the same location. In Sudbury, the ongoing struggle to balance the roles of mother, wife, and police officer, without family nearby to help out, made Houliston consider giving up her police career. Like many other women in policing who are doing the job far from home, she learned to rely instead on a strong support network of co-workers and friends to help out when needed, and was able to stay in the career she had worked so hard for.

In 2001, Houliston was promoted to detective constable, serving as the abuse issues coordinator for the Sudbury OPP detachment. She quickly became a passionate advocate for the victims of abuse, making connections and forming partnerships with community agencies, and paving the way for better police responses for victims of abuse.

In 2007, Houliston was promoted to the rank of detective sergeant as the Regional Abuse Issues Coordinator, and transferred to OPP Northeast Region Headquarters. Continuing her dedication to abuse issues, her hard work and advocacy did not go unrecognized, and in 2012, D/Sgt Laura Houliston received the prestigious Queen's Jubilee Medal for her work with victims of crime.

In 2012, Houliston was again promoted, this time to the rank of staff sergeant in the Career Development Bureau, OPP Headquarters. In this new role, she managed the placement and positioning of police constables across the region, and worked closely with managers on the selection process designed to identify the right people for positions within the organization. She also became a mentor and coach to officers preparing for various promotional processes.

In 2015, looking to get back into a frontline policing role, Houliston assumed the position of Staff Sergeant Detachment Commander, OPP Northeast Region, the first female ever to take on the position in that Region. As detachment commander, she is responsible for managing 44 constables, 5 sergeants, 4 administrative assistants, 3 clerks, and a volunteer police auxiliary unit of 14 members. Houliston's groundbreaking role as detachment commander is setting a new standard for women police officers to reach for.

Drawing from her personal life and her commitment to physical fitness, Houliston encourages her officers and staff to be active and lead a healthy lifestyle. Operating from a leadership style based on mutual respect, she is always available to the detachment members, and takes great pride in the professional policing her officers provide to the communities they serve.

Source: Staff Sgt. Laura Houliston (personal interview conducted by Det. K. Woodbury, January 19, 2017).

Similar to other police organizations around the world, Canadian police services have recognized the need to recruit and promote more female police officers. According to the National Center for Women in Policing (2002), increasing the numbers of women at all ranks of law enforcement is a strategy that will "reduce police excessive force, strengthen community policing reforms, and improve police response to violence against women" (p. 9). In particular, if police organizations are to truly reflect Sir Robert Peel's 1829 founding principle that "the police are the public and the public are the police" (Melville, 1901, cited in Schmalleger et al., 2004, p. 100), representation from women must increase markedly in the future.

If the RCMP and provincial and municipal police services are to continue increasing female representation in the future, there are important barriers to recruitment and retention of females that must be addressed (Franklin, 2008; Shelley, Morabito, & Tobin-Gurley, 2011; Walker, 1993). Cordner and Cordner (2011) found that discriminatory practices in hiring, in particular, physical fitness tests, can be used unfairly to eliminate female candidates. According to a 2012 study commissioned by the Canadian Association of Chiefs of Police (Maguire & Dyke, 2012), female police officers were less likely than male officers to express the belief that their police organization was supportive of them, and less likely to believe that problematic behaviour by other officers would be reported. Among the issues that policing organizations must confront for the future are their policies regarding equipment, work schedules, parental leaves, gender harassment, job performance, and job retention.

▶ WHAT DO YOU THINK?

Recruiters complain that most young women won't even consider a career in policing. What would make policing more attractive to women as a career?

Equipment

The RCMP, OPP, and other Canadian police services now accommodate individuals with smaller hands by determining the appropriate size of the pistol grip and issuing either a modified standard-issue firearm or a similar but smaller version to those who require it, typically women. Female police officers may also be issued with a smaller magazine pouch with the smaller-version firearm, which allows for more room around the waist of the officer. Women often have smaller waists than their male counterparts and thus have less room around the duty belt for the various tools of the trade. Women may choose to carry first-aid materials and gloves in the cargo pocket of their pants instead of on their belt to reduce the weight and to avoid having items in the small of their back.[2]

Work Schedules

Accepting the dual role that women must play requires that organizations recognize that many women continue to shoulder the burden of caring for home and children (Cordner & Cordner, 2011; Ranson, 2005). This responsibility requires consideration of work schedules to accommodate women's dual role, while at the same time meeting the work-related goals of both the female worker and the organization. As the proportion of women in policing grows, police organizations will need to introduce shorter shift schedules, job-sharing, and part-time work, as have other male-dominated occupations (Anker, 1998; Corsianos, 2009).

The standard schedule of 12-hour shifts, with four days on, four days off, is not conducive to female officers managing both a career and a family. At the same time, part-time work is almost non-existent in Canadian policing; most police organizations and police associations maintain that policing has no room for part-timers. Nevertheless, a few Canadian police organizations have accommodated requests for part-time status on a limited basis and are developing policies to address broader requests for part-time work among constables.[3]

Job-sharing is a work arrangement in which two employees agree with the employer to share the work hours of one position, each receiving half of the pay. The Calgary Police Service is one of the few Canadian police services that have developed a policy for job-sharing by officers, though on a restricted basis (Calgary Police Service, 2008). The OPP is currently drafting a job-sharing policy. Significantly, part-time and job-sharing policies are restricted by Canadian police services to current, generally long-standing employees; opportunities for part-time work and job-sharing are not advertised to potential recruits.

▶ WHAT DO YOU THINK?

Other occupations, for example medicine (nurses, physicians, etc.), have practiced job-sharing and part-time work for many years—and people working in this field must maintain a current licence and practice standards. Why can't a police officer work part-time, or job-share with another police officer?

Parental Leaves

Although parental leave has become an accepted practice in almost all workplace settings, in male-dominated workplace environments, use of parental leave may be viewed negatively. Other officers may view use of parental leave as evidence of an individual's lack of commitment to the work organization (Liff & Ward, 2001) and as increasing the workload for others (Bagilhole, 2002). At the same time, management may point to adverse financial impacts of parental leave, in terms of hiring, transferring, or equipping other officers to assume the positions of those on parental leave (Metcalfe & Dick, 2002). Certainly, women's experience shows that leaving the workplace for child-rearing purposes has a negative impact on career aspirations and promotion (Ranson, 2005). In fact, even short-term leaves and absenteeism related to child care are perceived negatively by traditionally male-dominated organizations (Collander & Woos, 1997).

Gender Harassment

Because females comprise only 21 percent of police officers overall, they too often find themselves isolated and vulnerable, as the only female on a platoon working alongside men, or the lone female in management supervising almost exclusively men. Consequently, like in other male-dominated work environments, female officers may be the subject of a variety of forms of gender harassment, including sexist locker-room talk (McKinnon & Ahola-Sidaway, 1995), questioning of their commitment and job competency, assertions of preferential treatment for females, assignment to menial duties, and exclusion from informal social activities at work and outside of work (Enloe, 2013; Gruber, 1998; Heidenshohn, 1992; Morash & Haarr, 1995; Seklecki & Paynich, 2007). Isolation, vulnerability, and exclusion from the so-called "boys' club" too often incur negative consequences for women's career advancement (Holdaway & Parker, 1998; Prokos & Padavic, 2002).

Job Performance

In three decades, researchers (Koenig, 1978; Sims, Scarborough, & Ahmad, 2003; Worden, 1993) have found no significant differences in the overall performance of male and female police officers, though the competency of female police officers continues to be called into question by male officers, and even the public (Prokos & Padavic, 2002). In fact, research shows that female officers are sometimes perceived to be more competent than their male counterparts (Ffrench & Waugh, 1998; Seagrave, 1997; Sichel, Friedman, Quint, & Smith, 1978) and are less likely to use force to resolve conflicts (Bazley, Lersch, & Mieczkowski, 2007).

Despite the research evidence, Prokos and Padavic (2002) found that policing continues to be perceived as a man's job, a perception reinforced through the hidden curriculum used to train new police recruits, which extols male values related to toughness, violence, weaponry, and action.

Job Retention

Research has demonstrated that women officers are more likely than men to leave the job early in their career (Boni, Adams, & Circelli, 2001; Doerner, 1995; Edwards & Robinson, 1999). The commonly cited reasons for the lower retention rates of women include harassment, negative attitudes of male co-workers and supervisors, family and childcare responsibilities, lack of support from management, blocked career opportunities, and inflexible work arrangements (Fleming & Lafferty, 2003; Metcalfe & Dick, 2002; Morash & Haarr, 1995; Ward & Prenzler, 2016).

In the RCMP, the OPP, and the Sûreté, and in most Indigenous police services, a lone female officer among a complement of male officers is not uncommon, especially in northern detachments. Some women feel they do not fit in, and their lack of female role models to look up to and learn from further compounds their sense of isolation.

SUMMARY

Police services in Canada recognize the need to increase the number of women constables and senior officers if they are to effectively police the communities they serve. If police services are to recruit and retain more female officers, they must change the very organization of police structures and police work to reflect the dual role, as family caregiver and career officer, that most female police officers must play. At the same time, long-standing negative, often misogynist, attitudes toward female officers must change.

The National Center for Women and Policing (2003) outlines six performance and organizational-related advantages to employing greater numbers of women police officers:

1. Female officers have proven to be as competent as their male counterparts in meeting the requirements of policing.
2. Female officers are less likely to use excessive force.
3. Female officers are more likely to embrace the community policing model.
4. More female officers will improve law enforcement's response to violence against women.
5. Increasing the presence of female officers reduces problems of sex discrimination and harassment within a law enforcement agency.
6. The presence of women can bring about beneficial changes in policy for all officers. (pp. 3–10)

Although women police officers have been demonstrated to perform as competently as their male counterparts, the abilities, skills, and life experiences that women bring to the job add a different dimension to policing: an emphasis on negotiation instead of the use of force; a stronger focus on child protection and prevention of violence against women; greater awareness of the dynamics of inequality and diversity; and demands for creativity and flexibility in the organization of the workplace (Dantzker, 2005; Fleming & Lafferty, 2003; Jurik & Halemba, 1984).

At the same time, the growth in the number of women in policing has led to increased opportunities for other groups in society—Indigenous people, visible minorities, even males who would not have met the formerly rigid height requirements.

Perhaps the most important of Sir Robert Peel's nine principles of policing is the seventh principle, which states:

> The police should at all times maintain a relationship with the public that gives reality to the historic tradition that the police are the public and the public are the police; the police are the only members of the public who are paid to give full-time attention to duties which are incumbent on every citizen in the interest of the community welfare. (Melville, 1901, cited in Schmalleger et al., 2004, p. 100)

As modern police services move toward truly reflecting the public they serve, and as more and more women, Indigenous people, and visible minority groups assume the various positions and ranks within the police services, the police will be the public and vice versa. And perhaps, as Peel hoped, law, order, and community will be one and the same for all. What will such a vision of policing look like?

NOTES

1. The exception was matters of civil law in Quebec.
2. This observation was made by the principal author, Kellie Woodbury, based on her own use of equipment on the job.
3. This information was provided to the principal author, Kellie Woodbury, from internal documents of the Human Resources Bureau of the Ontario Provincial Police.

DISCUSSION QUESTIONS

1. What factors were behind the first hiring of women police officers in Canada? How was the role of the first policewoman defined and why?

2. What factors make it difficult for present-day police agencies to recruit and retain women as police officers? How are police agencies in Canada attempting to address these factors? Are these police agencies being successful? Why or why not?

3. If Canadian police agencies were to hire more women, to the point where men and women were equally represented (50/50) among police officers, what would the structure, organization, and operations of police agencies look like? Would the public be better served by equal representation of men and women in policing? Why or why not?

4. Thinking about recent reports and court action regarding the sexual harassment of female police officers in the RCMP and other Canadian police services, why is it that sexual harassment of women police officers continues to be a problem? If you were the commissioner or chief of police, how would you go about dealing with these problems?

ADDITIONAL RESOURCES

Suggested Readings

Jackson, L.A. (2006). *Women police: Gender, welfare and surveillance in the twentieth century*. Manchester, UK: Manchester University Press.

Schulz, D.M. (2004). *Breaking the brass ceiling: Women police chiefs and their paths to the top*. Westport, CT: Greenwood.

Wells, S.K., & Alt, B.L. (2005). *Police women: Life with the badge*. Westport, CT: Greenwood.

Films and Videos

Crouch, L. (Producer), & Pequenza, N. (Director). (2005). *Women behind the badge* [3-part television documentary series]. Canada: A Telefactory production in association with TVO.

Kovanic, G.D. (Producer), Johnson, G. (Producer), & Simpson, M. (Director). (2000). *Flipping the world: Drugs through a blue lens* [Motion picture]. Canada: National Film Board.

MacDonald, J. (Producer), & Lank, B. (Director). (2004). *Women on patrol* [Motion picture]. Canada: National Film Board.

Websites

Calgary Police Service: www.calgarypolice.ca/recruiting/html/women_in_policing.htm
Canadian Police College: www.cpc.gc.ca
International Association of Women Police: www.iawp.org
National Center for Women and Policing: www.womenandpolicing.org/aboutus.asp
Ontario Provincial Police (OPP): http://www.opp.ca/index.php?id=128
Royal Canadian Mounted Police. Police Officer Careers: http://www.rcmp-grc.gc.ca/en/police-officer-careers

REFERENCES

After 65 years: Women. (1974). *The Review, 9*(2), 1–3.

Anker, R. (1998). *Gender and jobs: Sex segregation of occupations in the world*. Geneva: International Labour Office.

Archbold, C.A., & Schulz, D.M. (2012). Research on women in policing: A look at the past, present and future. *Sociology Compass, 6*(9), 694–706.

Armstrong, P., & Armstrong, H. (1990). *Theorizing women's work*. Toronto: Garamond Press.

Bagilhole, B. (2002). *Women in non-traditional occupations: Challenging men*. New York: Palgrave Macmillan.

Banihani, M., Lewis, P., & Syed, J. (2013). Is work engagement gendered? *Gender in Management: An International Journal, 28*(7), 400–423.

Barnes, M. (1991). *Policing Ontario: The OPP today*. Erin, ON: Boston Mills Press.

Bazley, T.D., Lersch, K.M., & Mieczkowski, T. (2007). Officer force versus suspect resistance: A gendered analysis of patrol officers in an urban police department. *Journal of Criminal Justice, 35*, 183–192.

Bikos, Lesley J. (2016). *"I took the blue pill": The effect of the hegemonic masculine police culture on Canadian policewomen's identities.* MA Research Paper. Paper 7.

Bolton, S.C., & Muzio, D. (2007). Can't live with 'em; can't live without 'em: Gendered segmentation in the legal profession. *Sociology, 41*, 47–64.

Boni, N., Adams, K., & Circelli, M. (2001). *Educational and professional development experiences of female and male police employees.* Payneham, South Australia: Australasian Centre for Policing Research.

Bronskill, J. (2016, October). RCMP earmarks $100M in compensation for sexual harassment against female Mounties. The Canadian Press. Retrieved from http://globalnews.ca/news/2986688/rcmp-to-settle-in-class-action-harassment-claims-from-former-mounties/.

Brown, J.M. (1998). Aspects of discriminatory treatment of women police officers serving in forces in England and Wales. *British Journal of Criminology, 38*, 265–282.

Busby, N. (2006). Affirmative action in women's employment: Lessons from Canada. *Journal of Law and Society, 33*, 42–58.

Calgary Police Service. (2008). Women in policing. Retrieved from www.calgarypolice.ca/recruiting/html/women_in_policing.htm.

Canadian Encyclopedia (2017). Rose Fortune. *The Canadian encyclopedia.* Retrieved from http://www.thecanadian encyclopedia.ca/en/article/rose-fortune/.

Carrigan, D.O. (1991). *Crime and punishment in Canada: A history.* Toronto: McClelland & Stewart.

CBC News. (2017, February 1). Calgary police officer's public resignation renews questions about harassment, intimidation on force. Retrieved from http://www.cbc.ca/news/canada/calgary/magnus-police-officer-resignation-harassed-intimidation-1.3961918.

Collander, D., & Woos, J.W. (1997). Institutional demand-side discrimination against women and the human capital model. *Feminist Economics, 3*(1), 53–64.

Cooke-Reynolds, M., & Zukewich, N. (2004). The feminization of work. *Canadian Social Trends,* 24–29.

Cordner, G., & Cordner, A.M. (2011). Stuck on a plateau? Obstacles to recruitment, selection, and retention of women police. *Police Quarterly, 14*(3), 207–226.

Corsianos, M. (2009). *Policing and gendered justice: Examining the possibilities.* Toronto: University of Toronto Press.

Dantzker, M.L. (2005). *Understanding today's police.* Monsey, NY: Criminal Justice Press.

Dodge, M., Valcore, L., & Klinger, D.A. (2010). Maintaining separate spheres in policing: Women on SWAT teams. *Women & Criminal Justice, 20*, 218–238.

Doerner, W.G. (1995). Officer retention patterns: An affirmative action concern for police agencies? *American Journal of Police, 14*(3/4), 197–210.

Edwards, C., & Robinson, O. (1999). Managing part-timers in the police service: A study of inflexibility. *Human Resource Management Journal, 9*(4), 5–18.

Enloe, C. (2013). Maculinities, policing, women and international politics of sexual harassment. *International Feminist Journal of Politics, 15*(1), 77–81.

Ericson, R.V. (1982). *Reproducing order: A study of police patrol work.* Toronto: University of Toronto Press.

Feldberg, R.L., & Glenn, E.N. (1979). Male and female: Job versus gender models in the sociology of work. *Social Problems, 26*, 524–538.

Ffrench, M., & Waugh, L. (1998). The weaker sex? Women and police work. *International Journal of Police Science and Management, 1*(3), 260–275.

Fleming, J., & Lafferty, G. (2003). Equity confounded? Women in Australian police organizations. *Labour and Industry, 37*(13), 37–49.

Franklin, C.A. (2008). Male peer support and the police culture. *Women & Criminal Justice, 16*(3), 1–25.

Frost, S. (1997). Gender equity analysis. In M.E. LeBeuf & J. McLean (Eds.), *Women in policing in Canada: The year 2000 and beyond—Its challenges* (Workshop proceedings, Canadian Police College, May 20–23, 1997, pp. 89–97). Ottawa: Canadian Police College.

Gill, C., Weisburd, D., Telep, C.W., Vitter, Z., & Bennett, T. (2014). Community-oriented policing to reduce crime, disorder and fear and increase satisfaction and legitimacy among citizens: A systematic review. *Journal of Experimental Criminology 10*, 399–428.

Goff, C. (2001). *Criminal justice in Canada* (2nd ed.). Toronto: Nelson Thomson Learning.

Government of Manitoba. (2014). *Women and policing in Canada: A status brief and discussion paper.* Manitoba Status of Women. Retrieved from http://www.gov.mb.ca/msw/publications/pdf/2014_women_in_policing_brief.pdf.

Griffiths, K.T., Whitelaw, B., & Parent, R.B. (1999). *Canadian police work.* Toronto: ITP Nelson.

Gruber, J.E. (1998). The impact of male work environments and organizational policies on women's experiences of sexual harassment. *Gender and Society, 12*, 301–320.

Hadfield, G.K. (1995). Rational women: A test for sex-based harassment. *California Law Review, 83*, 1151–1189.

Hasham, A. (2016, October 25). Police environment "poison" for women officers, tribunal told. *Toronto Star*. Retrieved from http://www.thestar.com/news/gta/2016/10/25/police-environment-poison-for-women-officers-tribunal-told.html.

Heidenshohn, F. (1992). *Women in control: The role of women in law enforcement*. Oxford, UK: Clarendon Press.

Higley, D.D. (1984). *OPP: The history of the Ontario Provincial Police force*. Toronto: Queen's Printer.

Holdaway, S., & Parker, S.K. (1998). Policing women police. *British Journal of Criminology, 38*, 40–60.

Huffman, M.L., Cohen, P.N., & Pearlman, J. (2010). Engendering change: Organizational dynamics and workplace gender desegregation, 1975–2005. *Administrative Science Quarterly, 55*(2), 255–277.

Janzen B.L., Muhajarine, N., & Kelly, I.W. (2007). Work-family conflict, and psychological distress in men and women among Canadian police officers. *Psychological Reports, 100*, 556–557.

Jurik, N.C., & Halemba, G.J. (1984). Gender, working conditions and the job satisfaction of women in a non-traditional occupation: Female correctional officers in men's prisons. *Sociological Quarterly, 25*, 551–566.

Kanter, R.M. (1976). The impact of hierarchical structures on the work behaviour of women and men. *Social Problems, 23*, 415–430.

Kanter, R.M. (1977). *Men and women of the corporation*. New York: Harper and Row.

Kelling, G.L., & Moore, M.H. (1998). The evolving strategy of policing. *Perspectives on Policing, 4*, 1–15.

Kelly, W., & Kelly, N. (1976). *Policing in Canada*. Toronto: Macmillan.

Koenig, E.J. (1978). An overview of attitudes toward women in law enforcement. *Public Administration Review, 38*, 267–275.

Lassalle, A.D., & Spokane, A.R. (1987). Patterns of early labor force participation of American women. *Career Development Quarterly, 36*, 55–65.

LeBeuf, M.E., & McLean, J. (2004). Women in policing in Canada. In S.E. Nancoo (Ed.), *Contemporary issues in Canadian policing* (pp. 318–335). Mississauga, ON: Canadian Educators' Press.

Lee, P.M., & Hayes James, E. (2007) She'-e-os: gender effects and investor reactions to the announcements of top executive appointments. *Strategic Management Journal, 28*(3), 227–241.

Legault, M-J., & Chasserio, S. (2013). Family obligations or cultural constraints? Obstacles in the path of professional women. *Journal of International Women's Studies, 4*(3), 108–125.

Lewis-Horne, N. (2002). Women in policing. In D.P. Forcese (Ed.), *Police: Selected issues in Canadian law enforcement* (pp. 98–109). Ottawa: Golden Dog Press.

Liff, S., & Ward, K. (2001). Distorted views through the glass ceiling: The construction of women's understandings of promotion and senior management positions. *Gender, Work and Organization, 8*, 19–36.

Linden, R., & Minch, C. (1984). *Women in policing: A review*. Ottawa: Ministry of the Solicitor General.

Lombardo, R., & Lough, T. (2007). Community policing: Broken windows, community building, and satisfaction with the police. *The Police Journal, 80*, 117–140.

Maguire, S., & Dyke, L. (2012). CACP 2012 survey of policing: CACP professionalism in policing research project. Canadian Association of Chiefs of Police.

McKenna, P. (1998). *Foundations of policing in Canada*. Scarborough, ON: Prentice Hall Canada.

McKinnon, M., & Ahola-Sidaway, J. (1995). "Workin' with the boys": A North American perspective on non-traditional work initiatives for adolescent females in secondary schools. *Gender & Education, 7*, 327–340.

Melville, W.L. (1901). *A history of police in London*. London: Methuen.

Metcalfe, B., & Dick, G. (2002). Is the force still with her? Gender and commitment in the police. *Women in Management Review, 17*, 392–403.

Mirchandi, K. (1999). Feminist insight on gendered work: New directions in research on women and entrepreneurship. *Gender, Work and Organization, 6*, 224–235.

Morash, M., & Haarr, R.N. (1995). Gender, workplace problems and stress in policing. *Justice Quarterly, 12*, 113–140.

Morash, M., & Haarr, R.N. (2012). Doing, redoing, and undoing gender: Variation in gender identities of women working as police officers. *Feminist Criminology, 7*(1), 3–23.

Murphy, S.A. (2006). Executive motivation: From the front lines to the boardroom? *International Journal of Police Science & Management, 8*(3), 232–245.

National Center for Women and Policing. (2002). *Recruiting and retaining women: A self-assessment guide for law enforcement*. Beverly Hills, CA: Author.

National Center for Women and Policing. (2003). *Hiring & retaining more women: The advantages to law enforcement agencies*. Beverly Hills, CA: Author.

Okhuysen, G.A., Lepak, D., Ashcraft, K.L., Labianca, G., Smith, V., & Steensma, H.K. (2013). Theories of work and working today. *Academy of Management Review, 38*(4), 491–502.

Phillips, S.D., & Imhoff, A.R. (1997). Women and career development: A decade of research. *Annual Review of Psychology, 48*, 31–59.

Police Service of Northern Ireland. (2008). Early policing in Ireland. Retrieved from http://www.psni.police.uk/index.htm.

Potts, L.W. (1983). Equal employment opportunity and female employment in police agencies. *Journal of Criminal Justice, 11*, 505–523.

Prenzler T., & Sinclair, G. (2013). The status of women police officers: An international review. *International Journal of Law, Crime and Justice 41*(2), 115–131.

Prokos, A., & Padavic, I. (2002). "There oughtta be a law against bitches": Masculinity lessons in police academy training. *Gender, Work and Organization, 9*, 439–459.

Rabe-Hemp, C.E. (2008). Female officers and the ethic of care: Does officer gender impact police behaviors? *Journal of Criminal Justice, 36*, 426–434.

Ranson, G. (2005). No longer "one of the boys": Negotiations with motherhood, as prospect or reality, among women in engineering. *Canadian Review of Sociology and Anthropology, 42*, 145–166.

Riccucci, N.M., Van Ryzin, G.G., & Lavena, C.F. (2014). Representative bureaucracy in policing: Does it increase perceived legitimacy? *Journal of Public Administration Research and Theory, 24*, 537–551.

Royal Canadian Mounted Police. (2016). Women in the RCMP. Retrieved from http://www.rcmp-grc.gc.ca/en/women-rcmp.

Royal Commission on the Status of Women in Canada. (1970). *Report of the Royal Commission on the Status of Women in Canada*. Retrieved from http://epe.lac-bac.gc.ca/100/200/301/pco-bcp/commissions-ef/bird1970-eng/bird1970-eng.htm.

Schmalleger, F., MacAlister, D., & McKenna, P.F. (2004). *Canadian criminal justice today* (2nd ed.). Toronto: Pearson Education Canada.

Schmidt, B.R. (2011). Women on the force. *Canada's History, 91*(4), 3441–3448.

Schuck, A.M. (2014). Female representation in law enforcement: The influence of screening, unions, incentives, community policing, CALEA, and size. *Police Quarterly 17*(1), 54–78.

Seagrave, J. (1997). *Introduction to policing in Canada*. Scarborough, ON: Prentice Hall Canada.

Seklecki, R., & Paynich, R. (2007). A national survey of female police officers: An overview of findings. *Police Practice and Research, 8*, 17–30.

Shelley, T.O., Morabito, M.S., & Tobin-Gurley, J. (2011). Gendered institutions and gender roles: The current state of women and policing. *Criminal Justice Studies, 24*(4), 351–367.

Sichel, J.K., Friedman, L.N., Quint, J.C., & Smith, M.E. (1978). *Women on patrol: A pilot study of police performance in New York City*. NY. New York: Vera Institute of Justice.

Silvestri, M., Tong, S., & Brown, J. (2013). Gender and police leadership: Time for a paradigm shift? *International Journal of Police Science & Management, 15*(1), 61–73.

Sims, B., Scarborough, K.E., & Ahmad, J. (2003). The relationship between police officers' attitudes toward women and perceptions of police models. *Police Quarterly, 6*, 278–297.

South, S.J., Bonjean, C., Corder, J., & Markham, W.T. (1982). Sex and power in the federal bureaucracy: A comparative analysis of male and female supervisors. *Work and Occupations, 9*, 233–254.

Statistics Canada. (2006). *Police resources in Canada 2006*. Ottawa: Canadian Centre for Justice Statistics.

Statistics Canada. (2016). *Police resources in Canada 2015*. Ottawa: Canadian Centre for Justice Statistics.

Sûreté du Quebec. (2016). 1975 Place aux policières. Retrieved from http://www.sq.gouv.qc.ca/mission-et-services/historique-de-la-sq/policieres-historique-sq.jsp.

Walker, G.S. (1993). *The status of women in Canadian policing*. Ottawa: Ministry of the Solicitor General.

Ward, A., & Prenzler, T. (2016). Good practice case studies in the advancement of women in policing. *Police Science & Management, 18*(4), 242–250.

Worden, A.P. (1993). The attitudes of women and men in policing: Testing conventional and contemporary wisdom. *Criminology, 31*, 203–241.

Women Working in the Courts

Introduction

As is the case with other areas of the Canadian criminal justice system, women's foray into the field of law has occurred relatively recently. Although some women broke ground early in the 20th century, the frequency with which women entered the legal profession did not reach parity with men until the mid-1980s. In the last 30 years, we have seen considerable progress made by women in various fields of law.

The jobs that women perform in the Canadian legal system are varied and interesting. Women are everywhere—women handle civil litigation and practise real estate law, criminal law, taxation law, family and divorce law, immigration law, and corporate and commercial law. In many of these areas, marked differences are still evident between men and women with respect to equality and work-related issues and challenges; however, readers should not infer that the issues to be discussed in this chapter are not experienced by women working in other fields in the criminal justice system. To the contrary, many similarities are shared by all women across the criminal justice system. By examining the challenges specific to women in the courts, we hope to illustrate the issues faced by many women working in the field of law.

Historical Overview of Women and the Practice of Law

On February 2, 1897, Clara Brett Martin became the first female to be called and admitted to the practice of law both in Ontario and in all of the British Commonwealth (Backhouse, 1985; Leiper, 2006). A year earlier, Family Compact[2] leader John Strachan stated that lawyers "will gradually engross all the colonial offices of profit and honour" (Backhouse & Backhouse, 2004, p. ix). Strachan was referring to the rise of "lawyering" in the colonial outposts, including Canada. He forecast a significant growth in the legal profession, envisioning the role of lawyers in society as occupying the upper echelons of business and commerce in all facets of the public and private sector. In some ways, Strachan's forecast has proven accurate. Regrettably, with respect to full equality and integration of women in the profession, his prediction has yet to be fulfilled.

Although little information appears to exist with respect to the early history of Clara Brett Martin, much has been written about her from the pivotal point when she entered Trinity College in Toronto, as an arts student, in 1888, to the end of her career as a prominent lawyer in Ontario (Backhouse, 1985). In both her undergraduate and legal studies, she faced monumental hurdles in her quest for equality:

> In 1867, an article in the Toronto *Globe* on the topic of "Higher Female Education" noted that Canadians were "for the most part, of one mind ... as to the rivalry of the boys' grammar

school, and [were] still less likely to claim for them the right of mingling in the classes of University or Trinity College....” The prospect of admitting women to university provoked disastrous prophecies of “desexed, enfeebled, and arrogant female students.” Critics expressed fears that the female co-ed would be “ill-suited” to take her “primary place” in the social order, and would threaten the “sanctity of the domestic circle.”

Male physicians also contributed to the furor by expressing concern over the debilitating effects of higher education on women, arguing that studying and working “weakened their developing wombs” which could cause infertility, the inhibition of lactation in nursing mothers, serious mental disturbance, and even pelvic distortion (presumably from sitting too much). (Backhouse, 1985, p. 3)

Clara Brett Martin’s career was a distinguished one that blazed the way for women to take up the practice of law, but it was short-lived. She died at age 49 of a heart attack after suffering ill health for a number of years as a result of a cold she caught during an important case (Backhouse, 1985).[3] Clara Brett Martin’s accomplishments have not been given the recognition they deserve. As Backhouse (1985) has stated: “tragically, the women who were to follow in her footsteps often failed to recognize her importance and adopted an all too frequent attitude of belittling and diminishing Clara Brett Martin’s accomplishments” (p. 40). Although she was clearly a woman who made significant headway in forging a path for other women to practise law in Canada, recent discoveries have cast a shadow on her personal attitudes and beliefs (Backhouse, 1992).

In the 1920s, another woman had the courage to almost single-handedly challenge the leading members of Canada’s legal establishment (Backhouse & Backhouse, 2004). In the pursuit of her family inheritance, Elizabeth Bethune Campbell became the first woman to argue a case in front of the Law Lords at the Privy Council.[4] In a case that stretched for more than a decade and touched on all facets of the male-dominated legal profession in Ontario, Campbell emerged victorious (Backhouse & Backhouse, 2004). Her pioneering spirit set the stage for women to slowly work their way into a profession that had, for the most part, been previously off limits.

Ontario’s Clara Brett Martin and Elizabeth Bethune Campbell paved the way for women across Canada to pursue a legal career in their respective provinces. For example, in 1911, Melrose Sissons, from Portage la Prairie, Manitoba, “made an application to the Law Society of Manitoba to be admitted as a student” (Kinnear, 1992, p. 412). Not surprisingly, given the tenor of the day, the Law Society of Manitoba refused her application. After considerable persistence, Melrose Sissons won her battle in the Manitoba legislature, and an amendment was passed in 1912 to effectively open the doors for the women of Manitoba to enter the practice of law. As shown in Table 12.1, by the early 1940s, the first women were practising law throughout Canada. Interestingly, although some of the early pioneers in Ontario and Manitoba faced considerable resistance to their quest to become lawyers, this struggle was not the case in Alberta:

Lillian Ruby Clements enrolled as a student-at-law in 1912. She would become the first woman admitted to the Alberta bar. The absence of formal opposition places her experience in sharp contrast to that of women in many other provinces, particularly to that of Clara Brett Martin. All other Canadian provinces found that, regardless of her level of legal training, a woman was not qualified to practise law because of her sex—a bar no amount of training could alter. Certainly, Ruby Clements never questioned her qualifications on the grounds of sex, nor did the Law Society of Alberta. (Petersson, 1997, p. 368)

Table 12.1   Women's Admission to the Bar and Amending Legislation

Province	Women's Admission	Year and Amending Legislation
Ontario	1897 Clara Brett Martin	1892: *Act to Provide for the Admission of Women to the Study and Practice of Law*, SO 1892, c 32 and SO 1895, c 27.
New Brunswick	1907 Mabel Penery French	1901: *Act to Remove the Disability of Women so Far as Relates to the Study and Practice of Law*, SNB 1906, c 5.
British Columbia	1912 Mabel Penery French	1912: *Act to Remove the Disability of Women so Far as Relates to the Study and Practice of Law*, SBC 1912, c 18.
Alberta	1915 Lillian Ruby Clements	1930: *Sex Disqualification Removal Act*, 1930, SA 1930, c 62.
Manitoba	1915 Melrose Sissons	1912: *Act to Amend "An Act to Amend the Law Society Act,"* SM 1912, c 32, s 2.
Saskatchewan	1917 Mary Cathcart	1912: *Act to Amend the Statute Law*, SS 1912-13, c 46, s 27.
Nova Scotia	1917 Frances Fish	1917: *Act to Amend the Barristers and Solicitors Act*, SNS 1917, c 41, s 2.
Prince Edward Island	1926 Roma Stewart	1918: *Act to Amend an Act to Incorporate a Law Society and Amending Acts*, SPEI 1918, c 14, s 6.
Newfoundland	1933 Louisa Maud Saunders	1910: *Act to Amend … [an act] Entitled "Of the Law Society, Barristers and Solicitors,"* SN 1910, c 16.
Quebec	1942 Elizabeth Monk	1941: *Act Respecting the Bar*, SQ 1941, c 56, s 1.

Source: Petersson, S. (1997). Ruby Clements and early women of the Alberta bar. *Canadian Journal of Women and the Law, 9*, appendix I, p. 393.

Three Waves of Women Lawyers in Canada

The first women to practise law in North America did so in the 1870s in the United States. The first women to be admitted to the bar in Canada followed shortly thereafter (see Table 12.1). In Mary Jane Mossman's (2005) analysis of women's entry into the law profession in Canada, she identified three distinct phases, or waves. The pioneering group of women represented the first wave of women to enter the field of law. Some of these first women were not able to officially practise law because they did not receive full accreditation and were not members of the bar. Not until various changes in legislation occurred were women able to fully participate in the practice of law in their respective provinces (Mossman, 2005).

According to Mossman, the second wave of women's entry into the legal profession occurred over a long period of time, from the 1920s to the 1970s in Canada.[5] This period was characterized by a gradual and fairly steady increase in the number of women being admitted to the practice of law in Ontario. However, proportionally speaking, the ratio of women to men in the field of law was still considerably skewed, with males far outnumbering their female counterparts. By 1970, a total of 313 women had been admitted to the bar in Ontario, and one-third of these admissions occurred from 1961 to 1970 (Mossman, 2005).

In the 1970s, a noticeable shift occurred both in the number of women applying to law school and in the number who continued on to practise law (Mossman, 2005). This rapid increase of women's entry into the profession was termed by Mossman as the third wave. In Ontario, by 1986, the ratio of women to men in law schools across the province was approaching parity. The University of Windsor law school has the distinction of being the first, in 1985, to reach this mark (Mossman, 2005).

General Statistics Regarding Women in the Legal Profession

In 1971, only 5 percent of the lawyers in Ontario were female (Ornstein, 2010). According to an article published in April 1992, 20 percent of people practising law in Ontario were women (Federal/Provincial/Territorial Working Group of Attorneys General Officials on Gender Equality in the Canadian Justice System [FPTWG], 1992). By 2014, this percentage had jumped to 53 percent (Federation of Law Societies of Canada, 2017). Statistics from the Federation of Law Societies of Canada (FLSC) indicated that 54.4 percent of those practising law in Canada in 2014 were women[6] (FLSC, 2017).

The influx of women into the field of law in Canada can be further illustrated by looking at articling students (55.8 percent female), and those lawyers with less than 5 years of working in the field (54.7 percent female). A breakdown of Ontario lawyers by sex and age provides more insight into the pattern of age distribution among women lawyers (See Figure 12.1). Far fewer lawyers (10.9 percent) are women in the age 60-to-64 group, while women dominate the under 30 group, where 58.5 percent of this group are women (Ornstein, 2010). It is interesting to note that the large increase seen in the percentage of women in the law in Ontario over the last decade has been largely due to the gains made by racialized women (Ornstein, 2010). Sixteen percent of lawyers under the age of 30 in Ontario are racialized women, compared to the 7 percent of this group who are racialized men (see Figure 12.2).

Examination of the kinds of practice that lawyers in Ontario pursue has indicated that 40.8 percent of women lawyers in Ontario were law firm employees, whereas only 26.9 percent of male lawyers were similarly employed (Ornstein, 2010). Further, it was noted that "gender related segmentation increases dramatically with age" (Ornstein, 2010, p. 25). That is, for lawyers under the age of 35, there is very little difference with respect to their job. However, for those between 35 and 44 years of age, far fewer women (20 percent) are law partners or law firm proprietors than are men (38 percent) (Ornstein, 2010). The divide grows even larger for those between 45 and 54 years: 30 percent of women are partners or proprietors, compared to 55 percent of men (Ornstein, 2010). In addition to the increase in the number of women working in firms, more and more women lawyers were working in government (FPTWG, 1992; Kay, Masuch, & Curry, 2004b; Ornstein, 2004). Just over 21 percent of women lawyers work for government in Ontario, compared to just over 10 percent of men (Ornstein, 2010). Approximately 15 percent of women lawyers work outside of government or law offices, compared to only 8.5 percent of male lawyers (Ornstein, 2010).

Statistics Canada reported that in 2006 nearly half of all employed persons in Canada over the age of 25 were women;[7] however, in stark contrast, only 39 percent of our nation's 77,690 lawyers were female (Ornstein, 2010). In a similar comparison, women represented 38 percent of all lawyers in Ontario in 2006, similar to the percentages of Ontario's women physicians (35.8 percent), university professors (38 percent), and middle-level managers (39.2 percent) (Ornstein, 2010).

FIGURE 12.1   Percentage of Women Lawyers by Age, Ontario, 1971–2006

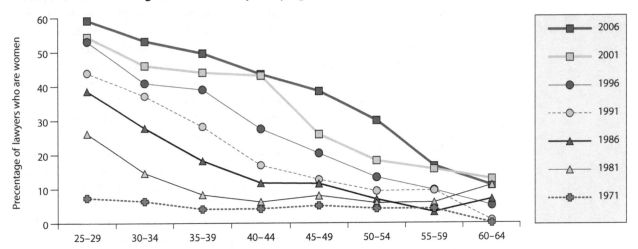

Source: Orenstein, M. (2010). *Racialization and gender of lawyers in Ontario: A report for the law society of Upper Canada.*
Toronto: The Law Society of Upper Canada, p. 19.

FIGURE 12.2   Racialization and Gender of Lawyers by Age, Ontario, 2006

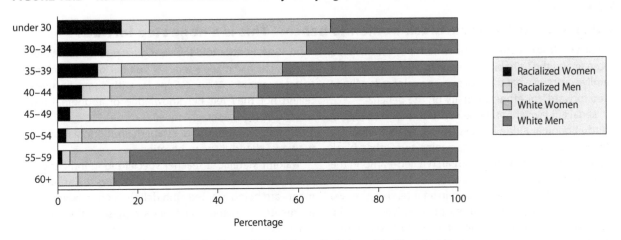

Source: Orenstein, M. (2010). *Racialization and gender of lawyers in Ontario: A report for the law society of Upper Canada.*
Toronto: The Law Society of Upper Canada, p. 20.

Income estimates suggest that what a lawyer earns in Ontario is affected by gender and race, with females and racialized lawyers earning less in salary than men and white lawyers respectively. The mean annual earnings for racialized lawyers in Ontario in 2005 was $101,800, while white lawyers made $176,100 on average that year. The median salary for racialized lawyers was similarly lower than that of white lawyers ($77,400 versus $115,000) (Ornstein, 2010). Men who worked 40 hours or more a week in 2005 made on average $190,800 (median $120,000) compared to $127,900 on average for women working the same number of hours (median income of $97,800) (Ornstein, 2010).

Across Canada, women make up only 37.3 percent of all federally appointed judges (Office of the Commissioner for Federal Judicial Affairs [OCFJA], 2017). While 44.4 percent of those serving on the Supreme Court of Canada are women, only 20 percent of judges appointed to the Federal Tax Court are women (OCFJA, 2017). Recent research looking at the importance of the judicial appointment process has uncovered some interesting results with respect to women's representation in provincial courts (Crandall, 2014). In a review of judicial appointments in Ontario from 1972 to 2012, Crandall (2014) found that following the introduction of a new judicial appointment system in 1989, the appointment of female judges increased by 5 percent. Further, Crandall (2014) noted that "the data indicate that the province's judicial nominating system has been more successful than the federal government's judicial review committee system at appointing women judges and that the Liberal Party and the New Democratic Party (NDP) are more likely to appoint women as judges in Ontario than the Conservative parties" (p. 188). The results of the study suggest that the active recruitment of women is critical to increasing their representation among the judiciary. Nova Scotia has recently made headlines by appointing the first Mi'kmaq woman and a third black woman to the provincial and family courts, as noted in Box 12.1.

BOX 12.1

N.S. appoints Mi'kmaq, black women to bench: "This is a huge step forward"

HALIFAX—Nova Scotia has appointed the first Mi'kmaq woman and the third black woman to the provincial and family courts, in what the province's premier calls a "huge step forward" for ethnic diversity on the bench.

Legal aid lawyer Catherine Benton becomes only the third aboriginal judge in Nova Scotia, while Ronda van der Hoek, a public prosecutor, joins two other black women—Corinne Sparks and Jean Whalen—among the 73 full-time judges in the province.

Premier Stephen McNeil said in an interview the two new judges will provide added perspectives from the black and indigenous population in a court system that needs to reflect the makeup of the general population.

"I believe this is a huge step forward. They have had distinguished careers in making sure minority voices are being heard, that Mi'kmaq rights are being protected, and their cultures will be reflected in the decisions they make," he said.

Benton is well known within legal circles as an advocate for racial and ethnic diversity in the courts, having pushed from the earliest days of her career for a stronger role for indigenous lawyers in the court system.

She worked as a researcher with the Union of Nova Scotia Indians and the Mi'kmaq Grand Council before getting her law degree from Dalhousie in 1993.

In 1994, Benton told the aboriginal publication Windspeaker she had made a series of fruitless job applications to firms around Atlantic Canada, with some partners telling her they felt her knowledge of aboriginal law wouldn't be an asset.

"I think it's important to establish an aboriginal justice network," she told the publication.

Naiomi Metallic, a teacher specialized in indigenous law at Dalhousie's Schulich law school, says the appointments are being greeted with delight among advocates for greater indigenous and black representation in the legal system.

"I'm elated .... We've been saying in the media there needs to be more diverse appointments and it appears that hasn't fallen on deaf ears," she said.

Van der Hoek, from Windsor, has practised law for 19 years and also worked with Nova Scotia Legal Aid in Windsor and Halifax after graduating from Dalhousie Law School.

She is the third black judge in the province's lower and superior courts.

Van der Hoek and Benton also bring the family and provincial courts a step closer to gender parity, with a total of 15 full-time female judges, compared to 20 full-time, male judges.

Robert Wright, a Halifax social worker who has been a member of provincial advisory committees for judicial selections, said the appointments are welcome.

But he cautions the justice system's treatment of racial minorities is still flawed, pointing to the release of police figures showing that black men were three times more likely to be street checked in Halifax in the first 10 months of 2016.

"Do (the appointments) demonstrate ... that the province clearly understands and is responsive and is completely on side with the issues of indigenous and African Nova Scotians? I would say no, we still have a long way to go," he said in interview.

However, McNeil said he intends to continue broadening diversity in both government and the courts.

"I look forward to continuing to make sure the institutions that matter, the judiciary and government, reflect who we are and that every Nova Scotian can see themselves in those institutions," he said.

Source: Tutton, M. (2017, January 23). N.S. appoints Mi'kmaq, black women to bench: "This is a huge step forward." The Canadian Press. Retrieved from http://www.news1130.com/2017/01/23/nova-scotia-justice-minister-appoints-first-mkmaq-woman-to-the-judiciary/.

Women Lawyers in Ontario

A number of publications have been devoted to an analysis of the role of women in the legal profession in Canada (Edward, Davies, Presser, & Stewart, 2013; Kay, Alarie, & Adjei, 2013; Kay, Masuch, & Curry, 2004a, 2004b; Madon & Doob, 2016; Ornstein, 2004). Across Canada, provincial law societies publish statistics about their members in their annual reports and in reports written by consultants hired by the law societies to address specific issues, such as diversity and equality (Kay et al., 2004a, 2004b; Ornstein, 2004). Reports are also published by various provincial county law associations, district law associations, and the Canadian Bar Association. An examination of published reports from the Law Society of Upper Canada (LSUC) provides a sense of women's current role in the legal profession in Canada, as illustrated using a sample of lawyers from Ontario. Although the LSUC studies are looking only at lawyers in Ontario (and thus are not representative of all lawyers in Canada), the kinds of issues faced by women lawyers in Ontario are likely to be shared by other women lawyers across the country. Ontario was of particular interest because of the many lawyers employed in the financial capital of Canada (Toronto) and in the largest centre of federal government (Ottawa).

Over approximately the past three decades, the Law Society of Upper Canada has commissioned a series of reports focused on women in the law. The first report, published in 1989, *Women in the Legal Profession*, was commissioned by the LSUC's Subcommittee on Women in the Legal Profession (Kay et al., 2004b). This report initially identified some significant differences in Ontario in the way women and men were represented across the various fields of law, their work settings, and their positions held (Kay et al., 2004b).

Following this first report, *Transitions in the Ontario Legal Profession* was commissioned. This study entailed a survey of the membership of the LSUC. The focus of this report was to look at "job changes, promotions, career switches, and departures from law practice" and to compare the career patterns of men and women (Kay et al., 2004b, p. 2). This survey was the first of four such surveys that, taken together, constituted a longitudinal approach to the study of a cohort of Ontario lawyers who were called to the bar between 1975 and 1990 (Kay et al., 2004b).

The second survey, published in 1996, *Barriers and Opportunities Within Law*, focused on women who had entered the practice of law in large numbers and who then faced significant barriers to advancement within the profession (Kay et al., 2004b). The study examined the relationships between gender and the various types of practice, earnings, partnership opportunities, fields of law, attitudes toward the profession, challenges to the profession, and job satisfaction (Kay et al., 2004b). The third survey, *Turning Points and Transitions: Women's Careers in the Legal Profession*, explored the survey data from 2002, integrating these data with data from the previous two surveys (Kay et al., 2004b). A fourth survey, completed in 2009, rounded out this longitudinal study. A final report, entitled *Leaving Law and Barriers to Re-entry: A Study of Departures from and Re-entries to Private Practice*, included data collected from almost 1,600 lawyers in Ontario (Kay et al., 2013).

These studies provide a picture of the emerging careers of both men and women lawyers over the past few decades in Ontario. Interestingly, the cohort of study corresponds to a time period during which women were entering the law profession in greater and greater numbers. The surveys (administered in 1990, 1996, 2002, and 2009) have provided very detailed information on lawyers in Ontario and the differences between men and women in this field.

Although we have seen "impressive advances in the status and mobility of women in the legal profession," these exist alongside "sizeable gaps that persist between men and women in remuneration, promotional opportunities, and levels of job satisfaction" (Kay et al., 2004b, p. 1). The authors noted the considerable challenges for both men and women in the field of law, including balancing career and family obligations, inflexibility of the workplace, discrimination, and blocked mobility (Kay et al., 2004b).

Men continue to be more likely to be partners than women in Ontario (Kay et al., 2004b). Only 65 percent of women working in law firms in Ontario are partners, compared with 78 percent of men. In addition, when the type of partner is explored, just more than half of the women are considered senior partners, whereas more than 70 percent of men are senior partners. Women (40 percent) are far more likely to be junior partners or to be considered salaried or part-time partners than are men (28 percent) (Kay et al., 2004b). No doubt related to these statistics is the observation that men tend to be more satisfied with the partnership policies at their firm than are the women.

Women are more likely to work as lawyers in government (16 percent) compared with men (12 percent). In terms of the various fields of law, women are more likely to work in "other" fields of law (23 percent), in family and divorce law (18 percent), and in corporate and commercial law (11 percent), whereas men are more often found working in civil litigation and real estate law (19 percent and 17 percent, respectively), and 14 percent of men work in corporate and commercial law (Kay et al., 2004b). For an illustration of the main fields of law practised by men and women in 2002, see Figure 12.3.

In terms of earnings, women's remuneration continues to pale in comparison with that of their male counterparts (Kay et al., 2004b), even when such factors as practice setting and years of experience are taken into account. In government settings, "men earn on average $123,818, compared with $119,757 among women," whereas "among law firm partners, men earn $296,830 and women earn $263,549" (Kay et al., 2004b, p. 107). Women are also not rewarded at the same rate as men in terms of professional responsibilities. Kay et al. (2004b) reported that women are not as likely to own their own business, to be in management, or to be in positions where they supervise others.

When questioned about their job satisfaction, women lawyers appeared to be less satisfied than male lawyers in Ontario (Kay et al., 2004b). In a later examination of the role of job satisfaction and leaving the legal profession, Kay et al. (2013) did not find any statistically significant gender differences. They did report that there was a relationship

FIGURE 12.3   Main Fields of Law Practised in 2002 in Ontario

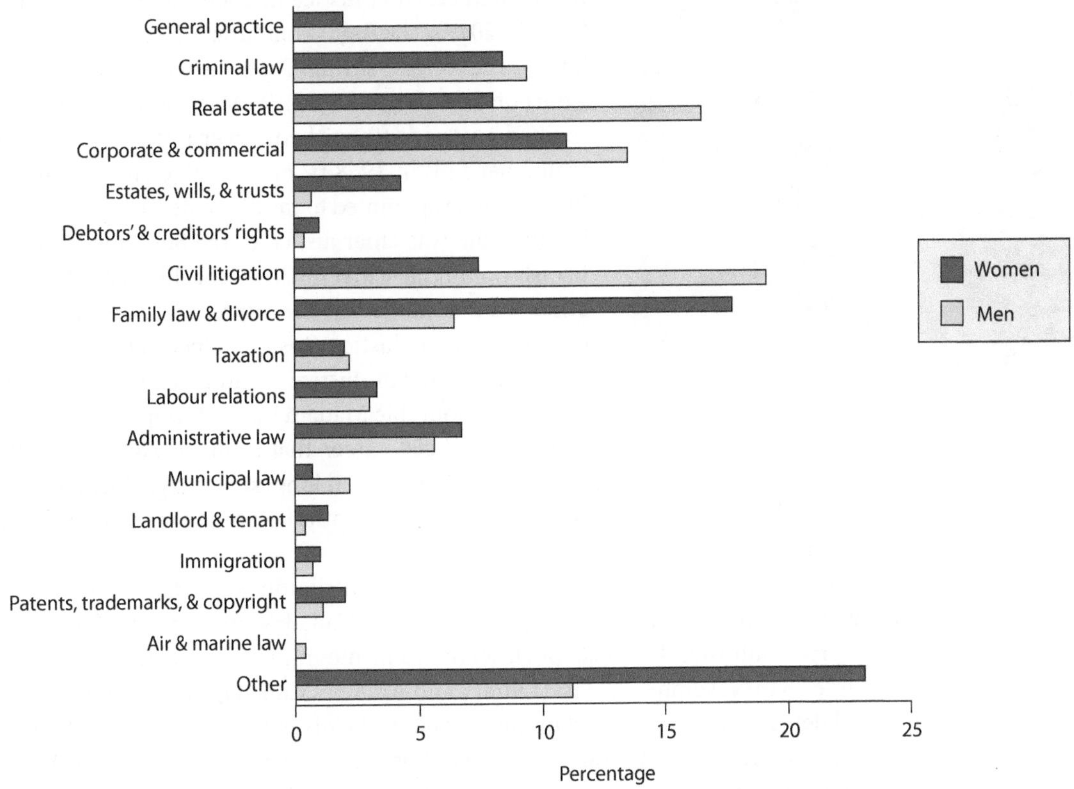

Source: Kay, F., Masuch, C., & Curry, P. (2004). *Turning points and transitions: Women's careers in the legal profession—A report to the Law Society of Upper Canada.* Toronto: Law Society of Upper Canada, p. 25.

between having satisfaction with "power-track" (characterized by earnings, promotions, and prestige) and a reduction in the risk that a lawyer would leave the profession. They found no such relationship with other measures (collegiality, content) of job satisfaction (Kay et al., 2013).

With respect to the main challenges confronting those working in the legal profession in Ontario, a number of issues tend to be of particular concern to women: balancing family and career, equality for women in the profession, alternative careers and part-time work arrangements, and expanding family responsibilities (Kay et al., 2004b). The LSUC reports looking at the role of women in the legal profession in Ontario suggest that despite some headway in gaining a foothold in this historically male-dominated profession, challenges continue to face women lawyers in Ontario (Kay et al., 2004b; Kay et al., 2013).

A Few More Firsts for Women in the Law in Canada

As noted in Chapter 1, the Supreme Court of Canada has final authority over all private and public law in Canada. This court has jurisdiction over matters in all of the areas of the law, including criminal and civil law and constitutional and administrative law. The Supreme Court of Canada comprises a chief justice and eight additional judges. For the

The Right Honourable Beverley McLachlin was the longest sitting Chief Justice of the Supreme Court of Canada (2000–2017).

first time in the history of the Supreme Court, a woman was appointed chief justice in 2000 (Supreme Court of Canada, 2017). The Right Honourable Beverley McLachlin was the longest sitting Chief Justice of the Supreme Court of Canada (2000–2017) (MacCharles, 2016), and she had a very distinguished career in the law. She obtained her LLB in 1968 from the University of Alberta. Prior to being appointed to the Supreme Court of Canada in 1989, she was chief justice of the Supreme Court of British Columbia. Chief Justice McLachlin sat with three other women judges on the Supreme Court: the Honourable Madam Justice Rosalie Silberman Abella, the Honourable Madam Justice Andromache Karakatsanis, and the Honourable Madam Justice Suzanne Côté. After a 36-year judicial career that spanned 28 years on the top court—17 of them as the country's first female, and longest-serving, chief justice—Chief McLachlin retired December 15, 2017, nine months before she reached the mandatory retirement age of 75.

Canadian history books will make note of the contributions of a famous Canadian female lawyer in politics: Kim Campbell, who was Canada's first (and, to date, only) female prime minister. Kim Campbell served as prime minister for about six months, from June 25 to November 3, 1993 (Library and Archives Canada, 2010). Following her political defeat, she accepted a fellowship at Harvard University, where she taught prior to appointment as Canada's consul general in Los Angeles, California, in 1996 (Library and Archives Canada, 2010). Kim Campbell has been described as a "sought-after speaker and authority on leadership, gender issues and democratization," and in 2014 was appointed as the founding principal of the Peter Lougheed Leadership College at the University of Alberta (Alary, 2014, p. 7).

Women Working as Lawyers in Canada: A Statistical Overview

Unfortunately, a dearth of information is available on specific statistics for women working as defence lawyers in Canada. Part of the problem in obtaining these sorts of estimates relates to the nature of the work. In particular, women practising as defence counsel are predominantly working on their own. Although the various provincial law societies and legal associations all produce annual reports, and some have commissioned specific reports related to equity and diversity, the level of statistical detail regarding their memberships varies considerably. As a result, the number of women in Canada working as defence lawyers is impossible to easily identify, unlike the situation for judges and Crowns, who are government employees, and thus detailed statistics on their numbers are readily available. Recently there has been an attempt to understand why the retention of women practising criminal law is problematic. Madon and Doob (2016) identified a number of challenges specific to women that may have an impact on their decision to leave criminal defence work. In particular, they found that there were financial difficulties (taking time off to have children, unpredictable incomes, low rates of pay, and delayed payment associated with legal aid certificates), unpredictable work hours, as well as the perception that judges and other court workers treated women differently than men that may tip the scale toward leaving this sort of practice (Madon & Doob, 2016).

According to estimates for 2000–2001, "female lawyers accounted for 43 percent of all permanent and contract lawyers (staff lawyers) employed by criminal prosecutions services," which represented an increase of 5 percent since 1998–1999 (Snowball, 2002, p. 5).

Other Occupations in the Criminal Justice System

In addition to lawyers and judges, some of the traditional jobs associated with the court process include court translators, probation officers, special court constables, paralegals, and law clerks (Goff, 2008). In recent years, changes in the court system have resulted in a number of new occupations linked directly or indirectly to the courts and courthouses.

Specialty courts, such as domestic violence courts and drug courts, have created new positions for support workers (Goff, 2008; Roberts & Grossman, 2008). Intake workers, liaison officers, and onsite support workers have also emerged in the field. Many of these jobs appear to be performed by women (Snowball, 2002). Women are particularly evident working in areas dealing with domestic violence and young offenders, and many are employed as staff in victim witness offices at courthouses and Victim Crisis Assistance and Referral Services (VCARS) at police stations. The jobs outlined above do not comprise an exhaustive list, but are intended to give the reader a sampling of the variety of jobs currently in the criminal justice field.

Women Lawyers in the Criminal Courts

Shakespeare's character of Portia is frequently referred to in discussions on the role of women lawyers in the courtroom (Leiper, 2006; van Wormer & Bartollas, 2007). As noted by van Wormer and Bartollas (2007), "besides Shakespeare's Portia, who, disguised as a young man, brought a soft touch to the law in her famous 'the quality of mercy is not strained' exhortation (Shakespeare, 1600/1970:4.1.182), few literary or historical examples of women advocates in court exist" (p. 341).

Take a moment to consider that statement. Whether you are a fan of Shakespeare or not, in films and literature, both fiction and non-fiction, few women lawyers exist as role models or heroines. Although Nancy Drew revolutionized the male-dominated detective world in fiction, no women appear to have been portrayed as groundbreakers in the legal field. Classic television programs, such as *Perry Mason* and *Matlock*, always showed women working alongside male lawyers in more traditional roles, as assistants or clerical support. This stereotype began to change in the late 1970s, with the introduction of secondary characters, such as Phyllide Erskin-Brown, QC, in *Rumpole at the Old Bailey*. Only in the last few decades or so have television programs, such as *How to Get Away with Murder*, *LA Law*, *Ally McBeal*, and *Law and Order*, and movies, such as *Legally Blonde*, *The Pelican Brief*, and *The Client*, routinely depicted and more explicitly focused on women working in the court system as lawyers and judges. In the recent style of reality TV, Judge Judy has entertained all with her sarcastic and in-your-face style of adjudicating disputes. This shift to show more women in the legal profession on television and in movies is reflective of, and parallels, the reality of the growth of women in this field.

Not reflective of the Canadian criminal justice system, however, is the American-style lawyering depicted in the mass media, which has led many people to assume that lawyers in Canadian criminal courts argue cases in a similar manner. Thus, Canadian lawyers are often subjected to questions about their roles based on people's understanding of US court proceedings. In Canada, however, lawyers follow a more conservative,

British-style approach to advocacy and litigation, which is a far cry from the drama seen daily on our televisions and in movie theatres.

Many interesting and rewarding jobs have been created as a result of the need for some lawyers to work on a part-time basis. More women lawyers are employed on a part-time basis than are men (Kay et al., 2004b). Of the following part-time positions, not all receive salaries or other forms of remuneration; as such, they do not appeal to all people:

- Benchers for the Law Society of Upper Canada[8]
- Commissioners for inquiries
- Ombudspersons
- Political positions and ministerial appointments
- Members of review boards and tribunals
- Small Claims Court judges
- Judicial advisory committee members
- Elected positions in the various associations that assist lawyers in provinces and the country, such as the County and District Law Presidents' Association (CDLPA) and the Canadian Bar Association (CBA), or, in Ontario, the Ontario Bar Association (OBA)

Challenges Faced by Women Working in the Courts

As noted at the beginning of this chapter, Clara Brett Martin was the first woman to be admitted to the bar in Ontario (Backhouse, 1985, 1992). Although she was clearly a pioneer in this field, her success did not come without a cost. Reportedly, Martin "had to put up with the curiosity and scrutiny of the profession and members of the public generally throughout her career" (Backhouse, 1985, p. 33). In one instance, a newspaper reporter for the *Toronto Star Weekly* made a point of emphasizing not her skills, but commented in a sexist manner that the arrangement of her office did not match that of a male lawyer (Backhouse, 1985).

Despite the rise in the number of women entering Canadian law schools, and their subsequent entry into the workforce, not all women continue to work in the legal profession. Proportionally more women leave the law profession than do men (Brockman, 1994; Kay, 1997; Kay et al., 2004a, 2004b; Sheehy & McIntyre, 2006). Some authors have hypothesized that significant retention issues might affect women differently from men (FPTWG, 1992; Hagan & Kay, 2007; Kay, 1997; Leiper, 2006; Mossman, 2005). Many challenges faced by women lawyers cut across the various fields of law; however, this chapter's focus is to explore these issues as they pertain to women working in the criminal courts.

▶ WHAT DO YOU THINK?

Why do you think so many women are leaving the law profession? What kinds of changes do you think that law firms could make that would encourage more women to remain in their chosen field? Follow this link to read the article by Andrea Lekushoff (2014) entitled "Where Have All the Female Lawyers Gone?" http://www.huffingtonpost.ca/andrea-lekushoff/female-lawyers-canada_b_5000415.html.

Career Development and Career Path

In recent years, women in Canada have been entering law school at the same rate as men and in some cases at an even higher rate (Brockman, 2001, cited in Krakauer & Chen, 2003; Wilson, 1993, cited in Krakauer and Chen, 2003; Ornstein, 2004). However, when working in the field, women continue to encounter gender-based barriers, which are thought to contribute to the higher rate at which women leave the practice of law (Krakauer & Chen, 2003). These gender-based barriers faced by today's women lawyers are not the kinds of legal hurdles that confronted Clara Brett Martin, but are thought to be more informal and structural in their form and, in many ways, more insidious (Brockman, 2001, cited in Krakauer & Chen, 2003). The barriers that women lawyers face in achieving equality with their male peers include but are not limited to "the allocation of work, opportunities for advancement, income differentials, lack of accommodation for family responsibilities, and sexual harassment" (Krakauer & Chen, 2003, p. 66).

Women appear to enter law school for reasons similar to those of men, but because women frequently make different choices at graduation, their career paths become more divergent from men as time passes (Kay, 1997; Krakauer & Chen, 2003; Leiper, 1997). Most men, on leaving law school, will article, qualify to practise law, work as an associate for six or seven years, and then become a partner in a law firm (Krakauer & Chen, 2003). This kind of linear career path is typical for male lawyers (Krakauer & Chen, 2003; Leiper, 1997). However, some have noted that career paths appear to be more fluid now, compared with the past (Kay, 1997; Kay et al., 2004b). In fact, Kay et al. (2013) report that "the careers of contemporary lawyers appear to be characterized by more job changes, discontinuity and movement between sectors of practice than is commonly assumed" (p. iii).

Women lawyers do not tend to have linear careers. Research has shown that women's career paths within the profession tend to be more lateral: they have more career interruptions and are more likely to be unemployed at some point in their career (Kay et al., 2004b; Krakauer & Chen, 2003). Women who work in large firms are more likely to have linear careers (Krakauer & Chen, 2003; Leiper, 1997). Research has shown that "female lawyers are underrepresented in the partnership ranks, overrepresented in the public sector, and more likely to be working in marginal positions or leaving law altogether" (Krakauer & Chen, 2003, p. 68). Female lawyers' integration into the field of law has been described as marginal at best (Kay, 1997). Male lawyers tend to make a career change to pursue a better opportunity, whereas women tend to make a career change for personal or family reasons (Krakauer & Chen, 2003).

Kay et al. (2013) examined the careers of male and female lawyers in Ontario, why they left the profession, and the barriers that they experienced when they returned to work in the law. Interestingly, they found that on average, the lawyers in their cohort of study had three professional positions across the course of their careers to date (Kay et al., 2013). Just over a third of their sample experienced some gaps between these professional positions. The average length of the gaps experienced by the women lawyers (6.14 months) was statistically significantly longer than their male counterparts (2.89 months) (Kay et al., 2013). There were gender differences in terms of the reasons given for the gaps, with women reporting that caring for children was the main reason, while men were more likely to report travel, unemployment, and furthering their education as the reasons for the gaps (Kay et al., 2013).

A rather large percentage (44 percent) of their sample reported that they left private practice at some time, with more women (52 percent) leaving than men (35 percent) (Kay et al., 2013). Additionally, it was clear from their analysis that women left private practice at a faster rate than did men (Kay et al., 2013). From their analysis, the researchers noted that there were four general themes that emerged when it came to explaining why the lawyers in their sample left private practice. The first general explanation was that of family responsibilities. Family pressures were paramount for many in making their decision to leave private practice. Further, it was not always the case that the lawyers left the profession to stay at home to raise children; rather, for some it was the need to strike more of a work/life balance that led to this decision (Kay et al., 2013). A second explanation for leaving related to the organizational structure of the firm. For example, it was noted that the pressure to increase revenues and billable hours was a reason for some to leave. A third reason given for leaving was to pursue other interests. In effect, these individuals were looking for a break from practising law that entailed a lifestyle change or a pursuit of a different career. The final reason given by some who left was burnout. For these individuals, the stress and negative impact on their health may have led to their decision to leave private practice (Kay et al., 2013). The authors noted that policy changes like flexible full-time hours and improved parental leave could reduce the risk that lawyers will leave private practice (Kay et al., 2013).

Some who leave private practice will return one day. Kay et al. (2013) found that 18 percent of women who left, and 15 percent of men, eventually returned to private practice. The barriers that they faced to re-entry into the profession could be lessened through the implementation of mentoring programs; educational programs and upgrading courses or seminars; more part-time and volunteer positions; recruitment and lawyer-firm matching services; increased workplace flexibility (job sharing, working from home); reduced or graduated fees for licensing, insurance, and memberships; and counselling (Kay et al, 2013).

Although the impact of gender on career choice has been studied, in comparison, relatively little research has looked at the impact of gender and race on career choice. Early in their careers, minority women can be seen to be "heavily overrepresented in entry-level positions in government, legal clinics, and legal education" (Krakauer & Chen, 2003, p. 70). According to a report published by the Canadian Bar Association (1993, cited in Krakauer & Chen, 2003), minority women who decided to pursue public service work thought that their career choices were more limited, right from the start of their careers, as compared with their white peer group (Krakauer & Chen, 2003). Their decision to work in the public sector was heavily influenced by their belief that they would face fewer barriers there than in the private sector (CBA, 1993, cited in Krakauer & Chen, 2003).

In a more recent study, Ornstein (2010) examined racialization and gender in lawyers in Ontario. While there has been an increase in the number of visible minority lawyers, the growth has lagged behind the growth of women in the profession by about 20 years (Ornstein, 2010). Estimates from 1986 show about 3 percent of lawyers between the ages of 25 and 34 were visible minorities. This percentage had increased to 20 percent in 2006 (Ornstein, 2010). Although their numbers are on the rise, Ornstein (2010) reported that both women and visible minority lawyers were less likely to be partners in law firms, and were more frequently found among law firm employees and associates, and working in the government. In addition, both women and visible minorities were found to earn less than white male lawyers (Ornstein, 2010). Further, the gap in income is even more exaggerated for visible minorities than for women. Racialized lawyers between the ages of 25 and 29 years earn $4,000 less (median difference) than white male lawyers. This gap jumps to a median difference of $40,000 by the time they are in the 40 to 44 years age bracket (Ornstein, 2010). Ornstein (2010) noted that this does not give a complete picture of the wage gap earnings for all visible minority groups, because "there are too few middle aged and senior visible minority and Aboriginal lawyers to accurately estimate their earnings" (p. 35).

▶ WHAT DO YOU THINK?

Why do you think that the growth in the number of racialized lawyers in Ontario has lagged behind the growth in women lawyers by 20 years? What are some possible explanations for this?

Some have questioned whether women lawyers might be treated as tokens within the law firms where they work (MacCorquodale & Jensen, 1993). Despite being a US study, MacCorquodale and Jensen's research is worth noting because the issues identified are likely salient for Canadian female lawyers. The researchers found evidence to support the existence of tokenism as illustrated by heightened visibility, polarization, and stereotyping. Because tokens are usually few in number and considered a novelty, they often have heightened visibility, which can put them under considerable performance pressure and can lead to either overachievement or underachievement (MacCorquodale & Jensen, 1993).

Polarization is seen as the differences that seem to be exaggerated between the dominant group and the tokens. An example of polarization can be seen in the loyalty tests that tokens may be subjected to and expected to tolerate: women lawyers may have to put up with sexist jokes, swearing, and sexual innuendoes (MacCorquodale & Jensen, 1993). Stereotyping may also occur, in that women lawyers may be expected to fill a certain role, such as that of pet, mother, or seductress. When this role is not fulfilled, she may be regarded as tough or bitchy (MacCorquodale & Jensen, 1993). In terms of heightened visibility, the women noted they were more likely to be complimented for characteristics not related to achievement (such as appearance and clothes) than for achievement-related characteristics (such as their legal reputation or the way they handled a case). Women were also more likely to be seen as "having less credibility in professional settings" (MacCorquodale & Jensen, 1993, p. 590). When it came to polarization, the women reported that they heard more sexist jokes and remarks than did the men. Evidence of stereotyping was found in the women's reports of being patronized, being called by their first names, and being questioned about whether they were lawyers (MacCorquodale & Jensen, 1993).

Earnings and Market Sector

On average, women lawyers earn less than male lawyers, which has been well documented in the literature (Hagan, 1990; Kay & Hagan, 1995; Kay et al., 2004a, 2004b; Robson & Wallace, 2001; Stager & Foot, 1988). Although similar wage discrepancies are also the case in other professions, this gender-based earnings differential seems more offensive in a profession that professes to seek "justice for all." Inspection of the mottos for a selection of law societies in Canada reveals their ideology of equality and justice: the Law Society of Upper Canada's "Let Right Prevail," the Law Society of British Columbia's "Law is the king of a free people," and the Law Society of Newfoundland and Labrador's "Pro lege, rege, grege"—For the law, the King, and the people.

Although women have made considerable strides in the law profession in Canada in the last 30 years, they still face many obstacles to equality, including their lower earnings. To the credit of the law societies in Canada, many have struck gender and equality committees and published reports in an attempt to address these disparities (Law Society of Alberta, 2006; LSUC, 2004, 2006). The purpose of these committees is to acknowledge the gender inequality and other issues related to diversity and to develop and implement policy and practice guidelines to address these inequities (LSUC, 1997, 2003).

As noted in the previous section, women who work in large firms tend to have a more linear career path (Krakauer & Chen, 2003; Leiper, 1997). The choice surrounding where a lawyer decides to work (large firm versus small firm versus sole proprietorship) is related to the expected remuneration. Many perceive that working in larger firms leads to more prestige—and more money (Kay & Hagan, 1995). While an articling student in a large Toronto firm might expect to be paid $1,300 per week, those in government articling positions might be paid between $700 and $900 per week, and those in legal clinics or small firms may earn only $400 or $500 a week (Navarrete, 2002, cited in Krakauer & Chen, 2003). These disparities in salaries continue throughout lawyers' careers, resulting in very large differences between the annual salaries of those who work in the large firms and those who choose a less prestigious career path, such as in government (Kay et al., 2004a, 2004b; Krakauer & Chen, 2003).

Robson and Wallace (2001) studied gender inequality in terms of lawyers' earnings in Canada. They proposed the human capital theory, in which the gender gap in earnings is likely due to "gender differences in education, training and experience and as the outcome of both efficiency and choice" (p. 76). Men's increased earnings are explained as reward because they put more investment toward developing their human capital and are rewarded for making the choice to put a greater priority on their careers (Kay & Hagan, 1995; Becker, 1991, cited in Robson & Wallace, 2001). On the other hand, women in the legal profession are seen to gravitate to jobs that, despite allowing for more of a balance in terms of work and family, "offer the lowest returns on their human capital investments" (Robson & Wallace, 2001, p. 76).

Research on lawyers in western Canada has shown that, although the sex of a lawyer does not have a direct effect on earnings, women lawyers are perceived to be disadvantaged in a number of areas related to the amount of money they can make (Robson & Wallace, 2001). Generally, a lawyer's income is determined by firm-specific variables, such as hours worked, protegé status, and general law experience (Robson & Wallace, 2001). Lawyers in small firms tend to earn less than those in larger firms, and exposure to corporate clients is associated with a higher income (Robson & Wallace, 2001). Not surprisingly, those working in the larger firms are more likely to have corporate clients and to specialize in the more prestigious types of law. Robson and Wallace (2001) found that women lawyers earned only 62 percent of their male counterparts' income. The researchers noted that women lawyers differed from the men in a number of areas: the women worked shorter hours, had less experience practising law, were less likely to have preschool-aged kids, and had less autonomy.

As Kay and Hagan (1995) summarized, a body of literature has documented the earnings differentials that have existed between male and female lawyers over the years. Although these studies highlighted the existence of pay inequity, they did not explore why such disparity existed:

> An early study by White (1967) sampled men and women from the graduating classes of 1956 through 1965 of 134 American law schools and discovered that "the males make a lot more money than do the females" (p. 1057). A study of Harvard law school graduates (Glancy 1970: 25) found fewer than 12 per cent of the women as compared to 57 per cent of the men earned in excess of $20,000 annually. Furthermore, a study (Vogt 1987) conducted in 1985 of seven north-eastern US law schools reports that among graduates 11 years out and in the same size firms, men earn on average $75,000 and women $46,500. In Canada, a five-year follow-up study (Adam and Baer, 1984: 39) of the 1974 graduates of Ontario law schools reports that women graduates earn on average about $3,000 a year less than their male counterparts. (Kay & Hagan, 1995, p. 280)

In a Canadian study, Hagan (1990) found that male lawyers earned more than women lawyers; when this difference was examined, gender discrimination accounted for more than one-quarter of this difference. Hagan (1990) noted support for the notion of gender-specific mobility ladders in the legal profession. In a modification of a taxonomy of class relations developed by Wright et al. (1982, cited in Hagan, 1990), Hagan proposed a way to conceptualize positions within the field of law. Hagan's resultant taxonomy looked at such factors as "ownership relations, number of employees, authority, participation in decision making, work autonomy, and hierarchical position" and conceptualized the various positions as rungs on a hierarchical ladder (p. 837).

The mobility ladder was thought to "be conceived as having steps which form a power hierarchy that extends across private practice, government and corporate settings" (Kay & Hagan, 1995, p. 284). The highest rung on the ladder consisted of the managing partners in large and medium-sized firms, the "managerial bourgeoisie" (Hagan, 1990, p. 837), who had ownership of the firm, sanctioned others, exercised task authority, formed the decision-making group for the firm, and supervised at least two levels of subordinates (excluding secretaries) below them. The next rung down comprised the "supervisory bourgeoisie" (p. 837), the non-managing partners in large and medium-sized firms. These individuals had no firm-related decision-making role, did not sanction others, and did not have task authority over those below them. The lowest rungs on the mobility ladder were held for what Hagan referred to as "semiautonomous and nonautonomous lawyers" (p. 838), who were not responsible for any kind of supervision of others and had only secretaries below them in the hierarchy.

The existence of gender-specific mobility ladders is related not only to career path but also to earnings, because the mobility ladders are thought to lead to an income hierarchy stratified by gender (Hagan, 1990). In his study of Toronto lawyers, Hagan found that men made $40,000 more than women and noted a widening of the gender gap as it related to income; that is, as men made more and more money, women's earnings also increased, but not at the same rate as men's.

In a more recent publication, Kay and Hagan (1995) investigated the gendered inequality of earnings in terms of human capital theory, labour segmentation theory, and

Marxist theories. Even after taking into account such factors as differences in specializations, positions within a firm, and different employment settings, a gendered gap in earnings was evident. As noted earlier, human capital theory postulates that the decisions that men and women make concerning their careers will influence their earnings: those who choose to invest more in their human capital will reap the rewards in an increased income, compared with those who choose to invest less in their human capital (Kay & Hagan, 1995).

A labour segmentation approach to earning differentials involves acknowledging the differences in types of employers. Dual labour market theories posit the existence of a core labour market, which offers greater pay, more job stability and security, good working conditions, and plenty of opportunity for advancement (Kay & Hagan, 1995). The secondary or less preferable peripheral labour market comprises more unstable work, where earnings are lower, benefits are fewer, working conditions are poorer, employee turnover is frequent, and staff have minimal opportunity for advancement (Kay & Hagan, 1995). In this conceptualization, women's lower earnings are reflective of their higher concentration in the peripheral labour market. On the other hand, a Marxist framework takes more of a relational approach to investigate the impact of power and authority.

Kay and Hagan (1995) noted their intention to "introduce an analysis of the role of authority and power dimensions to explanations of the gender differences in earnings" (p. 284). They proposed the existence of three market sectors for the law: private practice, corporate settings, and government. Within these sectors, the researchers found that women were less likely than men to work in private practice, equally as likely as men to work in corporate settings, and more likely than men to work in government (Kay & Hagan, 1995). In addition, they found women were more likely to work in large or mid-sized firms, but men were more likely than women to be found working as sole practitioners or in small firms (Kay & Hagan, 1995).

Kay and Hagan's results supported the human capital theory: men received more reward for their human capital acquisitions and were able to "reap greater income rewards from experience and from elite law school education than women" (Kay & Hagan, 1995, p. 304). They also found evidence of sex segregation both between and within the different market sectors of the profession, which, they noted, served to disadvantage women. So, although lawyers in the core labour market (private practice) were at an advantage over lawyers in the second tier (corporate settings), men in private practice showed economic gains over the women in this sector. Similarly, in the second-tier settings, both men and women showed economic gain over those in the peripheral sector (government). But again, men in the second tier showed economic gains over women in that same tier. Notably, the researchers observed an apparent "amplification of earning differentials with movements to higher positions of the mobility ladder" (Kay & Hagan, 1995, p. 304). That is, as women moved up the mobility ladder, the disparity between their earnings and those of men at the same level increased.

► **WHAT DO YOU THINK?**

The gender wage gap among lawyers is well known. Do you think there will ever be income parity between male and female lawyers? What do you think could be done to lessen or even eliminate the gender wage gap?

Job Satisfaction and Gender

The "paradox of the contented female worker" has been described as the observation that "although women have jobs with lower pay and less authority than men, they are equally satisfied with their jobs and employers" (Phelan, 1994, p. 95). This paradox has been investigated in samples of lawyers (Chiu, 1998; Hagan & Kay, 2007; Mueller & Wallace, 1996). Mueller and Wallace (1996) noted that such a paradox with respect to job satisfaction did not exist for female lawyers when the correct model specifications were made.[9] The researchers did, however, report a paradox with respect to pay satisfaction (Mueller & Wallace, 1996). Chiu (1998), in a sample of 326 American lawyers, found that the women lawyers (who had similar career expectations as the men) reported lower job satisfaction. Chiu concluded that the difference in job satisfaction was due to inequality in opportunity.

More recently, this notion of a paradox has been investigated by Hagan and Kay (2007), who pointed out the overall support in the literature for an apparent paradox with respect to job satisfaction among women lawyers (Chambers, 1989, cited in Hagan & Kay, 2007; Dinovitzer et al., 2004, cited in Hagan & Kay, 2007; Kay et al., 2004b). The researchers noted that although the literature is consistent in the findings that women lawyers tend to enter firms at the same rate as men, the similarities end there. Women are more likely than men to leave the job, leave earlier, be paid less, and are less likely to become partners (Brockman, 1994; Hagan, 1990; Hagan & Kay, 2007; Kay, 1997; Kay et al., 2004a, 2004b; Stager & Foot, 1988). In their research involving a sample of Toronto lawyers, Hagan and Kay (2007) found three indirect pathways that connected gender and job dissatisfaction and despondency. Using LISREL[10] analyses, the researchers made the following conclusions:

- Women lawyers have less occupational power, which relates to more despondency about their job.
- Women lawyers' perceived powerlessness serves to dampen their job satisfaction.
- Women are more likely to be concerned about the career consequences of having children, which results in despondency.

Hagan and Kay (2007) suggest that to fully explore the relationship between gender and job satisfaction among lawyers, studies of job satisfaction should include measures of despondency, because gender appears to be indirectly connected to job satisfaction through feelings of despondency. As the authors note, "women are more likely to respond to their professional grievances with internalized feelings of despondency than with externalized expressions of job dissatisfaction" (Hagan & Kay, 2007, p. 51).

Role Overload and Role Strain

Gomme and Hall (1995) identified aspects of qualitative and quantitative role overload that have contributed to role strain among prosecutors. According to the researchers, "role overload occurs where insufficient time exists in which to properly execute all necessary work-related tasks" (Gomme & Hall, 1995, p. 192). Quantitative overload occurs when insufficient time is available to complete the work because of the large volume of work to be done. In contrast, qualitative overload refers to the experience of being unable to complete one's work because the material resources available are insufficient to meet the demands of a very complex task within a limited time period (Gomme & Hall, 1995). Both forms of overload have been found to be associated with role strain—the negative psychological and physical consequences of role overload, such as difficulty sleeping, exhaustion, heart palpitations, anxiety, irritability, frustration, and burnout (Kemery, Mossholder, & Bedeian, 1987, cited in Gomme & Hall, 1995). The researchers note that the job of a prosecutor is very demanding and difficult, involving high case-loads, difficult witnesses, disturbing case material, and various administrative chal-lenges, complicated by a lack of control over one's schedule (Gomme & Hall, 1995). The deleterious effects of role strain are illustrated in the following quotation from a Crown attorney in the Maritimes:

> It's really frustrating—exhausting. It's always stressful. You're always there [in court]. There's always someone mad at you … . We're all here, we're all under stress—tremendous amounts of stress … . There are days I didn't want to go to work—just felt so sick—phys-ically sick from the anxiety and the stress of the work. But you push yourself.
>
> There should be more to life than tolerating. That, you know what I mean, there should be time for family and happiness.
>
> It does. It does. It affects your family life terribly. And it can affect you mentally too, especially over a period of time … . Your system breaks down. [There is] constant pressure from a job like this. (Gomme & Hall, 1995, p. 196)

Clearly, levels of stress associated with this kind of work can affect a prosecutor's performance. The issues raised by Gomme and Hall (1995) cut across gender lines and encompass more than just the experiences of prosecutors. Without a doubt, many de-fence lawyers and even judges have similar kinds of experiences.

Sexism, Harassment, and Discrimination

Although a great deal of what has already been discussed in this chapter would fall under the category of sexism, harassment, and discrimination (for example, women's earnings compared with men's and the longer time period for women to become a partner), some specific issues are worth mentioning explicitly. An American study published in the mid-1990s reported that sexist behaviours were found to be more frequent both in the private sector (as opposed to the public sector) and among those who were in token positions (Rosenberg, Perlstadt, & Phillips, 1993). Also, more sexist behaviours were reported to occur after women were on the job (with respect to salary, promotion, and types of jobs assigned to them) as opposed to during the recruitment and hiring process (Rosenberg et al., 1993). Interestingly, the authors noted that women with careerist orientations, those who "deny the importance of gender in stratifying the profession," reported more sexual harassment than did those with a feminist orientation (p. 420). For an examination of how some women lawyers have dealt with sexism in the law, see Box 12.2.

In a study of Ontario lawyers, Kay et al. (2004a) noted significant differences between men and women lawyers with respect to incidents of discrimination based on gender. The researchers found that women more often identified witnessing examples of dis-criminatory practices than did men. For example, women reported with greater frequency than men that women had:

BOX 12.2

Battling Sexism in Law

Female litigators don't just fight legal battles in the courtroom; they're also fighting the battle against sexism within the legal profession.

During a two-part panel discussion in Toronto Feb. 8 hosted by the Ontario Bar Association's Institute: Female Litigators: Staking Your Claim in the Courtroom, six female lawyers shared their experiences and strategies on overcoming sexist treatment on the job.

"I am as much worthy of respect as my male counterparts in this career," said Linda Fuerst, senior partner with Norton Rose Fulbright LLP, on the first of the two panels.

Whether sexism is experienced inside the courtroom, for instance, focusing on a female lawyer's appearance rather than her job as a litigator, as spoken of on the first of the two panels, or outside the courtroom during meetings with colleagues or clients, or through email correspondence, as spoken of in the second panel, it's proving to be an ongoing issue.

The speakers agreed that one of the best ways to overcome sexism inside the courtroom is to command authority and have a thorough knowledge of the case at hand. According to panellist Linda Rothstein, partner at Paliare Roland Rosenberg Rothstein, you have to protect your own integrity but also act in the best interest of the client.

"Men who are tall and had baritone voices sounded authoritative. I couldn't do that because I was short and female," said Fuerst.

Fuerst added that it's important to speak with confidence and to practice changing tone and intonation. It's important to act authoritative because when so much emphasis is placed on a woman's appearance in court, female lawyers need to command respect.

For instance, Rothstein said that early in her career, as she was delivering a motion, a judge stopped her to tell her that she had "lovely nails."

Outside the courtroom, the importance of having a mentor was stressed because whether a lawyer needs advice on how to react professionally to sexist behaviour or just have someone to debrief with, they're there to serve as a guide. Panellist Shantona Chaudhury of Pape Barristers said that inter-generational learning is key and believes that these can be the most important relationships in the profession.

Often, when experiencing sexism outside the courtroom, the verbal attacks on gender are subtle. According to Asha James of Falconers LLP, older male lawyers have tried to tell her how to deal with a client.

"Hey, honey, let me explain to you how this works," she said, quoting from a past experience.

Another strategy touched upon was taking on a leadership role and expanding one's sphere of influence. According to Law Society of Upper Canada Bencher Sandra Nishikawa, a big reason she ran for bencher was to help facilitate change in the industry and to help change the institutions that are part of the profession.

Nishikawa, a mother of three, said many female lawyers struggle with juggling childcare and motherhood with a career due to the fear of losing their clients and their position in their law firm when taking maternity leave. Often, mothers are perceived to not be serious about their legal career as their femininity becomes more evident, she said.

"Sometimes, you need to say, 'I need to leave to pick up my kids from daycare,'" Nishikawa said. "It seems to be more acceptable, even charming, when men do this."

Another benefit male colleagues have, according to the panellists and the session attendees, is ease at networking with other men. Often, men are able to bond with their clients and network due to mutual interests women might not share. For instance, male lawyers might build rapport with a client by taking them to play golf.

"I think men have a secret society. They golf together and they even go to the urinal together," said Fuerst. "As women, we could find other things and other common ground to build rapport with these male clients."

Above all, it was stressed that women in law need to look out for each other and propel each other forward, especially since there's a shortage of women who make it past the 10-year mark working in law.

"I'd like to share a quote that I've read before: There's a special place in hell for women that don't support other women. Build bonds with women in the profession rather than see them as just your competition," said Chaudhury.

Source: Kapralos, A. (2017, February 14). Legal feeds: The blog of *Canadian Lawyer* and *Law Times*. Battling sexism in law. Retrieved from http://www .canadianlawyermag.com/legalfeeds/3679/battling-sexism-in-law.html.

- been assigned tasks that were below their skill level;
- not been invited to work with a specific senior partner;
- been excluded from a social gathering;
- been denied work even when an interest had been expressed;
- been the recipient of comments about their appearance;
- heard derogatory comments about their family status;
- heard disrespectful remarks from judges or other lawyers; and
- experienced a lack of support from office staff.

In their longitudinal study of a cohort of Ontario lawyers, Kay et al. (2004b) found that over the course of the first three surveys, women were more likely to perceive sexual discrimination in the workplace than were men. Three times as many women (18 percent) as men (6 percent) believed they had been denied responsibility for a file because of their sex. Similarly, more women perceived they had been assigned a specific case because of their sex, and more women thought fewer opportunities were afforded to them because of their sex (Kay et al., 2004b).

Future Directions

From this chapter, readers should find it readily apparent that many challenges face women in the legal profession. If the profession is to see continued growth and equality, then some of these challenges will require creative solutions. Serious consideration will need to be given, both in private and public practices, to increased flexibility in the workplace to deal with expanding family responsibilities (child care and eldercare), to more flexibility with respect to the costs associated with practising law, and to a better use of technology. Great strides have been taken to accommodate the needs of accused persons and litigants, yet that same technology does not seem to have offered any assistance to the people working with them. If we can bring court to the jails in the interest of expediency and justice, can we not offer better assistance to the people working with the accused persons and litigants who find themselves in the system?

Additionally, a concern to be addressed in the very near future is the rising cost of obtaining a legal education. The dramatic rise in admissions to law schools in the third wave needs to continue to ensure a continuous flow of women into the practice of law (Mossman, 2005). Exorbitant tuition fees, lack of subsidies, and inflexibility in the law school curriculum will likely contribute to a decline in the number of women practising law in this country (LSUC, 2004).

The death of the Honourable Madam Justice Bertha Wilson in 2007, the first woman appointed to the Supreme Court of Canada, should help to remind those who enter the practice of law that the issues women face are similar regardless of when they start their journey. When Bertha Wilson enrolled in law at Dalhousie in 1955, Horace Read, the dean of the law school, was reported to have said to her, "Have you no appreciation of how tough a course the law is? This is not something you can do in your spare time. We have no room for dilettantes. Why don't you go home and take up crocheting?" (McPhee, 2007, p. 1). We are certainly glad that she did not. Clara Brett Martin and others paved the way for women to enter law school and the practice of law, and pioneers such as Justice Wilson ensured that we understand there are no limits to what women can achieve.

SUMMARY

It is sobering to think that a little more than 100 years ago, Canada had no women lawyers. Times have changed, and women are now an integral part of the practice of law. Their presence in the field does not, however, mean that their representation is equal to that of men. We know that as many women enter law school as do men. We know that they attend law school for the same reasons as men. They graduate and pursue jobs in the field, as do men. However, somewhere along the way, their equality with male lawyers ends. More women can be found working in lower-paid and less prestigious government positions, whereas more men work in more lucrative private practices. Although some women decide to work in law firms, examination of those who make partner shows that fewer women than men in law firms are partners. Even among those who are partners, fewer women than men are considered senior partners. Women lawyers earn considerably less than their male counterparts, even when taking into account their years of practice, the type of law practised, and the positions held.

What is clear is that, over the years, varying types of barriers have impeded women's progress in the field of law. Initially, legislation prevented their entry into the profession. Although such structural barriers no longer exist, women continue to face some significant challenges that may be seen to affect their progress in their chosen career. Factors related to the inflexibility of the job (hours of work and lack of part-time alternatives, for example), lower earnings, sexual discrimination, and sexual harassment may be related to the observation that more women than men leave the practice of law altogether.

As is the case in many other areas of the Canadian criminal justice system, the study of women in the legal field has not taken centre stage until fairly recently. Only in the last couple of decades have we seen an intensive push to investigate issues related to women in the legal profession. Academics and a number of law societies in Canada have taken the lead in this area. The commission of various studies and the publication of reports on issues relating to women lawyers have furthered our understanding of women's role in the legal profession in Canada. Continued focus on issues of gender and discrimination may enable women to one day attain equality with men in all aspects of the legal profession.

NOTES

1. The author wishes to thank Shelley Lechlitner for her contributions to the first edition's chapter of the same name, some of which is reproduced here.
2. The Family Compact refers to an elite group of wealthy Anglican conservatives who, as a group, had major influence in Upper Canada following the War of 1812.
3. Clara Brett Martin is believed to have been left permanently weakened by a cold she caught while working on the John Doughty–Ambrose Small case in 1920 (Backhouse, 1985).
4. In Canada, the Queen's Privy Council, which includes Cabinet ministers and members appointed by the Queen on the advice of the prime minister, exercises formal functions of law.
5. This increase was steady, apart from a period during the 1930s (Mossman, 2005).
6. Not including Nunavut where breakdown by sex was not available.
7. In 2006, 14,388,160 people in Canada over the age of 25 were employed in the labour force.
8. Successful candidates to these elected positions are involved in the many operations and functions surrounding the monitoring, educating, and disciplining of the lawyers in the province of Ontario.

9. For an in-depth discussion, see Mueller and Wallace (1996).

10. LISREL, a statistical program developed by Jöreskog and Sörbom, allows for the estimation of covariance structure models (Hagan & Kay, 2007).

DISCUSSION QUESTIONS

1. Fewer women than men are partners in law firms. Why do you think women are under-represented among partners in these firms?

2. Being a lawyer is associated with many stressors. In what ways can stressors be gendered?

3. John and Jane Doe went to law school at the same time. They both were called to the bar at the same time and accepted positions in mid-sized law firms in the same town at the same time. Ten years into their respective careers, John makes $20,000 a year more than Jane. How would human capital theory explain this difference?

4. Women's representation in the legal profession has changed drastically over the last 100 years. Discuss Mossman's three waves of women lawyers in Canada. What would a fourth wave look like?

ADDITIONAL RESOURCES

Films and Videos

Rowen, S. (Director & Producer). (2016). *Balancing the scales* [Documentary]. USA. Skydive Films and R&K Productions.

Websites

The Canadian Bar Association: www.cba.org
Law Society of Upper Canada: www.lsuc.on.ca
National Association of Women and the Law: www.nawl.ca

REFERENCES

Alary, B. (2014, April 15). Former PM to lead the way at Peter Lougheed Leadership College. University of Alberta. Retrieved from https://www.ualberta.ca/news-and-events/newsarticles/2014/april/former-pm-to-lead-the-way-at-peter-lougheed-leadership-college.

Backhouse, C. (1985). "To open the way for others of my sex": Clara Brett Martin's career as Canada's first woman lawyer. *Canadian Journal of Women and the Law, 1,* 1–41.

Backhouse, C. (1992). Clara Brett Martin: Canadian heroine or not? *Canadian Journal of Women and the Law, 5,* 263–279.

Backhouse, C., & Backhouse, N. (2004). *The heiress vs. the establishment: Mrs. Campbell's campaign for legal justice.* Vancouver: University of British Columbia Press.

Brockman, J. (1994). Leaving the practice of law: The wherefores and the whys. *Alberta Law Review, 32,* 116–180.

Chiu, C. (1998). Do professional women have lower job satisfaction than professional men? Lawyers as a case study. *Sex Roles, 38,* 521–536.

Crandall, E. (2014). Does the system of judicial appointments matter? Exploring women's representation on Ontario courts. *Canadian Journal of Women and the Law, 26*(2), 185–205.

Edward, M., Davies, B., Presser, J., & Stewart, I. (2013). *Final report and recommendations of the working group on women in criminal law.* Retrieved from http://www.criminallawyers.ca/wp-content/uploads/2015/01/CLAWomensWorkingGroupFinalReportAugust-2013.pdf.

Federal/Provincial/Territorial Working Group of Attorneys General Officials on Gender Equality in the Canadian Justice System. (1992). *Gender equality in the Canadian justice system background papers: Women working in the justice system.* Ottawa: Department of Justice.

Federation of Law Societies of Canada. (2017). 2014 Statistics. Retrieved from http://flsc.ca/resources/statistics/.

Goff, C. (2008). *Criminal justice in Canada* (4th ed.). Toronto: Nelson Canada.

Gomme, I., & Hall, M. (1995). Prosecutors at work: Role overload and strain. *Journal of Criminal Justice, 23,* 191–200.

Hagan, J. (1990). The gender stratification of income inequality among lawyers. *Social Forces, 68,* 835–855.

Hagan, J., & Kay, F. (2007). Even lawyers get the blues: Gender, depression and job satisfaction in legal practice. *Law and Society Review, 41,* 51–78.

Kapralos, A. (2017, February 14). Legal feeds: The blog of *Canadian Lawyer* and *Law Times.* Battling sexism in law. Retrieved from http://www.canadianlawyermag.com/legalfeeds/3679/battling-sexism-in-law.html.

Kay, F. (1997). Flight from law: A competing risks model of departures from law firms. *Law and Society Review, 31,* 301–335.

Kay, F., Alarie, S., & Adjei, J. (2013). *Leaving law and barriers to re-entry: A study of departures from and re-entries to private practice—A report to the Law Society of Upper Canada.* Toronto: Law Society of Upper Canada.

Kay, F., & Hagan, J. (1995). The persistent glass ceiling: Gendered inequalities in the earnings of lawyers. *British Journal of Sociology, 46,* 279–310.

Kay, F., Masuch, C., & Curry, P. (2004a). *Diversity and change: The contemporary legal profession in Ontario—A report to the Law Society of Upper Canada.* Toronto: Law Society of Upper Canada.

Kay, F., Masuch, C., & Curry, P. (2004b). *Turning points and transitions: Women's careers in the legal profession—A report to the Law Society of Upper Canada* (p. 25). Toronto: Law Society of Upper Canada.

Kinnear, M. (1992). "That there woman lawyer": Women lawyers in Manitoba, 1915–1970. *Canadian Journal of Women and the Law, 5,* 411–441.

Krakauer, L., & Chen, C. (2003). Gender barriers in the legal profession: Implications for career development of female law students. *Journal of Employment Counseling, 40,* 65–79.

Law Society of Alberta. (2006). Diversity and equality initiatives: 1991–2006. Edmonton: Author.

Law Society of Upper Canada. (1997). *Bicentennial report and recommendations on equity issues in the legal profession: Report to bicentennial convocation.* Toronto: Author.

Law Society of Upper Canada. (2003). Guide to developing a policy regarding workplace equity in law firms. Toronto: Author.

Law Society of Upper Canada. (2004). *Bicentennial implementation status report and strategy.* Toronto: Author.

Law Society of Upper Canada. (2006). *Equity and Aboriginal issues committee: Report to convocation.* Toronto: Author.

Leiper, J. (1997). It was like "wow!": The experience of women lawyers in a profession marked by linear careers. *Canadian Journal of Women and the Law, 9,* 115–137.

Leiper, J. (2006). *Bar codes: Women in the legal profession.* Vancouver: University of British Columbia Press.

Lekushoff, A. (2014, May 5). Where have all the female lawyers gone? Huffington Post. Retrieved from http://www.huffingtonpost.ca/andrea-lekushoff/female-lawyers-canada_b_5000415.html.

Library and Archives Canada. (2010). *Celebrating women's achievements: Kim Campbell.* Retrieved from https://www.collectionscanada.gc.ca/women/030001-1314-e.html.

MacCharles, T. (2016, September 19). Chief Justice Beverley McLachlin looks forward, not back. *Toronto Star.* Retrieved from https://www.thestar.com/news/canada/2016/09/19/chief-justice-beverley-mclachlin-looks-forward-not-back.html.

MacCorquodale, P., & Jensen, G. (1993). Women in the law: Partners or tokens? *Gender and Society, 7,* 582–593.

Madon, N., & Doob, A. (2016). *The retention of women in the private practice of criminal law: Research report.* Criminal Lawyers Association. Retrieved from http://www.criminallawyers.ca/wp-content/uploads/2016/03/CLA-Womens-Study-March-2016.pdf.

McPhee, J. (2007). A powerful flame extinguished. *Law Times, 18*(16), 1.

Mossman, M. (2005). Defining moments for women as lawyers: Reflections on numerical gender equality. *Canadian Journal of Women and the Law, 17,* 15–25.

Mueller, C., & Wallace, J. (1996). Justice and the paradox of the contented female worker. *Social Psychology Quarterly, 59,* 338–349.

Office of the Commissioner for Federal Judicial Affairs Canada. (2017). *Number of federally appointed judges as of January 5, 2017.* Retrieved from http://www.fja-cmf.gc.ca/appointments-nominations/judges-juges-eng.aspx#nwt.

Ornstein, M. (2004). *The changing face of the Ontario legal profession 1971–2001: A report to the Law Society of Upper Canada.* Toronto: Law Society of Upper Canada.

Ornstein, M. (2010). *Racialization and gender of lawyers in Ontario: A report for the Law Society of Upper Canada.* (pp. 19–20). Toronto: Law Society of Upper Canada.

Petersson, S. (1997). Ruby Clements and early women of the Alberta bar. *Canadian Journal of Women and the Law, 9,* 365–393.

Phelan, J. (1994). The paradox of the contented female worker: An assessment of alternative explanations. *Social Psychology Quarterly, 57,* 95–107.

Roberts, J., & Grossman, M. (2008). *Criminal justice in Canada: A reader* (3rd ed.). Toronto: Nelson Canada.

Robson, K., & Wallace, J. (2001). Gendered inequalities in earnings: A study of Canadian lawyers. *Canadian Review of Sociology and Anthropology, 38*, 76–95.

Rosenberg, J., Perlstadt, H., & Phillips, W. (1993). Now that we are here: Discrimination, disparagement, and harassment at work and the experience of women lawyers. *Gender and Society, 7*, 415–433.

Sheehy, E., & McIntyre, S. (2006). *Calling for change: Women, law and the legal profession*. Ottawa: University of Ottawa Press.

Snowball, K. (2002). *Criminal prosecutions, personnel and expenditures, 2000/01*. Ottawa: Canadian Centre for Justice Statistics.

Stager, D., & Foot, D. (1988). Changes in lawyers' earnings: The impact of differentiation and growth in the Canadian legal profession. *Law and Social Inquiry, 13*, 71–85.

Supreme Court of Canada. (2017). *The Right Honourable Beverley McLachlin, P.C., Chief Justice of Canada*. Retrieved from http://www.scc-csc.ca/judges-juges/bio-eng.aspx?id=beverley-mclachlin.

Tutton, M. (2017, January 23). N.S. appoints Mi'kmaq, black women to bench: "This is a huge step forward." The Canadian Press. Retrieved from http://www.news1130.com/2017/01/23/nova-scotia-justice-minister-appoints-first-mkmaq-woman-to-the-judiciary/.

van Wormer, K., & Bartollas, C. (2007). *Women and the criminal justice system* (2nd ed.). Boston: Pearson.

Women Working in Corrections

Introduction

Women work in many different capacities within Canada's correctional system. Their roles include, but are not limited to, correctional officers, clerks, wardens, deputy wardens, chaplains, parole officers, probation officers, primary workers, case management officers, psychologists, nurses, and doctors. Much of the day-to-day workload and the responsibilities of these staff remain a mystery to the general public because so much of what goes on is literally behind a fence or behind a stone wall. In comparison with other justice occupations (such as the police or lawyers), very few people have actually come into contact with correctional staff acting in their official capacity. For example, think of the last time you saw a police officer in uniform, spoke to a police officer on the phone, or saw a police cruiser in your neighbourhood. Now think of the last time you saw a correctional officer in uniform, spoke to a correctional officer on the phone, or saw a corrections vehicle in your neighbourhood. If you are like most Canadians, you have likely encountered a police officer, but have rarely, if ever, encountered a correctional officer.

For the most part, the general public is unaware of what prisons are like on the inside, a collective ignorance that reflects the kind of institution a prison is—a closed institution. Unless you live, work, or volunteer in a prison, you are unlikely to know what it is like inside. Tours of prisons have sometimes been made available to the general public, but they occur rarely (Outhit, 1999). Many people's only contact with the interior of a prison is through the news and media. Their perceptions of prison are shaped by the images portrayed through television, films, and print media. The general public has a natural curiosity and some confusion toward those who spend their days working with offenders. These feelings are especially pronounced when sensationalized cases are highlighted in the news. People wonder why anyone would want to work in what is sometimes a dangerous and toxic environment (van Wormer & Bartollas, 2000).

Over the years, numerous studies have focused on the lives of offenders, yet we know very little about the attitudes, behaviours, and experiences of the people who supervise offenders, and how they interact with offenders and with each other (Bensimon, 2005b). This chapter will introduce the reader to various components of the Canadian correctional system, the staff who work in corrections, and the challenges faced by women who choose to work in what has, for the most part, been a male-dominated regime.

The Correctional System

The correctional system in Canada comprises custodial services (both provincial or territorial and federal), community supervision services, and the national and provincial parole boards. In 2015-16, total expenditures for correctional services in Canada were $4.6 billion (Reitano, 2017). The federal system accounted for 51.5 percent of that total, and provincial and territorial correctional services accounted for the remaining 48.5 percent.

On average, it costs $283 per day to incarcerate a federal offender, whereas incarcerating a provincial offender is much cheaper, at $203 per day (Reitano, 2017). Historically, the costs to incarcerate federally sentenced women far surpassed the costs to incarcerate similarly sentenced men (Public Safety Canada [PSC], 2016). Estimates for 2013-14 show that it cost $219,884 annually to incarcerate a woman at a federal women's facility, whereas the costs to incarcerate a man ranged from $83,182 a year for a minimum security institution to $156,768 for a maximum security facility (PSC, 2016).

We can speculate why it costs so much more to federally incarcerate a woman than a man. Fewer women are incarcerated, yet they still require facilities, security, and staff to work in the institutions, and specially designed programs need to be developed and delivered to address the unique needs of incarcerated women. Comparatively speaking, supervising an offender in the community costs 70 percent less ($34,432 annually) than incarcerating that offender (on average, $115,310 annually) in a correctional facility (PSC, 2016).

Historically, two key indicators have been used to assess the workload of corrections: the average daily count of offenders and the annual admissions to corrections (Statistics Canada, 2005). In 2015-16, there was an average of 8,455 youth on any given day being supervised in a community program or in custody (Malakieh, 2017). The majority (89 percent) were being supervised in the community, with only 998 young offenders in a custodial facility. This represents a decrease in youths in custody of 27 percent since 2011-12 (Malakieh, 2017).

Correctional Personnel

The Correctional Service of Canada (CSC) employed approximately 18,000 staff in 2015-16 (Goodale, 2017). Correctional officers account for about 42 percent of the workforce, with parole and program officers making up about 14 percent (Goodale, 2017). CSC strives to maintain a workforce reflective of the Canadian public as a whole, employing persons from visible minority groups (9.1 percent), persons with disabilities (5.2 percent), and Indigenous people (9.5 percent). In terms of the CSC's employment of women, recent estimates suggest that women comprised 47.5 percent of the CSC's workforce (Goodale, 2017). Since women comprise slightly more than half (50.4 percent) of Canada's population, the CSC still has some headway to make in its hiring of women if it wants to be reflective of Canada's population (Milan, 2015).

Female Correctional Service Officers

According to the 2001 Census of Canada, just over 5,400 women were working as correctional service officers in Canada, representing 29 percent of the total number of correctional service officers that year (Statistics Canada, 2005). Box 13.1 features an interview with a female federal correctional officer. Over a ten-year period (from 1991 to 2001), the number of female correctional officers in Canada increased by 1,455, an increase of 7 percent of the total number of Canadian correctional officers (Statistics Canada, 2005). This increase was consistent with increases over the same time period in other justice-related occupations, such as judges, lawyers and notaries, paralegals, and probation and parole officers (Statistics Canada, 2005).

BOX 13.1

Interview with a Female Correctional Officer with Nearly a Decade of Experience in Federal Corrections

Why did you decide to become a federal correctional officer?

I had an unexpected career change and was feeling burnt out from working in various fields (youth, family, and First Nations communities). A friend suggested corrections, as there were similar skill sets required, but with the advantage that you punch a clock with offenders, whereas troubled teens were a 24-hour-a-day proposition.

So, I applied on a whim. A number of factors appealed to me: pension, decent salary, working with marginalized communities, and it was a government organization. At the time I was hired, CSC was coming out of a big hiring freeze, so I was one of quite a few hired that year.

What kind of education did you pursue prior to becoming a correctional officer? Did you need to acquire any additional qualifications or certifications prior to being hired? (e.g., first aid, etc.) What kind of training did you receive once you were hired?

I have a university degree, but I didn't have any other prior qualifications or certifications. Once I began the recruitment process, there was extensive training. I really had no idea what it all entailed. We underwent a month of online reading and testing and then reported for CTP—the Correctional Training Program—which is a three-month intensive training program. Less than half of our class made it through to graduation. It was stressful. At that time, we trained in our local region, but now I believe recruits all go to Depot—and the training is based on a military model.

I had to have a valid driver's license, first aid, and had to pass a fitness test called the CoPAT. We underwent a series of interviews, aptitude tests, and a security background check. References were checked and a final interview was held before being invited to train. This process took about eight months.

Training was five days a week and covered topics such as: law and policy, use of force policy training, mental health, suicide awareness and prevention, motivational-based interviewing, report writing, static and dynamic security training, firearms, arrest and control, self-contained breathing apparatus (SCBA), fire suppression, inflammatory sprays, and searching techniques.

What they *weren't* able to teach us was how a prison runs, because every prison is very unique. There are some basic underlying similarities but the devil is in the details. We toured a number of institutions and got a look at cells, control posts, armory, principal entrance, etc., but in my experience, it was completely overwhelming. At the time, there was no organized orientation training to the jail. Now there is a structured introduction with checklists and schedules as well as orientation officers who help new officers learn the ropes. I have been an orientation trainer and new officers now receive much more extensive onsite training, and after this, they are put on the roster and assigned to a mentor on their crew.

In my estimation it takes about a year for someone who is new to corrections to familiarize themselves with the operations of their roster in any particular jail. The learning curve is steep and patience from other staff can sometimes be limited. I had a very rough first six months until I fell into the groove.

What kinds of additional training have you been required to do?

We have ongoing training. Every year we requalify on things like use of force and firearms, SCBA, inflammatory sprays, arrest and control, restraint techniques. We have additional training on other topics like mental health and self-care as well.

As a woman working in a male institution, are there issues that you experience with cross-gender staffing?

Yes, to some extent. There are limitations to what a female can do in terms of escorts, strip searches, and urinalysis, because of the privacy concerns of the male offenders. Other than that, I think there is equal opportunity for advancement for females and males. I would estimate that women are equally represented at the management and executive level.

In your estimation, what is the ratio of male to female correctional officers at the institution where you work?

CX [correctional officer]—about 20 to 25 percent female. A lot of women move on to other things—like I did, to the parole office or they might become program officers. Working with offenders as line staff can be boring work much of the time. The people who are most successful have very rich lives outside of work.

Have you experienced incidences of sexism on the job? If so, how did you handle it?

HA! Oh my—it is inherent, pernicious. I have come to realize that I had lived in an ivory tower. The reality that I knew through my previous work, at school, and living in large urban centres was just not representative of the common experience of many women. I have been treated differently because I am a woman but not necessarily worse. In my experience, overt or degrading sexism has to be addressed head on. Mostly with an "excuse me???? Did you just say that?" or something or other. Straight and to the point. It is about setting boundaries.

In my opinion it is almost never to do with women being the "weaker" sex. Interestingly, in a prison, a guard's muscle mass is next to useless. Half of the offenders are in better shape than the most physically fit officer. Many offenders are obsessed with weight training, and they outnumber the staff. Being able to run is a highly valued commodity, but being able to use your words is the most valuable. Not stirring up trouble is the best of all, and women and men are equally able to do that.

Does your work interfere in any way with your home life? Is your family supportive of your career choice?

I keep a large separation between work and home. There just isn't a way to explain how a day in prison is to outsiders. It is surreal, and some days are hard. Any frontline worker knows what I am talking about: misery, tragedy, agony, torture, and hopelessness. It is a crucible of all that in a prison, every day. So, we try to make a difference where we can.

Source: Personal communication, April 9, 2017.

The History of Women Working in Provincial Corrections

As noted in Chapter 1, women have had a long history of working with incarcerated women. Because they could be paid less than their male counterparts, women were historically employed as matrons (Strange, 1985). Although they were mainly responsible for the female offenders, their jobs sometimes included such tasks as cooking and making beds (Ministry of Correctional Services, 1983, cited in McMahon, 1999). In some cases, a matron was employed by virtue of her husband's occupation (as a jail superintendent or governor). In these cases, women weren't always eager to assume the role of matron (Ministry of Correctional Services, 1983, cited in McMahon, 1999). In 1971, the Ministry of Correctional Services determined that husbands and wives would not be allowed to work together, effectively abolishing the practice of hiring the wives of correctional officials as matrons (Ministry of Correctional Services, 1983, cited in McMahon, 1999).

The history of women working strictly with male offenders is more limited and, as McMahon (1999) has pointed out, is not extensively documented. In her book, *Women on Guard: Discrimination and Harassment in Corrections*, McMahon (1999) extensively traced the history of women working in male provincial corrections. A shift appeared to occur in the 1970s. Prior to this time, most women employed in corrections filled stereotypically female roles (as nurses and in clerical positions). In more recent years, women have assumed roles traditionally reserved for men in correctional work. McMahon further pointed out that the paramilitary manner in which institutions were run prior to the 1970s encouraged an authoritarian structure that catered to males with a military background, effectively excluding women (who did not tend to have military experience) from the job pool. In a related finding, Jurik and Halemba (1984) noted that the majority of their male sample of correctional officers had previous law enforcement or military backgrounds, whereas none of the female sample of officers had any military background, and only one-third had a law enforcement background.

The first institution in Ontario to hire women as correctional officers was the Alex Brown Clinic/Ontario Correctional Institute (OCI) in Brampton in the 1970s (Ministry of Correctional Services, 1983, cited in McMahon, 1999). By the end of that decade, women were working as correctional officers in no less than 24 facilities (Ministry of Correctional Services, 1983, cited in McMahon, 1999). According to figures presented by McMahon (1999), by 1998 more than 1,000 women were working as correctional officers in Ontario, 969 of them in male institutions. Women's rise to management positions in male institutions did not occur in Ontario until the mid- to late 1970s, and it wasn't until 1982 that the first woman was hired as the superintendent of a male adult prison (Ministry of Correctional Services, 1983, cited in McMahon, 1999). Although no specific piece of legislation encouraged the hiring of women into traditionally male roles in the prison system in Ontario, both the Ontario government and the Ontario Ministry of Correctional Services were reported to have been proactive in their response to a series of federal and provincial reports, including the 1970 *Report of the Royal Commission on the Status of Women* (McMahon, 1999).

The History of Women Working in Federal Corrections

According to its mission statement:

> The Correctional Service of Canada (CSC), as part of the criminal justice system and respecting the rule of law, contributes to public safety by actively encouraging and assisting offenders to become law-abiding citizens, while exercising reasonable, safe, secure and humane control. (CSC, 2012)

Women have worked in the CSC for many years in traditionally female roles (Griffiths, 2004). However, in the early to mid-1980s, the CSC attracted a flurry of media attention when it first began integrating female correctional officers into male institutions (Across Canada, 1983; Cleland, 1986; Kershaw, 1985a, 1985b; Large, 1986). The inclusion of women into this prior bastion of male domination can be traced to developments in the late 1960s and early 1970s.

In 1969, the *Public Service Employment Act* became applicable to the Canadian Penitentiary Service (Canada, Public Service Commission [PSC], 1977). According to the *Public Service Employment Act*, section 12, a federal public service was not to discriminate on the basis of sex (Canada, PSC, 1977). However, up until that time, the penitentiary service had hired only men as guards in male institutions. Exemptions were applied for and received in 1973 and again in 1975 (Canada, PSC, 1977). However, in the mid-1970s, the rationale for this exemption was questioned. Complaints were filed with the Anti-Discrimination Branch of the Human Rights Commission, which, in 1975, was tasked to perform an in-depth investigation to identify the justifications for maintaining only men in guard positions. By 1977, a report was issued, and no justification was determined for limiting the guard positions to men; the practice of excluding women from these jobs was set to change (Canada, PSC, 1977). In 1978, the first eight women were hired as correctional officers in male penitentiaries within the Correctional Service of Canada (Sakowski, 1986).

In the early 1980s, the results from the "Female CX Pilot Project"[1] were published, suggesting that as long as women were introduced into the institutions in a methodical manner and were actively supported by management, they would have no problems integrating into the male institutions (CSC, 1980). An account of the experiences of the first women employed in the CSC in male institutions suggested otherwise (Sakowski, 1986). Similarly, a report from the Canadian Human Rights Commission published in 1981 suggested the integration was not a smooth one. Whereas the senior managers at institutions where female correctional officers were deployed exhibited "a positive or at least a neutral position" toward the presence of women in these positions, the union representatives expressed a less enthusiastic view (Canadian Human Rights Commission [CHRC], 1981, p. 4). The union representatives were neutral or negative about having women correctional officers in male institutions (CHRC, 1981). Key concerns included issues of inmate privacy and the testing of authority with female officers, including whether they could handle violent incidents (CHRC, 1981).

In 1984, Kingston Penitentiary was the first maximum security federal male prison to hire women as guards (Cleland, 1986). Within a year, it was not uncommon to find women working as guards in maximum security institutions (Cleland, 1986). In 1985, Millhaven Institution was the last federal prison in Ontario to prepare to hire women as guards. At that time, 120 females were employed in male federal institutions in Ontario, as guards and living unit officers (Kershaw, 1985b). In the mid-1980s, the federal correctional service was attempting to increase women's representation among junior guards and living unit officers to 19 percent by 1988. In order to assess the "policies, guidelines and practices" that would allow for flexibility in attaining this target, an operational and resource management review was undertaken in 1985 (CSC, 1985, p. 1).

Not surprisingly, a backlash against this increased representation of women was played out in the media. Concerns were expressed that women were being given priority in terms of hiring for correctional officer positions. In addition, the emphasis on a university education had some individuals upset about the so-called whiz kids with degrees who were being promoted over more seasoned guards without degrees (Kershaw, 1985a). According to a report in the media, an Ontario region official and a Kingston lawyer carried out a secret report that alleged "widespread sexual harassment of female officers at the Collins Bay Institution that included name-calling, grabbing, vicious gossiping, refusal by male guards both to talk to their female colleagues on the job and to adequately train them for certain posts" (Kershaw, 1985a, p. 1). Such a claim was counter to the conclusions previously drawn regarding the relative ease with which women could be integrated into male institutions (CSC, 1980).

By 1990, although one-third of those working in the CSC were women, upon closer inspection, these women tended to be employed in stereotypical kinds of positions (Jamieson, Beals, Lalonde & Associates Inc., 1990). Specifically, the report noted that the women in the CSC tended to be clustered in positions of administrative support. In 1990, only 12 percent of the CSC's operations sector employees were female, and only 10 percent of those at the executive level in the CSC were women (Jamieson et al., 1990). The surveyed women expressed disillusionment about their work and collectively felt "isolated from the positions of power within the organization" (Jamieson et al., 1990, p. i). In its final report on the employment barriers for women in the CSC, Jamieson, Beals, Lalonde & Associates Inc. (1990) noted that the largest barriers for women tended to be the attitudes and behaviours shown mainly by men in the male-dominated organizational culture of the CSC:

Many men and women believe discriminatory practices such as gender-biased selection boards, tokenism, sexual harassment, biased perceptions toward family life, and a persistent, underlying ethos that corrections work is men's business, are factors hampering the realization of equitable participation for women. (p. ii)

Federal Correctional Officer Recruits

Few researchers have looked at the attitudes and behaviours of correctional officers as recruits and early in their careers (Bensimon, 2005b). A longitudinal study on recruits, the first of its kind in Canada, sought to examine recruits' experiences of training, their beliefs, and their attitudes as they embarked on a new career in the Correctional Service of Canada (Bensimon, 2004, 2005a, 2005b). In addition to providing interesting data on recruits as a whole, Bensimon's (2004, 2005a, 2005b) work also affords a glimpse at some of the ways in which female recruits are similar to and different from their male counterparts.

A total of 233 participants completed the first series of testing, and some interesting descriptive statistics emerged regarding the female recruits (Bensimon, 2005a). Just less than half the group was female (47.2 percent). Most of the women were single (59 percent), 34.5 percent were married or living in common-law relationships, and approximately 6 percent were separated or divorced. The men did not have as high an education level as the women, and the mean age for the women was lower than that of the men. Similar to policing, correctional officer recruits tend to be in their late 20s or early 30s when they enter the profession. Their maturity is likely a benefit because of the significant life experiences that older recruits bring to their job.

Results of the longitudinal study indicated three areas where correctional officers (both male and female) showed very positive attitudes that did not change over time, from their first day of recruitment to the end of one year on the job. These three areas were empathy, desire to learn, and counselling or helping relationships (Bensimon, 2005b). These abilities were repeatedly endorsed by correctional officers as key skills that would enable them to do their job. In terms of significant differences between male and female officers, women tended to score higher on support for rehabilitation, empathy, and attitudes toward correctional work.

▶ WHAT DO YOU THINK?

Bensimon (2005b) found that women corrections recruits scored significantly higher on empathy than male recruits did. Do you think that having more empathy would be an asset or a liability for a correctional officer? Can you think of examples of when empathy would help them to do their job? How about situations where empathy might interfere with their ability to carry out their job?

The study identified the major disadvantages to the job: shift work, stress related to the anticipation of violence, and environment and negative atmosphere (Bensimon, 2005b). A decrease in positive attitudes toward role conflict reflected the monotony of a job that was routine and repetitive. The officers did not perceive themselves to be challenged, nor were they involved in a counselling role, because of the static nature of their work (Bensimon, 2005b). The officers indicated they believed their skills were being underutilized, and they expressed concern that it was difficult to manage the requirements of the new environment. Job stress was expressed as a strain in trying to meet the needs of a unique client group: people who may be in crisis, who are likely being imprisoned against their will, and who are being exposed (sometimes daily) to very stressful situations (Bensimon, 2005b).

Bensimon (2005b) stressed the importance of studying the attitudes and beliefs of correctional officers. In order for the CSC to be competitive in its retention of employees, correctional workers need to "feel supported, guided and fairly recognized at their full worth" (Bensimon, 2005b, p. 183). Without this sense of purpose in one's work, the tasks of a correctional officer can be described as routine, and even mundane. With respect to gender differences, interestingly, women tended to score more positively on dimensions of work motivation and attitudes, support for rehabilitation, and the importance of taking a human service orientation toward their work. That being said, issues of job stress and job satisfaction are of paramount concern to correctional personnel and administrators and will be discussed further in this chapter.

The CSC, recognizing that correctional staff encounter stressors on the job, has focused attention on ways to support staff. They have done this through an analysis of workplace wellness strategies employed in government departments (Bensimon, 2010), through literature reviews on working with offenders who engage in self-injurious behaviour (Power & Usher, 2014) and the impact on staff of working in the corrections environment (Scott & Ternes, 2015), and with the continuation of programs like EAP (Employee Assistance Program) and CISM (Critical Incident Stress Management) (CSC, 2002). There is now recognition that correctional officers are considered to be first responders, and as such may experience PTSD as a result of their work (see Box 13.2).

BOX 13.2

Correctional Officers Officially First Responders

The national vice-president of the Union of Canadian Correctional Officers is applauding legislation passed on Tuesday at Queen's Park that declares that correctional officers are now considered first responders—along with police, firefighters and paramedics—and sees post-traumatic stress disorder as a work-related illness.

Jason Godin, who's based out of Kingston, said in a telephone interview on Wednesday the legislation will allow correctional officers to receive treatment for PTSD much faster.

"They categorized in the bill who they considered first responders and it actually included correctional officers. We've been long arguing and fighting to get governments to recognize us as first responders," Godin said.

Bill 163 was passed unanimously in the legislature on Tuesday. It covers both federal correctional officers working in Ontario and their provincial counterparts.

According to a news release from the Ontario government, the legislation will presume that a PTSD claim is legitimate and the treatment will come soon after from the Workplace Safety and Insurance Board. Once a first responder is diagnosed with PTSD by either a psychiatrist or a psychologist, the claims process to be eligible for WSIB benefits will be expedited, without the need to prove a causal link between PTSD and a workplace event.

The legislation applies to more than 73,000 first responders in the province. Godin said Ontario is the second province in the country, after Manitoba, to add in a presumption for all first-responder occupations. Manitoba's legislation covers all occupations, Godin said.

Alberta is considering a similar bill for first responders but has yet to include correctional officers.

"You don't get any more first responder than us. We're the nurse, the firefighter, the police officer and paramedic all inside [the institution]," Godin said. "That's a big thing for us, and we're kind of excited about it, so it's good news."

"Hopefully, it'll help fast-track our members who have been diagnosed with PTSD so they're not sitting around idle and not sitting around waiting to get treated. The reason we have all these suicides with PTSD-responder occupations [is that] the guy ends up diagnosed with PTSD and he's sitting there waiting as he fights his appeal for a year."

Godin said his union, along with Ontario Public Service Employees Union officials, lobbied MPPs at Queen's Park for the first-responder designation for correctional service officers.

"It's a real acknowledgment that now governments are recognizing correctional officers as first responders," he said.

Godin said correctional officers obviously work in a violent environment.

"We walk the streets inside institutions and see horrific things."

He said that, in 2010, correctional officers across Canada did 1,800 medical interventions.

Officers don't have to just worry about their own safety, Godin said, but they also have to break up inmate assaults.

As well, locally in 2010, officers at Millhaven had to shoot two inmates, killing one of them and injuring the other.

"First, the officer had to shoot and take somebody's life, then the officers that were on the floor had to apply first aid to the inmates who were shot," Godin said. "So for us, we're really first responders in the truest sense."

He added that correctional officers suffer from PTSD at a high rate.

"Governments are clueing in now that they have to deal with PTSD on the front end immediately, and that's what we hope this legislation will be able to do."

Godin believes the new legislation will end up saving money for the system as fewer officers will be off sick awaiting treatment.

"The whole goal here is to treat the individual so we can help them get back to work."

Source: MacAlpine, I. (2016, April 6). Correctional officers officially first responders. *Kingston Whig-Standard*. Retrieved from http://www.thewhig .com/2016/04/06/correctional-officers-officially-first-responders.

Community Supervision

Probation and Parole Officers

Probation officers are tasked with "monitoring the conduct and behaviour of criminal offenders serving probation terms" (Government of Canada, 2006, p. 1). Parole officers are concerned with the reintegration of the offender into the community and supervise offenders who have been conditionally released from a federal institution[2] into the community to serve the remainder of their sentence (Government of Canada, 2006). Because of the human service orientation of probation and parole officer work, this career is especially attractive for those who are interested in the social service side of criminal justice work.

According to the Probation Officers Association of Ontario (POAO), the Ontario Ministry of Correctional Services employs approximately 800 probation and parole officers who are responsible for overseeing approximately 56,000 adult offenders residing in the community on any given day. The Ontario Ministry of Children and Youth Services employs approximately 384 probation officers who are responsible for supervising approximately 10,000 young offenders in the community (POAO, n.d.).

In Alberta, by comparison, there were approximately 475 (152 male, 323 female) full-time probation officers who were responsible for supervising a monthly average of 15,772 adult offenders and 1,481youth offenders under supervision in the province in 2015-16 (K. Murphy, personal communication with D.S. Tavcer, April 10, 2017). "Community Corrections and Release Program offers community-based programs to adult and youth offenders through a network of 43 community corrections offices and two attendance centres located in 36 separate geographic locations in Alberta" (Alberta Justice & Solicitor General, n.d., p. 1).

Unlike some other positions in the criminal justice system in Canada (such as correctional officer or police officer), probation and parole (P&P) officers require a university degree, which may explain why, on the whole, P&P officers tend to be better educated than other justice-related personnel. The degree requirement stems from the role that P&P officers play in the protection of the public and the need to ensure that candidates for the job are of the "highest calibre" (Ontario, Ministry of Community Safety and Correctional Services [MCSCS], 2006, p. 2). In addition, candidates need to have excellent written and verbal communication skills, counselling and assessment skills, and the ability to establish a rapport and maintain a relationship with their clients and stakeholders (Ontario, MCSCS, 2006). After new P&P officers are hired, they complete a basic training program that emphasizes the latest "research and principles of effective correctional intervention and programming" (Ontario, MCSCS, 2006, p. 3).

The job of a probation and parole officer requires them to stay current with both research in the field and the most up-to-date intervention methods (POAO, n.d.). A P&P officer's duties include the supervision of offenders who are in the community on parole, on probation, on a conditional sentence, or on a conditional supervision order (POAO, n.d.). P&P officers ensure that offenders comply with their restitution orders and complete their community service. Good written communication skills help in the preparation of pre-sentence, pre-disposition, and pre-parole reports. Because a large part of a P&P officer's job involves counselling offenders in areas such as life skills and employment skills, interpersonal communication skills are also needed. Case management skills are needed when acting as a link between institutions and the community and when assessing risk. In addition to liaising with victims for the purposes of education, referrals, and advocacy, P&P officers also need to act as liaisons with various community groups (POAO, n.d.).

Parole Boards

In Canada we have the Parole Board of Canada (PBC) and two provincial parole boards, in Ontario and Quebec (PBC, n.d.). The PBC is an administrative tribunal that operates as an independent body and is responsible for determining whether offenders are suitable for conditional release from federal penitentiaries and from facilities in provinces and territories where no parole board exists (PBC, n.d.). The PBC is also responsible for granting pardons to people who have been convicted of committing an offence in the past and who are now able to show that they are law-abiding citizens.

According to the Government of Canada website, in 2017, 67 people were employed as Parole Board of Canada members across Canada: just under half were employed part time and just over half were employed full time (PBC, 2017). From a cursory inspection of the names of the PBC members, approximately 30 percent of the PBC members were women. Just over 29 percent of those employed full time were women, and about 37 percent of those employed part time were women (PBC, 2017). The percentage of women on the PBC as full-time members differs across the various regions. Representation was highest for women in the Prairies, where more than 55 percent of the full-time members were women. In contrast, women's representation as full-time members varied from a low of 11 percent (in the Quebec region) to a high of 40 percent for the Pacific region. For Ontario and the Atlantic region, women comprised 33 percent and 20 percent of the full-time PBC members, respectively.

Barriers to Employment in the Correctional System

Occupational Interests

Approximately 35 years ago, at about the same time that careers in criminal justice for women were beginning to open up in the United States, Golden (1982) surveyed a sample of 288 criminal justice students for their interest in various criminal justice-related jobs. Golden found that female students showed a higher interest in positions considered to be more traditionally female, such as juvenile probation officer and youth service worker. Less interest was expressed by the women (compared with the men) for occupations traditionally considered to be male, such as patrol officer.

This kind of gendered occupational interest could pose a barrier to women whose specific interests might limit the options available to them, both in the criminal justice field overall and in the correctional system in particular. It would be interesting to attempt to replicate Golden's (1982) study to see whether any significant change has occurred in the last 35 years regarding the occupational interests of female criminal justice students.[3] One could hypothesize that a similar study would find less of a gendered influence on job preferences today, given the large influx of women into the criminal justice field over the last 35 years, in both the United States and Canada.

▶ **WHAT DO YOU THINK?**

What are your career interests? Are your career aspirations consistent with a gendered view of occupational interests? Do you think that there is a gendered difference in terms of career interests among your classmates? Why do you think this? Take an informal poll the next time you are in class and see whether your prediction is correct!

Role Traps and Stereotypes

Jurik (1988) noted that women who were employed as correctional officers needed to develop certain strategies to avoid both organizational and interactional barriers that might hinder their career advancement. Organizational barriers were defined as those "characteristics that shape worker attitudes and performance: the power structure, and the relative proportions of social types employed in the organization" (Jurik, 1988, p. 291). Interactional barriers, which are faced by women in non-traditional occupational roles, are caused by the sexist attitudes of the people they work with—subordinates, peers, supervisors, and clients. These attitudes may result in women being harassed and denied information critical to their organizational survival (Jurik, 1988).

Zimmer's (1986) typology of female correctional officers' work styles classified these women as falling into one of three roles: the institutional role, the modified role, or the inventive role. Women who tried to do their job in the same manner as the male officers were thought to be in the institutional role. Female correctional officers in this role might express themselves in the following manner:

> When I put on this uniform and this badge, I'm a prison guard and that's all the inmate needs to know. If he does what he's supposed to do, we'll have no trouble. If he decides to break the rules, then I'm here to enforce them—just the same as any other officer. Once the inmate understands that, there's no problem. (Zimmer, 1986, p. 111)

Those women who expressed doubt that they could perform the job in the way the men did, who sought the protection of their male colleagues, and who settled for what would be traditionally seen as women's roles in the institution would be classified as being in the modified role. These women seemed to embrace the notion that they could not be equal to men on the job and believed that this inequality did not just apply to themselves but was extended to all women. In this sense, they could be seen to be in direct opposition (in terms of their beliefs about women's appropriate roles in the institution) to those in the institutional role. The following quotation encapsulates a woman in this modified role:

> Any woman who starts to believe that she can compete with the men here is in serious trouble. Women aren't built the same as men—we're not built to fight. If an inmate decides to make trouble, there's just no way he's going to be stopped by a woman. (Zimmer, 1986, p. 122)

Women in the inventive role sought to work in posts where face-to-face inmate contact was high—for example, on housing units or on work details. These women would then be able to get to know the inmates better and to learn more about their backgrounds, their lives, and their problems. These women stressed the importance of knowing the inmate as an individual person, which would, in turn, enable them to better perform their job. The following is an example of how this strategy could work:

> I know the guys on this unit so well that when I come on duty I can tell right away who is mad at whom, who is upset, who got a bad letter from home, etc. Instead of letting them go at each other, I can usually stop trouble before it begins by giving them a chance to talk these things out. (Zimmer, 1986, p. 130)

Zimmer (1986) noted that no female guard would ever be forced to adopt one of these three roles, but they might, at different points in their careers, find themselves making a conscious decision about the kind of role they wanted to play in the institution. According to Zimmer, the choice an individual makes depends on a number of factors, including personality characteristics, situational circumstances, interactions with inmates, and subjective responses to on-the-job experiences (1986).

Interestingly, in a study by Belknap (2004) looking at women correctional officers in the United States, more of her sample (48.6 percent) self-identified as following the institutional style compared with Zimmer's sample (11 percent). More than half (51.4 percent) saw themselves as following the inventive style, similar to Zimmer's sample where 46 percent were assigned this style. None of Belknap's sample of women correctional officers self-identified as fitting the modified role, in contrast to Zimmer's (1986) study, in which 43 percent were assigned the modified role.

Zimmer's (1986) typology has been described as static because it does not address the day-to-day situations in which a worker handles a particular situation with inconsistencies or differences (Jurik, 1988). Although Zimmer's typology is an efficient way to conceptualize the various roles that a female correctional officer may favour, it does not fully capture why worker styles can change (Jurik, 1988). In comparison with Zimmer's views, Jurik (1988) favoured the conceptual reframing of the occupational styles to a more positive image, in which the worker projected a positive image on the workplace. Female correctional officers could then be seen as "replacing derogatory images with more positive presentations of self, that is, women as competent, collegial and promotable" (Jurik, 1988, p. 293).

Various role traps and stereotypes have been theorized to apply to female correctional workers (Kanter, 1977, cited in Jurik, 1988; Zimmer, 1986). About 30 years ago, some researchers applied the concept of tokenism to female correctional workers (Kanter, 1977, cited in Jurik, 1988). At that time, the number of women working in corrections was low compared with today. Token status was defined as being a member of a collection of people who represent less than 15 percent of a total group. Consequences of tokenism were thought to include high degrees of performance pressure and visibility within an organization, role encapsulation, and boundary heightening (that is, emphasizing the unique qualities about the members of a group, which can then be distorted to result in stereotyping) (Kanter, 1977, cited in Jurik, 1988). Although today women comprise much more than 15 percent of the workforce in corrections, these consequences may still exist for some women working in non-traditional occupations.

When stereotypes exist, they form role traps that maintain the distance between the tokens and the dominant group (Jurik, 1988). A number of informal stereotypes have been said to exist for women who work in occupations not traditionally filled by females: the pet, the seductress, the iron maiden, and the mother. The pet is described as a woman who is weak, innocent, and incompetent, akin to a little sister who needs some sort of protection from a male. The seductress is "sexually desirable, potentially available, often manipulative, and as incompetent as the little sister" (Jurik, 1988, p. 292). The iron maiden is a woman who is seen as being competent, but who is cold, harsh, and asexual. Lastly, the mother is "supportive, scolding, and incapable of independent action" (Jurik, 1988, p. 242). In all these stereotypes, the female correctional officer, as a woman working in a traditionally male role, is seen as having characteristics that make her an undesirable colleague.

The strategies that female officers have used to avoid role traps and stereotypes include casting a professional image, using humour, demonstrating unique skills, taking a team approach, and enhancing visibility through the use of sponsorship (Jurik, 1988). Each strategy has its pros and cons. Those who have a professional demeanour may effectively remove any problems related to the perception of female officer sexuality; however, they might be prone to "Queen Bee" syndrome, where very rule-minded behaviour may be seen in a negative light by co-workers and supervisors (Kanter, 1977, cited in Jurik, 1988, p. 297). Similarly, those who are able to use humour might find it an effective strategy, but it doesn't always work (Jurik, 1988).

By demonstrating a unique skill, a woman can establish competence in a way that allows others to appreciate her unique contributions to the workplace. As an example, a woman who has excellent communication and crisis management abilities might find that she is able to use these skills in an effective manner in the prison setting. The use of this unique skill may enable a female officer to enhance her profile in a manner that is less threatening to her male colleagues (Jurik, 1988).

Officers who are able to take a team approach may be seen to avoid role traps and stereotypes because the rapport among their colleagues is enhanced when, in tough situations, the team-oriented players are there to help the others. Lastly, making effective use of sponsorship involves "striking a balance between isolation and being too closely identified with a sponsor" (Jurik, 1988, p. 301). Informal mentoring can be an effective strategy; however, if an officer seeks too much sponsorship she may be viewed not as being competent but as being overly dependent on another officer. These kinds of strategies are individual-level adaptations, and even when such strategies are used, they are not always successful in avoiding negative stereotypes. In the absence of organized support to assist the integration of female correctional officers into men's facilities, women have often been left to make these kinds of individual-level adaptations on their own (Jurik, 1988).

Job Stress and Job Satisfaction

Job Stress

Stress needs to be considered from both an individual and an organizational perspective. Occupational or workplace stress has been described as any disturbance that affects individuals in terms of their social, psychological, or physiological functioning; it arises in response to a condition that exists in the environment or at work; and it poses a threat, perceived or real, to a person's safety or well-being (Armstrong & Griffin, 2004). Not only does stress negatively affect the individual but it can also have negative effects on the organization. When the staff of an organization is stressed, job satisfaction may be low, and the organization may experience high absentee rates, poor morale, internal conflicts, and difficulties retaining staff. Absenteeism has been associated with job stress, job satisfaction, organizational commitment, and personal characteristics (Lambert, Edwards, Camp, & Saylor, 2005).

Job Stress and Correctional Work

Although sources of stress for correctional officers in Canada are varied, the sparse research on Canadian correctional officers suggests that, for the most part, officers are able to adequately cope with the stressors they encounter (Griffiths, 2004). In his review of the stressors associated with correctional work, Griffiths identified some threats to personal safety that most correctional officers face daily, including violence and exposure to disease (HIV/AIDS, tuberculosis, and hepatitis).

Millson (2002) found that the largest predictor of stress among Canadian correctional officers was the perception of personal security. Variables related to the operation of the organization were also predictors of stress: staff empowerment, the impact of shift work, job security, and an understanding of work procedures (Millson, 2002). Others have found that a lack of respect or lack of support from senior management and the increased emphasis on inmate rights are sources of stress (Griffiths, 2004). Additionally, stressors related to the nature of the job itself (shift work, lack of training, the need to multi-task, negative effects on one's family) are common. Frequently, the institutional environment itself is viewed as a source of stress (Griffiths, 2004).

Most of the research on stress and correctional work has focused on the experiences of correctional officers (Cheek & Miller, 1983; Dollard & Winefield, 1994; Huckabee,

1992; Keinan & Malach-Pines, 2007; Pollak & Sigler, 1998). Research into stress levels among correctional supervisors found that stress levels were low for this group, and no differences were seen between the stress levels of male and female supervisors (Owen, 2006). In a Canadian study of stress levels among correctional officers in northern Ontario, similarly low levels of stress were reported (Pollak & Sigler, 1998). Contrary to this finding, most of the research on correctional officers has found that they experience considerable levels of stress on the job, as evidenced by their high rates of divorce and such serious health problems as hypertension and heart disease (Cheek & Miller, 1983; Huckabee, 1992; Lambert, Hogan, Camp, & Ventura, 2006). However, some have suggested that correctional officers tend not to acknowledge their stress because such an admission might imply weakness on their part (Cheek & Miller, 1983). Additional evidence suggests that, despite their high levels of stress and burnout, correctional officers appear satisfied with their work and do not plan on leaving their jobs in the future (Keinan & Malach-Pines, 2007).

In 1992, Robert Huckabee provided an overview of the research conducted to that date on stress in corrections. This work has been extensively referenced because it served as an effective summary of the research in the area and, more importantly, made some sage recommendations about the direction the field needed to move toward. Huckabee (1992) noted that research had, until that point, been very much "hit and miss"—that is, not well organized in terms of addressing specific patterns or themes (p. 479). He recommended the research become more systematic to address questions about how much stress was in correctional work, how it manifested itself, where it was located, what it correlated with, and how it could be reduced or eliminated (Huckabee, 1992).

Considerable research has been carried out looking at stress and correctional work in many countries, including the United States (Armstrong & Griffin, 2004; Auerbach, Quick, & Pegg, 2003; Cheek & Miller, 1983; Lambert et al., 2006; Owen, 2006; Tewksbury & Higgins, 2006), Canada (Pollak & Sigler, 1998), Israel (Keinan & Malach-Pines, 2007), South Korea (Moon & Maxwell, 2004), and Australia (Brough & Williams, 2007), to name a few. Early research in the area of stress and corrections tended not to focus on gender as a variable of interest; research that did focus on gender as a variable tended to be in the minority (Jurik, 1988), likely reflective of the low percentage of women employed in these predominantly male roles. Because increasing numbers of women are being employed in correctional work, more recent studies have been able to focus exclusively on women or to include enough women in their samples to allow for comparisons to be made with men in similar jobs (Armstrong & Griffin, 2004; Auerbach et al., 2003; Moon & Maxwell, 2004; Triplett, Mullings, & Scarborough, 1999).

Individuals who have more contact with offenders (such as custody personnel) are likely to have more job stress than non-custody personnel, who do not work directly with offenders (Lambert et al., 2006). Job stress has also been found to increase as the length of time working at a correctional facility increases (Lambert et al., 2006). The importance of supervisor support has also been identified as a key factor in addressing occupational stress in correctional officers (Brough & Williams, 2007).

In addition to higher levels of job stress, correctional officers have also reported much lower levels of job satisfaction than non-custody correctional personnel (Lambert et al., 2006). Their higher stress levels are not surprising, considering the obvious link between experiencing stressors on the job and feeling a sense of satisfaction at work.

In a meta-analysis, Dowden and Tellier (2004) analyzed 20 studies for an examination of job stress in correctional workers. This statistical technique allowed the researchers to aggregate the results of a group of studies (that had been conducted independently) to come to a conclusion regarding the results (Dowden & Tellier, 2004). Dowden and Tellier's results suggested demographic variables had an unimpressive effect on correctional stress, and when individual variables were examined, the researchers found that gender, education, marital status, and number of children were all very weak predictors. Much stronger predictors were found for work-related attitudes, such as participation in decision-making, commitment, and job satisfaction. These factors showed significant negative effects on stress. That is, those officers who were engaged in decision-making, who were committed to the organization, and who had higher job satisfaction were less likely to express work stress. They also found that intent to leave the job was a positive predictor of work stress: those employees who expressed a desire to leave their job were more likely to experience higher levels of job stress (Dowden & Tellier, 2004). Additionally, the researchers found that perceived dangerousness was also linked to significantly higher levels of work stress. In this meta-analysis, little support was found for the role of job characteristics.

Job Stress Specific to Women Working in Corrections

Huckabee (1992) highlighted some important considerations regarding women's experiences of stress in the correctional context, including experiences of harassment and discrimination (more from male co-workers than from male inmates) (Pogrebin & Poole, 1998; Zimmer, 1986). To compound the issue, an additional stressor that served to increase the negative experiences was supervisory inaction (Zimmer, 1986). Higher stress levels experienced by women correctional officers (compared with their male counterparts) may be explained by women's experiences of sexism on the job (Jurik, 1988; Lovrich & Stohr, 1993).

Some stressors specific to women have been identified in more recent literature. Women employed as juvenile correctional officers reported higher levels of stress resulting from both lack of agency support and everyday activities of the job (Auerbach et al., 2003). Women have also been reported to experience greater stress levels at work when behaviour-based work–home conflict was evident (Triplett et al., 1999). The higher levels of work–home conflict seen for women were not surprising, given the very different cultural expectations for women both at home and at work. As Triplett et al. (1999) noted, their findings suggested women are still struggling to find a way to deal with this work–home conflict. Women correctional officers (and younger officers) have been found to report significantly more health-related concerns than men and older officers (Armstrong & Griffin, 2004).

Job Satisfaction

Job satisfaction involves "a subjective, individual-level feeling reflecting whether a person's needs are or are not being met by a particular job" (Lambert, Hogan, & Barton, 2002, p. 116). Studies on job satisfaction among correctional workers tend to use global measures of job satisfaction, in which individuals are asked to form their own opinion about their overall level of job satisfaction (Lambert et al., 2002).

Job Satisfaction and Correctional Work

In recent years, researchers have shown an increased interest in studying factors that affect job satisfaction in correctional workers (Griffin, 2001; Jurik & Halemba, 1984; Jurik, Halemba, Musheno, & Boyle, 1987; Lambert et al., 2002; Lovrich & Stohr, 1993; Tewksbury & Higgins, 2006). The reason is pragmatic: when people have high levels of job satisfaction, they tend to engage in positive behaviours (such as support for rehabilitation and performance) (Lambert et al., 2002). On the other hand, low levels of job satisfaction have been associated with more negative kinds of behaviours, such as absenteeism and job turnover (Lambert et al., 2002). Organizations that want to attract and retain quality staff need to maximize job satisfaction. Correctional services is no different from any other corporation when it comes to these kinds of human resources issues. Therefore, it needs to increase job satisfaction among correctional workers. As with job stress, correlates of job satisfaction tend to fall into one of two groups: personal characteristics and work environment (Lambert et al., 2002). In correctional settings, factors related to work environment appear to have more of an effect on job satisfaction than personal factors (Griffin, 2001; Lambert et al., 2002).

Personal characteristics include background factors (educational level, specifics regarding a person's upbringing), demographic factors (gender, age, race, ethnicity), and other factors (family income, religion, distance from work), although the latter tend to be infrequently investigated (Lambert et al., 2002). These sorts of personal characteristics are the attributes that we take to our jobs, and they tend to shape the way we interpret the world around us.

Lambert et al. (2002), in their recent review of the correctional literature, noted that research that looked at job satisfaction and educational levels reported mixed results. However, they came to the tentative conclusion that a negative relationship existed between education level and job satisfaction among correctional officers. They reported no overall relationship between job satisfaction and race and no clear link between gender and job satisfaction. Although the reviewers reported that age and tenure related to job satisfaction, the results were also mixed (Lambert et al., 2002).

Work environment is more than the workplace setting; it consists of "the factors or characteristics that comprise the overall work conditions and situations for an employee, both tangible and intangible" (Lambert et al., 2002, p. 125).

Job stress and stressors have been studied most frequently for their possible relationship to job satisfaction. For the most part, the research literature has shown a negative association between these two variables: the greater the job stress, the lower the job satisfaction among correctional staff, especially correctional officers (Lambert et al., 2002). In addition, job autonomy and participation in decision-making are positively linked to job satisfaction, as are positive attitudes toward supervisors and administration (Lambert et al., 2002).

Job Satisfaction in Women Working in Corrections

The literature specific to women's job satisfaction in correctional settings is fairly sparse. However, researchers found that female correctional employees reported lower levels of job satisfaction than male correctional staff, which, they pointed out, was counter to the findings in much of the literature (Lambert et al., 2006). Most other studies have not reported significant relationships between gender and job satisfaction (Jurik & Halemba, 1984; Moon & Maxwell, 2004). In Lambert et al.'s (2002) review, gender did not appear to have any relationship with job satisfaction.

Griffin (2001) found that although male and female correctional officers shared similar levels of job satisfaction, the factors that influenced their job satisfaction differed. Females tended to believe that the work environment was safer than did the men, yet the women viewed themselves as being more vulnerable in this setting. Perhaps because the male correctional officers had embraced the stereotypical image of a dominant, aggressive, and authoritarian guard, they viewed the setting as more dangerous (Griffin, 2001). As reported in earlier studies, the women also valued the human service aspect of the work (Griffin, 2001; Jurik & Halemba, 1984). According to this study, women and men differ very little in their level of job satisfaction, but they do differ in why they find the job satisfying (Griffin, 2001). In this sense, gender may be seen to play a "moderating role in the relationship between organizational climate and job satisfaction" (Griffin, 2001, p. 228).

The Consequences of Job Satisfaction in Correctional Staff

Research has looked at the consequences of low and high job satisfaction on variables such as productivity, staff turnover, and absenteeism. High levels of job satisfaction have been associated with a number of positive outcomes, such as motivated workers and good productivity, whereas low levels of job satisfaction have been linked with negative outcomes, such as high absenteeism and job turnover (Lambert et al., 2002). In their review of the literature, Lambert et al. (2002) noted a relationship between low levels of job satisfaction and negative work behaviour. However, only turnover and, to a lesser extent, absenteeism were researched to any degree.

The conclusion from Lambert et al.'s (2002) thorough review of the literature pertaining to job satisfaction among correctional staff is that correctional administrators should be paying attention to job satisfaction. To be accountable, administrators should be concerned with retaining their well-trained staff members, because each trained employee represents a considerable financial commitment. In addition, high job satisfaction is associated with a plethora of positive outcomes for the organization. Lambert et al. (2002) recommended that to improve job satisfaction among correctional staff, administrators should focus on the work variables that can be changed, not the staff's personal characteristics.

Salient Issues for Staff in the Canadian Correctional System

Cross-gender staffing is an issue for staff regardless of whether a worker is a male employed in a female prison or a female employed in a male prison. The research into this issue in the United States is relevant to workers in Canadian prisons. Similarly, the dangers of working in a prison exist for both men and women, and many of the issues identified in American studies are also pertinent in a Canadian context.

Cross-Gender Staffing Issues

The debate regarding cross-gender staffing is not a new one, but was highlighted as an issue following the release of the Arbour report in 1996. In her report, Madam Justice Louise Arbour made a number of recommendations specific to the issue of cross-gender staffing. She recommended, among other things, that at least one federal women's institution not be staffed with any men in the living units. She further suggested that explicit protocols be put into place regarding male access to the living units to ensure that men were always paired with a female staff member when on patrol, that men not patrol the living units at night, and that men be required to announce their presence on a living unit or at a woman's cell or room. Justice Arbour recommended that the CSC's sexual harassment policy be extended to apply to both inmates and staff. In addition, recommendations were made concerning the design of the new prisons, to ensure appropriate levels of privacy for inmates, especially when bathing, using the washroom, and dressing and undressing. For areas where inmates were being closely monitored, she recommended the installation of modesty barriers.

In terms of cross-gender monitoring, Justice Arbour recommended that:

> a woman be appointed to monitor and report annually for the next three years following the opening of each new regional facility, to the Deputy Commissioner for Women on the implementation of the cross-gender staffing policy in the living units of the new institutions, and on related issues, including the effectiveness of the extension of the sexual harassment policy to the protection of inmates. (Canada, Commission of Inquiry, 1996, p. 253)

The recommendations specific to the cross-gender monitor included the suggestion that the monitor be independent from the CSC and have confidential access to both inmates and staff. The mandate of the monitor was to assess the system, not the individuals per se, and to recommend improvements to the system (Canada, Commission of Inquiry, 1996). Further, any reports generated should be made public, and the deputy commissioner for women should, after three years, make recommendations to the commissioner regarding the future of the cross-gender staffing policy, taking into account the findings of the monitor (Canada, Commission of Inquiry, 1996).

The first of three cross-gender monitoring reports was released in October 1998 (CSC, 1998).

The second report included an in-depth investigation into such issues as employment, staff training, sexual harassment, privacy, grievances, abuse of power, special needs offenders, and Indigenous women (CSC, 2000).

The third and final annual report of the cross-gender monitoring project was completed in 2000 (Lajeunesse, Jefferson, Nuffield, & Majury, 2000). This report recommended the screening of all personnel, women-centred training for all staff, and the availability of sufficient resources to accomplish both. The monitor also recommended that women never be left alone with men in unobserved areas and that the CSC complete a review to determine which (if any) positions should be designated female only. A series of recommendations was offered to better deal with allegations of sexual harassment and sexual misconduct. Recommendations were also made concerning the correctional investigator's role. The most striking recommendation in the final report was that there be "an end to the use of male staff members as front-line primary workers (PWs) in facilities for federally sentenced women inmates" (Lajeunesse et al., 2000, p. 1).

Around the same time that the monitor's report was being completed, the Canadian Human Rights Commission (CHRC) began a review of how women offenders were treated by the CSC (CHRC, 2003). This review was in response to a complaint laid by the Canadian Association of Elizabeth Fry Societies and the National Women's Association of Canada (CSC, 2005). In its report, the CHRC determined that the CSC should "vigorously pursue other alternatives before impairing the employment rights of men in such a fashion" (CHRC, 2003, p. 43). The CHRC noted that the CSC had undertaken a number of steps in an attempt to reduce the probability that staff would harass offenders, and the CHRC supported the continued use of a gender-neutral staffing policy by the CSC. The CSC implemented a special protocol for men in front-line positions, women-centred training was offered to staff, and the selection process for staff was improved.

The CSC began both an internal and external consultation process on the recommendations contained in the report of the cross-gender monitoring project (CSC, 2005). In its response to the report, the CSC made reference to the CHRC report, in which the employment of men as front-line workers was supported. The CSC also reported on the results of its consultations and indicated that the majority of those consulted disagreed with the monitor's assertion that men should not be allowed to be employed as front-line workers in women's facilities.

A number of initiatives were implemented to address cross-gender staffing concerns (CSC, 2005). The women-centred training program was updated to fit with the national operational protocol. A process was introduced to address issues related to the deployment of primary workers (to ensure that the staff was prepared to work in a women-centred environment). The CSC has also enhanced and standardized its selection process for primary workers and has developed a process to select assistant team leaders (CSC, 2005). Men continue to be employed as primary workers in federal women's prisons in Canada.

▶ WHAT DO YOU THINK?

Imagine that you are working as a correctional officer in a prison that houses members of the opposite sex (note: for the purpose of this question we will utilize a binary definition of gender: male and female). What are some of the concerns that might be raised about your working in this prison? What challenges would you face pertaining to mixed-gender staffing? Do you think it is reasonable to place any restrictions on aspects of your job based entirely on your gender, or would you consider this a violation of your human rights?

Sexual Relationships with Inmates

Although sexual relationships between correctional staff and inmates are isolated incidents, reports of this behaviour are publicized widely. The media has reported numerous stories of staff who have been accused of trading drugs for sex (Seglins & Noël, 2012) or lost their jobs because of inappropriate relationships with inmates (Blackwell, 2004; Dawson, 2000; Female Staff, 1994; High Proportion, 1994; Pritchard, 2016). Consider these headlines: "Boyfriends behind bars: It's not unusual for female guards to have relations with prisoners" (Blackwell, 2004), "Jail guard admits smuggling drugs to extort sex" (Pritchard, 2016), and "High proportion of female guards cited by probe of guard–inmate sex" (High Proportion, 1994). Neither the federal correctional system nor the provincial and territorial correctional systems condone any kind of a sexual relationship between staff and offenders. According to the commissioner's Directive Code of Discipline, in the federal system, a staff member is not to enter into any kind of a personal relationship with an offender. Engaging in this kind of behaviour is clearly a violation of professional standards.

Dangers of Working in the Correctional System

Through the media, we seem to be inundated with the message that prisons and jails are violent places to work. In reality, most people employed in corrections in Canada spend their lives working in prisons and are never harmed by offenders. However, that is not to say that injuries never occur or that dangers do not exist. Moreover, some evidence suggests that male and female correctional officers differ with respect to their fears and their perceptions of risk associated with their work (Gordon & Moriarty, 2005). In a study of youth correctional workers, female officers had higher levels of fear and their perception of risk was higher when surveyed about the potential occurrence of riots and being attacked by an inmate. Their perception of risk was also higher for a variable related to personal threats from offenders (Gordon & Moriarty, 2005).

Working in a correctional setting has more potential for danger and violence than working in an office or other community setting. A major concern for both men and women working in corrections is offenders' assaults on staff and on other offenders. In 2005-06, 243 staff members in the federal correctional system were injured on the job as a result of 357 inmate assaults on staff and 557 assaults on other offenders (CSC, 2007). On average, between 2011 and 2016, there were 310 assaults annually on staff in federal correctional facilities (Cottrill, 2017). Assaults on correctional officers increased by 39 percent from 2014 to 2015, and in Ontario, there was an increase from 505 incidents (assaults, attempted assaults, and threats) in 2014 to 654 in 2015 (Cottrill, 2017). Newspaper headlines like "Assaults nearly double at Nova Scotia jail, records show" (Tutton, 2015), and "Assaults on staff at Ontario prisons skyrocketing" (Mallen, 2014) capture the reader's attention. Approximately two-thirds of workplace accidents reported in CSC involve correctional officers (Stone, 2014). The national vice-president of the Union of Correctional Officers attributes the increase in work-related injuries to increases in violence in institutions (Stone, 2014). Possible reasons for the increase in violence toward staff include the higher percentage of offenders who reported gang affiliation at intake, high rates of substance abuse in offender populations, overcrowding, and understaffing. In the British Columbia correctional system, prior to 2002, the ratio of officer-to-inmate was one to twenty in the living units. A ratio of one to seventy-two is not unheard of now (Cottrill, 2017). Reports of double and even triple bunking have been reported at the Saskatoon Correctional Centre in Saskatchewan (Cottrill, 2017).

Post-Traumatic Stress Injuries (PTSI)

Recent news coverage (Adam, 2016; Mallen, 2014; Purdon, 2015; Stone, 2014) has highlighted workplace accidents, assaults, and the issue of post-traumatic stress disorder (PTSD) among prison guards. Assistant Deputy Minister Lori MacDonald (Department of Safety) reported that government surveys indicate "that about 36 percent of male correctional officers have identified as having post-traumatic stress disorder" (Galloway, 2016, p. 5). No rates of PTSD among female correctional officers in Canada were reported (Galloway, 2016). Public Safety Canada (PSC) recognizes that, over the course of their careers, public safety officers are exposed to various kinds of traumatic incidents that can put them at risk of developing operational stress injuries (OSIs) (PSC, n.d.). PTSI is a type of OSI. An OSI is a non-medical term that refers to "persistent psychological difficulties resulting from operational duties" (PSC, n.d., p. 5). By referring to this as PTSI instead of PTSD, there is a hope that there will be a reduction in stigma associated with these mental health issues. In addition, there is recognition that the impact of experiencing traumatic incidents at work can include drug and alcohol abuse, depression, anxiety, and different mental health challenges other than a diagnosis of PTSD (PSC, n.d.).

People who are diagnosed with PTSD may re-experience or relive the trauma in the form of flashbacks or nightmares. They may even become extremely upset when something reminds them of the traumatic event. People with PTSD might avoid places or people that remind them of the trauma. They may isolate themselves. They may feel numb, or even experience an increased sensitivity where they may feel on guard or irritable, or have trouble sleeping (PSC, n.d.). Research from France indicates that prison workers prone to PTSD show high levels of emotional exhaustion, stress, intrusion, avoidance, hyperreactivity, and depersonalization (Boudoukha, Altintas, Rusinek, Fantini-Hauwel, & Hautekeete, 2013).

Likely in response to concerns about OSI, CSC has piloted the Road to Mental Readiness (R2MR) program that was developed by the Department of Defence (Adam, 2016) and plans are in place to roll out R2MR as part of its national training standard (Goodale, 2017). In this way, the CSC hopes to ensure that employees are prepared mentally for the challenges inherent in their work. Workplace wellness has been identified as an important issue by the CSC, given that nearly 45 percent of all federal public service disability claims are for depression, stress, and other types of mental illness (May, 2010, cited in Bensimon, 2010).

Work–Family Conflict

Work–family conflict (WFC) has been described as "a multi-dimensional, bi-directional concept" (Lambert et al., 2006, p. 372). This conflict takes on two distinct forms: work on family conflict and family on work conflict. In work on family conflict, issues and problems related to the workplace have a negative effect on the person's family life. For family on work conflict, the opposite occurs: issues and problems related to family life spill over into the person's work life. In either case, conflict is created.

WFC can be further divided into time-based conflict, strain-based conflict, and behaviour-based conflict (Netemeyer, Boles, & McMurrian, 1996). In time-based conflict, the amount of time that employees spend at work (or home) interferes with their home (or work) responsibilities in some way. Those working in correctional settings may experience time-based conflict because the nature of the job requires 24-hour-a-day shift scheduling and mandatory overtime to accommodate staffing shortages or crisis response (Lambert et al., 2006). Strain-based conflict is an issue for those working in a correctional setting, when the effects of the job (fatigue, tension, irritability, or shock, for example) spill over into family life (Lambert et al., 2006). Lastly, behaviour-based conflict can result when the requirements of the job (barking orders and taking physical control of inmates, for example) conflict with how one should respond to and treat family members (Lambert et al., 2006). Research has shown that job satisfaction among correctional staff can be significantly affected by both behaviour-based and strain-based conflicts. Time-based conflicts, behaviour-based conflicts, and family on work conflicts have been found to have significant effects on organizational commitment (Lambert et al., 2006).

Perceptions of Competency and Sexism

In the past, female correctional officers were viewed by their male co-workers as being innately inferior (Zimmer, 1986). They have also been tokenized and viewed as sex objects by their peers (Pogrebin & Poole, 1997). Some of the women who were among the first to break into this male-dominated occupation allege that they experienced so much abuse from their co-workers that they now suffer from post-traumatic stress disorders (Lu, 2001). In an Ontario case in which compensation was being sought for job harassment, the plaintiffs reported abuses that included criticism over their weight, being called derogatory names, being forced to ask for a washroom key, having their cars tampered with, being exposed to pornography on the job, and having sanitary napkins displayed in an attempt to mock the women (Lu, 2001). In a landmark case in Quebec, Claudine Lippe was awarded almost $143,000 for the sexual harassment that she experienced during the two years she worked as a jail guard. The Quebec Public Security Department was ordered to pay her this money as compensation and for moral damages resulting from the sexual harassment that she endured on the job (Cornacchia, 1998). To date, there do not appear to be any class action suits in the corrections field similar to the case study of the RCMP included at the beginning of Chapter 11.

Negative experiences were documented among the pioneering women who first worked in federal male institutions in the late 1970s and into the early 1980s (Sakowski, 1986). These women suffered from both systemic and individual harassment. As an example of systemic harassment, because the majority of the women had not been issued uniforms when they began work, they had to wear civilian clothes to work. They did not have their own washroom; they had to use a washroom open to the public. There were no showers and no change room designated for them. They were constantly monitored by middle management (whereas their male counterparts were not).

The most disturbing cases of harassment by individuals were the abuses that women were subjected to by their co-workers. Comments were made about their "lack of 'appropriate' male genitalia … degrading comments referring to tits and ass" and "the underlying motive behind the harassment appeared to be the resignation en masse of the women" (Sakowski, 1986, p. 53). After five years on the job, the three women who remained in the job (out of the original eight) noted that although the harassment was no longer as overt, it was far from over (Sakowski, 1986). Despite each of the women having applied for a transfer or a promotion on at least one occasion, none had been approved, yet male officers with far less experience had been routinely promoted (Sakowski, 1986). The women commented that the only equality they had truly achieved was economic, but it was at the expense of their self-esteem and their emotional health. In a more recent study in the United States, researchers found that there were three factors that women working in corrections believed had a negative effect on their chance for promotion: 1) the perception that they could not do the job as well as men, 2) sexual harassment at work, and 3) balancing of responsibilities at work and home (Matthews, Monk-Turner, & Sumter, 2010).

Sexism may appear in a variety of ways and can be either intentionally or unconsciously expressed (Jurik, 1988; Lovrich & Stohr, 1993; Pogrebin & Poole, 1997). Regardless of how sexism is expressed, systemic sexism is often identified as being at the root of women's difficulties when they work in what have been traditionally defined as male roles (Pogrebin & Poole, 1997). As Pogrebin and Poole (1997) have noted, the sex typing of different jobs tends to follow one basic tenet: men and women are different and so they should be doing different things.

This sort of stereotypical thinking leads to the stigmatization of those (usually women) who are seen to be in violation of the aforementioned occupational segregation. In turn, this attitude reinforces the sex-role stereotyping that occurs in the workplace (Pogrebin & Poole, 1997), which accomplishes a number of objectives: women are kept busy in supportive and ancillary roles and are kept at a distance from any real positions of authority, independence, or achievement (Pogrebin & Poole, 1997). The woman who chooses to challenge the sex-role stereotypes in the workplace risks having her abilities, skills, and overall competence evaluated negatively by her peers, subordinates, and supervisors (Pogrebin & Poole, 1997).

Discrimination and Harassment of Women in the Canadian Correctional System

No discussion of the issues that face women working in corrections would be complete without some reference to discrimination and harassment. Harassment of women working in corrections must be acknowledged because, as in other traditionally male occupations, it has been so systemic. A distinction that is not often made in the literature is between gender harassment and sexual harassment (Belknap, 2004); yet, we need to acknowledge the differences between these two types of harassment. Gender harassment has been described as any non-sexual slur against either women or men based on their gender, whereas sexual harassment refers to offensive behaviours or comments that are sexual in nature (Belknap, 2004).

A key facet of Canada's conceptualization of human rights is the understanding of equality between men and women. However, despite the focus that the Status of Women Canada (SWC) has placed on this very issue in the 40 years since its inception, "women are still unequal" to men in this country (Status of Women Canada, 2007, p. 3).

Women are more likely than men to have a university degree, they are less likely than men to earn an advanced degree (only 39 percent of PhDs are held by women), and, although more women are entering the workforce than in the past, they tend to be clustered in traditionally female occupations (Ferguson, 2016; Moyser, 2017). Of working women in 2015, 56 percent were employed in occupations that involved the "5 Cs" (caring, catering, clerical, cashiering, and cleaning) (Moyser, 2017). Women earn less money than men in this country: in 2015, women earned 88 cents for every dollar earned by men, primarily as a result of wage inequality between the sexes (Moyser, 2017). This is illustrated in the average hourly wages, where women in 2014 earned $25.38 per hour while men earned $28.92 per hour (Moyser, 2017).

The level of sexual harassment that exists in correctional systems is difficult to estimate. According to Griffiths (2004), researchers who conducted internal surveys within the CSC "found a high incidence of sexual harassment, discrimination, and abuse of authority in many federal institutions" (p. 234). He indicated that at one federal institution in particular, a startling 62 percent of the female employees had been harassed by a co-worker (Griffiths, 2004). Rates of more than 50 percent were reported for the Ontario and Pacific regions (Griffiths, 2004). Some women even reported having threatening notes placed on their car windshields (Griffiths, 2004).

SUMMARY

Up until the 1970s, women occupied predominantly stereotypically female kinds of jobs within the correctional system in Canada. With the emergence of women into more traditionally male jobs, that of correctional officer, for example, the last bastion of male domination in the correctional system was breached. Much progress has been made in the last 30 years, but equality with men has not been achieved in the correctional service.

Historically, women have faced some unique barriers to working in corrections. Included among these were their own occupational interests—that is, women's tendency to favour jobs that were more traditionally female within the justice system. Also, various role traps and stereotypes could hinder a woman's career advancement in corrections. Researchers studying job stress and job satisfaction in correctional work have suggested that correctional officers are, for the most part, able to effectively cope with the myriad of stressors they face daily (Griffiths, 2004). Women, in particular, have reported higher stress levels that relate to the lack of agency support, the everyday activities of the job, and higher levels of work–home conflict (Auerbach et al., 2003; Triplett et al., 1999). In addition, women correctional officers have reported more health-related concerns than their male counterparts (Armstrong & Griffin, 2004).

A number of salient issues face those who work in Canada's correctional systems, regardless of whether they are male or female, including cross-gender staffing, sexual relationships with inmates, physical dangers, and PTSD. Other issues, such as those that relate to work–family conflict, perceptions of competency and sexism, and discrimination and harassment, may be experienced by both men and women, but are likely to be of greater concern to women than to men.

Women's involvement in correctional work is a comparatively recent phenomenon. The gains made to date will likely continue to be built upon as more and more women explore the career opportunities that exist in provincial, territorial, and federal correctional services in Canada.

NOTES

1. The abbreviation CX refers to a correctional officer.
2. For information about parole officers and federal institutions visit: www.csc-scc.gc.ca.
3. Lindsey Pecaric replicated Golden's study for her undergraduate thesis at Nipissing University. The results of the study have not yet been published. She found evidence of gendered occupational interests among undergraduate criminal justice majors.

DISCUSSION QUESTIONS

1. It was not until the 1970s that women in Canada could be employed as correctional officers in male institutions. Why did it take so long?
2. How do female correctional recruits differ from male recruits in terms of their attitudes toward the job of correctional officer? What do these differences mean in terms of the day-to-day operation of a prison?
3. What are the role traps for female correctional officers that Zimmer (1986) outlined? Do you think that these traps still exist today?
4. "The job stress that is associated with being a correctional officer is the same for men as it is for women." Do you agree with this statement? Discuss.

ADDITIONAL RESOURCES

Suggested Reading

Griffiths, C. (2014). *Canadian corrections* (4th ed.). Toronto: Nelson Education.

Films and Videos

Correctional Service of Canada. (2015). *Beyond the fence: A virtual tour of a Canadian penitentiary* [Virtual tour]. Retrieved from http://www.cbc.ca/news/multimedia/government-offers -virtual-tour-of-federal-prison-1.3038025.

Greenwald, B. (Director). (1998). *High risk offender* [Documentary]. Canada, National Film Board.

Websites

Correctional Service of Canada: www.csc-scc.gc.ca

Ministry of Community Safety and Correctional Services: www.mcscs.jus.gov.on.ca

Parole Board of Canada: https://www.canada.ca/en/parole-board.html

Probation Officers Association of Ontario: www.poao.org

REFERENCES

Across Canada women have edge for prison guard jobs. (1983, October 5). *The Globe and Mail*, p. 12.

Adam, B.A. (2016, April 24). PTSD high among prison workers, union says. *Saskatoon StarPhoenix*. Retrieved from http://thestarphoenix.com/news/local-news/ ptsd-high-among-prison-workers-union-says.

Alberta Justice and Solicitor General. (n.d.). *Community corrections*. Retrieved from https://www.solgps.alberta .ca/programs_and_services/correctional_services/ community_corrections/Pages/default.aspx.

Armstrong, G., & Griffin, M. (2004). Does the job matter? Comparing correlates of stress among treatment and correctional staff in prisons. *Journal of Criminal Justice*, *32*, 577–592.

Auerbach, S., Quick, B., & Pegg, P. (2003). General job stress and job-specific stress in juvenile correctional officers. *Journal of Criminal Justice*, *31*, 25–36.

Belknap, J. (2004). Women in conflict: An analysis of women correctional officers. In B. Raffel Price & N. Sokoloff (Eds.), *The criminal justice system and women* (pp. 543–561). Boston, MA: McGraw-Hill.

Bensimon, P. (2004). *Correctional officer recruits and the prison environment: A research framework*. Ottawa: Research Branch, Correctional Service of Canada.

Bensimon, P. (2005a). *Correctional officer recruits during the college training period: An examination*. Ottawa: Research Branch, Correctional Service of Canada.

Bensimon, P. (2005b). *Correctional officers and their first year: An empirical investigation*. Ottawa: Research Branch, Correctional Service of Canada.

Bensimon, P. (2010). *Wellness at work: A matter of choice for a better future*. Ottawa: Research Branch, Correctional Service of Canada.

Blackwell, T. (2004, January 8). Boyfriends behind bars: It's not unusual for female guards to have relations with prisoners. *National Post*, p. A5.

Boudoukha, A.H., Altintas, E., Rusinek, S., Fantini-Hauwel, C., & Hautekeete, M. (2013). Inmates-to-staff assaults, PTSD and burnout: Profiles of risk and vulnerability. *Journal of Interpersonal Violence*, *28*(11), 2332–2350.

Brough, P., & Williams, J. (2007). Managing occupational stress in a high-risk industry: Measuring the job demands of correctional officers. *Criminal Justice and Behavior*, *34*, 555–567.

Canada, Commission of Inquiry into Certain Events at the Prison for Women in Kingston. (1996). *Commission of inquiry into certain events at the Prison for Women in Kingston* (the Arbour Inquiry). Ottawa: Public Works and Government Services of Canada.

Canada, Public Service Commission. (1977). *A study of the existing sex restrictions in the correctional group CX: An emotional and controversial issue*. Ottawa: Public Service Commission.

Canadian Human Rights Commission. (1981). *Review of Correctional Service Canada's special employment program to integrate women into the correctional officer occupational group (CX-COF and CX-LUF) in male penitentiaries*. Ottawa: Author.

Canadian Human Rights Commission. (2003). *Protecting their rights: A systematic review of human rights in correctional services for federally sentenced women*. Ottawa: Author.

Cheek, F., & Miller, M. (1983). The experience of stress for correction officers: A double-bind theory of correctional stress. *Journal of Criminal Justice, 11*, 105–120.

Cleland, D. (1986, December 10). More female guards expected in Canadian prisons, hearing told. *Kingston Whig-Standard*, p. 1.

Cornacchia, C. (1998, November 16). A victory for Quebec women: Claudine Lippe wins landmark victory in sexual harassment case after complaining that fellow jail guards made her working life hell. *Montreal Gazette*, p. E1.

Correctional Service of Canada. (1980). *Employment of female correctional officers in male institutions*. Ottawa: Correctional Service of Canada.

Correctional Service of Canada. (1985). Flexibility in attaining national targets for female correctional/living unit officers. In *Operational and Resource Management Review* (Review #148). Ottawa: Affirmative Action Division, Personnel Branch, Correctional Service of Canada.

Correctional Service of Canada. (1998, September 9). *The cross-gender monitoring project first annual report* [News release]. Ottawa: Author.

Correctional Service of Canada. (2000, February 2). *The cross-gender monitoring project second annual report* [News release]. Ottawa: Author.

Correctional Service of Canada. (2002). *Commissioner's Directive 253: Employee assistance program*. Ottawa: Author.

Correctional Service of Canada. (2005). *The cross-gender monitoring project: CSC's response to the third and final annual report*. Retrieved from http://www.csc-scc.gc.ca/publications/fsw/gender4/CGM_response-eng.shtml.

Correctional Service of Canada. (2007). *Correctional Service Canada: Report on plans and priorities*. Ottawa: Public Safety and Emergency Preparedness Canada.

Correctional Service of Canada. (2012). *Our mission*. Retrieved from http://www.csc-scc.gc.ca/about-us/index-eng.shtml.

Cottrill, J. (2017, February 22). Trouble in the big house. *OHS Canada: Canada's Occupational Health and Safety Magazine*. Retrieved from http://www.ohscanada.com/features/trouble-big-house/.

Dawson, F. (2000, February 28). Female guard investigated for having sex with inmate: Lesbian love affair is said to have been going on for some time. *Vancouver Province*, p. A4.

Dollard, M., & Winefield, A. (1994). Organizational response to recommendations based on a study of stress among correctional officers. *International Journal of Stress Management, 1*, 81–101.

Dowden, C., & Tellier, C. (2004). Predicting work-related stress in correctional officers: A meta-analysis. *Journal of Criminal Justice, 32*, 31–47.

Female staff out of jobs after jail sex. (1994, February 20). *Vancouver Province*, p. A38.

Ferguson, S.J. (2016). Women and education: Qualifications, skills and technology. In *Women in Canada: A gender-based statistical report*. Ottawa: Statistics Canada. Retrieved from http://www.statcan.gc.ca/pub/89-503-x/2015001/article/14640-eng.pdf.

Galloway, G. (2016, July 27). PTSD affects 36 per cent of male prison officers, federal data reveal. *The Globe and Mail*. Retrieved from http://license.icopyright.net/user/viewFreeUse.act?fuid=MjQ4OTM5OTY%3D.

Golden, K. (1982). Women in criminal justice: Occupational interests. *Journal of Criminal Justice, 10*, 147–152.

Goodale, R. (2017). *Correctional Services Canada 2015-16: Departmental performance report*. Ottawa: Ministry of Public Safety and Emergency Preparedness Canada. Retrieved from http://www.csc-scc.gc.ca/005/007/092/005007-4500-2015-2016-eng.pdf.

Gordon, J., & Moriarty, L. (2005). Who's afraid of Johnny Rotten? Assessing female correctional staff's perceived fear and risk of victimization in a juvenile male institution. In R. Muraskin (Ed.), *It's a crime: Women and justice* (pp. 661–678). Upper Saddle River, NJ: Pearson Prentice-Hall.

Government of Canada. (2006). Probation and parole officers. In *Career handbook 2006*. Retrieved from http://noc.esdc.gc.ca/English/CH/QuickProfile.aspx?ver=06&sub=0&ch=03&v=4155.1.

Griffin, M. (2001). Job satisfaction among detention officers: Assessing the relative contribution of organizational climate variables. *Journal of Criminal Justice, 29*, 219–232.

Griffiths, C. (2004). *Canadian corrections*. Toronto: Thomson Nelson.

High proportion of female guards cited by probe of guard-inmate sex. (1994, March 3). *Montreal Gazette*, p. A13.

Huckabee, R. (1992). Stress in corrections: An overview of the issues. *Journal of Criminal Justice, 20*, 479–486.

Jamieson, Beals, Lalonde, & Associates Inc. (1990). *Employment barriers for women: Final report*. Ottawa: Correctional Service of Canada.

Jurik, N. (1988). Striking a balance: Female correctional officers, gender role stereotypes, and male prisons. *Sociological Inquiry, 58*, 291–305.

Jurik, N., & Halemba, G. (1984). Gender, working conditions and the job satisfaction of women in a non-traditional occupation: Female correctional officers in men's prisons. *The Sociological Quarterly, 25,* 551–566.

Jurik, N., Halemba, G., Musheno, M., & Boyle, B. (1987). Educational attainment, job satisfaction, and the professionalization of correctional officers. *Work and Occupations, 14,* 106–125.

Keinan, G., & Malach-Pines, A. (2007). Stress and burnout among prison personnel: Sources, outcomes, and intervention strategies. *Criminal Justice and Behavior, 34,* 380–398.

Kershaw, A. (1985a, August 10). The changing of the guard "whiz" kids with degrees lead to prison staff woes increasing danger, stress two recent reports. *Kingston Whig-Standard,* p. 1.

Kershaw, A. (1985b, December 13). Millhaven is ready to take applications from women for guard jobs. *Kingston Whig-Standard,* p. 1.

Lajeunesse, T., Jefferson, C., Nuffield, J., & Majury, D. (2000). *The cross-gender monitoring project: Third and final annual report.* Winnipeg: Thérèse Lajeunesse and Associates Ltd.

Lambert, E., Edwards, C., Camp, S., & Saylor, W. (2005). Here today, gone tomorrow, back again the next day: Antecedents of correctional absenteeism. *Journal of Criminal Justice, 33,* 165–175.

Lambert, E., Hogan, N., & Barton, S. (2002). Satisfied correctional staff: A review of the literature on the correlates of correctional staff job satisfaction. *Criminal Justice and Behavior, 29,* 115–143.

Lambert, E., Hogan, N., Camp, S., & Ventura, L. (2006). The impact of work-family conflict on correctional staff: A preliminary study. *Criminology and Criminal Justice, 6,* 371–387.

Large, B. (1986, March 1). Women guarding men. *Kingston Whig-Standard,* p. 1.

Lovrich, N., & Stohr, M. (1993). Gender and jail work: Correctional policy implications of perceptual diversity in the work force. *Policy Studies Review, 12,* 66–84.

Lu, V. (2001, March 2). Women guards in male jails: "They were trying to humiliate us." Compensation being sought for job harassment. *Toronto Star,* p. A1.

MacAlpine, I., (2016, April 6). Correctional officers officially first responders. *Kingston Whig-Standard.* Retrieved from http://www.thewhig.com/2016/04/06/correctional-officers-officially-first-responders.

Malakieh, J. (2017). Youth correctional statistics in Canada, 2015/16. *Juristat.* Retrieved from http://www.statcan.gc.ca/pub/85-002-x/2017001/article/14702-eng.pdf.

Mallen, S. (2014, December 3). Assaults on staff at Ontario prisons skyrocketing. Global News. Retrieved from http://globalnews.ca/news/1734283/assaults-on-staff-at-ontario-prisons-skyrocketing/.

Matthews, C., Monk-Turner, E., & Sumter, M. (2010). Promotional opportunities: How women in corrections perceive their chances for advancement at work. *Gender Issues, 27,* 53–66.

McMahon, M. (1999). *Women on guard: Discrimination and harassment in corrections.* Toronto: University of Toronto Press.

Milan, A. (2015). *Women in Canada: A gender-based statistical report.* Ottawa: Statistics Canada. Retrieved from http://www.statcan.gc.ca/pub/89-503-x/2015001/article/14152-eng.pdf.

Millson, W. (2002). Predictors of work stress among correctional officers. *Forum on Corrections Research, 14*(1), 45–47.

Moon, B., & Maxwell, S. (2004). The sources and consequences of corrections officers' stress: A South Korean example. *Journal of Criminal Justice, 32,* 359–370.

Moyser, M. (2017). Women and paid work. In *Women in Canada: A gender based statistical report.* Ottawa: Statistics Canada. Retrieved from http://www.statcan.gc.ca/pub/89-503-x/2015001/article/14694-eng.pdf.

Netemeyer, R., Boles, J., & McMurrian, R. (1996). Development and validation of work-family conflict and family-work conflict scales. *Journal of Applied Psychology, 81,* 400–410.

Ontario, Ministry of Community Safety and Correctional Services. (2006). *Careers in corrections: Becoming a probation and parole officer.* Retrieved from www.gov.on.ca.

Outhit, J. (1999, November 25). Neighbors warming to prison for women; Residents who once opposed the Grand Valley Institution give it a high rating during tour. *Kitchener Record,* p. B3.

Owen, S. (2006). Occupational stress among correctional supervisors. *Prison Journal, 86,* 164–181.

Parole Board of Canada (PBC). (n.d.). *Parole Board of Canada.* Retrieved from https://www.canada.ca/en/parole-board.html.

Parole Board of Canada (PBC). (2017). *List of Parole Board of Canada board members by region.* Retrieved from https://www.canada.ca/en/parole-board/services/board-members/list-of-parole-board-of-canada-board-members-by-region.html.

Pogrebin, M., & Poole, E. (1997). The sexualized work environment: A look at women jail officers. *Prison Journal, 77,* 41–47.

Pogrebin, M., & Poole, E. (1998). Women deputies and jail work. *Journal of Contemporary Criminal Justice, 14,* 117–134.

Pollak, C., & Sigler, R. (1998). Low levels of stress among Canadian correctional officers in the northern region of Ontario. *Journal of Criminal Justice, 26,* 117–128.

Power, J., & Usher, A. (2014). *Working with offenders who self-injure: Fostering staff resilience in high stress situations* (Research Report R-276). Ottawa: Correctional Service of Canada.

Pritchard, D. (2016, July 3). Jail guard admits smuggling drugs to extort sex. *Winnipeg Sun.* Retrieved from http://www.winnipegsun.com/2016/07/03/jail-guard -admits-smuggling-drugs-to-extort-sex.

Probation Officers Association of Ontario (POAO). (n.d.). What we do. Retrieved from http://www.poao.org/about/.

Public Safety Canada (PSC). (n.d.). *Post-traumatic stress injuries and support for public safety officers.* Ottawa: Public Safety Canada. Retrieved from https://www.publicsafety .gc.ca/cnt/mrgnc-mngmnt/mrgnc-prprdnss/ptsi-en.aspx ?wbdisable=false.

Public Safety Canada (PSC). (2016). *2015 Corrections and conditional release statistical overview.* (Cat. No. PS1-3E-PDF). Ottawa: Public Safety Canada. Retrieved from https://www.publicsafety.gc.ca/cnt/rsrcs/pblctns/ ccrso-2015/ccrso-2015-en.pdf.

Purdon, N. (2015, July 24). PTSD taking its toll on Canada's prison guards. CBC News. Retrieved from http://www .cbc.ca/news/canada/ptsd-taking-its-toll-on-canada-s -prison-guards-1.3166791.

Reitano, J. (2017). Adult correctional statistics in Canada, 2015/16. *Juristat.* Retrieved from http://www.statcan.gc .ca/pub/85-002-x/2017001/article/14700-eng.pdf.

Sakowski, M. (1986). Women guards in Canada: A study of the first women to work in a federal penitentiary for male offenders. *Resources for Feminist Research, 13,* 52–53.

Scott, T., & Ternes, M. (2015). *Assessing the impact of working in correctional environments: A literature review* (Research Report R-377). Ottawa: Correctional Service of Canada.

Seglins, D., & Noël, B. (2012, November 19). Prison guard accused of trading drugs for sex. CBC News. Retrieved from http://www.cbc.ca/news/canada/prison-guard -accused-of-trading-drugs-for-sex-1.1211354.

Statistics Canada. (2005). *Criminal justice indicators 2005.* Ottawa: Author.

Status of Women Canada. (2007). *Report on plans and priorities, 2006–2007.* Ottawa: Author.

Stone, L. (2014, December 2). Workplace accidents among Canada's prison guards on the rise, documents reveal. Global News. Retrieved from http://globalnews.ca/ news/1704183/workplace-accidents-among-canadas -prison-guards-on-the-rise-documents-reveal/.

Strange, C. (1985). The criminal and fallen of their sex: The establishment of Canada's first women's prison, 1874–1901. *Canadian Journal of Women and the Law, 1,* 79–92.

Tewksbury, R., & Higgins, G. (2006). Examining the effect of emotional dissonance on work stress and satisfaction with supervisors among correctional staff. *Criminal Justice Policy Review, 17,* 290–301.

Triplett, R., Mullings, J., & Scarborough, K. (1999). Examining the effect of work-home conflict on work-related stress among correctional officers. *Journal of Criminal Justice, 27,* 371–385.

Tutton, M. (2015, February 1). Assaults nearly double at Nova Scotia jail, records show. *The Globe and Mail.* Retrieved from http://www.theglobeandmail.com/news/ national/assaults-nearly-double-at-nova-scotia-jail -records-show/article22740740/?service=print.

van Wormer, K., & Bartollas, C. (2000). *Women and the criminal justice system.* Boston: Allyn & Bacon.

Zimmer, L. (1986). *Women guarding men.* Chicago: University of Chicago Press.

Glossary

anomie: A term used to describe societal conditions that negatively impact people. It emphasizes the importance of societal norms in regulating a person's goals. Durkheim's writings on this topic outline how social transformations (alienation and economic depression, for example) may stimulate anomic societal conditions (leading one to commit crime or opt out of participating in society).

cascading: The process of placing offenders in progressively lower security facilities as they respond positively to rehabilitative programs and near their release date. Although cascading is frequently desirable, it is not always possible.

clinical judgment: A predominantly qualitative decision made by a corrections professional regarding the recidivism risk posed by an offender.

criminogenic need: A factor or behaviour that is related to criminal behaviour or recidivism.

decarceration: The opposite of incarceration. The decarceration movement strives to remove people from prisons. The Elizabeth Fry societies in Canada are proponents of decarceration.

exchange of service agreement (ESA): Within the Canadian penal system, an agreement between a province or territory and the federal government that allows for the incarceration of provincial or territorial inmates in federal institutions or vice versa.

feminism: (1) The belief that women and men are, and have been, treated differently by our society; (2) the belief that women have frequently and systemically been unable to participate fully in all social arenas and institutions; and (3) the desire to change that situation.

habeas corpus: An order by a judge instructing a detaining authority (usually the police) to produce the detainee in a court of law so that the judge can determine whether the individual is being lawfully detained or should be set free.

healing lodge: A facility designed to meet the needs of Indigenous offenders by offering services and programs that reflect Indigenous culture, beliefs, and traditions.

learned helplessness: A mental state in which a person accepts that nothing they do can control or stop the painful situation(s) and subsequently become unable or unwilling to avoid those painful encounters even if they are "escapable."

male privilege: The experience of subtle and overt advantages, as well as the absence of subtle and overt discrimination, in daily life simply by virtue of being male.

Marxism: A 19th-century political theory advanced by Karl Marx and Friedrich Engels suggesting that society is divided into economic classes.

misogyny: A word of Greek origin that is defined as a hatred of or hostility toward women.

neutralization: An offender's rationalization that seeks to mitigate the effects of a crime. For example, a fraud offender passing bad cheques might tell herself that the money from the cheques was used to buy groceries to feed her children. In her mind, the damage from the fraud is mitigated by the good from the groceries.

NIMBY (not in my backyard): A belief that change in one's neighbourhood will deteriorate the property value of homes and businesses.

patriarchal structure: A heterosexual union in which the husband works outside the home in a position of authority and a wife is delegated responsibility for keeping the house and socializing and controlling the children.

positivist school: One of the two major schools of criminology. Assumes the root causes of crime are from factors outside the control of the offender (such as biological or physiological issues).

post hoc: After the fact.

prima facie: On the face of things.

rape culture: A set of beliefs that encourages male sexual aggression and supports violence against women in the form of words, jokes, advertising, media, objectification, and gendered norms.

recidivism: The repetition of a criminal behaviour by an individual who has already been convicted and punished for a previous offence. Because recidivism can be viewed as a measure of rehabilitative failure, it is also a measure of the effectiveness of rehabilitation programs and deterrents.

segregation unit: An area of a prison where inmates are kept separate from the rest of the prison population.

static security: The reliance on physical security measures (cameras, fencing, and alarms, for example) to control the inmate population of a prison.

strain theory: A criminological view that an individual's social setting generates certain goals and expectations. The failure of individuals to achieve these goals, and thus the inability to achieve the social treatment they expect, results in strain and creates alienation and negative relationships with others. When others are seen as blocking the means to achieve their goals, some alienated individuals resort to criminal behaviour.

White Ribbon Campaign: A campaign founded in 1991 by a group of men seeking to end violence against women, in response to the 1989 massacre at Montreal's École Polytechnique. The White Ribbon Campaign now operates in more than 55 countries.

Index

Credits

PART I

Chapter 1

Page 15 (Photo): © Howard Sandler. Dreamstime.com.

Page 21 (Box 1.1): Ottawa: Public Works and Government Services of Canada, p. 76. Link to Arbour Report: http://www.caefs.ca/wp-content/uploads/2013/05/Arbour_Report.pdf, questions@tpsgc-pwgsc.gc.ca. Used with permission.

Chapter 2

Page 34 (Figure 2.1): Created by D. Scharie Tavcer and Joanne Sutherland.

Page 36 (Box 2.3): Coren, M. (2007, July 28). End the blather. Toronto Sun. Available at: http://www.torontosun.com. Reprinted by permission of Sun Media Corporation.

Page 45 (Figure 2.2): Source: DeKeseredy, W.S., Ellis, D., & Alvi, S. (2005). Deviance and crime: Theory, research and policy. Cincinnati: Taylor and Francis, p. 45. Used with permission. Copyright Clearance Centre.

Page 46 (Figure 2.3): Source: DeKeseredy, W.S., Ellis, D., & Alvi, S. (2005). Deviance and crime: Theory, research and policy. Cincinnati: Taylor and Francis, p. 46. Used with permission. Copyright Clearance Centre.

Page 50 (Figure 2.4): Created by D. Scharie Tavcer.

PART II

Chapter 3

Page 59 (Photo): The Canadian Press/Waterloo Regional Record.

Page 84 (Photo): Used with the express permission of Association of Elizabeth Fry Societies (CAEFS).

Page 85 (Box 3.1): National Union of Public and General Employees. (2003). Two fraud cases: Conrad Black and Kimberly Rogers. Retrieved from www.nupge.ca. Reprinted by permission of NUPGE.

Chapter 4

Page 97 (Box 4.2): Tory bill proposes violent youth be tried as adults. (2007, November 19). *CTV.ca News*. Retrieved from www.ctv.ca. Reprinted by permission of CTVglobemedia.

Page 103 (Box 4.3): Yearwood-Lee, E. (2003, December 7). Viciousness of youth attacks increases while numbers remain static. Canadian Press. Available at www.thefreeradical.ca/Violent_crime_statistics_Canada.htm. Reprinted by permission of The Canadian Press.

Page 104 (Box 4.4): Accused in Virk case goes on trial for 3rd time. (2005, February 22). *CTV.ca News*. Retrieved from www.ctv.ca. Reprinted by permission of The Canadian Press.

Chapter 6

Page 149 (Box 6.3): Blanchette, K., & Taylor, K. (2005). *Development and field test of a gender-informed security reclassification scale for women offenders* (Research Report R-167). Ottawa: Correctional Service of Canada. Used with permission.

PART III

Chapter 7

Page 171 (Photo): The Canadian Press/Colin Perkel.

Page 188 (Figure 7.2): Calgary Newsroom, 18 May 2016. Calgary Saw Domestic Violence Rise in 2015. Retrieved from http://newsroom.calgary.ca/calgary-saw-domestic-violence-rise-in-2015. Used with permission.

Page 189 (Figure 7.3): Power and Control Wheel from Domestic Abuse Intervention Programs. https://www.theduluthmodel.org/wp-content/uploads/2017/03/PowerandControl.pdf. Used with permission of Duluth.

Chapter 8

Page 204 (Box 8.1): Gray, J.E., Shone, M.A., & Liddle, P.F. (2008). Canadian mental health law and policy 2nd ed. Toronto: Butterworths.

Chapter 9

Page 243 (Photo): The Canadian Press/Dave McCord.

Page 247 (Box 9.3): Morin, S. (1999). Federally sentenced Aboriginal women in maximum security: What happened to the promises of "Creating choices"? Ottawa: Correctional Service of Canada.

PART IV

Chapter 11

Page 291 (Box 11.3): Used with the permission of Sgt. Penny Hermann. Media Relations NCO / sous-officière des relations avec les médias "O" Division / Division "O."

Page 292 (Box 11.4): Used with the permission of Inspector Laura Houliston, Manager, Criminal Operations, North East Region.

Chapter 12

Page 305 (Figure 12.1): Copyright 2010, The Law Society of Upper Canada. Reproduced with permission of Law Society of Upper Canada.

Page 306 (Box 12.1): Michael Tutton, The Canadian Press (January 23, 2017). N.S. appoints Mi'kmaq, black women to bench: "This is a huge step forward." Retrieved from http://www.news1130.com/2017/01/23/nova-scotia-justice-minister-appoints-first-mkmaq-woman-to-the-judiciary/. Used with the permission of The Canadian Press.

Page 309 (Figure 12.3): Copyright 2012, The Law Society of Upper Canada. Reproduced with permission of Law Society of Upper Canada.

Page 310 (Photo): Photo by Fred Lum/ The Globe and Mail Digital Image/ CPimages.

Chapter 13

Page 334 (Box 13.2): MacAlpine, I. (April 6, 2016). Correctional officers Officially First Responders. The Kingston Whig-Standard. Retrieved from http://www.thewhig.com/2016/04/06/correctional-officers-officially-first-responders. Licensed by Postmedia.